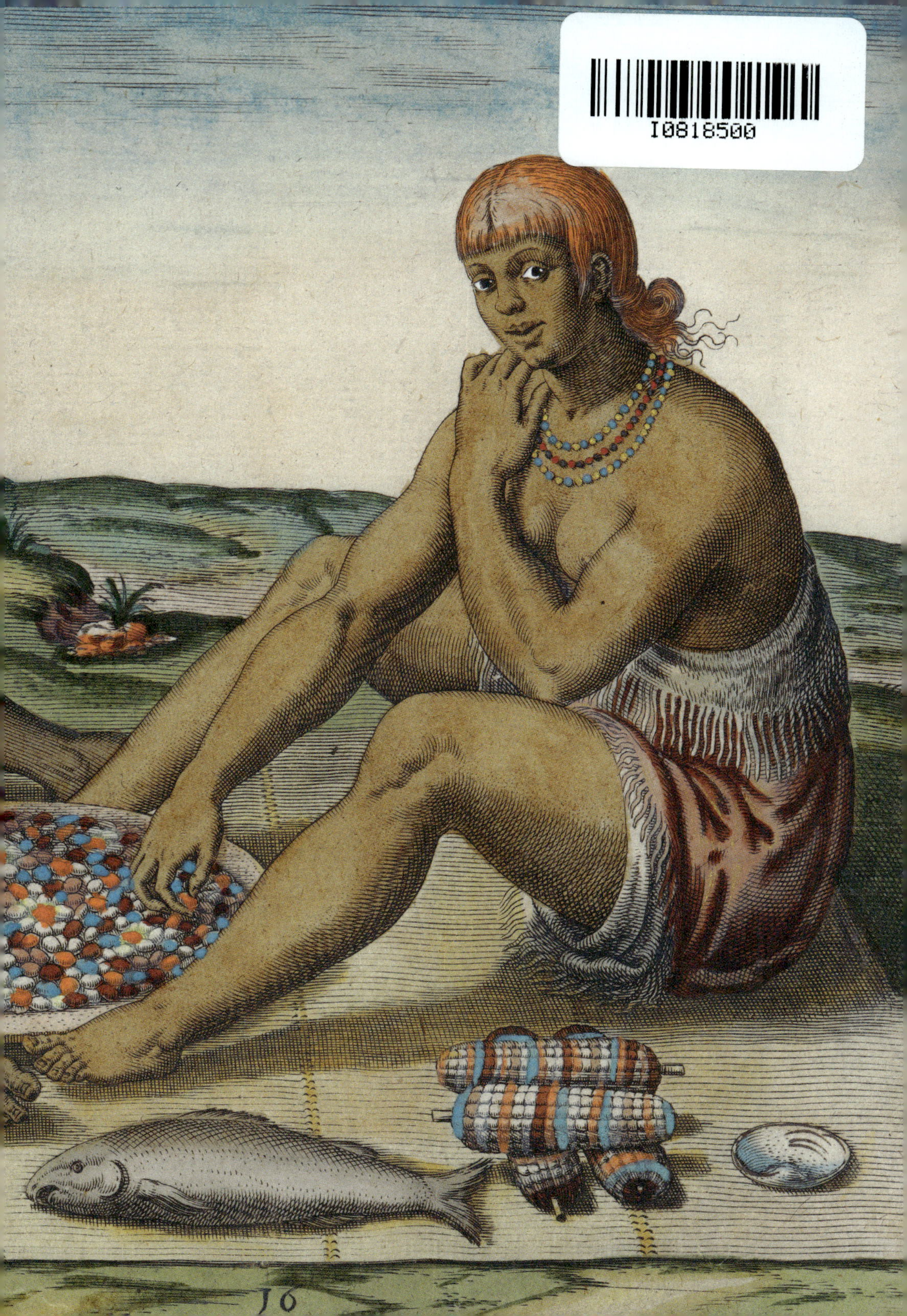
I0818500
16

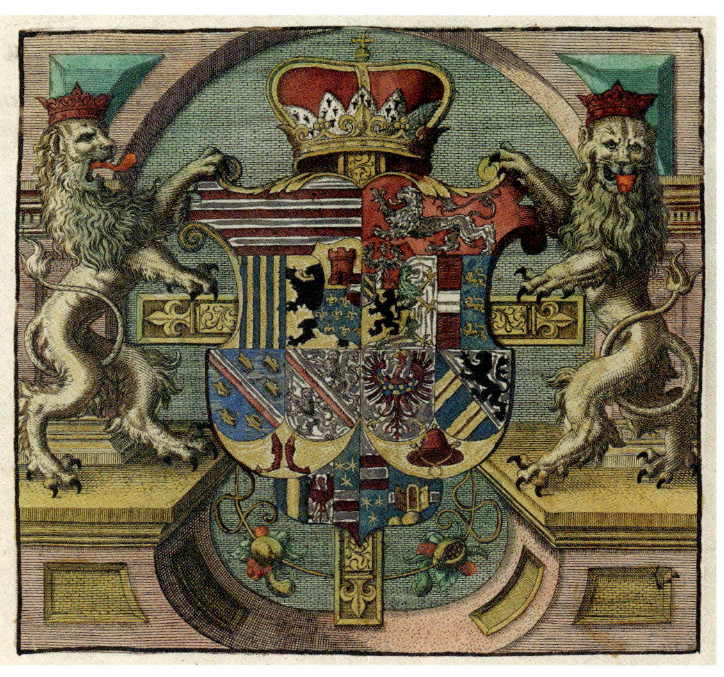

EFFIGIES

THEODORI DE BRY LEODIEN.

CRYPTICI NOBILISSIMI.

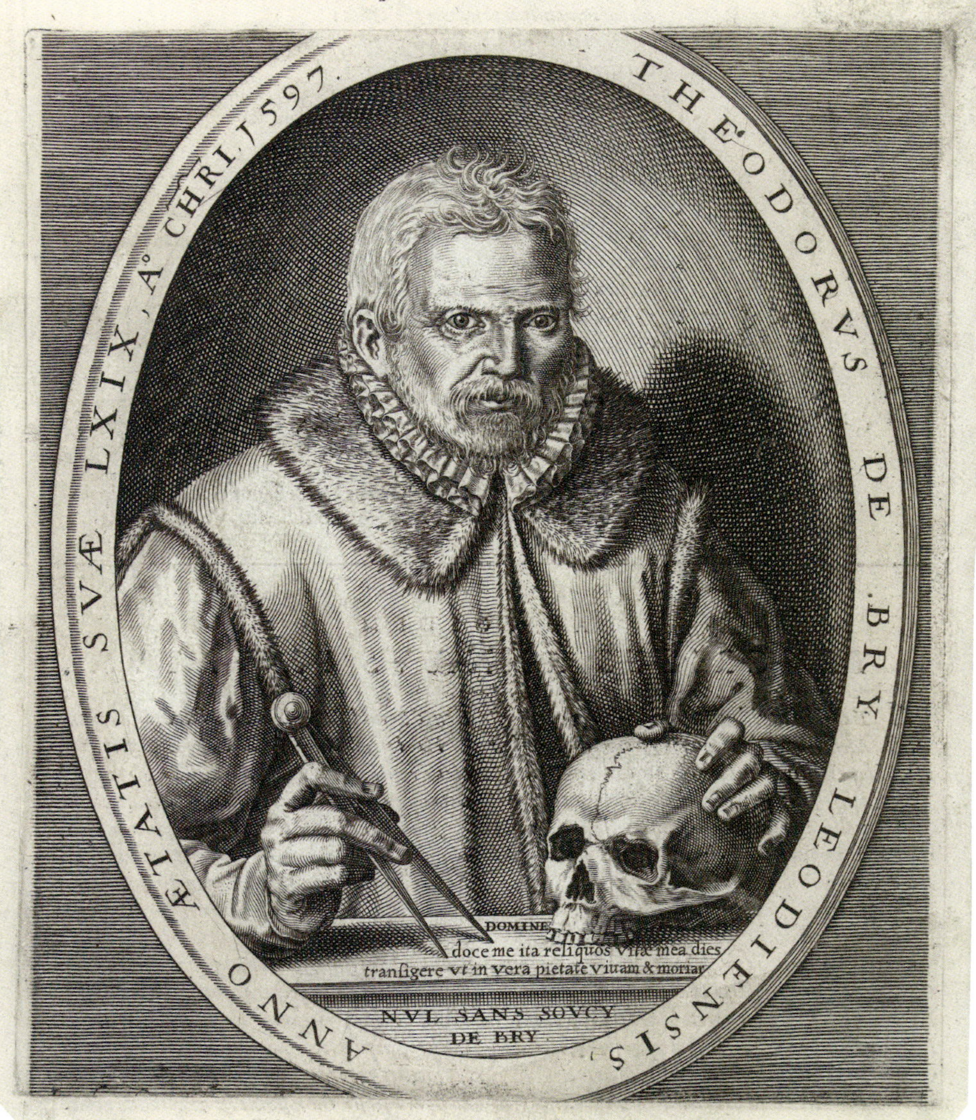

MICHIEL VAN GROESEN (ED.)
LARRY E. TISE

Theodore de Bry

The New World

Virginia, Florida, the Caribbean, Mexico and Central America, Brazil, Peru
1590–1602

The copies used for printing belong to the
JOHN HAY LIBRARY & JOHN CARTER BROWN LIBRARY,
BROWN UNIVERSITY, PROVIDENCE
STAATS- UND STADTBIBLIOTHEK AUGSBURG

Directed and produced by
BENEDIKT TASCHEN

TASCHEN

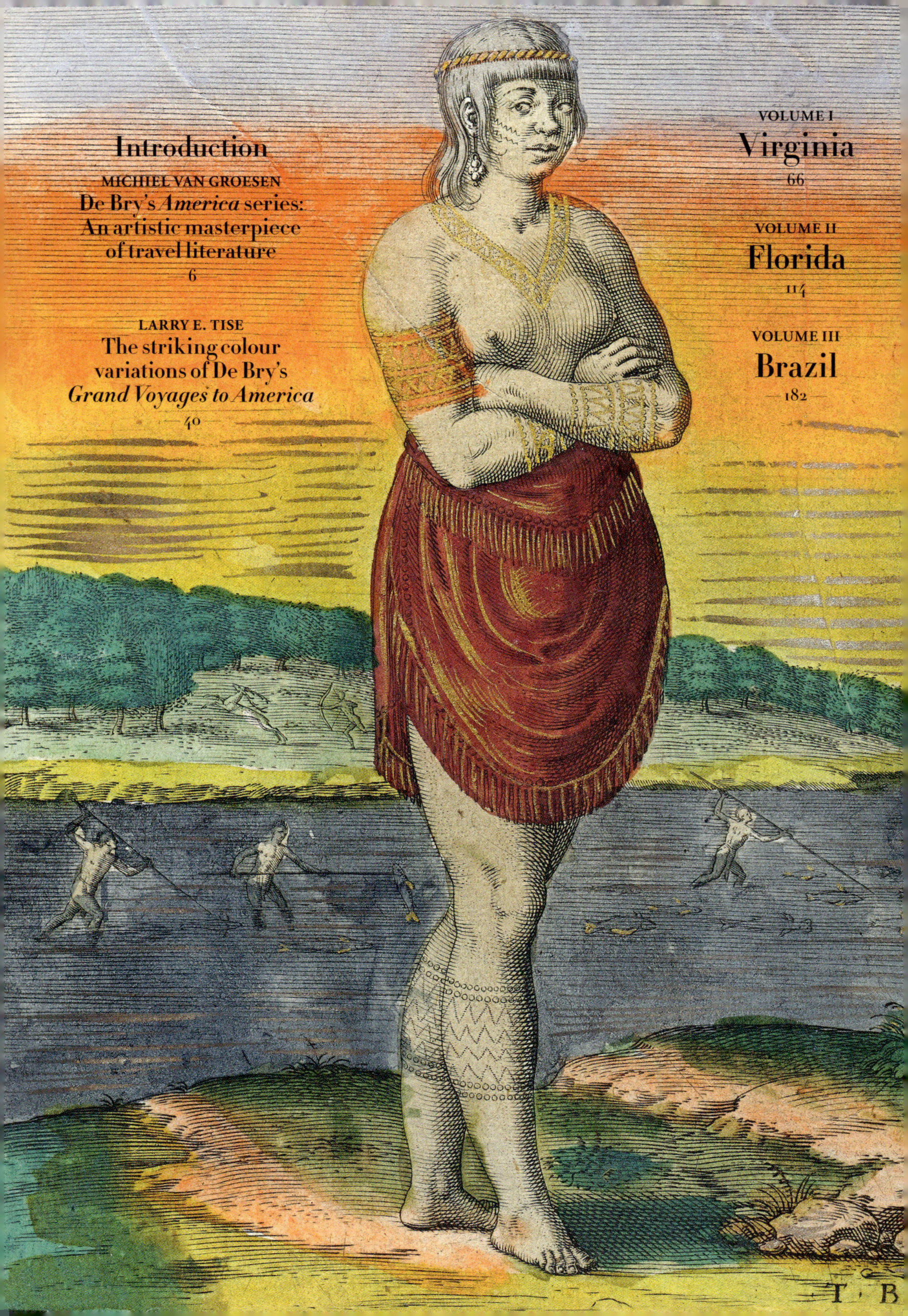

Introduction

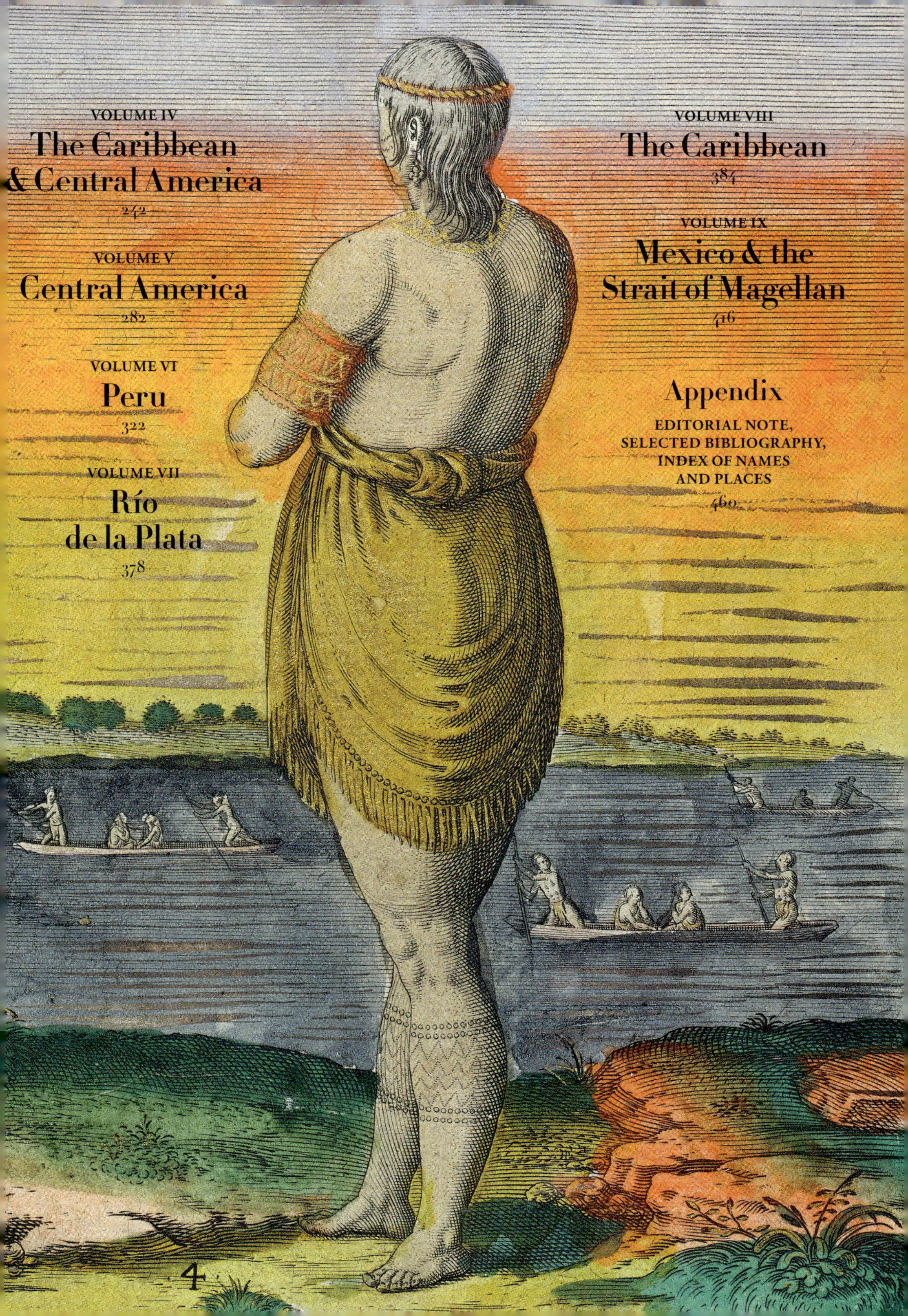

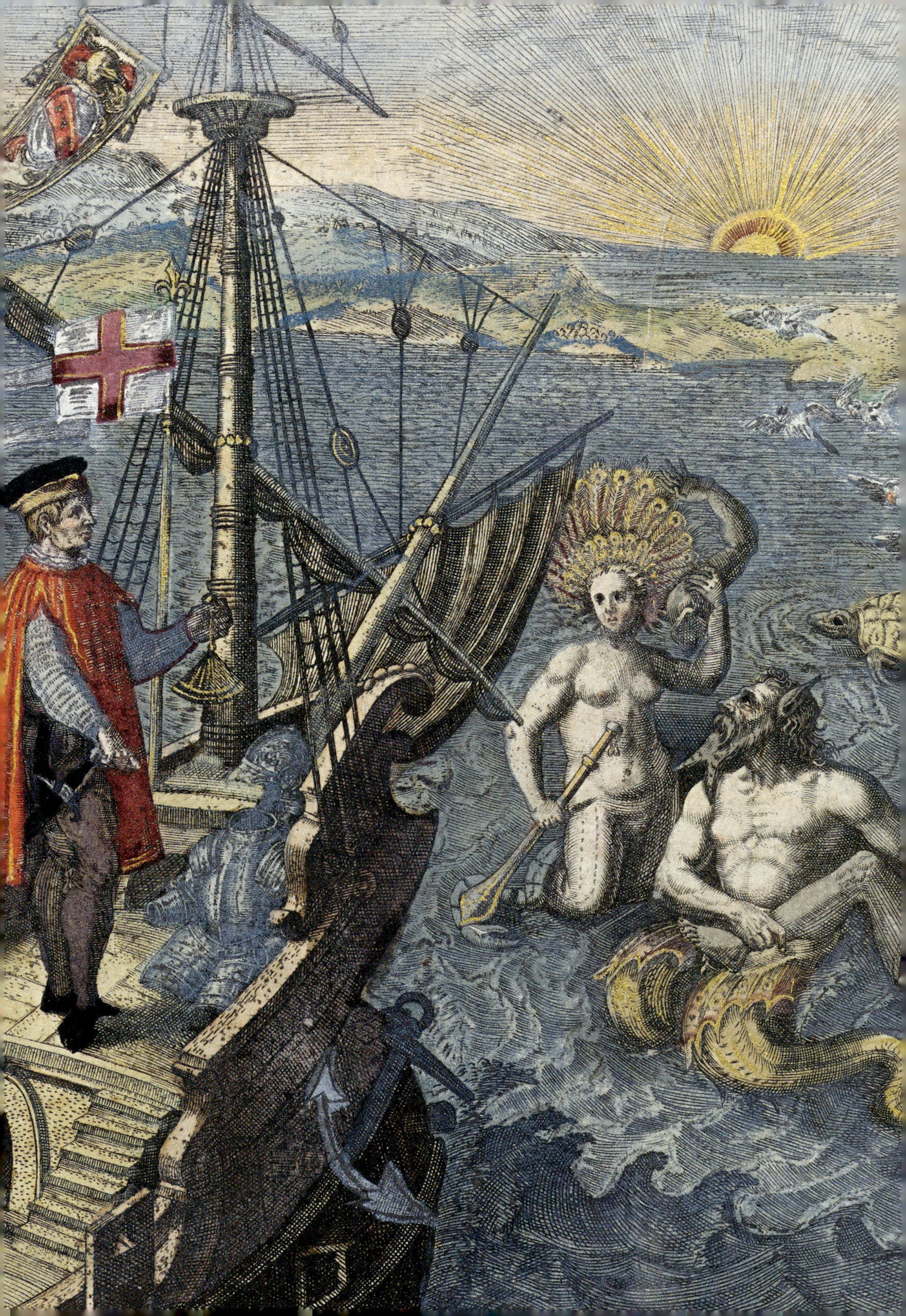

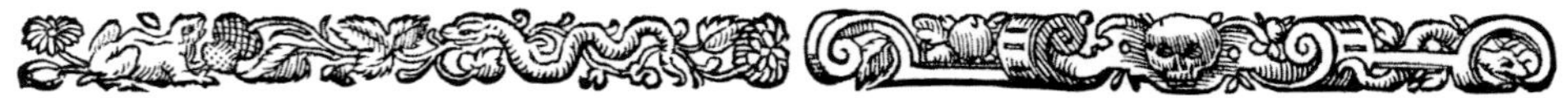

De Bry's *America* series: An artistic masterpiece of travel literature

MICHIEL VAN GROESEN

The monumental collection of voyages assembled by Theodore de Bry and his heirs is one of the most impressive book series ever produced. It was published in Frankfurt am Main between 1590 and 1634, by Theodore himself, his two sons Johan Theodore and Johan Israel, and Johan Theodore's son-in-law Matthaeus Merian, and brought together texts and images to present a comprehensive European view of Asia, Africa and America. As a true premodern coffee-table book, it consists of 25 folio volumes divided into two largely identical series – the 13-volume *America* series, which included accounts of the New World, and the 12-volume *India Orientalis* series, dealing with Africa and Asia. Overall, the collection contains around 50 European travel accounts from the late 16th and early 17th centuries. All these reports had already been published before, in Dutch, English, French, Spanish, Portuguese or German. After having been selected by the De Brys for inclusion they were translated into German and Latin, and subsequently embellished with just under 600 large copper-plate engravings. In today's way of speaking, these illustrations were the collection's unique selling point. The De Brys had introduced the technique of including copper engravings in printed books in Frankfurt, the centre of the early modern book world, and even by the time they concluded their series on these voyages few publishers could match their skill in producing high-quality illustrated editions. The De Brys themselves, however, never travelled, and for their engravings they relied on images found in the original accounts they used, or else on their own imagination. Indeed, more than 40 percent of the engravings in the collection appear to have been invented from scratch in their Frankfurt workshop, thereby creating an idiosyncratic view of the world across the Atlantic and of the Orient which helped to legitimate European colonisation for the next two centuries.[1]

The combination of texts and high-quality images (for example pp. 13, 28, 29), and the sheer size of the collection, meant that it became a prestigious collectors' item as soon as it was published. Already in the 1640s, when revised editions and abridgements were still coming off the presses in Frankfurt, early volumes had become difficult to obtain, and the interest of collectors has never waned. Thomas Jefferson, the third president of the United States, was elated when in 1789 he finally managed to purchase a set of the 13 *America* volumes at an auction in Amsterdam. Bibliophiles such as the Englishman Thomas Dibdin referred to the collection only in the most

Christopher Columbus among nautical deities (detail)
From: *America*, foreword to vol. IV

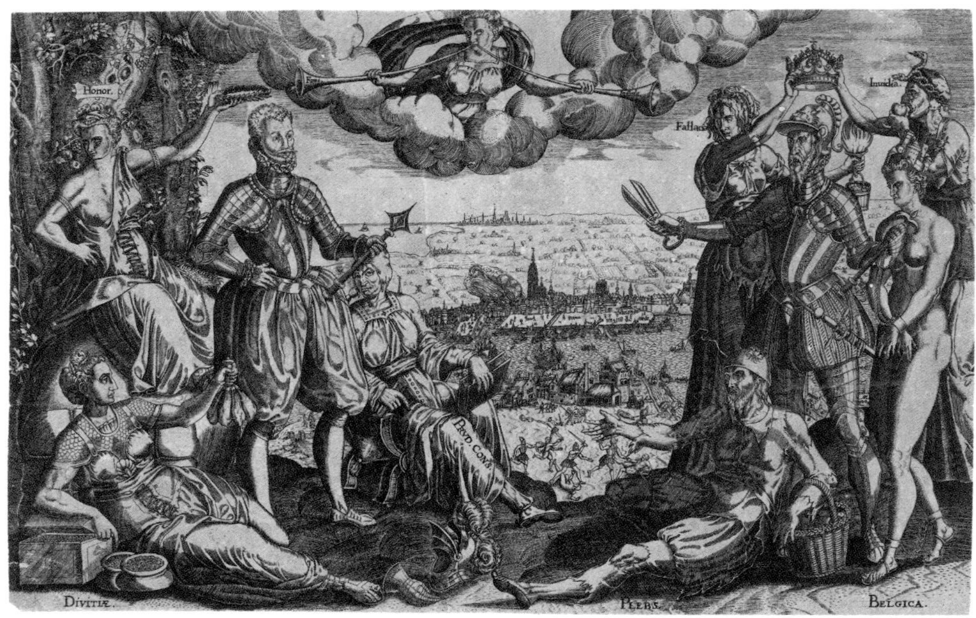

lyrical terms. "What a bibliographical chord I am striking," Dibdin wrote in 1824, "in the mention of the Travels of De Bry! What a *Peregrination* does the possession of a copy of his labours imply! What toil, difficulty, perplexity, anxiety, and vexation attend the collector – be he young or old – who sets his heart upon a perfect De Bry! How many have started forward on this pursuit, with gay spirits and well-replenished purses, but have turned from it in despair, and abandoned it in utter hopelessness of achievement!" In the two centuries since Dibdin's words, very little has changed. Complete sets of the De Bry collection are nowadays found almost exclusively in academic libraries. When they come up for auction, a 'good' copy of the *America* series – still the most sought after, then as now – commands a price which, depending on its quality, can reach up to 500,000 dollars.

The copper engravings are the main reason the collection is still in demand. Its images of the New World in particular were frequently copied by other engravers at the time, and are still being routinely used to decorate the dust-jackets of scholarly books which do not necessarily discuss the De Bry collection at all, such is their acclaim. It is the texts, however, which hold the key to understanding the objectives of the De Brys in producing their flagship publication. Whereas the eye-catching illustrations are identical in each of the two versions of the collection, the German

Theodore de Bry (attr.), **William of Orange and the Duke of Alva before the Spanish Fury at Antwerp**, 1577
Copper engraving, 20.6 x 33 cm, (8⅛ x 13 in.). Amsterdam, Rijksmuseum

Theodore de Bry, **Frontispiece**
From: Lucas Jansz. Waghenaer, *The Mariners Mirrour*, London, 1588. London, British Library

Pages 10/11
Lucas Jansz. Waghenaer, **Map of the south-west coast of England**
From: *De Spieghel der Zeevaerdt*, 1584. London, National Maritime Museum

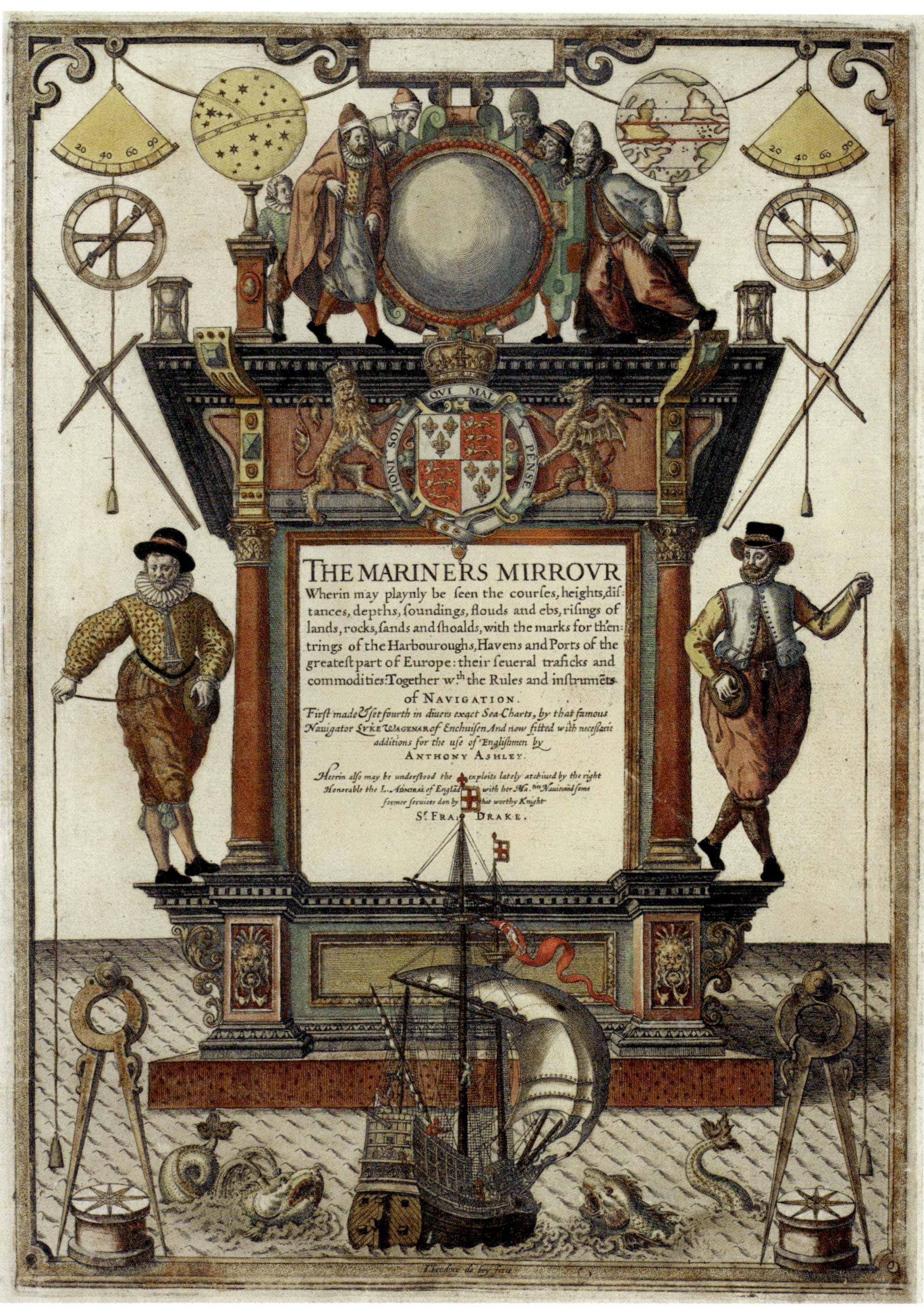
HONI SOIT QVI MAL Y PENSE
THE MARINERS MIRROVR
Wherin may playnly be ſeen the courſes, heights, diſ-
tances, depths, ſoundings, flouds and ebs, riſings of
lands, rocks, ſands and ſhoalds, with the marks for th'en-
trings of the Harbouroughs, Havens and Ports of the
greateſt part of Europe: their ſeueral traficks and
commodities: Together w.th the Rules and inſtrumēts
of NAVIGATION.
First made & ſet fourth in diuers exact Sea-Charts, by that famous
Nauigator LVKE WAGENAR of Enchuiſen And now fitted with neceſsarie
additions for the uſe of Engliſhmen by
ANTHONY ASHLEY.
Heerin alſo may be underſtood the exploits lately atchiued by the right
Honorable the L. ADMIRAL of Englād with her Ma.ties Nauie and some
former ſeruices don by that worthy Knight
S.r FRA: DRAKE.

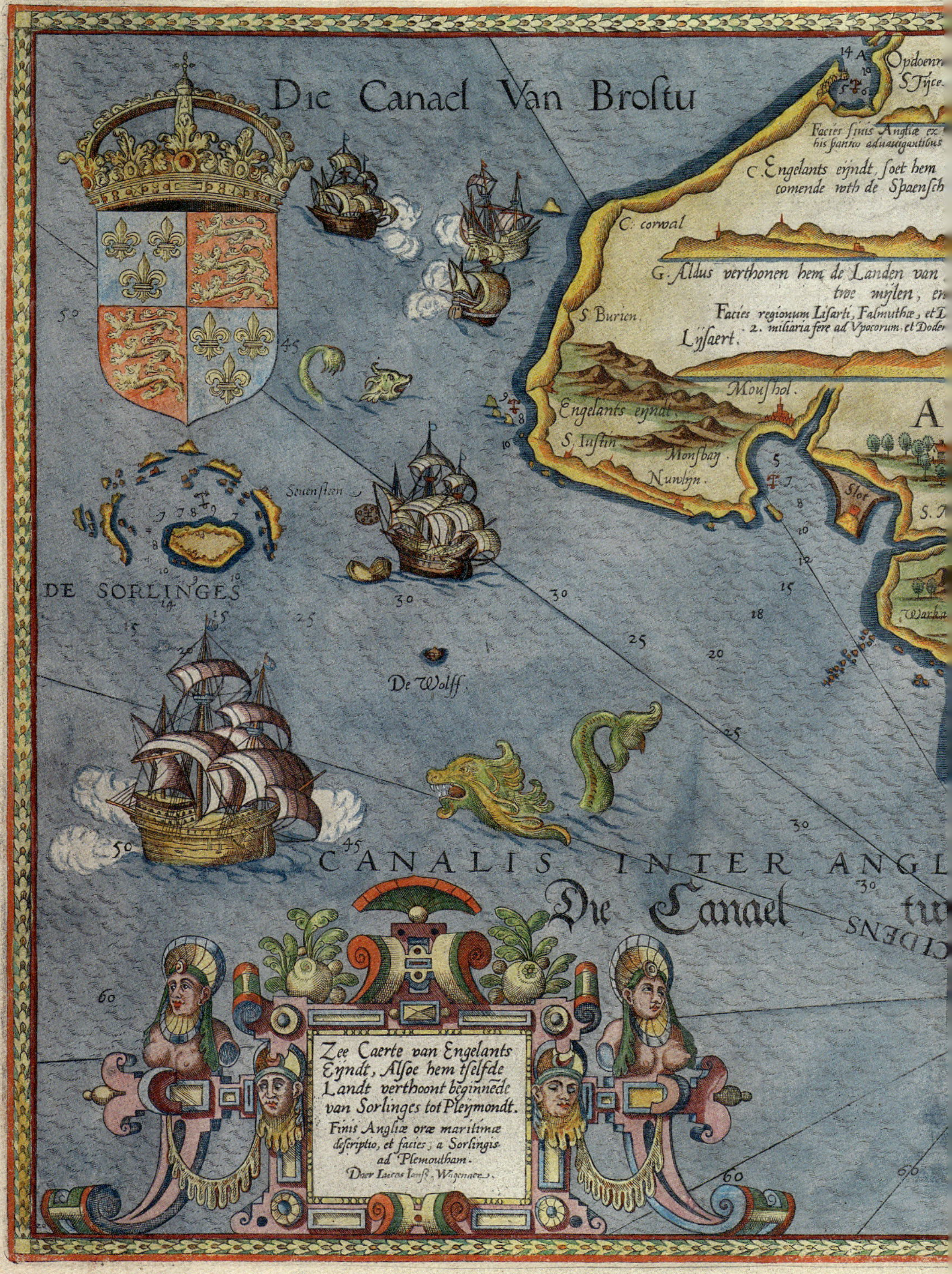

Die Canael Van Broſtu
C. corwal
S. Burien
Lyſaert.
Engelants eyndt
S. Iuſtin
Monſbay
Nunbyn.
Mouſhol.
Slot
Seuenſteen
DE SORLINGES
De Wolff
CANALIS INTER ANGL
Die Canael
Zee Caerte van Engelants Eyndt, Alſoe hem tſelfde Landt verthoont beginnēde van Sorlinges tot Pleymondt.
Finis Angliæ oræ maritimæ deſcriptio, et facies, a Sorlingis ad Plemoutham.
Door Lucas Ianſz Wagenaer.

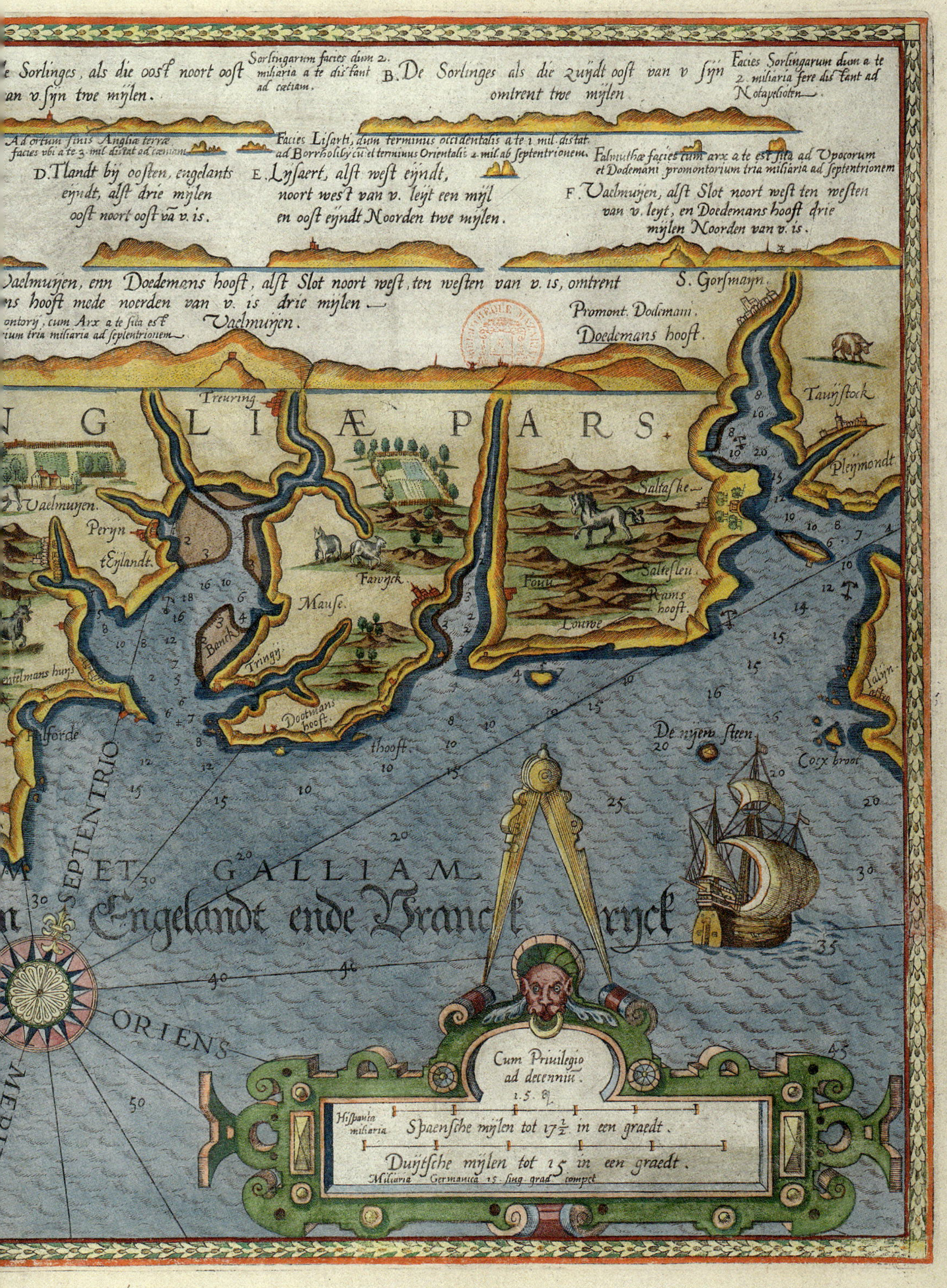
Sorlinges, als die oost noort oost
van v syn twe mylen.
Sorlingarum facies dum 2. miliaria a te dis tant ad caetiam.
B. De Sorlinges als die zuydt oost van v syn
omtrent twe mylen
Facies Sorlingarum dum a te 2. miliaria fere dis tant ad Notapeliotem.
D. Tlandt bij oosten, engelants eyndt, alst drie mylen oost noort oost va v. is.
E. Lysaert, alst west eyndt, noort west van v. leyt een myl en oost eyndt Noorden twe mylen.
F. Vaelmuyen, alst Slot noort west ten westen van v. leyt, en Doedemans hooft drie mylen Noorden van v. is.
Vaelmuyen, enn Doedemans hooft, alst Slot noort west, ten westen van v. is, omtrent
drie mylen
Vaelmuyen.
S. Gorsmayn.
Promont. Dodemani.
Doedemans hooft.
ANGLIÆ PARS.
Treuring
Tauystock
Pleymondt
Saltaske
Vaelmuyen.
Peryn
tEylandt.
Farwyck
Mause.
Fouy
Saltesleu
Rams hooft
Louwe
Bank
Tringy
Dootmans hooft.
thooft
De nyew steen
Corx hroot
SEPTENTRIO
ET GALLIAM.
Engelandt ende Vranckryck
ORIENS
Cum Privilegio ad decenniū.
1.5.8
Hispania miliaria
Spaensche mylen tot 17½. in een graedt.
Duytsche mylen tot 15 in een graedt.
Miliaria Germanica 15 sing. grad. compet.

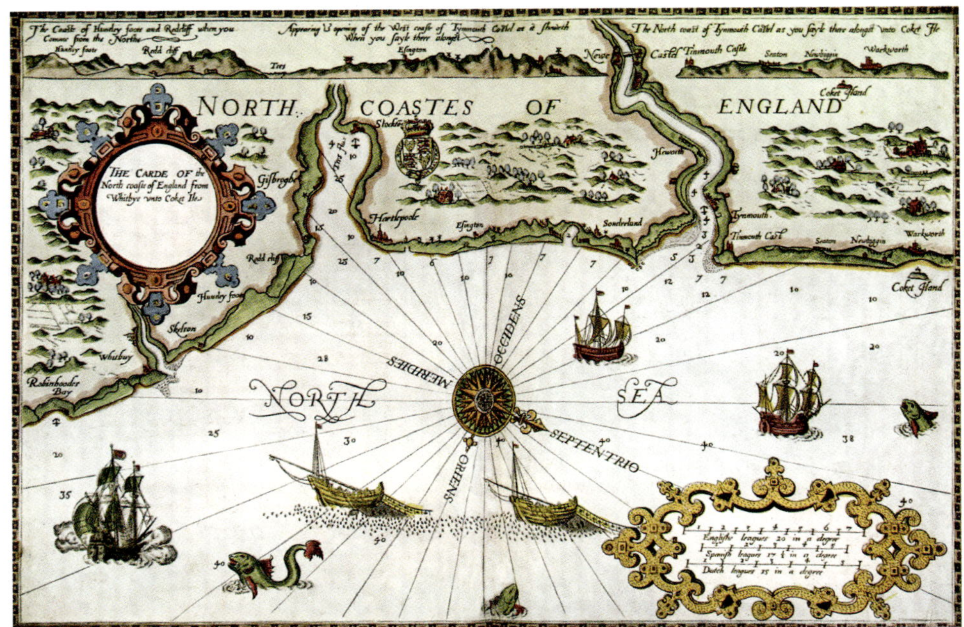

and Latin translations of the textual parts reveal significant differences. When compared, they reveal an editorial strategy on the part of the De Brys that was not solely intended to disseminate the notion of European supremacy – a tale being told by the texts and images combined in both translations. The textual differences show that the De Brys carefully adjusted their representations to reach their different intended readerships in an era that was marked by strong religious divisions. The German editions were aimed at a Protestant audience, and criticised the colonial efforts of Catholic imperial powers such as Spain and Portugal. The Latin editions, on the other hand, were sold to customers in Catholic countries such as France, Italy and in southern Germany, as well as in Spain and Portugal. For this segment of the book market, the De Brys carefully adjusted the texts to present a milder view of Iberian colonialism. Commercial considerations thus ousted ideological ones. The De Brys – whose business success depended on the sales figures of their collection of voyages – wanted to sell their books to customers right across Europe. Their editorial strategy worked: the censors of the Inquisition in Spain and Portugal, who meticulously checked printed books from abroad for heterodox ideas, explicitly allowed the volumes of the De Bry collection to be sold throughout Spain and Portugal.

This TASCHEN edition of the De Bry collection of voyages contains the first nine volumes of the *America* series. They were originally published by Theodore de Bry and his two sons between 1590 and 1602 and are, for various reasons, considered the best volumes in the entire series. They are intended to be read and understood collectively. After volume IX, the *America*

Theodore de Bry, **Map of the north coast of England**
From: Lucas Jansz. Waghenaer, *The Mariners Mirrour*, London, 1588. London, British Library

Illustration depicting Noah's Ark
From: *America*, foreword to vol. II

BENEVOLO LECTORI.

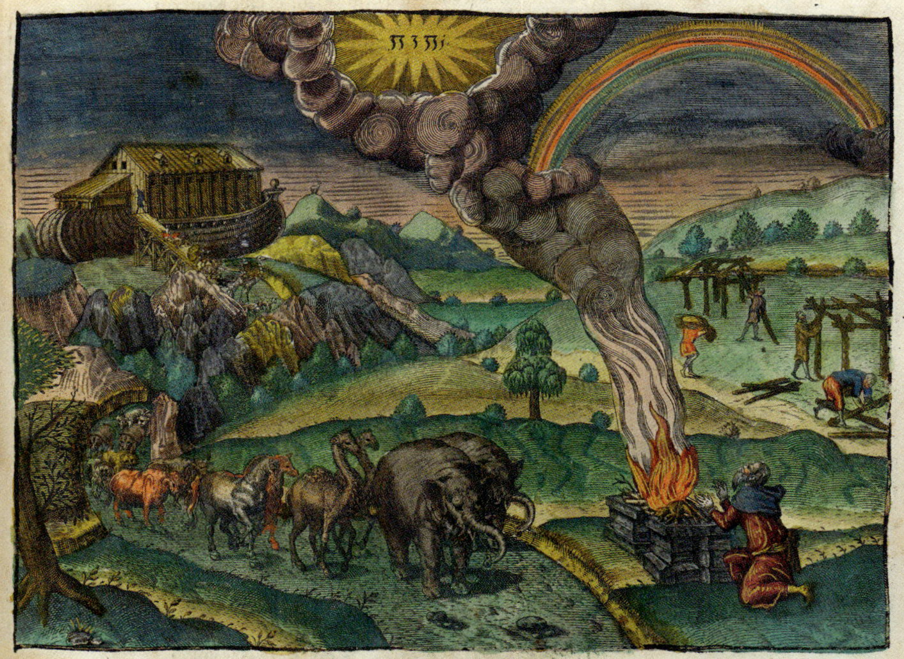

NOLI exiſtimare, benevole Lector, *Virginiæ*, quã ante aliquot menſes publicam fecimus, & hanc *Floridæ*, quam tibi nunc proponimus, Hiſtorias nobis dumtaxat eſſe conceſſas, ut voluptatem ex earum lectione & intuitu caperemus; tametſi, ut verum fateamur, ea res magnoperè animos etiam afficiat: ſed potius, ut obſervatis immenſis & admirandis Dei operibus, illi gratias agamus pro accepto beneficio, quòd ſe nobis patefacere, & ſalutis viam nos docere dignatus ſit, cùm animadvertimus miſeros iſtos Floridæ & vicinarum Provinciarum incolas (qui tamen ab uno ex Noë liberis haud dubiè originem duxerunt, à *Cham* verò potius, ut credibile eſt, quàm ab ullo ex reliquis) cognitionis Dei adeo eſſe ignaros. Alioqui ſane eleganti corporis ſymmetria donati ſunt, magni, robuſti, audaces, agiles: ſummi tamen diſſimulatores & infidi. Luridum & ſordidum colorem habent, quem corporis inunctione oleo quodam, & Solis ardoribus contrahunt: nam recéns nati ſatis ſunt albi.

)(3

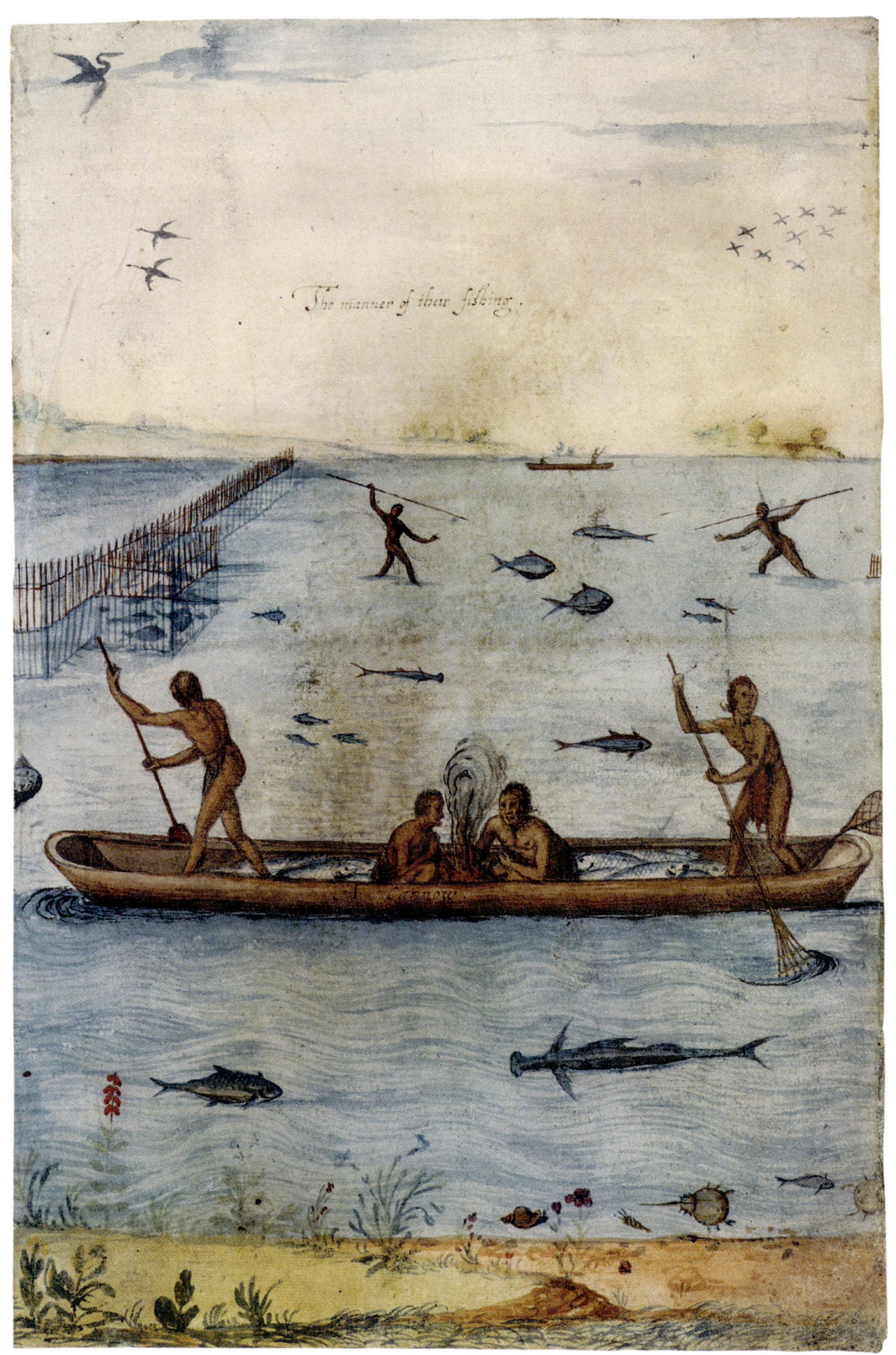
The manner of their fishing.

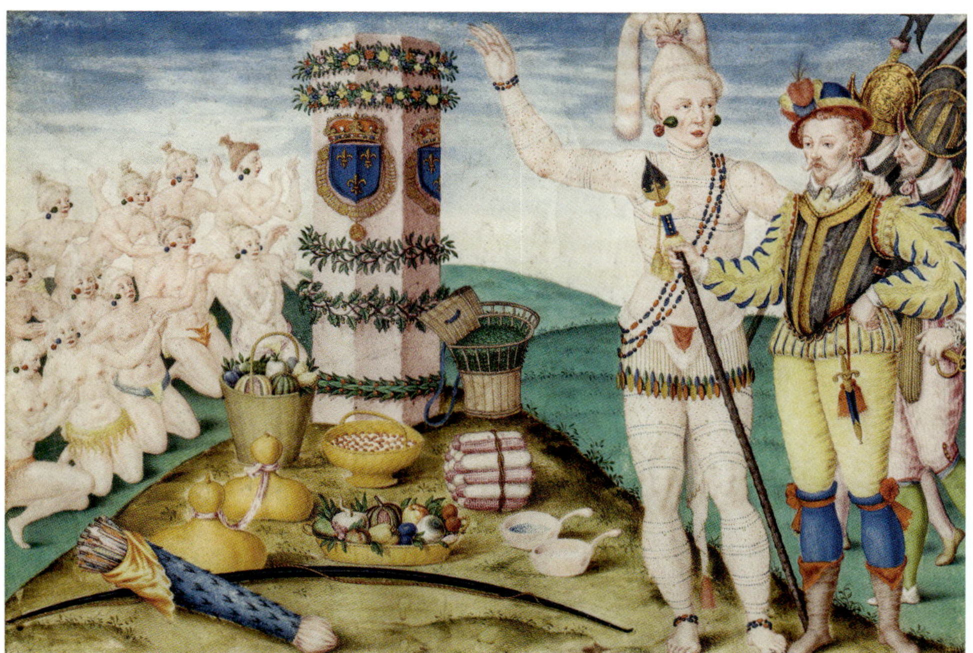

series was abandoned for 16 years, and was only resumed on the eve of the Thirty Years' War when the financial prospects of booksellers in Frankfurt were rapidly deteriorating. Every aspect of the collection is on show in this harmonious set of nine volumes. In the rest of this introduction, I shall discuss the background of the De Bry family, the various stages in the making of the collection, the editorial strategy gradually developed by the De Brys and the team of collaborators they relied on to produce such an exclusive book series. In the final sections I will consider the contents of the texts, the changes made to some of the images and the tasks involved in turning texts and images into a beautifully crafted book, such as binding and colouring. After the introduction, I have set out a short synopsis of each of the nine volumes, detailing the particulars of the various travel accounts included.

The origins and development of the collection

Theodore de Bry (page 2) was born in 1527 or 1528 in the Prince-Bishopric of Liège, in the southern Netherlands. Trained as a goldsmith in the workshop of his father, he left his hometown around 1558 and moved to Strasbourg. When he wrote, shortly before his death in 1598, about his decision to leave Liège, Theodore claimed that, "stripped of all my belongings by the accidents, deceptions and ill treatment of fortune and by the attacks of various robbers, I was forced to contend in the face of adverse chance that it was only by my art that I might fend for myself". In the late

John White, **The natives' manner of fishing**, c. 1587
Watercolour drawing, 35.2 x 23.5 cm (13⅞ x 9¼ in.). London, The British Museum

Jacques Le Moyne, **Athore showing Laudonnière a column bearing the crest of the King of France**, c. 1564
Watercolour drawing, 17.5 x 26 cm (6⅞ x 10¼ in.). New York Public Library

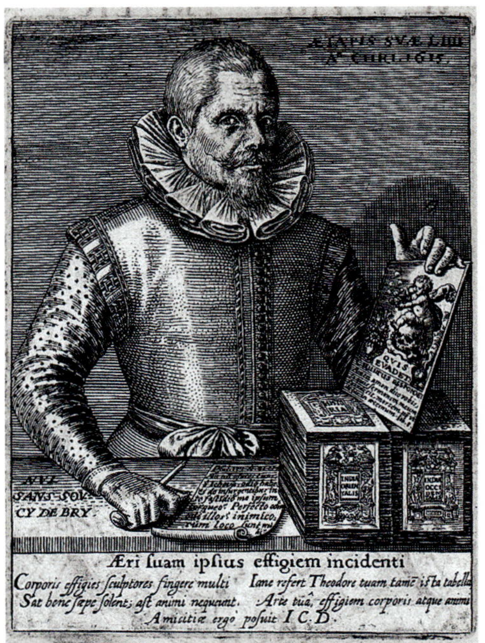

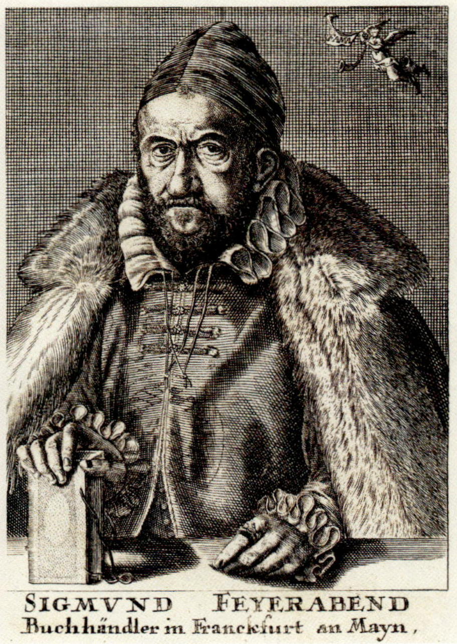

1550s, De Bry already had evangelical sympathies – his Calvinist zeal would only increase as he got older – but his emigration was not solely inspired by religious motives. Strasbourg was a Lutheran city and extended a nominal welcome to Calvinists, but already by 1563 the city council had closed the only Reformed church (although private worship continued to be tolerated). Commercial incentives were probably more important for De Bry, since Strasbourg was a much more attractive location for an ambitious goldsmith than Liège. Here, inspired by the Huguenot engraver Étienne Delaune, De Bry gradually began to shift his focus to copper engraving, although his occupation remained that of a goldsmith according to guild records. In the early 1560s, Theodore married Strasbourg-born Katharina Esslinger, and the couple went on to have four children together before Katharina died in 1569 or 1570. Johan Theodore (b. 1563) and Johan Israel (b. 1565) later followed in their father's footsteps and took up his trade. During his years in Strasbourg, Theodore established commercial connections with fellow Netherlanders in Frankfurt am Main, and when he remarried in 1570 it was to a daughter from Europe's book capital, Katharina Rölinger.

In 1577, after the Pacification of Ghent had quietened religious tensions in the Netherlands, Theodore and his family moved to Antwerp – the commercial hub of northern Europe which attracted great numbers of Calvinist merchants and artisans. Theodore joined the goldsmiths' guild, and in the early 1580s his two sons became apprentices in their father's workshop. In Antwerp, they lived close to the main printing house of 16th-century Europe, run by Christopher Plantin and

Johan Theodore de Bry, **Self-portrait**
From: Robert Fludd, *Amphitheatrum anatomicum*, Frankfurt, 1623. London, Wellcome Collection

Theodore de Bry, Jan Sadeler I, **Sigismund Feyerabend**, 1587
Copper engraving, 15.7 x 11.9 cm (6⅛ x 4¾ in.). Paris, private collection

his family, and it was during his eight-year stay in the city that Theodore began making copper engravings for the first time. Copper engraving was a well-developed art in the Low Countries, and Antwerp artists were in great demand. Theodore's oldest surviving copper engravings, of political developments in the Netherlands at a time of increasing religious tension, reveal his talent for this work (p. 8). His two sons probably embraced the trade right away – certainly, no goldsmiths' works with their names survive. In 1584, when Antwerp was besieged by Catholic troops, Theodore used his newly acquired skills to find a new place to live. Between 1585 and 1588, he and his family resided in London, where he made copper engravings for an important English navigation manual, *The Mariners Mirrour* (pp. 9, 12). It was also here, at the age of 60, that he found inspiration to produce the collection to which his name would forever be attached.

Two encounters set Theodore on course for the making of his masterpiece. In 1586, he met the Huguenot artist Jacques Le Moyne de Morgues. An accomplished draughtsman, Le Moyne had been to Florida in the 1560s as part of the expedition of the French captain René de Laudonnière. He had survived attacks by Spanish forces, and returned to the Old World with a set of watercolours of the natural world he had seen and the indigenous peoples (p. 15). When Theodore first approached Le Moyne and expressed his desire to turn the illustrations into copper engravings, Le Moyne rejected the idea. After his death the following year, however, Theodore returned to Le Moyne's widow and obtained the drawings at the second attempt. Perhaps the reason he was successful that time was because one of the most influential figures in Elizabethan England, Richard Hakluyt, had mediated on his behalf. Hakluyt had written a treatise entitled *The Discourse of Western Planting* (1584), and had promoted the first English attempts to establish a permanent English colony in North America. One of these settlements at Roanoke Island (in today's North Carolina) became known as "the Lost Colony" because the settlers who remained in the area they had christened "Virginia" were never found when a second English expedition, carrying various provisions for them, arrived in the New World in 1587. Amongst the early English voyagers was John White, an artist every bit as accomplished as Jacques Le Moyne who made his own watercolour drawings of native life in the Roanoke region (p. 14). These images presented an overly optimistic view of the colony, and were intended for Hakluyt to use in England with the aim of attracting large numbers of prospective settlers. In order to publicise the efforts of the English in Virginia, and to lay claim to the territory, Hakluyt turned to the most skilful copper engraver available and working in England at the time, the 60-year-old immigrant from Antwerp.

In the first volume of the *America* series, which was published in 1590 in Frankfurt after Theodore and his sons had moved there two years previously, De Bry paid homage to Hakluyt who "first Incouraged me to publishe the Worke". Hakluyt almost certainly had a hand in one important decision Theodore made for volume I of his collection. He persuaded him to begin his series with the drawings by John White rather than those De Bry had obtained earlier from Jacques Le Moyne, and for this reason volume I consisted of Thomas Harriot's account of "Virginia", first published in English in 1588. This volume was the only one in the whole collection which appeared in not two but four different languages: German, Latin, French and English. Such a multilingual approach fitted Hakluyt's international ambitions, but from a Frankfurt bookseller's perspective it was untenable. When Theodore turned his attention to producing volume II – combining René de Laudonnière's account of Huguenot Florida with the watercolours by Jacques Le Moyne – he opted to publish German and Latin editions only. Laudonnière's account had appeared in French as recently as 1586, while attempting to appeal to the peripheral English book market from Frankfurt more than once was probably considered commercially unfeasible by De Bry. To

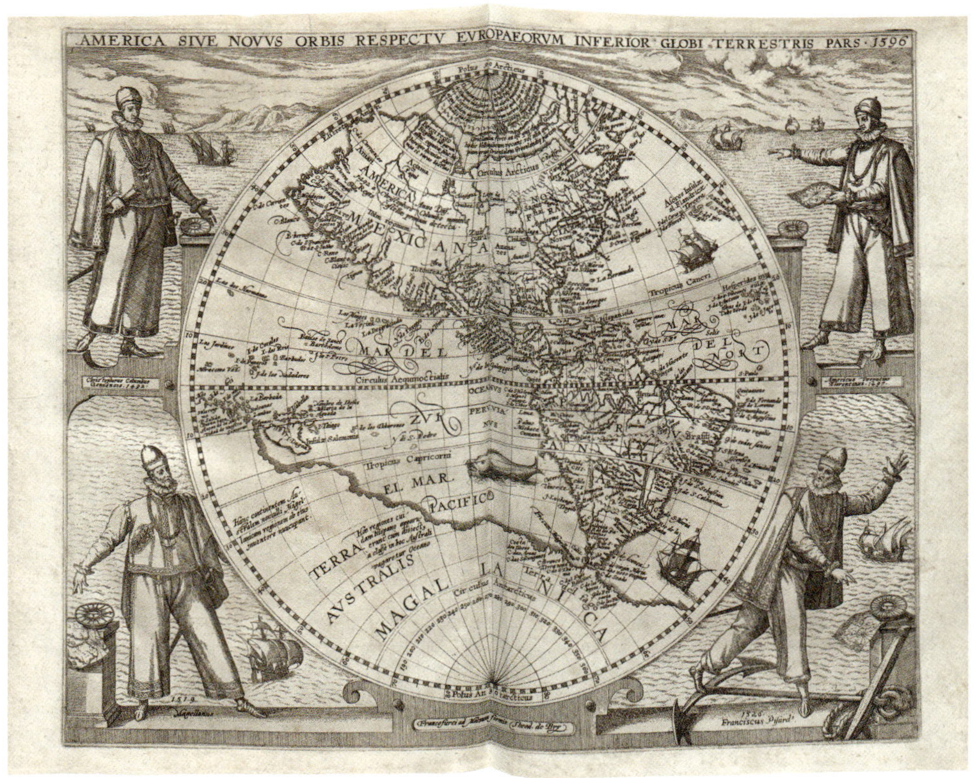

Hakluyt's disappointment, De Bry and his sons continued their project but without issuing English and French translations. As a result, the relationship between De Bry and his English patrons (or the partners he worked with) quickly soured.

Theodore's immediate inspiration was the leading Frankfurt bookseller Sigismund Feyerabend (p. 16, right). In one of the last works he published (he died in April 1590, three weeks after De Bry's first *America* volume had appeared), the experienced Feyerabend had prepared possible customers for the upcoming collection of voyages: "Although many books and histories have appeared in recent years about such countries, their situation, their wealth and poverty, their strange customs, plants and animals," Feyerabend wrote in the preface to a book he published on China, "they have only been printed in foreign languages such as Spanish and Italian. Such books are written especially on the Indies, New Spain, Peru, America and Brazil". These regions were exactly the ones that would feature in the first six volumes of the De Bry collection which were probably already on the drawing-board by the time Feyerabend wrote these words. Feyerabend must have recognised the potential of the De Brys as booksellers, even though Theodore and his sons had little previous experience in the book market. Their skills as engravers, and their incorporation of copper-plate engravings in printed books for the German market, boded well. As a token of his gratitude, De Bry included Feyerabend's name on the title-pages of the first three volumes of the *America* series. Until

World map depicting Terra Australis
From: *America*, appendix to vol. IX

his own death eight years later, Theodore continued with the publishing methods of his predecessor, producing a blend of richly illustrated prestigious volumes of the collection of voyages alongside small, relatively cheap, multilingual emblem books aimed at a lower segment of the market.

Tensions within the De Bry family enterprise

The collection of voyages was the flagship publication of the family firm. All 25 volumes carried on their title-page the names of one or more members of the De Bry family. It was they who copied or devised the illustrations, they who requested privileges from the authorities as was required for the publication of their books, and it was they who sold copies of the books in their bookshop. Although they published many other titles, as can be seen from the single-sheet catalogue for the firm that was set up as a placard in the window of their bookshop, the most prominent place in the display was invariably reserved for the collection of voyages. No internal records of the De Bry firm have survived, but based on acquisitions registered in the account books of colleagues in the book world around 1600, about 60 percent of the De Brys' revenues was generated by the sale of volumes from the collection of voyages. In 1603, when the bookshop moved to the Zeil, one of the main shopping streets in Frankfurt, they named it "Zum Indianischen König" (At the Indian King's), an allusion to the subject matter of the travellers' tales with which their names were associated. In 1615, when Johan Theodore de Bry engraved a self-portrait, he proudly depicted himself beside two large stacks of paper, recognisable by their title-pages as copies of the *America* and *India Orientalis* series (p. 16, left).

Behind the veil of unity, however, as displayed on the collection's title-pages, there was increasing animosity between Theodore and his two sons. Weakened by gout and old age, Theodore had been assisted by his sons in producing the collection from the moment the family moved to Frankfurt. The engraving of Adam and Eve at the start of the first volume, devised by the Flemish artist Jodocus van Winghe and transferred to copper by Theodore De Bry, was proudly signed "Theodore de Bry fe[cit]" in the first edition of 1590. When the second German edition of the same volume appeared in 1600, however, two years after his father's death, Johan Theodore had appropriated the engraving by adding (whether out of bitterness or pedantry) "Jo." to the signature, so that it now read "Jo. Theodore de Bry fe[cit]". Had he made the engraving in the first place, but not received the credit he deserved? Johan Theodore was unquestionably the most talented artist of the family, and unlike his father, he had started making copper engravings at an early age. He was more skilful with the burin than his younger brother, moreover, and this led to a sharp division of responsibilities between the two. Johan Theodore would make the illustrations and the books, while Johan Israel – until his death in 1609 – took care of financial and bureaucratic matters, requesting privileges, taking rivals to court when they had breached these privileges, and dealing with censorship applications. Even so, both their names appeared on the title-pages as equals.

One of the applications for publication in the 1590s reveals another possible reason for the rift between father and sons. In 1595, Johan Israel asked the Frankfurt city council for permission to publish a book entitled *Opera misericordia ad corpus penitentia*, written by the Jesuit Julius Roscius. The (Lutheran) council in Frankfurt rejected the request, and when Johan Israel applied for permission again, the authorities rejected it a second time on the grounds that they considered it to be 'papist' literature. For Theodore de Bry, who had lived through years that were characterised by considerable religious turmoil, the projected publication of a work by a Jesuit author may have been too much for him to accept. One month later, he complained in a letter about the behaviour of his sons: "I do not receive any assistance from my two sons," he wrote in disgust to a colleague in Leiden, "their ingratitude altogether outweighs their support". The failed application for

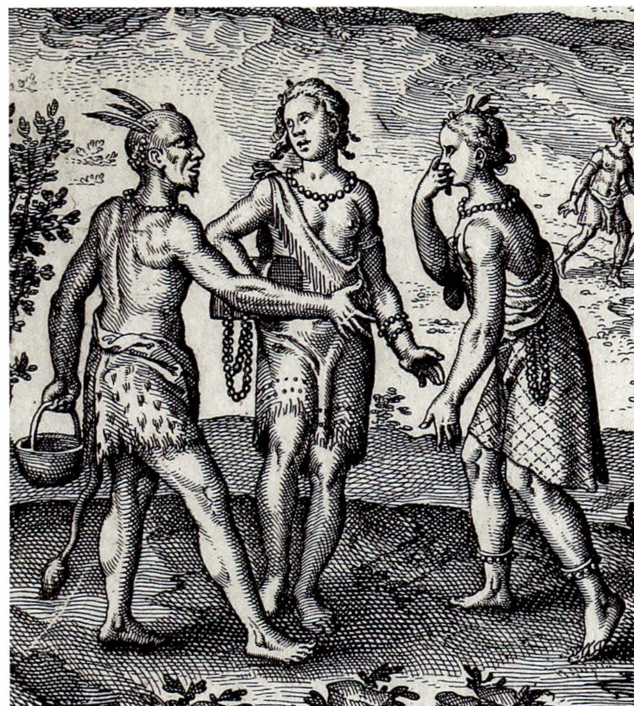
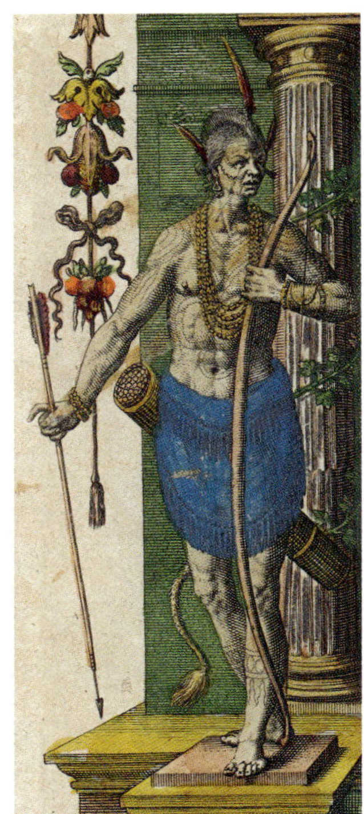

permission to publish proved to be a watershed moment in the history of the family firm, and later that same year, the first books with the imprint of the two brothers appeared, without any mention being made of their father. In their own branch of the family firm the brothers proceeded to publish the Jesuit work under their own names alone – albeit in Montbéliard, not in Frankfurt. From now on, the brothers used a different strategy in order to obtain permission for the books they wanted to produce, and in their routine employment of translators they henceforth made sure that one of them was the Lutheran schoolmaster Gotthard Artus, who also served as the censor on behalf of the Frankfurt authorities, a convenient combination of roles. In the course of the next two decades, Artus would thus typically approve of the publications he had himself translated.

The disharmony within the family firm also had implications for the collection of voyages. In 1597, the De Bry brothers published the first volume of the *India Orientalis* series and again this only carried their names – and not that of their ailing father – on the title-page. For the continuation of the extremely successful and lucrative *America* series, which by now extended to seven volumes, the brothers maintained their working arrangement with their stepmother, who as Theodore's second wife was entitled to part of his inheritance. In consequence, volumes VIII (1599) and IX (1601/02) were published with the imprint of the widow and sons of Theodore de

Rear-view of a Native American, showing a tail (detail)
From: *America*, Frankfurt, 1618, vol. X, part 2, plate 1. Providence, Brown University, John Carter Brown Library

Native American depicted with a tail (detail)
From: *America*, vol. I, frontispiece

Bry. But the two brothers appear to have made no effort to select new accounts for the continuation of the *America* series, which in part explains its premature conclusion in 1602. By the time Johan Theodore returned to the *America* series to publish volume X in 1618, both his brother and – crucially – his stepmother had died, which meant that he alone would own the rights to the entire collection as the only surviving heir to his father's artistic and commercial legacy. Geopolitical developments, on the other hand, worked in the brothers' favour, since in the late 1590s most of the new travel accounts which appeared were published in Amsterdam, and presented the narratives of Dutch navigators sailing to the East Indies; the De Brys gratefully extended their own *India Orientalis* series, which they published without the involvement of their father's widow.

Practical obstacles to publication

It is probably fair to conclude that from the very start, Johan Theodore de Bry played a leading role in the production of the collection of voyages. For a project of this size, however, many different skills were required. Once a travel account had been selected for incorporation – a process that was likely determined by the availability of newly published accounts more than anything else – it took the De Brys around 12 months to produce their own edition. First, the text needed to be translated, from Dutch, English, French, Spanish, Portuguese or Italian into German and Latin. Initially the De Brys turned to a small circle of humanists with whom they were on friendly terms to find their translators, probably in order to give their emerging collection some status among a learned, scholarly audience. The botanist Carolus Clusius (Charles de l'Escluse), a big name in the Republic of Letters, translated some of the early *America* volumes into Latin, and readers from as far away as Spain then came to know the collection in relation to the reference to C. C. A. (Carolus Clusius Atrebatensis, i.e., Charles de l'Escluse from Arras) on the first volume's title-page, and thus referred to the book in letters to Clusius as "your work". Clusius was living in Frankfurt at the time, and continued to assist with editorial tasks for the De Brys after he took up a professorship in Leiden in 1593. However, the De Brys preferred to work with local translators, in order to keep a close eye on how matters proceeded. By the late 1590s they had settled for the aforementioned Gotthard Artus, who translated the volumes not only into Latin, but also German. Their collaboration proved to be a lasting one.

The De Brys themselves did not own a printing press, and so had to hire printers to produce the volumes for them. Here there was less continuity, whether because some of the printers died after having worked on a few of the volumes, or because others were perhaps too busy with other jobs to be available for what must have been the complex task of combining printed texts, for which they required a normal press, with copper engravings, which required an intaglio press. Not all printers were equipped to deal with such work, and some of the volumes show the traces of neglect on the printers' part – something for which Theodore de Bry explicitly apologised to readers in the preface to one of the early volumes. In the end the De Brys settled for regular working arrangements with Johann Wechel (in the early 1590s, an associate of Sigismund Feyerabend), Matthias Becker and Wolfgang Richter, who lived next door to their bookshop on the Zeil. Sometimes the name of the printer is not mentioned at all.

Even though the De Brys, certainly Theodore and Johan Theodore, were capable of engraving the images, they occasionally hired others to do engraving work for them. It is difficult to trace who transferred which illustrations to copper, as generally the engravings were not signed, probably as a tacit rule in the way the family firm was run. The first volume though, as in so many ways, provides an exception. The designs for these engravings were made by Jodocus van Winghe, with the same task probably being fulfilled by Johan Theodore for most of the later volumes. Theodore de Bry signed his own work in transferring the designs to copper, using the monogram T. B., while some of the other engravings were done by the Netherlandish artist Gijsbert van Veen. As well as indicating a certain inexperience in making a book on the part of the De Brys, these signatures probably also point to the haste involved (and thus the many hands that were required) in producing volume I. Every volume had to be finished in time for the Frankfurt book fair, which was held twice a year (during Lent and in September), and where new volumes would be certain to attract the interest of fellow booksellers from all corners of Europe. As time went on, the De Brys improved in making sure they would meet the deadlines, and no further signatures are found on the engravings other than those by Georg Keller, a long-term employee of the firm who appears to have specialised in bird's-eye views and was (occasionally?) allowed to add his monogram G. K. Apprentices in the De Bry workshop probably contributed to the collection's engravings as well, and one signature that was added for later work suggests that the great Adam Elsheimer designed the title-page of *America* IV (which in turn would explain the subsequent interest of the painter Rubens for exactly this design – he purchased a copy of the collection in 1613). In the 1610s, as Johan Theodore was growing older, his talented son-in-law Matthaeus Merian assisted him or even took on some of the engravings himself.

One final (and very specific) task was for someone to write captions for the copper engravings, which were typically included as a separate section at the end of each volume. This was a part of the work to which the De Brys attached considerable importance. They initially employed Clusius (de l'Escluse) to write the captions for them (in Latin), which partly explains the prominent mention of his name on the title-pages of some of the early *America* volumes. Artus too wrote captions as part of his translating work for some of the later volumes, but in the 1590s in particular, the De Brys tried to attract big names from the Republic of Letters to their collection – as well as some of the other publications they produced. A letter from Carolus Clusius to the French author Jean-Jacques Boissard mentions that the De Brys had approached the famous humanist Justus Lipsius to write short commentaries to a work by (the not so famous) Boissard in order to enhance the publication's appeal. Lipsius, somewhat bemused, declined, while Boissard lamented that he was at the mercy of a publishing family whose only interest was in making money – something with which Clusius agreed. The authors of the travel accounts that were included in the collection of voyages played no role whatsoever in the production of the collection. Many of them in fact had already died by the time the De Brys produced their versions, while others had published their original accounts with other publishers in Amsterdam, Paris or Milan – editions the De Brys duly purchased, translated and adapted without the authors even knowing it.

John White, **A tomb for their Weroans, or chief lords**, *c.* 1587
Watercolour drawing, 29.5 x 20 cm (11⅝ x 7⅞ in.). London, The British Museum

The Tombe of their Cherounes or cheife personages, their flesh clene taken of from the bones saue the skynn and heare of theire heads wch flesh is dried and enfolded in matts laide at theire feete. their bones also being made dry ar couered wth deare skynns not alteringe their forme or proportion. With theire Kywash, which is an Image of woode keeping the deade.

9

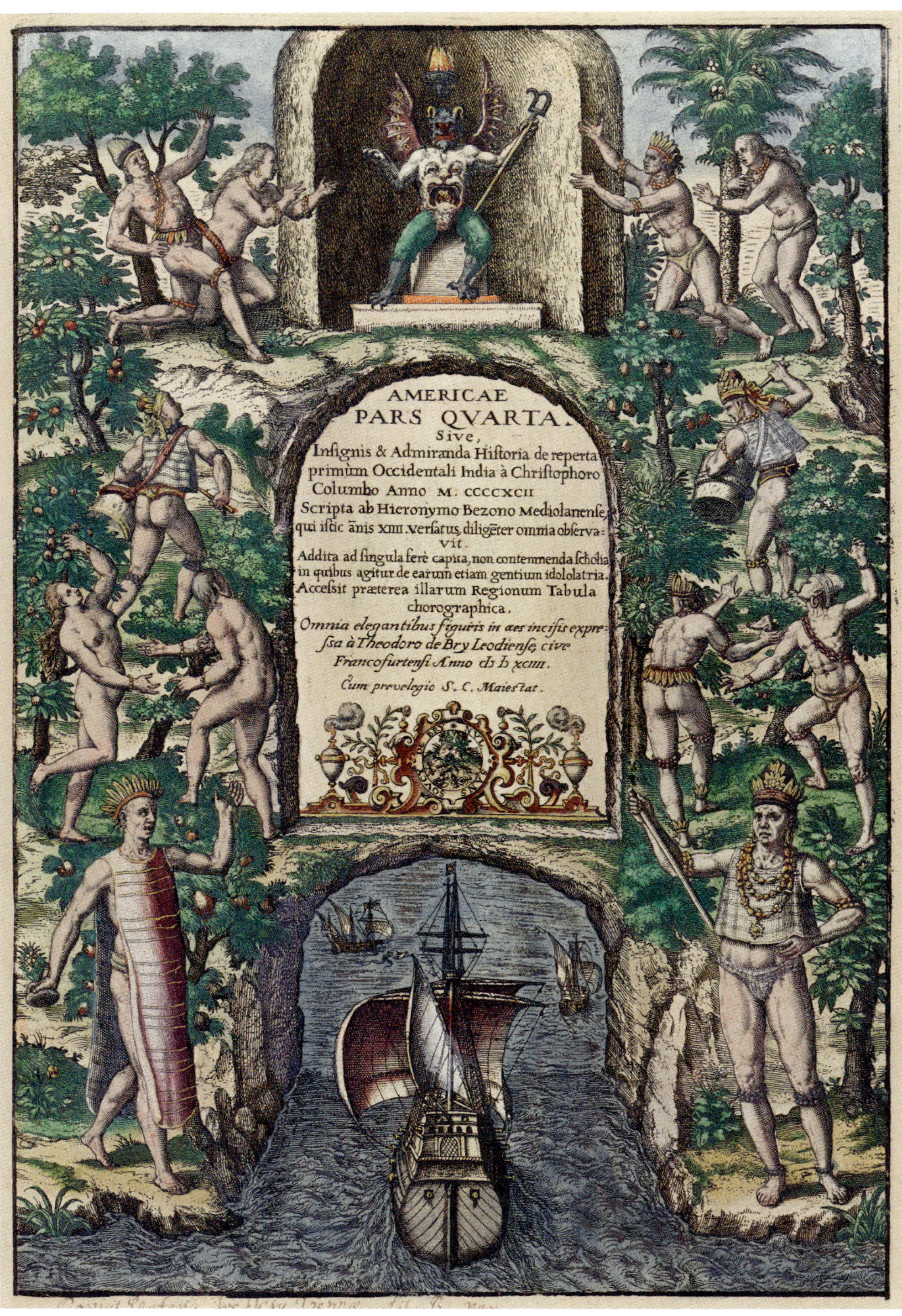
AMERICAE
PARS QVARTA.
Sive,
Insignis & Admiranda Historia de reperta
primùm Occidentali India à Christophoro
Columbo Anno M. CCCCXCII
Scripta ab Hieronymo Bezono Mediolanense,
qui istic ãnis XIIII. versatus, diligẽter omnia observa-
vit.
Addita ad singula ferè capita, non contemnenda scholia
in quibus agitur de earum etiam gentium idololatria.
Accessit præterea illarum Regionum Tabula
chorographica.
Omnia elegantibus figuris in æs incisis expre-
ssa à Theodoro de Bry Leodiense, cive
Francofurtensi Anno ciↃ IↃ XCIIII.
Cum previlegio S. C. Maiestat.

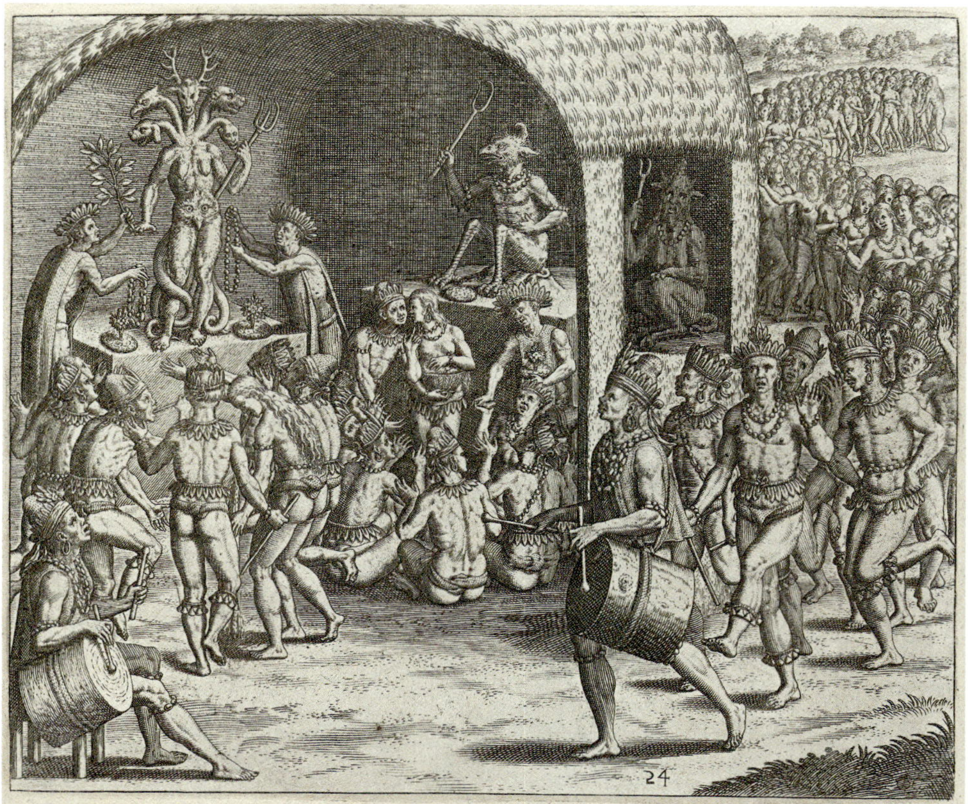

'Visual manipulation': Refining an editorial and commercial strategy

The processes of translation, modification and manipulation were all closely intertwined, and bring us to the heart of the editorial strategy behind the collection of voyages. Few of their contemporaries will have noticed the changes made in the De Bry workshop, because in order to detect them what is required is to compare the De Bry editions with the original accounts (often in a different language), or to compare the German and Latin translations of the De Bry editions, which would have been almost certainly too expensive for even a well-to-do customer. I have not encountered a single 17th-century reader or institution in possession of complete sets of both translations, and very few who owned the De Bry collection as well as versions of the works on which they were based. Moreover, some of the adjustments were so subtle that they would not have been detected on first reading, and perhaps not at all. Because the engravings were identical in the German and Latin versions, the impression that the two texts were also identical was widespread, and continued to persuade scholars this was so even into the 21st century.

Frontispiece illustrated with a devil
From: *America*, vol. IV

The veneration of diabolical figures by Native Americans
From: *America*, vol. IV, plate 24

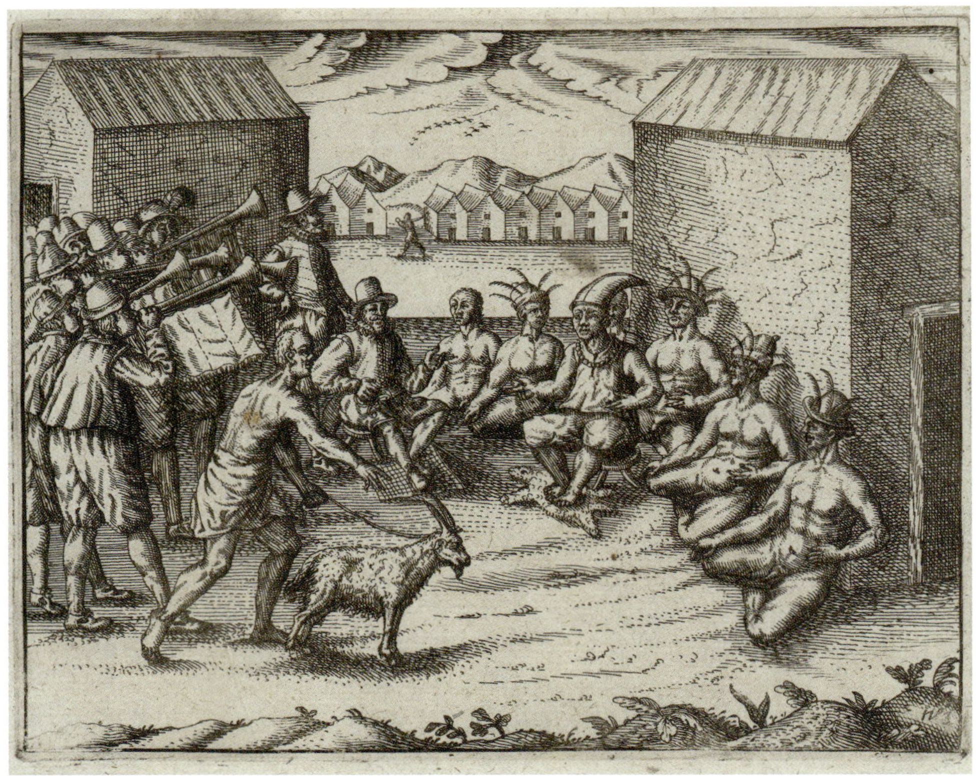

When it comes to their representations of foreign lands, the De Brys employed several means of manipulating them, almost always with the objective of highlighting the discrepancy between civilised (and Christian) travellers from Europe, and the wild, uncultured heathens from Africa, Asia and America. Their most obvious method was to invent or 'improve' the illustrations. What exactly would be done in such cases depended on what images were available in the original accounts. For volumes I and II, with the splendid watercolours of John White and Jacques Le Moyne at their disposal (as well as Richard Hakluyt looking over their shoulders), they changed very little. One image they did add to volume I, and which was lifted and exaggerated in size from a drawing by White (p. 23), was that of the pagan idol "Kiwasa", an image they labelled as "terrifying" in the caption that accompanied it. Within a sequence of illustrations that emphasised the appeal of Virginia, as Hakluyt and White would have envisaged it, the image of the pagan idol served as a stark reminder that although the land may have been fertile, the presence of those viewed as indigenous heathens was something would-be colonists would have to consider before signing up. In another significant adjustment, the De Brys then decided to lift this most alien and exotic of images from the inside of the volume and place it on the title-page, where it was given additional emphasis by being positioned at the top of the composition, and by being worshipped by two "Virginians" (one of them the man referred to as a "sorcerer" in the text of the volume) – a composition that was wholly devised in Frankfurt. The title-pages were important, because they served as advertisements, announcing to prospective readers what stories they could expect to find inside once they had purchased the volume. In this way a set of texts and images

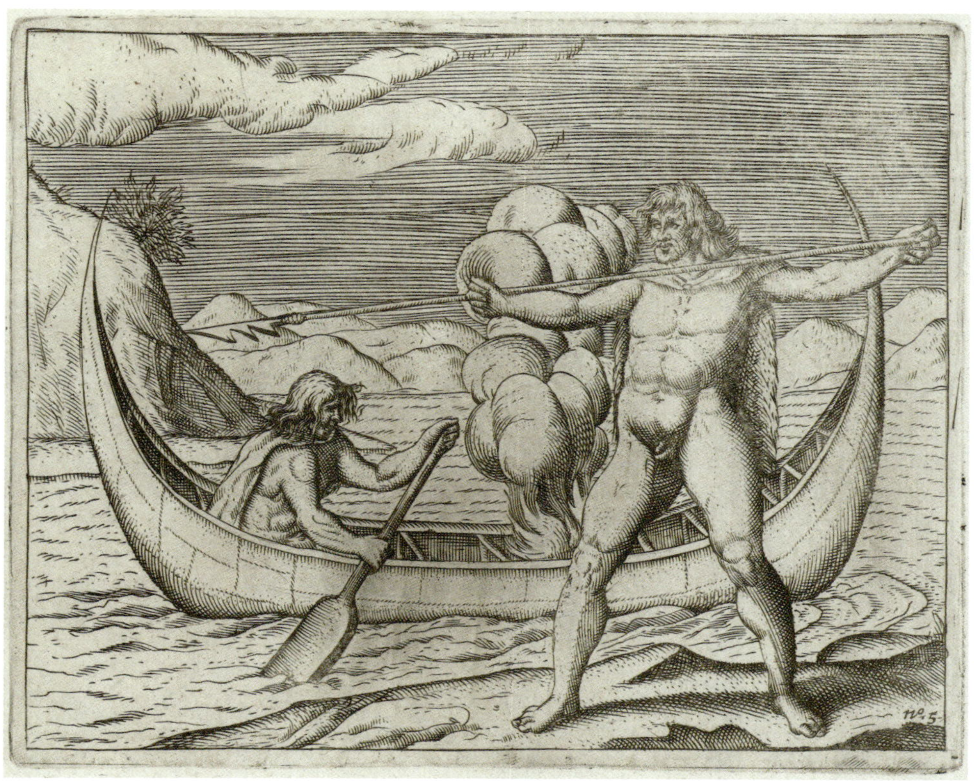

that paid next to no attention to religion was now fronted by a title-page that emphasised the New World's inherent 'otherness'.

Beneath the pagan idol and its two worshippers the De Brys depicted a 'typical' man and woman of the region, in a manner that resembled 16th-century costume books in which men and women from the same (European) city or province were depicted side by side. Both these individuals were also on show inside the book, and closely resembled the original images by White – although the fact that they were naked may have led to raised eyebrows or outright disgust in 1600. The depiction of the man is particularly interesting. Based on the image that appeared on the title-page, customers in the De Bry bookshop could have been forgiven for thinking that the man had a tail (p. 20, right). Although in certain respects this would have been understood as sensational information, it also touched upon mythical stories that had been told since the days of Columbus, about native people on the island of Cuba who also had tails. Only when the rest of the book was examined (and had thus been bought) would the reader have been able to see that the tail belonged to an animal, whose skin was bound around the man's waist so that he could put the arrows he

A visit to an African king. Engraving, 13.8 x 18 cm (5⅜ x 7⅛ in.)
From: Barent Jansz, *Wijdtloopigh Verhael*, 2nd ed., Amsterdam, 1617. Amsterdam, Rijksmuseum

The giants of Tierra del Fuego. Engraving, 14.5 x 18.5 cm (5¾ x 7¼ in.)
From: Barent Jansz, *Wijdtloopigh Verhael*, 2nd ed., Amsterdam, 1617. Amsterdam, Rijksmuseum

XVIII.

QVOMODO HOLLANDI REGVLVM QVENDAM LITTORALIS tractus Guineæ inuiserint.

IV.

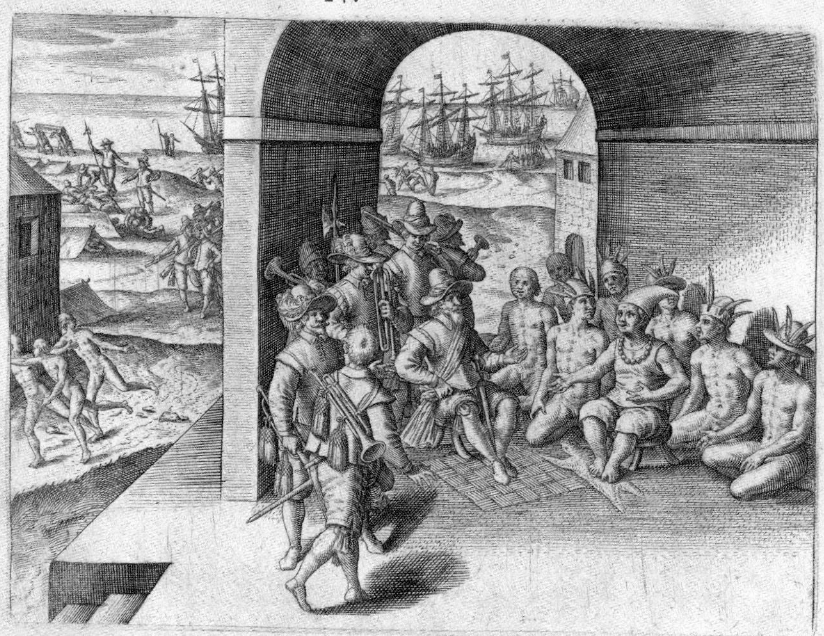

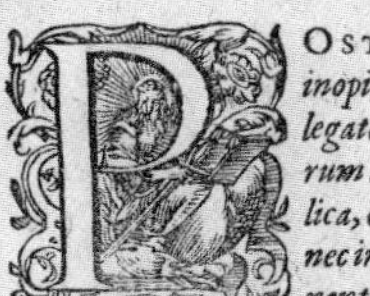POSTQVAM *Hollandi, cum maxima vndæ potabilis, rerumq́ necessariarum aliarum inopia cōflictati, multis suorum infirmatis & decumbentibus littus Guineæ attigissent, legatos suos cum interprete, ad loci eius Regulum amandarunt. Rex itaque de Hollandorum appulsu edoctus, habitu suo superbissimo ad illos prodiit. Induerat enim se palla Gallica, & caligis ex purpureo panno sartis, & tæniis ex auro spurio constratis, cæteroquin nec indusio, nec tibialibus, nec calceis amicitus. Caput illius longa, eaque in apicem desinente vitta, ex panno croceo, aut rubro cæruleoq́ texta, opertum erat. Hoc habitu ante Hollandos pressa humilique sella desidebat, pedibus eius ouina pelle substratis. Post ipsum omnes eius nobiles, in totum nudi consederant. Hollandico itaque præfecto ad Regulum ingresso, rex illum in consimili sella storea instrata considere iussit. Quo facto, quod opus erat, per interpretem tractabatur. Intereà vero Almirans omnes infirmos ex nauibus in terram exponi, ibidemq́ probè curari iusserat, dum plerique rursus conualescerent. Illic mortuos, terræ mandabant. Isti homines, ad Hollandorum quidem aspectum primum valdè agrestes & formidolosi erant. Posteà autem assuescentes magis, ita mitescebant, vt cum illis de omnibus probè tractari posset.*

ee 3

XXII.

HOLLANDI IN FRETO MAGELLANICO IVXTA INSULAM QUANDAM GRANDES & PORTENTOSOS HOMINES INUENIUNT.

VIII.

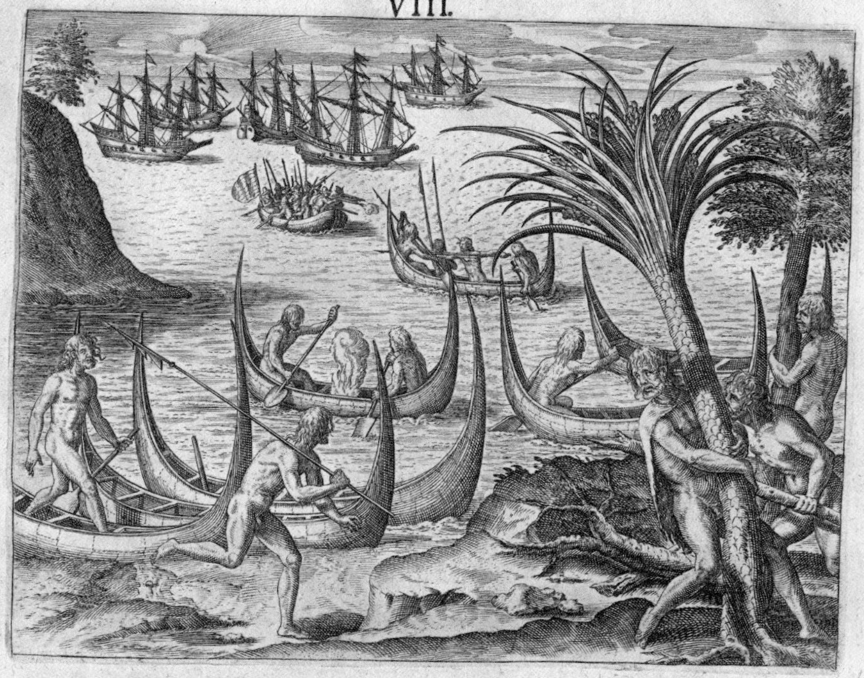

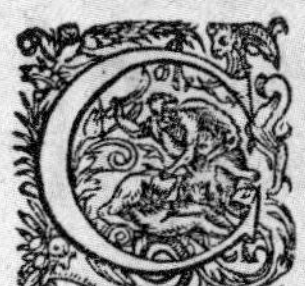

CVM aliquando Hollandi in freto Magellanico vna aut altera ſcapha verſus inſulam quandam remos agerent, inſperato ipſis ſeptem lintres, vaſtis horrendisq́ & illis nudis hominibus pleni occurrerunt, quorum longitudo decem vel vndecim pedum erat. Cutis horum ſubfuſca viſebatur: ipſi verò toti nudi capillos è capite longos promiſſosq́ fundebant. Hi ad Hollandos inuadendos, cum ſeſe auidè inſtruerent, animo eorum percepto, Hollandi in eos Muſquettis ſtrenuè defulminarunt, & ex omni numero tres derepentè morti dederunt. Quod videntes Barbari, remis incitatis, feſtinò in terram ſe receperunt, euulſisq́ è terra arboribus, contra Hollandos aduenturos ſeſe obuallarunt, cum ſpiculis, tum ſaxis interim minitabundi. Attamen Hollandi, cum perſequi hos Gigantes & fruſtraneum & nimis periculoſum putarent, eos miſſos fecerunt. Barbari autem, cum tempore quodam tres ex Hollandis fortuitò comprehendiſſent, inuſitata & miſerabili laniena eos commactarunt. Hæc figura quoque ſcapharum, quas illi vſurpant, formam exprimit.

ff 3

used for hunting there. The ploy of depicting what looked like a man with a tail on the title-page can be seen to have been entirely deliberate, however, by comparing volume X of the *America* series, where Johan Theodore de Bry, in designing a new image of a "Virginian" man to accompany the travel account of John Smith, depicted him too with a tail – this time clear for everyone to see because the man's back was turned towards the viewer (p. 20, left). The bundle of arrows, which had entitled the De Brys to 'play' with the tail in the first place, had now completely disappeared.

The techniques of visual manipulation became blunter still in volume III of the *America* series, for which the De Brys used the (already quite popular) accounts of Brazil by the German soldier Hans Staden and the Huguenot minister Jean de Léry. Both these original reports contained a few illustrations, but these were very crude woodcuts that allowed little opportunity for detail. Exploiting all the options offered by copper engraving, the De Brys greatly extended the number of images to 30 to provide an extremely graphic account of cannibalism in Portuguese *America*. These images, more than any others from the De Bry firm, must have resonated in Europe, because they were in turn copied and adapted time and again so as to publicise and confirm the stories of man-eaters in Brazil. The order of the images in the part of each volume where the copper engravings appeared could also be controlled in a meaningful way. The Italian traveller Girolamo Benzoni's account, used by the De Brys for *America* IV, V and VI, was essentially a condemnation of Spanish cruelties in the New World – something that was very familiar to many (Protestant) Europeans who had also suffered from 'tyranny' in the name of the Spanish rulers. Here too the De Brys significantly extended the repertoire of images found in the original publications they used, but also made a point of ending the series of engravings in volume IV with a damning representation of religious practices – this time Native Americans wearing feathers and venerating a five-headed idol and two devilish creatures in a temple built for their worship (p. 25). Once again it was the uncivilised Indians – not the Spaniards who were the protagonists of Benzoni's text – who populated the volume's title-page. So too, pride of place was given at the top of the composition to a diabolical creature that must have made most European readers shiver (p. 24).

Volume IX shows two completely different sides of the same method of visual manipulation. This volume was based on two accounts, the first written by the Spanish Jesuit José de Acosta (mainly on Mexico), the second by the Dutch ship's surgeon Barent Jansz, on Tierra del Fuego and the Strait of Magellan. Acosta's account, the well-known *Historia natural y moral de Las Indias* (1590), contained no illustrations, which meant that the De Brys had to invent the images in Frankfurt. The account by Barent Jansz, like so many Dutch journals, did include images, and although in this particular case they were woodcuts, Dutch journals were generally attractive for the De Brys because their images had been made by artists who were extremely skilful – thus reducing the workload in the Frankfurt workshop. The original images on this occasion, however, did not convey the message of otherness and European dominance as graphically as the De Brys desired. Their modification of the original image of the (mythical) Patagonian giant is very clear-cut.

Page 28
How the Dutch visited the coast of Guinea
From: *America*, vol. IX, plate 18

Page 29
The Dutch overwhelm a settlement of giants
From: *America*, vol. IX, plate 22

Peter Paul Rubens, **Triumphal Arch of the 'Mint'**, 1635
Etching, 48 x 32 cm (18⅞ x 12⅝ in.). Amsterdam, Rijksmuseum

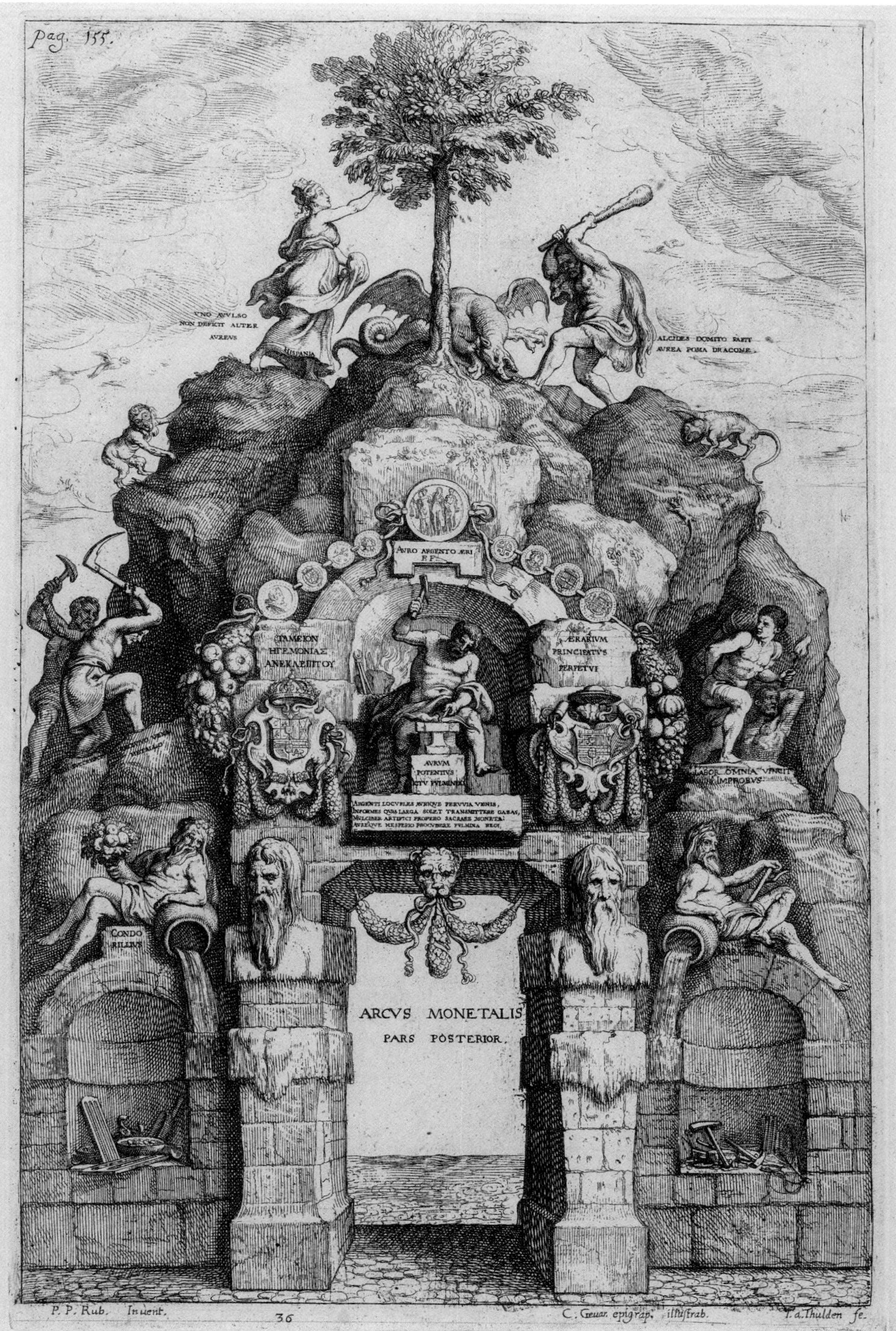

Pag. 155.
VNO AVVLSO
NON DEFICIT ALTER
AVREVS
HISPANIA
ALCIDES DOMITO RAPIT
AVREA POMA DRACONE.
AVRO ARGENTO AERI
F.F.
ΤΑΜΕΙΟΝ
ΗΓΕΜΟΝΙΑΣ
ΑΝΕΚΛΕΙΠΤΟΥ
AERARIVM
PRINCIPATVS
PERPETVI
AVRVM
POTENTIVS
ICTV FVLMINIS
LABOR OMNIA VINCIT
IMPROBVS
ARGENTI LOCVPLES AVRIQVE PERVVIA VENIS,
INFORMES QVAS LARGA SOLET TRANSMITTERE GAZAS,
MVLCIBER ARTIFICI PROPERO SACRARE MONETA:
AVREAQVE HESPERIO PROCVDERE FVLMINA REGI,
CONDO
RILLVS
ARCVS MONETALIS
PARS POSTERIOR.
P. P. Rub. Inuent.
36
C. Geuar. epigrap. illustrab.
T. a. Thulden fe.

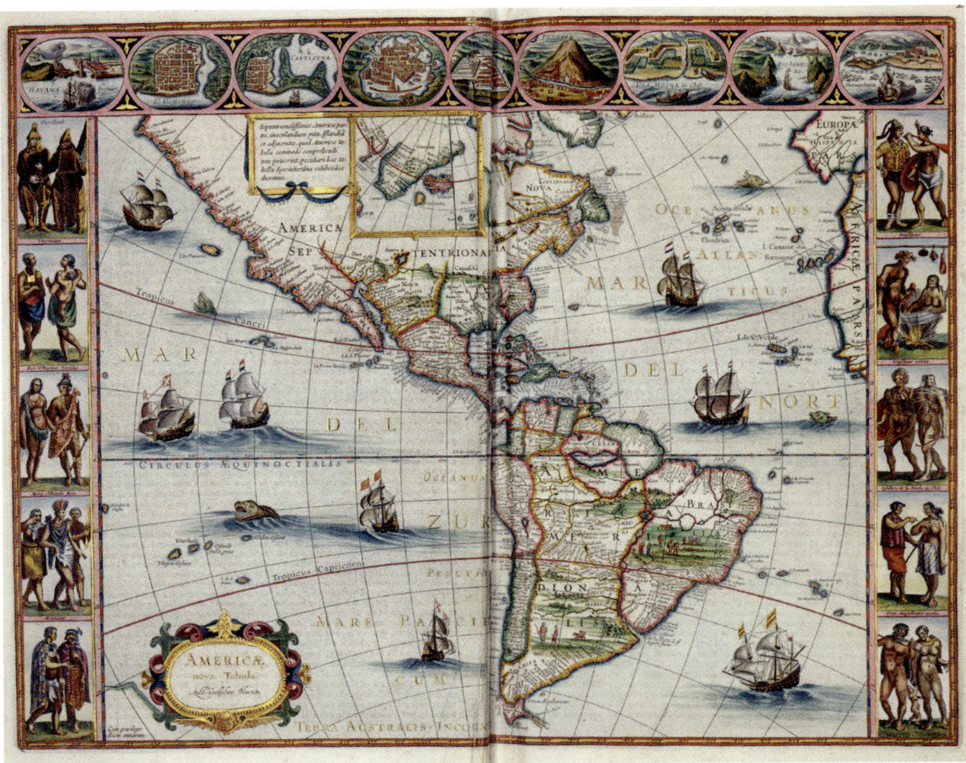

Whereas in Jansz's book the woodcut of the impressive Patagonian might have instilled fear in European hearts (p. 27), the corresponding De Bry image turned the tables on the Patagonians – focusing instead on how fearful (rather than fearsome) the native inhabitants were when faced with European guns and naval prowess (p. 29). The sensational story of Patagonian giants in the original Dutch travel account was thus not stripped of its appeal, but the underlying message being conveyed by the De Brys to their German and Latin readers was entirely the opposite of what Dutch readers had been treated to two years earlier. Volume IX also reveals the indiscriminate way in which the De Brys portrayed the inhabitants of the world across the Atlantic. Different peoples from Acosta's work, who might live thousands of kilometres apart, were depicted side by side in the same engravings by the De Brys. Women in Gabon, western Africa, concocted in the De Bry workshop to accompany Barent Jansz's journal, had identical facial features, hairstyles and clothing to women living in Tierra del Fuego. Through the eyes of the De Bry collection, the non-European world was inhabited by a homogeneous group of uncivilised, uncultured Others.

Most striking, perhaps, is the way in which the texts were adjusted to confirm the image being carefully crafted in the engravings. When Barent Jansz arrived in Gabon, he gave a detailed

Willem Blaeu, **Map of the Americas**, 1617
From: Joan Blaeu, *Atlas Maior*, Amsterdam, 1662–65, vol. XI
Copper engraving, 41 x 55 cm (16⅛ x 21⅝ in.). Vienna, Österreichische Nationalbibliothek

account of the diplomatic encounter between the Dutch captain Sebald de Weert and the native ruler Jansz referred to as the "king" of the region. In Jansz's account, the Dutch captain was solemnly received by the king who was "surrounded by his nobility". The accompanying woodcut showed a circle of men sitting on the ground behind their leader, awaiting the Dutch representative. The De Brys decided, quite literally, to undress the men sitting in the circle, with the result that their genitals were clearly displayed for all European readers to see (p. 28). This small but significant change was confirmed by the textual captions to the adapted image, where both in the German and the Latin two small words were added: "gantz nacket" and "tota nuda", both meaning "totally naked", cannot be traced to any part of the original account, and were simply invented in the Frankfurt workshop to create an all-round negative picture of the West African elite. Furthermore, the second edition of Jansz's work, published subsequently in 1617, would go on to implement this change, demonstrating the influence and reception of the *America* series (p. 26). This type of editorial precision, a sort of representational cosmetic surgery, can be found throughout the collection of voyages. Sometimes the changes were added to the full texts in the course of translation, or else when reworking the translations into captions for the illustrations, while at other times the text remained identical to the original account only to be accompanied by minutely manipulated illustrations.

It is difficult to gauge whether these changes had an effect on contemporary readers, although we may presume they did so if only on a subconscious level. There is strong evidence, however, that the editorial strategy paid off – evidence which can be found in Spain. The Spanish Inquisition, like its counterpart in Rome, systematically vetted foreign books for heterodox or Protestant views. The *Histoire d'un voyage faict en la terre du Brésil*, written by Jean de Léry, was one such account to attract the attention of the inquisitors in Madrid. De Léry's text was extremely critical of Catholics in French Brazil who had wrecked the dream of a Huguenot refuge in the New World. His account, written in the late 1550s, was only published in 1578 (in French), at the nadir of the Wars of Religion in France, and was part of a series of vehemently polemical, anti-Catholic publications. When it was translated into Latin in Geneva by the Calvinist hardliner Urbain Chauveton, it acquired even greater notoriety in Catholic circles since Chauveton added explanations, based on Scripture, that criticised Catholicism. This 1586 Latin edition was (understandably) banned by the Inquisition in Spain, yet was the very edition used by the De Brys for their Latin version of De Léry's account that formed part of *America* III, which spared them the trouble of finding a translator, but which did mean they were in danger of being censured by the Inquisition as well – something they could ill afford for commercial reasons. They therefore meticulously combed the text, deleting the most polemical passages, and did so successfully. The Spanish inquisitors who inspected the De Bry edition explicitly noted that they had used the prohibited edition reworked by Chauveton, but added that in spite of this, the De Bry collection *would* be permitted in Spain if certain minor sentences were crossed out by booksellers and customers. A remarkable (and unintended) endorsement of a careful strategy of modification and manipulation!

The impact and legacy of the *America* series

As a result of the De Brys' efforts, their collection became a truly unique publication. It was different from other collections of voyages which had appeared in the 16th century, most notably the *Navigationi e Viaggi* of the Venetian humanist Giovanni Battista Ramusio which, although largely lacking illustrations, had served as a template for the De Brys. Subsequent collections of voyages, including the famous *Pilgrimes* by Samuel Purchas and the early 18th-century collection of religious customs and ceremonies by Bernard Picart, were all heavily influenced by the De Bry volumes. The

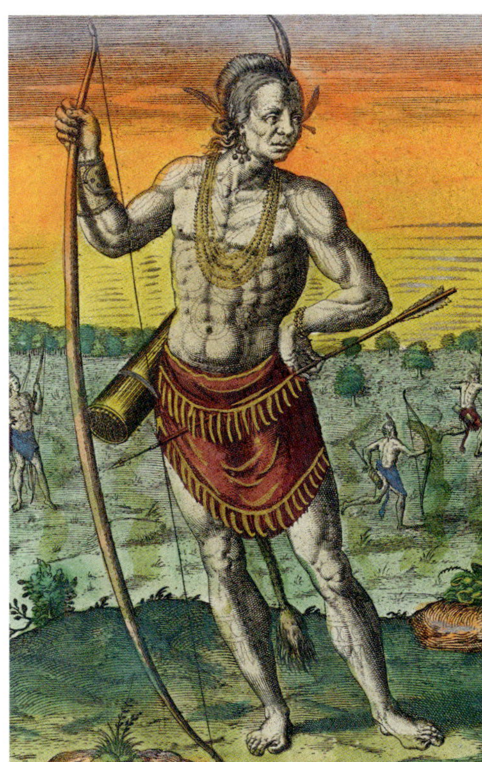

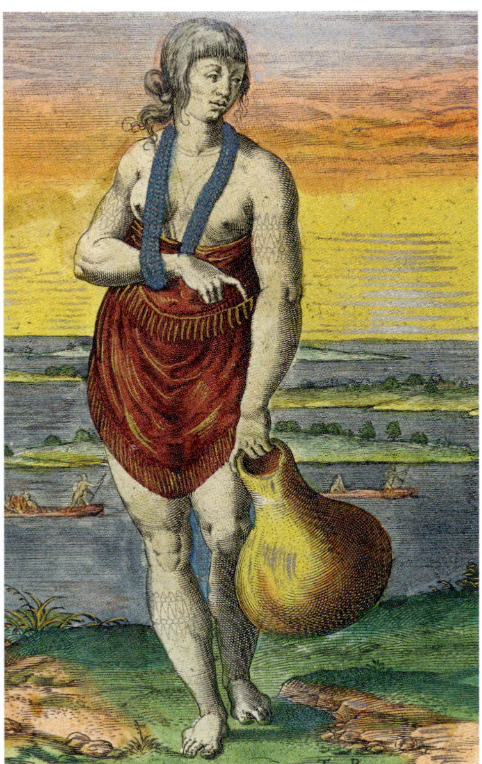

collection that most resembles the De Brys' work, a 26-volume series by the Netherlandish bookseller Levinus Hulsius, has long been considered a rival to the De Bry enterprise, being published in Nuremberg and Frankfurt between 1598 and 1660. On closer examination though, the Hulsius collection shows itself to be essentially a smaller version of the De Bry collection – a paperback to the De Brys' more luxurious hardback volumes. Ever since the first decade of the 17th century, the Hulsius family appear to have been indebted to the De Brys, as their more modest collection began to include the same accounts, and the same illustrations, as its prestigious counterpart. When the De Brys succeeded with an aggressive takeover of the Hulsius collection, this completed their editorial strategy as it addressed the only point of concern that remained, the fact that their own collection, had expanded to such an extent that it was only affordable to the elite.

The influence of their collection's imagery on the iconography of the Americas in the 17th and 18th centuries was profound. Almost every European publication that featured visual material on the New World and which appeared in print before 1750 includes illustrations which are derived, directly or indirectly, from the copper engravings made in Frankfurt around

A great lord of Virginia, equipped with bow and arrow (detail)
From: *America*, vol. I, plate 3

A chief lady of Pomeiooc, carrying a flask (detail)
From: *America*, vol. I, plate 8

1600 – including the work of prominent artists such as Rubens, who crafted a triumphal arch which represented the gold mines at Potosí for the joyous entry of Cardinal-Infante Ferdinand, the new governor of the Southern Netherlands, in Antwerp in 1635 based on one of the *America* series title-pages (p. 31). The ethnographic portraits of Native Americans in the margins of the map of America (p. 32) by the Amsterdam cartographer Willem Blaeu, from the early 17th century, were all directly or indirectly derived from the De Bry designs. Even as far away as India, the *America* series made an impact. A beautifully coloured gouache of a hunter and his wife from the 1620s or 1630s, in the collection of the British Museum and crafted by an artist in the Mughal style, reveals the impact of Theodore de Bry's designs of Virginia transplanted to the world of the Indian Ocean, a stunning example of the transcontinental exchange of knowledge in the early modern era (pp. 34, 37).

For the very top of the market, in Europe, the De Brys could produce extraordinary copies of their collection. Complete editions or single volumes could be printed on parchment rather than paper, or books could be delivered bound in red Moroccan leather, as was done for one of their most reliable patrons, the Calvinist Landgrave Maurice of Hesse-Kassel, although most customers preferred to look after their own binding. The earlier volumes could be printed in a somewhat larger format, although in the same way as the additional translations into English and French, this was probably part of an overly ambitious initial business model. Most tellingly, however, one thing that was not possible was for customers to buy the sections of the volumes containing the illustrations without the accompanying texts. The volumes in the collection were for sale only as complete units, not separated into smaller parts to meet individual customers' taste.

Another thing that the De Brys did not do was to provide coloured versions of their collection of voyages. Close inspection of the coloured copies of the sets which survive in national and university libraries today reveals that there was no template for the colours – no colouring scheme in other words. Part of the reason this may now seem surprising is that today skin colour is perceived by many people as a significant cultural and ethnic denominator – the potential basis for stereotypes *par excellence*. In a collection of voyages that presented often degrading representations of non-Europeans, and which helped to shape 17th-century stereotypes, colouring could easily have been an integral part of the De Brys' editorial strategy. There are no indications, however, that this was the case. No archival references exist relating to the colouring of copies in Frankfurt, no names of colourists are known who associated with the De Brys, there are no surviving copies from the 17th century that are recorded as being coloured, and – perhaps most significantly – no references from bibliophiles before 1800 to 'sought-after' copies in colour. The desire of modern collectors to refer to copies they know or – better still – possess as 'original hand-coloured' can sometimes risk determining (and quite possibly manipulating) the way we look at hand-coloured copies of the De Bry collection today. Such a market-driven interest should not obscure the historical facts, however, even though coloured books were frequently found in 16th- and 17th-century Europe, and atlases and maps – which can make credible claims for having been hand-coloured at the time of production – were closely related to the travel accounts the De Brys used for their collection. Ultimately, the claim that the De Bry volumes were coloured at the time remains unsubstantiated, and this work was certainly not carried out in their workshop as part of a predetermined plan of colouring. Perhaps for the De Brys, in the context of their commercial approach, going to great lengths to produce hand-coloured copies just wasn't worth it. It was the only exclusive 'asset' missing from the books in the eyes of collectors in later generations, and many no doubt decided to have this omission amended on their own account. Yet to do it thoroughly required expertise and, in the majority of cases, still more money. Perhaps as a result of this, I know of no extant copy of the De Bry collection that has been coloured beyond volume VI of the *America* series. In this TASCHEN edition, volumes I to VI are based on the hand-coloured volumes held at the John Hay and the John Carter Brown Libraries at Brown University, Providence, Rhode Island. Volumes VII to IX have been added in their original black-and-white. Together, these nine volumes offer everything that made the De Bry collection so appealing for contemporary and modern readers alike.

Mughal school, 17th century, **A Hunter and his Wife**, *c.* 1620–30
Gouache, 35 x 24 cm (13¾ x 9½ in.). London, The British Museum

Pages 38/39
Epigram of a globe showing the Americas, with vignettes of Christopher Columbus and Amerigo Vespucci
From: *America*, vol. IV

[1] This essay is based on research undertaken for my book on the De Bry collection, *The Representations of the Overseas World in the De Bry Collection of Voyages (1590–1634)* (Leiden: Brill, 2008).

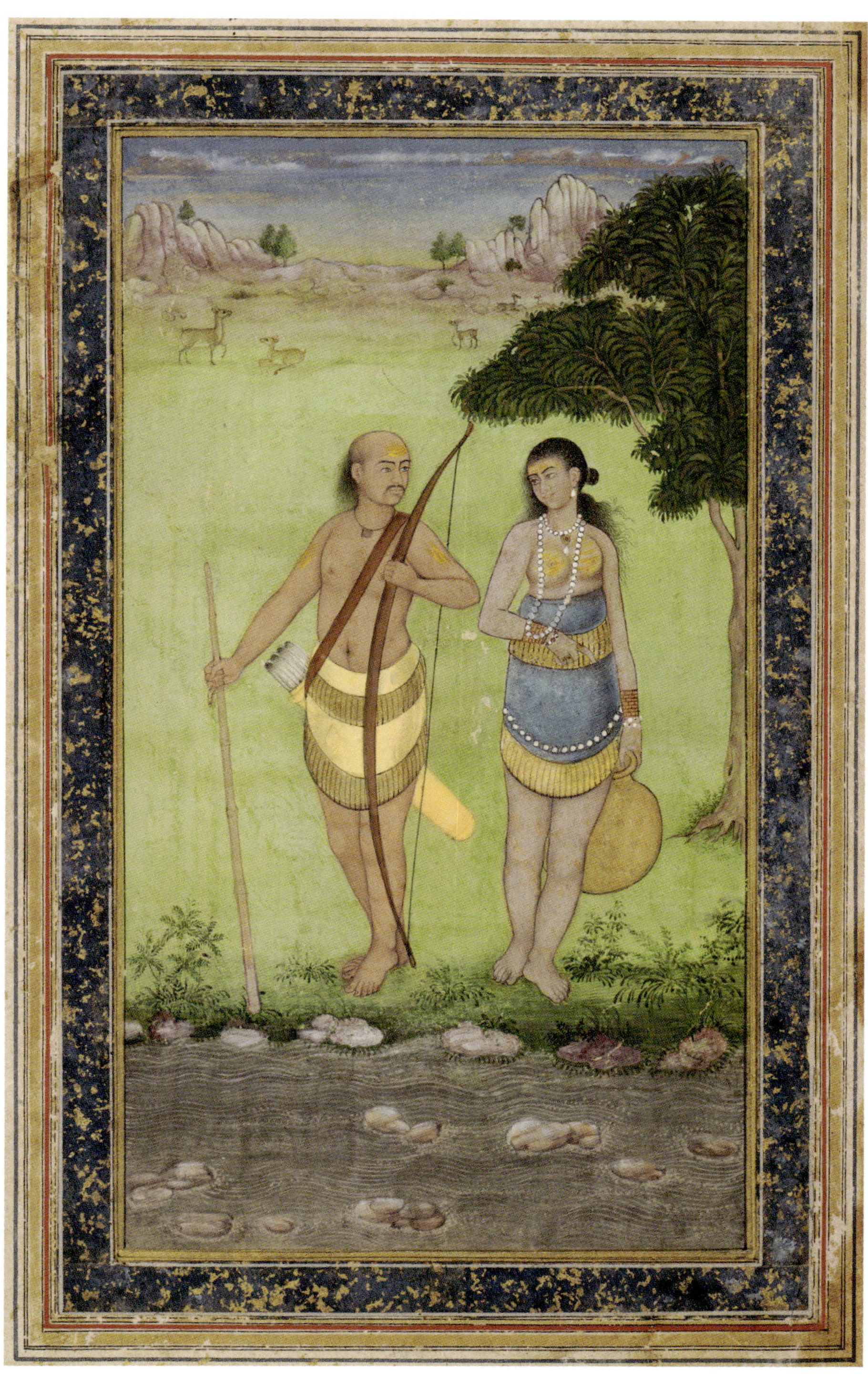

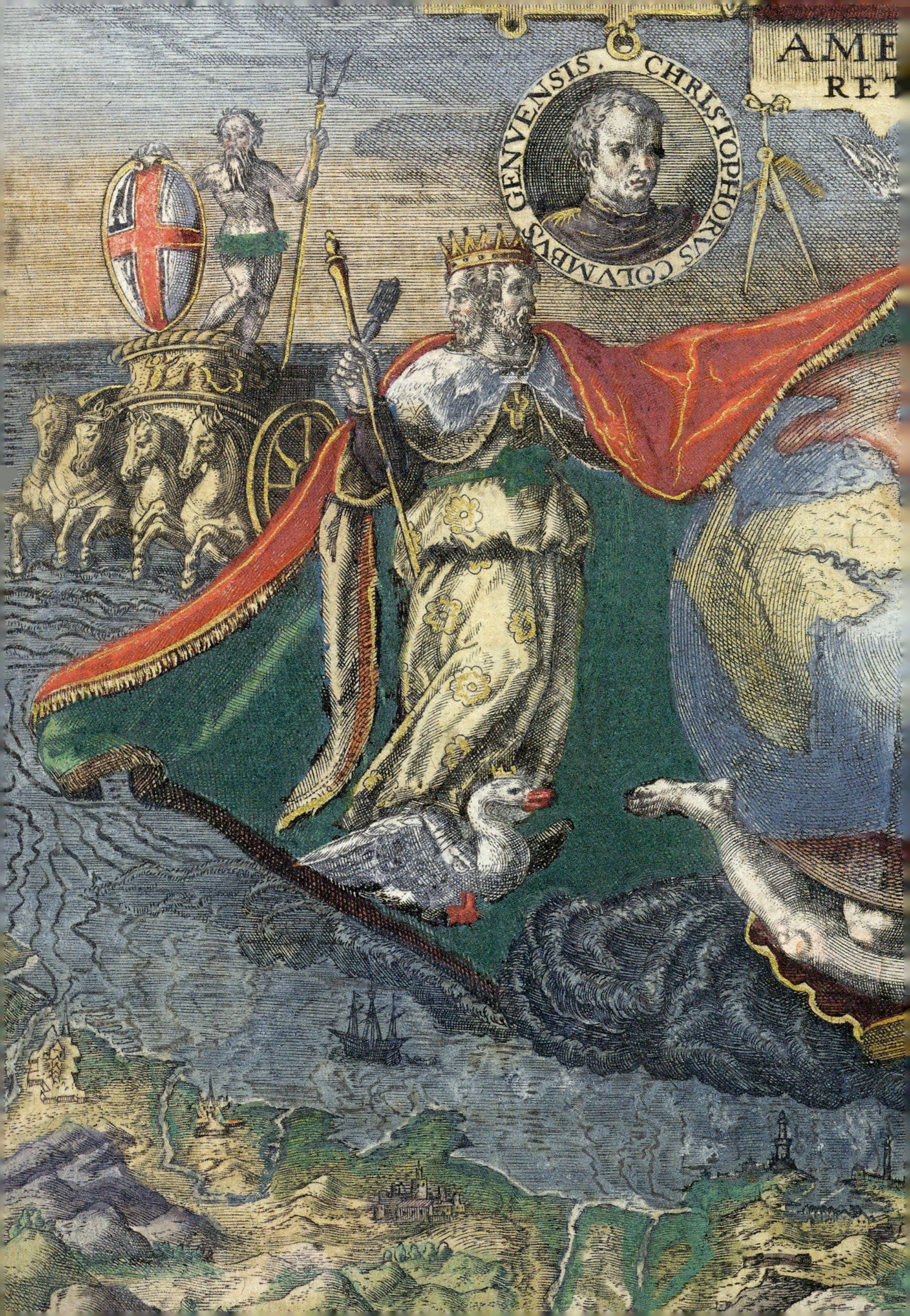
CHRISTOPHORVS COLVMBVS GENVENSIS.

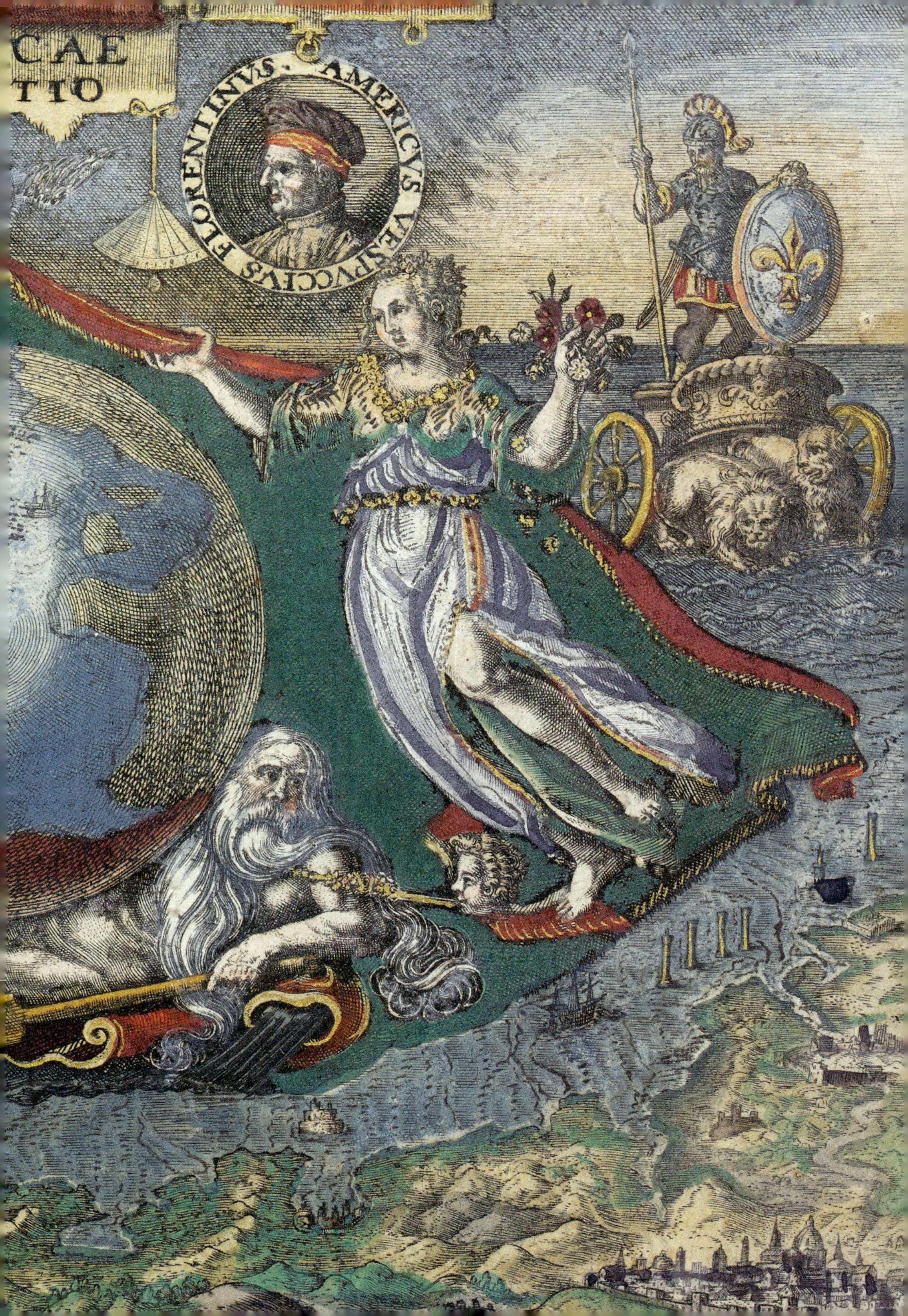
CAE
TIO
AMERICVS VESPVCCIVS FLORENTINVS

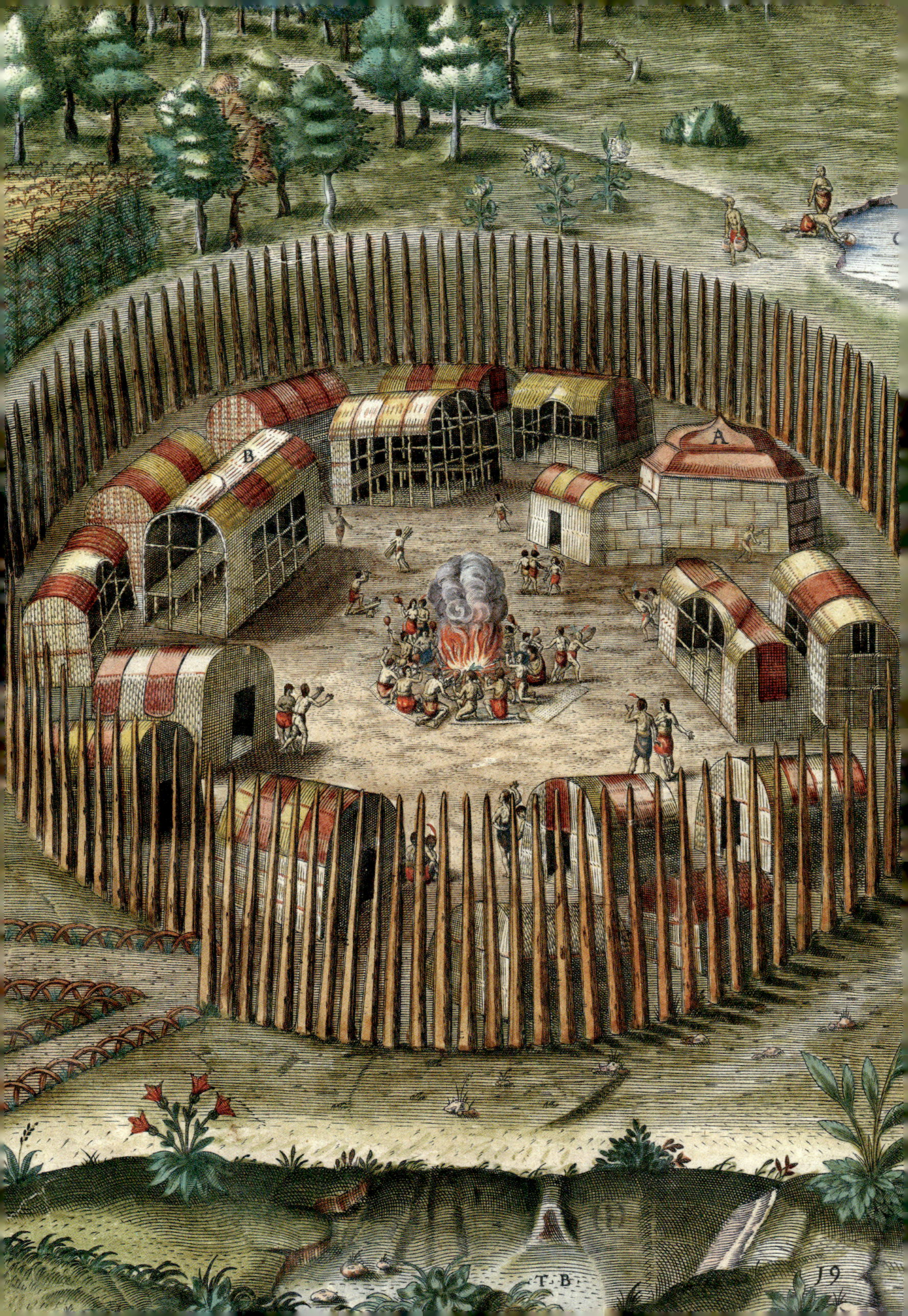
A
B
T B
19

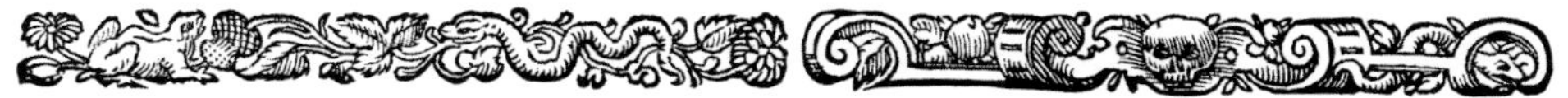

The striking colour variations of De Bry's *Grand Voyages to America*

LARRY E. TISE

When Theodore de Bry published in 1590 the first volume of his ambitious *Grand Voyages to America* (known at the time as *India Occidentalis*), he and his sons also presented Europeans with their first set of colouring books focused on the Americas and Native Americans. His first innovation was to introduce the art of copper-plate engraving to interpret original artistic impressions of the peoples and places of Virginia, Florida, Brazil, Mexico, Peru, the West Indies and other realms of the New World. His second contribution was to place before the eyes of readers panels of illustrative images begging to be further elaborated with colour. This was an era when Christian worshippers could view depictions of the ancient prophets or the Stations of the Cross in the living colours of stained-glass windows. At the same time, they could peer into churches and cathedrals at the pages of brilliantly illuminated Bibles. The invitation to colour in similar fashion the faces and clothes of mysterious Native Americans could not be resisted, nor to embellish with colour the scenes where European explorers encountered them. Just as the black outlines of enticing figures imprinted on white paper would eventually become the stock in trade of children's colouring books in the 19th century, De Bry's graphic depictions of strange peoples inhabiting unknown lands beyond vast oceans bestirred nimble imaginations then as now (pp. 6, 10/11).

In addition to introducing the medium of the engraver's art to readers of the late 16th century, De Bry told his readers that he was presenting the first-hand sketches and drawings of talented artists who had travelled into these foreign climes. From the eras of Alexander the Great and the Roman empire-builders, it had been recognised as wise procedure for conquerors to take along scribes, draughtsmen and artists to record their military engagements and geographic explorations. The role of these unarmed craftsmen was to validate claims of conquest and to gather information for further examination and analysis by investors and advisors to kings. Artists depicted the ports, armaments and military capabilities of other peoples. In the case of the Americas, where there was vital interest in finding rare metals, dyes and tradable goods, artists played an additional role of sketching geological landscapes, plants and animals. They also produced invaluable maps of seaways, ports, rivers and the location of native populations, not to mention the settlements and fortifications of colonial rivals (pp. 8, 9).

The town of Pomeiooc
From: *America*, vol. I, plate 19, Latin ed. Newport News, Virginia, Mariners' Museum

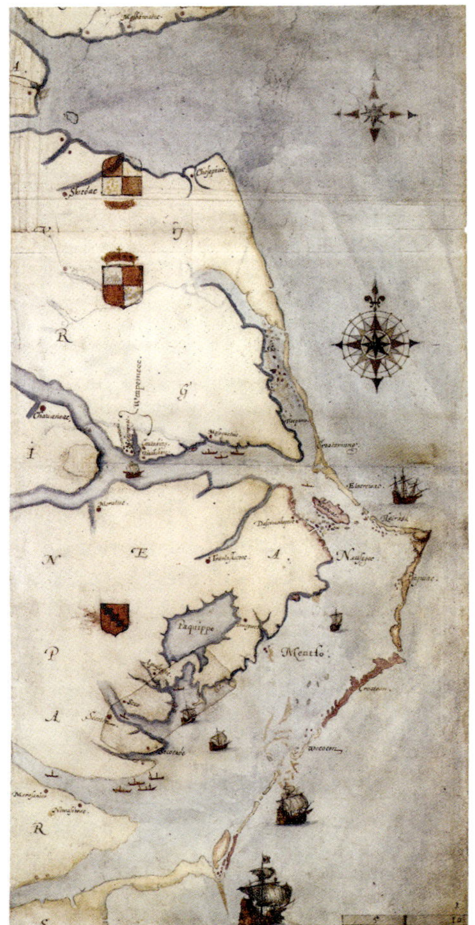

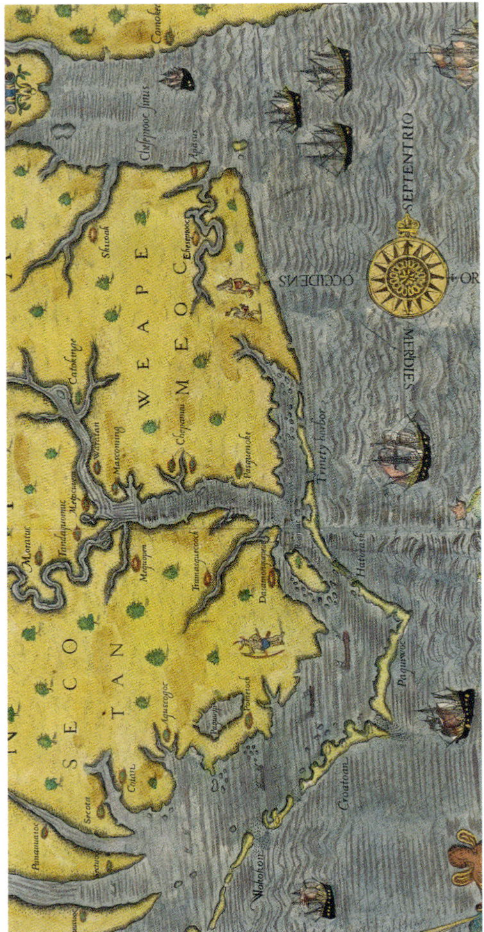

For the first two volumes of the *Grand Voyages*, Theodore de Bry was fortunate to encounter the original artists themselves in the same neighbourhood of London in the late 1580s. While he was contemplating a transition in trades from goldsmith to printer, he met the English artist John White who had travelled with other explorers, notably Thomas Harriot, on Sir Walter Raleigh's second exploration of Virginia in 1585. On that same trip to London De Bry met the exiled French artist Jacques Le Moyne de Morgues, who two decades earlier had accompanied an ill-fated attempt by Frenchmen to establish a settlement in Spanish Florida. Both artists had produced a large and ample stock of watercolours, which De Bry smartly obtained for his use in launching the most wide-ranging venture of publishing exploration narratives into the Americas of the Renaissance era. These illustrations, supplemented by Latin and German translations of both narrative texts and image captions – often with indications both of colour elements and of the details depicted – were taken up by De Bry and his engravers who then inscribed the skin furrows, tattoos, bodily shadows and facial expressions of Native Americans. Much of this text contained the kinds of practical information and pictorial elements needed by a colourist to apply hues and tints. Yet, with only black and white frames in which to apply colour and with only linear indications of willowy clouds, billowing smoke, tongues of water rivulets, plunging arrows and spears and wafting ship sails, much more was left to the imagination of whoever might be employed as the colourist for these volumes.

We do not know the identity of the early colourists for these first American colouring books. Nor do we know how many books were coloured – especially contemporaneous with the period of publication. Since only the first volume, Thomas Harriot's *Briefe and True Report of the New Found Land of Virginia* [*Admiranda Narratio*] (1590), was published in four languages – Latin, German, and smaller print runs in English and French – we know there were very few of the latter issues for colouring. Since the 13 volumes that comprise the *Grand Voyages* were published in spurts and intervals over a period of 44 years (1590–1634), and with less dramatic original art in the later volumes, there was much less inclination to render those volumes published after the 1590s (volumes I–VIII) in colour. Moreover, since the hand-colouring of most of the volumes seems to have been realised at the instance of patrons and collectors, there have always been many more examples in private libraries than in public repositories. Even those in research libraries are frequently difficult to find because of the many arcane systems of cataloguing the numerous De Bry volumes and editions (at least 186 versions among all volumes) and the absence of descriptive detail in library catalogues (i.e., that some volumes are hand-coloured!).

And yet, despite the odds and limitations, there are a number of well-known, beautiful and even thrilling hand-coloured copies of De Bry volumes in all of the language versions. They are scattered around Europe and the United States – especially in private collections donated to or eventually acquired by important libraries, such as the Bodleian in Oxford, the British Library in London, the University of Leiden in the Netherlands, the Military Library at Vincennes in Paris, the Houghton Library at Harvard University, the John Carter Brown and Hay Libraries at Brown University (whose original hand-coloured volumes are reproduced in this work), the Firestone Library at Princeton University, the John Work Garrett Library at Johns Hopkins University, the Mariners' Museum at Newport News, Virginia and the North Carolina Collection at UNC Chapel Hill. Other private collectors and antiquarians have also made their copies available for analysis and comparison. Sadly, a few book and print dealers over the past two centuries have dismantled hand-coloured De Bry volumes to sell individual engraved maps and images at a higher premium than the books themselves. Some of these demolished books are often displayed at book and map fairs around the world.

In analysing hand-coloured De Bry volumes and images it is instructive to know – thanks to the extensive research of Michiel van Groesen – that the Theodore de Bry & Sons firm evidently

John White, **Map of the east coast of America illustrating Virginia**, *c.* 1587
Watercolour drawing, 47.8 x 23.5 cm (18⅞ x 9¼ in.). London, The British Museum

Map of Virginia (detail)
From: *America*, vol. I, plate 2

neither employed a staff colourist nor contracted a Frankfurt colourist to illuminate their many illustrated imprints. Since most books of this period were created on demand by folding, binding and trimming previously printed sheets to fill the orders of individual patrons, it is more likely than not that the colouring of an individual volume or set of De Bry volumes was handled by a colourist retained by the purchaser and not by the publisher or printer. This seems to have been the general practice with regard to the individually issued volumes of De Bry's *Grand Voyages* – and was perhaps also the case in the 1620s and later when the firm of De Bry & Sons used its supply of existing printed sheets combined with second or third states of some engravings to form newly bound books containing from two to five volumes of the earlier works.

The complicated printing and distribution history of the *Grand Voyages* imprints makes the analysis of hand-coloured volumes quite difficult. It is still possible, however, to learn much from the bibliographic history of some of the hand-coloured books and from the comparison of hand-colouring practices in those copies that are available for examination. For example, it is worth noting that – at least in the case of volume I, Harriot's *Briefe and True Report of the New Found Land of Virginia* (1590) – there are distinctive and marked differences in the application of colours to the four language variations (pp. 12–15). German imprints are heavily and densely coloured with dark colours of green, red and black (p. 13). The hair and skin colours of the Algonquin Indians on the Virginia coast are dramatic – the men are dark and menacing, the women supple, blonde and with blue eyes, inviting us to come hither. Smoke billowing from the many fires is foreboding and eerie; the skies are gloomy and threatening. French imprints, in contrast, are audacious with lighter, more luminescent tones (p. 14). The men are still dark, but hardly sinister. The women are of pinkish hues, clothed in bright colours, red-haired and tweaking our fancy. Smoke rises from purposeful fires; clouds augur a rosy day. English imprints are drab, filled with lazy colours that dull our senses (p. 12). This world seems lifeless. The Algonquin men and women together are limp, still characters, sitting in pose and not seeking to interact with us at all. Colours are weak and seem watered-down.

An old man in his winter clothing (detail)
From: *America*, vol. I, plate 9

Page 46
The Native Americans sitting to dine
From: *America*, vol. I, plate 16, English ed. Princeton University, New Jersey, Firestone Library

The Native Americans sitting to dine
From: *America*, vol. I, plate 16, German ed. Chapel Hill, University of North Carolina

Page 47
The Native Americans sitting to dine
From: *America*, vol. I, plate 16, French ed. Cambridge, Harvard University, Houghton Library

The Native Americans sitting to dine
From: *America*, vol. I, plate 16

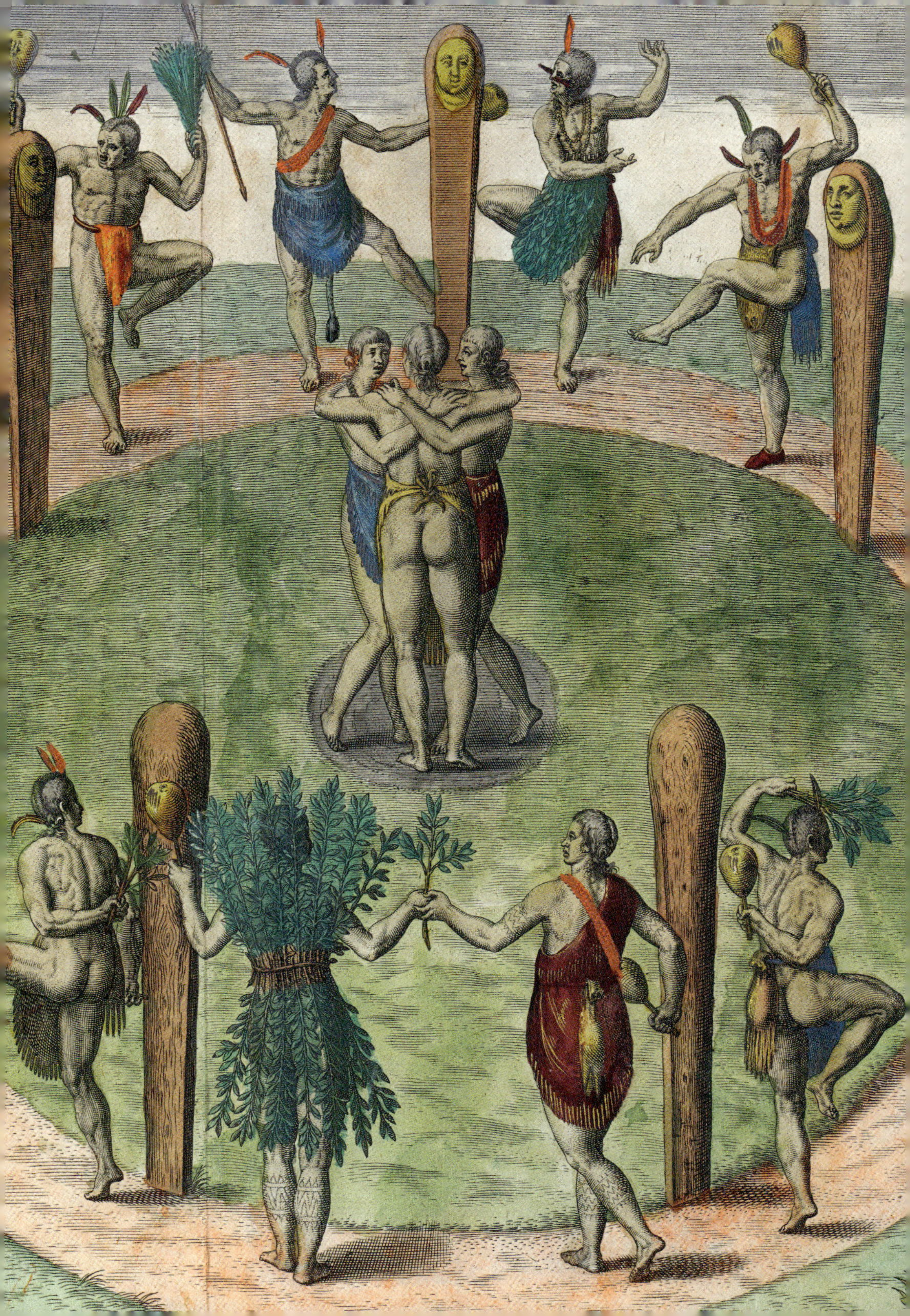

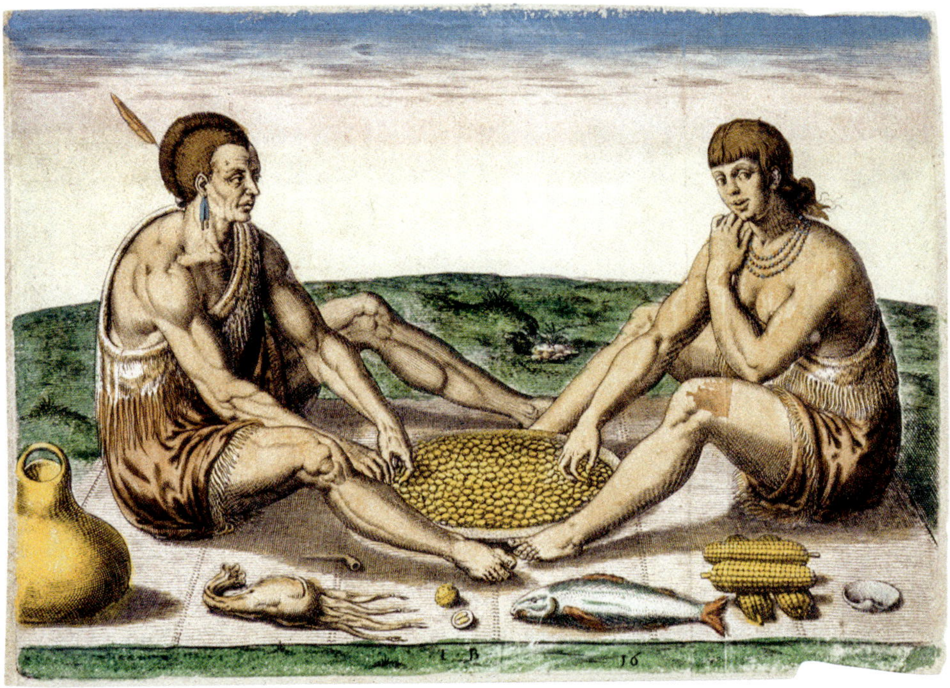

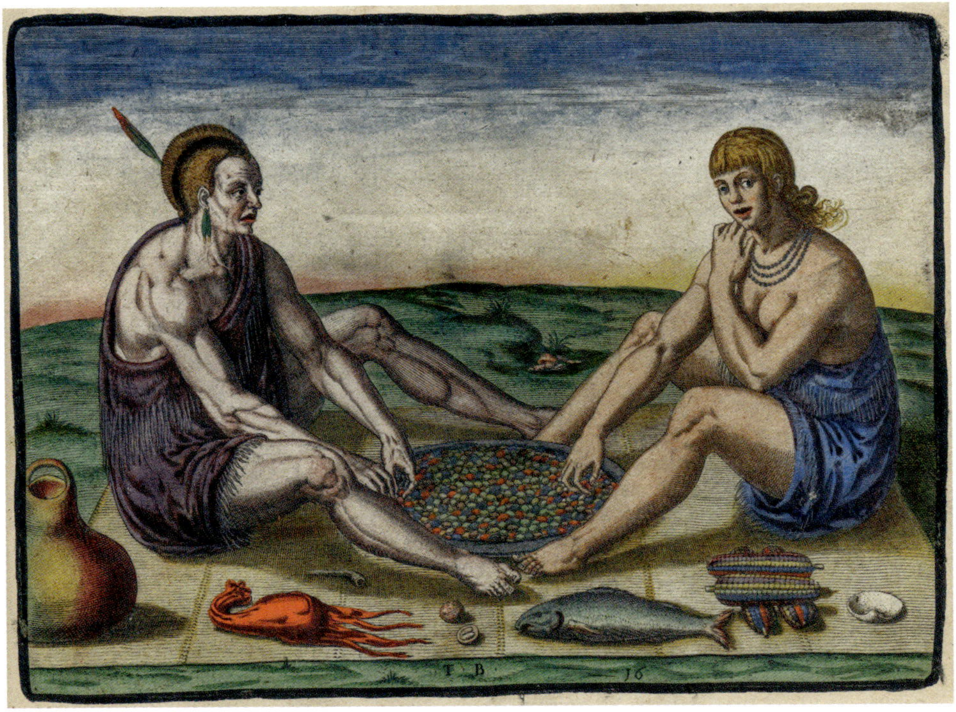

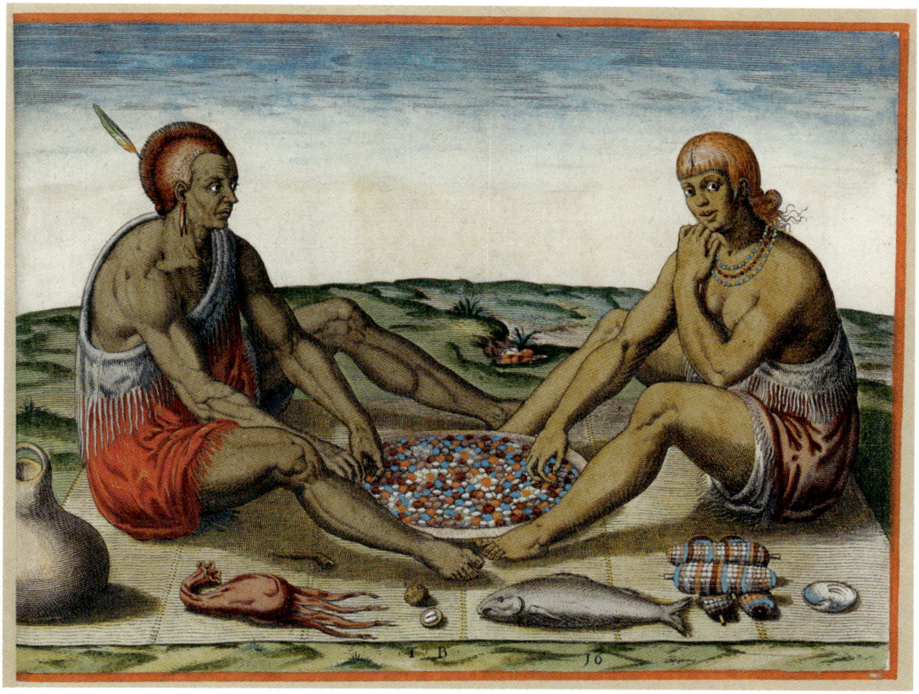

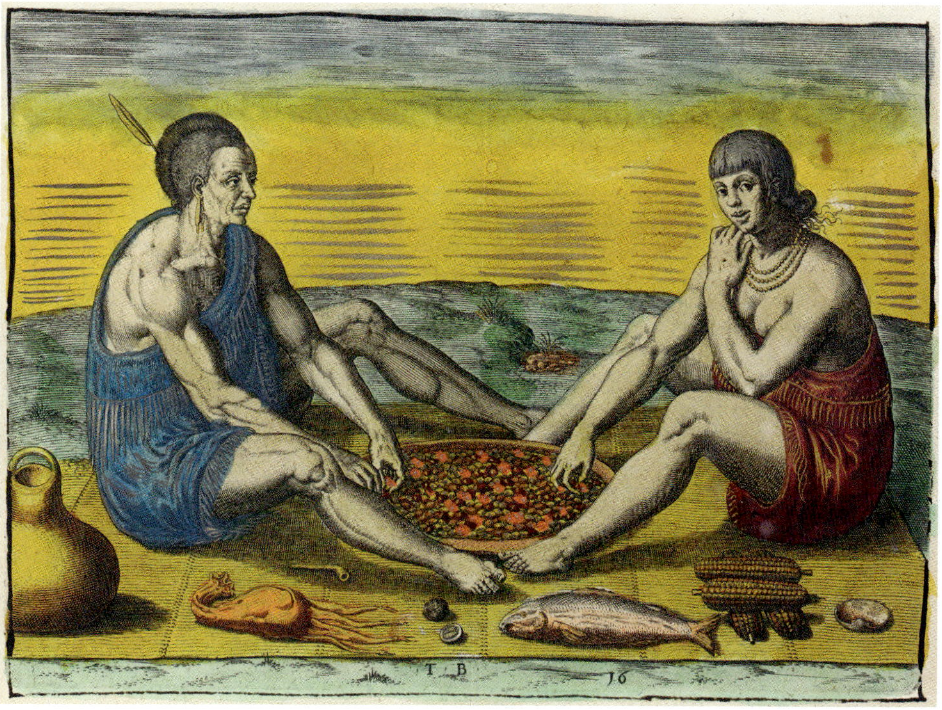

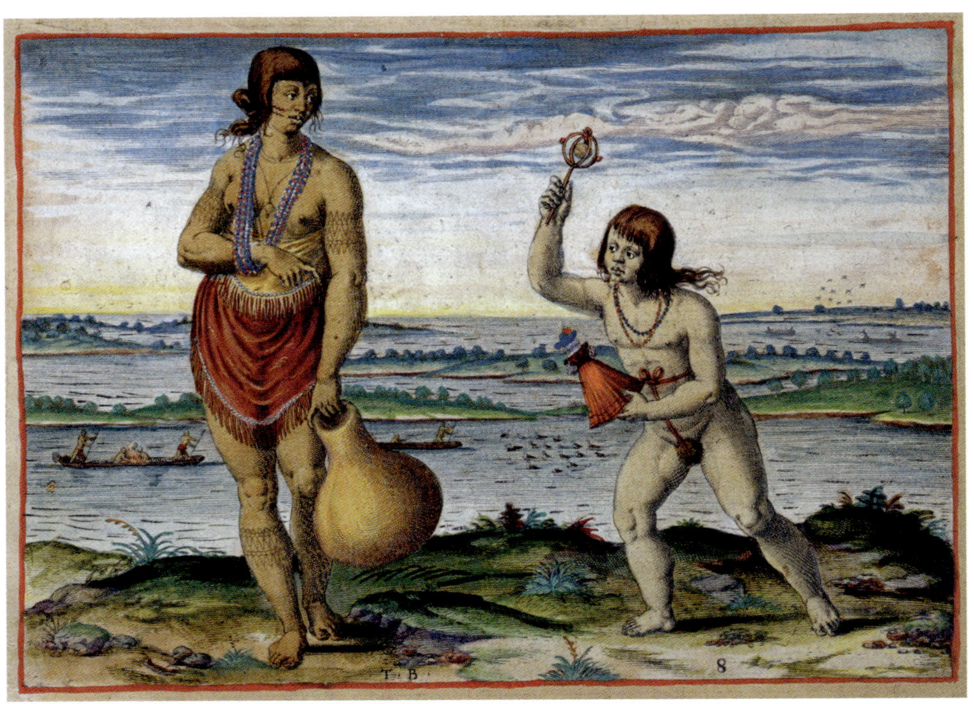

Blank spaces between imprinted lines are filled with colour, but they do not illuminate the images or features contained in the engravings. Nor do they help us understand the content of the engravings.

These variations in colour treatments cannot be merely accidental. They reflect quite different interpretations of the Indian world portrayed in Theodore de Bry's engravings. This observation raises the question of whether there is any relationship between hand-colouring and historical reality: to what extent does the work of the hand-colourist reflect the native Indians and their world – or the interactions of Europeans with that world? We have no documentation that any colourist travelled to the Americas. Thus colourists could only have obtained their insights into a colour protocol from the artists themselves or the artists' works used as sources for the engravings. Otherwise, they could have gained insights from the narrative text accompanying the original art. John White (the artist for volume I) was living in Ireland during the years De Bry was publishing the engravings based on his work; Jacques Le Moyne died before volume II was created. The length of time and space between other artists and the books based on their work by De Bry was even more distant.

In the case of John White's art, however, we are fortunate to have a well-authenticated set of the original artwork – created upon the artist's return from America in 1586; or, at least, copies of the original art created by the artist himself. We only need to place a few of White's original works, carefully preserved in the British Museum in London, beside the hand-coloured engravings based on his art to detect a wide gulf between his real-life sketches of Indians and the flamboyant renderings of European engravers and colourists (cf. pp. 57 and 90, 58 left and 108). The coloured engravings present us with well-toned and muscular males and shapely female figures of almost heroic proportions (pp. 48, 60/61). The figures and their surroundings in White's original watercolours are smaller, gaunter, ageing, depleted and colourless beings (pp. 51, 58).

However, at least in the case of the hand-coloured English engravings, we have a direct link between colouring and reality. Three of the hand-coloured English variations can be dated and the creator of those variations (but not the exact colourist) is known and can be well verified. William Strachey, a clever poet and author associated with John Donne, Ben Jonson and perhaps William Shakespeare, ventured to Virginia during its founding years of 1610/11. While there, he served as Secretary to the Virginia Company and travelled among Algonquin villages. Forever on the brink of financial ruin, he returned to England in 1612 and spent his remaining years seeking a patron to publish his well-documented account of Virginia, which he titled *The Historie of Travaile into Virginia Britannia*. Between 1612 and 1618 he prepared three autographed manuscript versions of this narrative, each illustrated with a full set of hand-coloured engravings from De Bry's 1590 edition of Harriot. Whether he coloured them himself or supervised the work of a colourist, the three versions are nearly identical, and their colours are the closest approximations of the tints in White's drawings of any set of De Bry engravings yet encountered (pp. 52, 53).

Comparing the colour treatments of De Bry volumes is a complicated procedure. Despite the growing availability of high-density photographic scans of images old and new, even the most sophisticated scans are only approximations of the actual colours in these four-century-old books. In addition to varying methodologies of scanning, the best scans are presented to us through electronic media seemingly always on their way to obsolescence. To achieve an intelligent comparison one almost inevitably needs to have engravings on their original paper and with their colouring side by side for experienced human analysis. Given the fact that known coloured books are widely spread across considerable institutional, national and geographic barriers, the opportunities for simultaneous physical comparisons are extremely limited. However, in one instance where it appeared that two historically separated Latin versions of the 1590 Harriot book might have been coloured by the same hand, it was possible to bring them together on a single table and, by visual analysis, to confirm that they seemed indeed to derive from the same colourist. But even in that case – and despite the obvious rigours and regimens of the skilled colourist – dramatic differences could be detected between the colouring rituals observed in the culminating engravings of each book. It appeared that the colourist tired in the marathon of colouring two dozen engravings and meandered off his or her practised path (pp. 62, 63).

An important lesson arises from the process of looking at panels of engravings in a single work. It becomes clear that the colourist of De Bry volumes did not colour the entirety of a single engraving and then move on to the next as a strategy of accomplishing the task. The colourist, it appears, selected a colour for sky, skin, bark, grass, trees, dirt, water, smoke and the like and applied colour to all of these elements in a single pass through the entire set of engravings. The same methods also applied to hair, dress, jewellery, tattoos and other adornments as well. While the colourist might vary the colours of hair and dress among several male and female figures, these treatments seem to be almost at random through most of the books. Even when a single engraving shows the front and back of a single person, the colourist almost always coloured the same individual in a single engraving in a different manner without regard to context. Skin and hair colours do not match, nor do the colours of clothing. This somewhat rote historical method of applying colours trains the observer to look for flaws in the rendering of colour schemes.

One is also apt to look for other hand-colouring characteristics that distinguish the works of master colourists from fledglings. Those volumes with the most elegant handling frequently include

A chief lady of Pomeiooc
From: *America*, vol. I, plate 8, Latin ed. Newport News, Virginia, Mariners' Museum

such dramatic touches as the colouring of initial letters in chapter texts and in captions for engravings. They might also include the colouring of De Bry's endlessly repeated stock of head-plates and foot-plates at the onset of chapters or as punctuating fillers in the white spaces at the culminating chapter ends. Another detail that often distinguishes the work of early, experienced colourists is the enclosure of engraving scenes within a frame of black, red or even pink lines. Additionally, great colourists can be depended upon to interpret virtually every detail of a focal scene, such as the first arrival of a European ship on an American shore or native Indians at worship.

Colourists also displayed their special talents in the colouring of De Bry's many pioneering maps. Since the originals of the maps he used have rarely survived in any other form, they are important testaments of information and insights into a world otherwise unknown either to the engraver or to the colourist. While the engraver gave shape and data to these maps, the colourist took on the job of interpreting these fundaments by expressing political boundaries for native peoples that did not really exist; by highlighting boundaries between land and waters with deeper hues of the same colour; and by adding a colour contrast to accentuate the engraver's hints of three-dimensional depth or of cresting waves of water. The most capable colourists caused maps of places previously unknown to readers to cohere, to elicit a broader understanding of features in the newly explored land, and to make indelible imprints in the minds of observers. By expressing European ideas about national boundaries through colours, they hinted (misleadingly) that Indian 'nations' in America claimed territorial limits as did the kings and princes of the Old World (pp. 54, 55).

The same effect occurs when the colourist achieved a balance of colour elements in a scene that the artist and engraver intended to depict an important event as opposed to presenting a portrait or a landscape. Vivid and luminescent colours transform black-and-white images of an Indian ritual dance into living, limb-tossing figures rising aloft in graceful motions. While the engraver has converted the dancers from the nimble and smooth-bodied Indians depicted by John White and Jacques Le Moyne into the typical muscular and sculpted human forms of European art, the colourist is still able to animate the native dancers by highlighting dress, ornament and hand-held shakers or rattles fashioned from gourds. The colourists also introduced thin lines of gold trim to enliven the clothing and jewellery of native Indians. But when depicting encounters between European commanders and native Indians, they used gold highlights, black dress and gun metal enhancing greys to demonstrate a presumptive superior power of colonial intruders over partially clad natives depicted in cowering postures. Legions of Indians bearing nothing but animal skins and primitive weapons are shown as powerless to contend with the guns, artillery and gleaming swords of the European invaders. Whether these encounters occurred in Virginia, Florida, Mexico, Guyana or Brazil, the narrative of European conquest over warlike, but helpless heathen peoples was the same – expressed through both the story told by De Bry and his engravers, and the colourists who assumed the task of illuminating the engravings.

John White, **The wife of a native chief of Pomeiooc**, *c.* 1587
Watercolour drawing, 26.3 x 14.9 cm (10⅜ x 5⅞ in.). London, The British Museum

Page 52
John White, **The town of Secota**, *c.* 1587
Watercolour drawing, 32.4 x 19.9 cm (12¾ x 7⅞ in.). London, The British Museum

Page 53
The town of Secota
From: *America*, vol. I, plate 20, English ed. Princeton University, New Jersey, Firestone Library

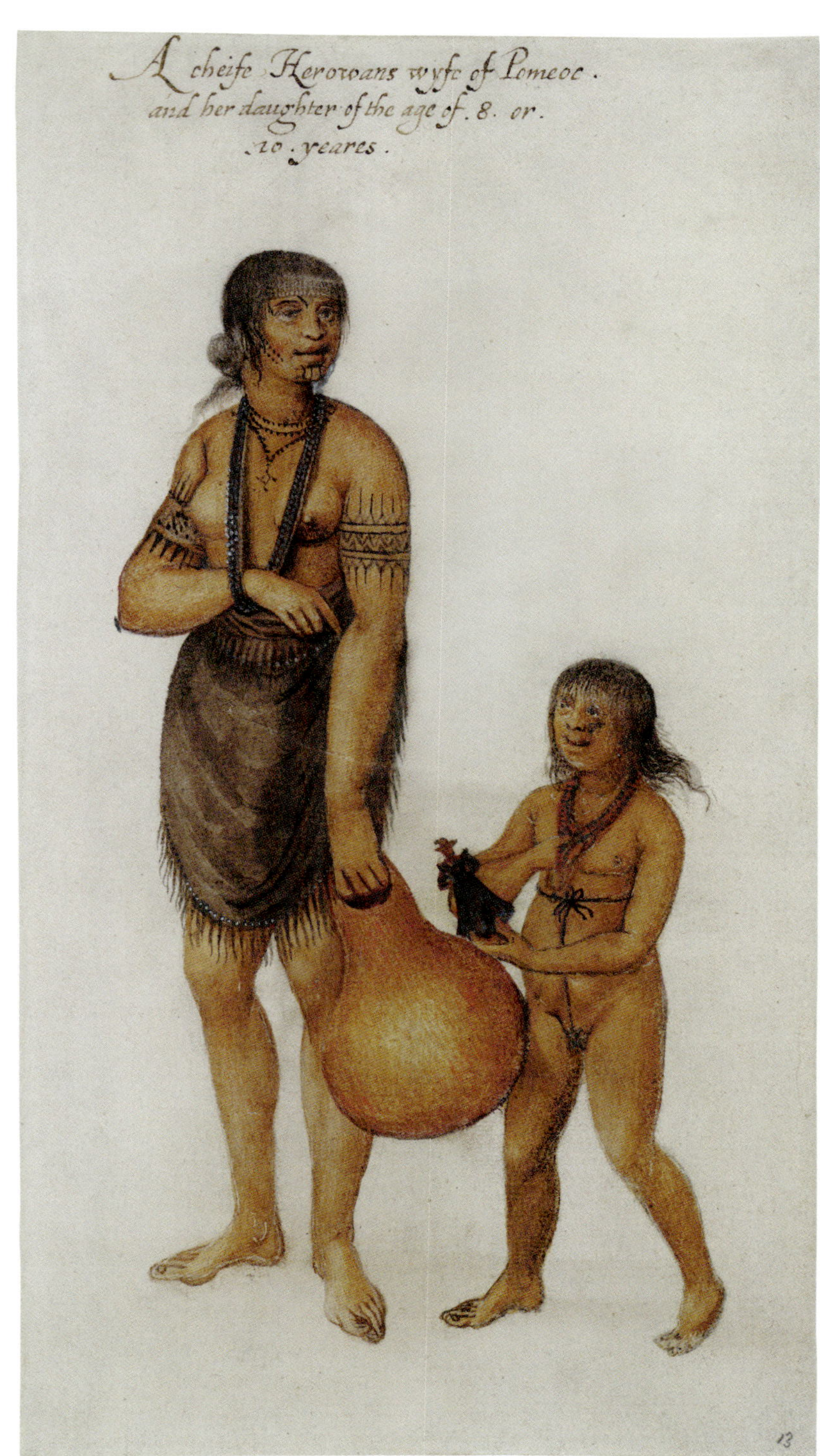
A cheife Herowans wyfe of Pomeoc.
and her daughter of the age of. 8. or.
10. yeares.
13

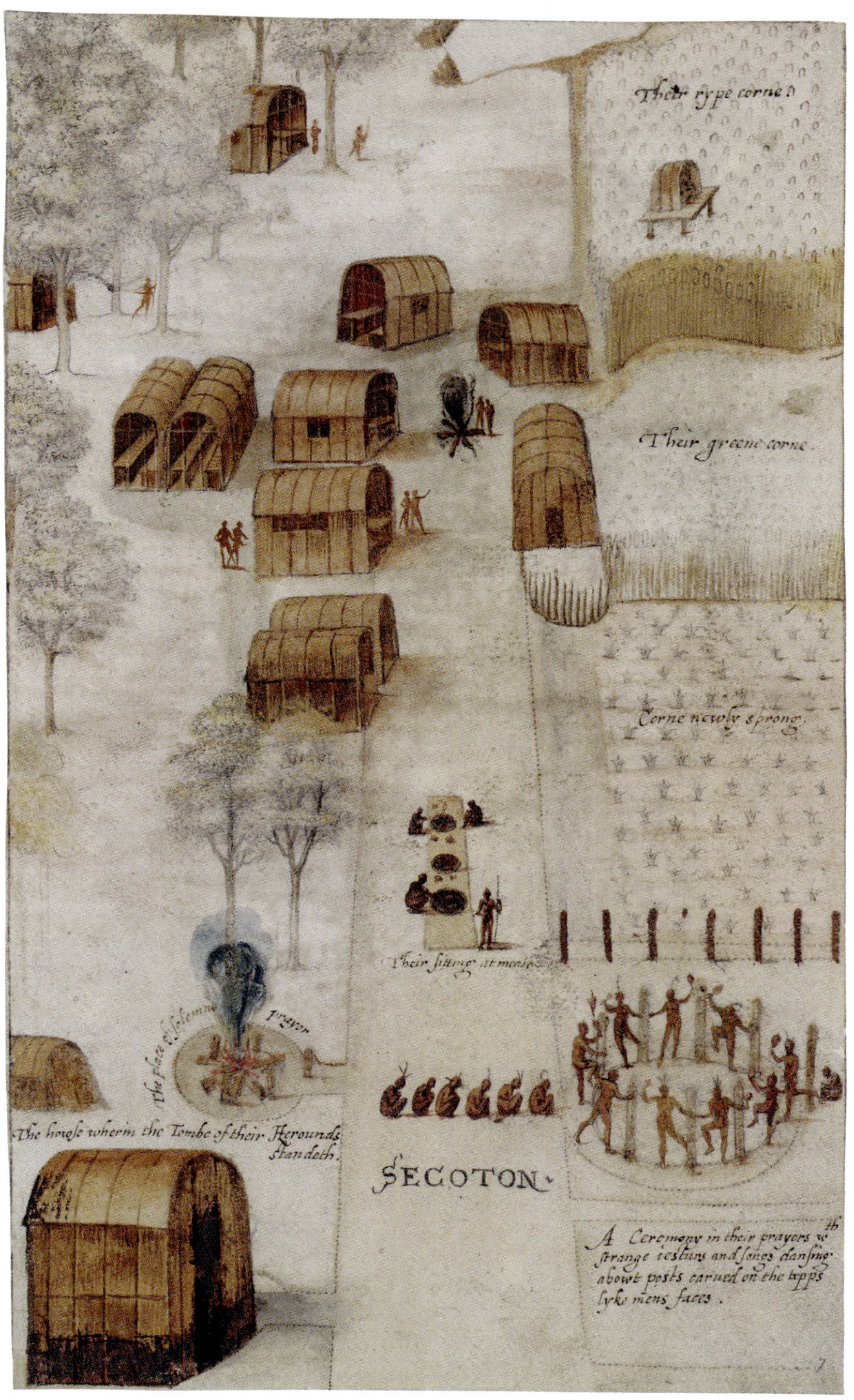
Their rype corne.
Their greene corne.
Corne newly sprong.
Their sitting at meate.
The place of solemne prayer
The house wherin the Tombe of their Herounds standeth.
SECOTON.
A Ceremony in their prayers wth strange iestures and songs dansing about posts carued on the topps lyke mens faces.

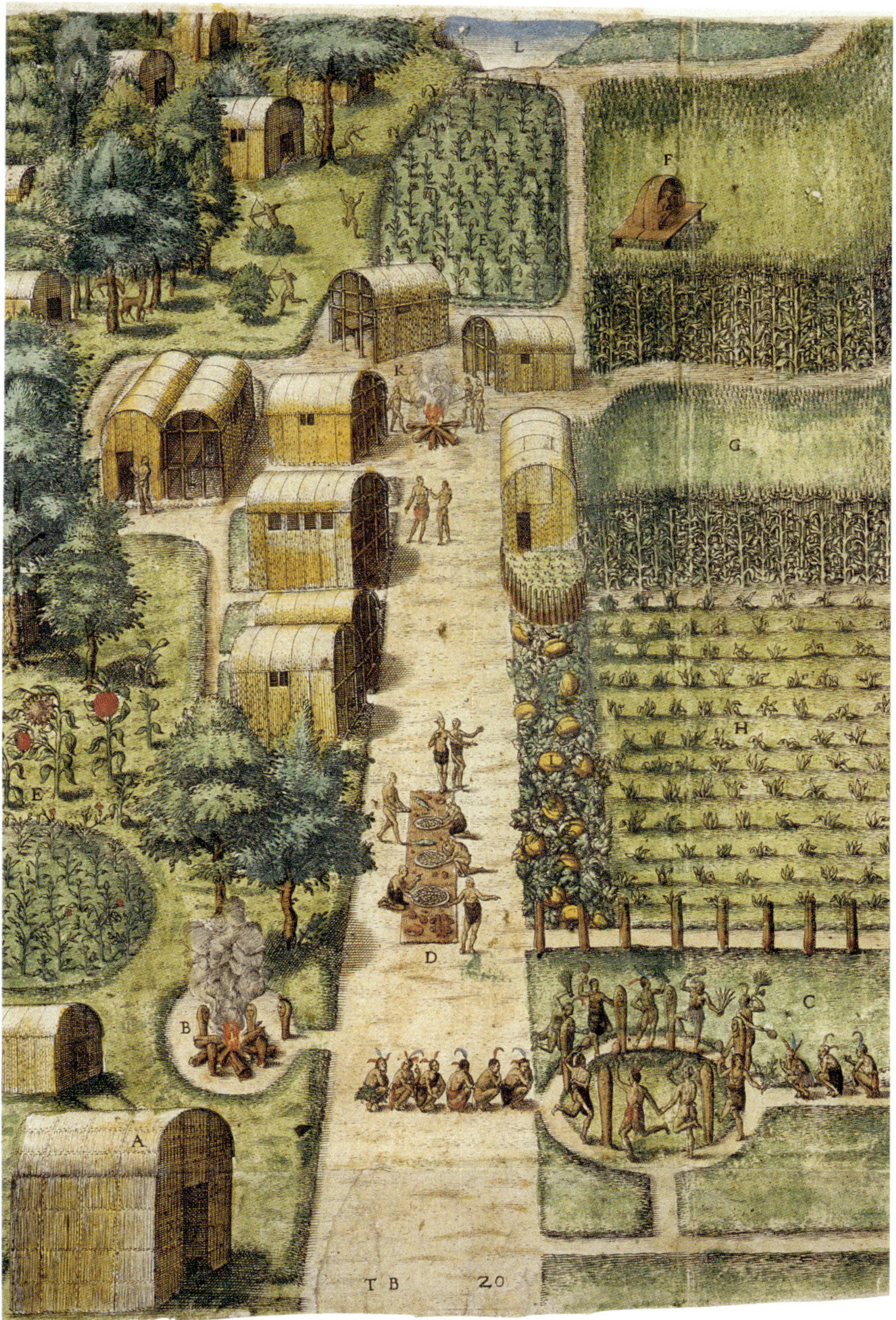
L
F
E
K
G
H
E
D
C
B
A
TB 20

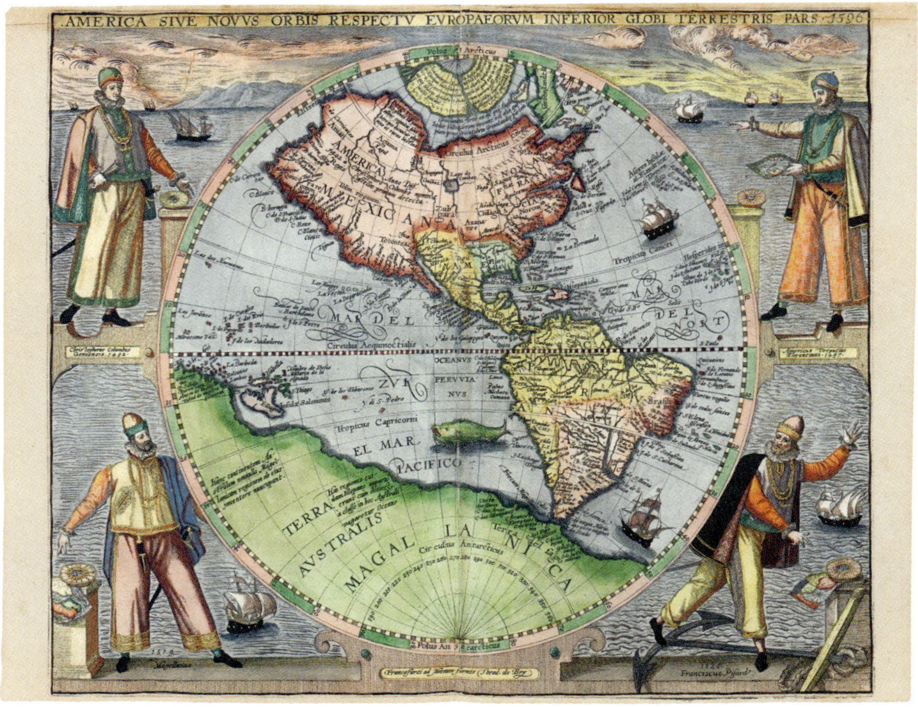

Hand-coloured versions of De Bry's *Grand Voyages* are exceedingly rare and thus very precious. Since it appears that most if not all hand-coloured volumes in the series were post-production, custom-ordered creations, the surviving examples which may originally date back to the 16th and early 17th centuries are as varied and capriciously designed as was the wont of their original owners. Whether the people who commissioned the colouring were bibliophiles, collectors or proud princes, nearly all hand-coloured volumes remained hidden in private libraries until the 19th century. When the United States began emerging as the industrial workplace of the world and a new centre of wealthy entrepreneurs, a small corps of eager book dealers opportunistically curried the whims and vanity of

World map depicting Terra Australis
From: *America*, vol. VI

Map illustrating Florida and Central and South America
From: *America*, vol. IV, German ed. The Hague, Koninklijke Bibliotheek

Jacques Le Moyne, Theodore de Bry, **Map showing Florida and Cuba**, 1591
Engraving, 35.5 x 45.7 cm (14 x 18 in.). Private collection

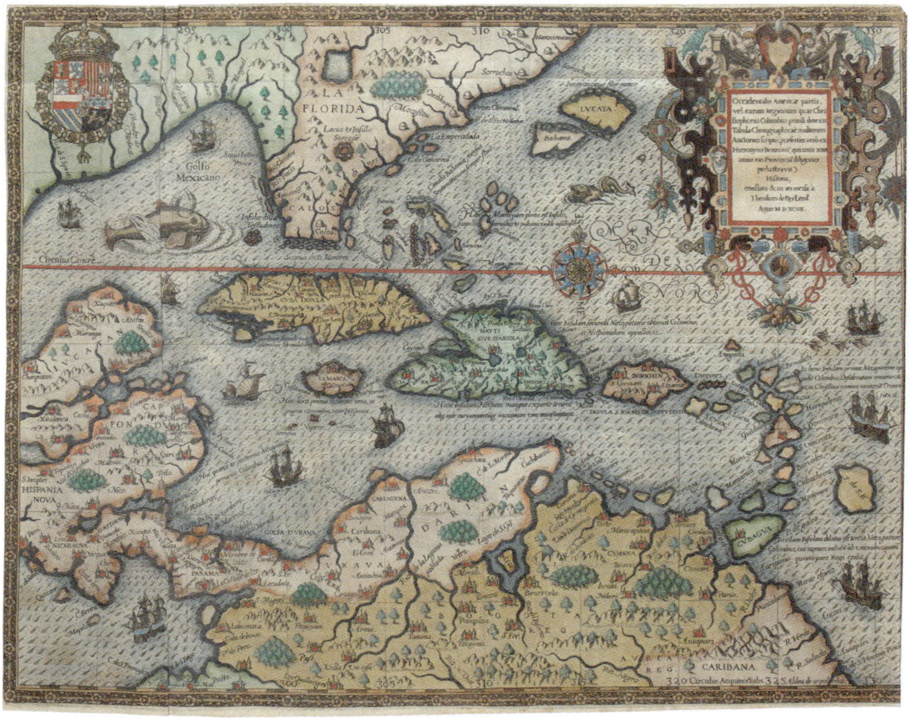

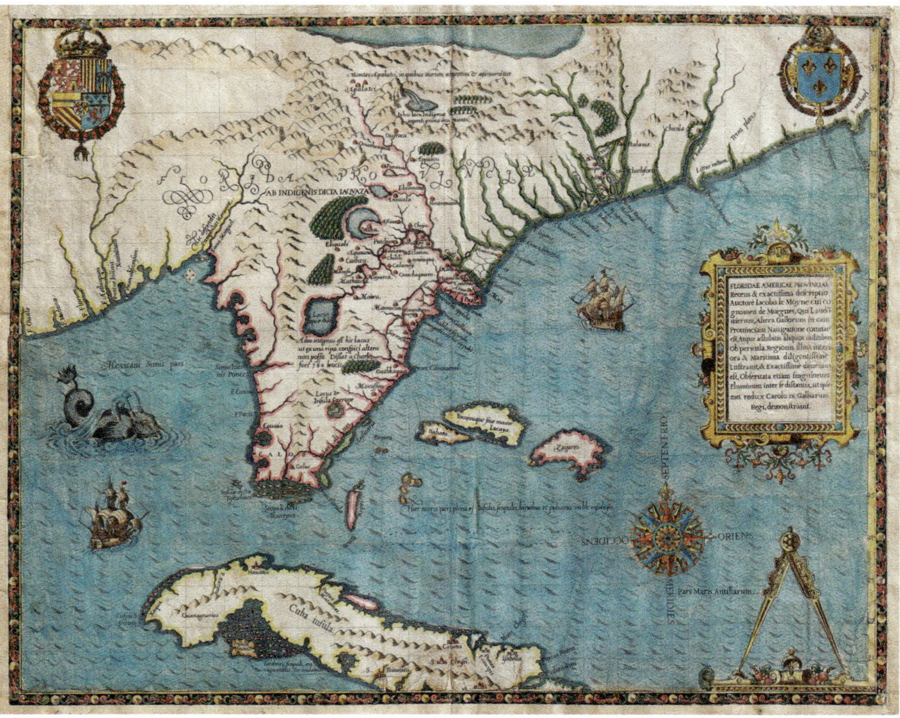
FLORIDAE AMERICAE PROVINCIAE
Recens & exactissima descriptio
Auctore Iacobo le Moyne cui co
gnomen de Morgues,
Prouinciam Nauigatione comitatus
est,
Ob pericula,
ora & Maritima diligentissime
Lustrauit, & Exactissime
est, Obseruata etiam singulorum
Fluminum inter se distantia,
met redux Carolo ix. Galliarum
Regi, demonstrauit.
Cuba insula
Pars Maris Antillarum
ORIENS
OCCIDENS
SEPTENTRIO
MERIDIES
AB INDIGENIS DICTA

these individuals by presenting them with an absorbing array of rare books. Every gentleman worth his salt needed to possess a library, they argued; and what was more logical to appear in such a library than a set of those great books that depicted in graphic images the exploration and conquest of the Americas? John Carter Brown (1797–1874) in Rhode Island, James Lenox (1800–1880) in New York and William L. Clements (1861–1934) in Michigan bought the idea and lavished fortunes on the acquisition of often multiple 'perfect' copies of De Bry's pioneering works. For these collectors, a perfect book with De Bry engravings was one that had exemplary copies of each engraving, though some of them might have been added or replaced from other books.

As American collectors and the libraries and colleges they endowed rose in prominence, the bulk of De Bry's works that came on the market in the 19th and 20th centuries gravitated to the United States. By the opening decades of the 20th century most of the known hand-coloured De Bry books were held in either European libraries formed prior to the middle of the 19th century or in acquisitive American libraries. Many of these books also crossed the Atlantic during the reconstruction years following World War II, when several private and institutional libraries across Europe had to be liquidated.

Since hand-coloured De Bry books are works of both history and art, it was inevitable that their value would escalate dramatically as the world market for important art ballooned at the end of the 20th century. Whereas those collectors and libraries who had acquired hand-coloured De Brys in the middle of the 20th century might need to expend 10–20,000 US dollars, by the early 21st century such an acquisition required 10 to 20 times that investment. As the value of these works inflated, antiquarian book dealers mined old family estates looking for additional hand-coloured volumes. And as in the case of important works of art, buyers of hand-coloured De Bry volumes more often than not encountered a cloak of confidentiality invoked by dealers to protect the identity of their sources. In many such cases, however, it was just as likely that the dealer could not elicit from the seller the actual provenance of the hand-coloured volumes being offered.

Hand-coloured De Bry works of any age pose a special problem for everyone involved in the study, appreciation or ownership of these beautiful books. Oil-painters in the era of the Renaissance used pigments and solvents that are inorganic in nature and thus can be somewhat reliably dated through X-ray analysis. De Bry books, however, were coloured primarily with organic materials that could be easily reproduced by the painter. Considering that these colours were applied to paper made for Theodore de Bry and his sons at Frankfurt in the 16th or 17th century, the cotton fibre medium is already dated. Since organic materials do not reveal their age in X-ray diffraction, one cannot easily determine whether the colour was applied in the 16th century or the 21st, yet one can quadruple or quintuple the value of such historic volumes merely by adding colour and claiming that the colour is original. This presents a clear and troubling dilemma for buyers, dealers, libraries, collectors and researchers interested in this important phase of the historic hand-colouring of images printed on paper.

It is much easier to analyse hand-coloured maps of the Renaissance era than books of that period such as the De Bry volumes. Cartographers of the Renaissance era frequently applied colour to their printed maps in their own shops by employing spouses, relatives and children. Moreover, the colours they consistently used are easily recognisable. Some of them also used stencils to speed up the process of adding specific colours. But we have found no evidence of such practice in the De Bry books. The number and variety of the engravings in these books made the use of stencils impractical. Nevertheless, the expanding profession of art and paper conservation promises that new analytical tools making use of colour spectrum analysis and the molecular structures of colours on paper will increase our analytical capabilities.

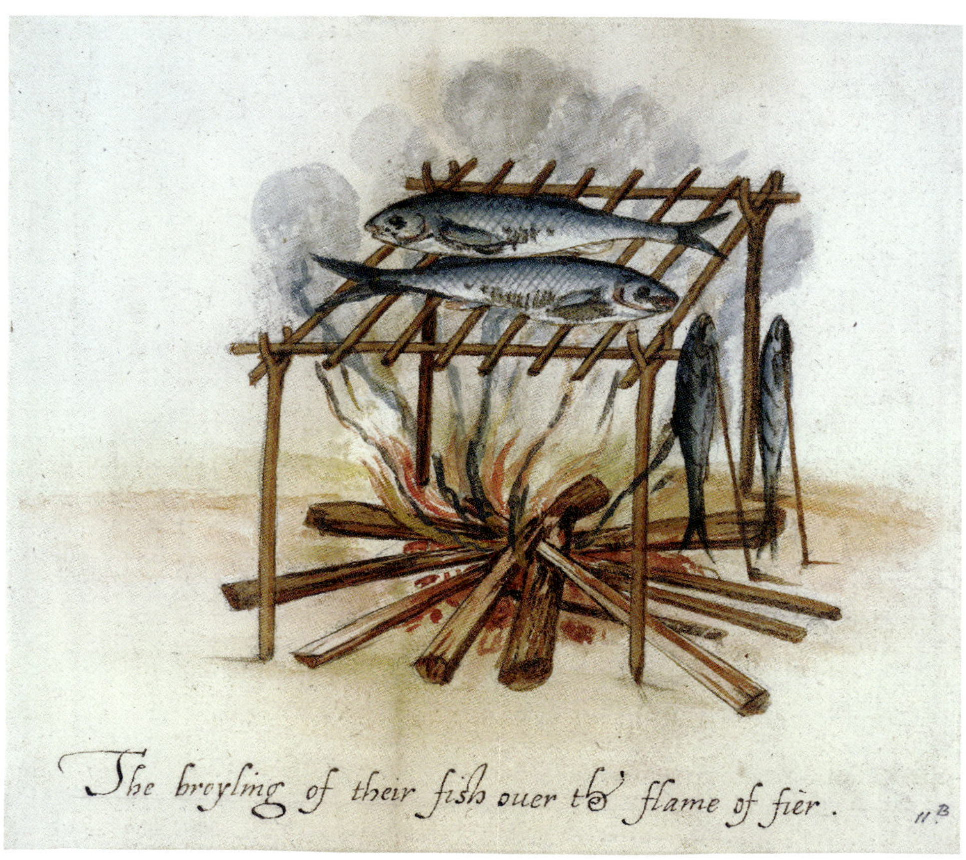

Meanwhile, there are other tools available to curators and collectors to provide a safeguard against acquiring a fraudulently coloured De Bry book. As book historians know, every book from the era of early printing has its own story and provenance. This is because every book had a composition and fabrication character that was unique. If a book has been rebound and trimmed and its pages are spotlessly clean, the would-be investor should be wary. If a seller proclaims that the book has 'original' hand-colouring, one should be doubly on guard. If the dealer cannot provide documentation that the book was identified in historical records (archival documents, estate inventories, bibliographic descriptions) as being hand-coloured prior to World War II, then one might take a further cautionary note. This is because 19th-century bibliographers were assiduous in their search for rare books and especially for the iconic De Bry volumes. Such nervous and compulsive bibliophiles as E. D. Church, Joseph Sabin and Henry Stevens left few stones unturned in their search to encompass the world of De Bry publications.

When one encounters an early hand-coloured book of De Bry engravings, there is little in the composition of books in general that is more beautiful to behold. One's first reaction is that of sublime engagement in the images on the page. The impression is not one of perfection (these

John White, **The cooking of fish over a fire**, *c.* 1587
Watercolour drawing, 14.6 x 17 cm (5¾ x 6¾ in.). London, The British Museum

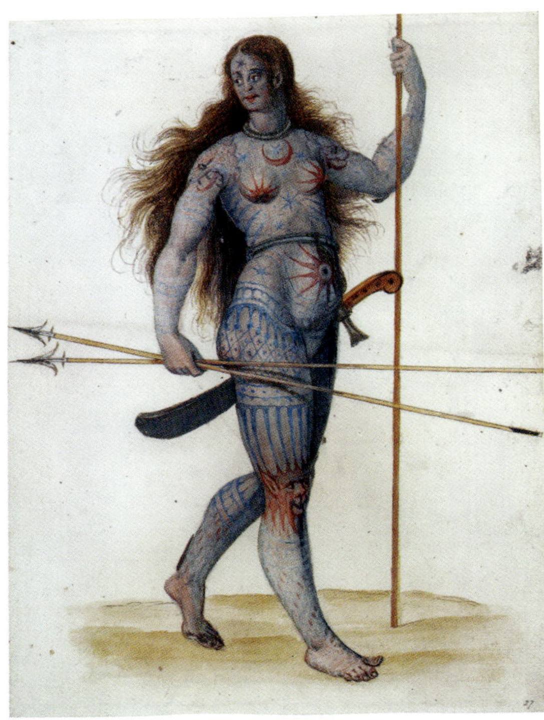

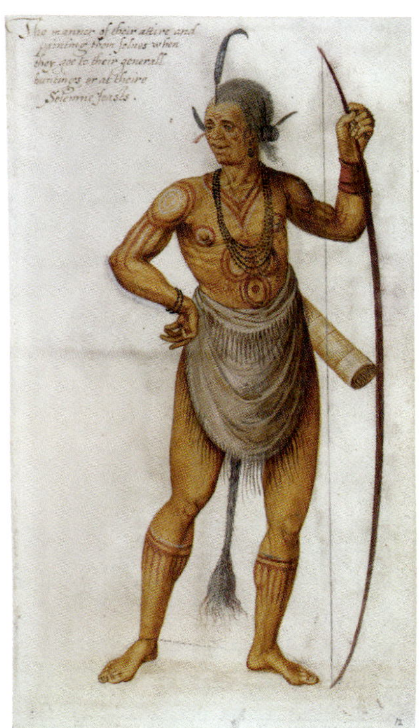

books are not sacred scriptures), nor of overpowering exhibitions of gold and royal reds or purples; but rather an arresting blend of rose, orange, brown, black, green and yellow. Heavy greens bleeding through the cotton fibres and splotches of colours around details of jewellery, beads and bodily tattoos are indications of amateurish applications of colour. Conversely, too much perfection in the application of colours in a rigorous routine might also suggest a fraudulent effort to replicate early hand-colouring. The expansion of colouring beyond the engravings themselves to initial letters, head-plates and foot-plates is suggestive of professional attention. In the best examples of early colouring, the coloured engravings tell the story and not the ambitious and distracting colours themselves.

One might well ask who made the decisions about colour schemes and the application of colours to particular features of the engravings? Many heads have puzzled over this aspect of hand-coloured maps, prints and books. Our best guess is that, in almost all circumstances, the colourist was the person in charge of choosing palettes, determining skin and hair colours, and in making skies and fires either ominous or intriguing. It was the colourist who interpreted the images and words on the printed page, and the best colourists were those skilled craftsmen who saw their work not as decorating De Bry engravings, but rather as playing a contributing role in elaborating the stories that the engravings told, their captions, and the substance of the books in which they appeared. When one encounters the craft and art of early colourists, one becomes more engaged in the story they help elucidate than in beholding the exquisiteness of the hand-coloured pages. One can cosy up to the story of one of these beautifully coloured books – whether the scene we are beholding is a portrait of a Native American, a landscape of a newly explored territory or a depiction of a bloody and disturbing encounter between European conquerors and indigenous peoples.

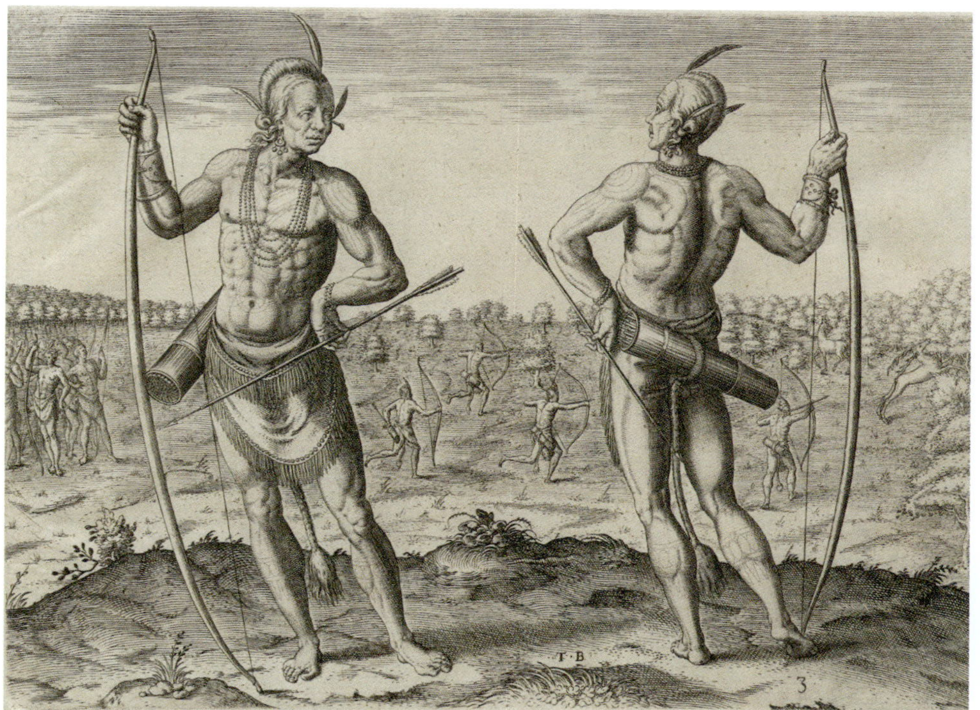

The best test of the power of hand-colouring in De Bry volumes is to spend a few hours examining the pages of one of these hand-coloured books and then turn to a volume that has not been coloured (pp. 60/61, 59). The effect verges on a slight case of mental confusion or brain trauma. Turning from one to the other is akin to losing sight and vision. The experience is not the same as going from a movie projected in colour to one presented in black-and-white images; engravings are much more complex displays of action, details and interpretation than a frame of film. The most successful colourist illuminates the masterful work of the engraver and adds another level of nuance and energy, drawing readers almost magnetically into the image as if they were standing before the original works of great masters in the halls of our finest art museums. But in the case of a well-produced book with an accurate replication of their colours, as is presented here, one can enjoy an engagement with these works of art in the confines of one's own home.

John White, **A woman belonging to the Picts**, *c.* 1587
Watercolour drawing, 23 x 17.9 cm (9 x 7 in.). London, The British Museum

John White, **A native Weroan or chief**, *c.* 1587
Watercolour drawing, 26.3 x 15 cm (10⅜ x 5⅞ in.). London, The British Museum

A Weroan or great lord of Virginia
From: *America*, vol. I, plate 3, Latin ed. East Carolina University, North Carolina, Joyner Library

Pages 60/61
A Weroan or great lord of Virginia
From: *America*, vol. I, plate 3, French ed. Cambridge, Harvard University, Houghton Library

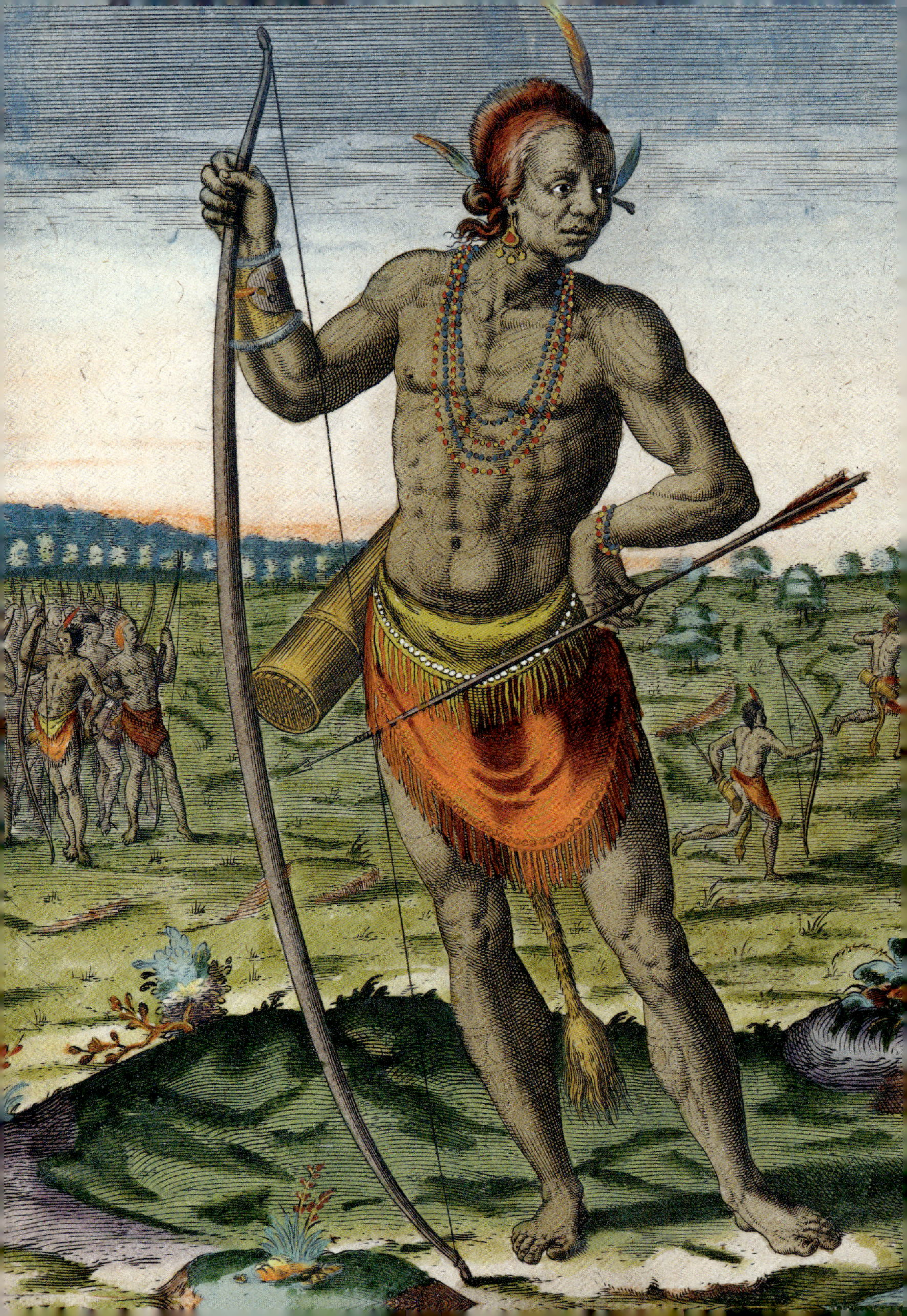

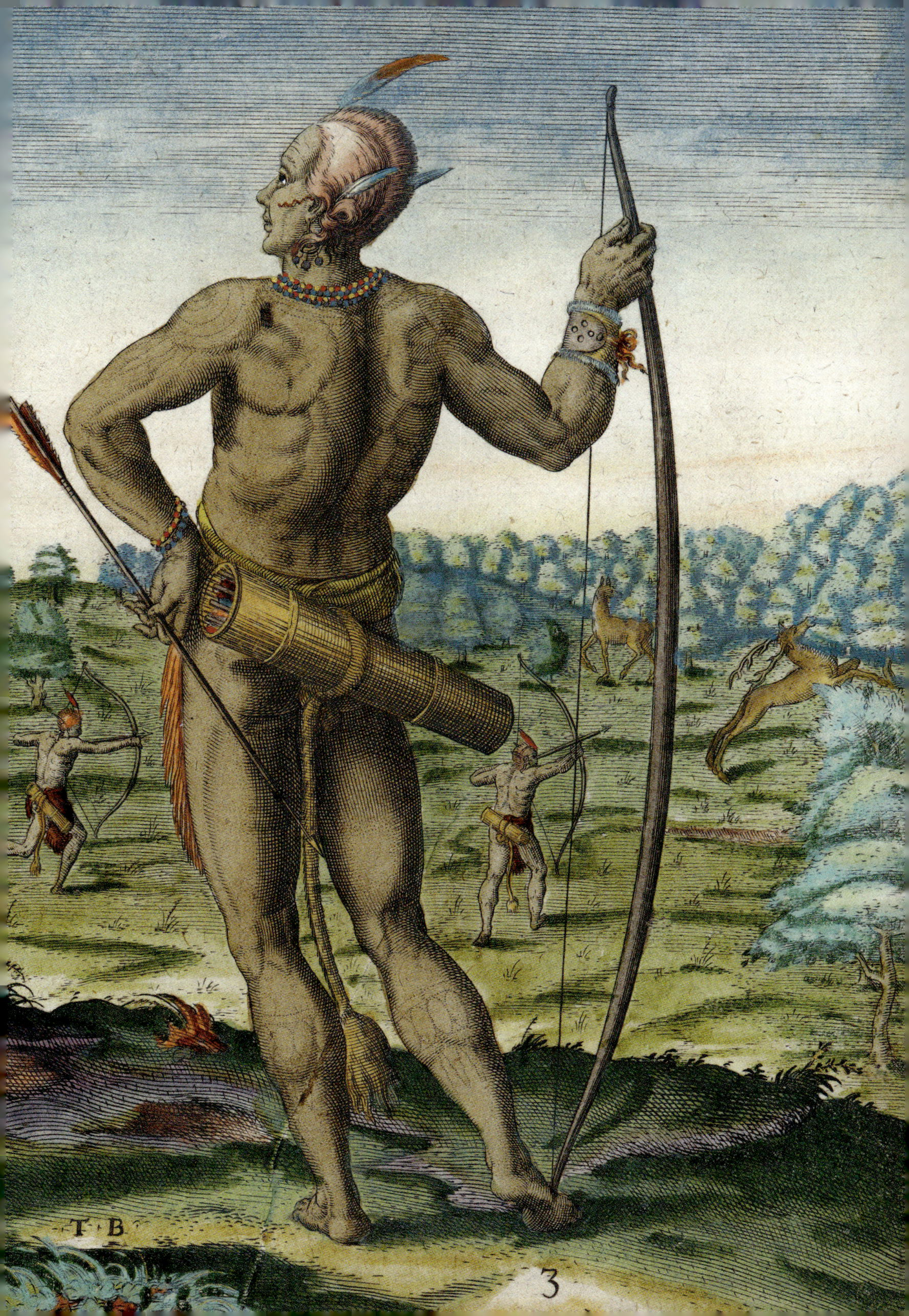
T·B
3

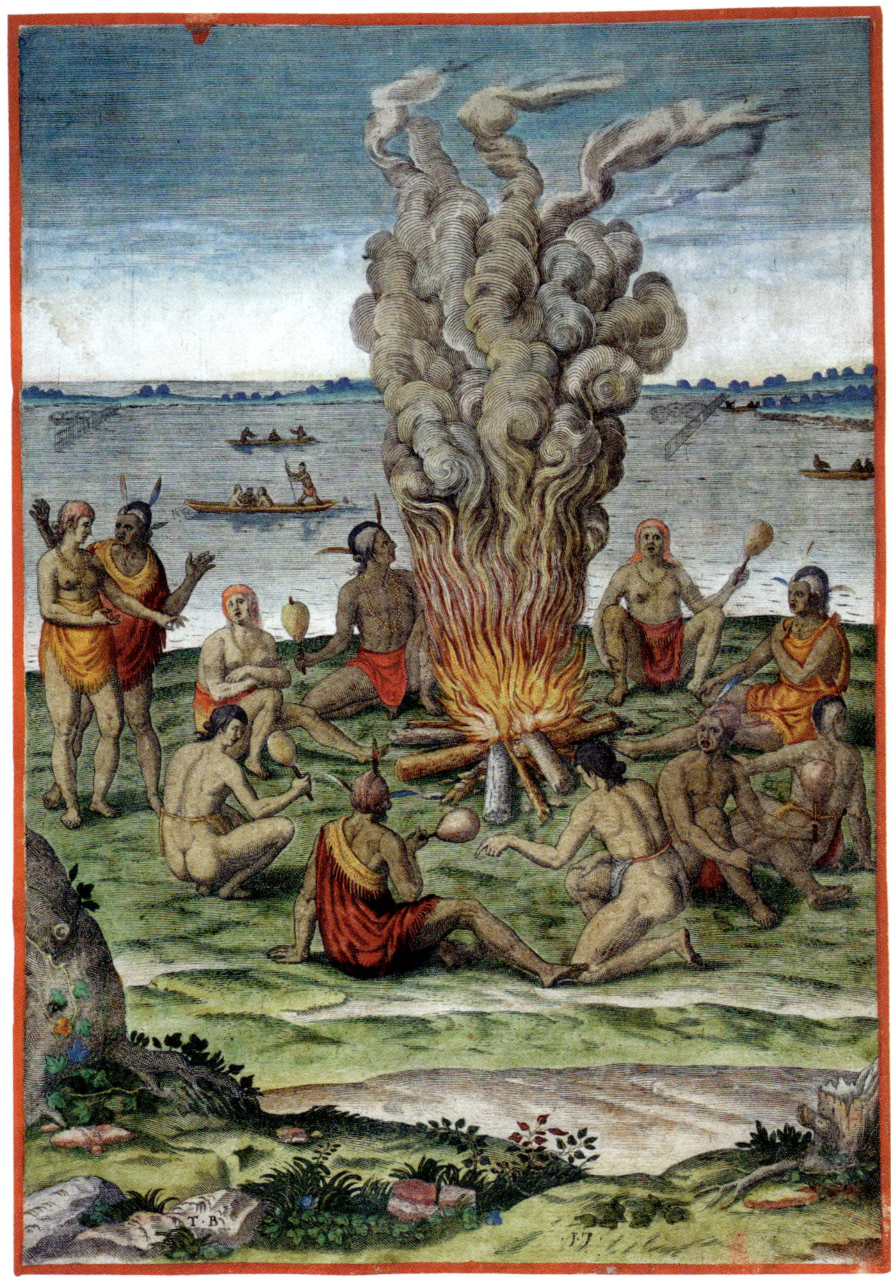

The Native Americans pray with rattles
From: *America*, vol. I, plate 17, Latin ed., Norfolk, Virginia, Virginia Cartographical Society

The Native Americans pray with rattles
From: *America*, vol. I, plate 17, Latin ed., Newport News, Virginia, Mariners' Museum

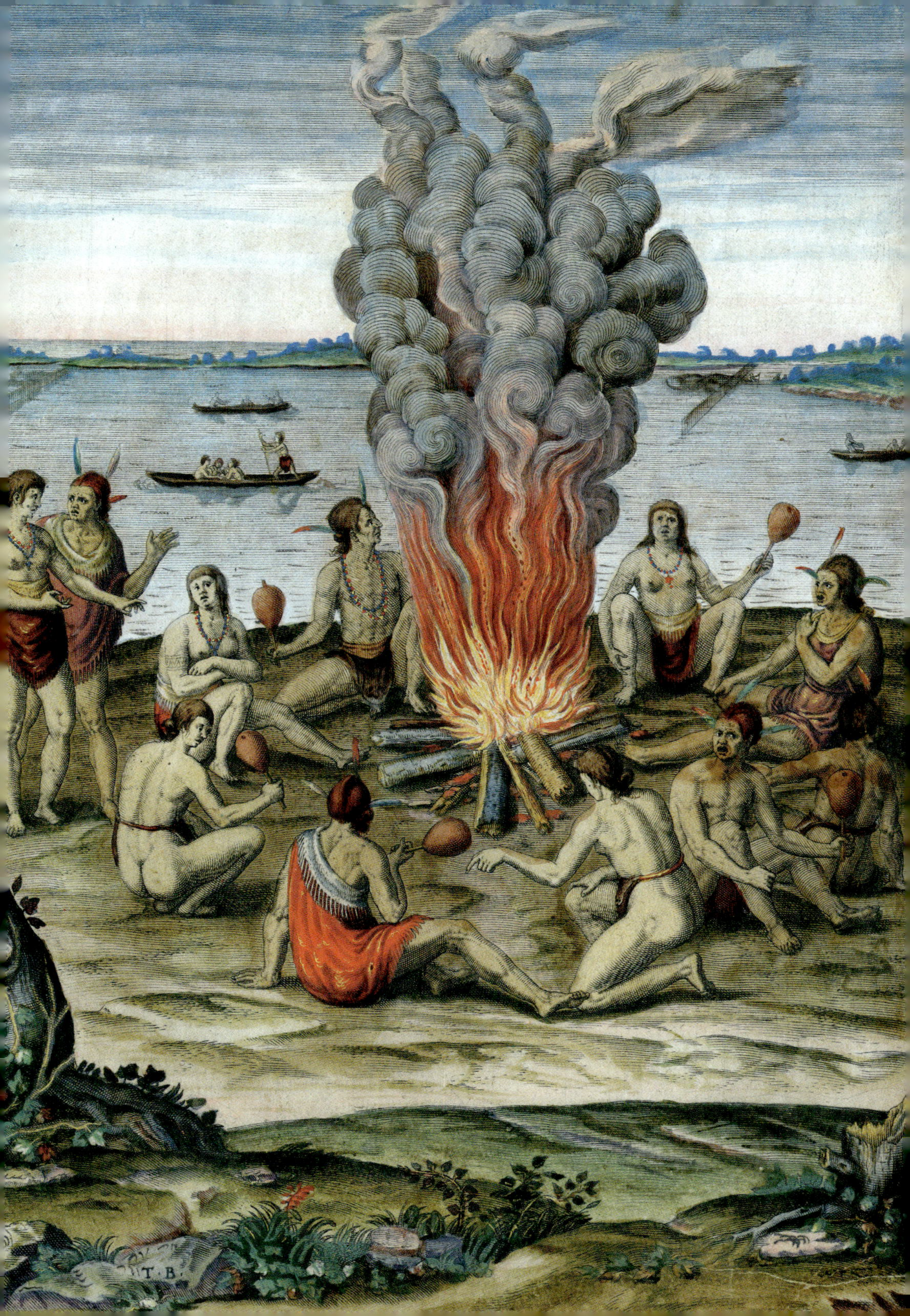
T.B.

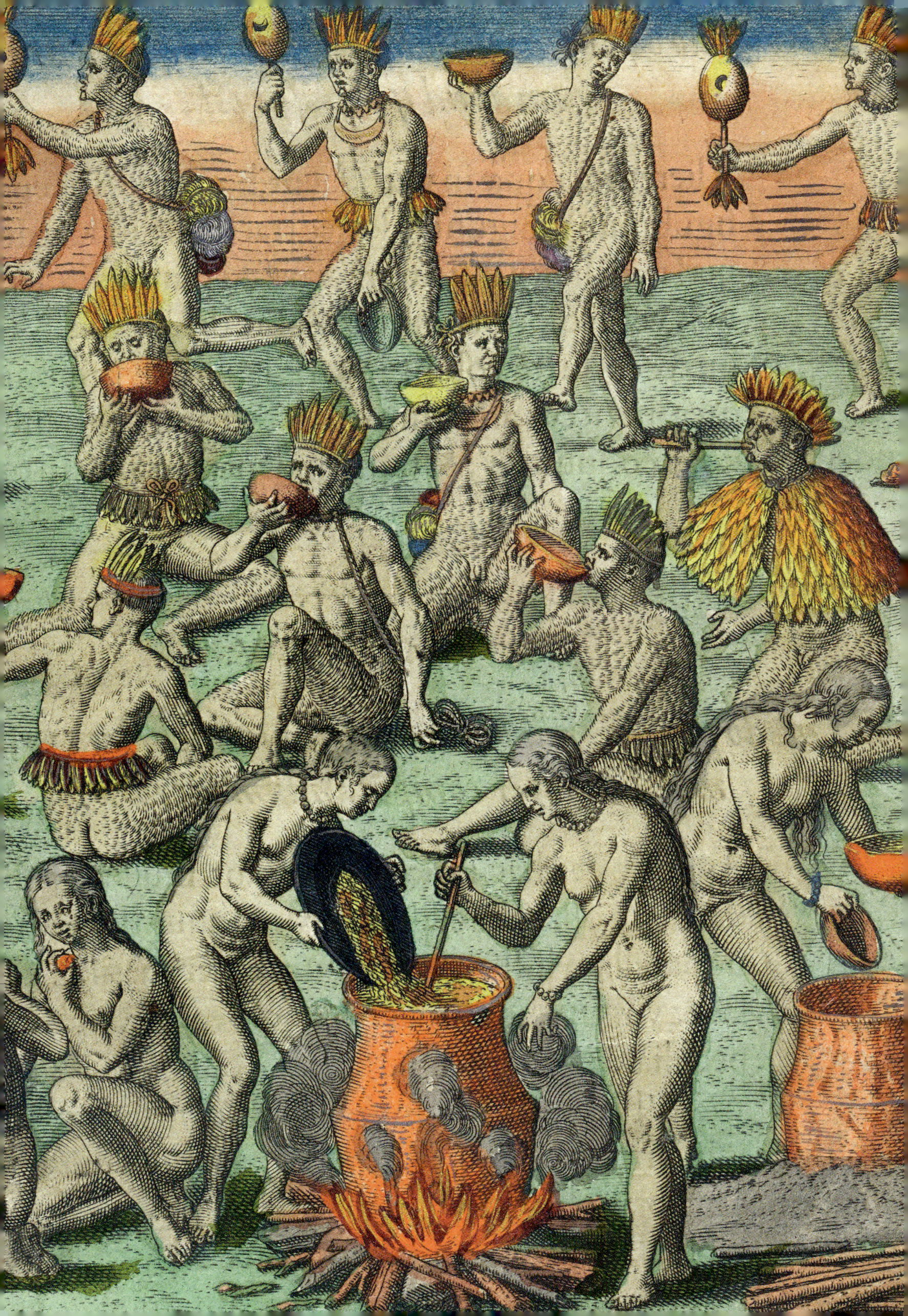

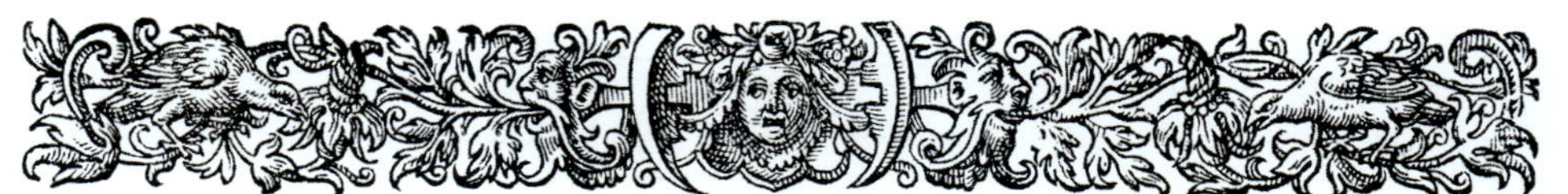

Theodore de Bry

America

PLATES AND COMMENTARIES

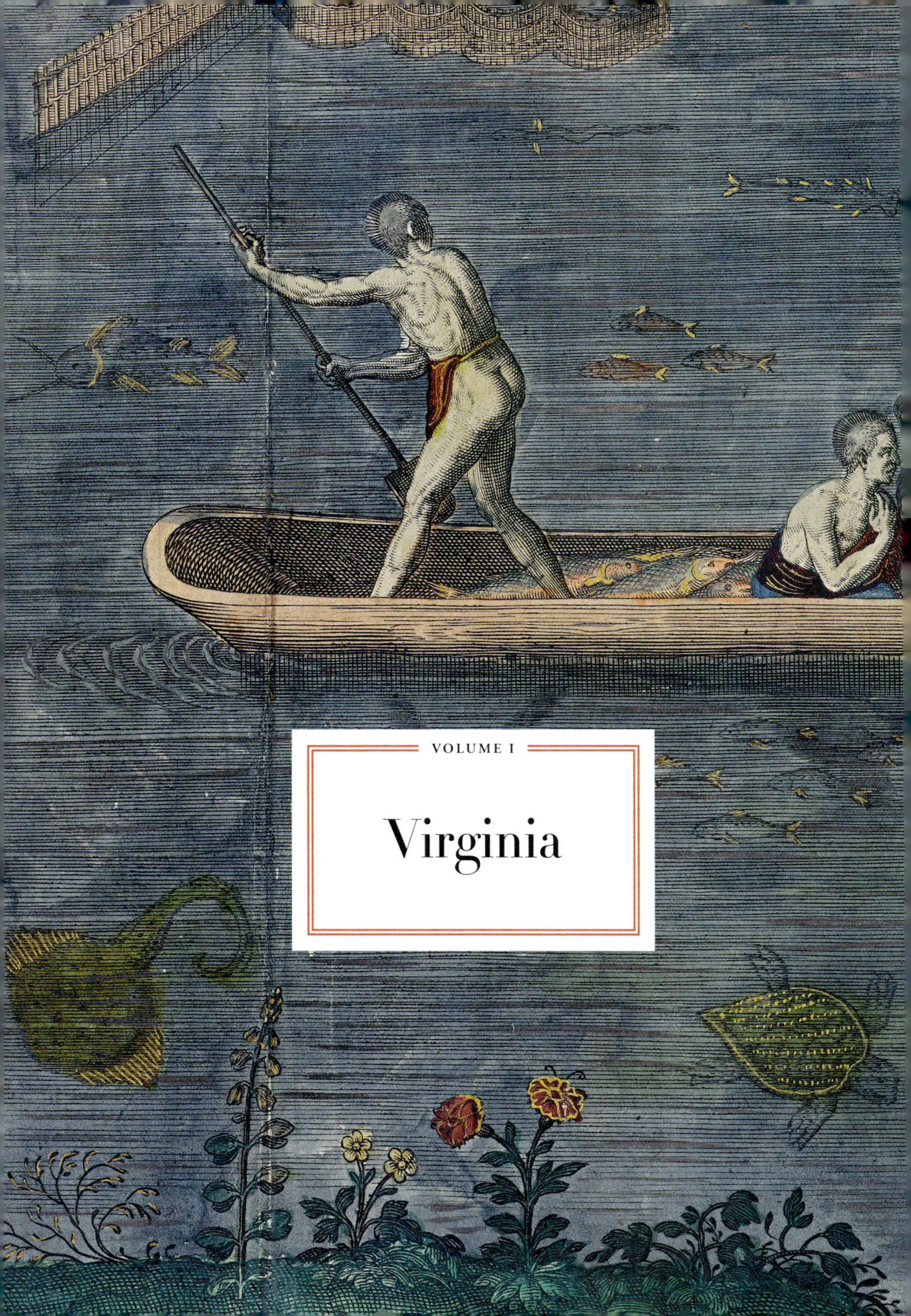

VOLUME I

Virginia

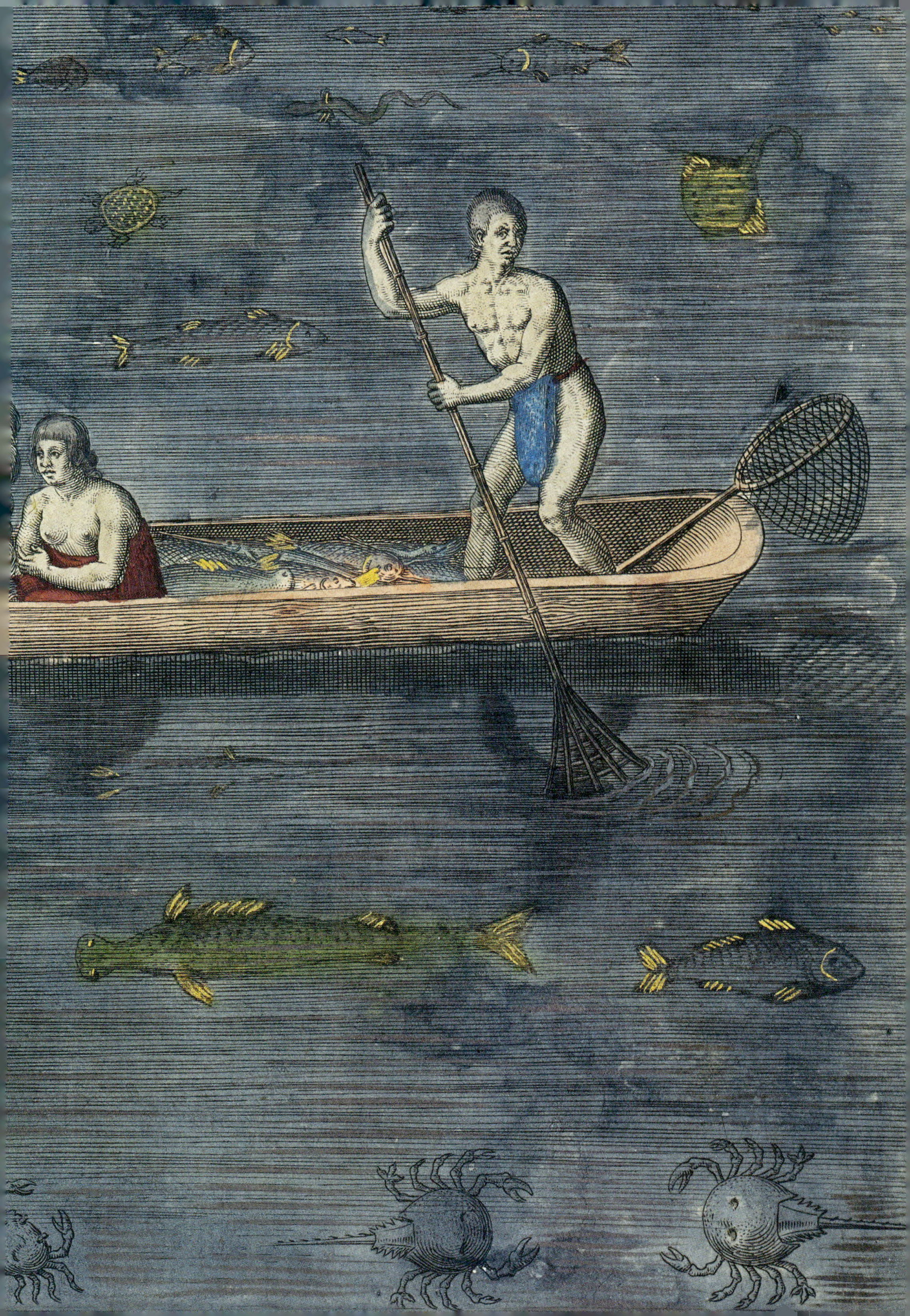

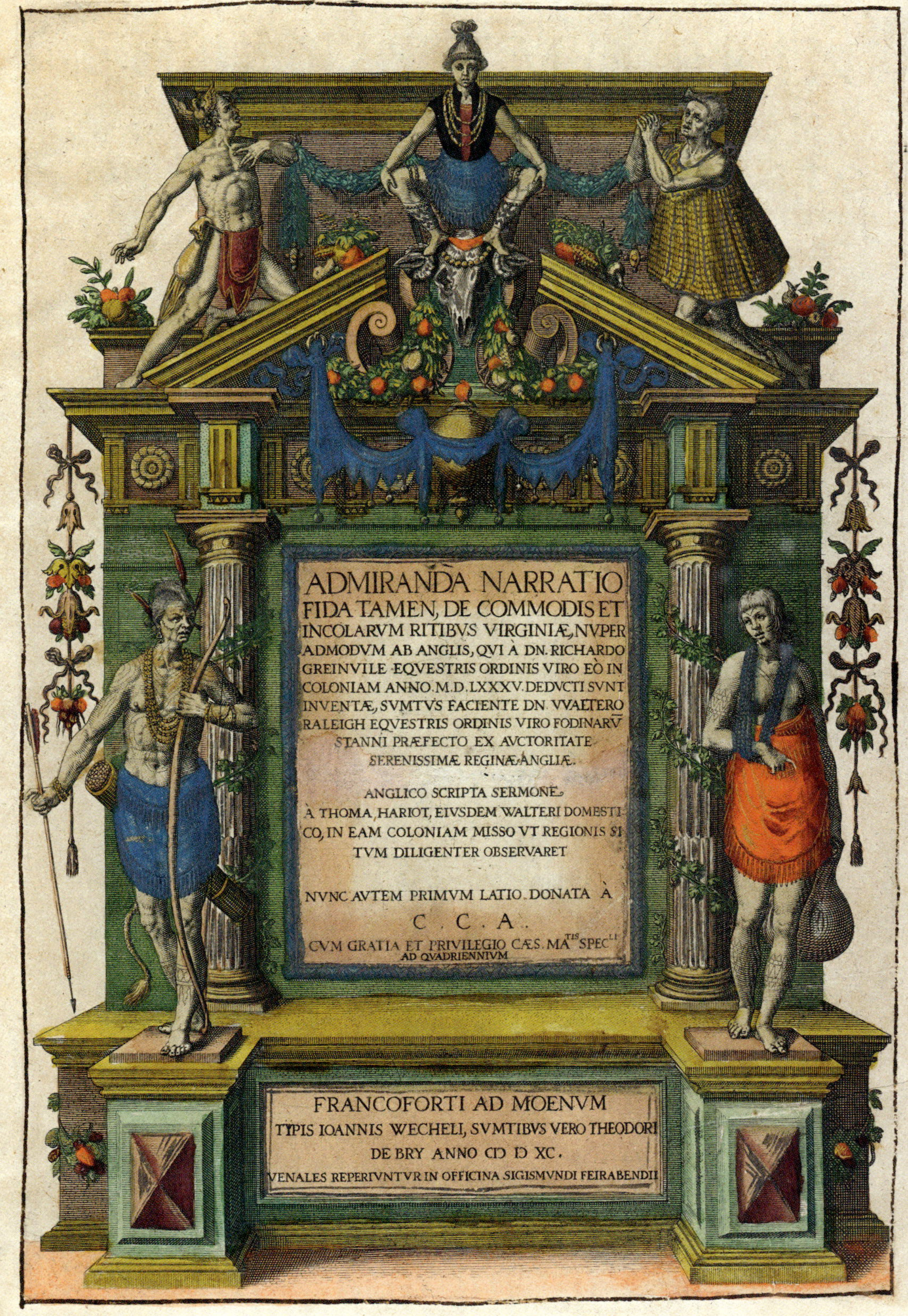

ADMIRANDA NARRATIO
FIDA TAMEN, DE COMMODIS ET
INCOLARVM RITIBVS VIRGINIÆ, NVPER
ADMODVM AB ANGLIS, QVI À DN. RICHARDO
GREINVILE EQVESTRIS ORDINIS VIRO EÒ IN
COLONIAM ANNO. M.D.LXXXV. DEDVCTI SVNT
INVENTÆ, SVMTVS FACIENTE DN. VVALTERO
RALEIGH EQVESTRIS ORDINIS VIRO FODINARV̄
STANNI PRÆFECTO EX AVCTORITATE
SERENISSIMÆ REGINÆ ANGLIÆ.

ANGLICO SCRIPTA SERMONE
À THOMA HARIOT, EIVSDEM WALTERI DOMESTICO, IN EAM COLONIAM MISSO VT REGIONIS SITVM DILIGENTER OBSERVARET

NVNC AVTEM PRIMVM LATIO DONATA À
C. C. A.

CVM GRATIA ET PRIVILEGIO CÆS. MA^TIS SPEC^LI
AD QVADRIENNIVM

FRANCOFORTI AD MOENVM
TYPIS IOANNIS WECHELI, SVMTIBVS VERO THEODORI
DE BRY ANNO CIↃ IↃ XC.
VENALES REPERIVNTVR IN OFFICINA SIGISMVNDI FEIRABENDII

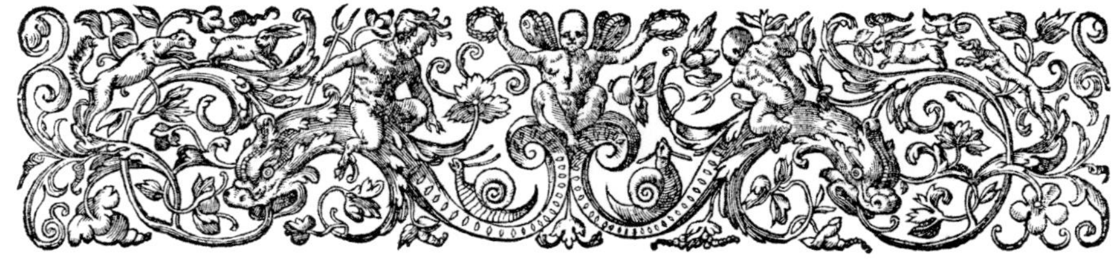

Volume I

Based on: Thomas Harriot,
A Briefe and True Report of the New Found Land of Virginia (London, 1588)
and John White's watercolours of the same settlement

Until recently, *America* I, the first volume of the collection of voyages, has been regarded as archetypal, a blueprint for the series devised by Richard Hakluyt in London and produced by Theodore de Bry and his sons in Frankfurt am Main, the book capital of early modern Europe. The truth, however, could not be more different, since *America* I is in fact more exceptional than any of the 25 volumes in the collection. It was printed in four languages (German, Latin, English and French) while the other 24 were printed only in German and Latin, and was based on an unpublished set of watercolours, whereas almost all of the other volumes were derived from travel accounts with either a few low-quality illustrations or none at all. It was also printed in a larger format than any of the subsequent volumes in the *America* series, and – perhaps most obviously – laid out more lavishly than all the other volumes, with the illustrations often printed as 'spreads' across two pages, rather than being strictly confined (as later) to a single page, with a title at the top and a caption underneath.

There are clear indications in this volume that Theodore de Bry was still in the process of working out how to structure the overall collection. His introduction includes a warning to would-be competitors that his illustrations contained hidden marks, in order that he would be protected from others seeking to circumvent the four-year copyright De Bry had secured for his publication, which had required significant investment. In reality, few publishers possessed the know-how or the

Frontispiece of volume I

Pages 66/67
Detail of volume I, plate 13

Page 71
Detail of volume I, plate 3

Pages 72/73
Map of Virginia showing Native American settlements

means to copy De Bry's work, and similar warnings are not found in any of the later volumes. That his ambitions extended beyond the publishing of just a single volume was clear from the start, and volume I, dealing with the experiences of English settlers in the Roanoke colony in the province they called "Virginia" (the present-day North Carolina), contains plenty of explicit cross-references to René de Laudonnière's account of Florida, a copy of which was in De Bry's possession. Several of the captions to De Bry's illustrations mention Floridian customs, and the sequence ends with an image of a Floridian pagan idol – a deliberate organisational choice which the De Brys would repeat in subsequent volumes. Another comparison, between late 16th-century Native Americans and Picts, the indigenous inhabitants of early medieval Britain, was probably inspired by Hakluyt's ambitions to attract settlers to Virginia, but this was not repeated by the De Brys in later volumes.

Volume I, more than any other part of the collection, provides a good impression of the sheer amount of work as well as the number of specialised contributors required for the publication of a single volume. Richard Hakluyt has been mentioned as the man who conceived the general idea of a multilingual, illustrated collection of voyages, but several other people in England were also involved in the making of volume I. The London apothecary James Garet and the naturalist Richard Garth provided translations of Harriot's travel account for Carolus Clusius to work with, the only translator credited on the Latin title-page. In 1589, the year before volume I came off the presses, as many as four different Latin translations of Harriot's account were in circulation. The German translation was provided by a certain Christian P., while for the later volumes, the Latin edition took precedence, with the German edition being derived from the Latin text. Sigismund Feyerabend, Frankfurt's leading publisher in the final third of the 16th century but who did not live to see the first *America* volume in print, supervised the De Brys in the process of making a book – something Theodore and his sons had never done before. Johann Wechel, who printed the book, was a close associate of Feyerabend and continued to work with the De Brys for volumes II and III. Alongside Theodore de Bry himself, who signed his engravings with the monogram T. B., other engravers who contributed to the collection included the Flemish artist Gijsbert van Veen and the German Jacob Kempener, another Feyerabend associate. Johan Theodore almost certainly contributed artwork as well. And finally someone – possibly Johan Israel or Theodore himself – acquired a privilege for the volume, which protected it from being copied, at least theoretically.

Just before the volumes were actually published, the De Brys made an effort to dedicate them to various patrons who in return for such an acknowledgement of their public support for the arts and sciences would provide financial backing or at least the guaranteed sale of a certain number of copies. Since there were four editions of volume I, for the four different languages, the De Brys attempted to find a corresponding number of patrons, something they would continue to do in later years for the bilingual volumes. Volume I was dedicated to Sir Walter Raleigh, the Elizabethan patron of Hakluyt and mastermind behind the early voyages to North America (English); Maximilian, Archduke of Tyrol (Latin); Christian I, Elector of Saxony (German); and William IV, Landgrave of Hesse-Kassel (French). The last two were also honoured in De Bry's dedications to volume II of the *America* series, for the Latin and German editions respectively, and can thus be regarded as crucial early supporters of the undertaking. The dedication of the Latin edition to Maximilian of Austria is significant, in that it foreshadowed the De Brys' practice to dedicate their Latin translations to highly placed Catholic noblemen in order to mitigate some of the visibly anti-Catholic ideas to be found in some of the travel accounts included in the collection.

Since volume I, unlike all the subsequent volumes, was also published in English, the captions which follow this introduction are not translations but modernised versions of the English edition of *America* I.

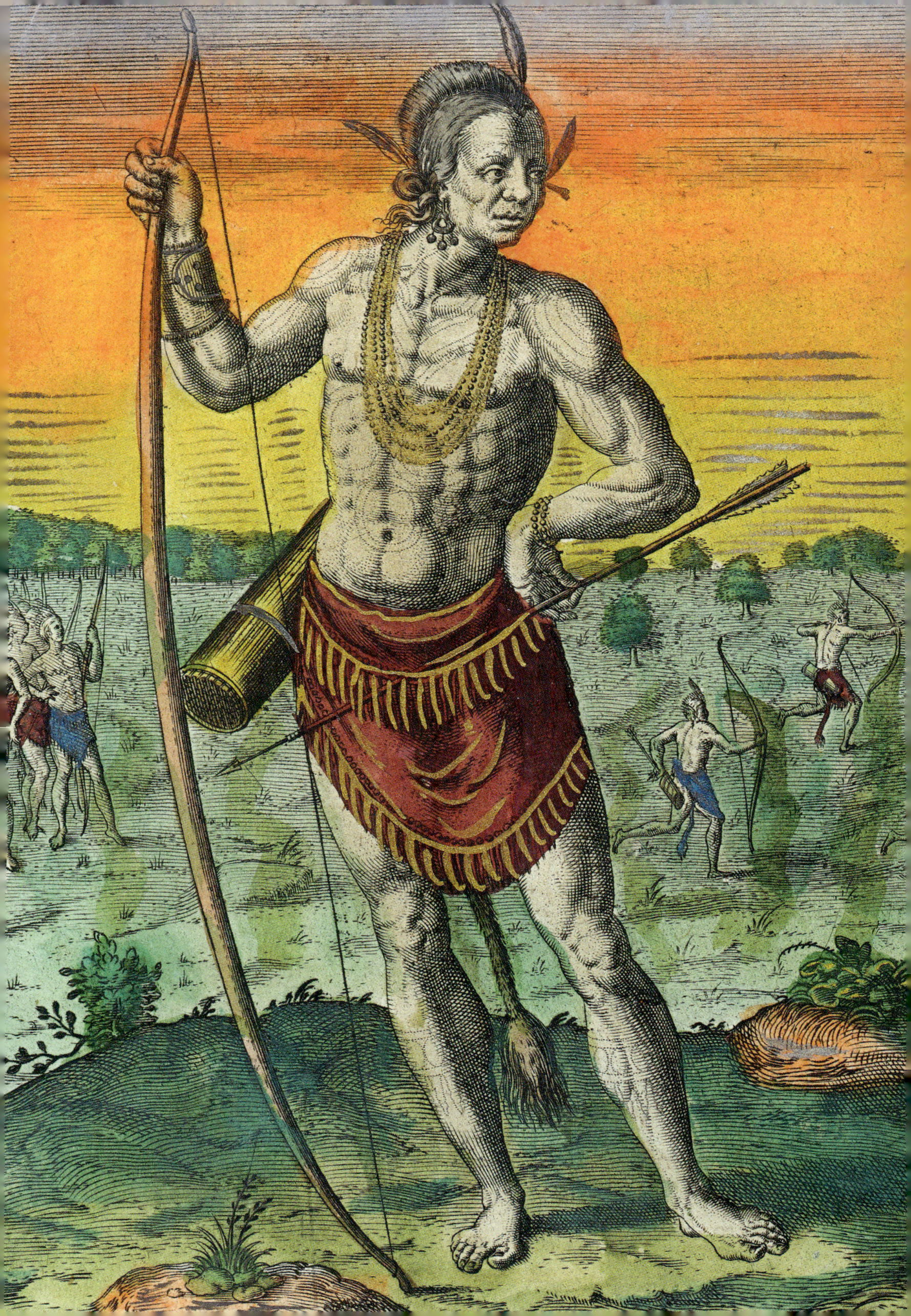

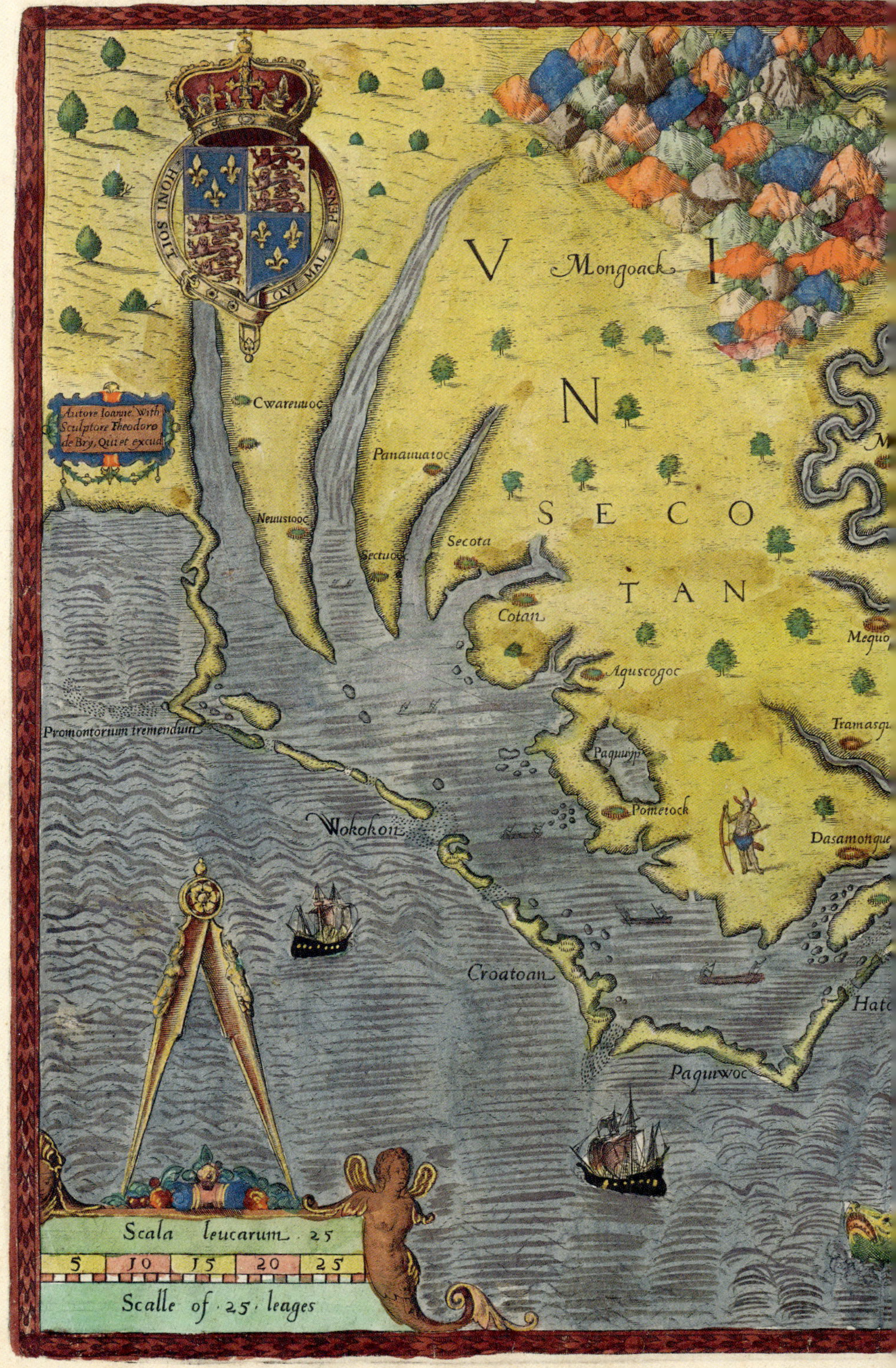

HONI SOIT QVI MAL Y PENSE
Autore Ioanne With Sculptore Theodoro de Bry, Qui et excud.
V
I
N
SECOTAN
Mongoack
Cwareuuoc
Panauuaioc
Neuustooc
Secota
Sectuooc
Cotan
Aguscogoc
Meguo
Tramasq
Promontorium tremendum
Paquuip
Pometock
Dasamonque
Wokokon
Croatoan
Hat
Paquiwoc
Scala leucarum 25
5 10 15 20 25
Scalle of 25 leages

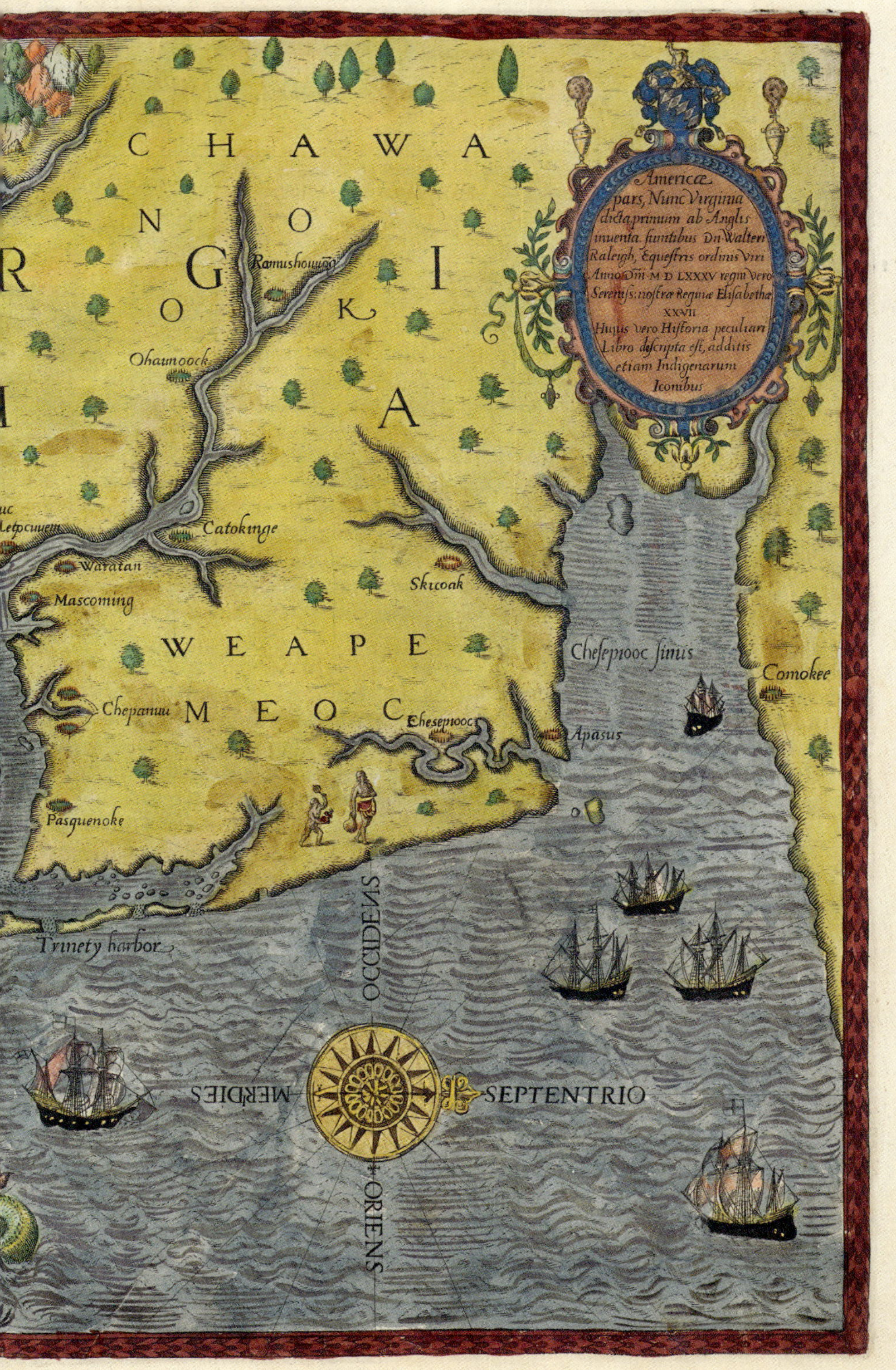

Americæ pars, Nunc Virginia dicta, primum ab Anglis inuenta, sumtibus Dn. Walteri Raleigh, Equestris ordinis Viri Anno Dñi M D LXXXV regni vero Serenis: nostræ Reginæ Elisabethæ XXVII Hujus vero Historia peculiari Libro descripta est, additis etiam Indigenarum Iconibus
CHAWA
N O
R G I
O K
A
Ramushouuog
Ohaunoock
Catokinge
Waratan
Mascoming
Skicoak
W E A P E
Chepanuu M E O C
Chesepiooc
Apasus
Chesepiooc sinus
Comokee
Pasquenoke
Trinety harbor
OCCIDENS
MERIDIES
SEPTENTRIO
ORIENS

PLATE 1

Adam and Eve

The decorative frontispiece from the foreword shows Adam and Eve in the Garden of Eden picking the forbidden fruit from the tree of knowledge of good and evil.

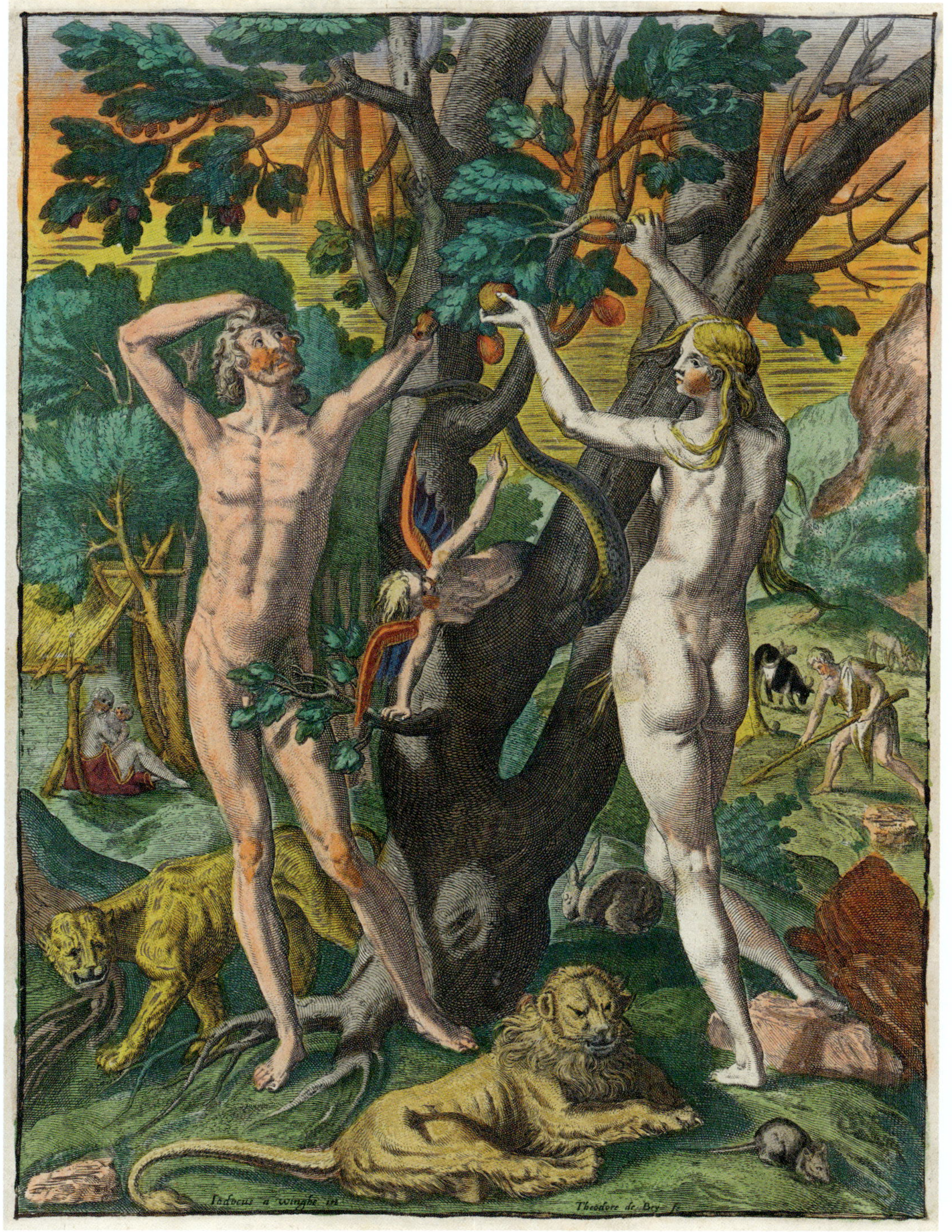
Iodocus a winghe in
Theodore de Bry f.

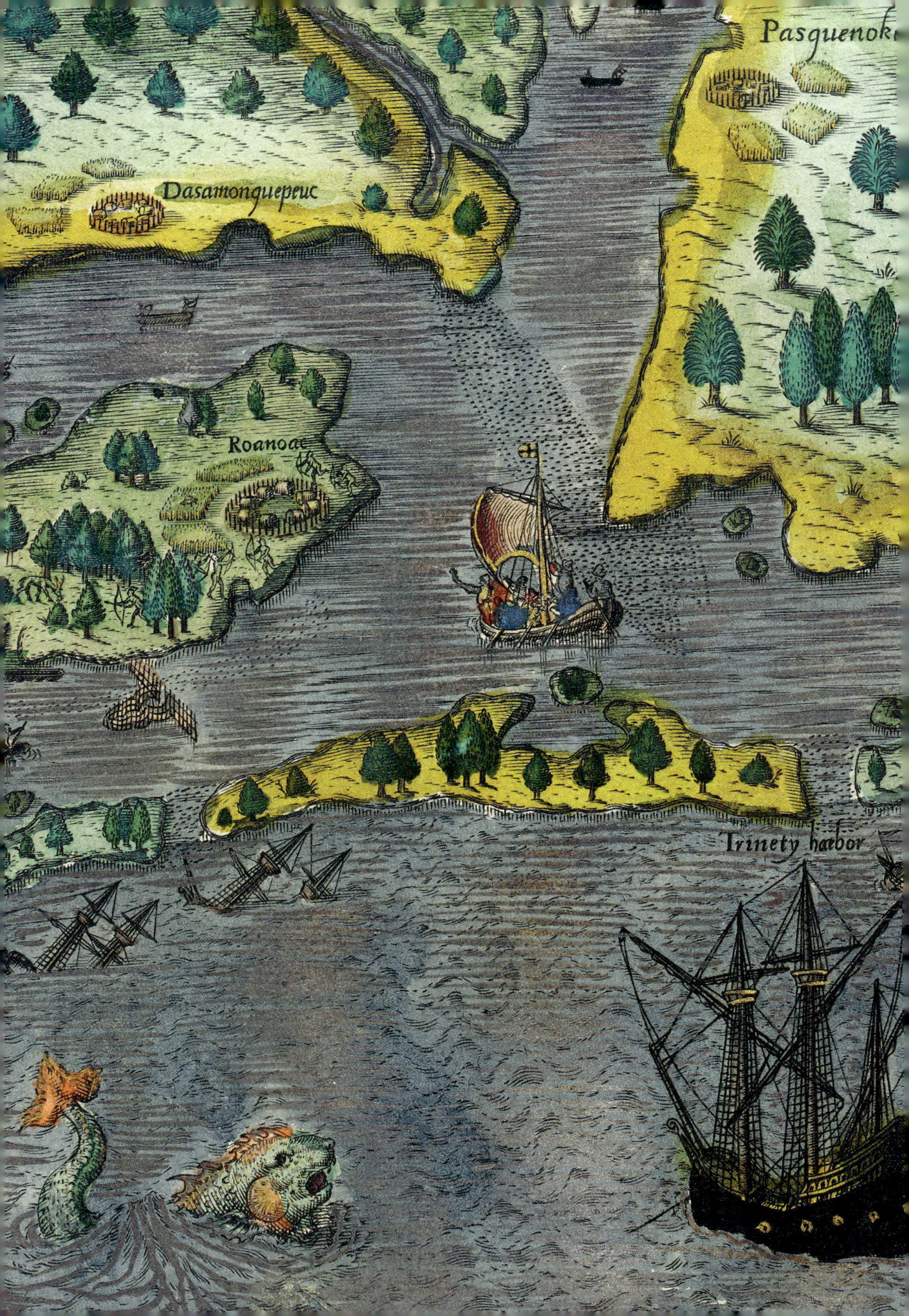
Pasquenok
Dasamonquepeuc
Roanoac
Trinety harbor

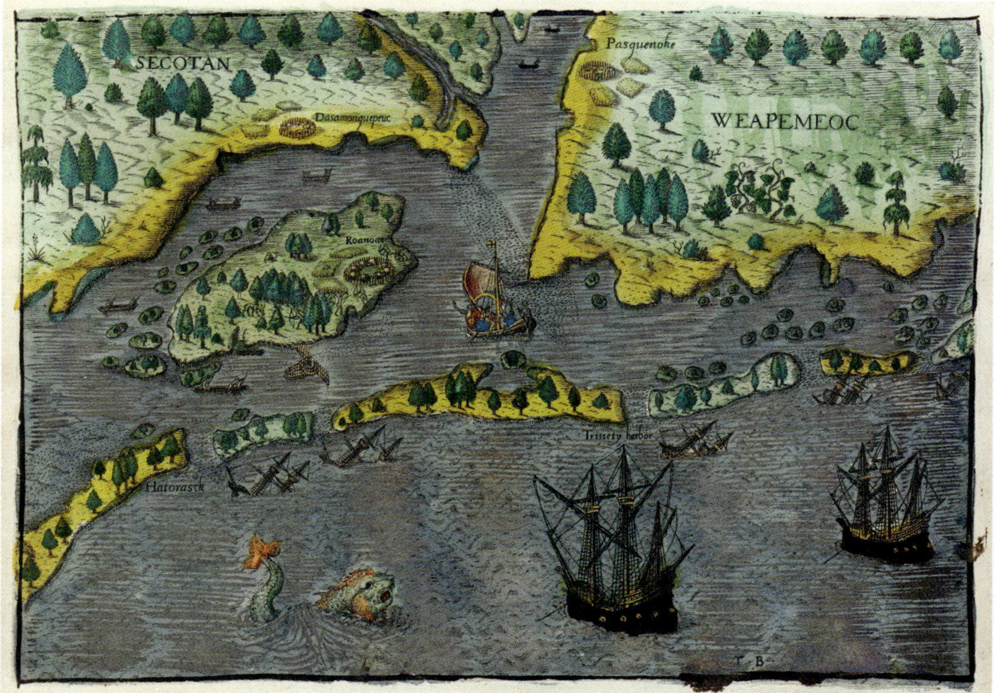

PLATE 2

The arrival of the English in Virginia

The coast of Virginia is so packed with islands that the point of entry to the mainland is hard to find. Although these islands are separated from each other by a variety of inlets, which at first seem to yield convenient access to the mainland, we established to our great peril that they were shallow and full of dangerous banks, and would never allow passage, until we made trials in many places with our small boats. Finally, we found a way through after our men had made a diligent search. After we had entered the channel we discovered a mighty river emptying into the sound over against those islands, but even so we could not sail very far up because it was too shallow, its mouth being filled with sand brought there with the tide. Therefore sailing further, we came to a good large island. As soon as they saw us, the islanders began to cry out in a loud and horrible manner, like people who had never seen men wearing outfits such as ours before, and so continued to make noises like wild beasts or like men who have lost their minds. But once we had managed to call them back gently, we offered them glasses, knives, dolls and other trifles, and these things appeared to delight them very much. All at once they then stood still, and, now perceiving our goodwill, they welcomed us. Then they took us to their village on the island called Roanoke, and led us to their Weroan or prince, who entertained us quite courteously, although everyone there was amazed at their first sight of us.

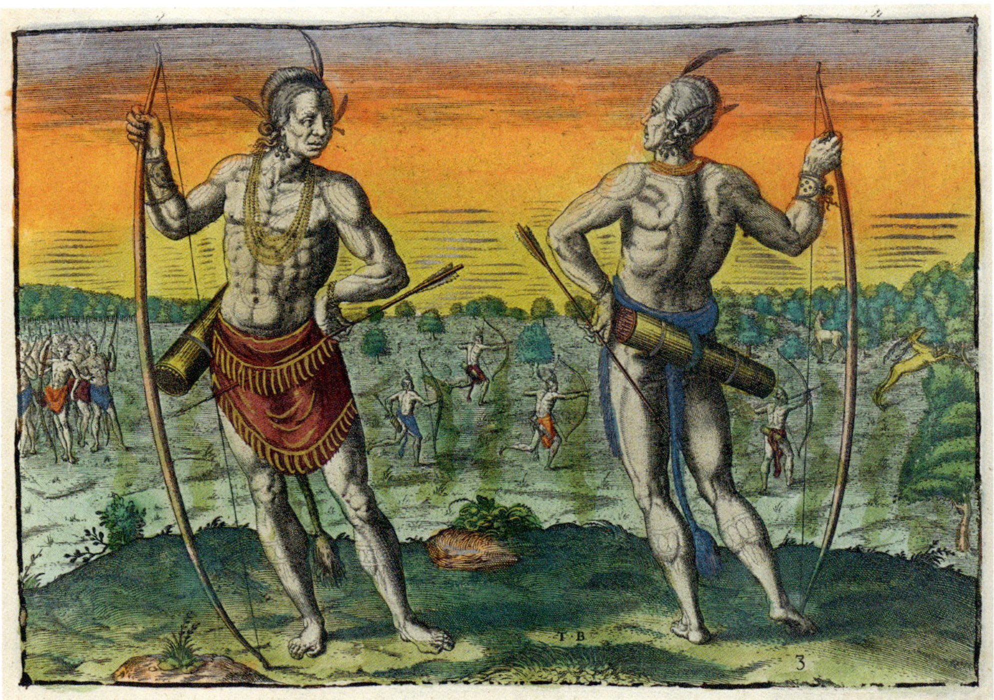

PLATE 3

A Weroan or great lord of Virginia

The princes of Virginia are dressed in such a manner as is shown here. They wear their hair long, and tie up the end of it in a knot under their ears. They cut the hair on the top of their head from the forehead to the nape of their neck like a coxcomb, sticking a longish beak of some bird at the front of the crest upon their forehead, and another short one on either side next to their ears. They also hang large pearls from their ears or something similar, such as the claw of some great bird, and many of them like to do this. Moreover, they either pounce, or paint their forehead, cheeks, chin, body, arms and legs, although in a different fashion from the inhabitants of Florida. Around their neck they wear a chain of pearls or beads of copper, which they value highly, and wear similar bracelets on their arms. Lower down their chest and around their belly there appear certain spots, and it is from these marks that they let themselves bleed when they are sick. They cover themselves with the skin of some beast which has been very carefully dressed and in such a way that the tail hangs down behind them. They carry a quiver made of thin rushes and hold their bow ready strung in one hand, and an arrow in the other, so that they may defend themselves without delay. In this manner they go to war, so too to their solemn feasts and banquets. They take much pleasure in hunting deer, which are plentiful in their country, for it is fertile, temperate and full of thick woods. There are also many rivers full of all sorts of fish. When they go to battle they paint their bodies in the most fearsome manner imaginable.

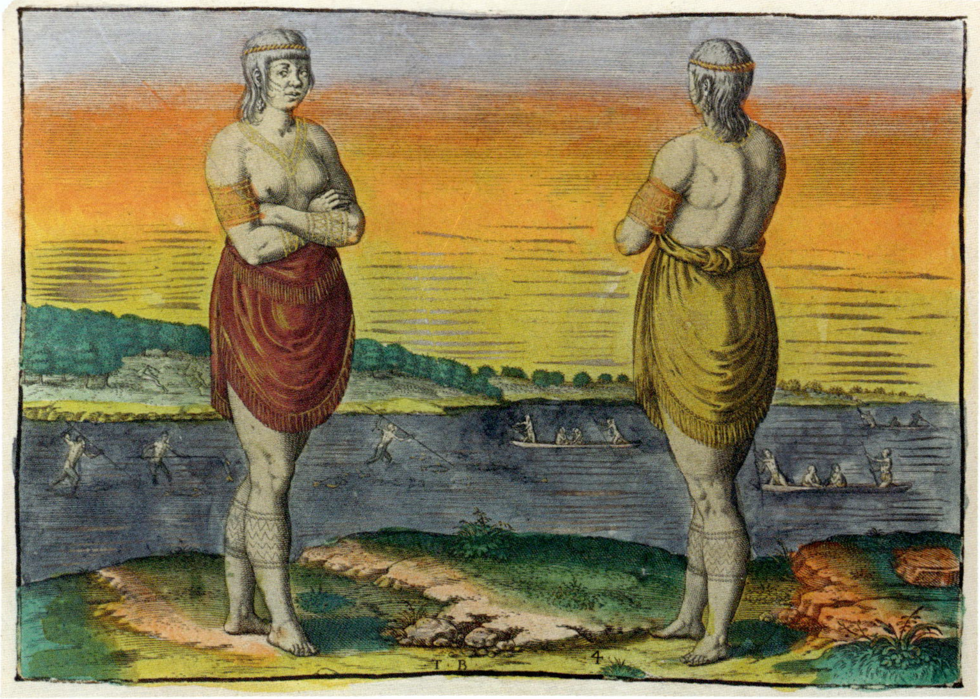

PLATE 4

One of the chief ladies of Secota

The women of Secota are quite well proportioned. They usually keep their hands held downwards, and are very beautifully dressed in deerskins, which hang down from their navel to the middle of their thighs, and also cover their private parts. The rest of their body is all bare. The front part of their hair they cut short while the rest is not overly long, and is thin, soft and falls down to their shoulders. Upon their head they wear a wreath. Their foreheads, cheeks, chin, arms and legs are pounced, and around their neck they wear a chain, either pierced or painted. They have small eyes, plain, flat noses, a narrow forehead and a broad mouth. For the most part they hang chains of long pearls from their ears, or others made from some smooth bones. Their nails, however, are not long like those of the women of Florida. They take pleasure in walking into the fields, and along the rivers, to watch the deer being hunted and the fish being caught.

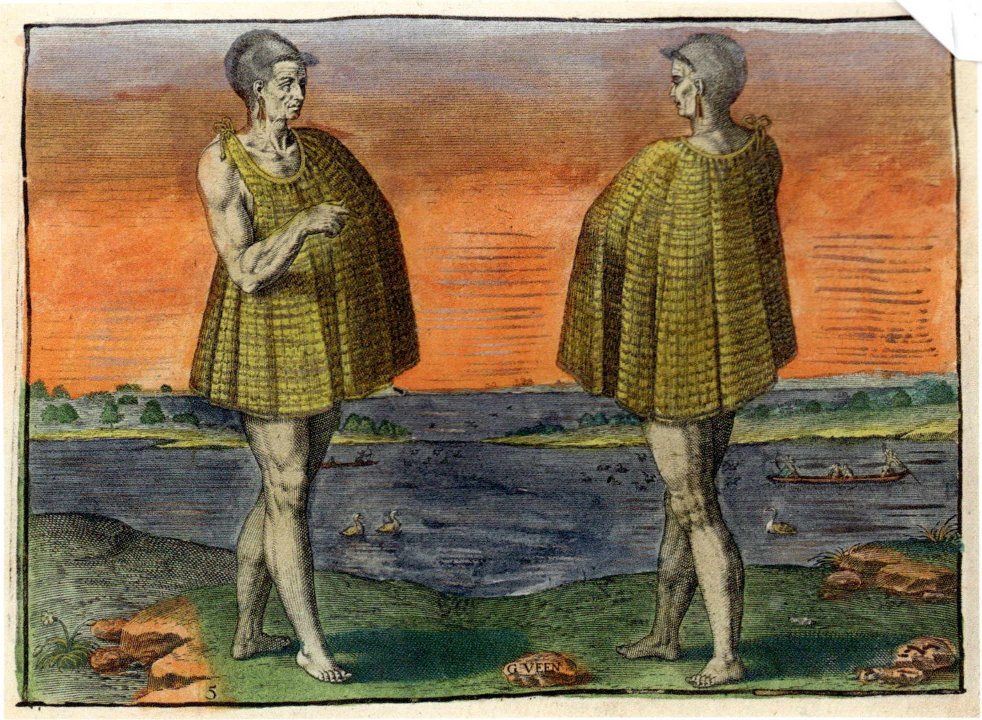

PLATE 5

One of the religious men of Secota

The priests of the aforementioned town of Secota are older and more experienced than the other people. They wear their hair cut like a crest, on the top of their head as others do, but the rest of it is cut short save the part that grows above their forehead, so that it resembles a periwig. They too wear various things hanging from their ears, and wear a short cloak made of finely dressed hares' skins quilted with the hair lying outwards. The rest of their body is naked. They are skilled enchanters, and for their pleasure they frequent the rivers, to kill with their bows and arrows wild ducks, swans and other birds.

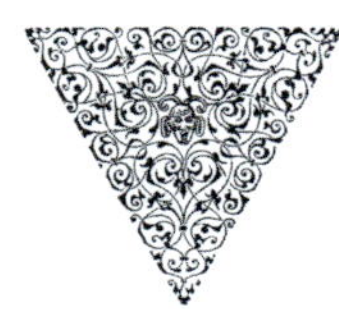

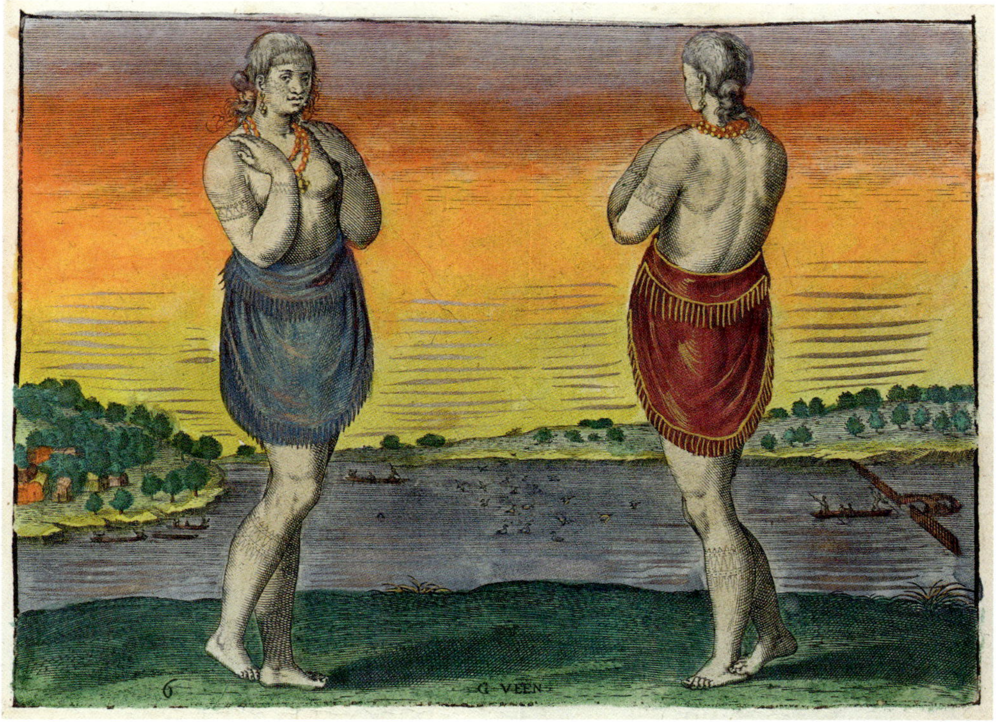

PLATE 6

A young and gentle woman of Secota

Virgins of good families closely resemble the women of Secota described earlier, save that instead of a chain around their neck they wear certain thick, round pearls, strung together with little beads of copper or polished bones between them. They pounce their forehead, cheeks, arms and legs. Their hair is cut with two ridges above their forehead, and the rest is trussed up with a knot behind. They have broad mouths, and well-shaped black eyes; they often rest their hands upon their shoulders, and cover their breasts in token of their virtuous modesty. The rest of their body is naked, as may be seen here. They too delight in seeing fish being caught in the rivers.

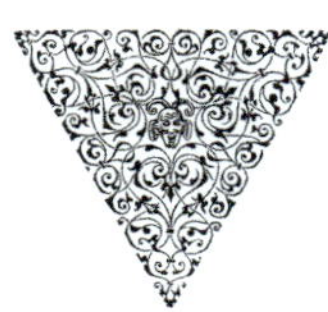

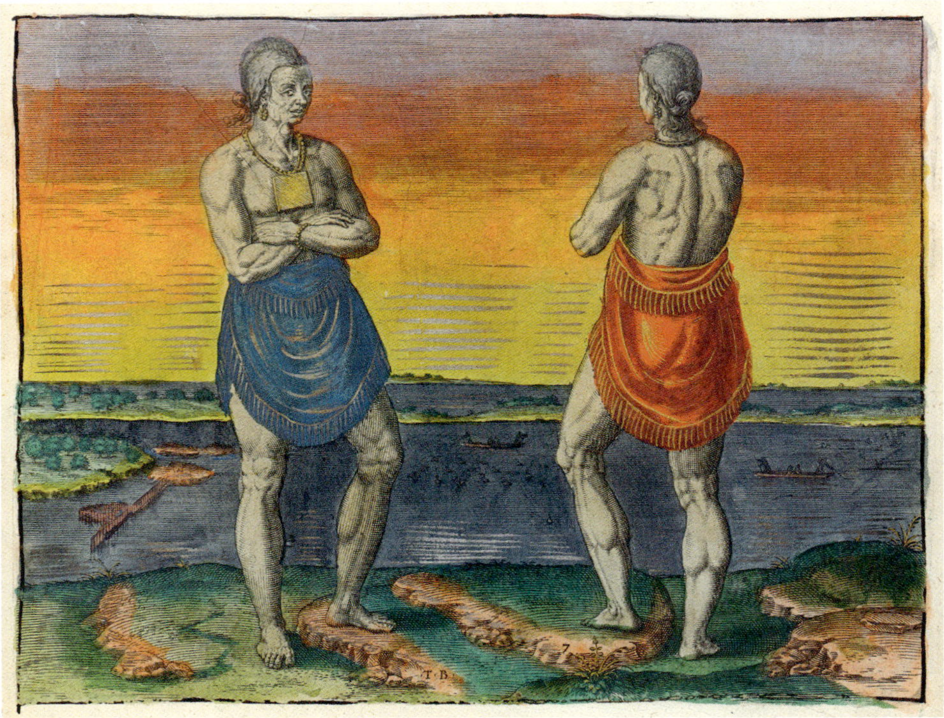

PLATE 7

A chief lord of Roanoke

The chief men of the island and town of Roanoke wear their hair cut like a coxcomb, as the others do, but the rest of it they wear long like the women and truss it up in a knot at the back of their neck. From their ears they hang pearls strung upon a thread, and wear bracelets on their arms made of pearls, or small beads of copper or a smooth bone called minsal. They do not paint or pounce their bodies, but as a sign of authority and dignity they wear a chain of great pearls, copper beads or smooth bones around their necks, and a flat fringe of copper pieces attached to a string, from their navel to the middle of their thighs. They cover themselves front and back as the women do with a deerskin that has been very well dressed, and is also fringed. Moreover, they fold their arms when they walk, or when they talk, as a sign of wisdom. The isle of Roanoke is very pleasant, and has plenty of fish by reason of the water that surrounds it.

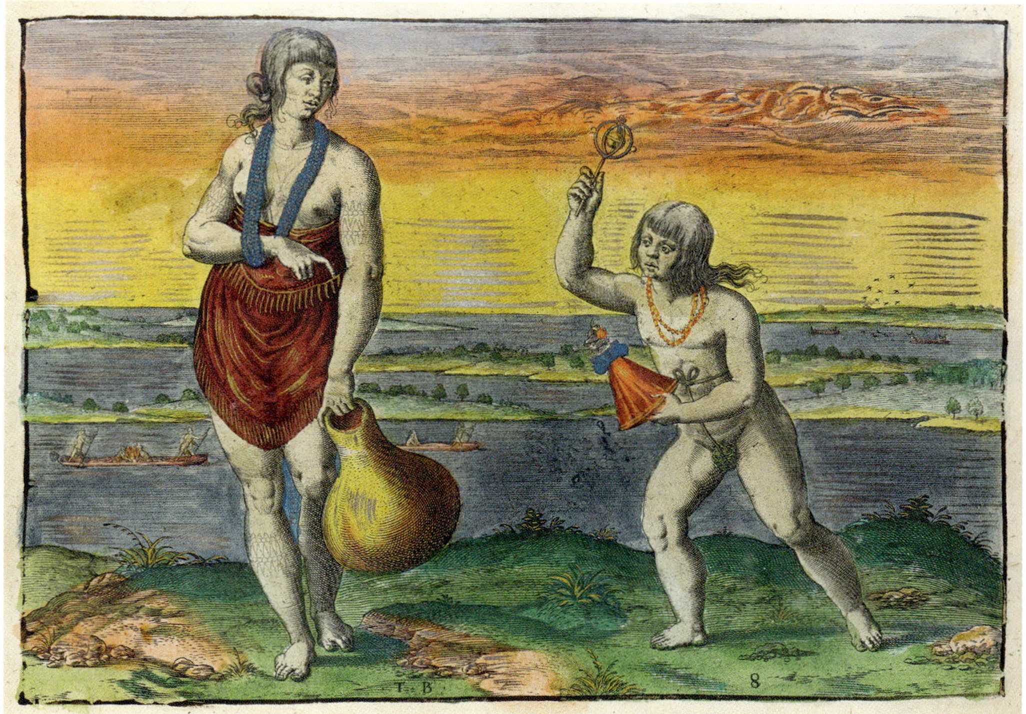

PLATE 8

A chief lady of Pomeiooc

About 20 miles from this island, near the lake of Paquippe, there is another town called Pomeiooc, which is close to the sea. The appearance of the chief ladies of this town differs very little from what is worn by those who live in Roanoke. Indeed, here they wear their hair trussed up in a knot, as the virgins do who were mentioned before, and have their skin pounced in the same way; however, they wear a chain of great pearls, or beads of copper or smooth bones, in five or six loops around their necks, and place one arm in this long necklace, while in the other hand they carry a gourd full of some kind of pleasant liquor. They tie a deerskin doubled around them that reaches higher up towards their breasts, and hangs down before them almost to their knees, while they are almost altogether naked behind. Commonly their young daughters of seven or eight years old wait upon them, and these wear about them a girdle of skin, which hangs down behind and is then drawn between their legs and bound above their navel, with green moss from the trees to line it and in this way the skins cover their private parts. When they are 10 years old, they wear deerskins in the same way as the older girls do. They are greatly delighted with dolls which we brought from England.

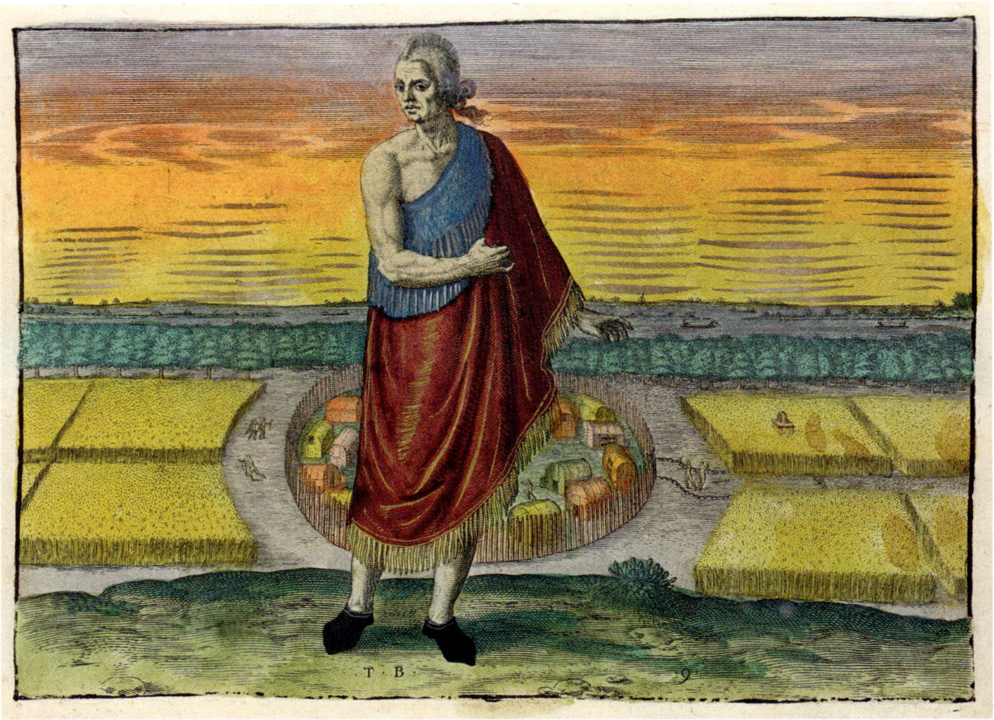

PLATE 9

An old man in his winter clothing

The older men of Pomeiooc cover themselves with a large skin which is tied around their shoulders on one side and hangs down below their knees, leaving their other arm naked and out of the skin so that they can use it more freely. These skins are dressed with the hair left on, and lined with other furred skins. The young men suffer no hair at all to grow upon their face and as soon as any grows they get rid of it, but when they are older they let it grow, although these hairs are always very thin. They also wear their hair bound up at the back, and have a crest on their heads like the others. The country here is so fertile and good that England cannot be compared to it.

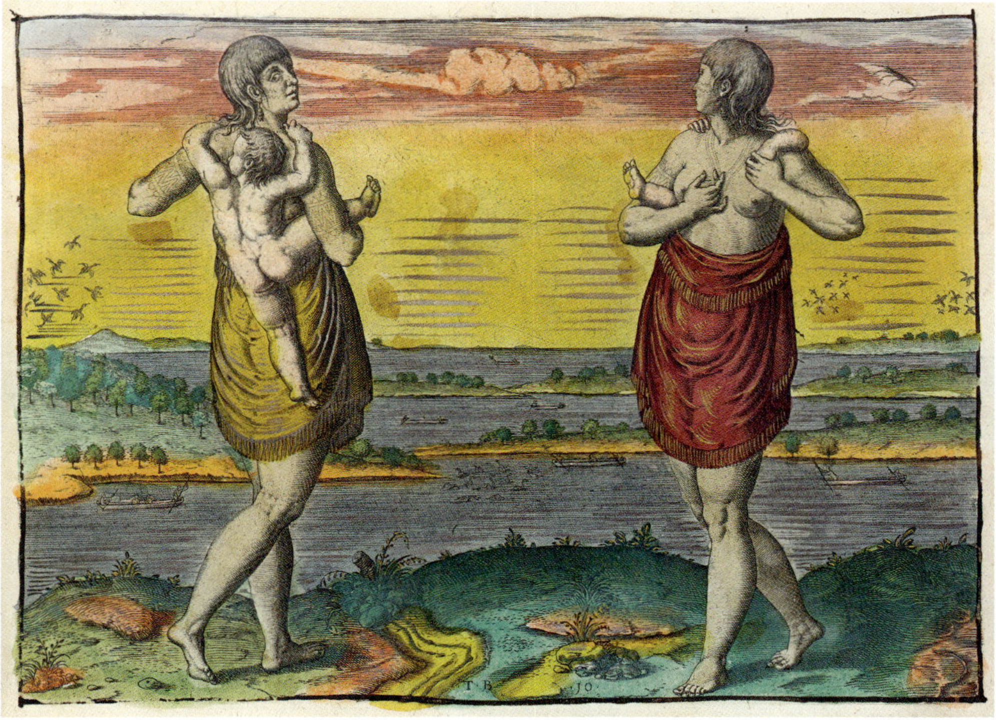

PLATE 10

Their manner of carrying their children, and the outfits of the chief ladies of the town of Dasomonquepeuc

In the town of Dasomonquepeuc, four or five miles from Roanoke, the women are dressed, and pounced, in the same way as the women of Roanoke, although they do not wear wreaths upon their head and nor do they paint their thighs with small dots. They have a strange manner of carrying their children. Our women carry their children in their arms at the level of their breasts, but these women take their son by his left hand and carry him around on their back, holding the right thigh in their right arm in a strange fashion, as can be seen here.

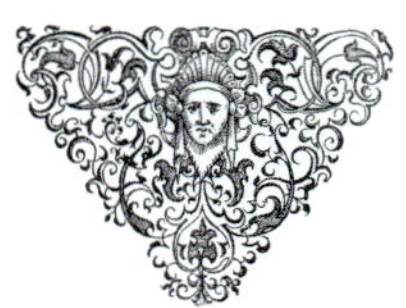

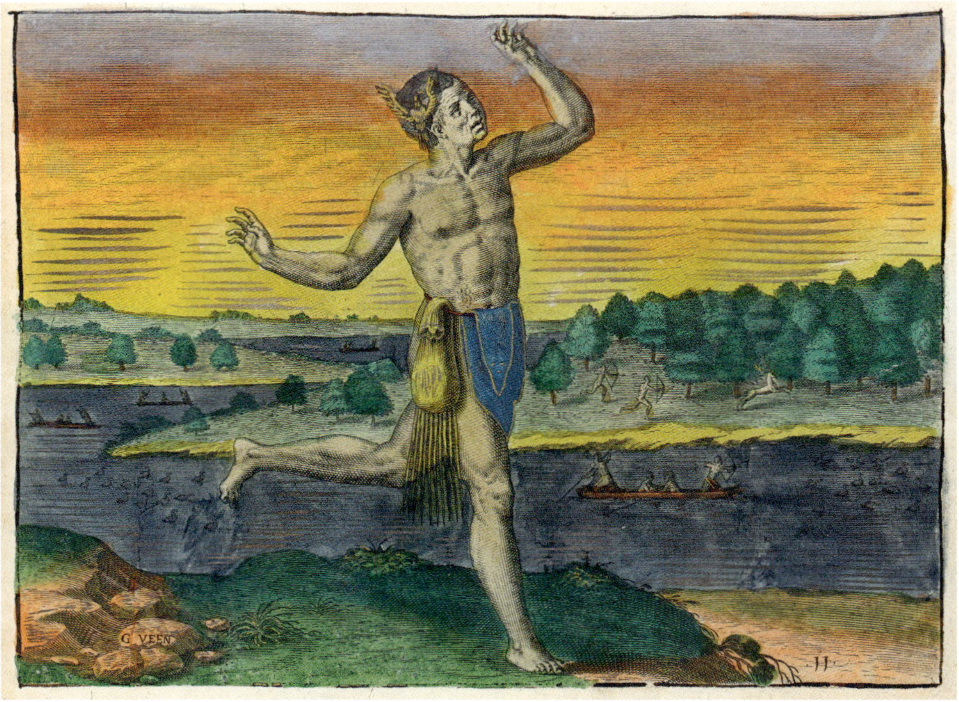

PLATE 11

The conjurer

There are many conjurers or jugglers here who use gestures, and in their enchantments often work against nature. This is because they are very familiar with devils, of whom they enquire what their enemies are doing, or other such things. They shave their head completely save the crest which they wear as others do, and fasten a small black bird above one of their ears as a badge of their trade. They wear nothing but a skin which hangs down from their girdle, and covers their private parts. By their side they wear a bag as can be seen here. The inhabitants put great faith in their speech, which often they find to be true.

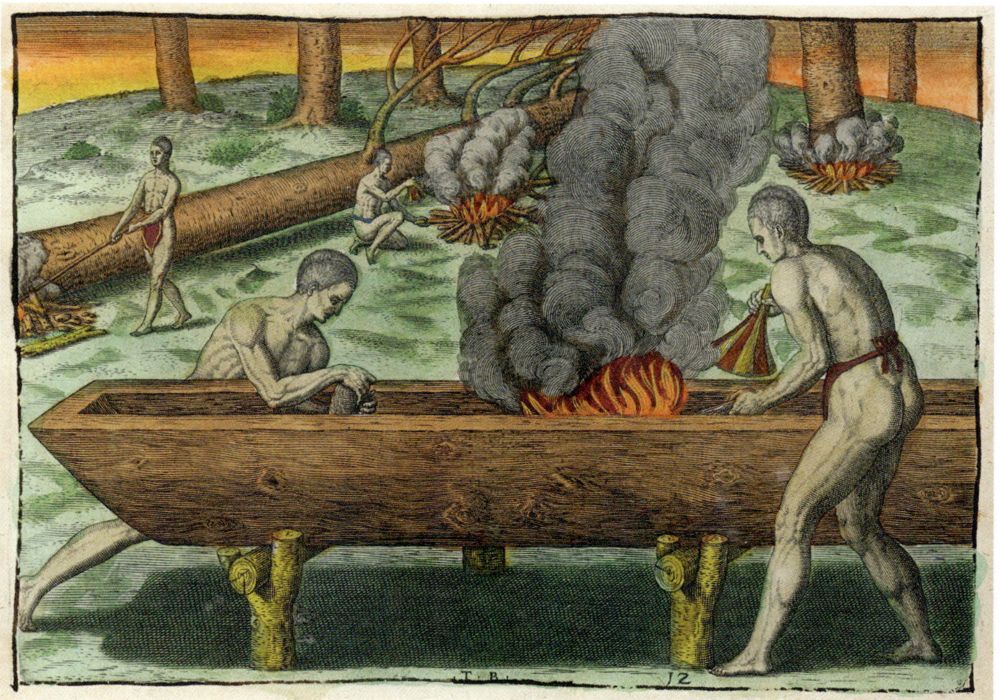

PLATE 12

The manner of making their boats

The manner of making their boats in Virginia is most wonderful. For even though they do not have any iron tools, or yet others like we do, they know how to make boats just as well so that they can sail with them where they like on their rivers, and fish as we do. First they choose a tall, thick tree, according to the size of the boat they want to make, and start a fire on the ground, kindling it little by little with dry moss from the trees and chips of wood, in such a way that the flames should not rise too high, and burn too much of the height of the tree. When it is almost burnt through and ready to fall they make a new fire, which they allow to burn until the tree falls of its own accord. Then with the new fire they burn off the top of the tree and the branches in such a way that the trunk is reduced to the right length, and then raise it up on poles resting on forked posts. Then they remove the bark using certain shells, and continue in this way such that the innermost part of the trunk will become the lowest part of the boat. On the other side they make a fire as long as the length of this main part of the tree. Where they think it has been burned enough they put out the fire and scrape away at the wood with shells, then making a new fire they burn it again, and so continue sometimes burning and sometimes scraping until the boats have the desired depth. God endows these savage people with sufficient reason to carry out this work to serve their needs.

PLATE 13

Their manner of fishing in Virginia

They also have a special way of catching fish in their rivers. Because they have no iron, they fasten on to the end of their long rods the hollow tail of a certain sea creature such as a crab, and use this day and night to catch fish, and raise them up into their boats. They also know how to use the prickles and spines of other fish. Again, they also make weirs, by placing reeds or twigs in the water, which they arrange in such a way that the construction grows narrower and narrower, as appears here. Never before had we seen such a cunning way of catching fish, many different sorts of which are found in their rivers and which are unlike ours, but taste very good. It is a wonderful sight to see these people, sometimes wading, sometimes sailing in their rivers which are quite shallow, free from all care of gathering riches for posterity, pleased with their state and living together happily on those things which God in his goodness has given them, although without giving him any thanks. For so savage is this people, and deprived of the true knowledge of God. Indeed they have none other than is mentioned before in this work.

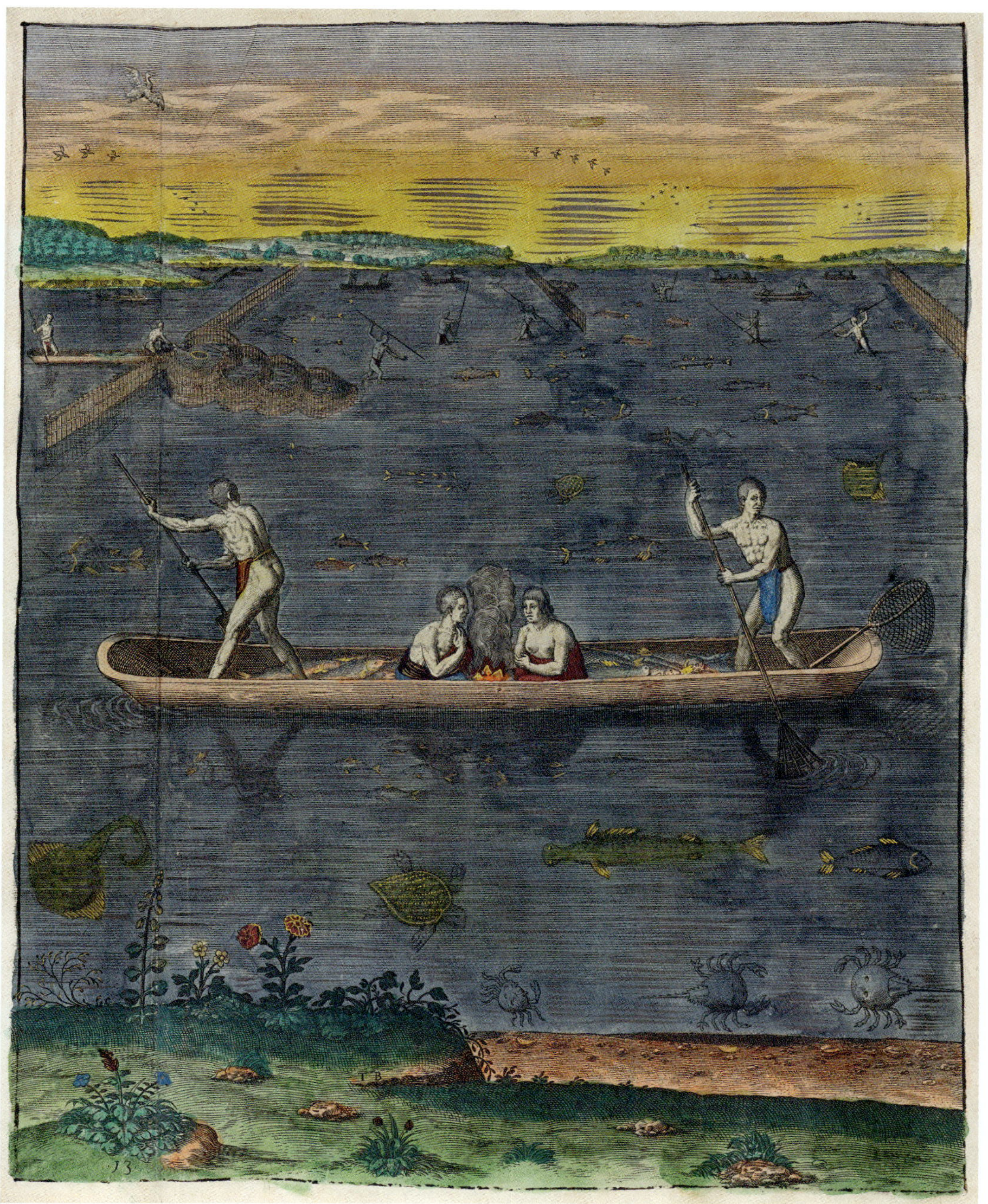

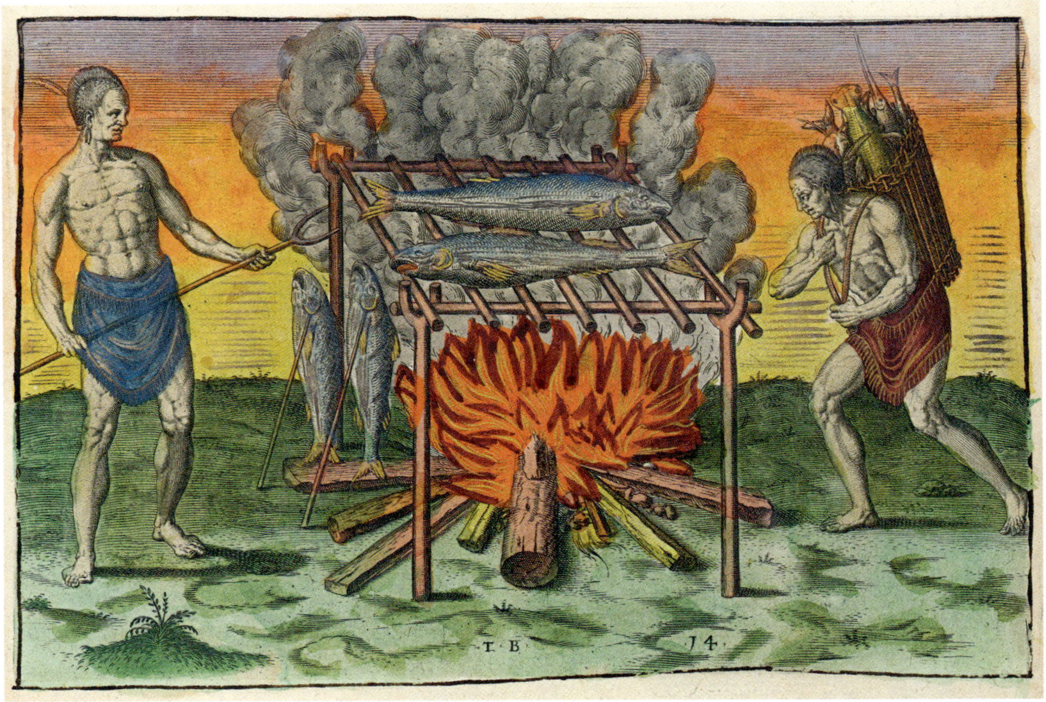

PLATE 14

The broiling of their fish over a fire

After they have caught enough fish, they take them to a place fit to prepare them. Here they stick four stakes in the ground in a square, and lay four posts on top of them and others athwart these as on a rack, at a reasonable height. Laying their fish upon this rack, they make a fire underneath to broil them, yet not after the manner of the people of Florida, who do this only very briefly and harden their meat in the smoke only to preserve it during the winter. For these people, preserving nothing for storage, they broil and consume everything at once. And when they desire more, they roast or boil again. If the rack is too small to hold all the fish, they hang the rest next to the fire on sticks set up in the ground nearby, and in this way finish the rest of their cooking. They take care that the food is not being burned. When the first fish have been cooked they put others on top which have just been caught, continuing the layering of their meat in this fashion until they think they have enough.

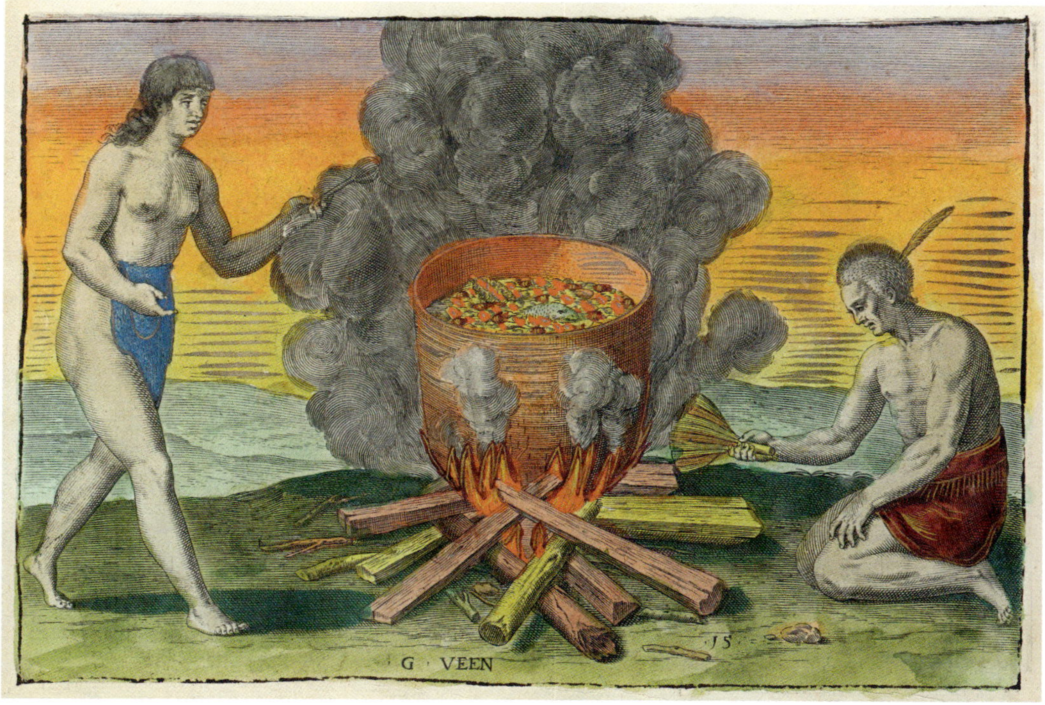

PLATE 15

The boiling of their food in earthen pots

Their women make earthen vessels that are so large and fine that our potters can make none better, and they carry them from place to place as easily as we can move our brass kettles. After they have set them down on a small heap of earth to prevent them from falling over, they put wood underneath them all around the base while one of them watches so that the fire burns equally all the way round. They or their womenfolk then fill the vessel with water, and put in fruit, meat and fish, and let everything boil together like a gallimaufry, which the Spaniards call olla podrida. Then they put it on dishes, and place it before those who are present, and they all enjoy a good meal together. Even so, they are moderate in their eating and thus avoid illness. I wish we might follow their example, for if we did we should be free from many kinds of diseases which we fall into by sumptuous and unseasonable banquets, continually devising new sauces, and provocations to gluttony to satisfy our unsatiable appetites.

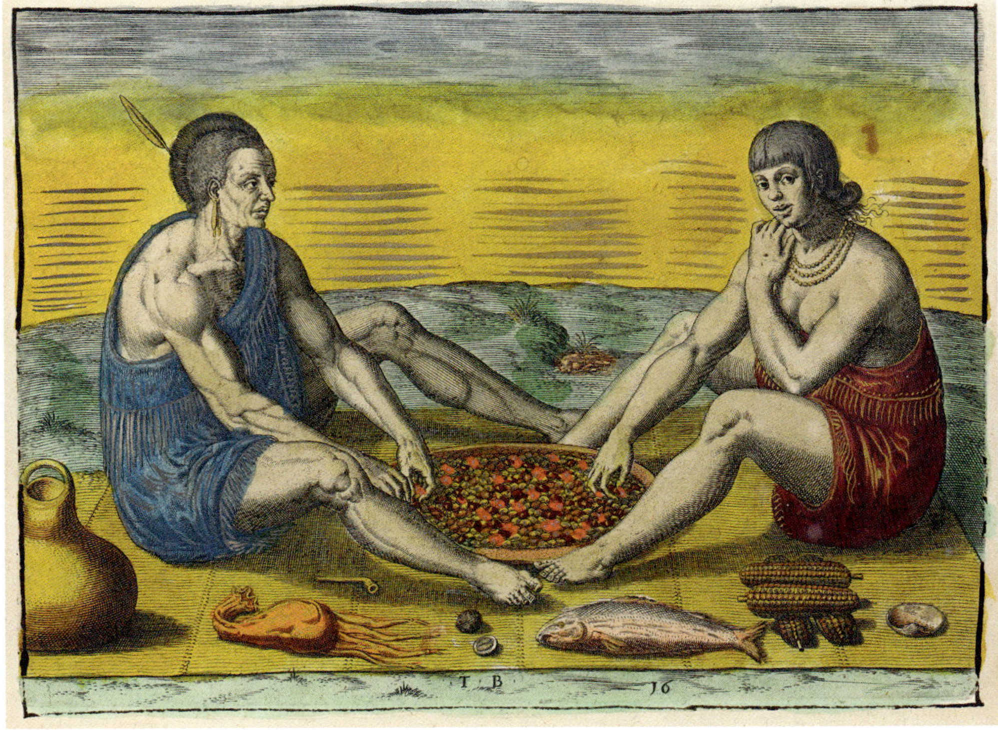

PLATE 16

Their manner of sitting to dine

Their manner of eating is such that they place a mat made of stiff grass on the ground and set their food in the middle, and then sit down around it, the men on one side and the women on the other. Their food is boiled maize which has a very good taste, deer meat, or the meat of some other animal, and fish. They are very restrained in their eating and drinking, and consequently they live very long because they do not oppress nature.

PLATE 17

Their manner of praying with rattles around the fire

When they have escaped some great danger on sea or land, or return from war, they build a great fire and the men and women sit together around it, holding a type of fruit in their hands like a round pumpkin or a gourd. After the fruit and seeds have been removed they fill it with small stones to make a noise and fasten it upon a stick, and so, singing in their own manner, they proceed to enjoy themselves, as I myself observed and noted down while being among them. For it is a strange custom, and worth the observation.

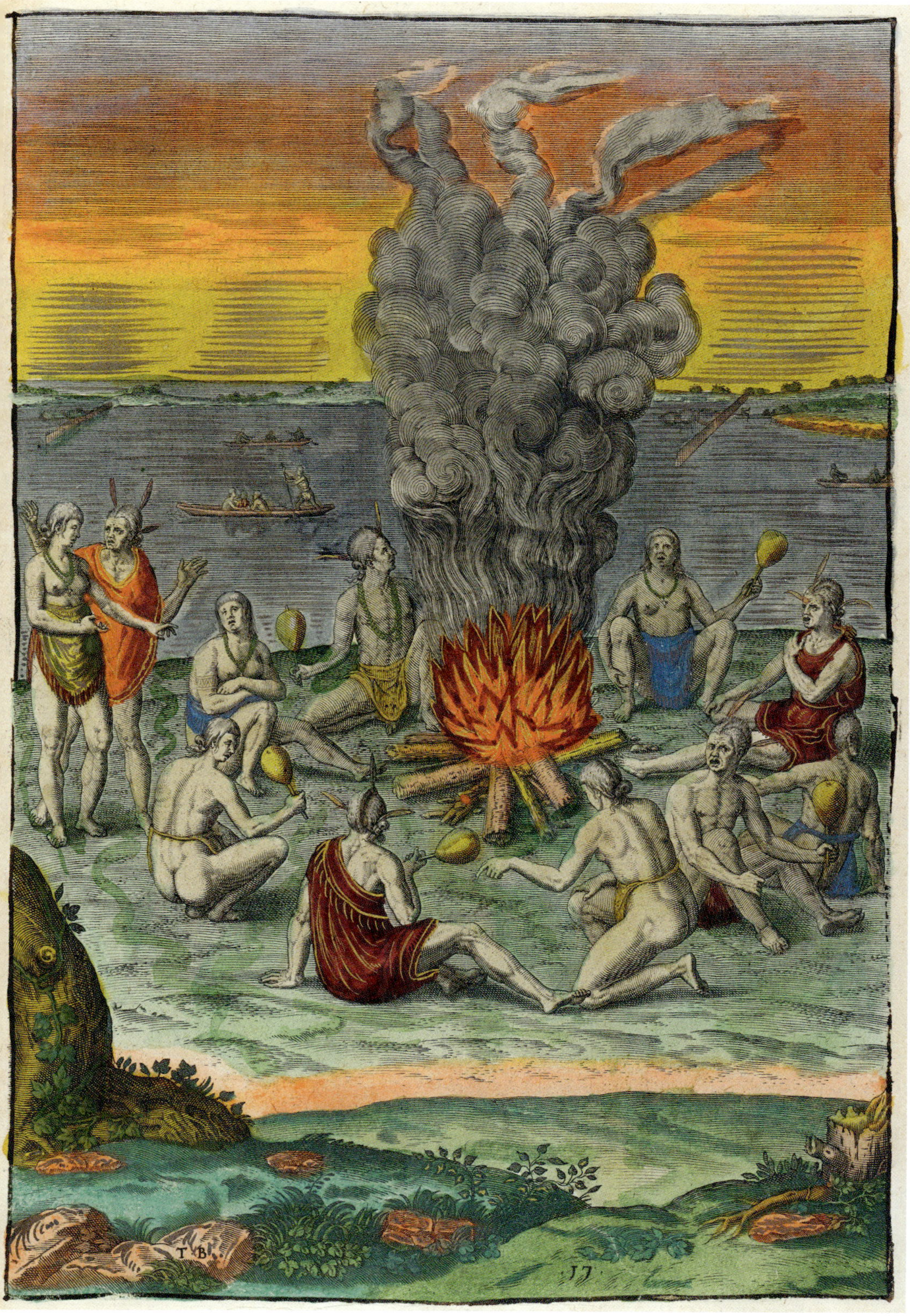
T B
17

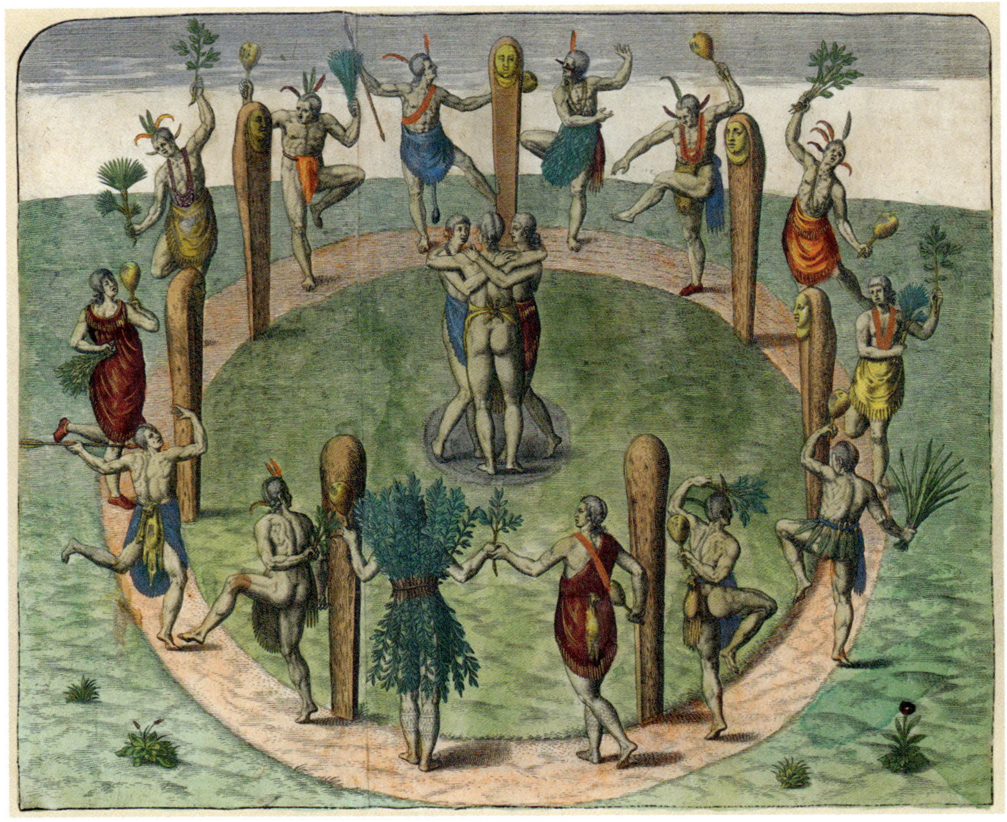

PLATE 18

Their dances which they perform at their high feasts

At a certain time of the year they make a great and solemn feast which their neighbours in the adjoining towns also attend, with every man dressed in the most strange fashion he can devise and making special marks on their back to declare what place they come from. The place where they meet is an open area, where they have planted a number of posts in the ground carved with heads like the faces of nuns covered with their veils. Then when everything is in order they begin to dance, sing and use the strangest gestures that may possibly be imagined. Three of the most beautiful virgins from the assembled company stand in the centre, embracing one another as part of their dancing. All this is done after the sun has set so as to avoid the heat of day. When they are tired of dancing, they retire from the circle, and return again later until all their dances are ended, enjoying themselves in this manner as is expressed in the previous picture.

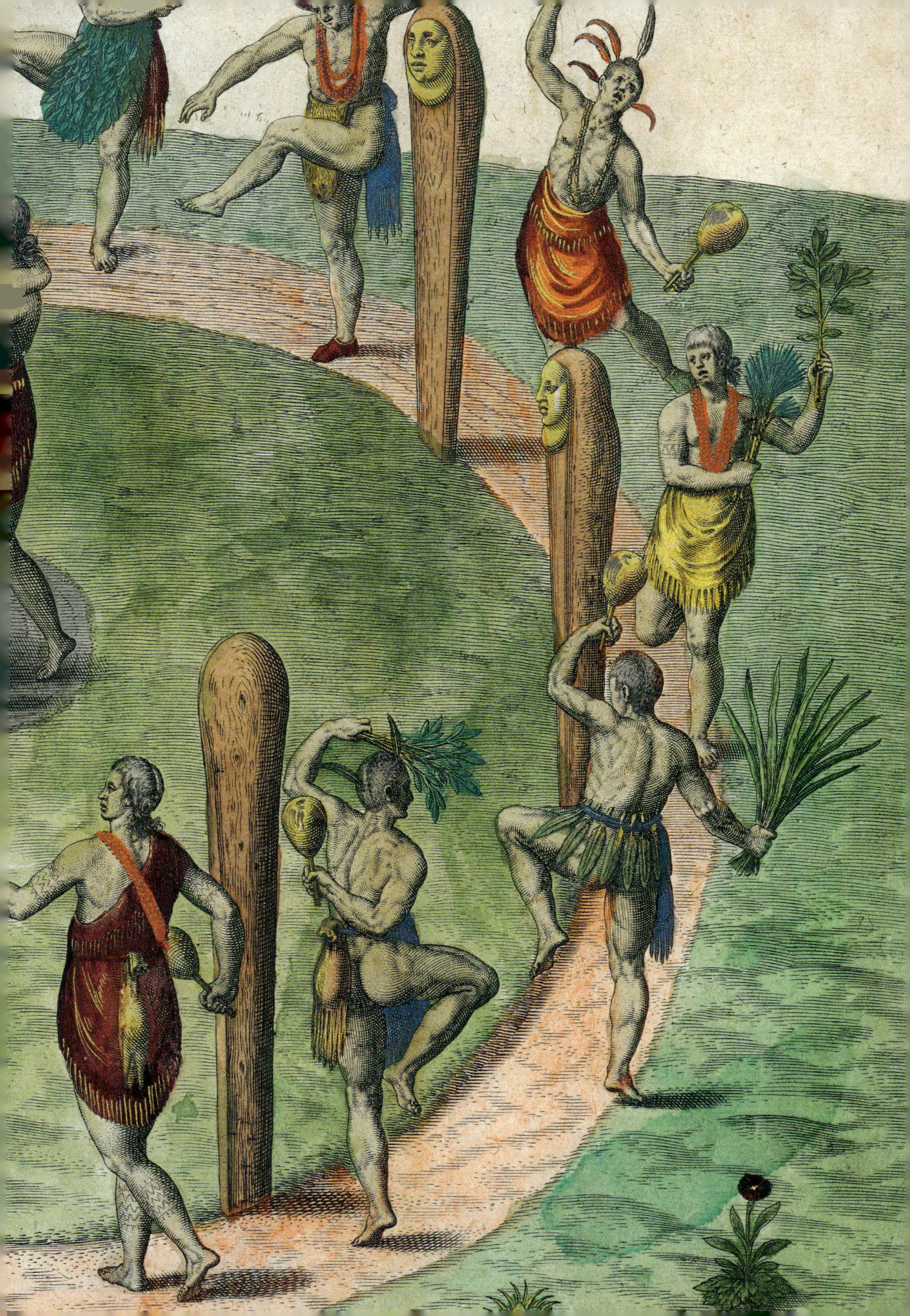

PLATE 19

The town of Pomeiooc

The towns of this region are similar to those in Florida, although they are not as well fortified nor are they attended to with great care. They are built with poles stuck into the ground, but these are not very secure. The entrance is very narrow, as can be seen in this picture, which was made according to the form of the town of Pomeiooc. There are only a few houses inside, apart from those which belong to the king and his nobles. On one side is their temple, separated from the other houses and marked with the letter A: it is round and covered with skin mats, with curtains outside the windows, and light comes in only through the door. On the other side is the king's lodging marked with the letter B. Their dwellings are built using posts fastened together, and covered with mats which they roll up as high as they choose, and so let in the light and other things. Some are also covered with the boughs of trees, in each case as the owner prefers. They hold their feasts and make good cheer together in the centre of the town. If the town is far from water they dig a great pond, marked with the letter C, and fill it with as much water as they need.

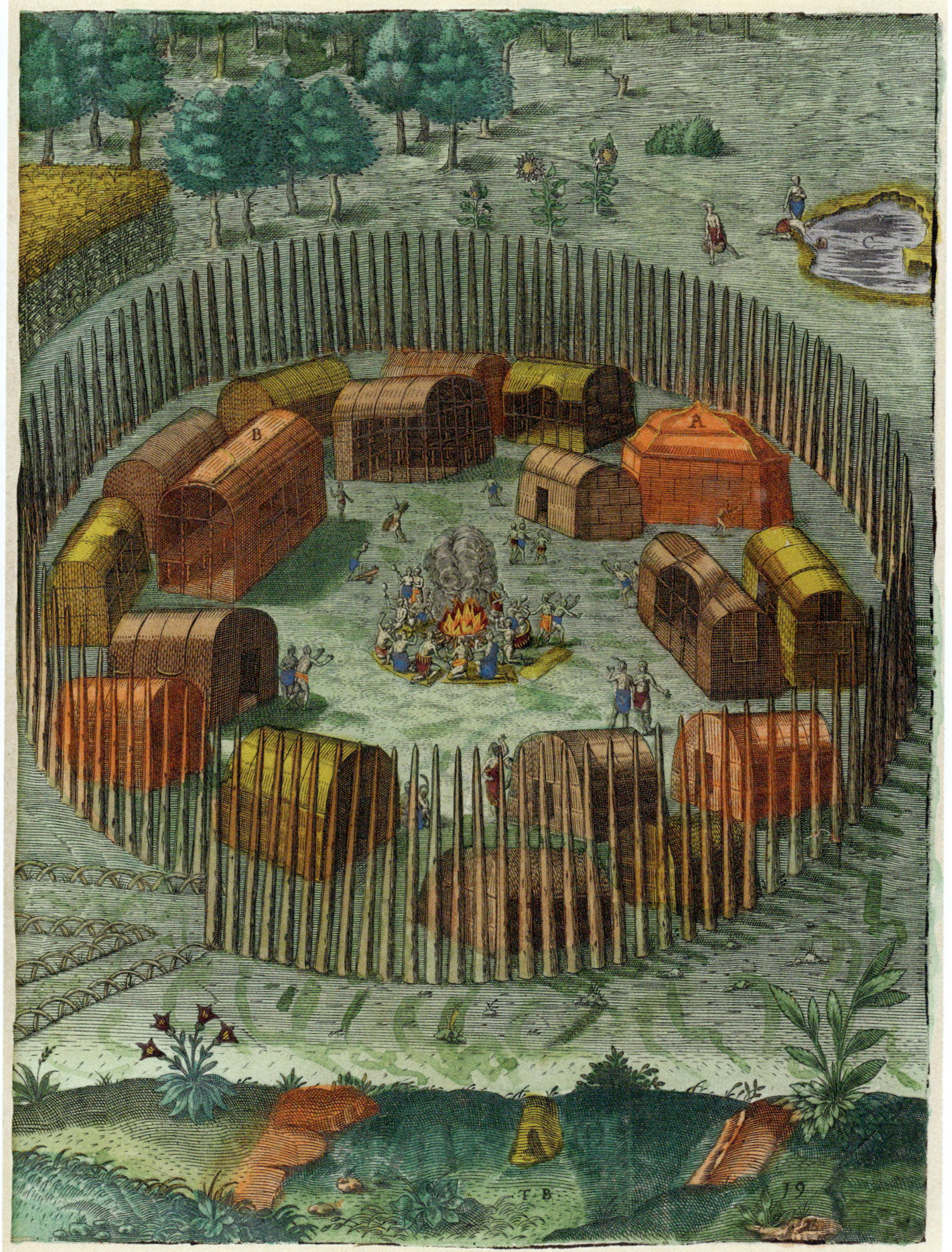
B
A
C
T B
19

PLATE 20

The town of Secota

The towns they build which are not enclosed with a stockade are usually better than those that are, as can be seen in this picture which shows the town of Secota. The houses are scattered here and there, and there is a garden marked by the letter E where tobacco grows, which the inhabitants call Uppowoc. They also have groves where they catch deer, and fields where they sow their corn. In their cornfields they build a sort of platform on which they place a small shelter similar to a round chair, signified by F, where they place someone to watch out for there are great numbers of birds and beasts. For this reason the watchman makes continual cries and noise. They sow their corn with a certain distance between each plant, as noted by H, otherwise one stalk would choke the growth of another and the corn would not reach maturity, G. For the leaves of this corn are large, like the leaves of great reeds. They also have several flat areas, C, where they meet with their neighbours, to celebrate their main solemn feasts as was discussed above; and a place D, where after they have ended their feast they make merry together. Opposite this place is a round plot B where they assemble to make their solemn prayers. Not far from this place there is a large building A where the tombs of their kings and princes are. Likewise they have a garden marked by the letter I where they sow pumpkins. And also a place marked K where they make a fire at their solemn feasts, and outside the town a river L where they fetch their water. Devoid of riches then, these people live cheerfully and at their ease. But they celebrate their feasts at night, and therefore keep very large fires to keep away the darkness.

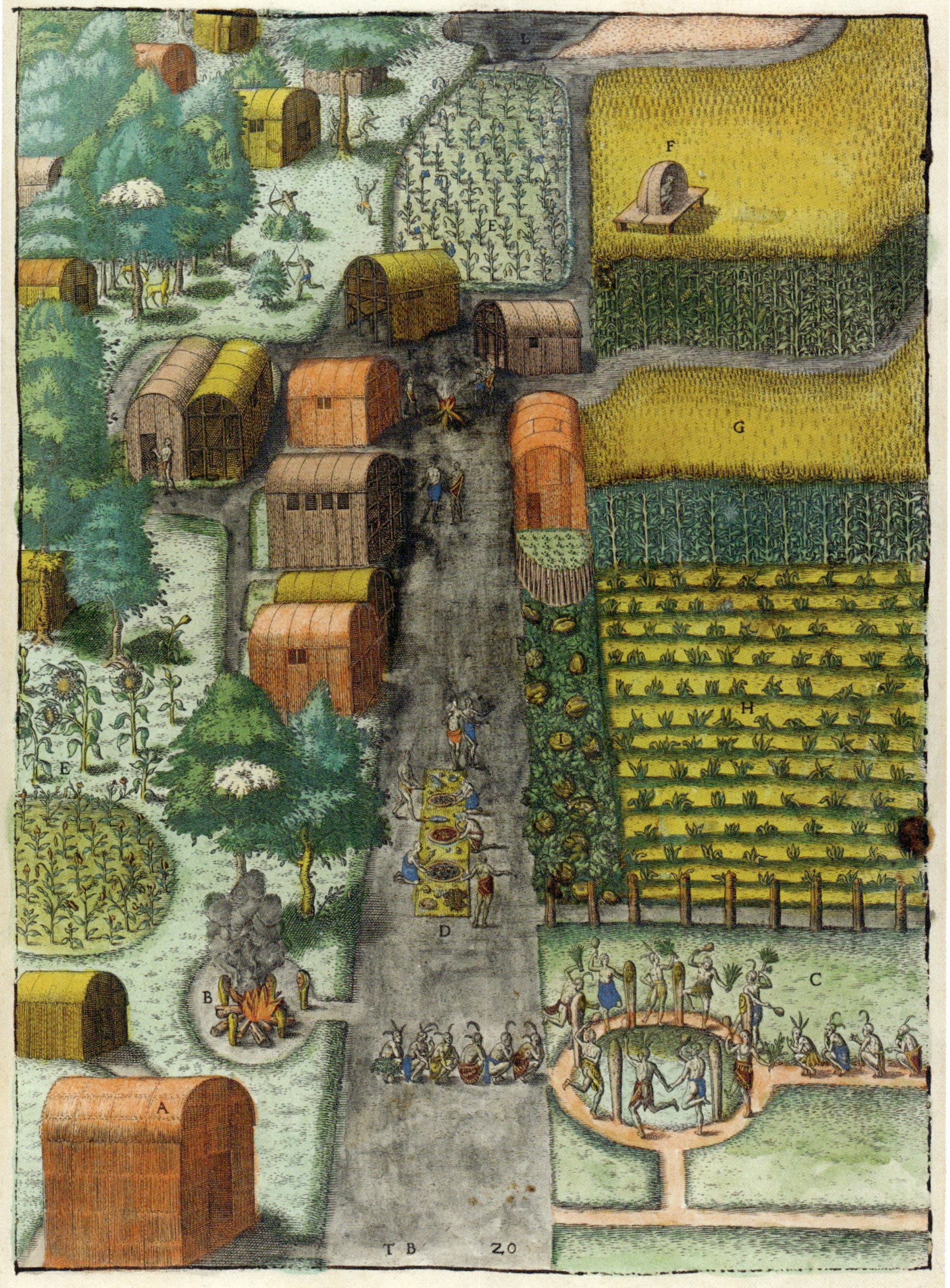
L
F
E
G
E
H
I
D
B
C
A
T B
20

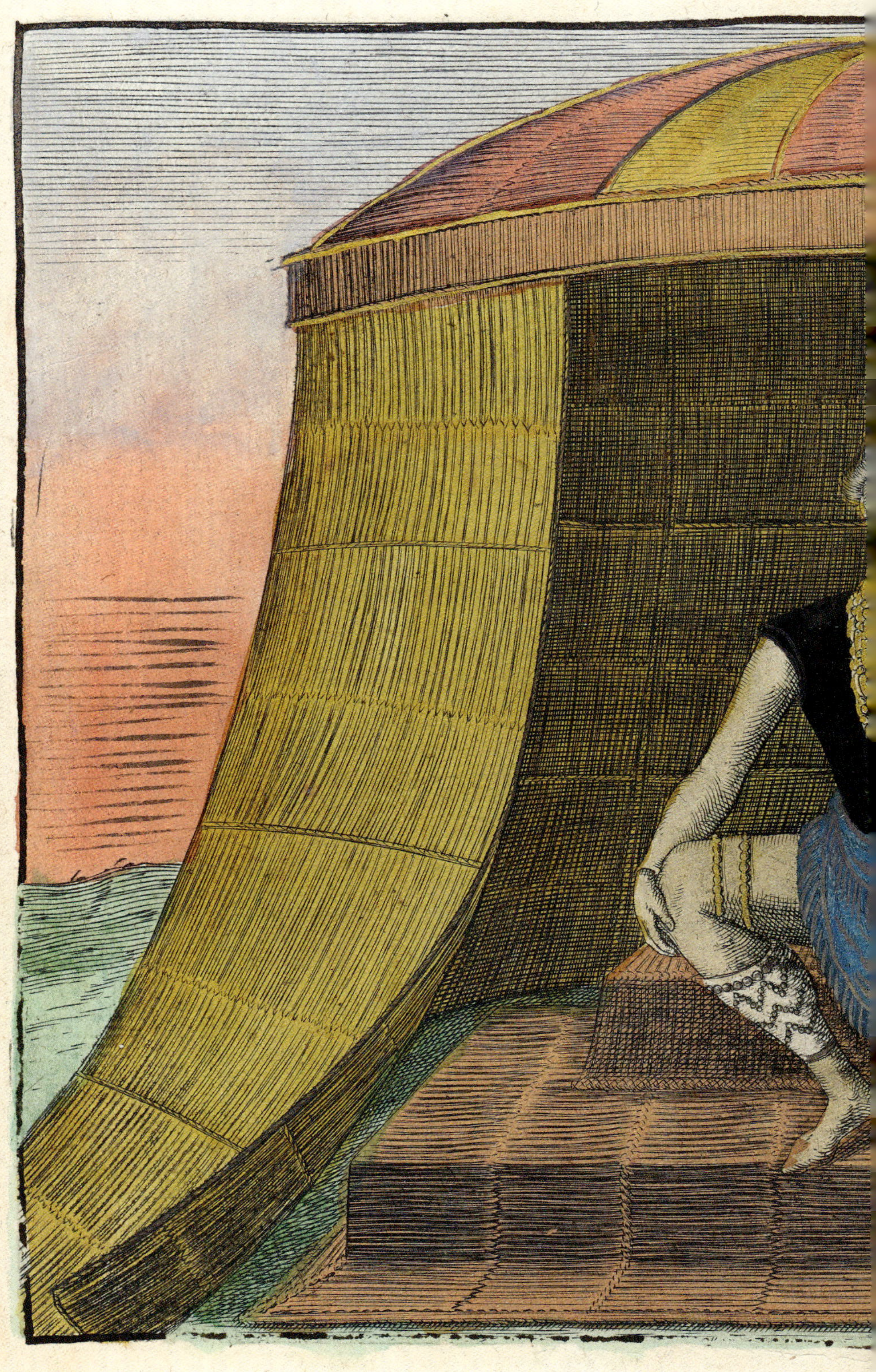

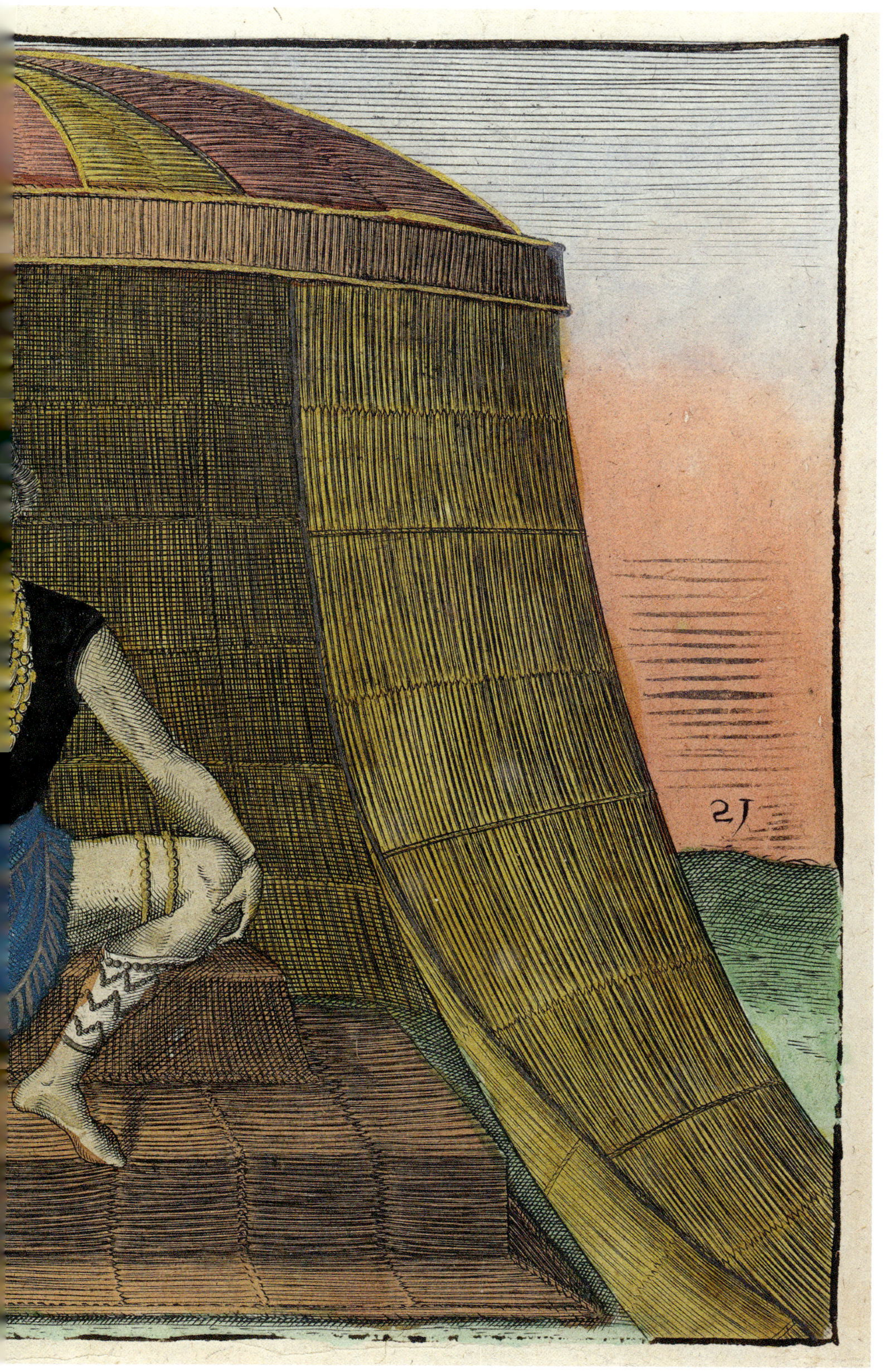
21

PLATE 21, PAGES 100/101

Their idol Kiwasa

The people of this country have an idol, which they call "Kiwasa": it is carved out of wood some four feet in length and its head is like those of the people of Florida; the face is of a flesh colour, rendered using the best white, while the rest is all black although the thighs are also spotted with white. He has a chain around his neck of white beads, between which are round beads of copper which these people value more than gold or silver. This idol is placed in the temple of the town of Secota, as the keeper of the corpses of their kings. Sometimes there are two of these idols in their churches, and sometimes three, but never more, and they place them in dark corners where they look terrifying. These poor souls have no other knowledge of God although I think they are very eager to know the truth. For when we knelt down to make our prayers to God they tried to imitate us, and when they saw that we moved our lips they did the same. For this reason it is very likely that they might easily be brought to the knowledge of the gospel. God in his mercy grant them this grace.

PLATE 22

The tomb of their Weroans, or chief lords

They build platforms nine or ten feet high as can be seen here under the tombs of their Weroans, or chief lords, which they cover with mats, and lay out the corpses of their Weroans in the following way: first the entrails are removed; then, paring away the skin, they cut all the flesh clean off the bones and dry it in the sun, and once it is well dried, they wrap it in small mats and place it at the feet of the bodies. Then the bones (still held together with the ligaments not yet rotted away) are covered again now with leather, and the carcass is fashioned so that it seems the flesh has not been removed at all. Each corpse is wrapped in its own skin and placed in order beside the corpses of the other chief lords. Next to the dead bodies they set their idol Kiwasa, of which we spoke in the previous chapter, for they believe that this idol protects the dead bodies of their chief lords so that nothing may harm them. Moreover, under the platform one of their priests has his lodging, and it is he who mumbles his prayers night and day and is in charge of the corpses. For his bed he has two deerskins spread on the ground, and if the weather is cold he makes a fire to warm himself. These poor souls are thus instructed by custom to pay reverence to their princes even after their death.

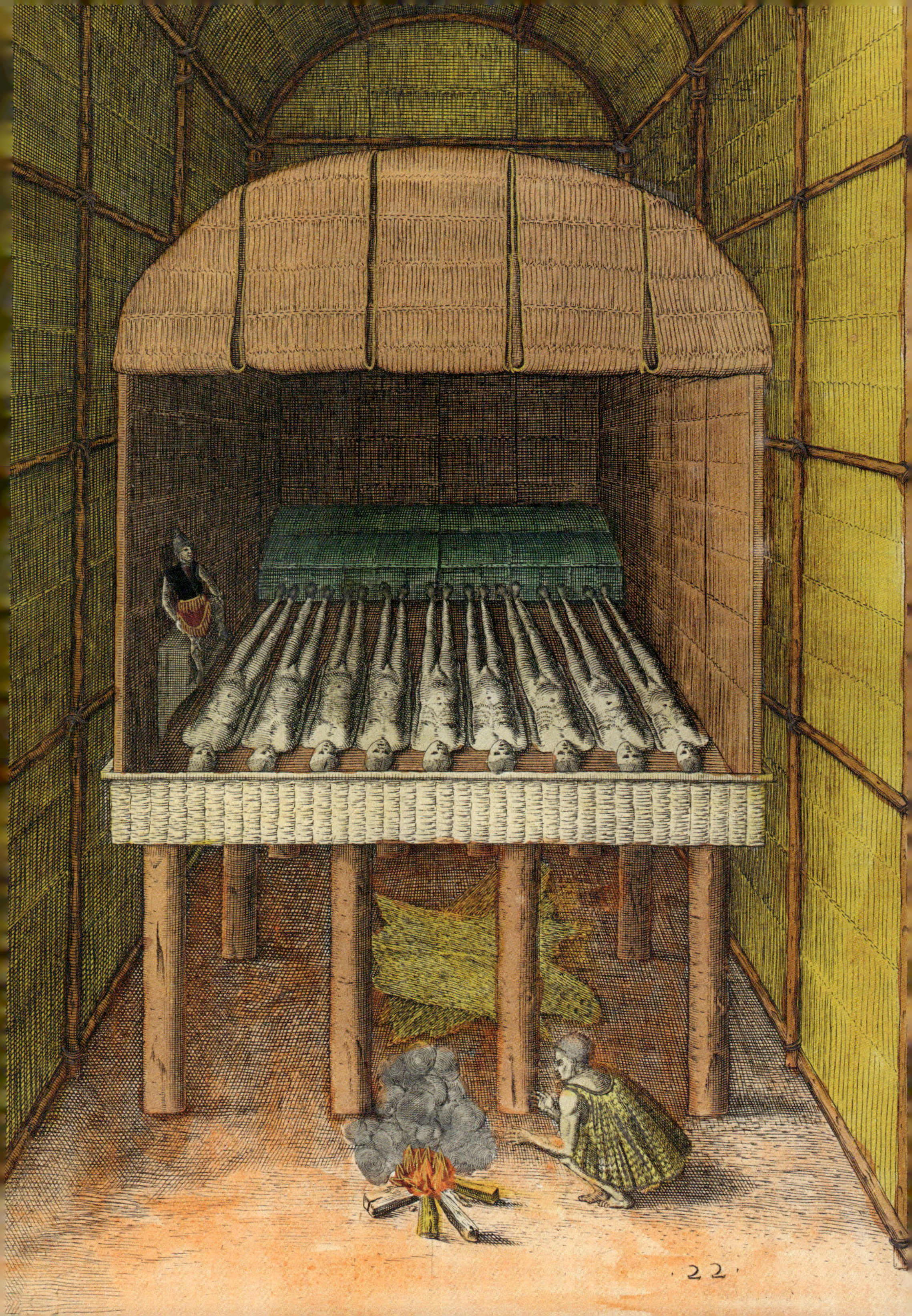
22

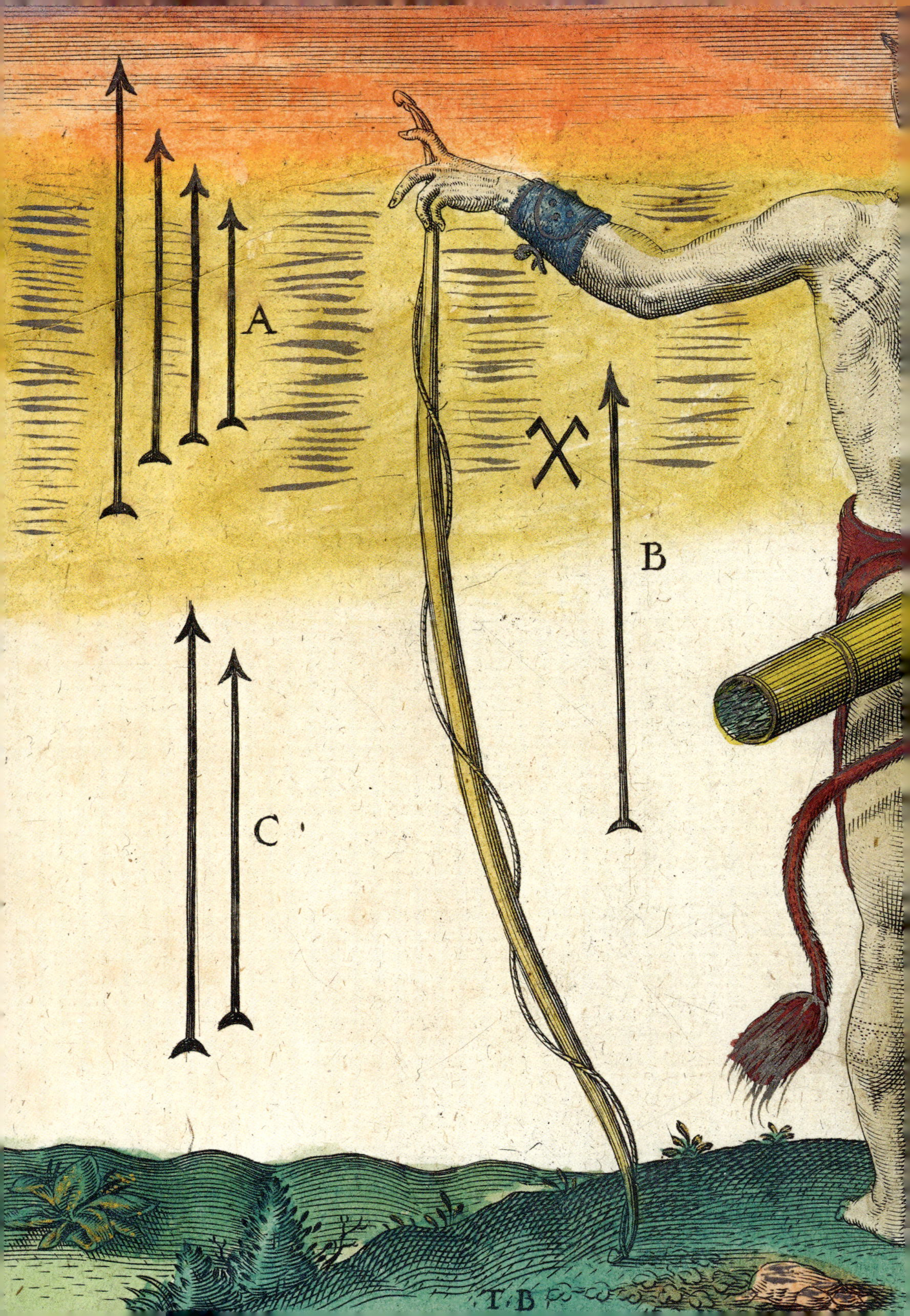
A
B
C
T. B

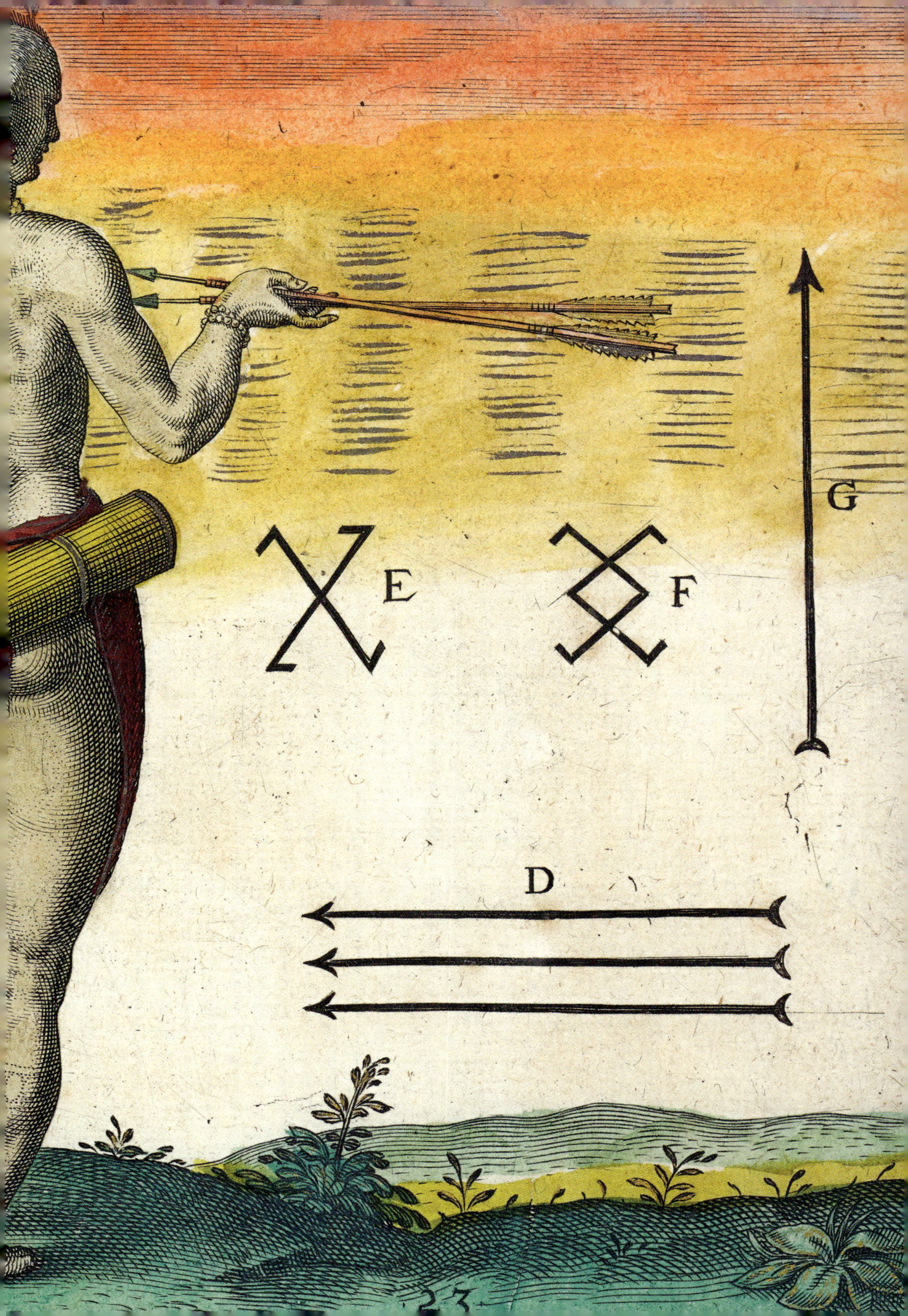
G
E
F
D

PLATE 23, PAGES 104/105

The marks of sundry of the chief men of Virginia

The inhabitants of all this country for the most part have raised marks on their backs, so that others may know which prince's subjects they are, or what place they come from. For this reason we have set down these marks in this picture, and have added the names of the places, so that they might more easily be discerned. This manner of working God has endowed them with, although they are very simple and basic. And to confess a truth, I cannot remember that I ever saw a better or quieter people than them.

The marks which I observed among them are here put down in the order following. The mark which is expressed by A belongs to Wingino, the chief lord of Roanoke. That which is marked by B is the mark of Wingino's sister's husband. Those which are noted with the letters C and D belong to diverse chief lords in Secota. Those which have the letters E, F and G are certain chief men of Pomeiooc and Aquascogoc.

FIVE ADDITIONAL ENGRAVINGS CONCERNING THE PICTS, INDIGENOUS INHABITANTS OF GREAT BRITAIN

PLATE 1

The true picture of a Pict

In times past the Picts, inhabitants of one part of Great Britain which is now named England, were a savage people and painted their whole body after the manner described below; they let their hair grow as far as their shoulders other than the hair of their forehead, which they cut. They shaved their beard but left the moustache, and upon their breast was painted the head of some bird, and the rays of the sun, while upon their belly was painted some fearful and monstrous face, spreading its beams right on to the thighs. On the knees were painted the faces of lions, and shellfish on their legs. On their shoulders were griffon heads, and coiled around their arms were painted serpents. Around their neck they wore an iron ring, and another around the middle of their body, around the belly, and at their side hung a Turkish sword on a chain; on one arm they carried a small shield made of wood, and in the other hand a pike, whose iron had vanquished a number of their enemies, the heads of whom they made sure to carry off with them after battle.

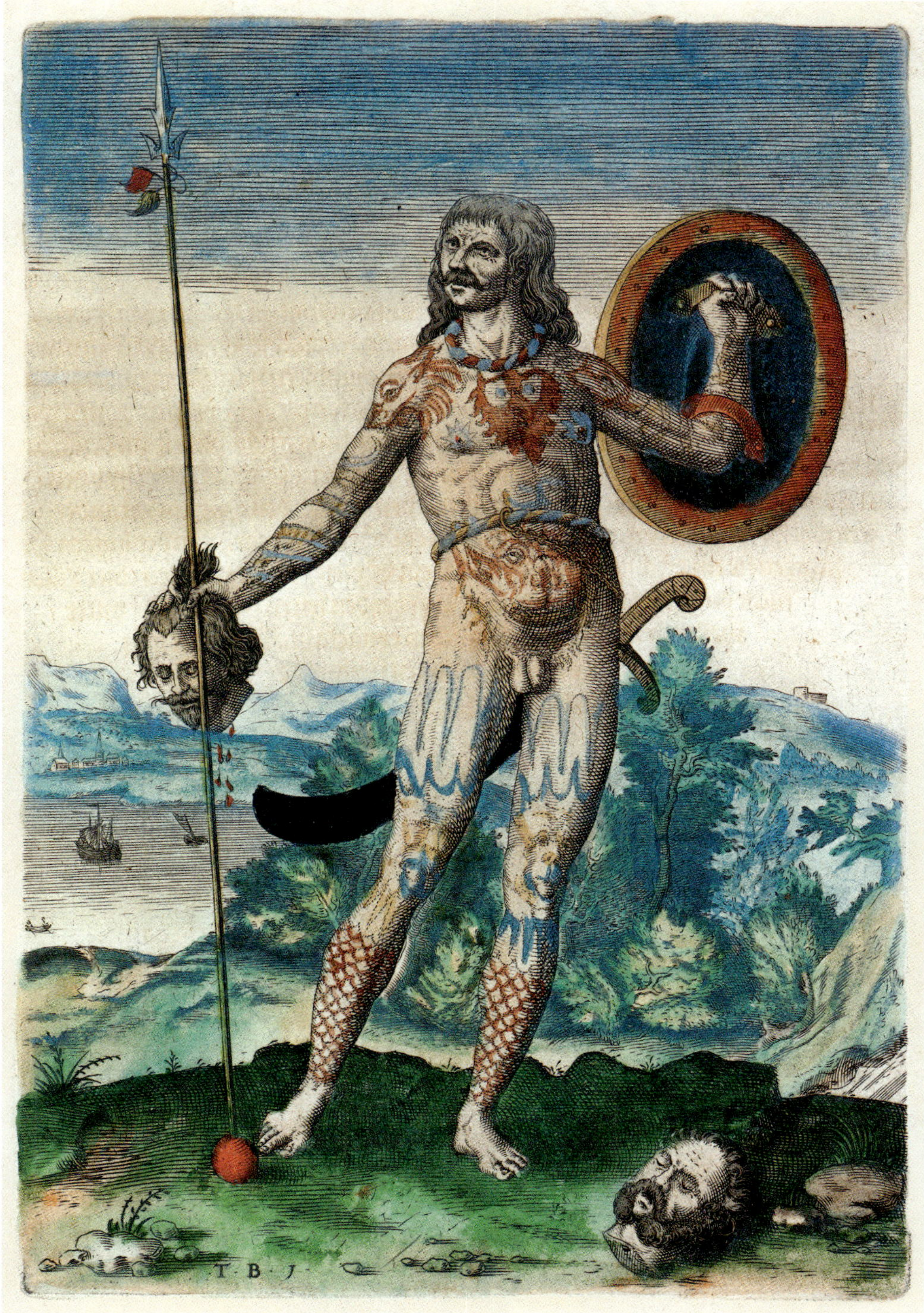

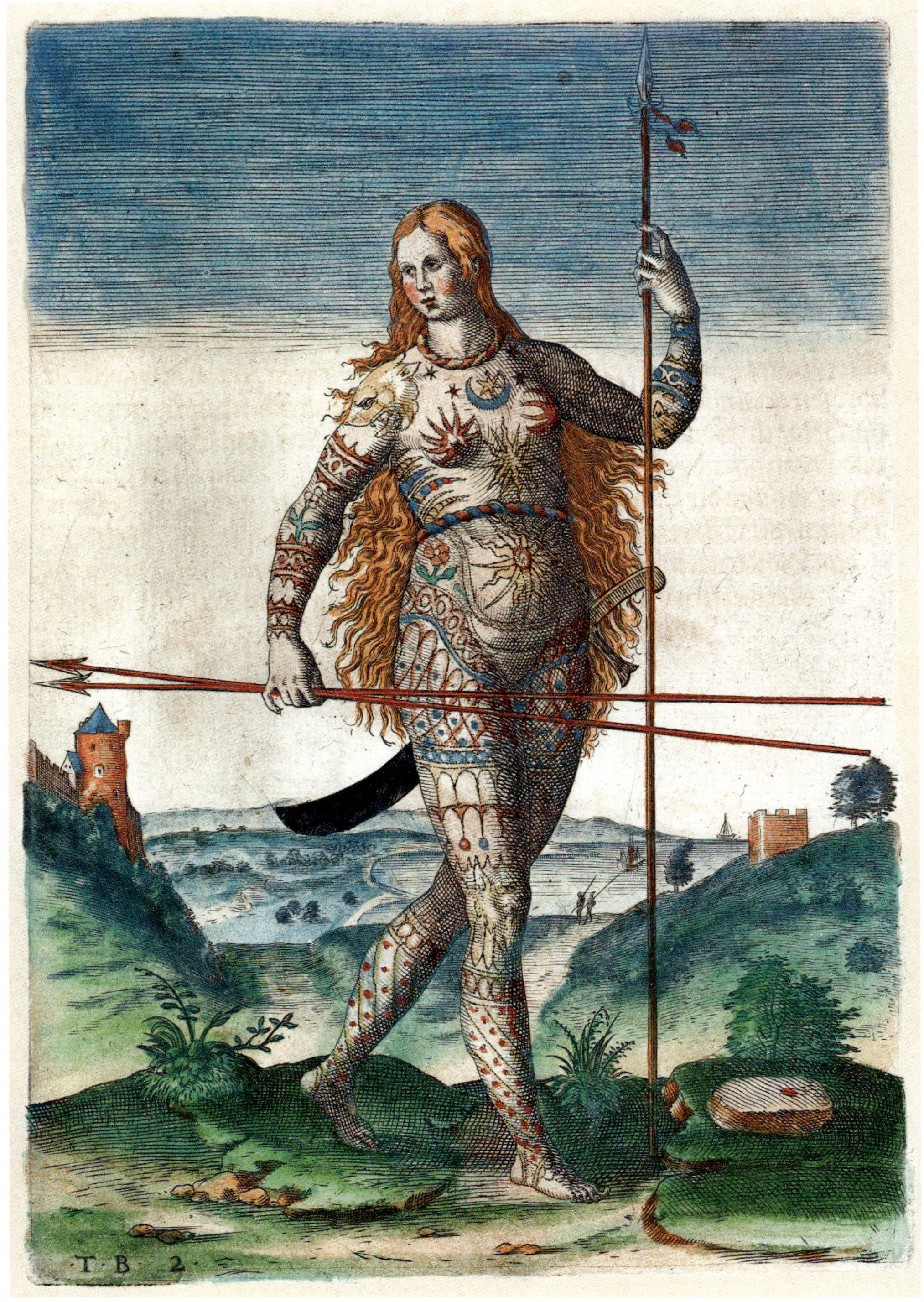
T B 2

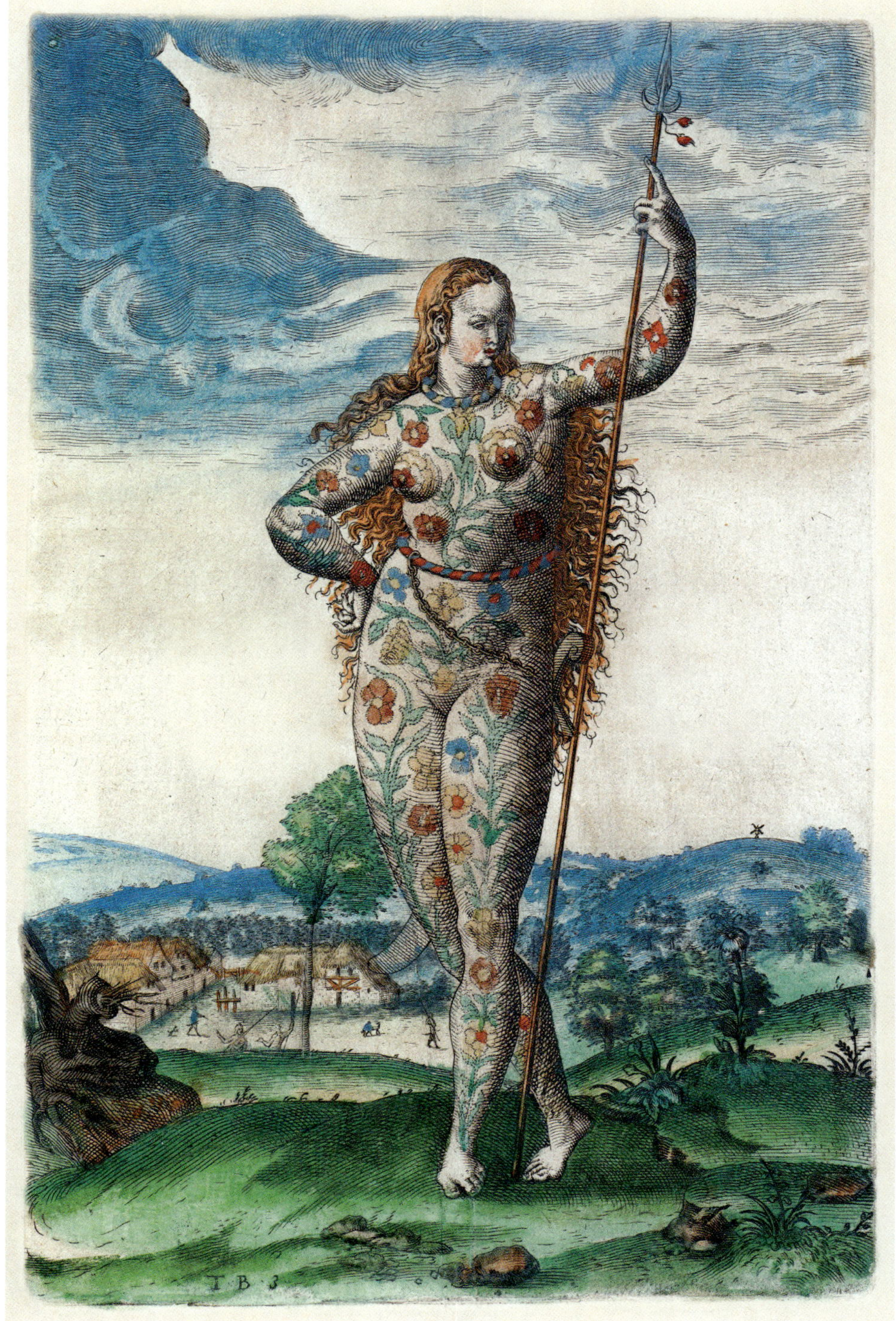
TB.

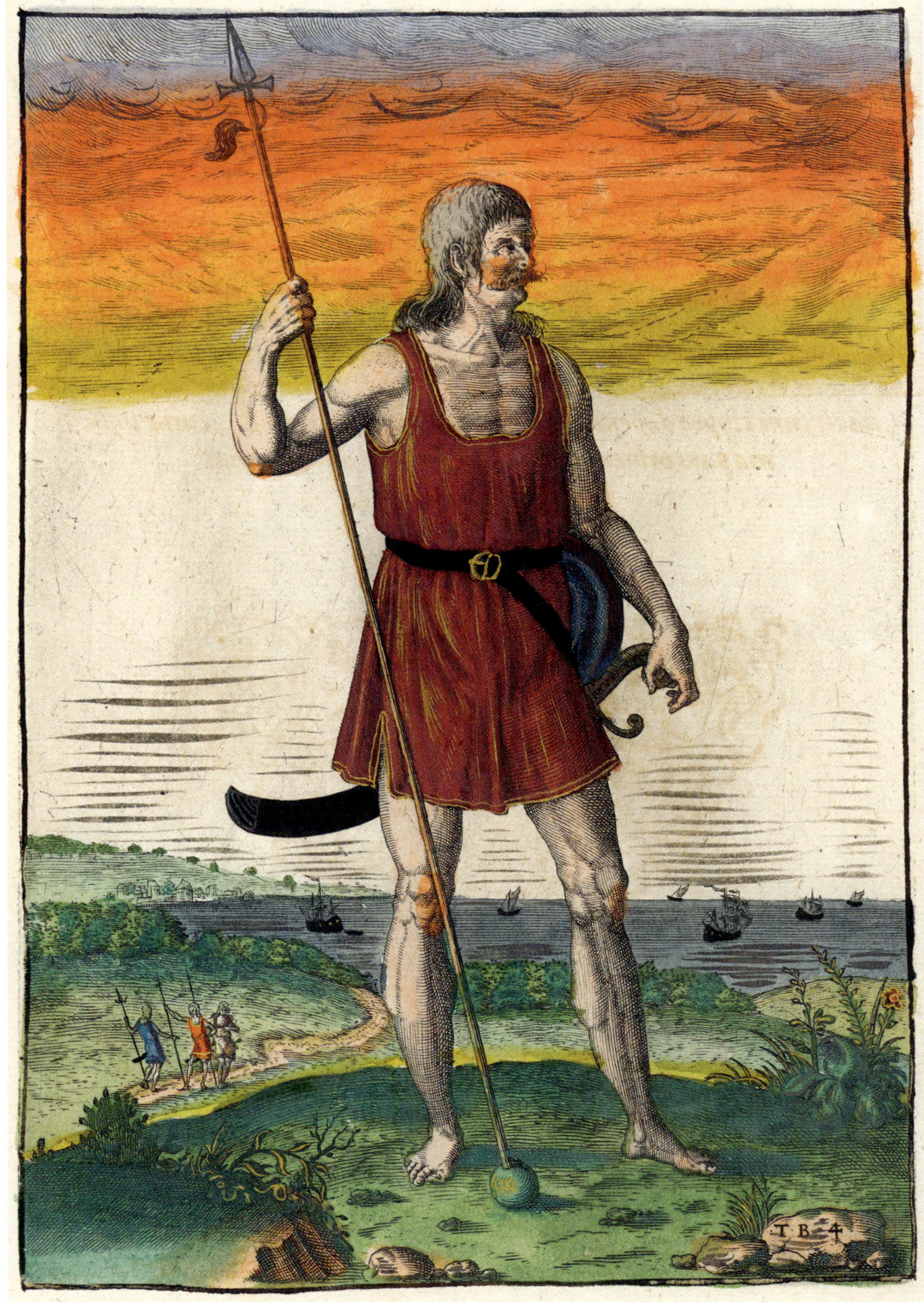
T.B.4

PLATE 2, PAGE 108

The true picture of a Pictish woman

The women of the Picts were no less boldly painted for war than the men. They were painted after the manner described below, having their heads uncovered and letting their hair fly freely. Their shoulders were painted with griffon heads, the lower parts of their body and thighs with lion faces, or some other beast as came best to their fancy; on their breast was a kind of half moon, with a great flare, and four lesser beams on both sides, then more beams of the sun, and amongst all this a great lightning star upon their breasts. The whole belly is covered with a sun, while the arms, thighs and legs are all well painted with diverse figures. They too wore an iron ring around their neck, like the men did, and a girdle like this one with the sword hanging at one side, while holding a pike or a lance in one hand and two darts in the other.

PLATE 3, PAGE 109

The true picture of a young daughter of the Picts

The young daughters of the Picts also let their hair fly free, and also went about with their entire body painted so much so that no one could see much difference, unless it was because they had another style of painting, for the daughters painted themselves with sundry kinds of flowers, and of the fairest types they could find; they were equipped with such kinds of weapon as the women wear as may be seen here, a thing truly worthy of admiration.

PLATE 4

The true picture of a man of the neighbouring nation to the Picts

There was in the aforenamed Great Britain another nation that lived alongside the Picts, who dressed themselves with a kind of cassock or cloth jerkin, while the rest of their body was naked. They had long hair and moustaches, but again the chin was shaved. They wore a large girdle, from which hung a crooked sword, together with the small shield, and carried a pike or lance in one hand which had a round bowl at the lower end, as can be seen here.

PLATE 5

The true picture of a woman of a neighbouring nation to the Picts

Their women were much the same in appearance, but their dress was open at the breast, and fastened with a little hook, as our women fasten their petticoat. They let their breasts hang out, and as for the rest they carried such weapons as the men did, and were as good as men at fighting wars.

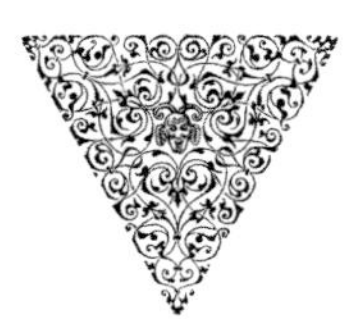

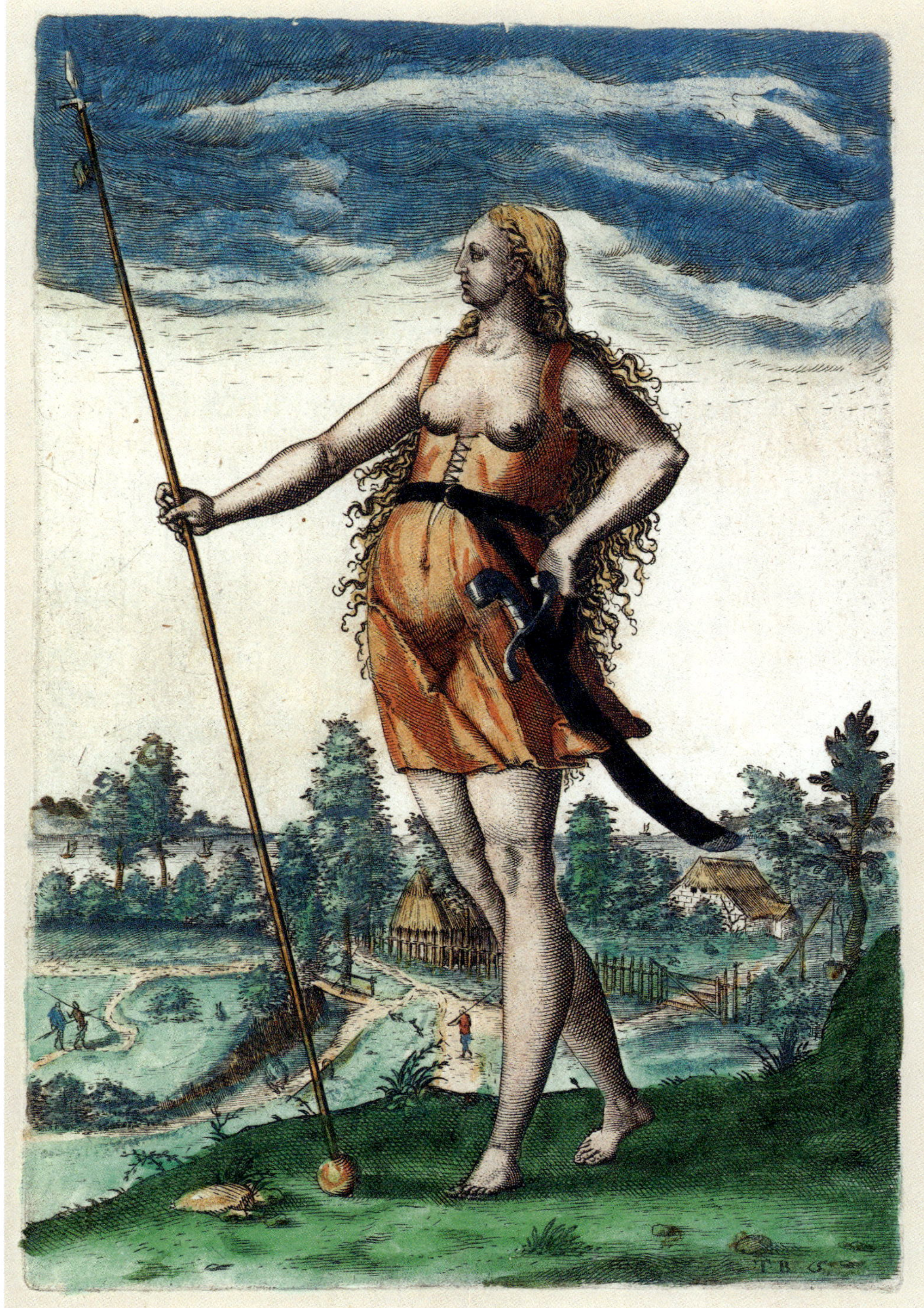

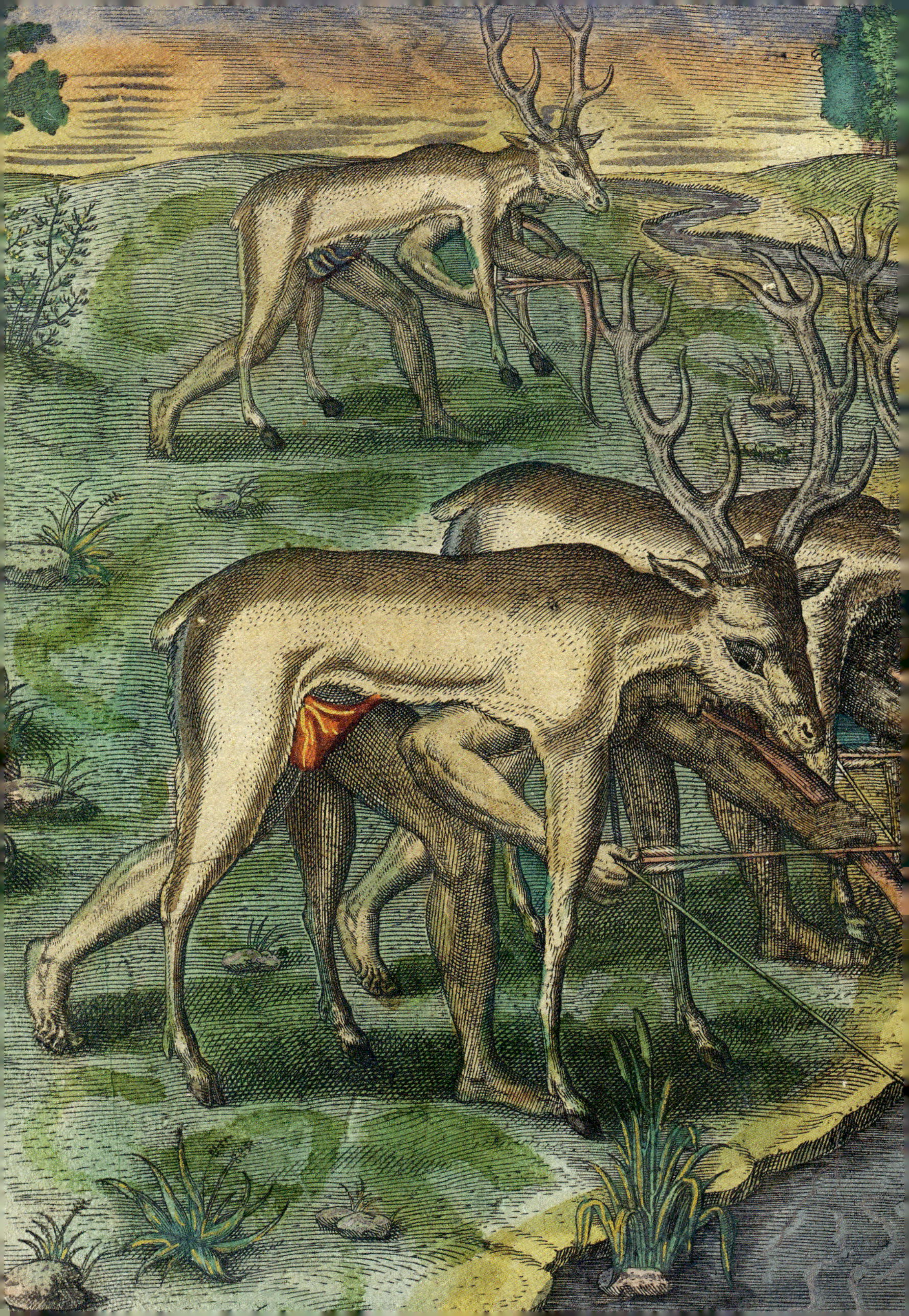

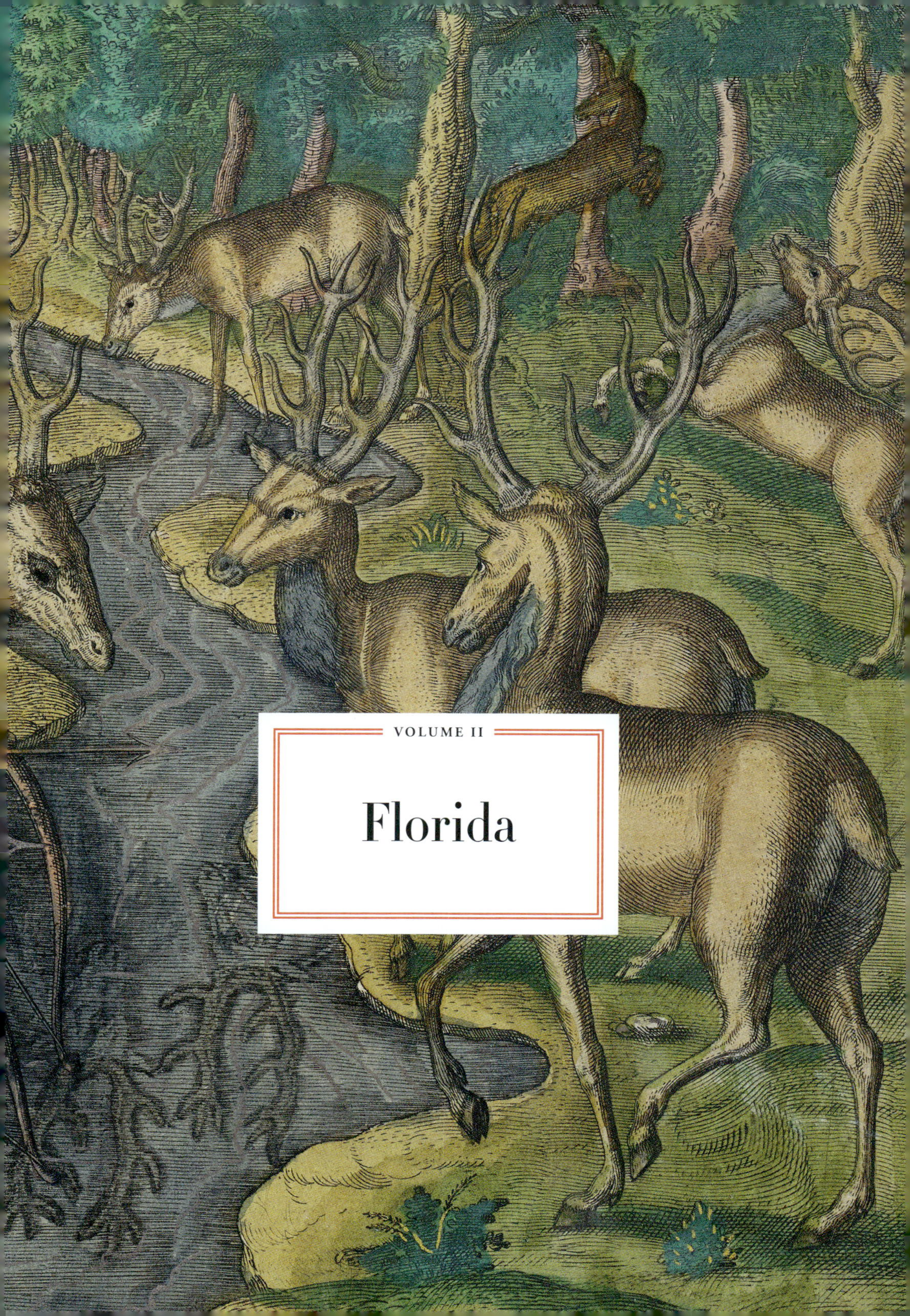

VOLUME II

Florida

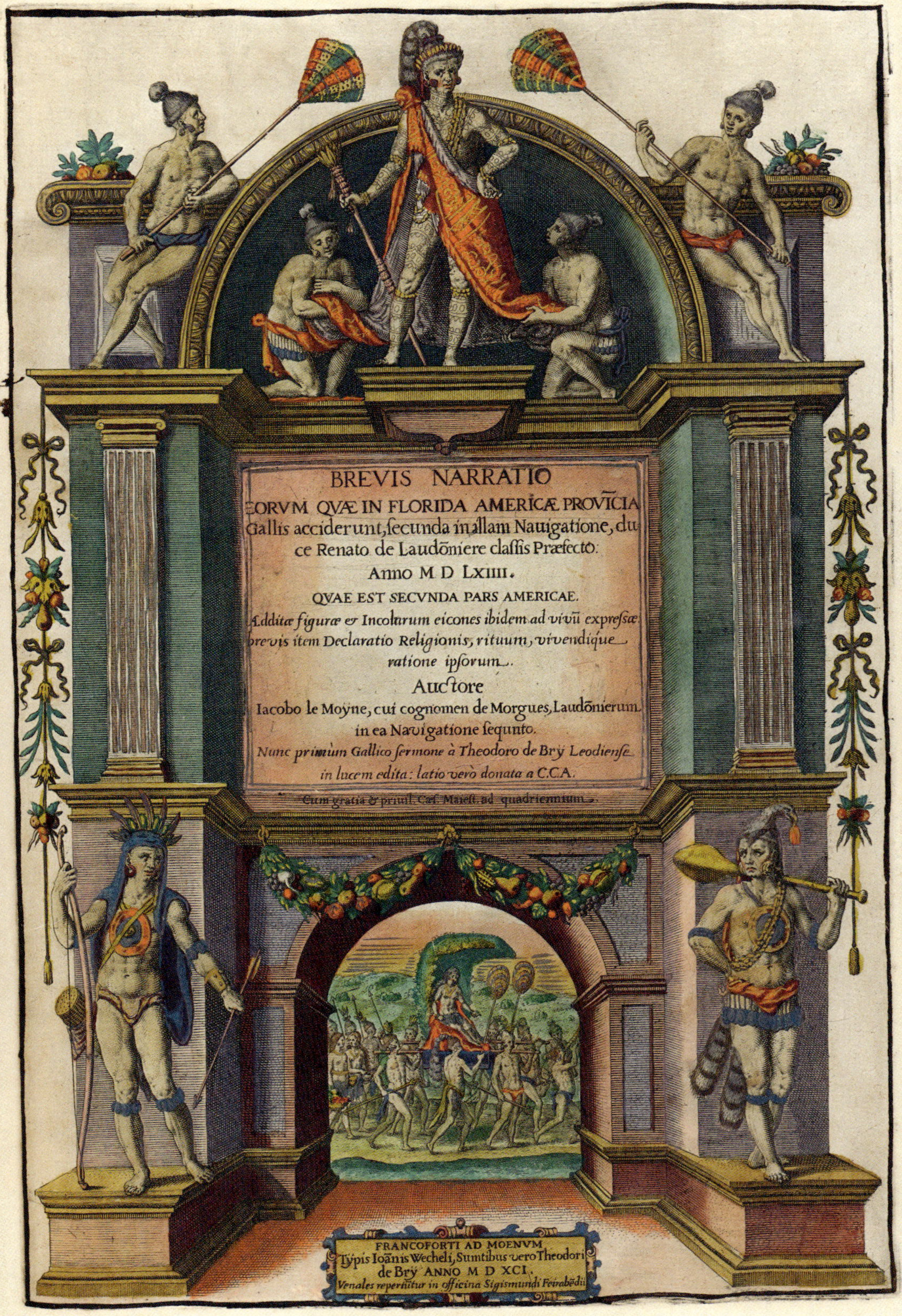

BREVIS NARRATIO
EORUM QUÆ IN FLORIDA AMERICÆ PROVĪCIA
Gallis acciderunt, secunda in illam Nauigatione, du-
ce Renato de Laudōniere classis Præfecto:
Anno M D LXIIII.
QUAE EST SECUNDA PARS AMERICAE.
Additæ figuræ & Incolarum eicones ibidem ad vivū expressæ
brevis item Declaratio Religionis, rituum, vivendique
ratione ipsorum.
Auctore
Iacobo le Moyne, cui cognomen de Morgues, Laudōnierum
in ea Navigatione sequuto.
Nunc primùm Gallico sermone à Theodoro de Bry Leodiense
in lucem edita: latio verò donata a C.C.A.
Cum gratia & priuil. Cæs. Maiest. ad quadriennium.

FRANCOFORTI AD MOENUM
Typis Ioānis Wecheli, Sumtibus vero Theodori
de Bry ANNO M D XCI.
Venales reperiūtur in officina Sigismundi Feirabēdii

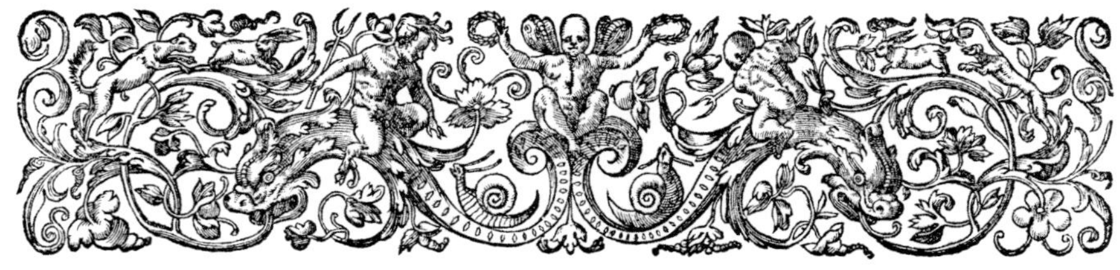

Volume II

Based on: René de Laudonnière,
L'Histoire notable de la Floride (Paris, 1586)
and Jacques Le Moyne de Morgues's watercolours of the same region

The watercolour sketches by Jacques Le Moyne, obtained at the second attempt from the artist's widow by Theodore de Bry in London in 1586 and 1587, were first intended to be used for the opening volume of the series. However, Richard Hakluyt, whose mediation between De Bry and Le Moyne's widow resulted in the engraver actually acquiring the coveted illustrations, persuaded De Bry to begin his series with the politically more significant attempts at the colonisation of North America by the English. For this reason the accounts of the French, although they preceded those of the English by two decades, instead became the subject of volume II. The most significant change the De Brys made in comparison with volume I was the abandonment of the French and English editions, thereby settling for a bilingual series – a model that was retained until the 25th and final volume appeared in 1634. The reason for focusing solely on Latin and German versions was probably to a large extent financial, since producing four different translations was a difficult and time-consuming process. Laudonnière's account, moreover, had originally been published in French – thus taking away the need for a special edition aimed at a French audience – and had already been translated into English by Hakluyt in 1587. The English market for books was comparatively small anyway, and the De Brys found success in the following years in reaching an international readership (including in France and England) with their Latin translations.

The narrative presented by Laudonnière in his account published in 1586 is a text containing several layers, beginning with the first French expedition to Florida in early 1562, on the eve of the

Frontispiece of volume II

Pages 114/115
Detail of volume II, plate 25

French Wars of Religion. This expedition was led by the Huguenot officer Jean Ribault, and can therefore be seen as the continuation of the French Protestant search for peace in the New World in the face of increasing religious intolerance at home, the first episode of which was discussed by the De Brys in *America* III. After Ribault returned to France, Laudonnière, his lieutenant, initiated a second voyage to Florida in 1564, later followed by a further expedition by his former commander. Ribault was then killed during a Spanish attack under Pedro Menéndez de Avilés on Fort Caroline, near present-day Jacksonville, in 1565. Hundreds of Frenchmen died in this attack, which can be regarded as one of the earliest interimperial conflicts in the New World. Le Moyne and Laudonnière himself were among the few survivors, and eventually managed to make their way back to France. Several years later, assisted by the Timucua Indians whose friendship Ribault and Laudonnière had courted, the French nobleman Dominique de Gourgues took revenge for the massacre in Florida by murdering the Spanish garrison in Fort Caroline. The French, however, never regained control of the region. Laudonnière's narrative, published 20 years after these events, included accounts of all four French expeditions to Florida in the 1560s.

It is interesting to see, especially in the light of Girolamo Benzoni's narrative which provides the contents of *America* IV, V and VI, that the De Brys did not emphasise the conflict between Protestants and Catholics in the New World at a time when religious intolerance in Europe was the rule. Here already, in volume II, the tendency is clear to keep the collection neutral and hence attractive to readers from various religious denominations. Instead, the story that was developed followed the French gradually taking control of Florida, first by finding a suitable place to create a permanent settlement, then by building a fort there in line with European customs and finally by understanding the culture of the Timucua Indians of the region and seeking to construct alliances with the most powerful groups. Ribault and Laudonnière arrived in Florida at a time of ongoing struggles between different Timucua chiefs, and the French – in their own interests – sought to intervene in the war and shepherd it to a conclusion which would prove satisfactory for both parties.

The decisive aspect in the De Brys' choice to focus on the encounter between Europeans and Floridians, rather than on the cross-confessional Franco-Spanish conflict, may have been the watercolours by Jacques Le Moyne. Unlike the illustrations by John White, which can be found in different versions in the collection of the British Museum, the original designs by Le Moyne have not survived, with the exception of his spectacular depictions of the natural world. For this reason it is difficult to establish whether the De Brys followed Le Moyne's originals faithfully when making their engravings. The style of the engravings and their subject matter suggests they did, and this conclusion would also make sense in the early years of the collection since the De Brys were still trying to find their footing in Frankfurt, and were still coming to terms with the art of making books. It is nevertheless also conceivable that they made modifications to Le Moyne's designs as they saw fit, something that was done regularly for subsequent volumes, or even that they invented several compositions to emphasise aspects of the account they thought would interest their readers. Often the De Brys' newly devised illustrations were loosely based on related images, which makes it even more difficult to distinguish eyewitness observations from fabricated compositions, as many of the later volumes demonstrate.

Detail of volume II, plate 23

Pages 120/121
Map of Florida showing Native American settlements

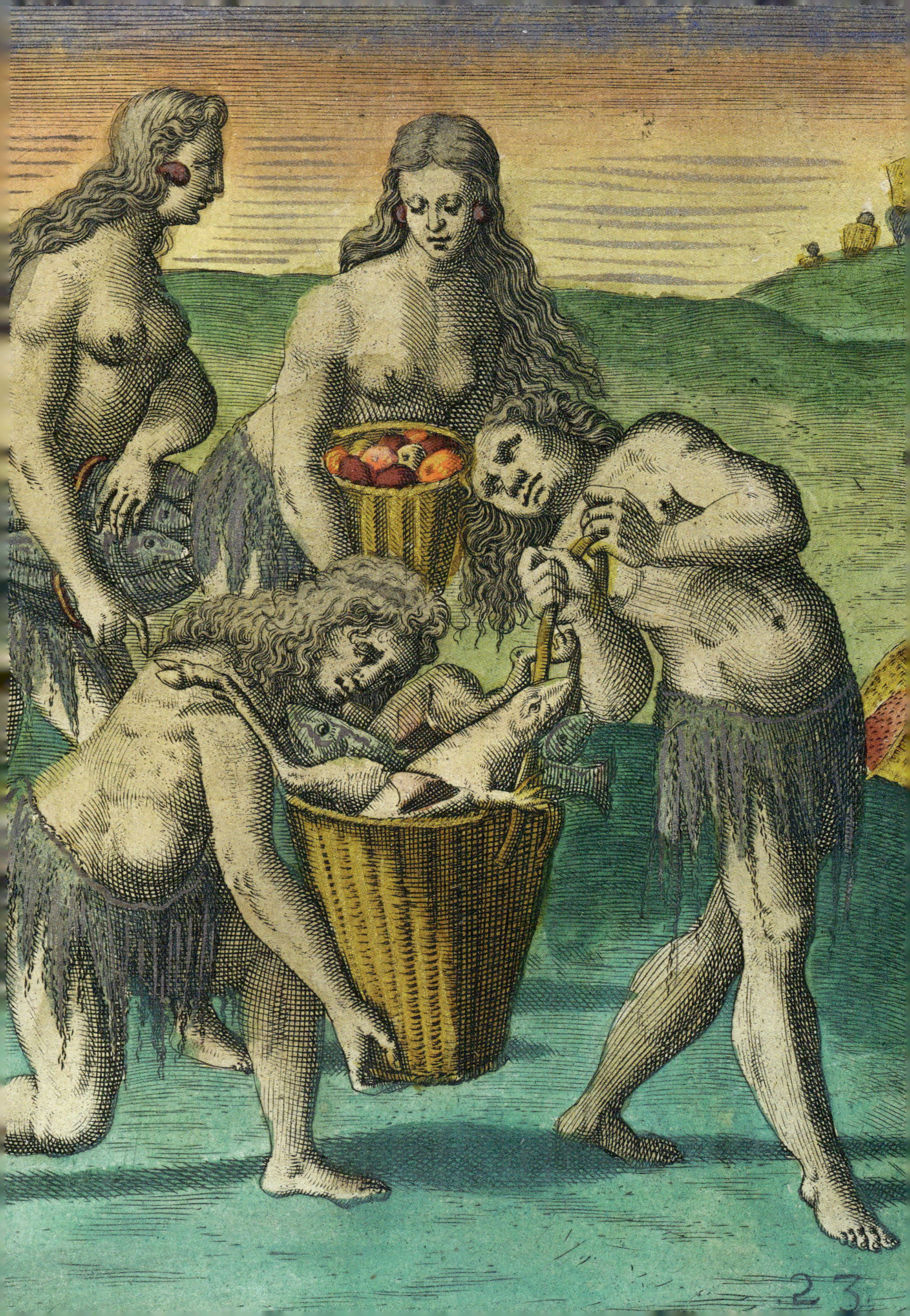
23

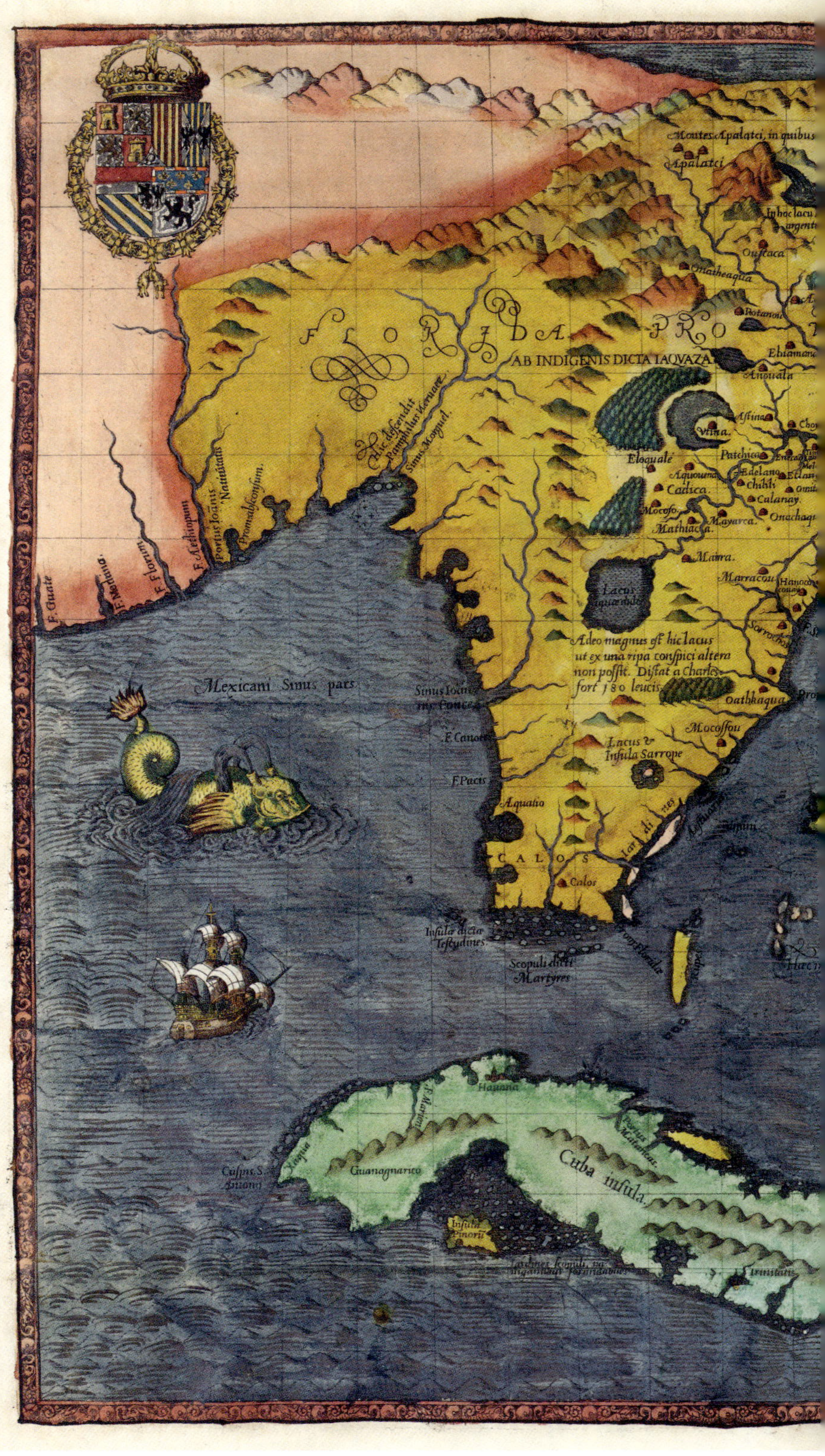

FLORIDA
AB INDIGENIS DICTA IAQVAZA
Apalatci
Onatheaqua
Potanou
Anouala
Astina
Vtina
Eloquale
Patchica
Edelano
Aquouena
Cadica
Chilili
Calanay
Mocoso
Mathiaca
Mayarca
Marracou
Adeo magnus est hic lacus ut ex una ripa conspici altera non possit. Distat a Charlesfort 180 leucis.
Oathkaqua
Mocossou
Lacus & Insula Sarrope
Hic descendit Pamphilus Narvaez
Mexicani Sinus pars
F. Canoe
F. Pacis
Aquatio
CALOS
Calos
Insula dicta Testudines
Scopuli dicti Martyres
Portus Ioanis
F. Florum
Havana
Guanagnarico
Cuba insula
Insula Pinorii
Trinitatis

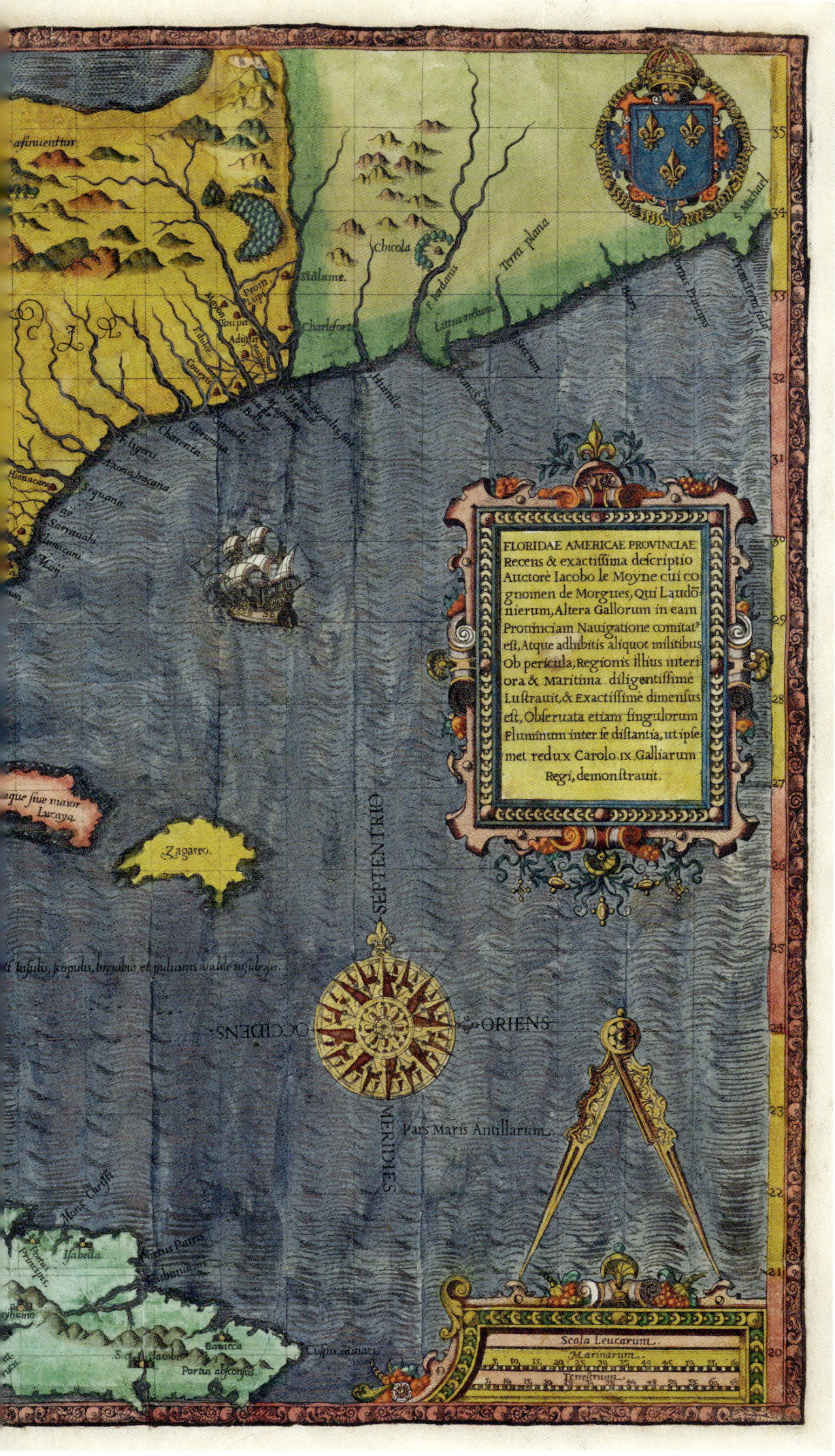

FLORIDAE AMERICAE PROVINCIAE
Recens & exactissima descriptio
Auctorè Iacobo le Moyne cui co-
gnomen de Morgues, Qui Laudõ-
nierum, Altera Gallorum in eam
Prouinciam Nauigatione comitatꝰ
est, Atque adhibitis aliquot militibus
Ob pericula, Regionis illius interi-
ora & Maritima diligentissimè
Lustrauit, & Exactissimè dimensus
est, Obseruata etiam singulorum
Fluminum inter se distantia, ut ipse-
met redux Carolo IX Galliarum
Regi, demonstrauit.
Stálame.
Chicola
Charlefort
Terra plana
Littus rectum
S. Michael
Portus Principis
Humile
Charenta
Garumna
Zagareo.
Lucaya
SEPTENTRIO
OCCIDENS
ORIENS
MERIDIES
Pars Maris Antillarum
Scala Leucarum
Marinarum
Terrestrium
Isabella
Portus Patris
Portus absconsus

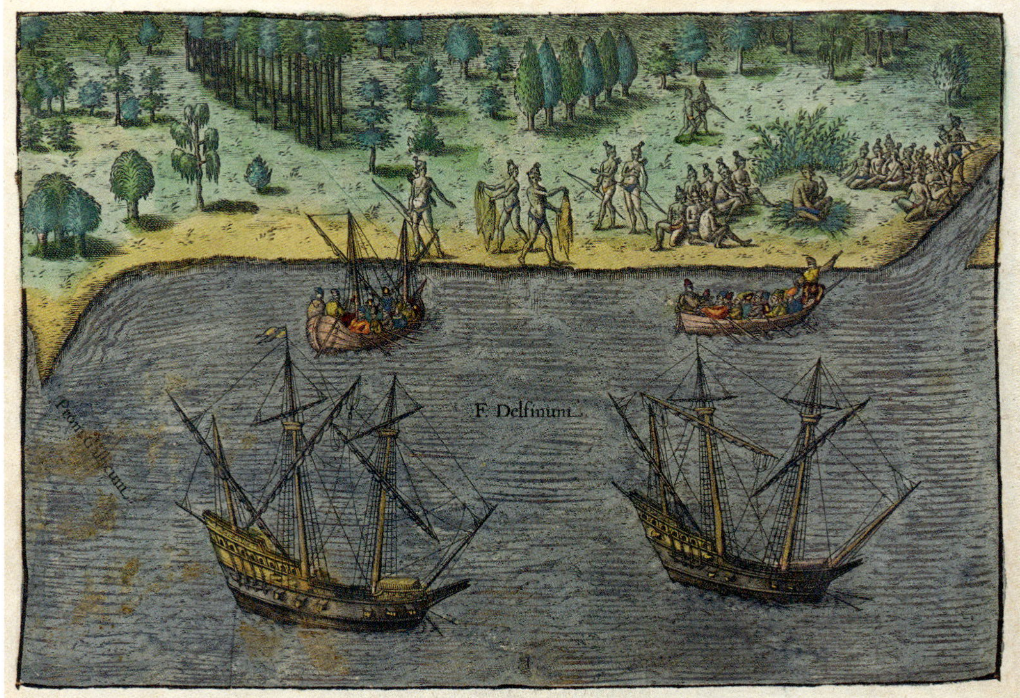

PLATE 1

The promontory where the French landed, called by them the French promontory

During their first voyage to Florida, the French arrived near a well-wooded headland, slightly elevated from the coastline. In honour of France the commander of the fleet named this place, which is about 30 degrees from the equator, the French Cape. Coasting northward, the French discovered a deep and beautiful river at whose mouth they cast anchor in order to examine it in more detail the next day. On his second expedition, Laudonnière called it the River of Dolphins because he had seen large numbers swimming there. When they disembarked they saw many Indians coming to give them a kind and friendly welcome, even making them presents of the skins they wore. After accepting many gifts from the commander of the expedition the Indians brought them to their king, who had not risen up, but remained seated on branches of laurels and palms. This king made our captain a present of a large animal skin decorated all over with very lifelike drawings of animals of the forest.

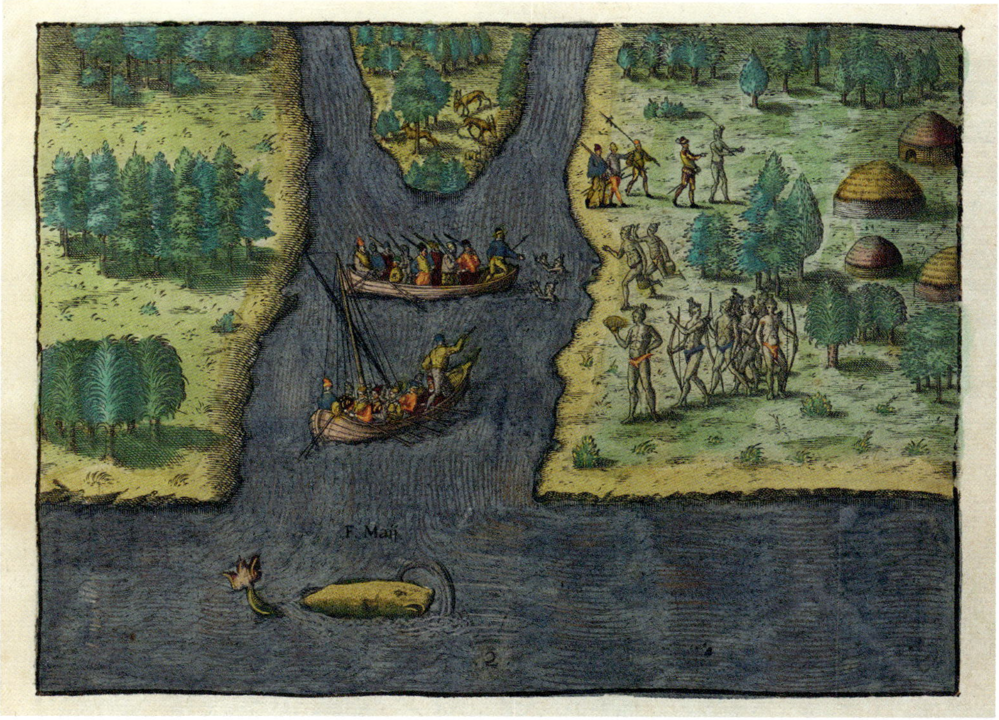

PLATE 2

The French sail to the May river

Embarking once more, the French sailed on further. As they came to land they were greeted by another group of Indians, some of whom waded into the water up to their shoulders offering little baskets of maize full of red and white mulberries, while others offered help so that they might come ashore. Having landed, the Frenchmen saw the Indian chief, who was accompanied by his two sons and a company of his men armed with bows and quivers of arrows. After exchanging greetings our men proceeded into the forest hoping to discover many wonderful things. But they saw nothing except for some trees bearing red and white mulberries whose tops were covered with innumerable silkworms. The French named this river the May, because they sighted it on the first day of that month.

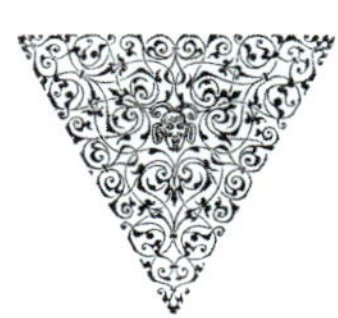

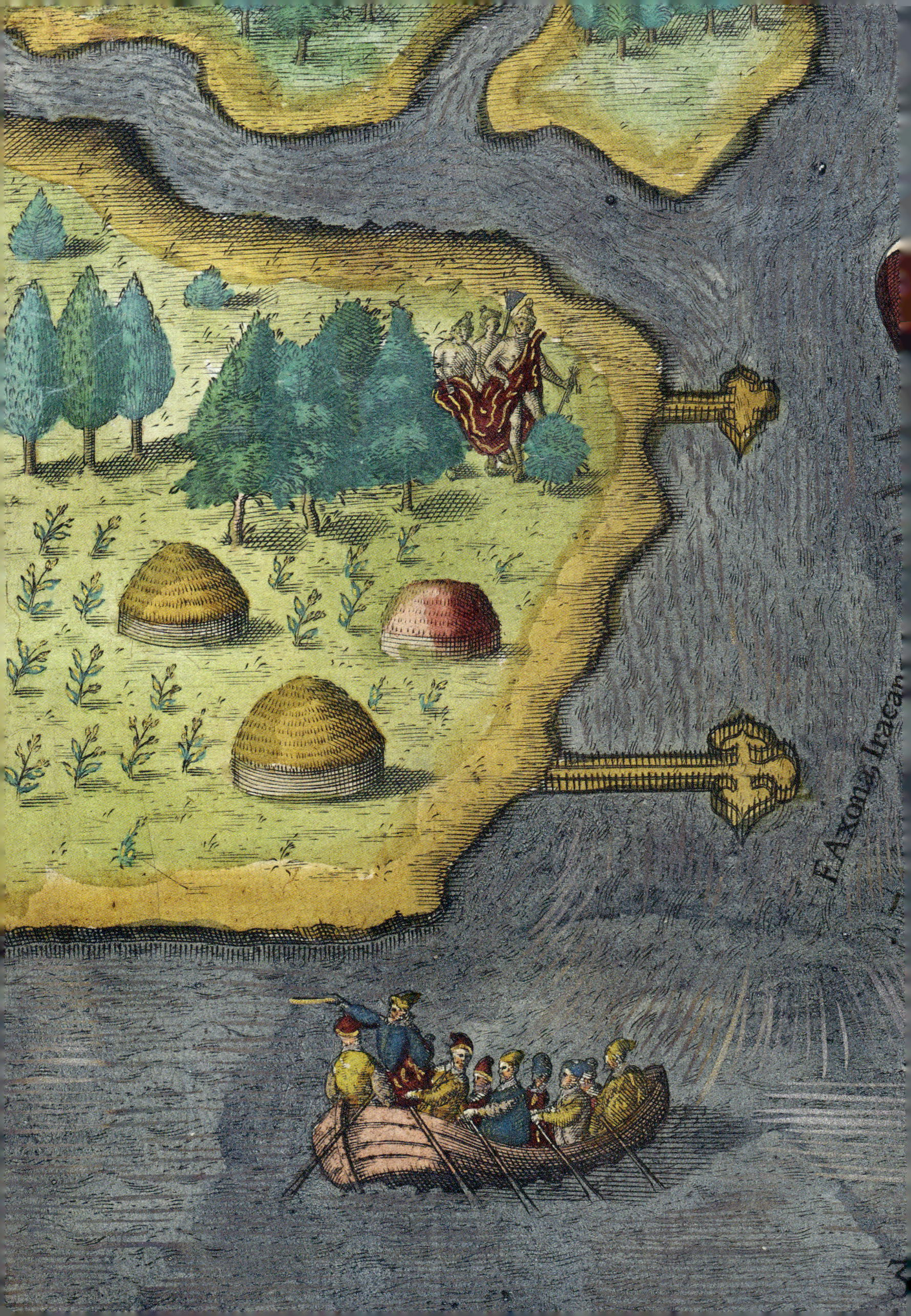
F. Axona, Iracan

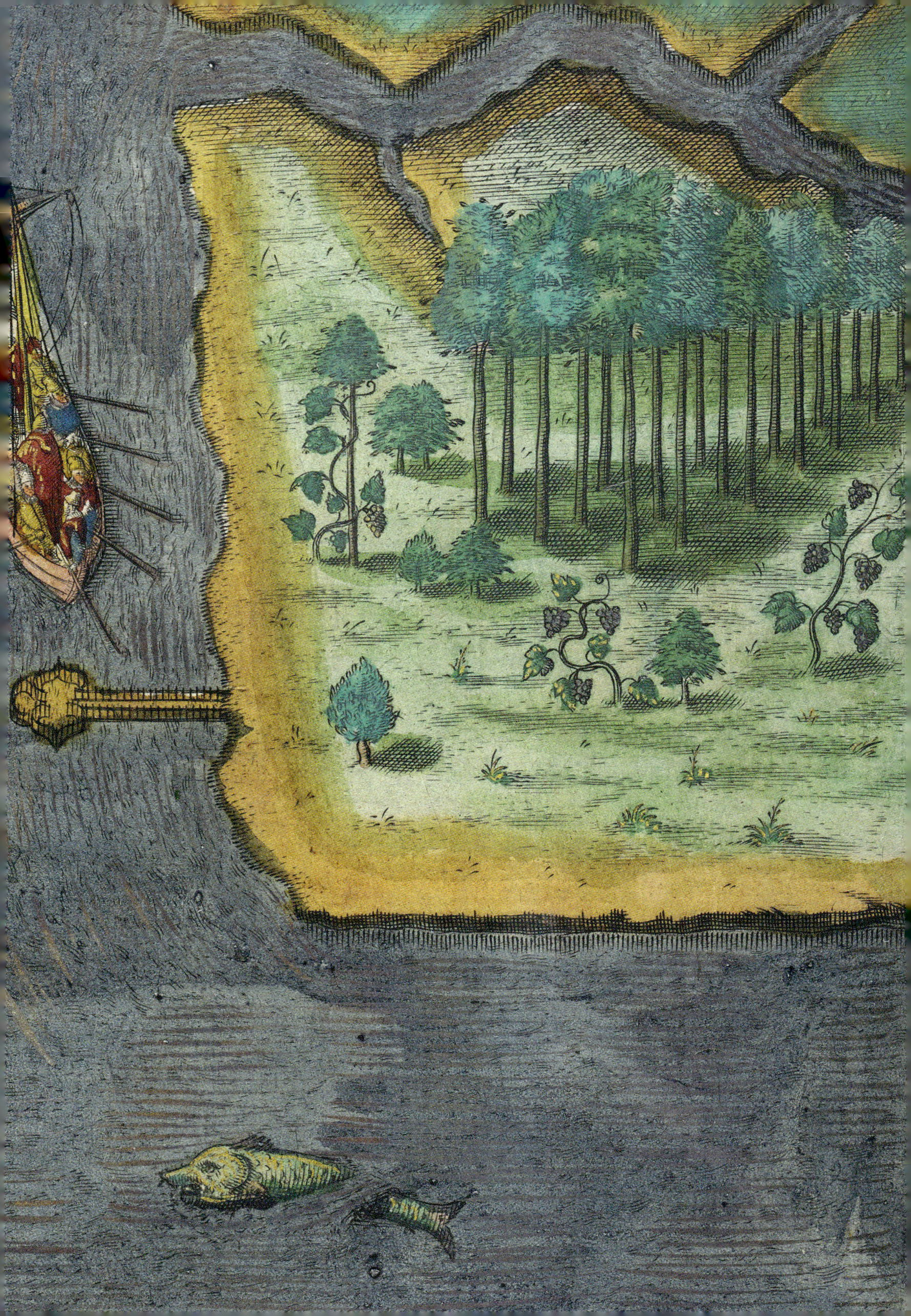

PLATE 3, PAGES 124/125

Leaving the May river, the French discover two other rivers

A little afterwards they went on board again, hoisted anchors, and sailed further on along the coast until they entered a beautiful river, which the commander himself chose to explore in company with the chief of that region and some of the natives, and which he named the Seine because it resembled the river Seine in France. It is about 14 leagues from the May river. Returning to the ships, they sailed further north; but, before going far, they discovered another fine river, and sent two boats to explore it. Here they discovered an island, whose chief was no less friendly than the other. This river, six miles from the Seine, they named the Aine.

PLATE 4

Six other rivers discovered by the French

Sailing on, about six miles further on they discovered another river, which they called the Loire; and subsequently five others, which they named the Charente, Garonne, Gironde, Beautiful and Great respectively. Having carefully explored all these, and having discovered along these nine rivers within the space of less than 60 miles many singular things, but still not being contented, they proceeded yet further north until they arrived at the Jordan river, which is perhaps the most beautiful river of the entire northern region.

PLATE 7, PAGES 128/129

The French left in Fort Charles suffer from scarcity of provisions

Not long after Ribault had left Florida, the men he left behind in Fort Charles (the fortress he built on an island in a stream entering the greater river of Port Royal from the north) began to find that provisions were running out. After discussing how to remedy this, they decided to apply to the chief Ouadé and his brother Couëxis. Those who went on this mission were sent in Indian canoes by the inland waters, and at a distance of some 10 miles discovered a large and beautiful river of fresh water, where they saw many alligators, much bigger than those in the Nile. The banks of this river were lined with large cypresses. After a short delay here they went on to the chief Ouadé, and being received by him in a very nice way, they presented him with the objective of their journey, and prayed him not to abandon them in these difficult circumstances. When he heard this, the chief sent messengers to his brother Couëxis for maize and beans. The latter responded instantly; early next morning the messengers came back with food, which the chief ordered on board the canoes. The French, very pleased with the chief's generosity, wanted to leave, but he would not allow this, keeping them with him, and entertaining them for the day. The following morning he showed them his fields of maize, and intimated that they would not be short of food as long as that field existed. Having now been dismissed by the king, they returned by the way they had come.

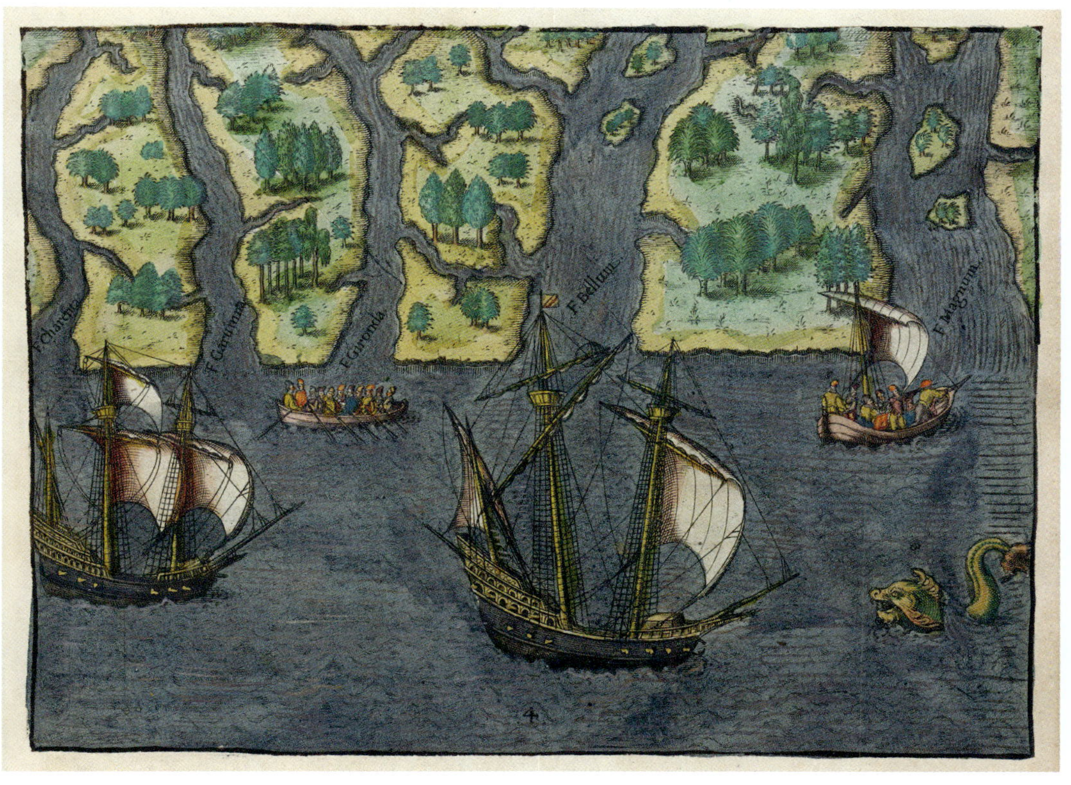
F. Charenta
F. Garumna
F. Gironda
F. Bellum
F. Magnum
4

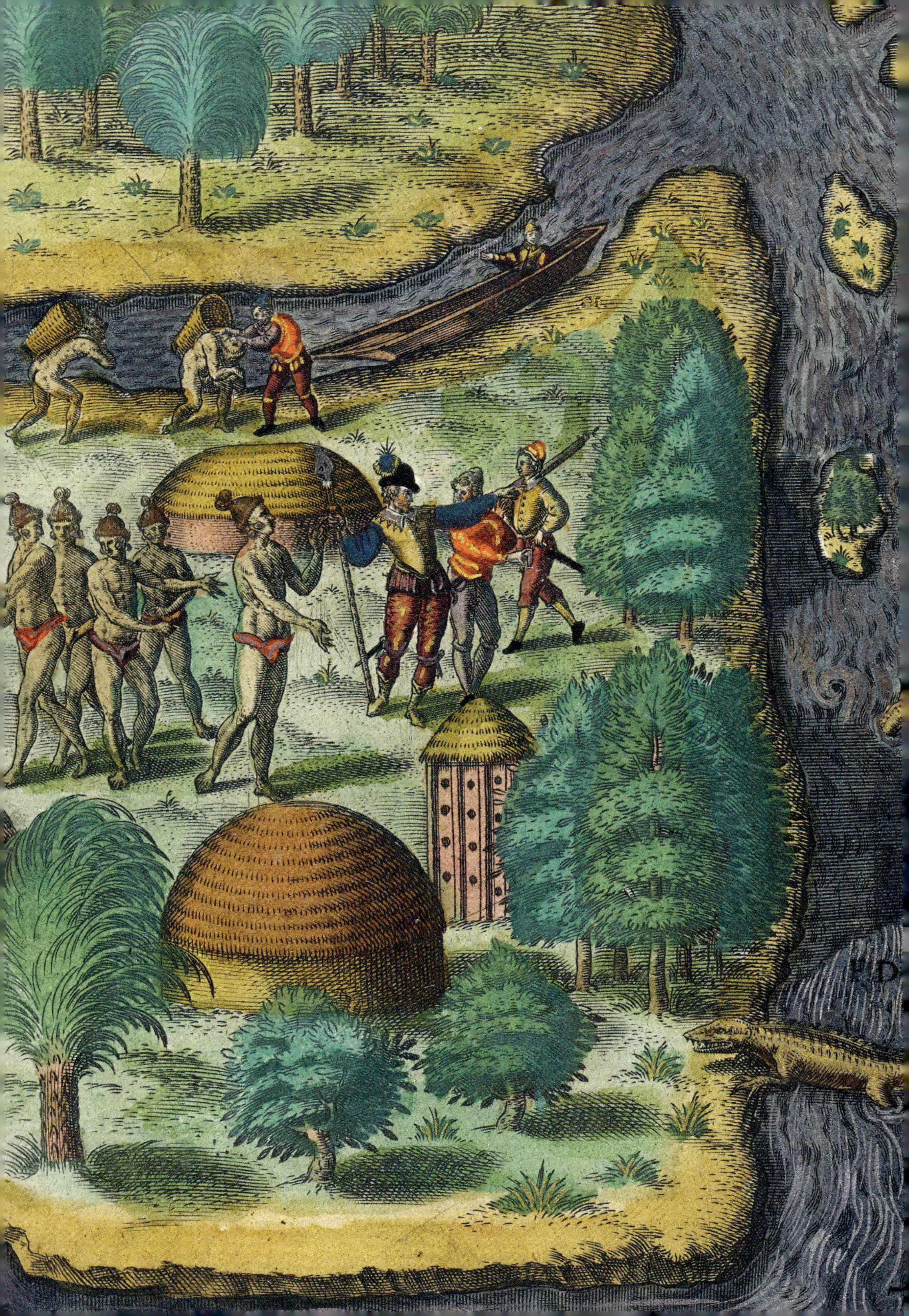

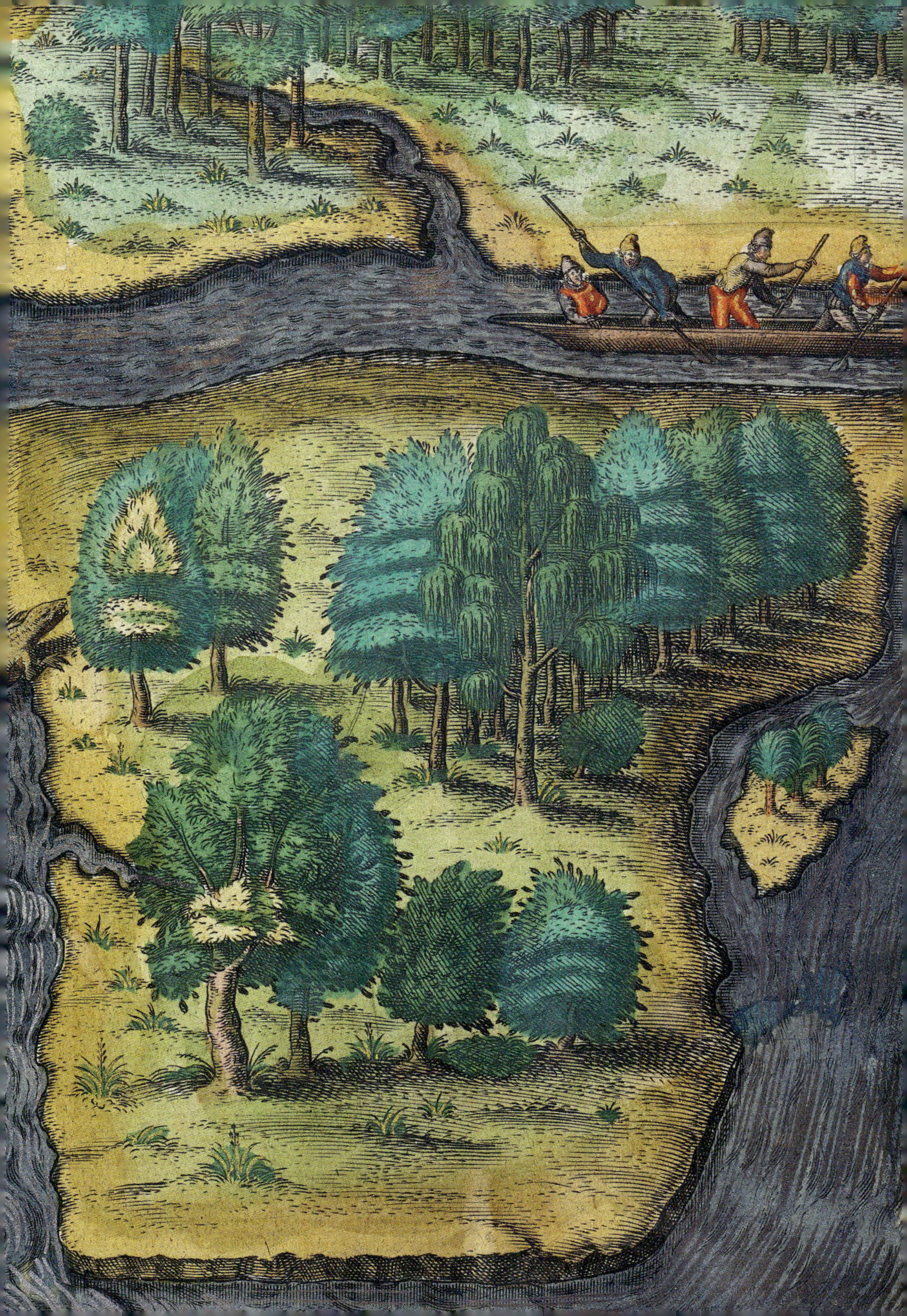

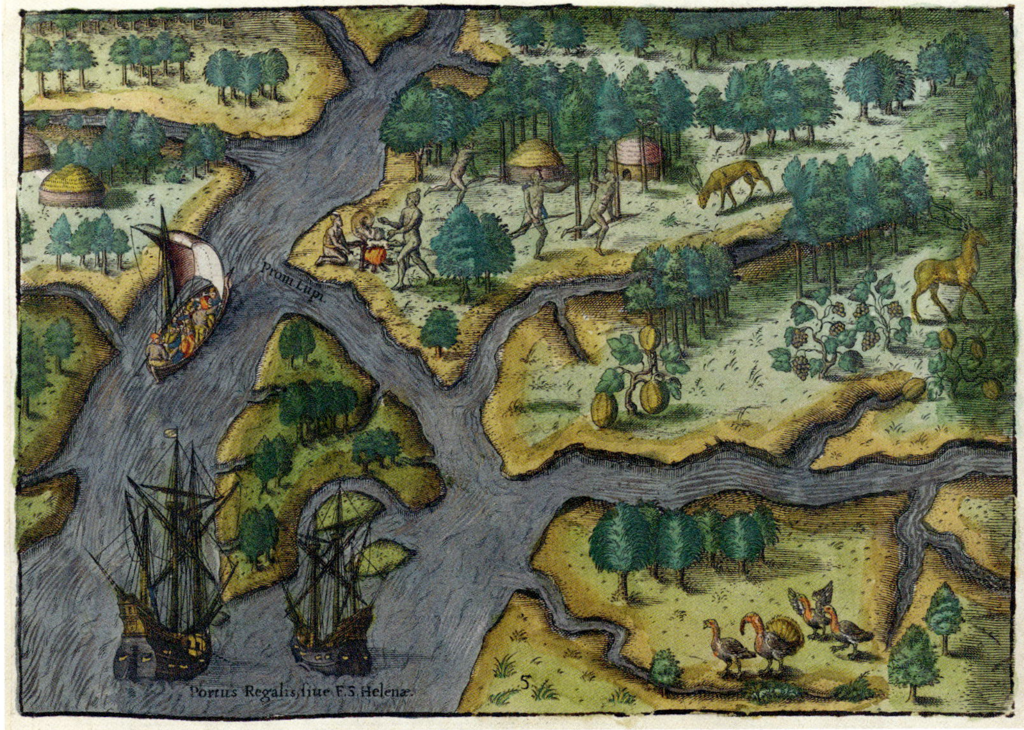

PLATE 5

The French reach Port Royal

Resuming their voyage as before, they discovered a river which they called Bellevue; and after sailing three or four miles further, they were informed that they were close to yet another river, surpassing all others in size and beauty. When they had reached it, they found it so impressive a stream that they called it Port Royal. Here they took in sail, and anchored in 10 fathoms. The commander, upon landing with several soldiers, found the country very beautiful, with many oak, cedar and other trees. As they went on through the woods, they saw Indian peacocks or turkeys flying past, and deer going by. The mouth of this river is three French leagues wide, and is divided into two branches, one turning westward, the other to the north. This latter is thought by some to connect with the Jordan river; the other returns to sea, as the inhabitants have confirmed. These two branches are two miles wide, and halfway between them is an island pointing towards the river delta. Then, embarking again, they entered the branch to the north in order to examine its possibilities. And after proceeding about 12 miles, they saw a group of Indians who immediately fled, leaving a young lynx which they were roasting. For this reason, the place was called Lynx Point. Going still further, they came to another branch of the river, which the commander determined to follow, leaving the main stream.

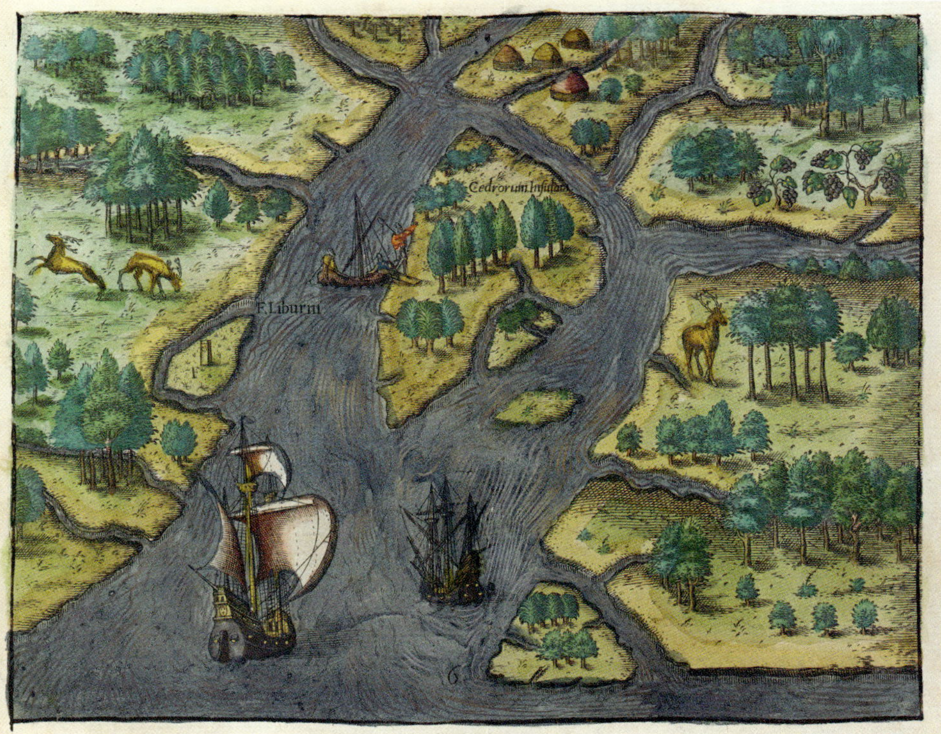

PLATE 6

The French commander erects a column with the coat of arms of the king of France

The commander, however, having returned to his ships, and having stayed on board one night, ordered into one of the boats a landmark carved in the form of a column, and having cut upon it the arms of the king of France, which was intended to be erected in some particularly agreeable location. This they found about three miles to the west, where they discovered a small creek, which they entered and, after following it for some time, found that it flowed into the main river again, thus forming a small island. The commander ordered the column to be erected here, on a small mound. Then they noticed two deer of a large size they had not seen before, and which they could easily have killed with the arquebuses had not the commander forbidden it in admiration. Before returning to the boats, they named this small island Libourne. Embarking again, they explored another island in the vicinity, but here they found very little apart from some large cedars. They named it Cedar Island, and then returned to the ships. The small island on which they erected the column is indicated in the plate by the letter F.

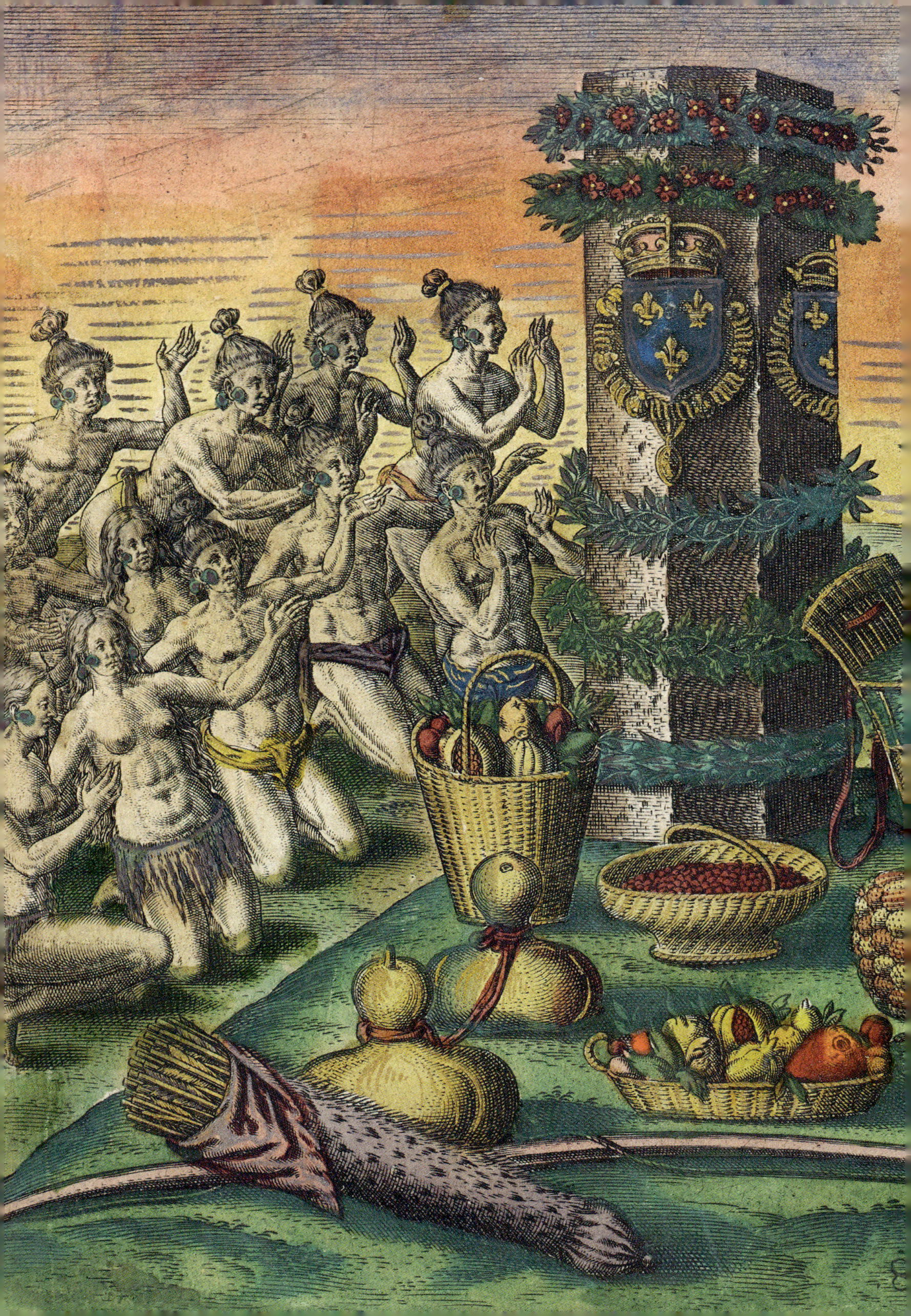

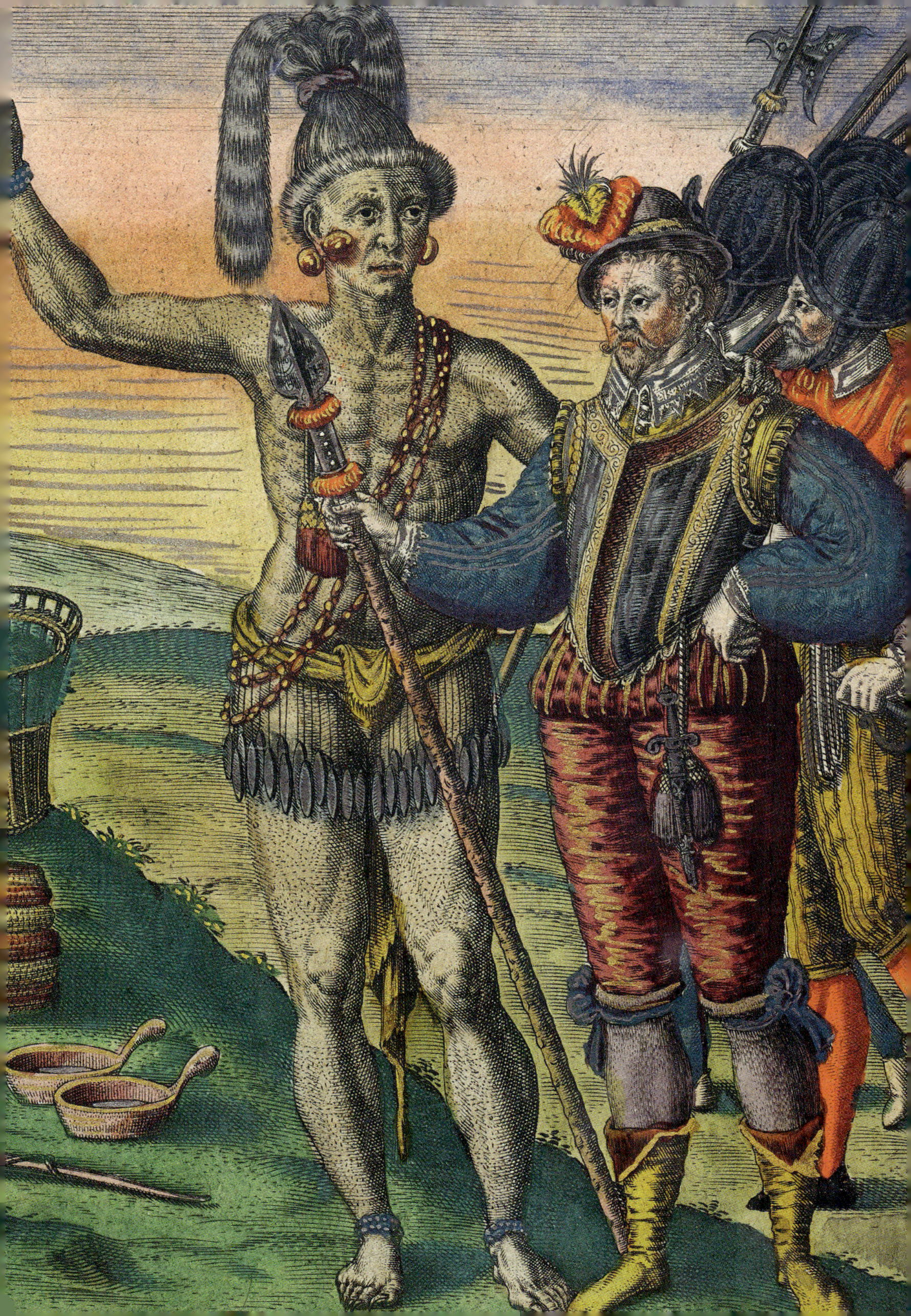

PLATE 8, PAGES 132/133

The natives of Florida worship the column erected by the commander on his first voyage

When the French landed in Florida on their second voyage under Laudonnière, he went ashore with 25 soldiers, after obtaining a safe passage from the Indians, who had gathered in numbers to see them. Their chief, Athore, lived four or five miles from the coast. After gifts had been exchanged, accompanied by all sorts of friendly interactions, the chief said he wanted to show them something remarkable. The French agreed, although they were cautious as the chief was accompanied by many of his people. He then led them straight to the island where Ribault had erected the stone column with the heraldic device of the king of France. Upon arrival, they noticed that the Indians were worshipping the column as an idol. The chief himself, having saluted it in the same way as his subjects revered him, kissed it. His men followed his lead, and we were invited to do so as well. Before the monument were various offerings of fruits and edible roots that grew there, bottles of perfumed oil, bows and arrows. After witnessing the ceremonies of these poor savages, the French returned to their companions and decided on the best place to build a fortress. Athore is very handsome, prudent, honourable, strong and of very great stature, being more than half a foot taller than the tallest of our men. He had married his mother, and had several children with her whom he showed to us, striking his thigh as he did so. After this marriage, his father Saturioua decided to leave his mother.

PLATE 9

The French select a location for building a fort

After exploring many of the rivers in the country, the French ultimately decided that the May river was the best place to build a fort, because maize and other food was most abundantly available there, in addition to the gold and silver that they had found on the first visit. They sailed there, and after following the river towards a mountain, they selected this place as better than any other they had visited before. On the next day, as the sun rose, they went to work after having prayed to God and having said grace for having found this rich province. After a triangular outline had been measured out, they all started – some digging the earth, some constructing fences of wood, some building the defensive wall. Every man was busy working with spade, saw, axe or some other tool, and did so diligently to make sure everything proceeded rapidly.

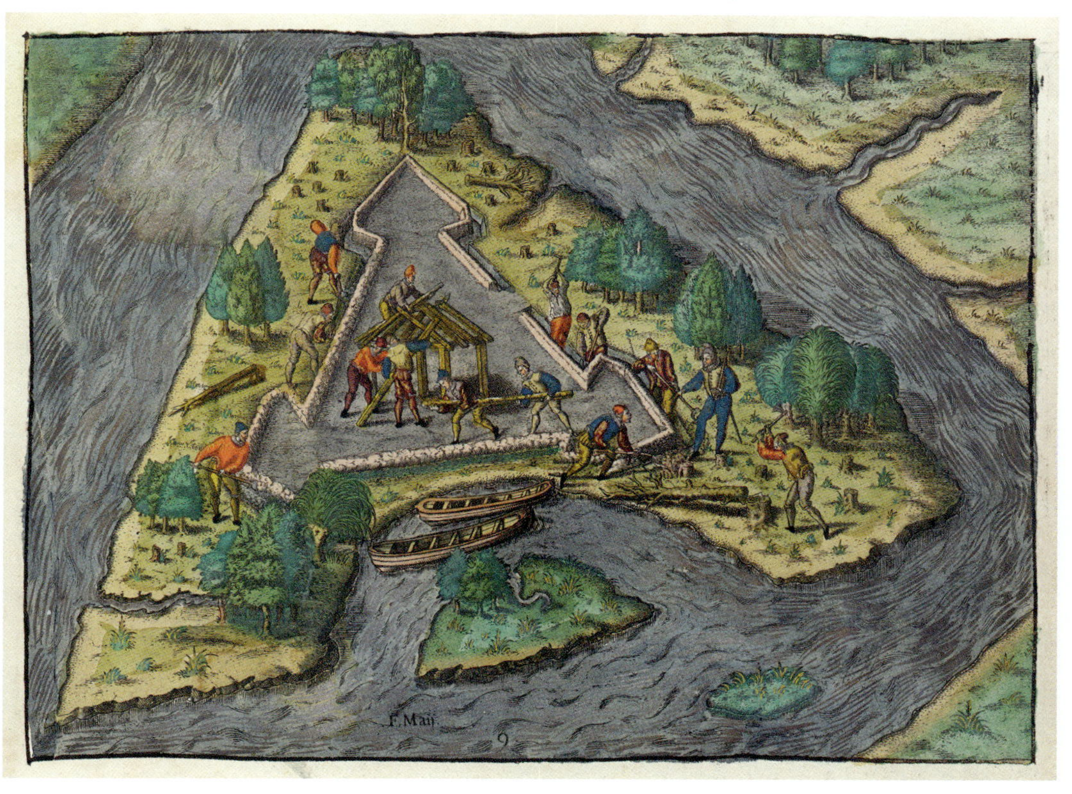
F. Maii.
9

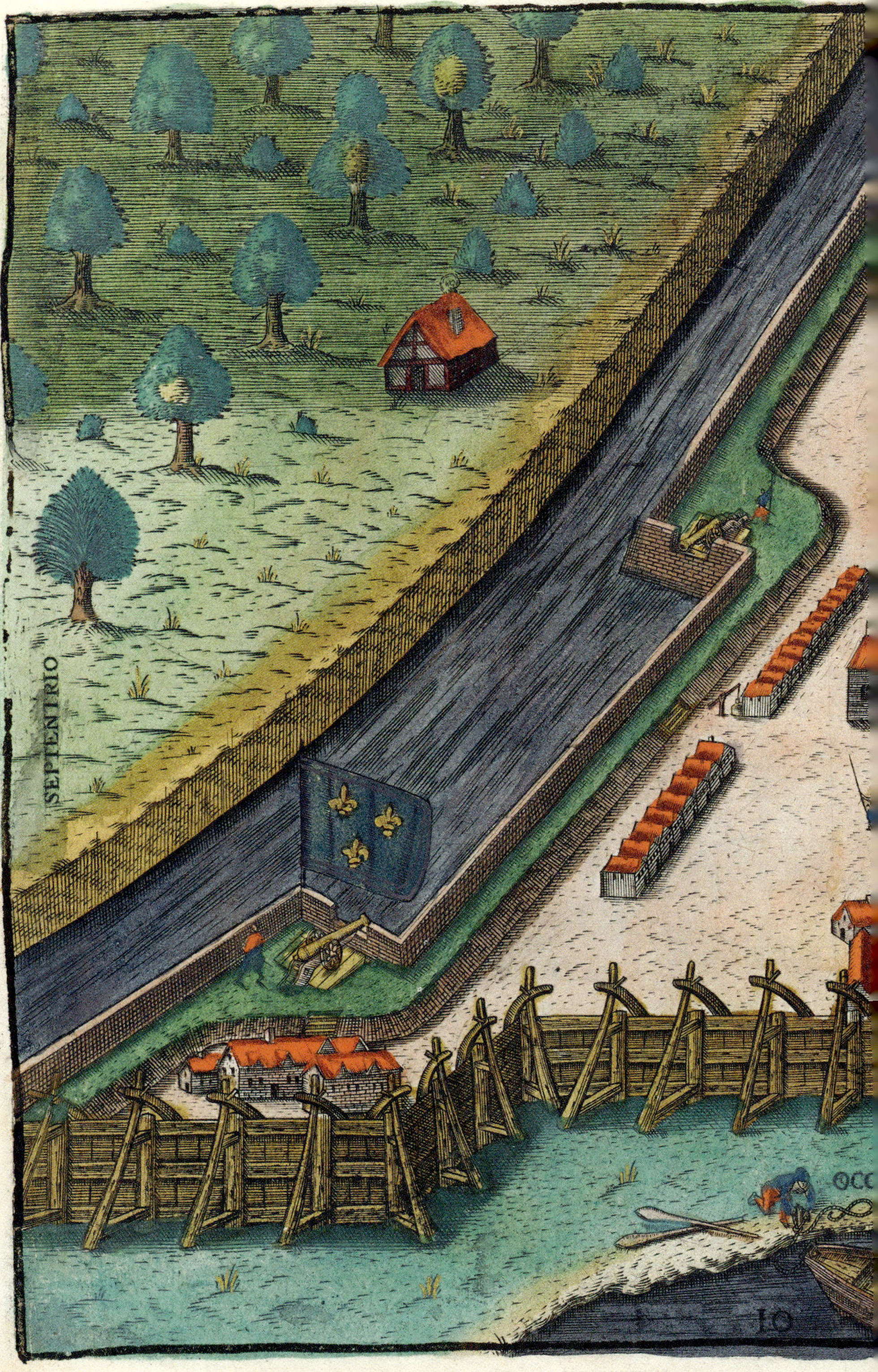

SEPTENTRIO
OCC
IO

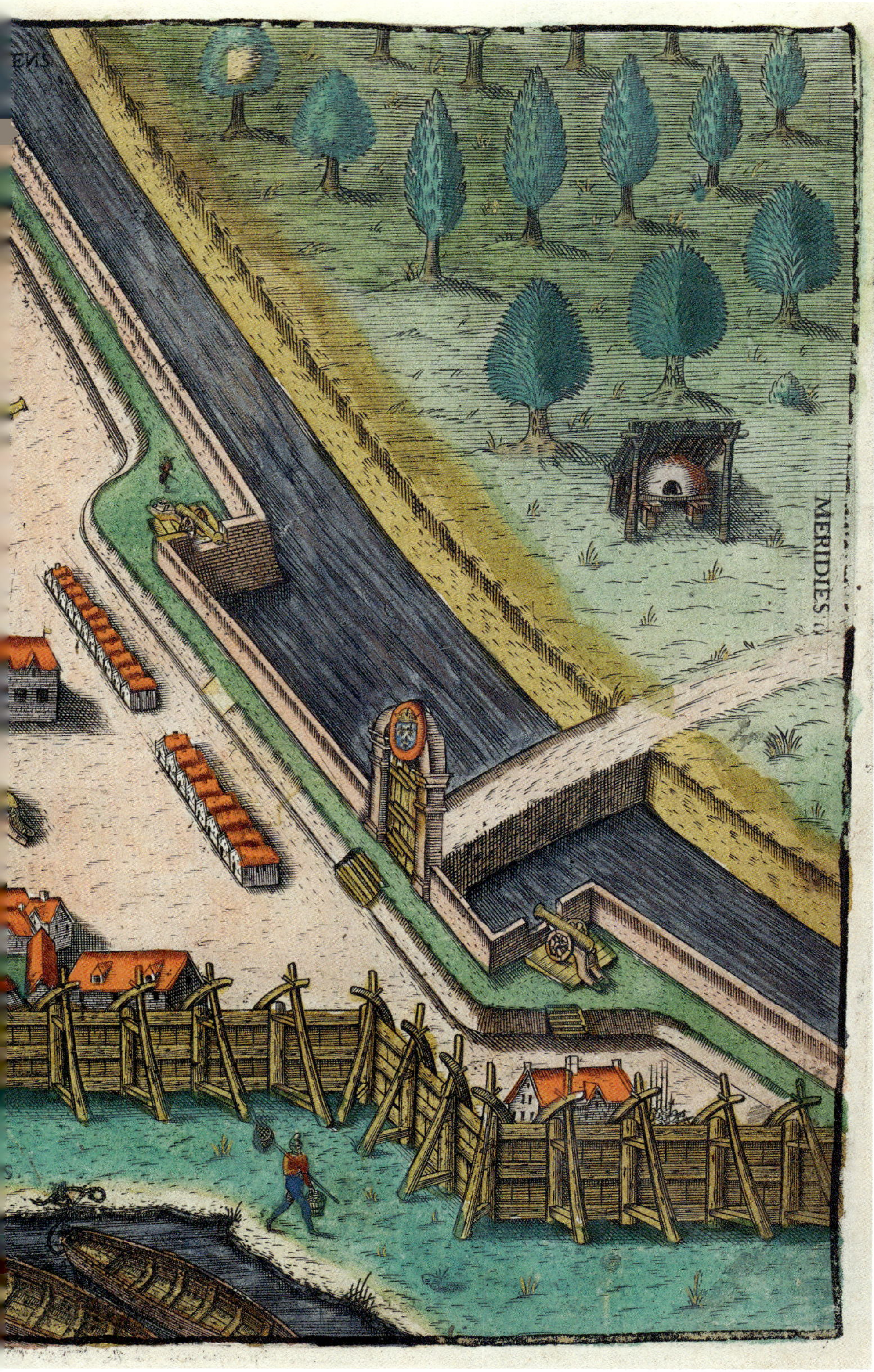
MERIDIES

PLATE 10, PAGE 136/137

Picture of Fort Caroline

Thus they erected a triangular fort, named Fort Caroline. The base of the triangle, looking west, was defended by a small moat, and a wall nine feet high. The side next to the river was raised with planks and fences. On the southern side, the building resembled a citadel, which housed a granary to store provisions. The whole was made of wood and mud, except for the upper two or three feet of the wall which was made of grass. Inside the fort was a large open space 18 yards long and 18 yards wide. Midway along the southern side of this open space were the barracks, and on the northern side was a high building, which was later blown away by the wind. Experience taught us that here, where the winds are so strong, it is better to build low houses. There was another open space, also fairly large, one side of which was covered by the granary, while on the other side stood the house of Laudonnière, looking out over the river with a small square before it. The main door opened on to the larger open space, and the back door on to the river. At a distance, an oven was built, for as the houses were thatched with palm-tree branches, they could easily catch fire.

PLATE 11

Ceremonies performed by Saturioua before going out to war

During the second voyage the French concluded a treaty with a powerful local chief, Saturioua, and agreed that they were allowed to erect a fort and would be allied with him in wars against other groups, and further that occasionally they would give him some arquebusiers. Some three months later he sent messengers to Laudonnière asking for the soldiers, as he was on the verge of going out to war. Laudonnière, however, sent Captain La Caille with some men to inform Saturioua in a courteous way that he could not provide him with any soldiers because he wanted to make peace between the two groups. The chief was angry, as now he could not begin his expedition despite having everyone and everything ready. He assembled his men in a low-lying place, where Laudonnière's soldiers were also present. The troops sat down, with the chief in the centre. The chief, after rolling his eyes in anger, uttered several deep noises and made various gestures, and suddenly everyone raised a horrid yell; his soldiers then repeated this yell, striking their hips and rattling their weapons. Then the chief took a platter of water, and raised it towards the sun in worship, praying for a triumph over the enemy and for enemy blood to flow just like the water from the platter. And then he flung the water up into the air, and as it fell down on to his men he said: "As I have done with this water, so I pray that you shall do with the blood of your enemies." Then he poured water on to the fire and said: "So may you be able to extinguish your enemies and bring us their scalps." Then they all rose up, and set out along the river.

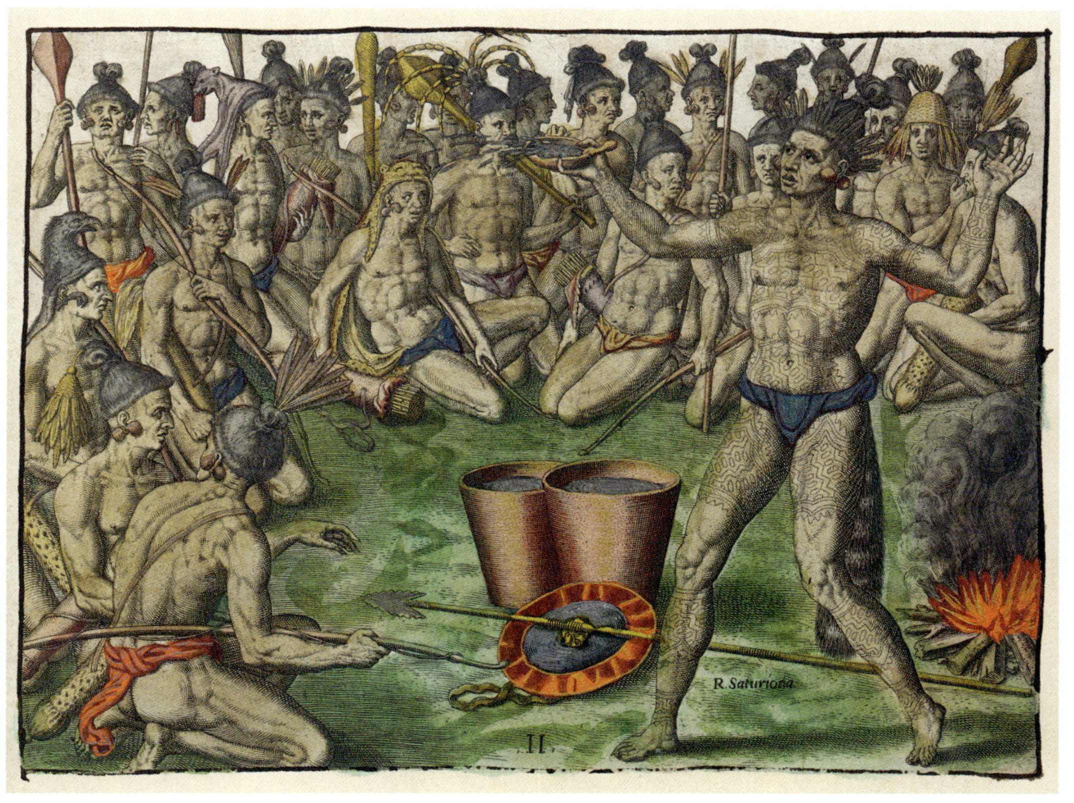
R. Saturiona
II.

PLATE 12

Outina, going at the head of his army, consults a sorcerer

Laudonnière, having received some of the men of the chief Outina, sent them back to their chief, which led to an alliance and promises of mutual friendship. The treaty was important because the only road to the Apalatcy Mountains, where gold, silver and copper are found, was through the lands of this chief. As part of this alliance, however, Outina asked Laudonnière for some arquebusiers, as he wanted to wage war on an enemy. Laudonnière sent 25 soldiers, under lieutenant D'Ottigny. The chief received them with great delight, and was sure of the upcoming triumph, since the arquebusiers' reputation had struck everyone with terror. The chief, having completed his preparations, ordered his army to march. Their first day's journey was easy, but the second very difficult because of several large swamps. Finally they reached enemy territory, where the chief stopped his troops and summoned a sorcerer, more than 120 years old, to report on the enemy camp. The sorcerer prepared a place in the middle of the army, and asked D'Ottigny's servant for the shield he was carrying. He then placed it on the ground, and drew a circle and several other signs. Then he knelt down on the shield and began to recite unintelligible phrases in a deep voice, making many wild gestures. After 15 minutes, he assumed an appearance that was so frightful that it was barely human, twisting his limbs so that the bones snapped out of position. He returned at once to his normal position, but in a very fatigued and bewildered state. Finally, stepping out of the circle, he saluted the chief and told him the number of his enemies, and where he would encounter them.

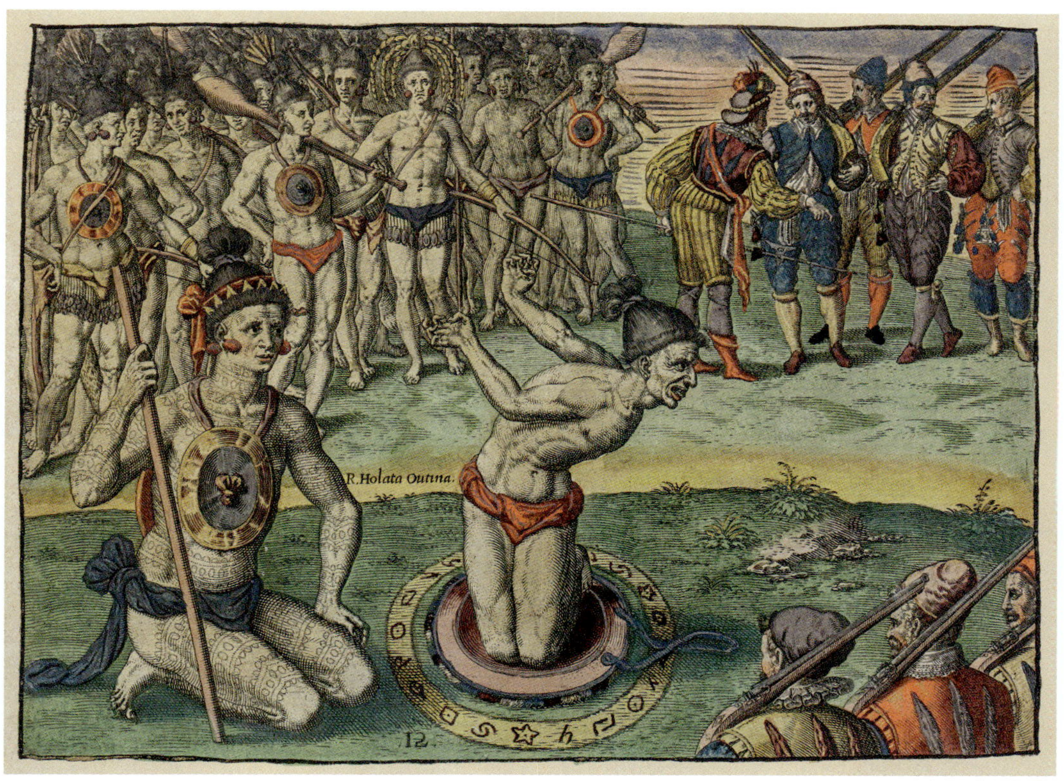
R.Holata Outina.
12.

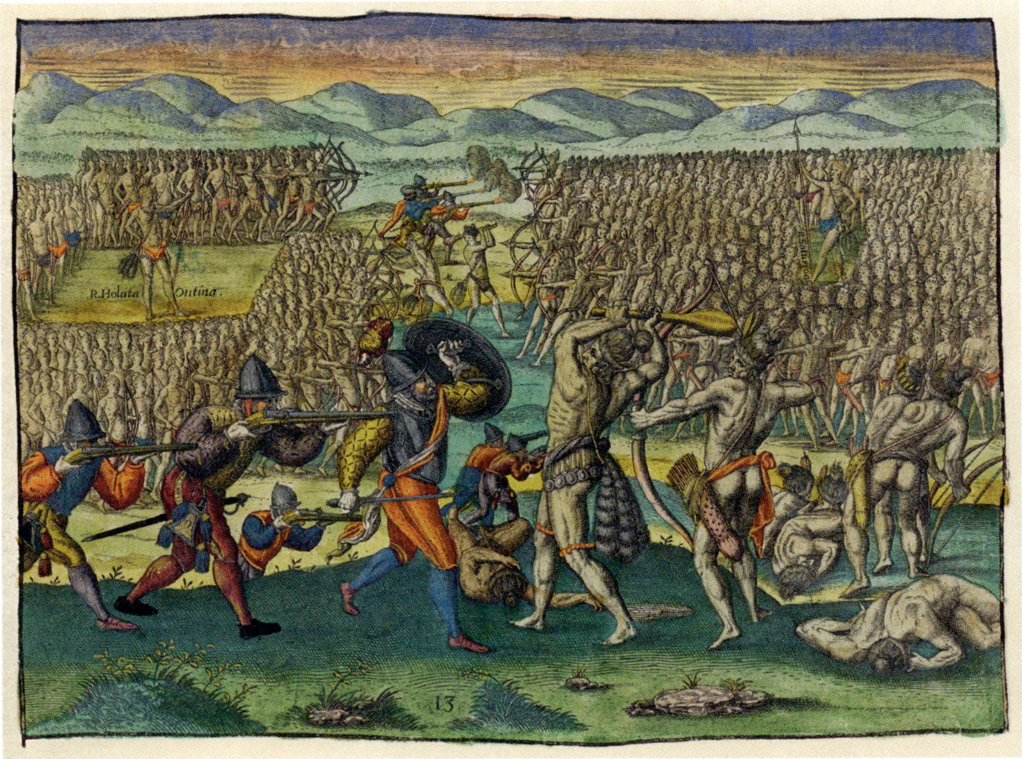

PLATE 13

Outina, supported by the French, gains a victory over his enemy Potanou

So frightened was he by the sorcerer's words that the chief no longer thought of attacking, but rather of how he could return home safely. D'Ottigny, however, indignant at having marched along without result, told him he would lose his respect if he did not dare risk his luck. At length these threats and insults forced him to attack. With their consent, he put the French in the front line, and indeed it is certain that had they not sustained the whole brunt of the battle and massacred so many of the enemy, causing King Potanou's army to flee, Outina would have been beaten. The magician was surely inspired by a spirit, for all he predicted was correct. Outina, content with the flight of his enemy, recalled his men and ordered them to return home, much to the irritation of D'Ottigny, who would have preferred to follow up his victory.

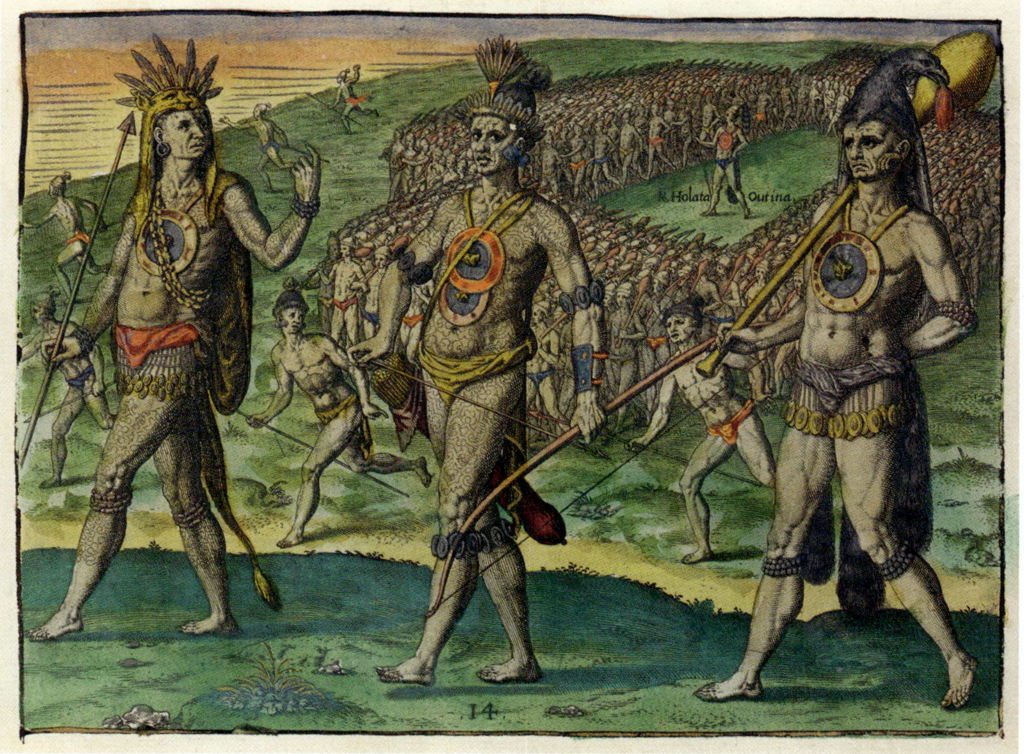

PLATE 14

Order of march observed by Outina on a military expedition

When Saturioua left for war, his soldiers advanced in chaotic fashion. His enemy Olata Outina, considered the king of kings, superior to all others in terms of riches and number of subjects, marched with his troops in military formation. The wings of the army are composed of young men, the fittest of whom, also painted red, are used as scouts to look for enemy troops. Like dogs looking for wild beasts, they hunt their enemies by scent, and when they find traces of them they swiftly return to their army to report. In the same way that our soldiers pass orders by trumpets and drums, they use heralds who have certain cries for when to stop, or to advance, or to attack or make some other move. They stop at sunset and never fight at night. When they set up camp, they divide into squads of 10, the bravest apart. The king chooses a place in the fields or in the forest to pass the night and after he has eaten and gone to sleep the masters of the camp place 10 squads of the bravest men in a circle around him. About 10 yards away some 20 other squads form another circle around the first, and 20 yards further away there is another circle of 40 and this formation continues to increase according to the size of the army.

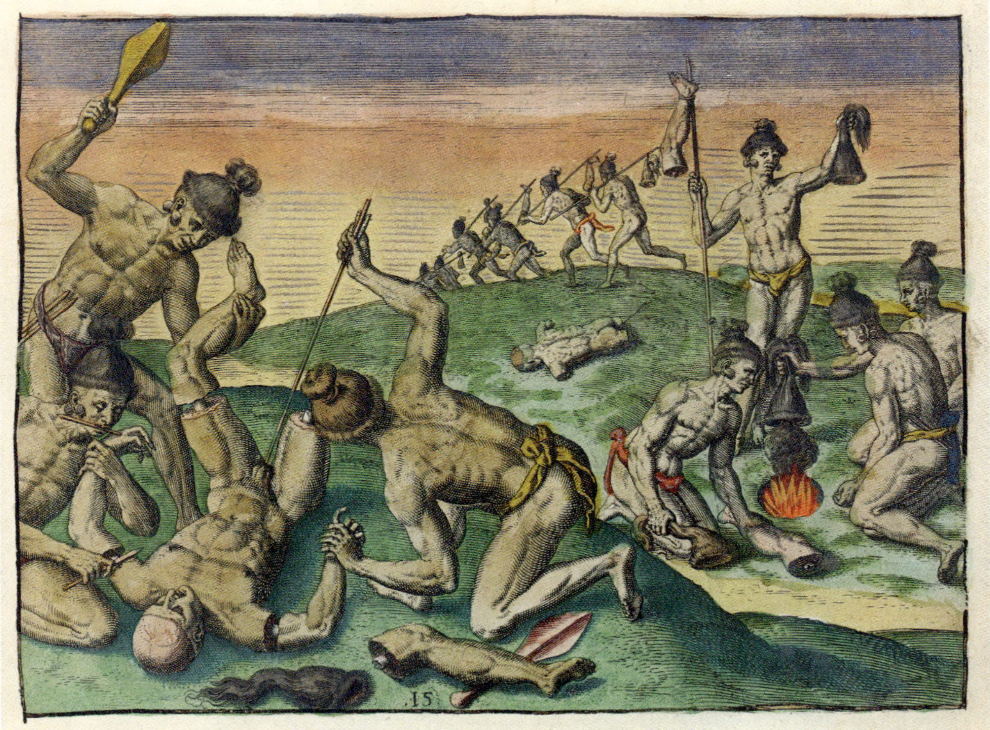

PLATE 15

How Outina's men treated the slain of the enemy

During the entire period the French had dealings with the great chief Olata Outina in the war against his enemies, no pitched battle was fought. It all happened in ambushes and skirmishes, fresh troops constantly replacing those who retired. Whoever put the enemy to flight first was credited with victory, even when his casualty rate was very high. In these battles those who fall are instantly dragged off by men specifically charged with this duty. With a sliver of reed, sharper than any steel blade, they cut the skin with the hair from the skull, the longest hairs being twisted into a plait, the hair from the forehead being rolled up with that of the back of the head. Immediately afterwards (if possible), they dig a hole and make a fire of smouldering moss which they carry around in leather sacks. Once the fire is lit, they dry the scalp until it becomes hard like parchment. At the end of the fight, they cut the arms of their victims off at the shoulder and their legs at the thighs. The bones laid bare are crushed to pieces, which, drenched in blood, are dried on the fire. Then they return home victoriously with the skin of the heads at the ends of their spears. What astonished me (for I was among those sent by Laudonnière under D'Ottigny) was that they never left the place of battle without piercing the mutilated corpses of their enemies right through the anus with an arrow, protected by their friends.

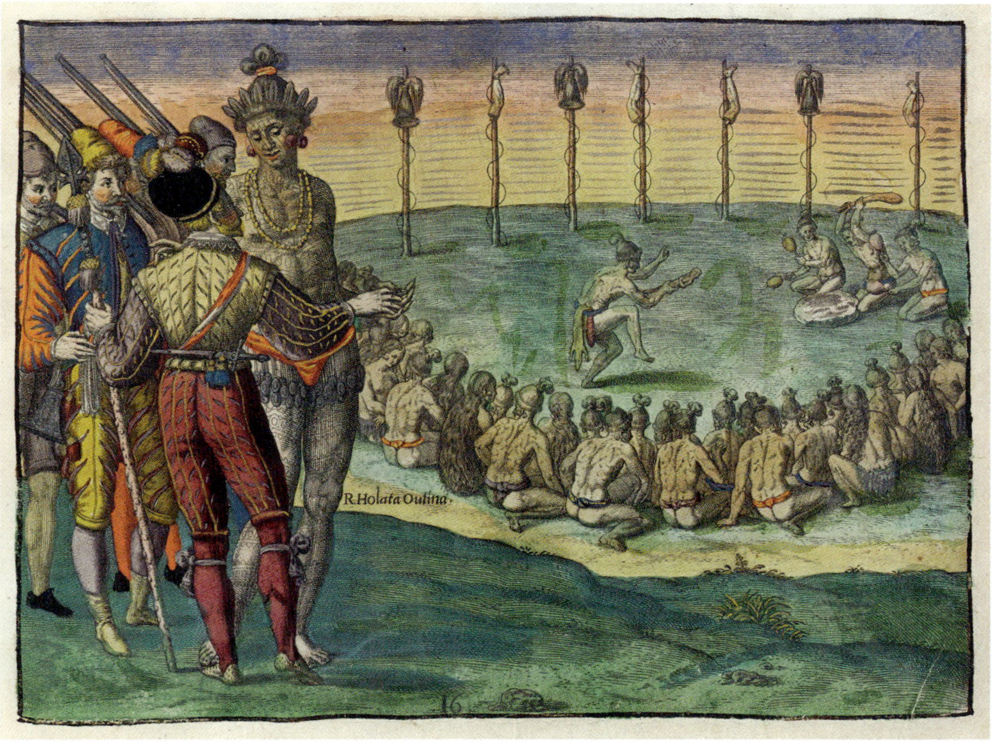

PLATE 16

The trophies and ceremonies that they have after returning from war victoriously

When they return home, they have a certain place where they assemble. Here they ceremoniously bring the legs, arms and skins of the heads of their victims, and stick them on large stakes. When they all sit in a circle, a conjurer appears carrying a small idol. He curses the enemies with a great multitude of angry words. Three men in the circle sit on their knees, one of whom drums with a large stick on a flat stone as a means of answering the conjurer's every word. Next to him, on either side, are two men holding a piece of fruit in each hand which looks like a pumpkin. After having dried it, they remove the heart and the seeds, and fill it up with little stones. Then they put it on a small stick, and rattle and sing, as their ancestors did, to answer the conjurer's mumbling.

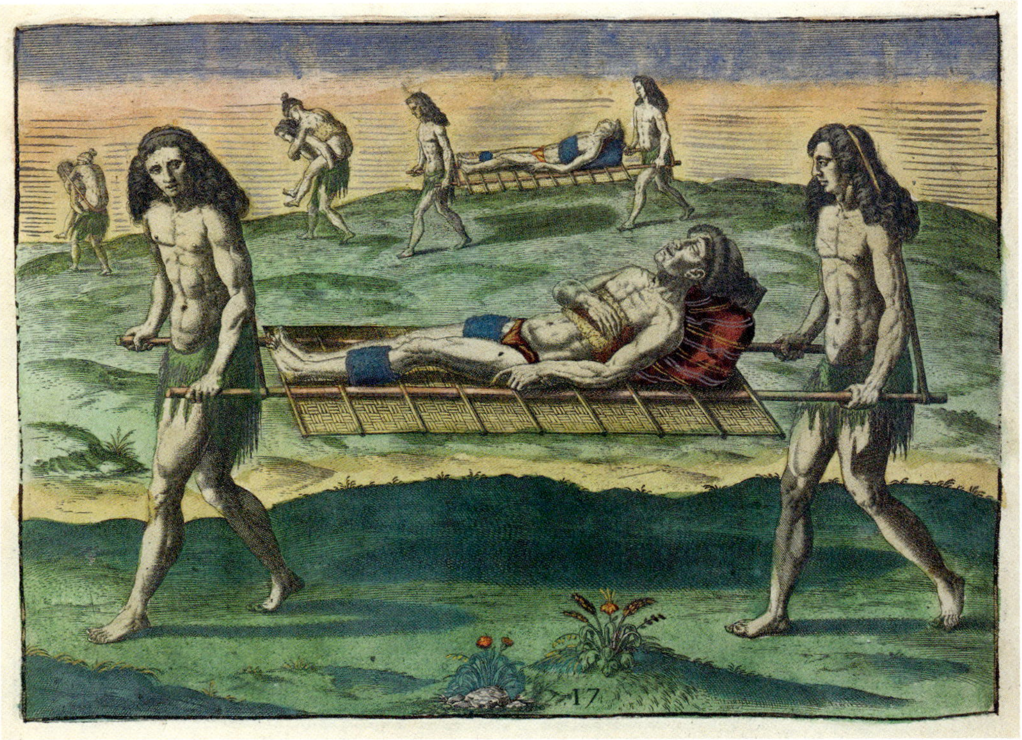

PLATE 17

Manner in which their hermaphrodites are employed

In this country there are numerous hermaphrodites, a mixture of both sexes. They are considered detestable by the Indians, but as they are big and strong they are used to transport loads instead of beasts of burden. When the kings set out to war, the hermaphrodites carry the supplies. They place the Indians, dead from either war or disease, on a stretcher made of two poles covered with a mat of thin woven canes. The head rests on a fur; a second fur is wound around the stomach; a third around the hips; a fourth is placed around the calves. Next they place belts of leather, about three or four fingers wide, at both ends of the poles and put them on their heads, which are very hard; then they carry their dead to their place of burial. Persons with infectious diseases are carried to specifically designated places on the shoulders of the hermaphrodites who provide them with food until they are healthy again.

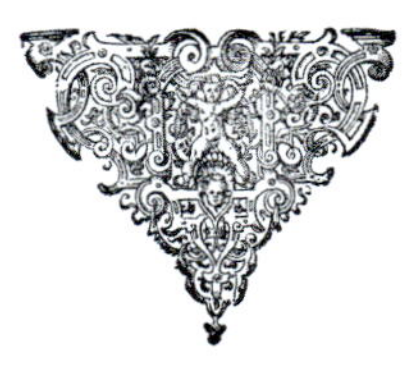

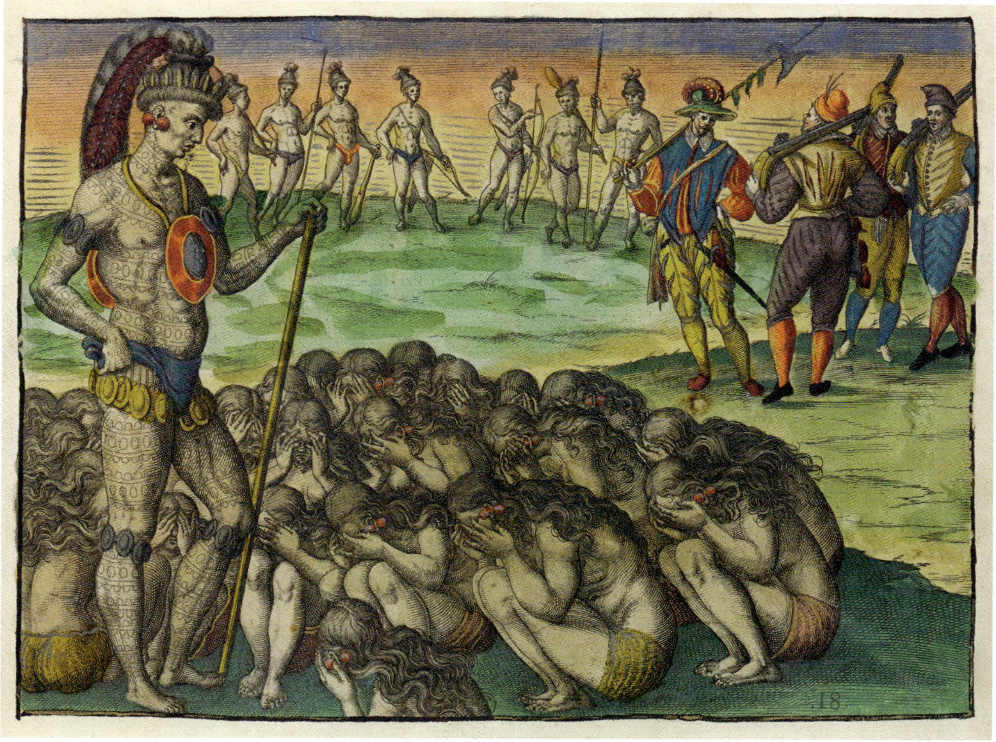

PLATE 18

The chief applied to by women whose husbands have died in war or of disease

The women whose husbands have died in battle or from illness gather on a day that appears to them most suitable to go to their king. They approach him, overcome with grief, sit down on their heels and, covering their faces with their hands, they cry and scream. They ask the king to avenge their deceased husbands, to provide them with means to live and to permit them to marry again after a certain legal period of time. The king, taking pity, grants their requests. They return home, weeping and wailing, as evidence of the love they felt for their husbands. After having spent several days in mourning they carry their husbands' weapons and drinking cups to their tombs, then they start to weep once more and perform other funeral ceremonies.

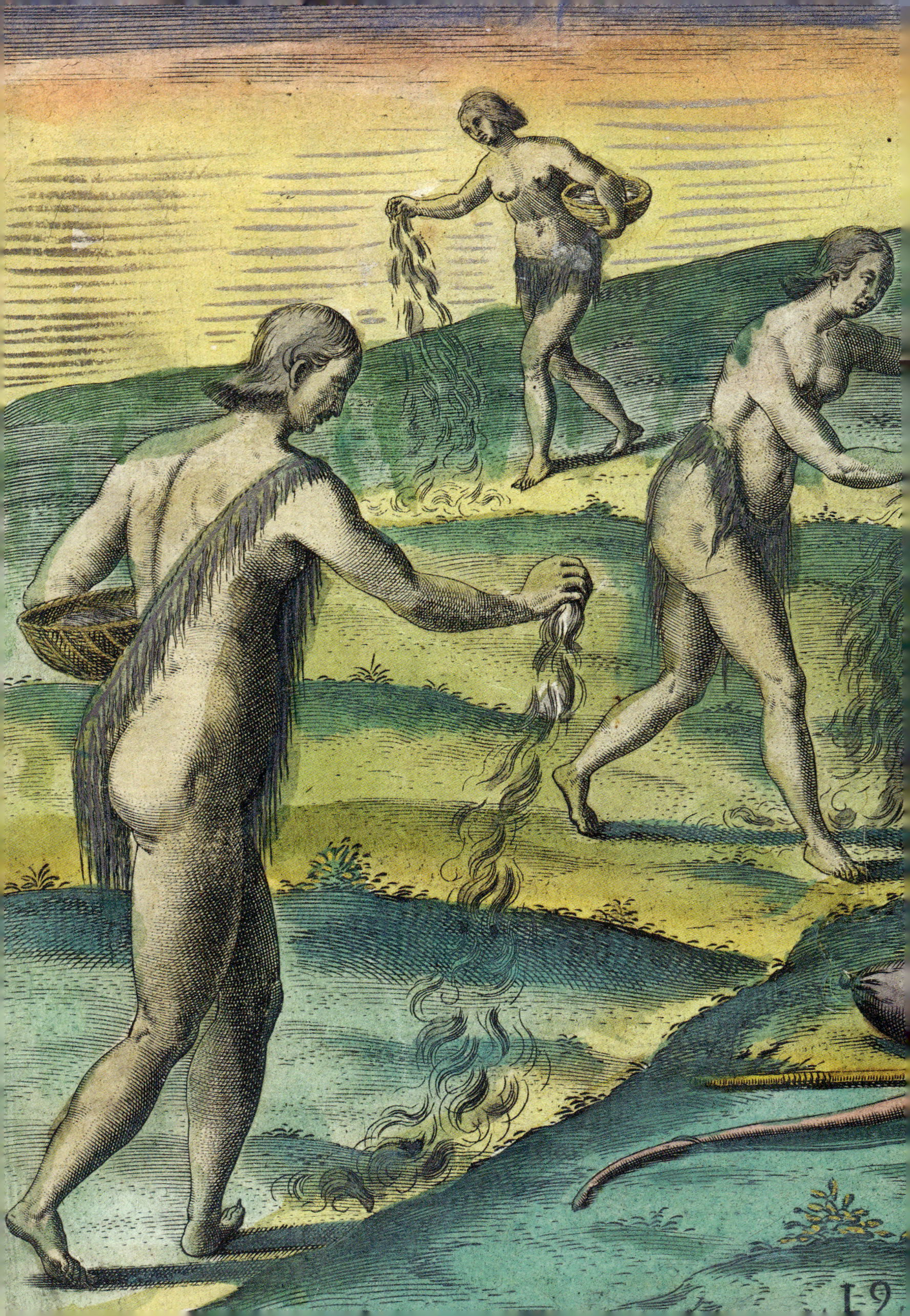

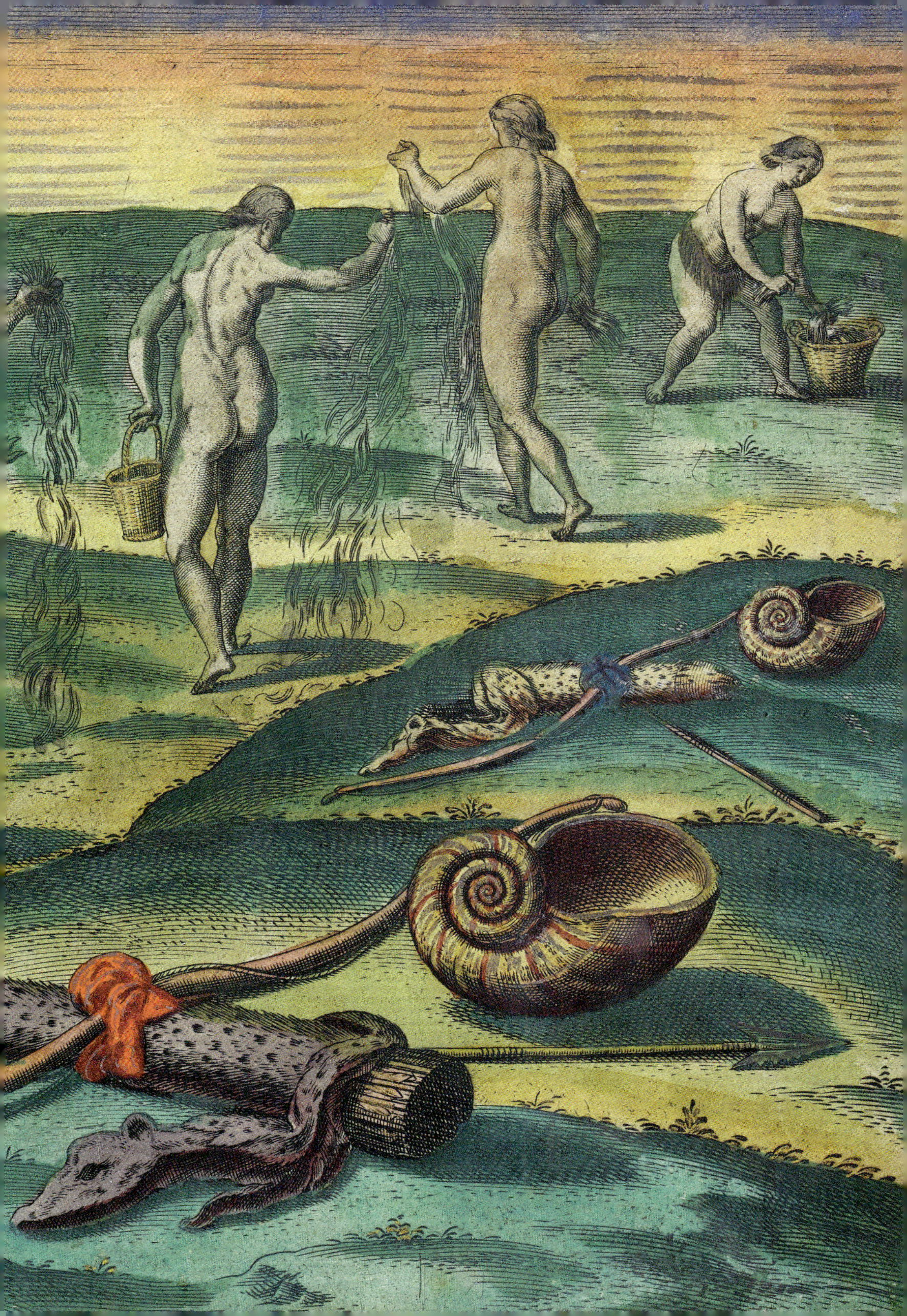

PLATE 19, PAGES 148/149

Ceremonies of women mourning for their deceased husbands

After coming to the graves of their husbands, they cut off their hair below the ears and scatter it across the graves, and then cast upon them the weapons and drinking-shells of the deceased as memorials of brave men. When they return home, they are not allowed to marry again until their hair covers their shoulders. They let their nails grow long on both fingers and toes, cutting them only on the sides, in order to make them very sharp, particularly the men. When they catch one of the enemy, they gouge their nails into his forehead, and tear off the skin so as to wound and blind him.

PLATE 20

Way of treating the sick

The Indians construct a long broad platform where they place a sick person, with his face up or down according to his complaint. With the help of a sharp instrument, a hole is made in the forehead. Blood is sucked from this hole into the mouth and spat into an earthen vessel. Women who are suckling boys or suffering from some disease drink this blood, especially when it is that of a strong young man, so that it may improve their milk and make their children fitter and stronger. For others who are sick, lying face down, they provide smoke by throwing certain seeds on the fire. Entering through the mouth and nose, this smoke circulates around the entire body and induces vomiting to expel the cause of the sickness. The Indians possess a certain plant named petum in Brazil, and which the Spanish call tapaco. The dried leaves of this plant are put in a pipe and set on fire. The Indians inhale the smoke so deeply from the narrowest part of the pipe that it comes out through the mouth and nose, thus dispelling the humours. They are also extremely susceptible to venereal disease, for which they have special remedies provided by nature.

PLATE 21, PAGE 152/153

Mode of tilling and planting

The Indians cultivate the earth very diligently. They make hoes with fish bones and fit them with wooden handles. With these they can dig the soil quite easily. Once the earth has been well broken up and levelled, the women sow beans, millet or maize. To do this they are assisted by people who precede them with a stick, and make holes in the soil where the seed is thrown. When the sowing is completed, they leave the field alone. The winter season is quite cold in this region and lasts three months, from 24 December to 15 March. Being naked, the Indians seek shelter in the forests. Once winter is over, they return home, anticipating the growing of the crops. After they have gathered the harvest, they store the corn for the year's uses, and do not trade with any of it except perhaps for some exchange of household articles.

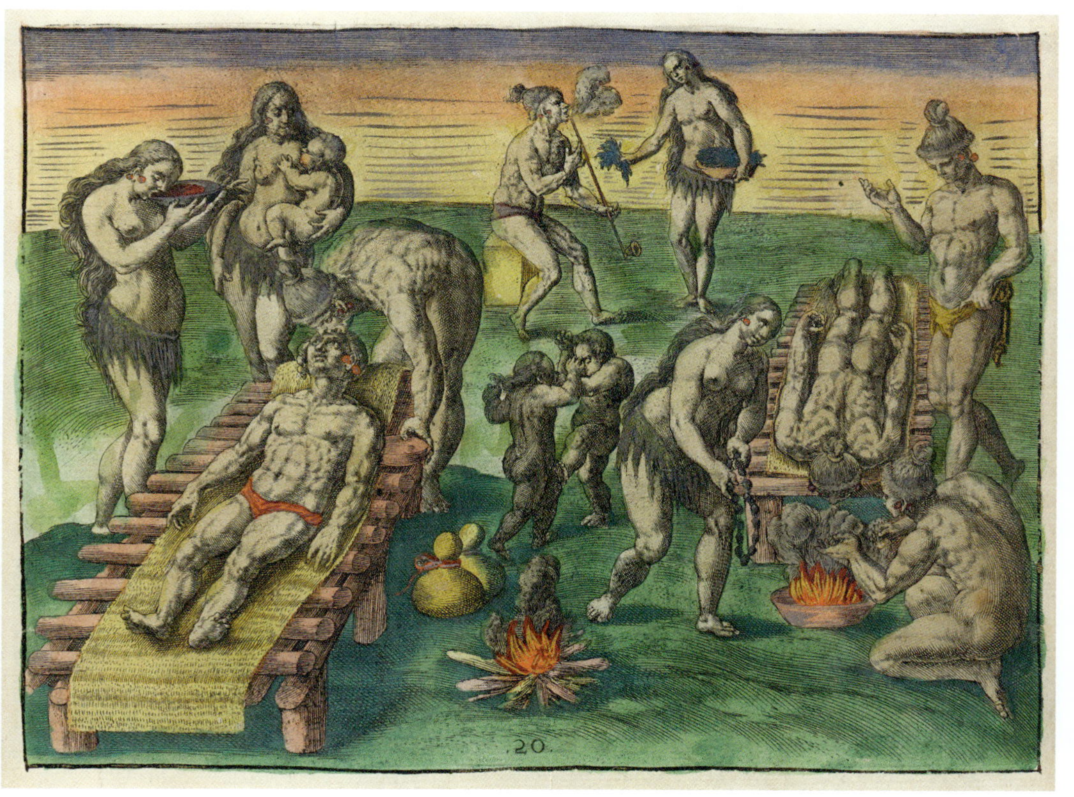
20.

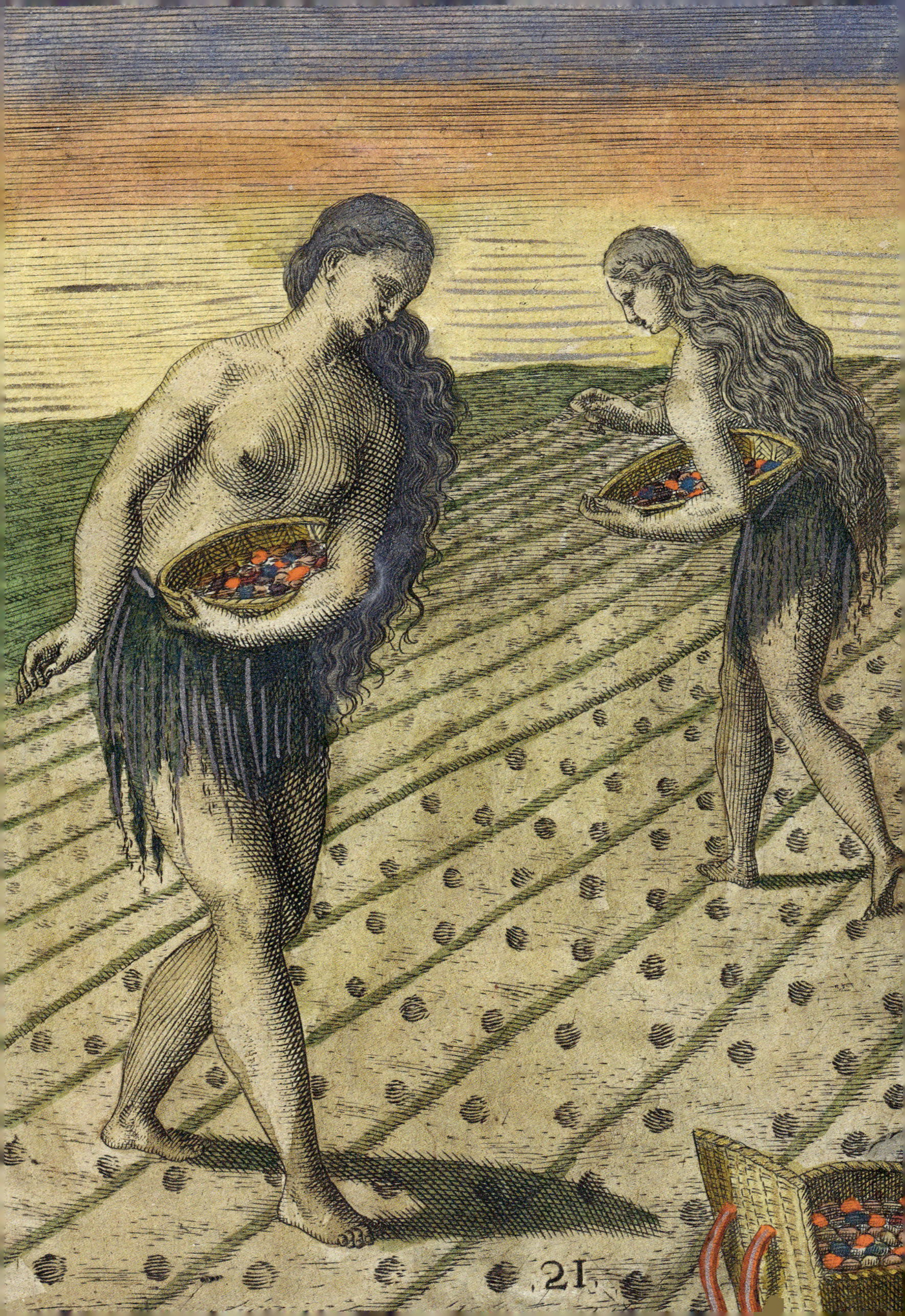
21

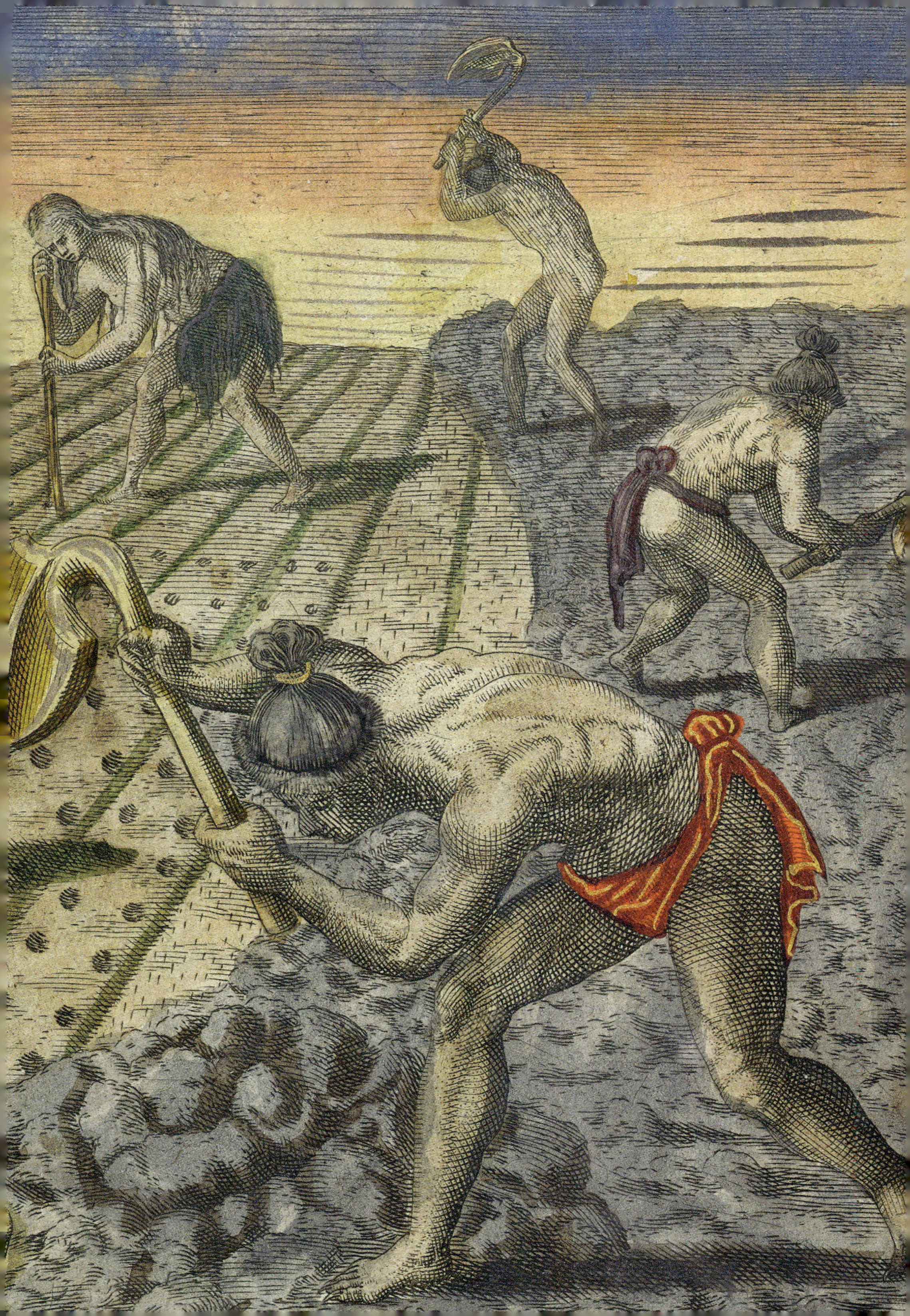

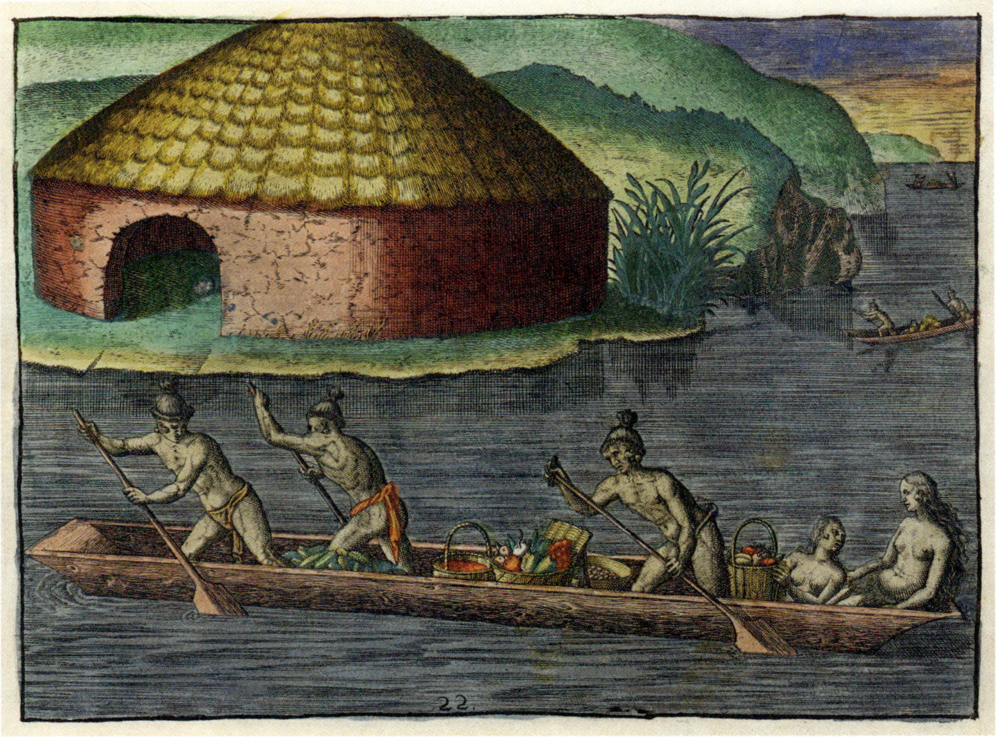

PLATE 22

Industry of the Floridians in depositing their crops in the common granary

There are many islands in this region which produce an abundance of various fruits which they harvest twice a year and take home in boats. Then they stack them up in large storehouses which are built of mud and small stones. They are roofed with thick branches and soft earth, suitable for this purpose. These storehouses are usually built under a hill or rock close to a river. In order to prevent the fruit from rotting, the sunshine is not allowed to enter the building. Apart from the fruit, the Indians store other food they wish to keep here. They go and take it whenever they need it in good harmony. It would be nice if such a lack of avarice prevailed among Christians, whose minds would then be less tormented.

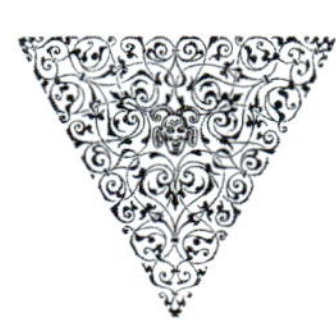

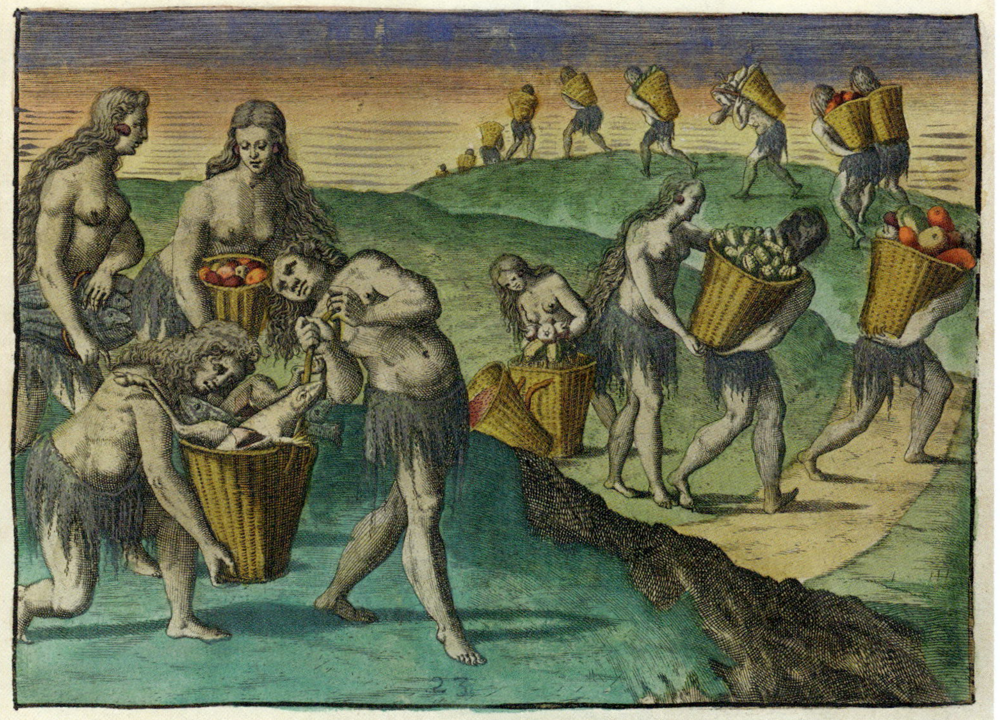

PLATE 23

Bringing in wild animals, fish and other stores

At the same time every year they gather all sorts of wild animals, fish and even alligators. These are put in baskets, and hermaphrodites carry them on their shoulders to the storehouse. They do not resort to this supply unless they are in desperate need. In this case, full notice is given to all so as to avoid antagonism, because they live in the greatest harmony. Only the chief is at liberty to take as he pleases.

PLATE 24, PAGES 156/157

Mode of drying fish, wild animals and other provisions

So as to preserve the flesh of animals, they prepare them in the following way: four strong forked stakes are planted in the ground. Across these are laid more sticks, forming a rack to place the animals and fish on. A fire is lit below in such a manner that the meat may be dried by the smoke. The Indians take great care with this procedure so that provisions do not spoil. I suppose that they prepare all this for the winter months when they are in the forests since in these months we were never able to obtain anything from them.

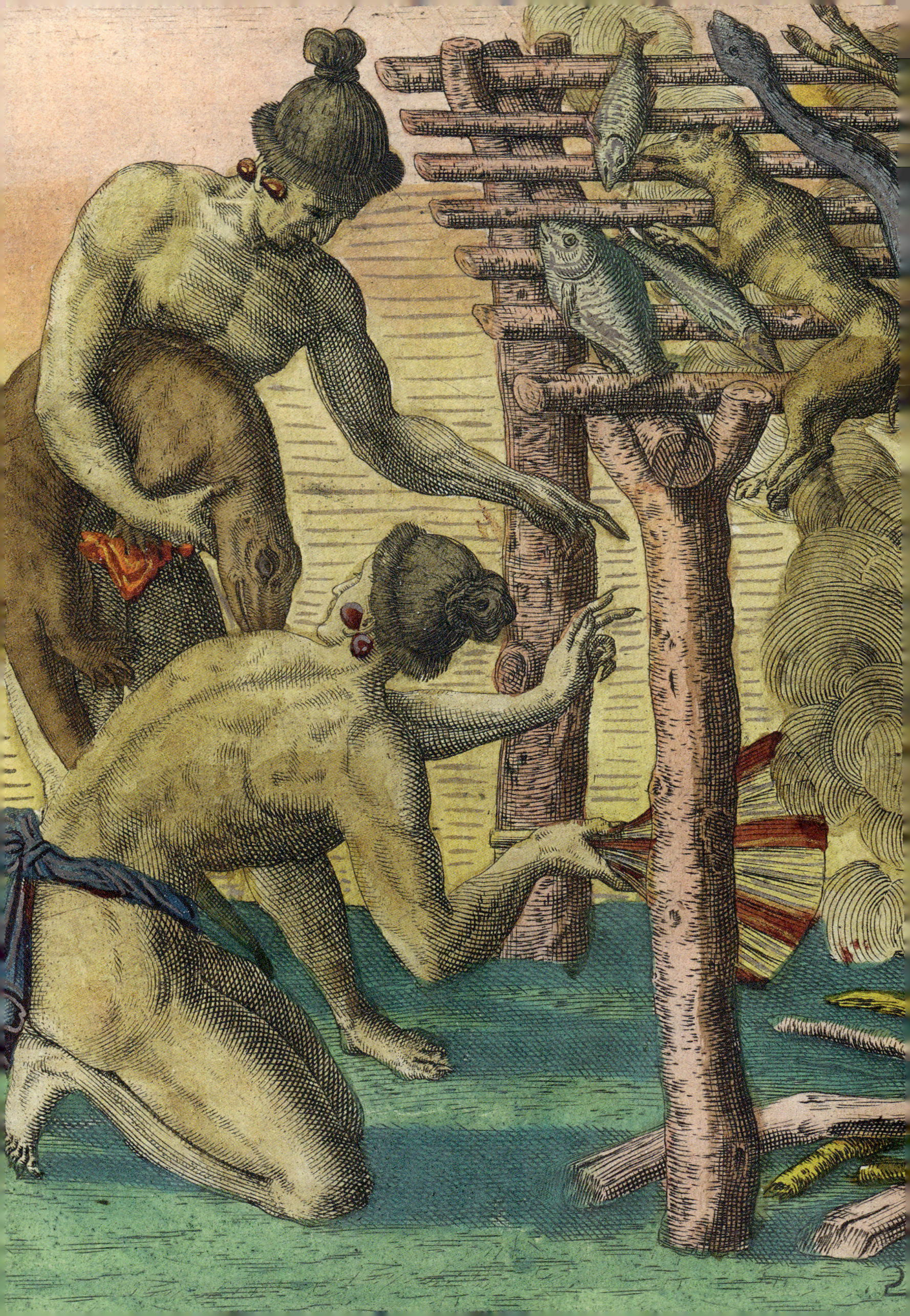

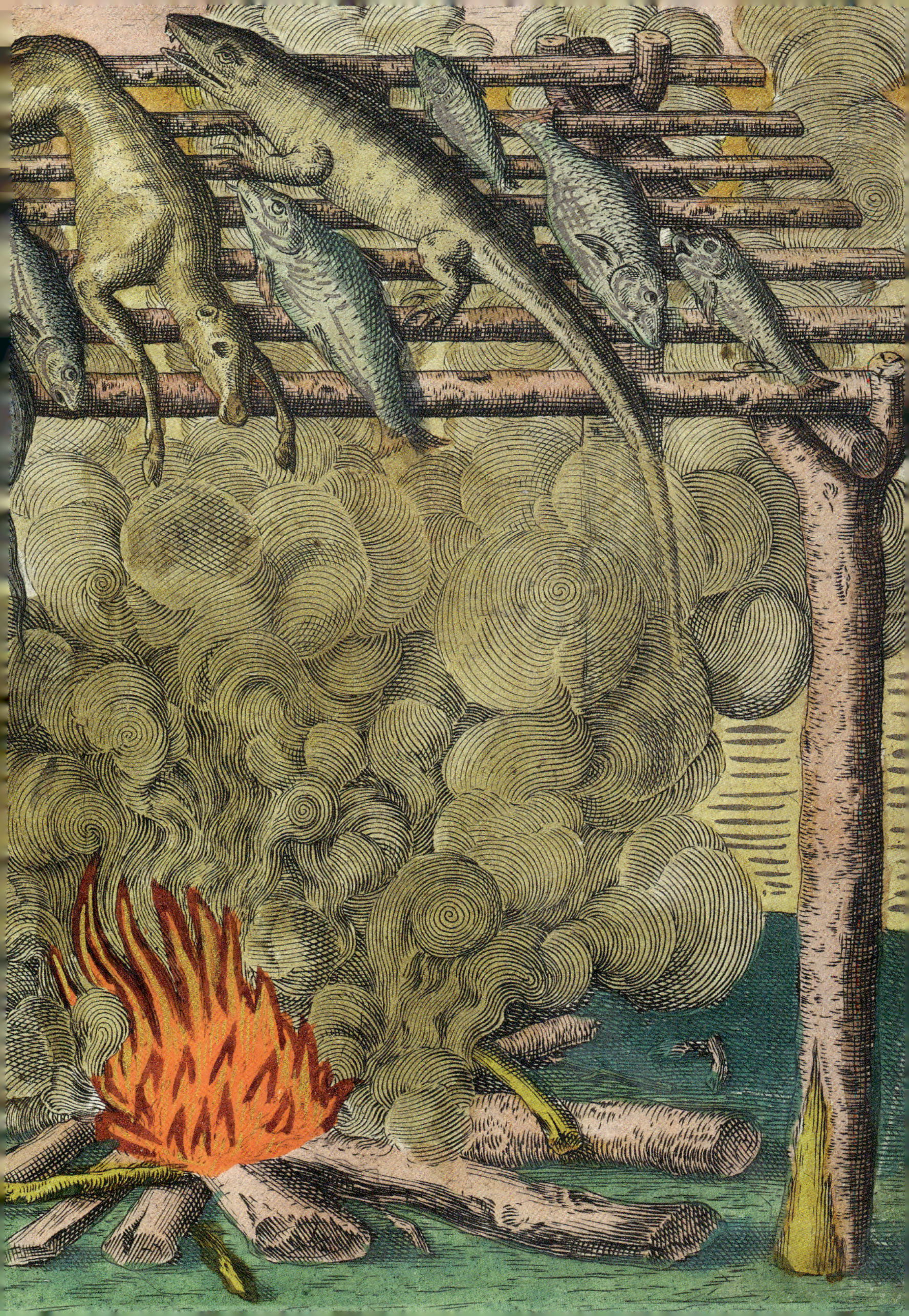

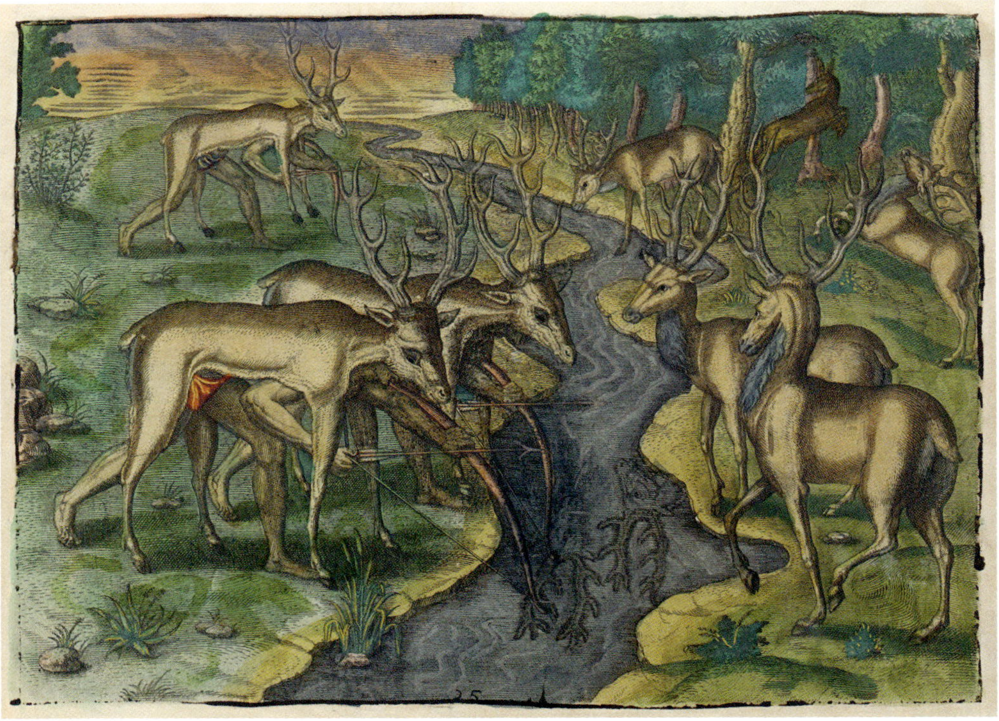

PLATE 25

Their manner of hunting

The Indians have a way of hunting deer that was completely new to us. They put on the skins of the largest which they have caught before, with the deer's head on top of their own in order to see through the eyes as through a mask. This way they can approach the deer without frightening them. They make use of the time when the animals come to drink at the river, and with their bows and arrows ready they easily shoot them, as there are also very many in this region. Usually, however, they protect their left arm with the bark of the branch of a tree to keep it from being grazed by the bow-string – a practice which they have learned through experience. They know how to prepare deer-skins, not with iron tools but with shells in a surprisingly successful way. I do not believe anyone in Europe could do this as well.

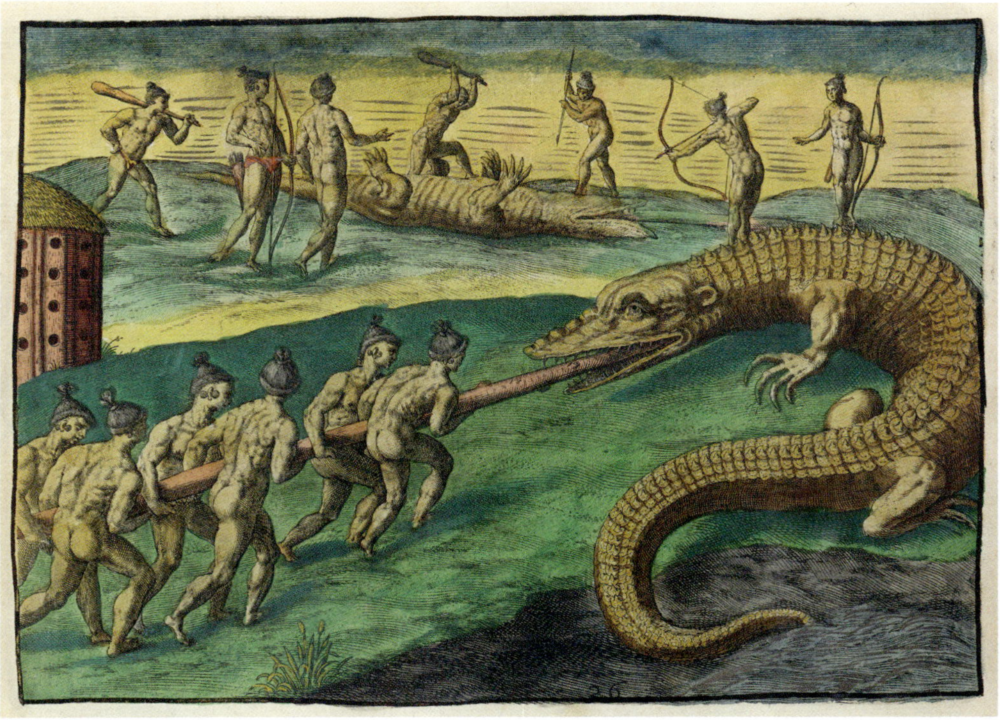

PLATE 26

Killing alligators

Near a river they build a little hut full of cracks, and here they position a watchman who can see the alligators coming from a distance. When the alligators are hungry, they leave the rivers and crawl on to the islands for prey. If they find nothing, they make an awful noise that can be heard from half a mile away. Then the watchman calls the rest of the men. They take the trunk of a tree, 10 to 12 feet long, and go out to find the beast who is crawling with his mouth wide open, ready to catch one of the men if he can. Very quickly, they push the pole, with the small end first, into the open mouth of the alligator as far as they can. The roughness of the tree ensures it does not come out again so easily. They twist the alligator on his back, and with clubs and arrows pierce his belly which is very soft. His back, especially if it is a mature alligator, is impenetrable, and full of hard scales. This is their way of hunting alligators. Still they need to remain watchful of them day and night, as we do against our most dangerous enemy.

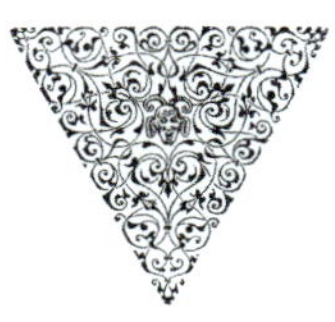

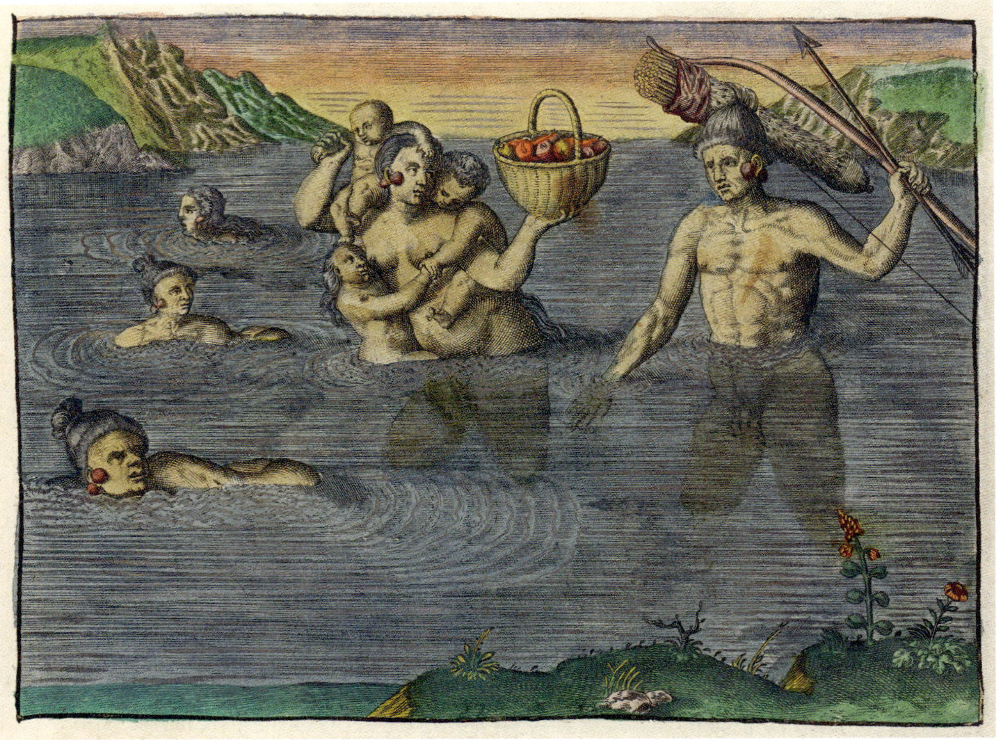

PLATE 27

Floridians crossing over to an island to take their pleasure

The country abounds in delightful islands, the rivers are shallow, and the water, which does not come higher than a man's chest, is clear and pure. When the Floridians want to enjoy a day out with their families on one of the islands, they cross the river by swimming, at which they are very skilful, or if they have young children, by wading. The mother can carry three children all by herself, the smallest on one shoulder, the others holding on to her, or under her arms. In her other hand, meanwhile, she holds a basket full of fruit or other provisions. When the enemy might be around, the men bring bows and arrows, and to keep them dry they attach them to their hair, and hold up one bow already strung and an arrow for immediate defence.

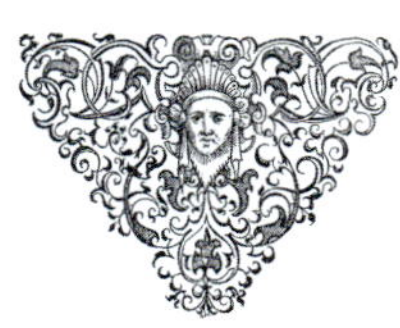

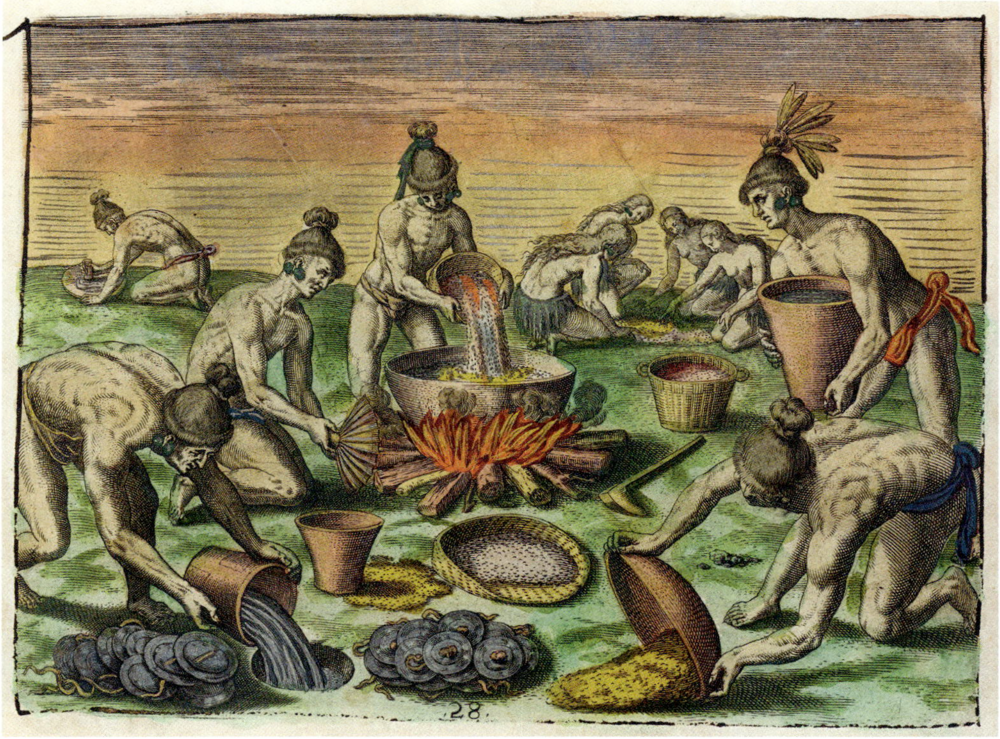

PLATE 28

Preparations for a feast

When the season of celebrations arrives, they employ cooks who are chosen for this purpose. First they take a large round vessel which they make and burn in order to boil water in, just as well as our kettles, and place it over a fire. One of them employs a fan very efficiently, holding it in his hands. The main cook puts all the ingredients into a great pot while others put water for washing food into a hole in the ground. Another brings water in a kind of bucket, another pounds on a stone aromatic herbs for seasoning, while the women are preparing the meat. Even though they have exuberant feasts, they are moderate in eating, and consequently they reach a great age. One of their lower chiefs told me that he was 300 years old, and that his father, whom he pointed out to me, was 50 years older still. The latter, I admit, looked like just skin and bones. All of this may well make Christians ashamed of their indulgence both in eating and drinking, which shortens their lives. They deserve to be brought under the tutorage of these savages and of brute beasts, to teach them moderation.

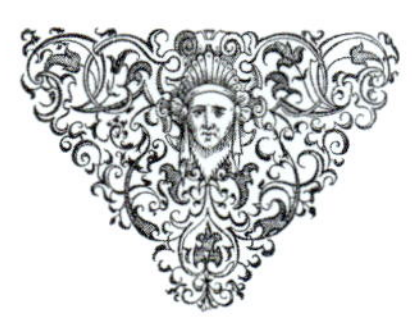

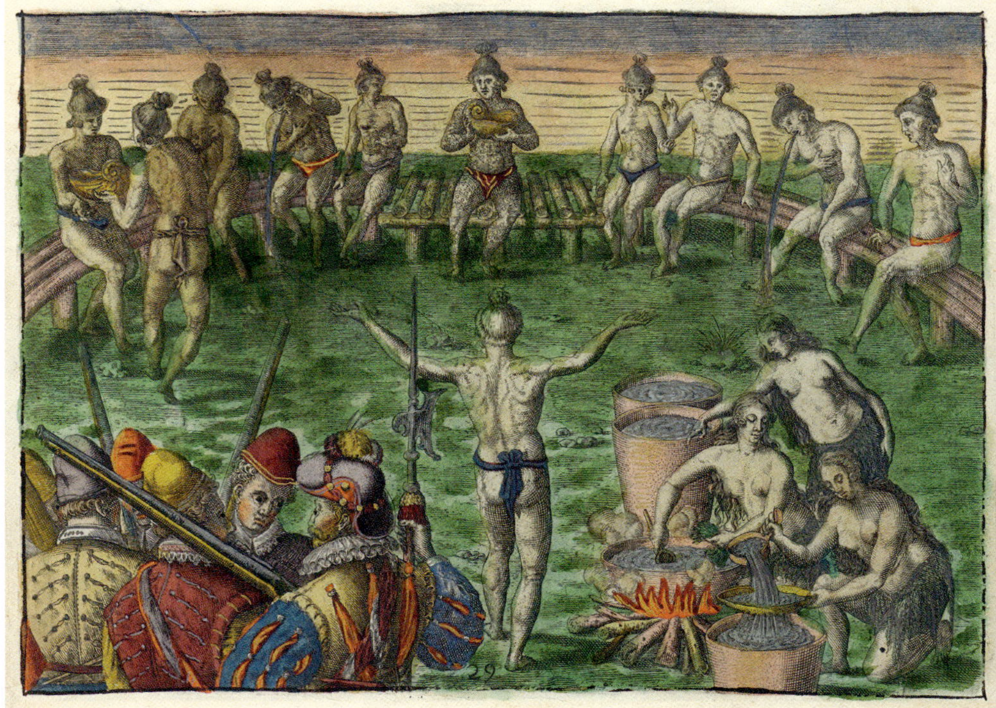

PLATE 29

Proceedings of the Floridians in deliberating on important affairs

On certain days of the year the king assembles with his nobles in a place specially prepared for this. There is a large bench here constructed in a half-circle with a prop of nine tree trunks in the centre, which is the throne of the king; the others come each in turn to salute him. Once everyone has saluted the king, they sit down on the bench. When important issues are being debated, the chief calls first upon the priests and upon the elders to give their opinion. The Native Americans, in fact, never make any decisions without first having listened to and discussed all the available opinions. Then the king orders the women to prepare a drink made from the leaves of a certain plant passed through a strainer. Then an Indian prays to the king and those who are going to partake of this hot beverage, which is passed round in a big shell, first to the king and afterwards, in strict order, to the others. This drink is so highly esteemed, that no one is allowed to drink it unless he has proved his skill in battle. It causes sweating almost immediately after it has been swallowed, and those who throw it up are never entrusted with any difficult task or military responsibility; for on campaigns the Native Americans often have to go three or four days without food, but having once managed to drink this liquor, it is possible to go 24 hours afterwards without food or drink. When going on an expedition, the hermaphrodites carry nothing but this drink, contained in gourds. This is because casina nourishes and fortifies the body without causing drunkenness.

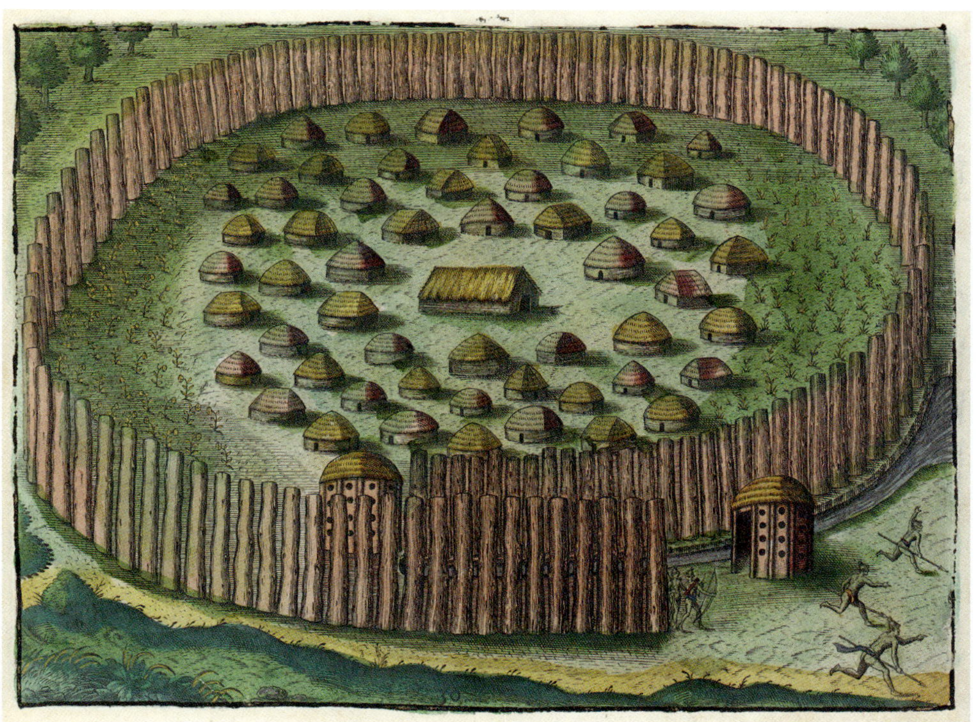

PLATE 30

Constructions of fortified towns among the Floridians

This is how the Indians construct their towns: they choose a place near a rapid stream and level it as much as possible. Next they make a circular ditch and fix in the ground thick round poles the height of two men. At the town's entrance they make the opening of the circle narrower, in the form of a spiral so that this entrance does not allow access to more than two men at once. The course of the stream is diverted to this point. At the beginning and end of this passage a circular building is erected, full of holes which are constructed very nicely. In each, watchmen who are expert at smelling the enemy from afar are stationed. As soon as they detect the enemy, they rush out, shrieking, to find him. The inhabitants of the town then run out to defend their fortress, armed with bows and arrows and clubs. The king's house is in the middle, and has been a little sunk into the ground to avoid the sun's heat. All around it are the houses of the nobility, lightly built and roofed with palm branches. They make new houses with the same materials, if, on their return from their winter lodgings, they find they have been burnt down by the enemy.

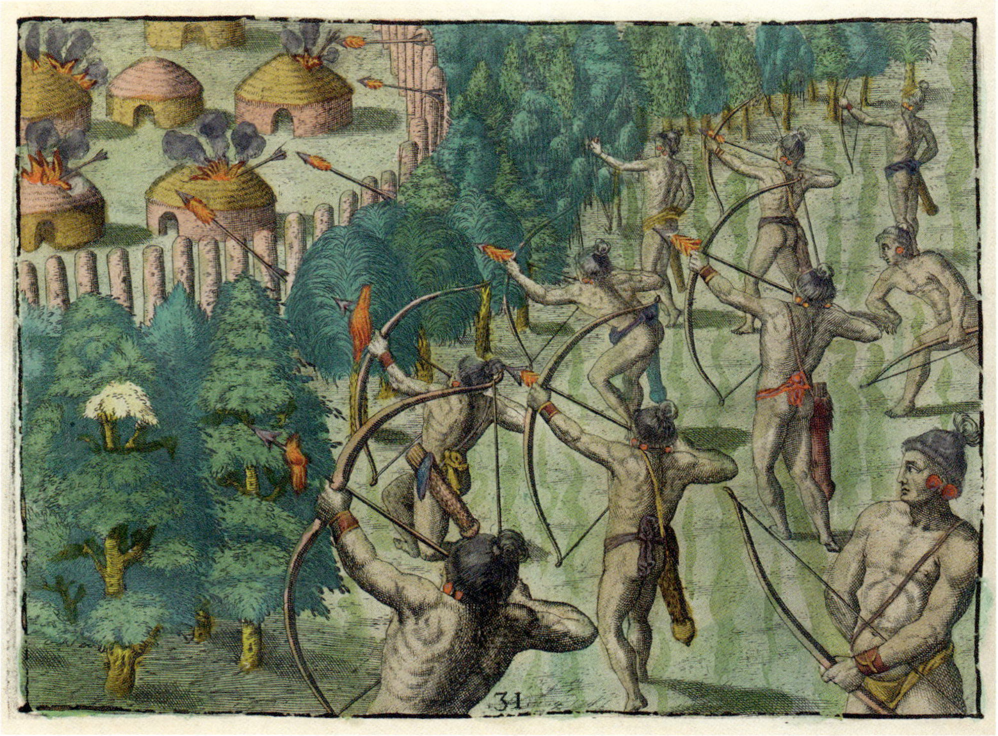

PLATE 31

How they set fire to an enemy town

The enemy, eager for revenge, will occasionally approach them at night, very silently, to find out if the watchman is asleep. If this is the case, they approach the back of the town, set fire to some dry moss from trees which they prepare for this purpose, and attach it to the tip of their arrows. Then they fire these into the town so as to set fire to the roofs of the houses which are made of palm-tree branches which are very dry because of the summer heat. As soon as they notice that the roofs are on fire, they run away as fast as they can before they are discovered, moving so rapidly that it is hard to catch them. Meanwhile the fire is giving the townsfolk enough to do. These are the strategies the Indians use in wartime. Still the damage is relatively small, little more than just the labour required to rebuild the houses.

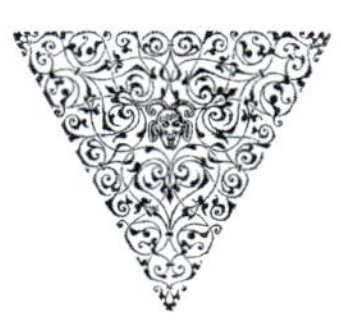

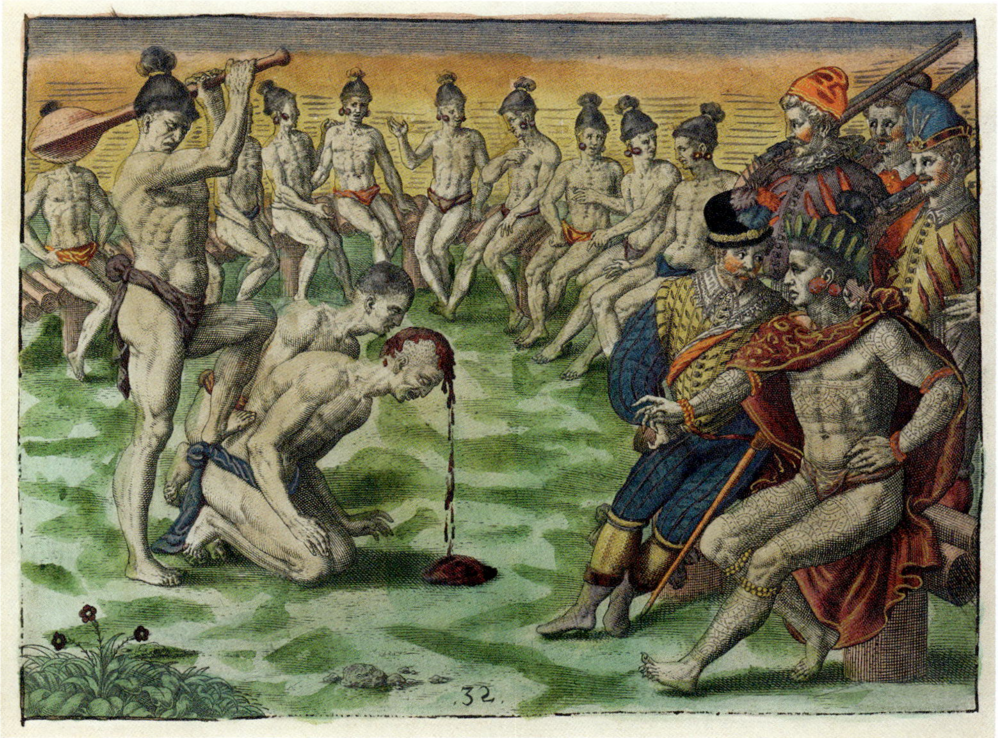

PLATE 32

How watchmen are punished for sleeping at their posts

When a town is burnt as a result of the negligence of the watchmen, they are punished in the following way: the chief is seated on his throne with the most senior Indians sitting on a semicircular bench and the executioner forces the guilty men to kneel down before them. Taking a club of ebony filed to an edge on both sides, he puts his left foot on their backs and strikes them such a blow with the club that he almost splits their skulls in two. This same penalty is meted out to any who are accused of what is considered to be a capital offence. We were present at two such executions.

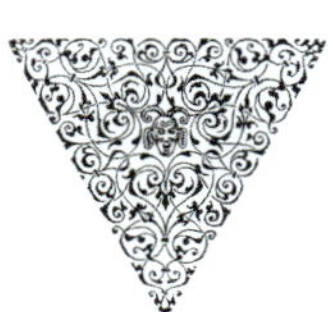

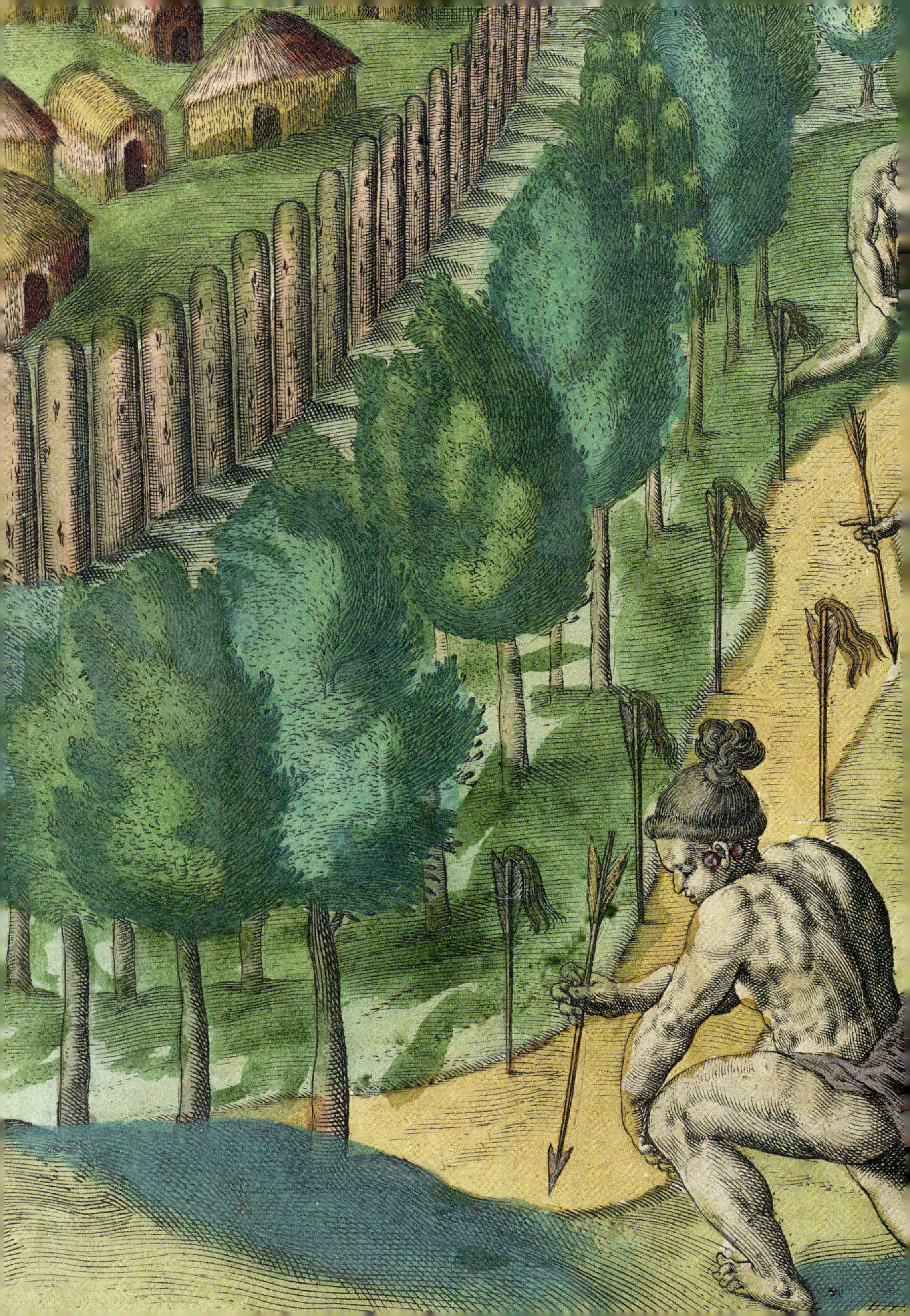

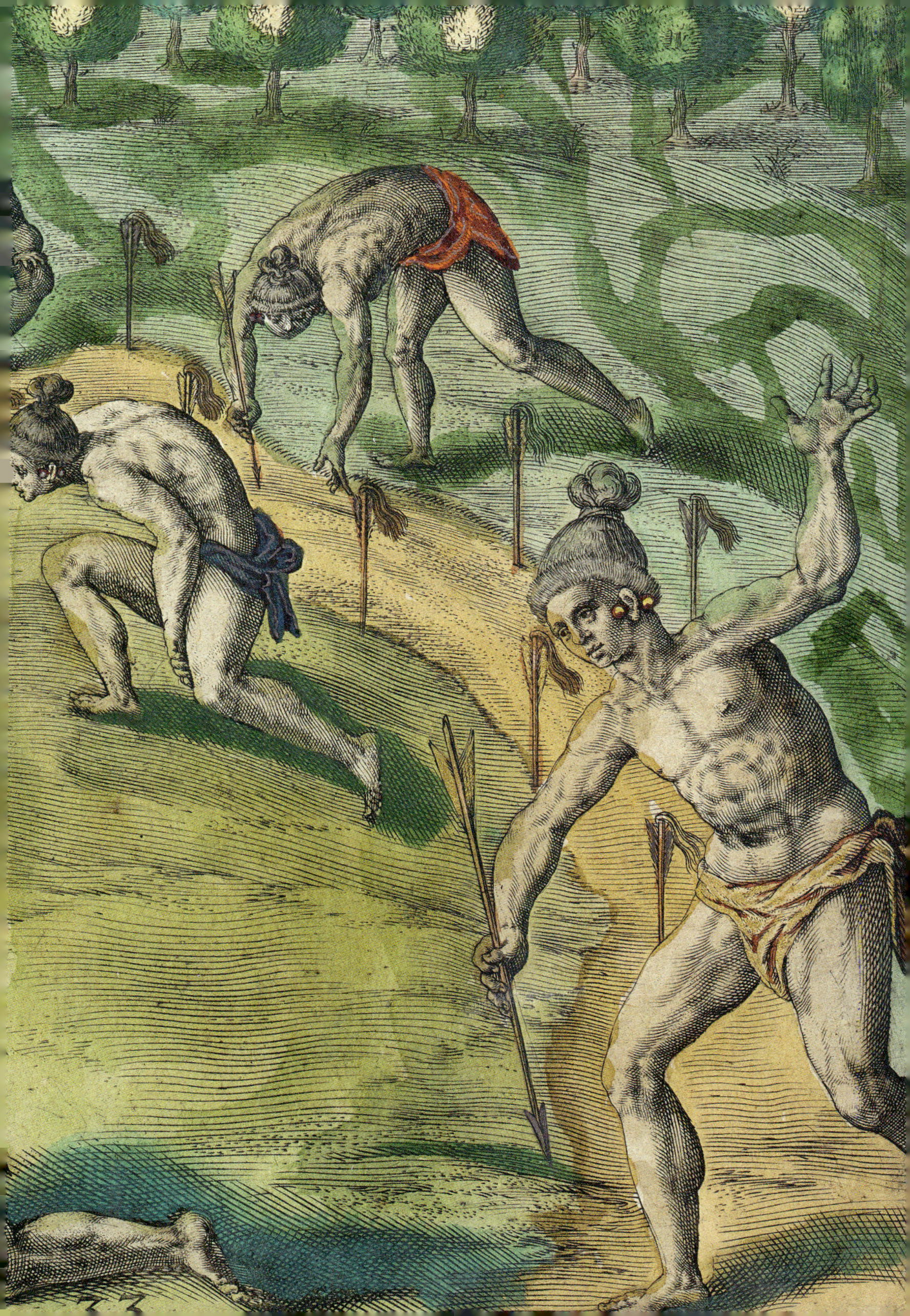

PLATE 33, PAGES 166/167

How they declare war

If a chief declares war against his enemy he does not send a messenger, but orders some arrows, having locks of hair fastened at the notches, to be stuck up along public paths. This we witnessed after we captured Outina, and led him around the towns under his authority to furnish us with provisions.

PLATE 34

Firstborn children sacrificed to the chief in solemn ceremonies

Their custom is to sacrifice their firstborn sons to the chief. When the day for sacrifice is announced to the chief, he goes to a place that is built for this purpose and sits on a bench there. In the middle of the area is a wooden stump, about two feet high, where the mother sits on her heels with her face in her hands, bewailing the loss of her child. The oldest of her female relatives offers the boy to the chief. Then the women who accompany the mother form a circle, and dance for joy without joining hands. The woman who holds the child dances in the middle, singing praise to the chief. Then six Indians chosen for this purpose gather in a designated place in the area, among them the sacrificer who is decorated with great magnificence, holding a club. When the ceremonies are finished, he takes the child and kills it on the wooden stump in honour of the chief, for all to see. On one occasion this ritual sacrifice was performed in our presence.

PLATE 35, PAGES 170/171

Solemnities while consecrating the skin of a stag to the sun

Every year at the end of February, Outina's subjects would take the skin of the largest stag they could find, keeping the horns on it, and put it full of the best roots that grow there, and embellish it around the horns, neck and other parts of the body with the best fruits. They subsequently carry it to a very large low-lying space, with song and dance, where they put it on top of a very large tree, with the stag's head and breast towards the rising sun. Then they pray to the sun to grow them the same high-quality roots and fruits offered to him. The chief, with his sorcerer, stands closest to the tree and prays. The other people, further back, respond. Then the chief and all the others salute the sun, and leave the stag there until next year, when they repeat the ceremony.

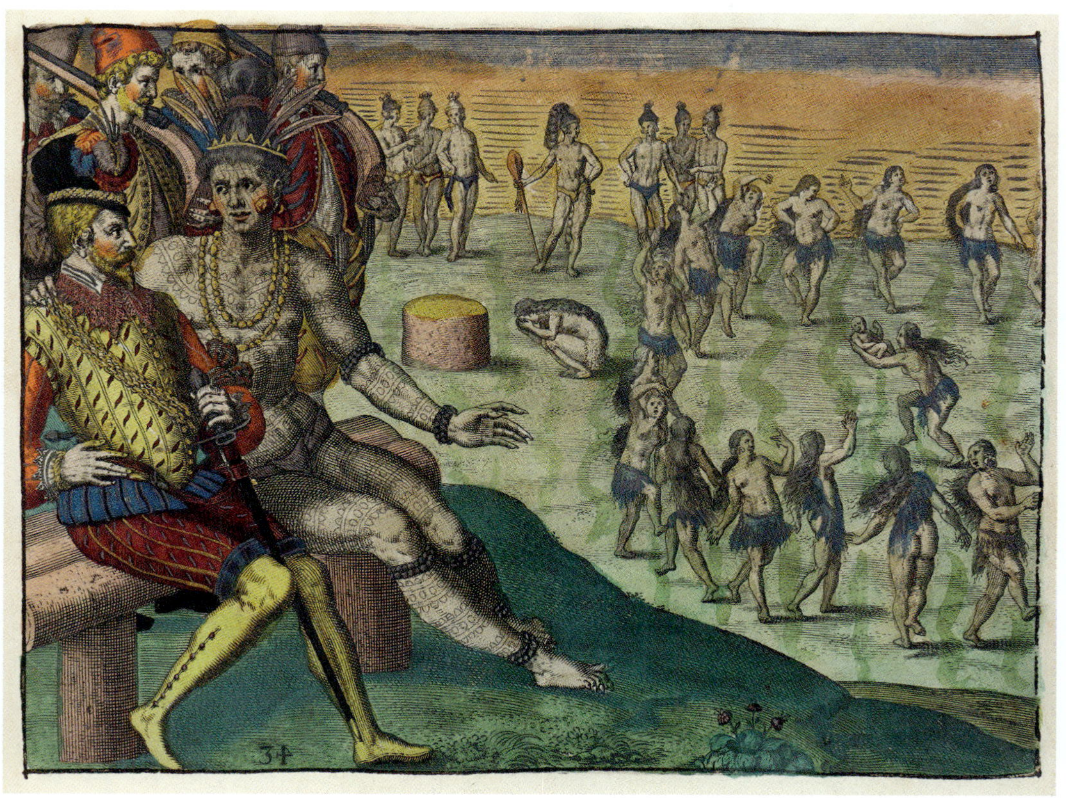
34

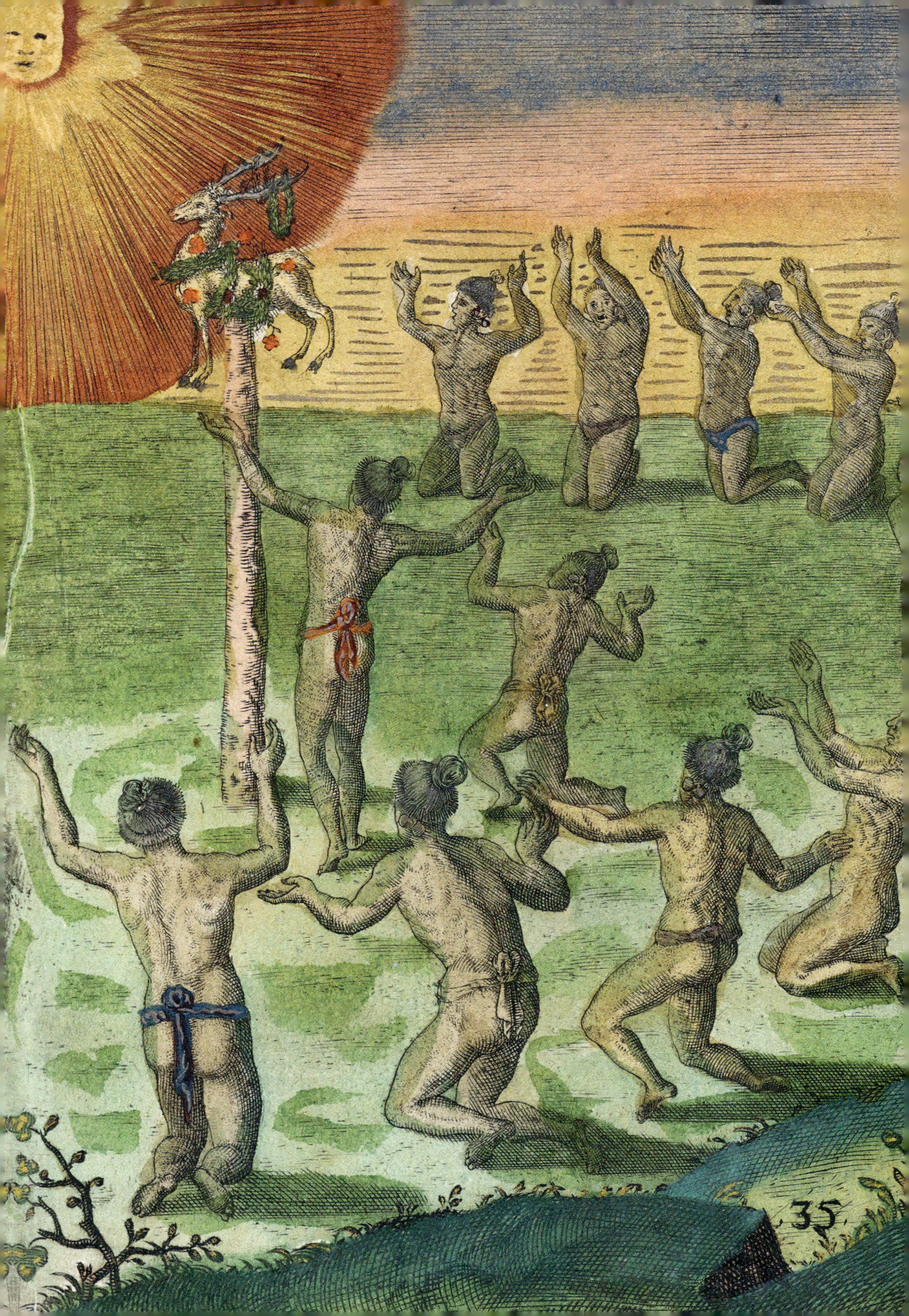
35

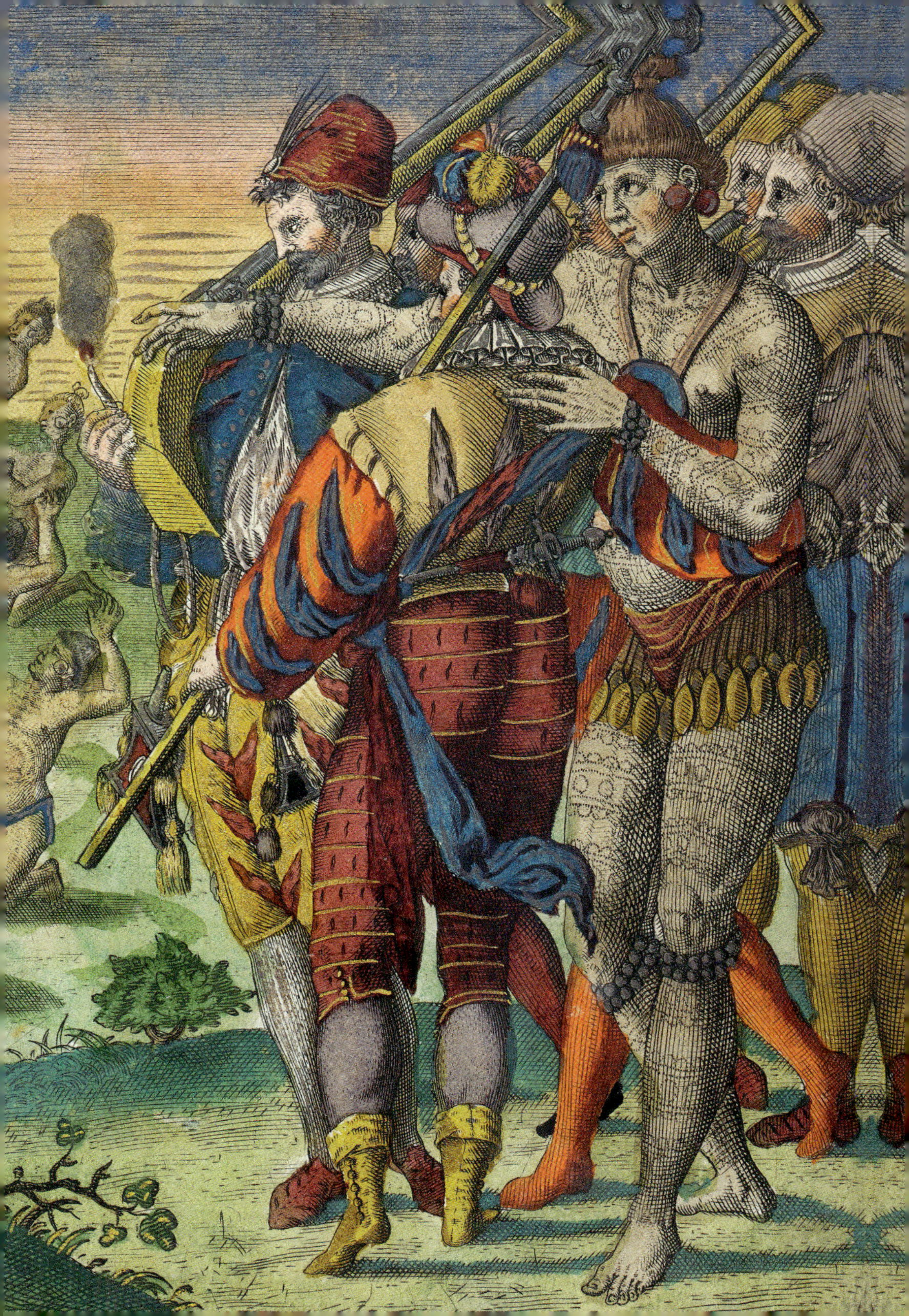

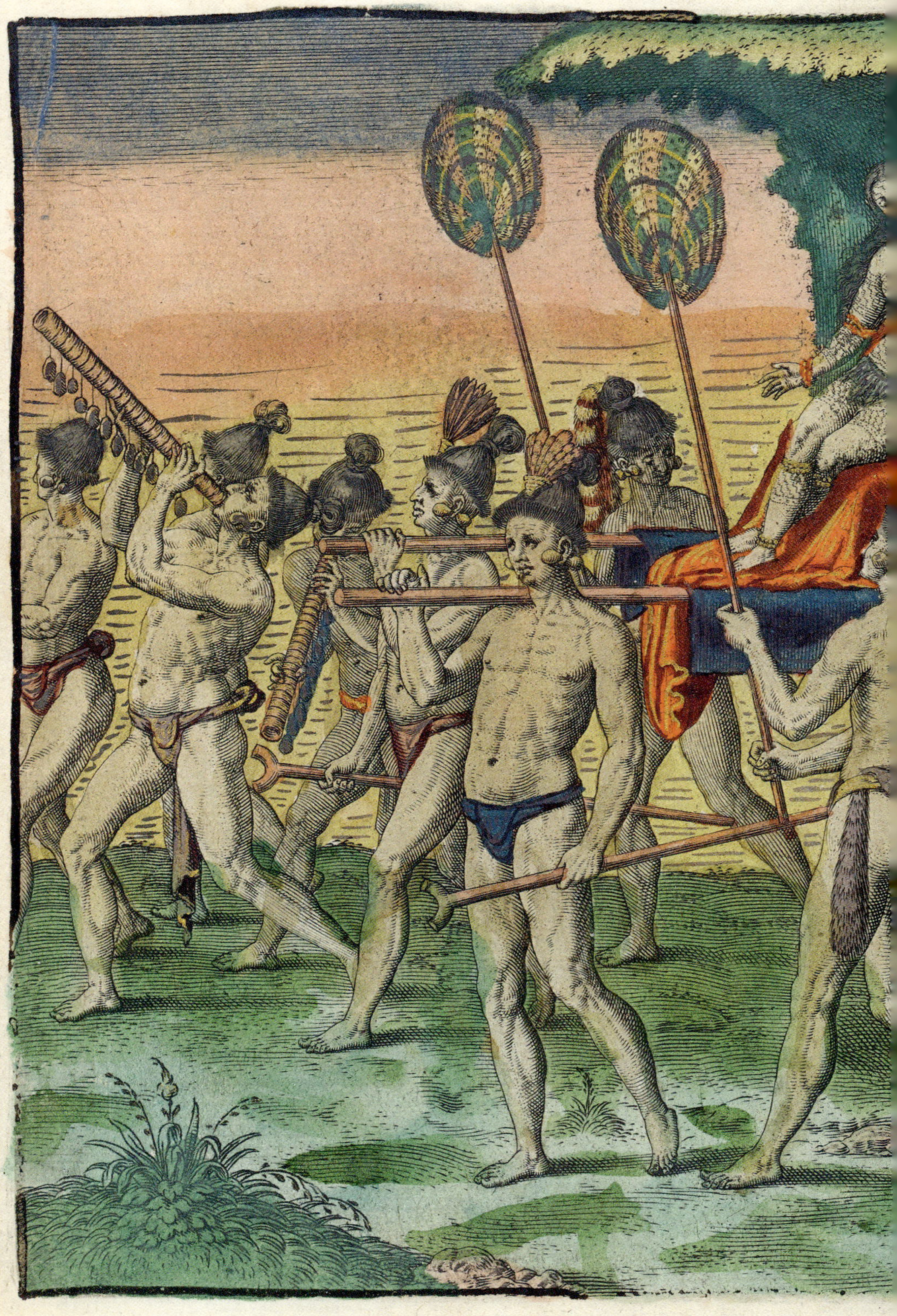

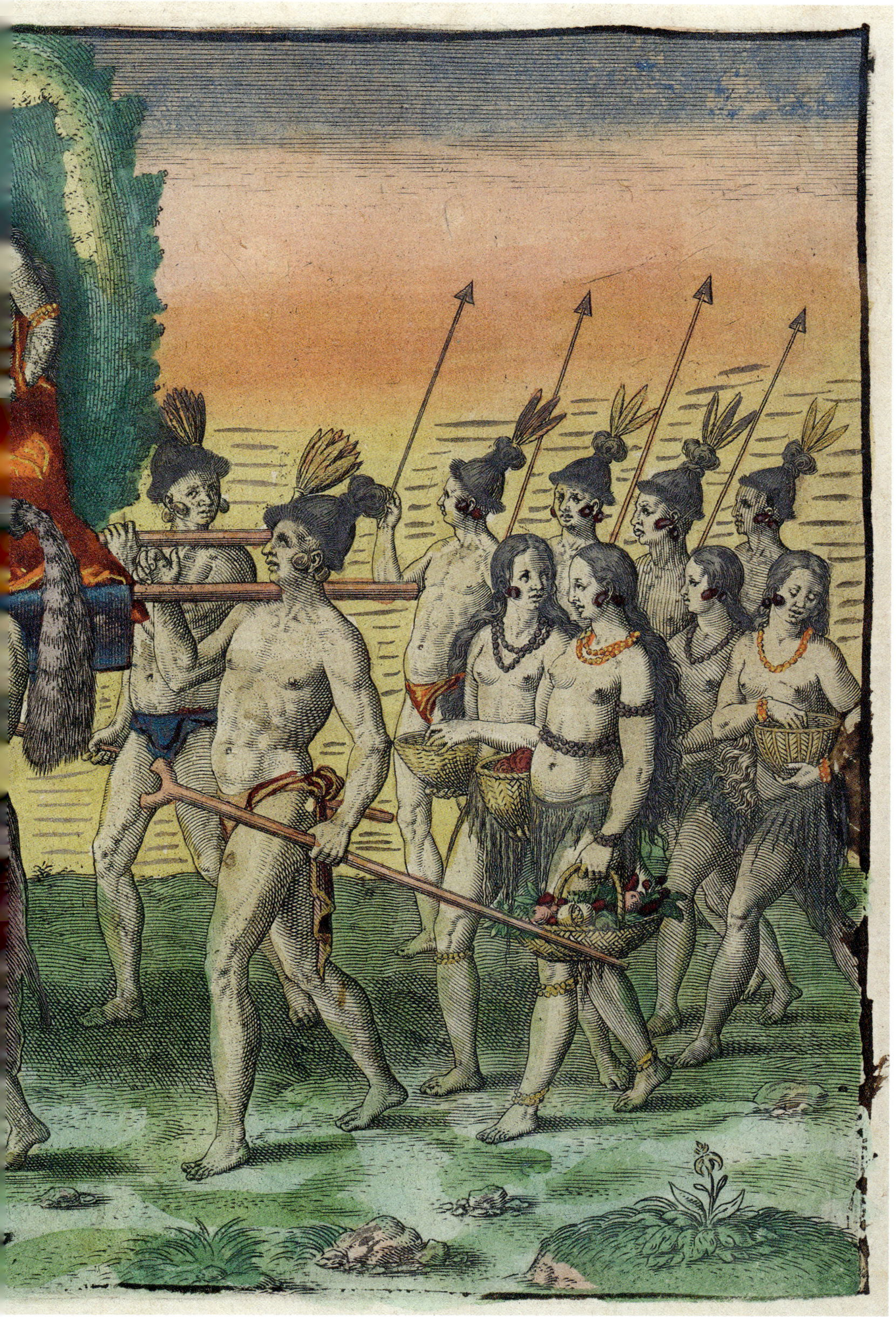

PLATE 37, PAGES 172/173

The display involved when a queen elect is brought to the king

When a king chooses a wife, he orders the tallest and most beautiful of the other chiefs' daughters to come to him. Then a seat is constructed on two poles covered with some special animal skin in such a way that it bends over forwards to provide shade. When the queen elect has been seated here, four men lift the poles and carry them on their shoulders, each carrying a forked branch to support the pole. Two more men walk alongside them, each carrying a kind of umbrella to protect the queen elect from the sun. Other men lead the way, blowing their trumpets made of wood, which are small at the tip and broader at the end. They are decorated with small oval balls of gold, silver and brass to generate a better sound. Then follow the most beautiful girls that can be found, elegantly decorated with necklaces and bracelets of pearls, each carrying a basket of delicious fruits, and belted below the waist and down to the thighs with the moss of certain trees to cover their private parts. Finally come the bodyguards.

PLATE 38

Solemnities as the king receives a queen

It is with great pomp and ceremony that the queen is led to the king in a place especially designed for that purpose. There a large platform made of logs has been built, with benches for the nobility on either side. Seated on the right, the king welcomes the queen who takes her place on his left, and he tells her why he has chosen her to be his wife. The queen, holding a fan in her hand, answers the king as graciously as her education has taught her. Next the young girls, now wearing a different costume, form a circle without touching each other. Their hair floats over their shoulders and down their backs, a wide belt encircles their hips and a kind of purse hides their intimate parts; pendants of gold and silver tinkle when they dance and sing the praises of the royal couple. When one of them moves her hand the others do so too. Men and women have the tips of their ears pierced and there insert little inflated fish bladders, as bright as pearls, painted red and which look like garnet. It is astonishing that such savage people have created such tasteful devices.

PLATE 36, PAGES 176/177

The youth at their exercises

Their youth are trained in running, and a prize is offered for running longest without stopping. They frequently practise with bow and arrows. They also play a particular ball game: in the middle of an open space, a tree of eight or nine feet high is erected, with a square made from woven twigs at the top. This has to be hit with the ball, and he who strikes it first gets a prize. They also like entertaining themselves with hunting and fishing.

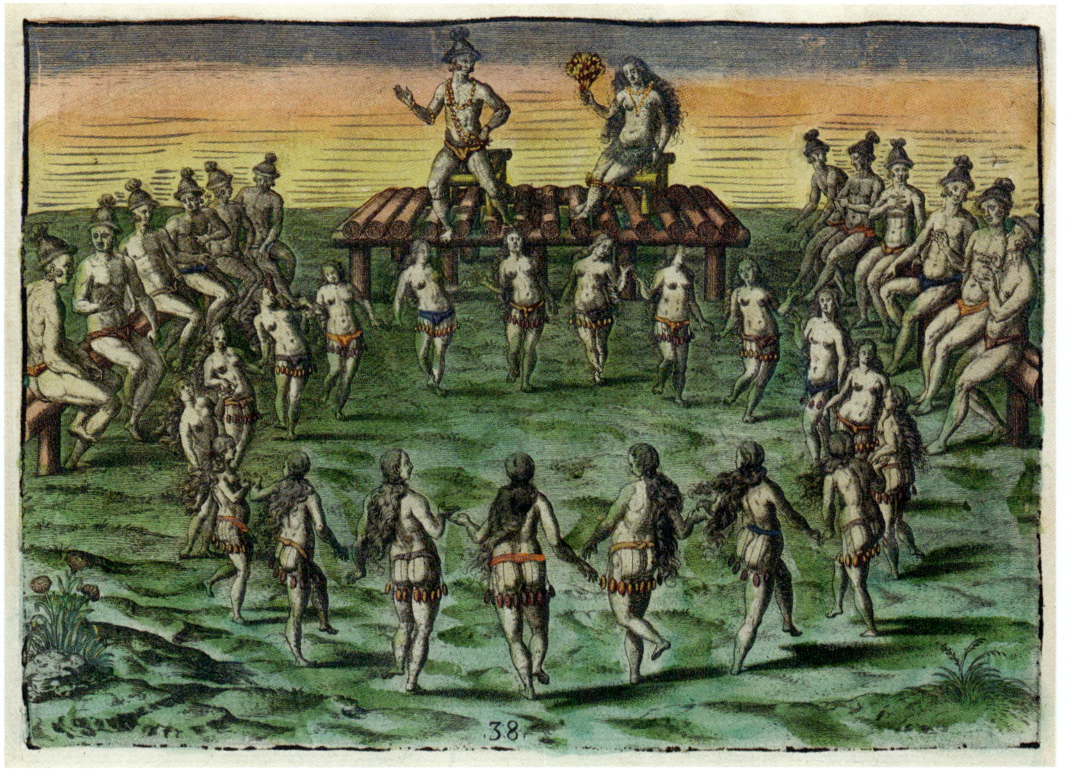
38

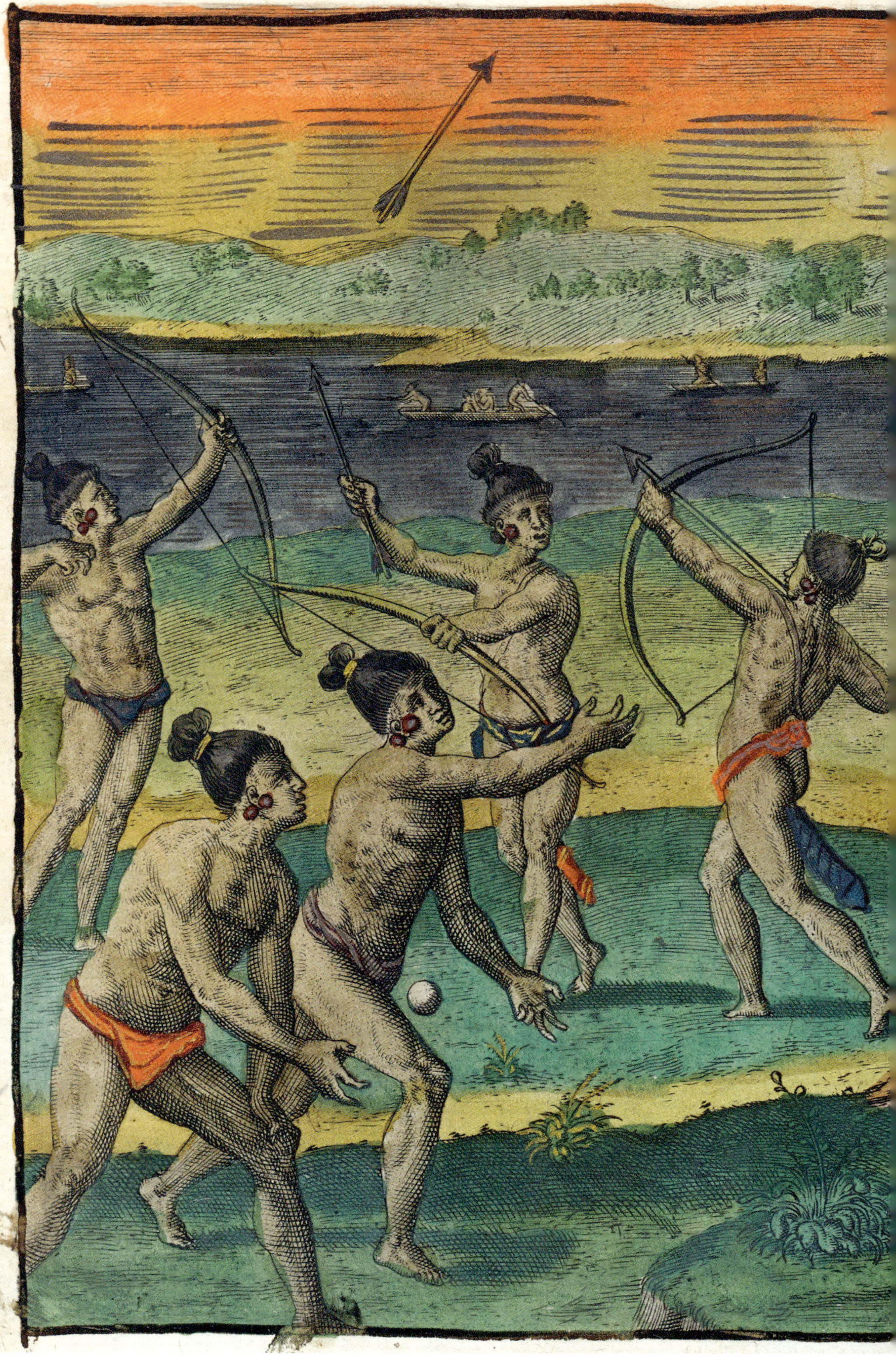

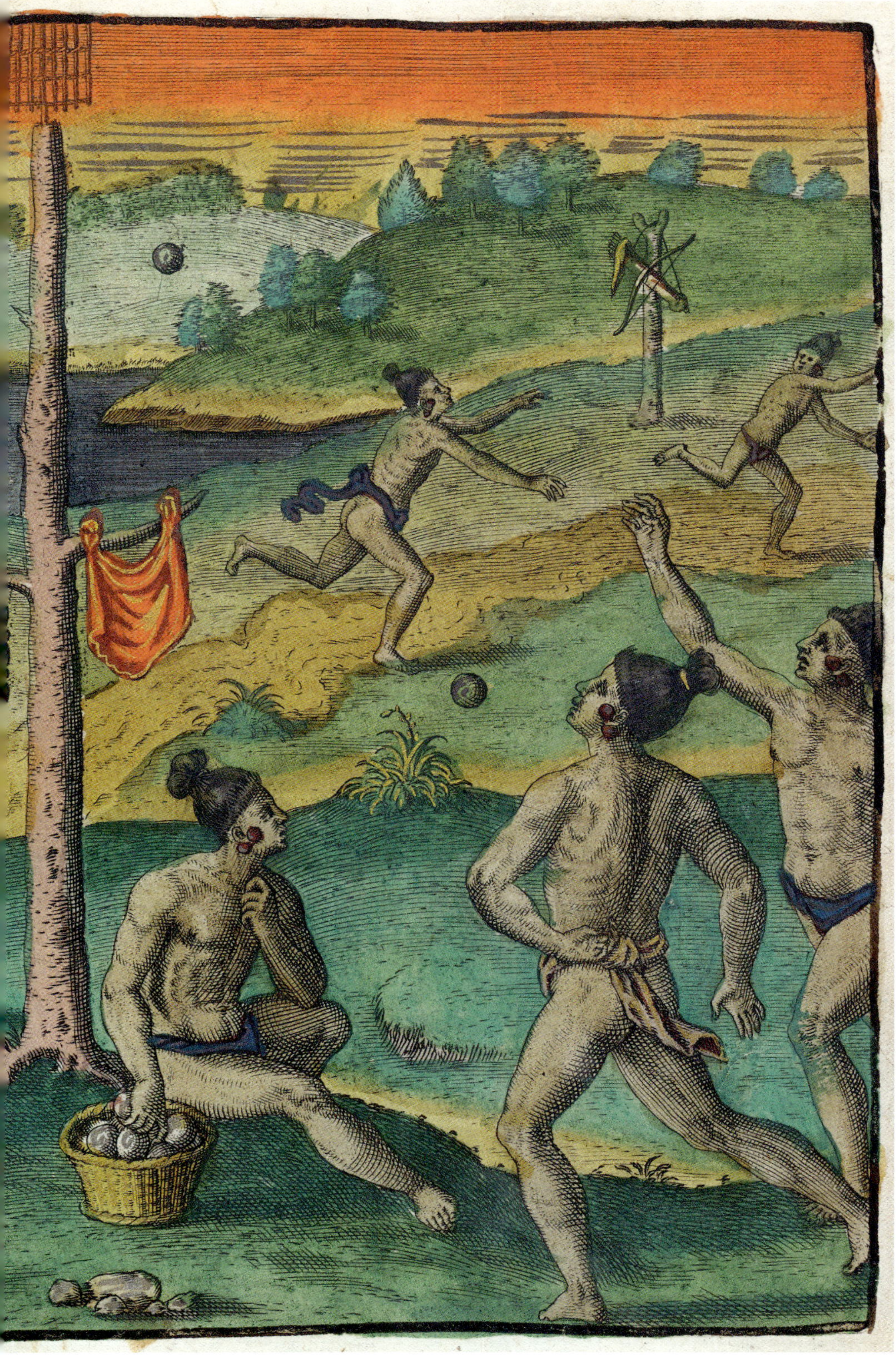

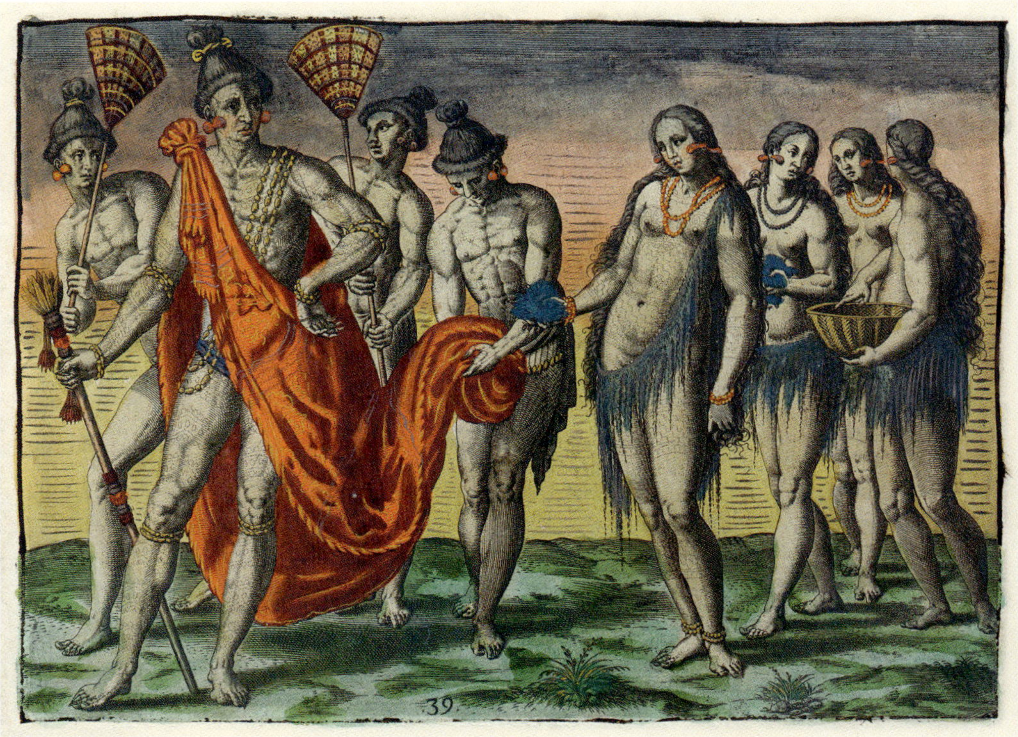

PLATE 39

The king and queen taking a walk for their amusement

Sometimes the king desires to walk in the woods in the evening accompanied only by his principal wife, wearing a deer's hide so elegantly prepared and colourfully painted that nothing more beautifully crafted can be seen anywhere. Two young men walk alongside him, carrying fans to keep him cool. A third, ornamented with little gold and silver balls hanging around his belt, walks behind him to hold up the deer's hide to keep it from dragging on the ground. The queen and her maids are adorned with belts around the shoulders and body, with slender chain-like attachments that are turquoise-coloured, and so beautiful in texture that they resemble silk. The trees on which the moss grows from which the belts are made are beautiful to see, because the moss sometimes hangs from the highest branches all the way to the ground. While hunting in the woods around Saturioua's residence with some of my men, I once saw him and the queen decorated in this manner.

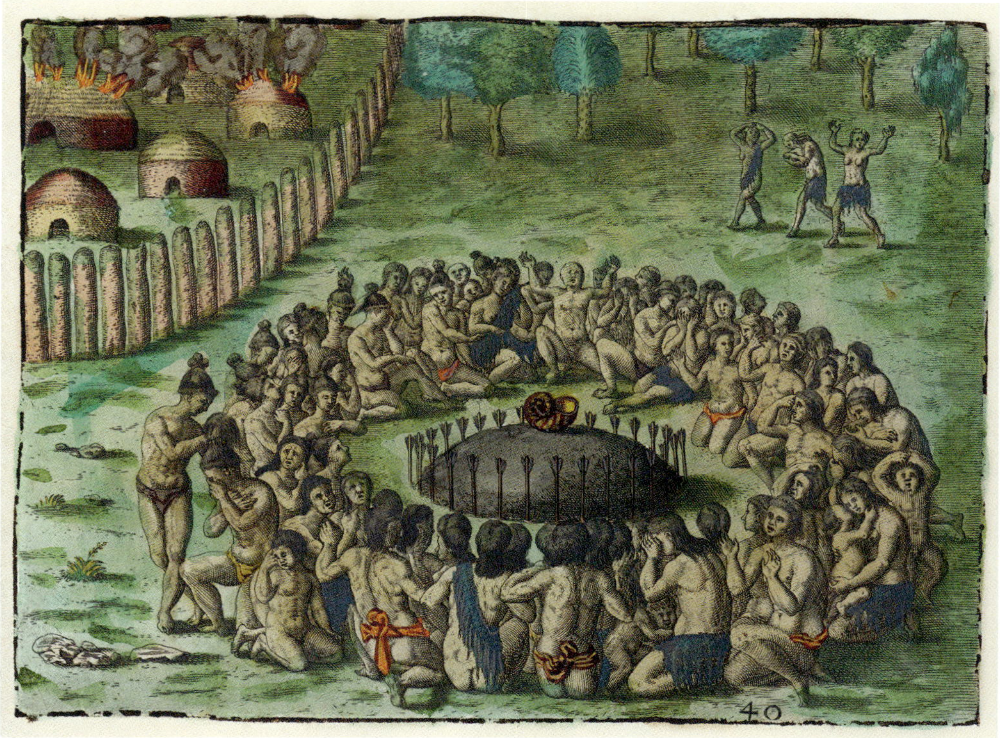

PLATE 40

Ceremonies at the death of a chief or priest

When a chief in this province dies, he is buried with great solemnity. His drinking vessel is placed on the grave, and many arrows are planted in the earth surrounding the mound. His subjects mourn for three days and nights without food or drink. All the other chiefs, his friends, mourn in the same manner. And both men and women, as a token of respect, cut off more than half of their hair. In addition, three designated women continue to mourn for him with great wailing three times a day, at dawn, noon and twilight, for six months. His entire household is gathered in his house, which is then set on fire. Similarly, when their priests die, they are buried in their own houses, which are then set on fire and burned with all their possessions.

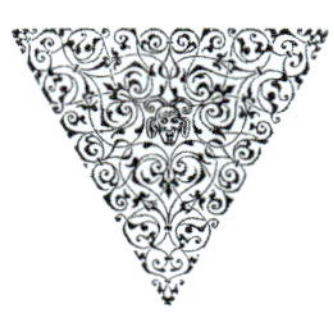

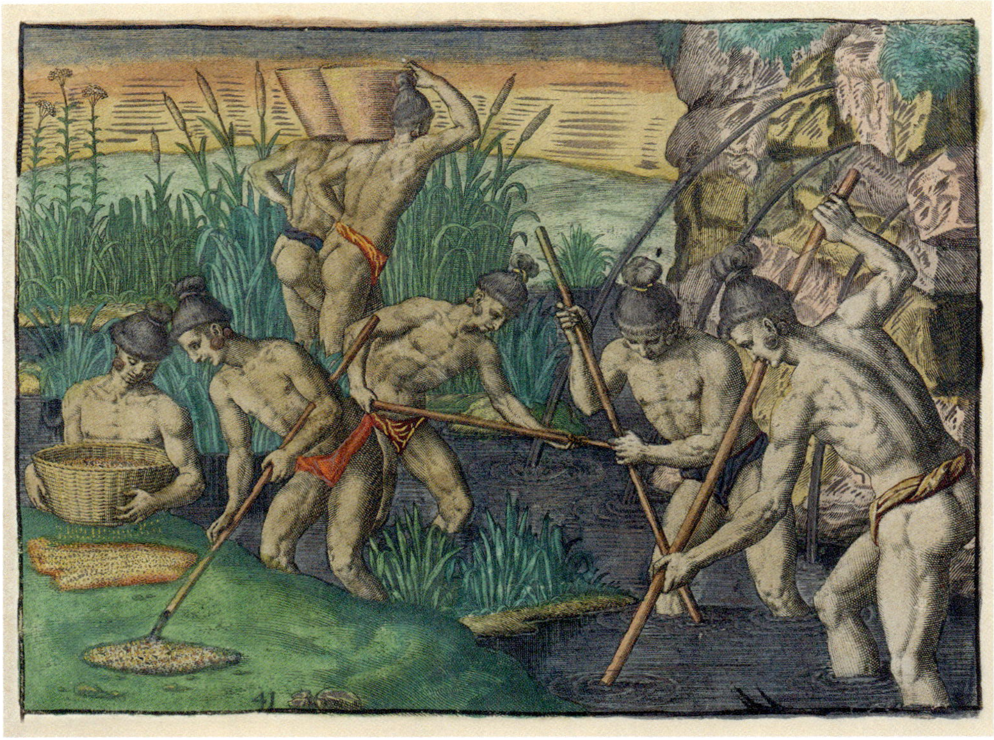

PLATE 41

Mode of collecting gold in streams running from the Appalachian Mountains

A little further from the place where our fort was built are great mountains the Indians call Appalachian in which three rivers arise, in the sands of which much gold, silver and copper are found. The natives dig ditches in these streams, into which the sand brought down by the current falls. Then they collect it and carry it away to a place by itself, and after some time collect again what is in the ditches. Then they bring it in large canoes to the May river which runs to the sea. The Spaniards have been able to use the wealth thus obtained for their own benefit.

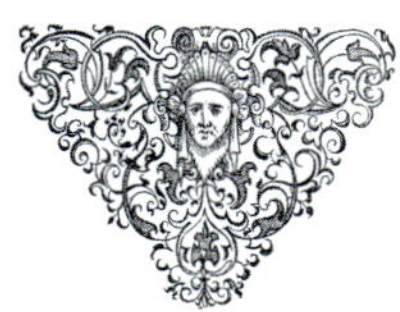

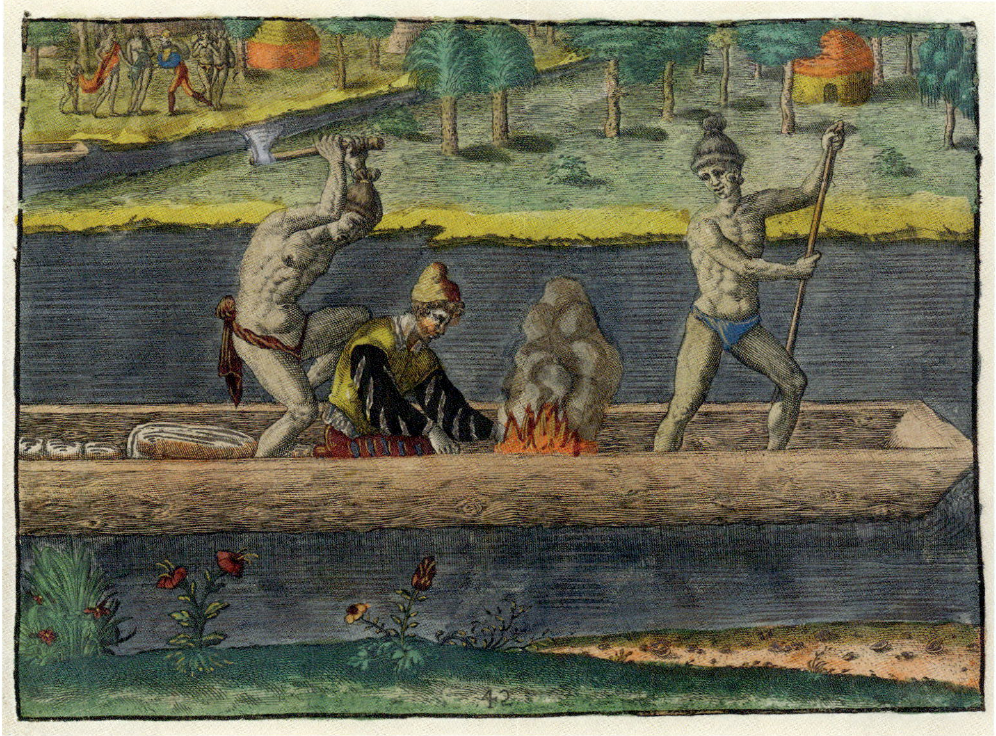

PLATE 42

Murder of Pierre Gambré, a Frenchman

I have spoken in my brief account of a certain Pierre Gambré, a Frenchman whom Laudonnière allowed to trade throughout the province. He was successful enough not only to become wealthy, but also to marry into the family of one of the chiefs of the country. Hoping to see his old friends at the fort, he finally got permission from his relative to go, but only if he returned within a certain number of months. A canoe and two Indians were given to him to assist him. The goods which he obtained were stowed in the boat, and his Indian companions killed him while he was bending down to make a fire. This was done partly out of revenge, as he had beaten one of them while the chief was away, and partly out of greed for the riches which Gambré had assembled in the boat. These the Indians took with them.

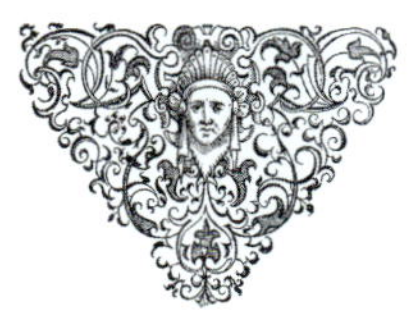

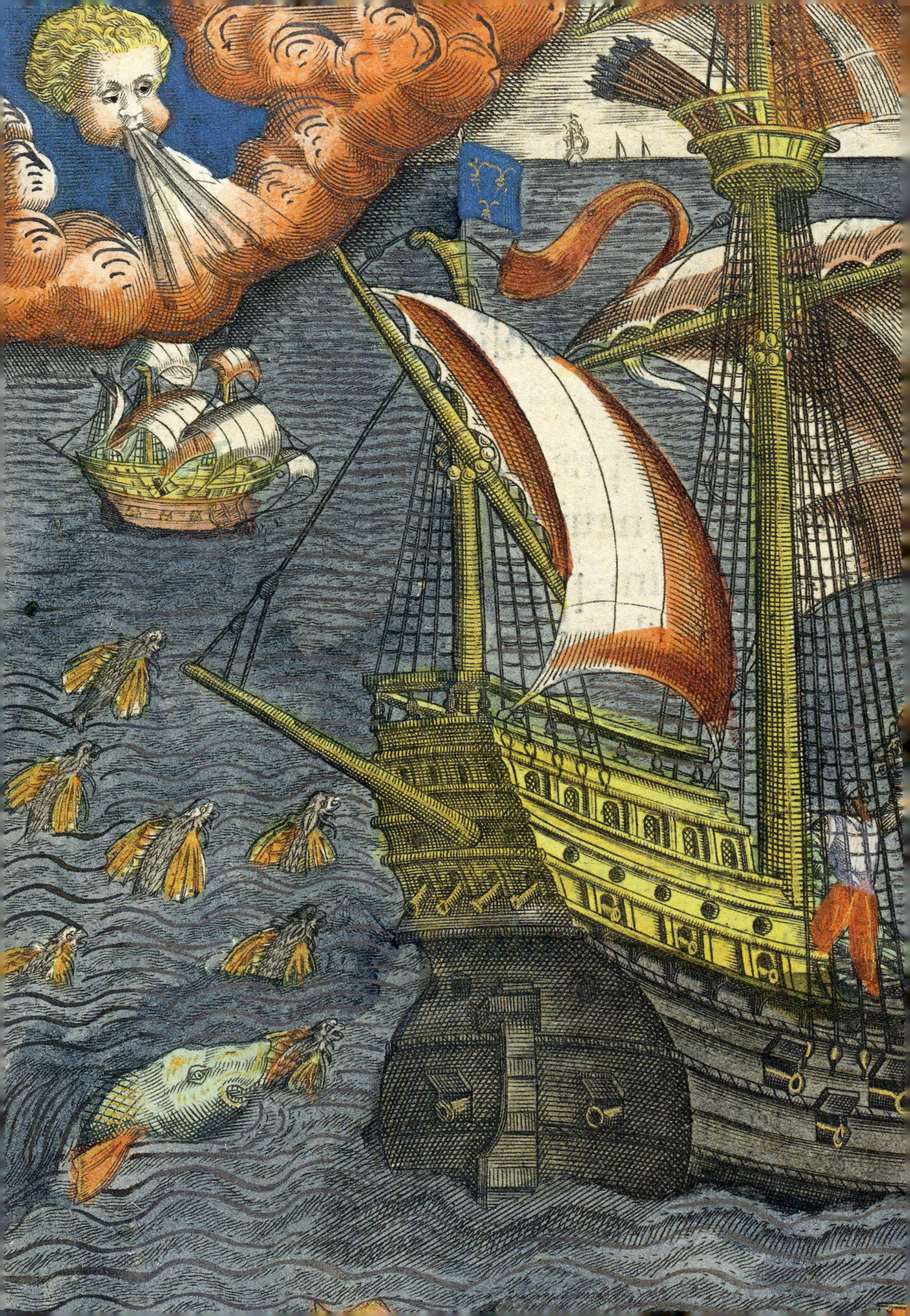

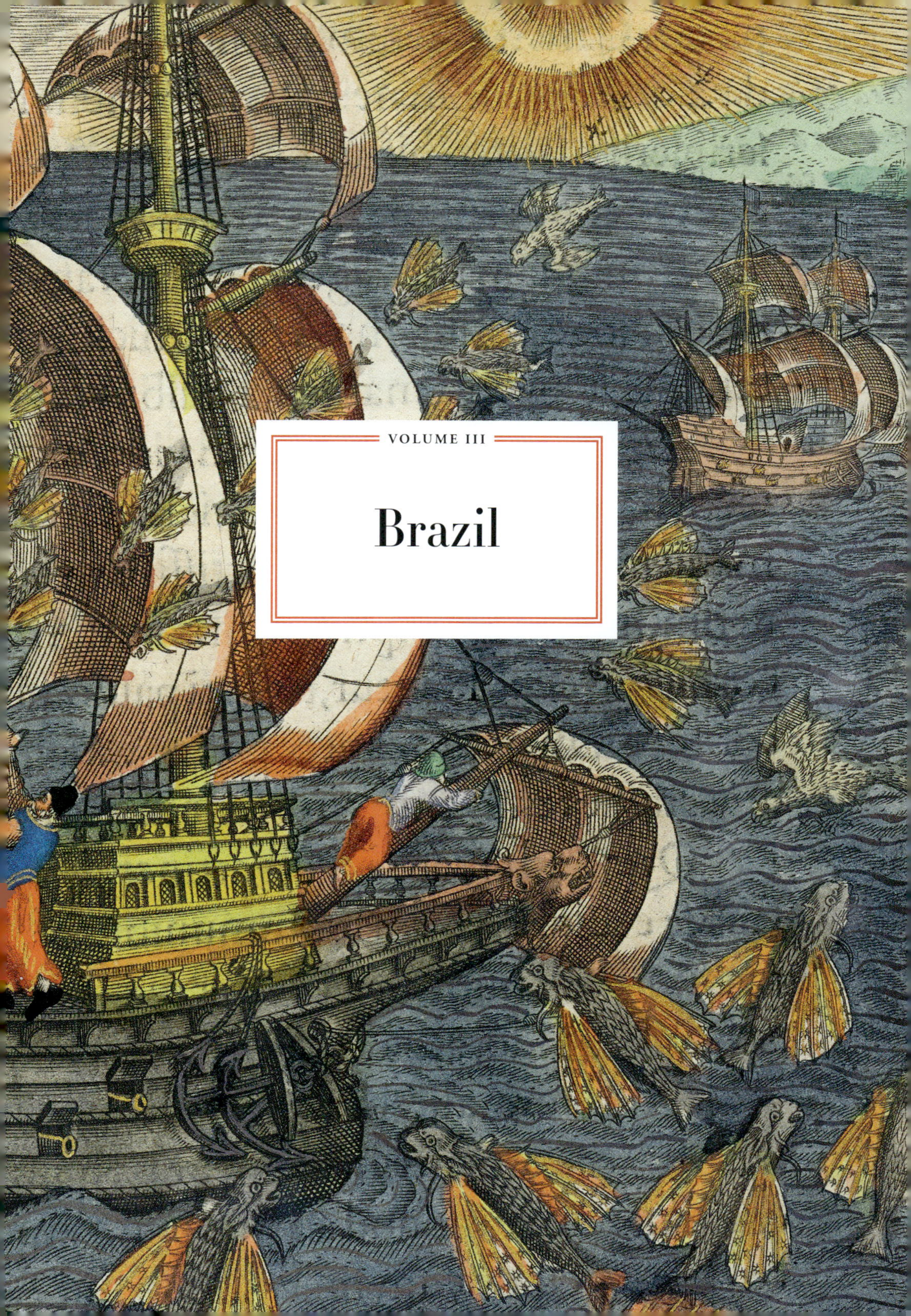
VOLUME III
Brazil

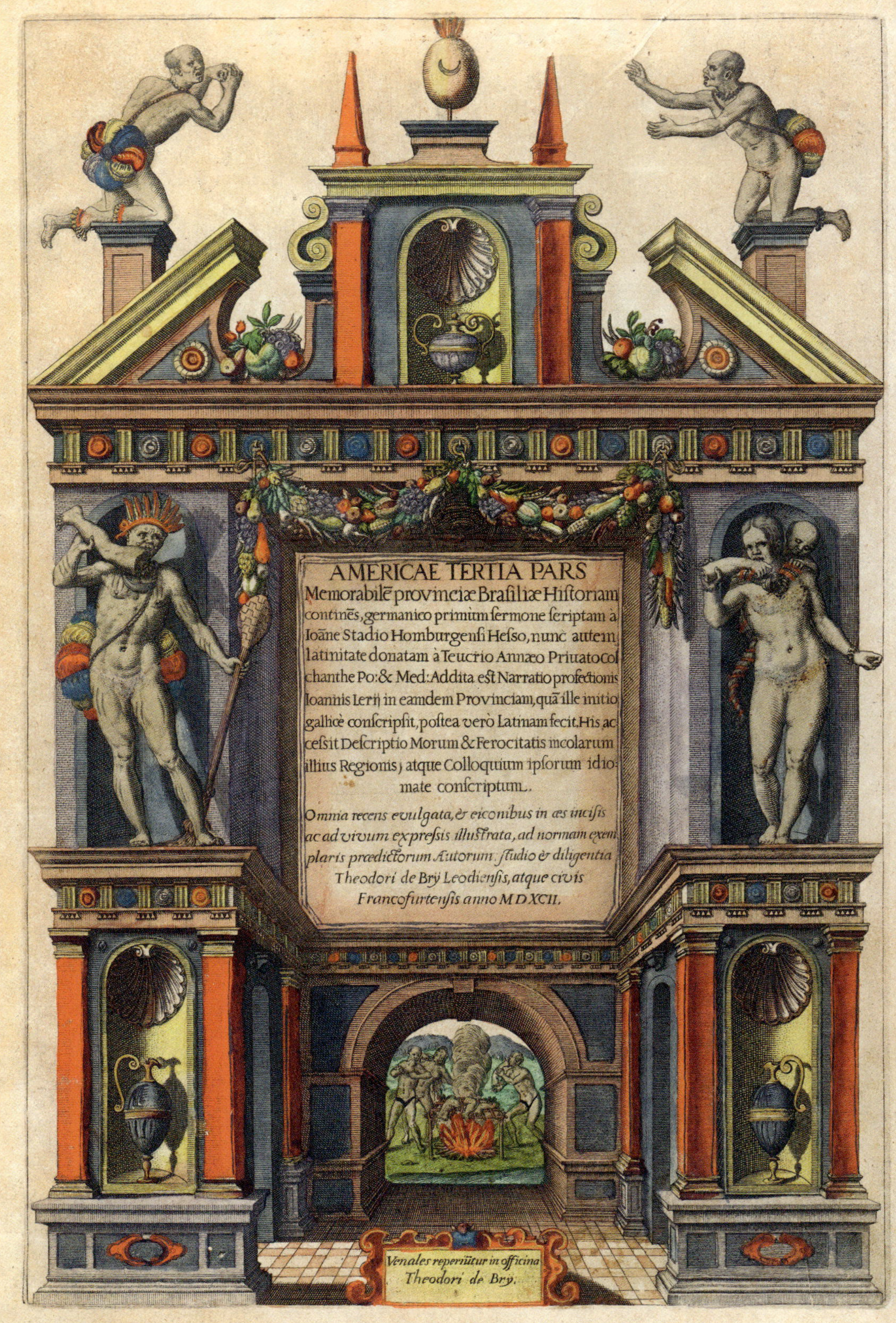
AMERICAE TERTIA PARS
Memorabilẽ provinciæ Brasiliæ Historiam
continẽs, germanico primùm sermone scriptam à
Ioãne Stadio Homburgensi Hesso, nunc autem
latinitate donatam à Teucrio Annæo Priuato Col
chanthe Po: & Med: Addita est Narratio profectionis
Ioannis Lerij in eamdem Provinciam, quã ille initio
gallicè conscripsit, postea verò Latinam fecit. His ac
cesit Descriptio Morum & Ferocitatis incolarum
illius Regionis, atque Colloquium ipsorum idio-
mate conscriptum.
Omnia recens evulgata, & eiconibus in æs incisis
ac ad vivum expressis illustrata, ad normam exem
plaris prædictorum Autorum: studio & diligentia
Theodori de Bry Leodiensis, atque civis
Francofurtensis anno MDXCII.
Venales reperiũtur in officina
Theodori de Bry.

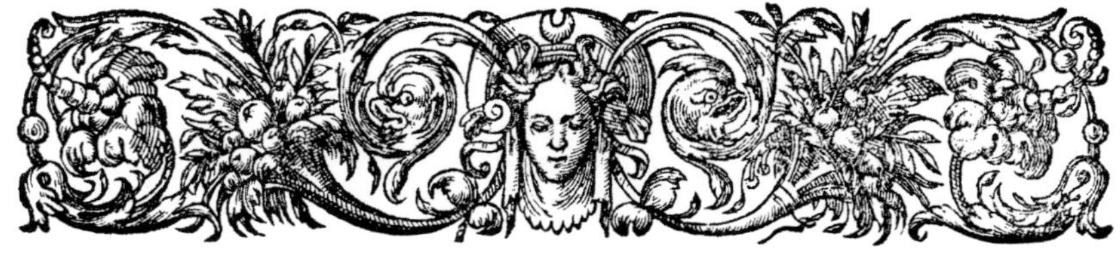

Volume III

Based on: Hans Staden, *Warhafftige Historia* (Marburg, 1557),
and Jean de Léry, *Histoire d'un voyage faict en la terre du Brésil* (La Rochelle, 1578),
both key works on Portuguese Brazil in the second half of the 16th century

Both the accounts which provided the contents for *America* III were already the equivalent of bestsellers in the early modern book world before the De Brys published their versions of them. Hans Staden, from Homberg in Hesse, set out on his voyage to Brazil in the service of the Portuguese monarchy to defend the colony against invasions from other European powers. But it was Staden's eyewitness account of his captivity with the cannibalistic tribes of the Tupinambá Indians in Brazil which explains his book's unrivalled popularity in Europe since it was first published in German in 1557. It was translated and published in various languages, and this in turn likely explains its appeal to Theodore de Bry. Unlike the travel accounts he obtained in England with the help of Richard Hakluyt, the selection of Staden's narrative, probably planned even before the making of volume I, is the first major editorial choice that must be ascribed to De Bry himself.

The second account in this volume, Jean de Léry's *Histoire d'un voyage faict en la terre du Brésil*, was an obvious companion to Staden's text. Just like Staden, De Léry went to Brazil in the latter part of the 1550s, and he too described at length his encounters with the Tupinambá. His expedition was part of a collective attempt to create a Huguenot refuge in the Americas on the eve of the religious wars in France, and was itself one of the main reasons why the Portuguese felt the need to strengthen their defences, and in turn the reason why Staden was sent to the South Atlantic in the first place. The French settlement lasted only five years (1555–1560), however, because the same religious turmoil which was to cause so much havoc in France had already created divisions in "Antarctic France". The settlement's designated leader, the nobleman Nicolas Durand de Villegagnon, turned out to be a Protestant only in name, and reverted to Catholicism in Brazil. The second party of Huguenots to arrive in La France Antarctique, which included De

Frontispiece of volume III

Pages 182/183
Detail of volume III, plate 27

Léry, thus encountered hostility from inside the colony; this led to a heated war of words, and the quick demise of the settlement, the remnants of which were easily wiped out by the Portuguese in 1560. De Léry's account appeared only in 1578, at the height of the French civil war, in order to emphasise the treacherous nature of French Catholics, and it was for this reason that it too was reprinted many times in cities across Protestant Europe, most notably in strongholds of the Reformed Church such as Geneva, and later Amsterdam.

Although the two accounts in volume III were in several important ways alike – they were printed, illustrated and already well-known among a European readership interested in the New World – they presented the De Bry workshop with two radically different propositions. Staden's account had obvious potential for its spectacular illustrations of cannibalistic practices, and De Bry's rendering of the climax of the man-eating process Staden had witnessed – with the victims being slaughtered for consumption, their limbs torn off and placed on a rack over the fire while their decapitated heads were prepared for the pot – became one of the most emblematic images not only of the De Bry collection, but also and more generally in the European imagination of the Americas in the colonial period. De Léry's account contained all the divisive matter that characterised polemic religious writing of the late 16th century, something that was certain to split the readership of the De Bry collection because of its very nature and which was almost impossible to neutralise as part of an editorial strategy that was intended to reach a cross-confessional audience. But at the same time the De Brys were adamant that they must include De Léry's treatise, representing as it did one of the most well-informed anthropological descriptions of Native Americans written in early modern Europe. It was later used by the respected French author Michel de Montaigne for his essay on cannibalism.

The De Brys eventually succeeded in making De Léry's account acceptable even for Catholic inquisitors in Spain and Portugal, but their path to success was a crooked one. As a result volume III is arguably the best example of the various intricacies of the translation process as employed in the De Bry workshop. De Léry's original account already had a strongly polemical tone, but the Geneva edition of 1586, which the De Brys used and which had been edited and translated into Latin by the staunch Calvinist Urbain Chauveton, was considered unacceptable by the Inquisition in Portugal, where accounts of Brazil came under close scrutiny. The De Brys heavily edited the account, leaving out some 22 pages altogether, while at the same time including transcriptions of two letters by the French Catholic friar Nicolas Barré which were meant to offset De Léry's Protestant discourse. For the German edition, published the following year, Barré's Catholic views were omitted, although the process of careful textual manipulation was continued, leaving out several of the exact passages which, despite the efforts taken with the Latin edition, had still offended the Catholic authorities. The De Brys had, in other words, further upgraded their self-censorship of De Léry's controversial account in order to avoid entering into a war of words with Catholic readers in southern Europe, an indication of the meticulous handling of the selected travel accounts in the Frankfurt workshop.

Detail of volume III, plate 17

Pages 188/189
Map of South and Central America showing Native American settlements

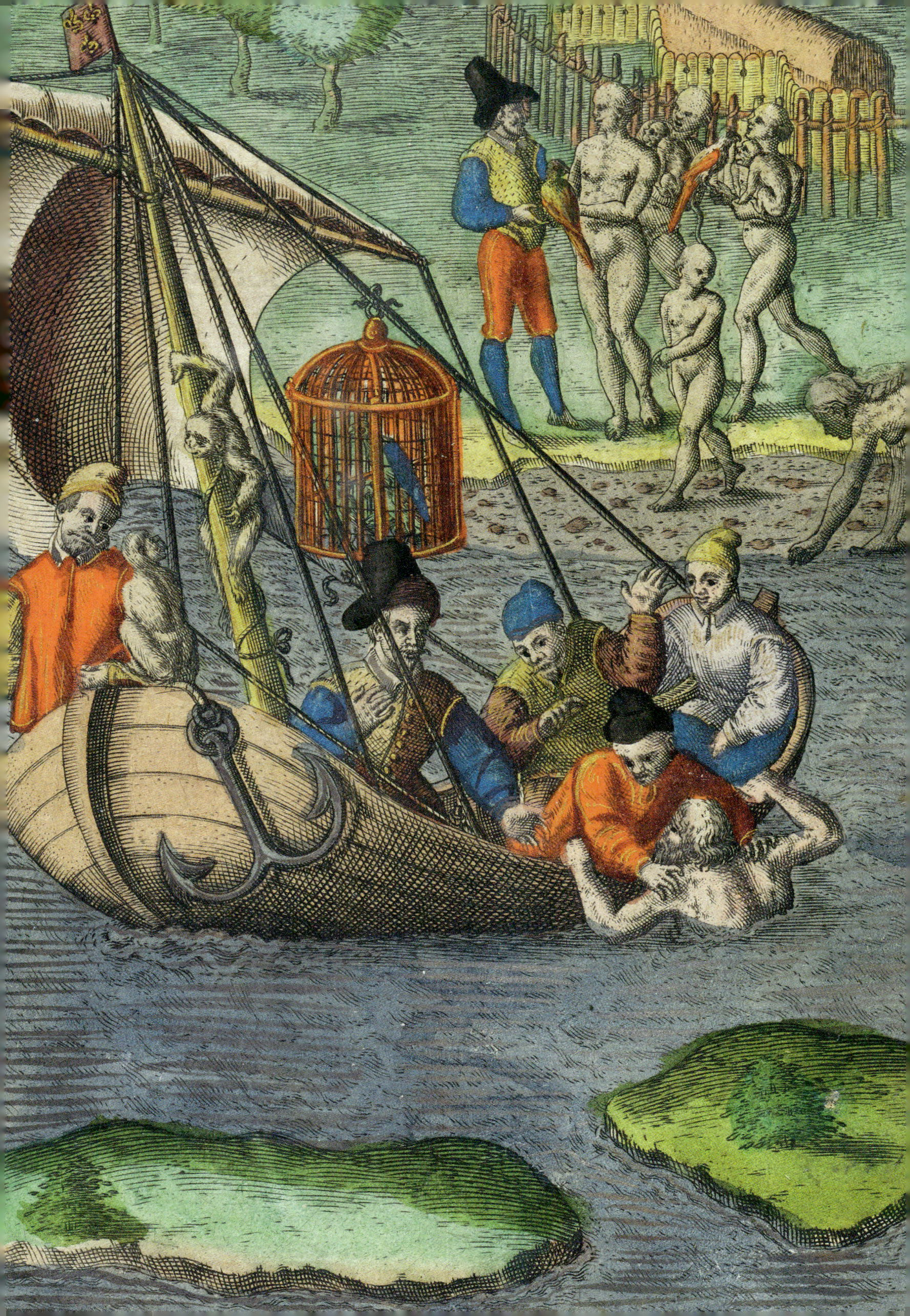

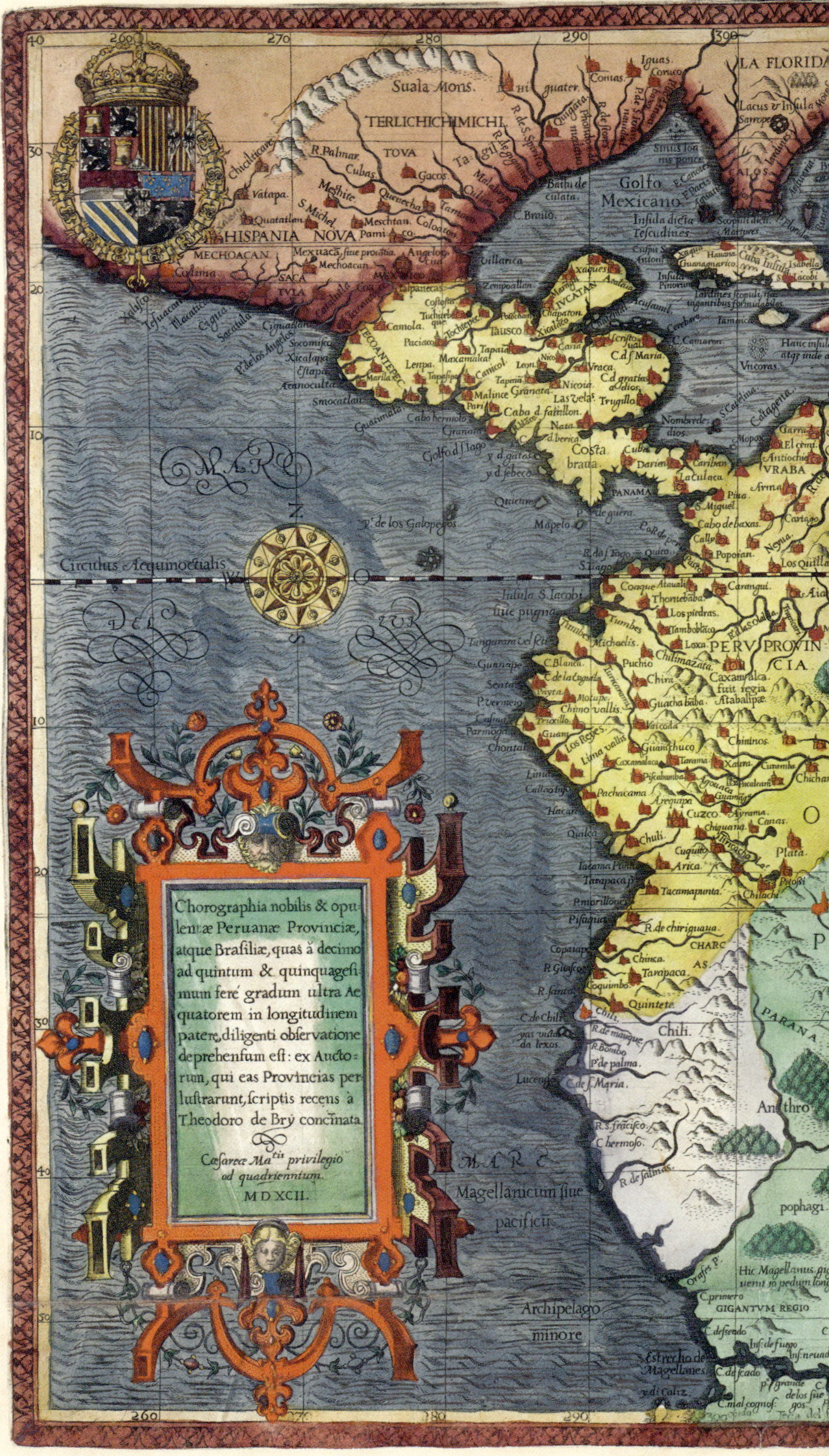
Chorographia nobilis & opulentæ Peruanæ Provinciæ, atque Brasiliæ, quas à decimo ad quintum & quinquagesimum fere gradum ultra Aequatorem in longitudinem patere, diligenti observatione deprehensum est: ex Auctorum, qui eas Provincias perlustrarunt, scriptis recens à Theodoro de Brÿ concinnata.
Cæsareæ Ma^tis privilegio ad quadriennium.
M D XCII.
LA FLORIDA
Suala Mons.
TERLICHICHIMICHI
HISPANIA NOVA
MECHOACAN
Golfo Mexicano
IVCATAN
Costa braua
PANAMA
VRABA
Circulus Aequinoctialis
MAR DEL ZVR
PERV PROVINCIA
Chili.
MARE Magellanicum siue pacificu
Archipelago minore
Estrecho de Magellanes
GIGANTVM REGIO
PARANA
Anthropophagi
Hic Magellanus gigã uenit in pedum longi

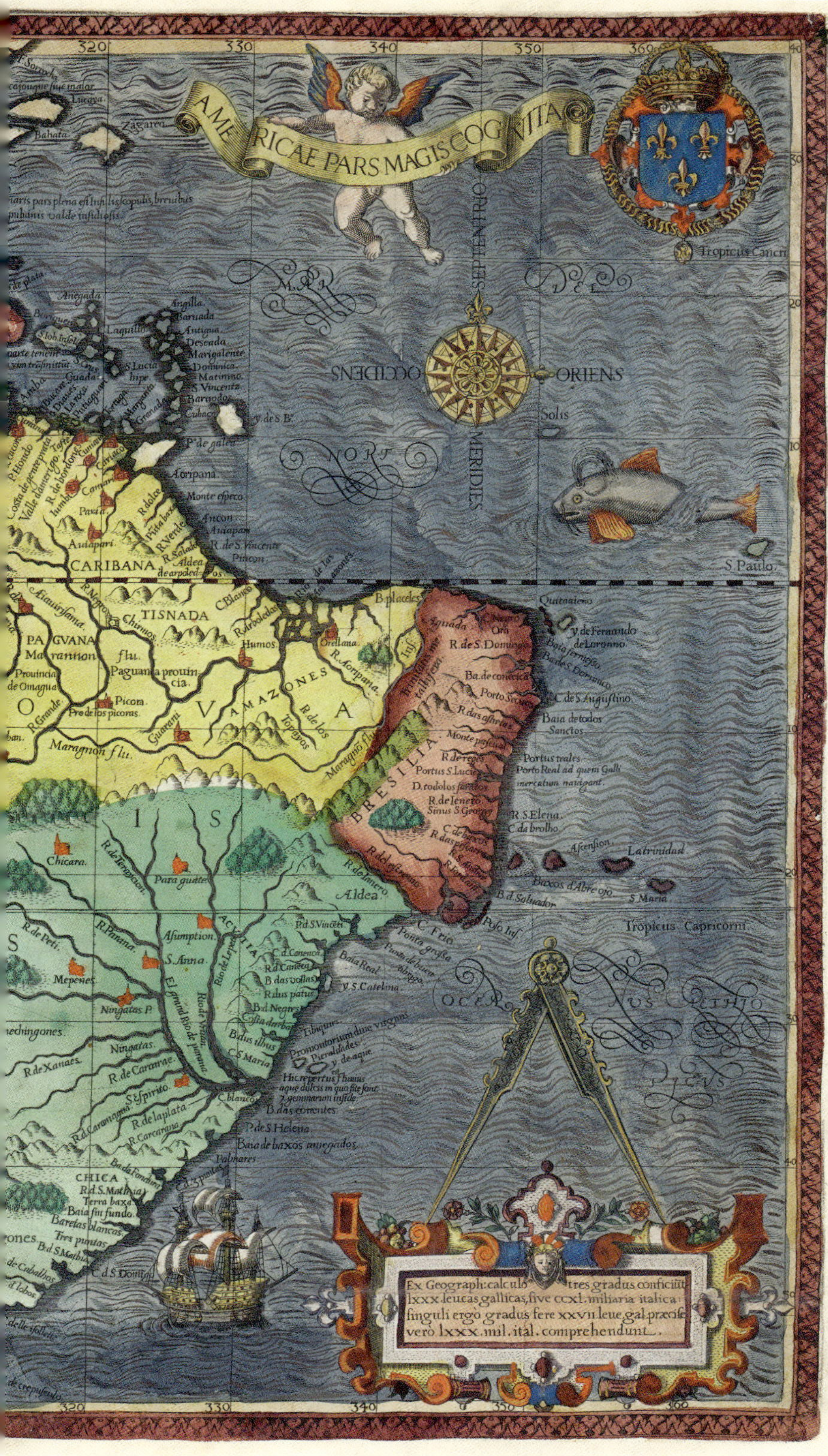
AMERICAE PARS MAGIS COGNITA
SEPTENTRIO
OCCIDENS
ORIENS
MERIDIES
Tropicus Cancri
Tropicus Capricorni
Solis
S.Paulo
CARIBANA
TISNADA
Marannon flu.
Paguana prouincia.
AMAZONES
BRESILIA
Aldea
Asumption.
S.Anna.
CHICA
Latrinidad
Ascension
y. de Fernando de Loronno
C. de S.Augustino
Baia de todos Sanctos
C. Frio
Ex Geograph: calculo tres gradus conficiunt lxxx. leucas gallicas, sive ccxl. miliaria italica: singuli ergo gradus fere xxvii leue gal. praecise verò lxxx. mil. ital. comprehendunt.
320
330
340
350
360

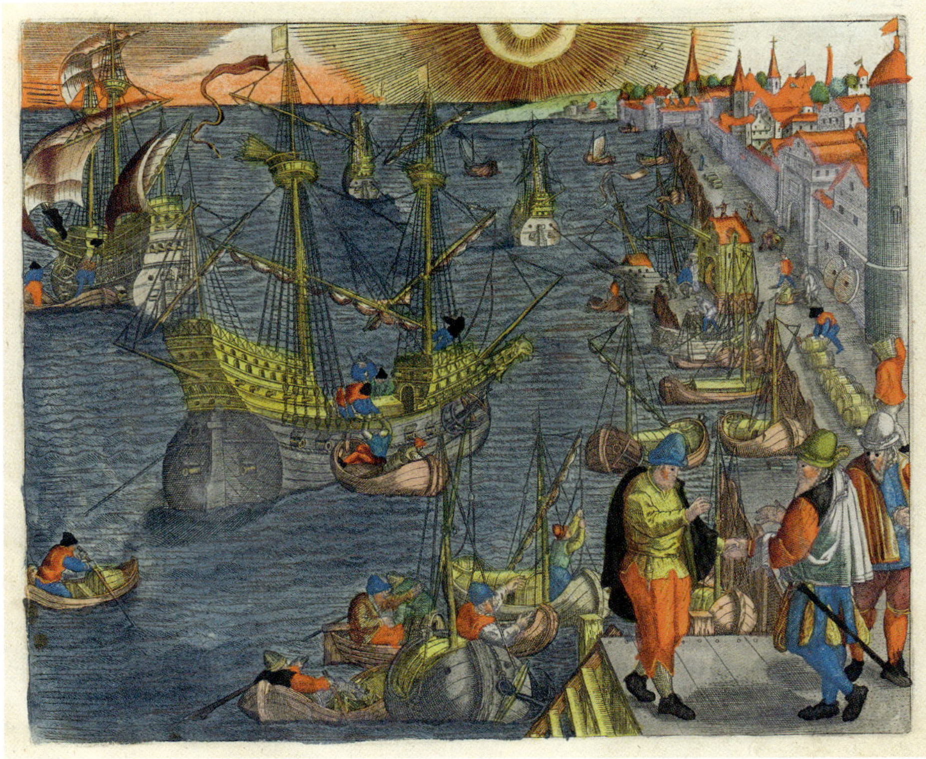

PLATE 1

The beginning of Hans Staden's voyage to Brazil

I, Hans Staden from Homberg, decided I would go and see the Indians, if God willed it. With this in mind I travelled from Bremen to Kampen in Holland and joined up with ships that were carrying salt to Portugal. We arrived in the city of Setúbal after four weeks at sea. From there I went to Lisbon, which was five miles away. I took up lodging with a German innkeeper named Leuhr. I told him about how I had left my fatherland to travel to the Indies. He told me, however, that I had dallied too long and that all of the king's ships had long since set sail for the Indies. I asked him then if he could help me join another expedition, since he knew the language. He got me a position as a rifleman on a ship. The captain's name was Pintado and he wanted to sail to Brazil for trade. He also planned a furlough along the way in order to make deals with the white Moors. Furthermore, he hoped to make deals with the savages in Brazil, for whom he carried goods in a French ship. He carried with him some prisoners of the king whose punishment had been set, but who were nonetheless permitted to see the new country. Our ship was equipped with all of the armaments needed on a sea voyage. There were three Germans on the ship: Hans, from Bruchhausen, Heinrich Brant, from Bremen, and me.

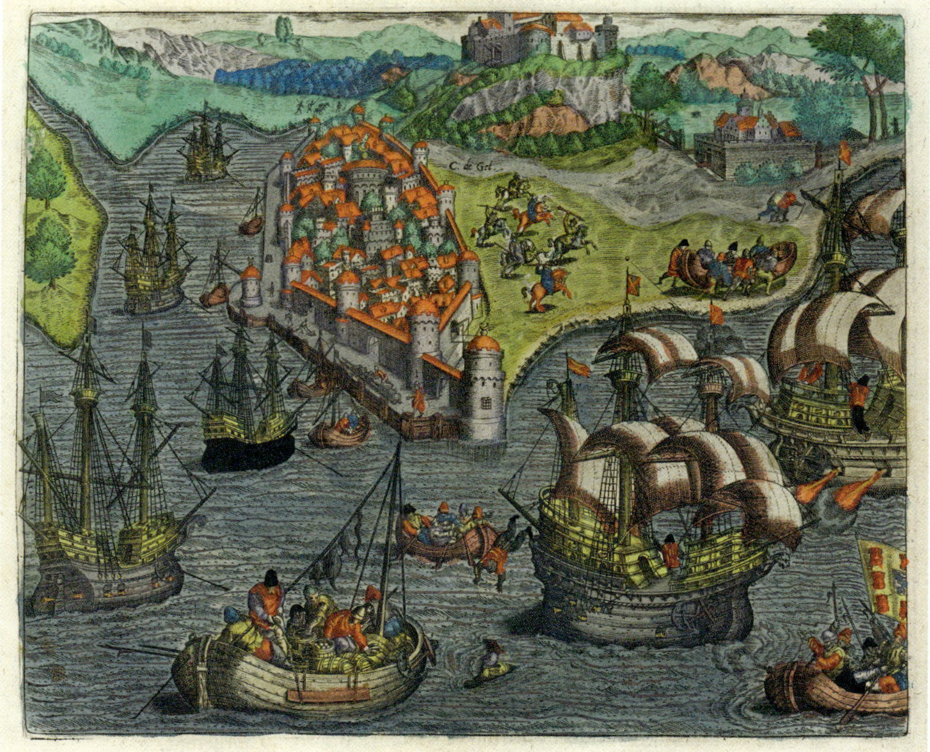

PLATE 2

Description of the first voyage out of Lisbon

We travelled to Cape de Gel to see if we could acquire more goods. The intentions were for nothing, however, and the wind there worked against us. On the night before All Saints' Day, we left the Barbary Coast with a great storm wind towards Brazil. When we were 400 miles out to sea, we came upon many fish and so we brought out our lures. Some of these fish were what mariners call albacore, which were very large. Others, slightly smaller, were bonitos. Others were the size of herrings and had fins on either side like a bat. After this, we came to the equatorial region, where it was very hot since the sun was directly over us at noon. There was no wind for several days and at night there was loud thunder with rain and wind that would quickly die down, so we could not catch it even if we hurried. When the wind finally came, it was in a storm that blew against us for several days, and then we began to suffer from hunger. We called upon God for good wind. Then there came a night when we experienced a big storm and we were all suffering. There appeared to us multiple blue lights on board the ship. Once the waves crashed on deck, the lights vanished. The Portuguese crew members said the lights were a sign of good weather ahead sent from God to console us. We gave thanks to God then with a collective prayer. There was good weather at daybreak and we got a good wind. It was clear to all of us then that the lights must have been a marvellous work of God. We sailed seaward on the good wind on 28 January. We entered the harbour of Pernambuco. The Portuguese had established a small town here called Marin.

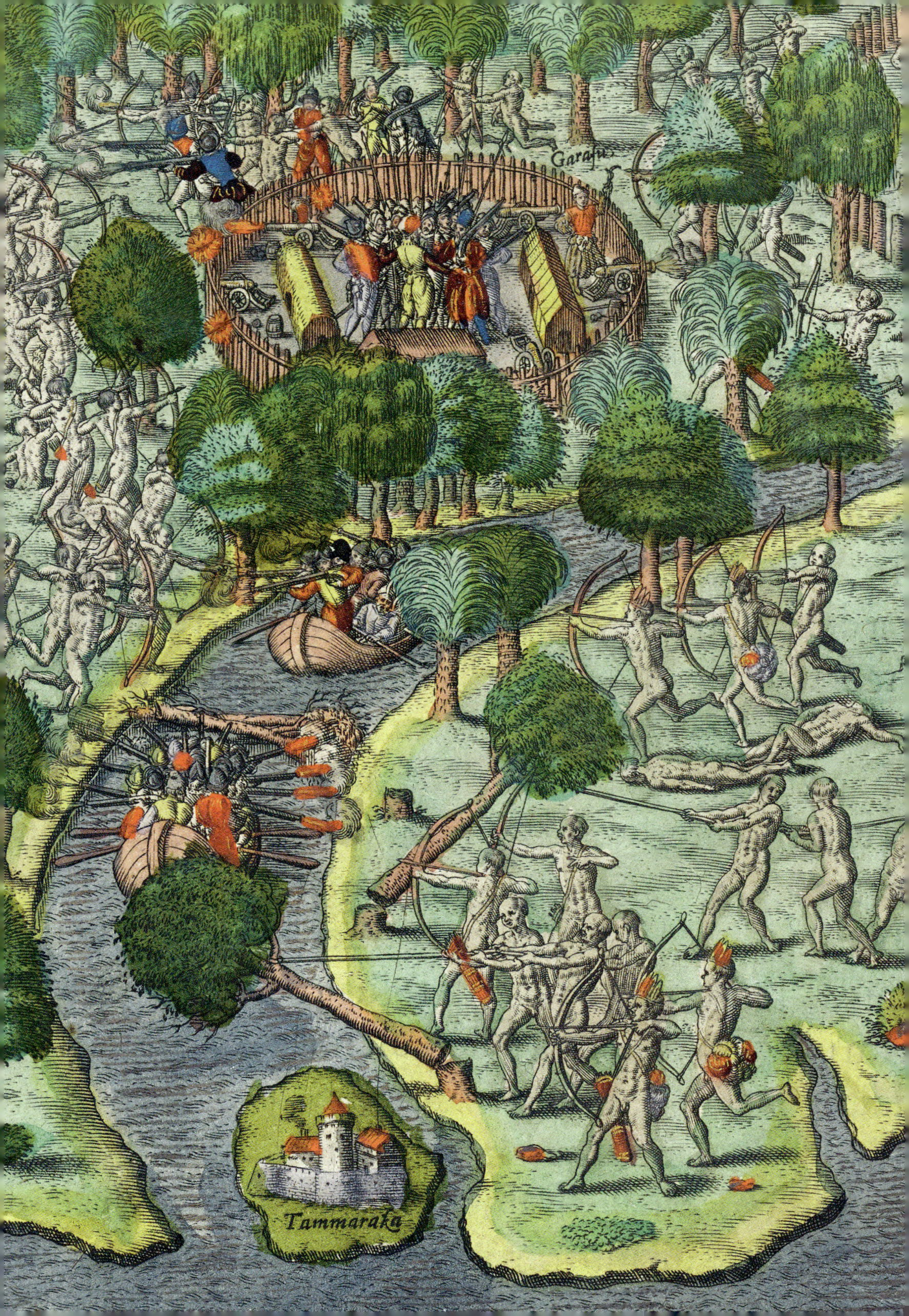
Garasu
Tammaraka

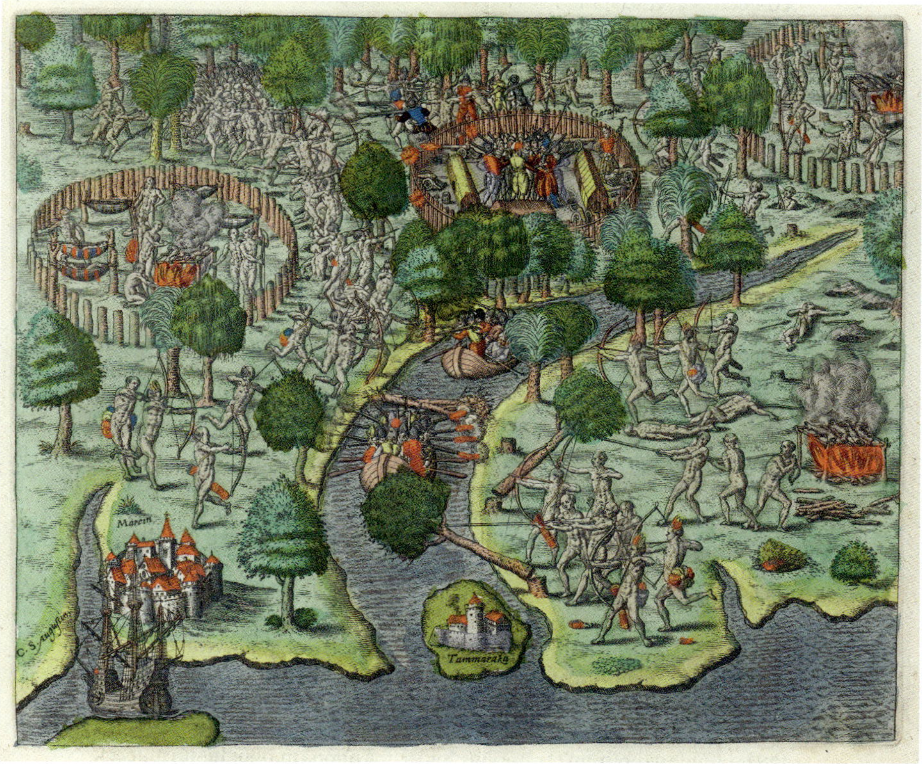

PLATE 3

Description of the savages' fortifications and how they attacked us

The town where we were staying was surrounded by forest where the savages had two fortifications. At night, they could hide among the dense trees. If we went out after them, this is where they waited for us. Besides this, they had also dug holes in the ground around our town, where they would wait during the day. They emerged out of them sometimes to have a skirmish with us. When shot at, they would all fall down and give the impression that their defences were down. They besieged us, however. We couldn't charge or retreat. They came for the town, firing their arrows high into the air so that they would fall upon us there. They also shot arrows directly at us. Some of the arrows were wrapped in cotton and wax and set on fire so that our houses would burn down. They intended to eat us if we were defeated.

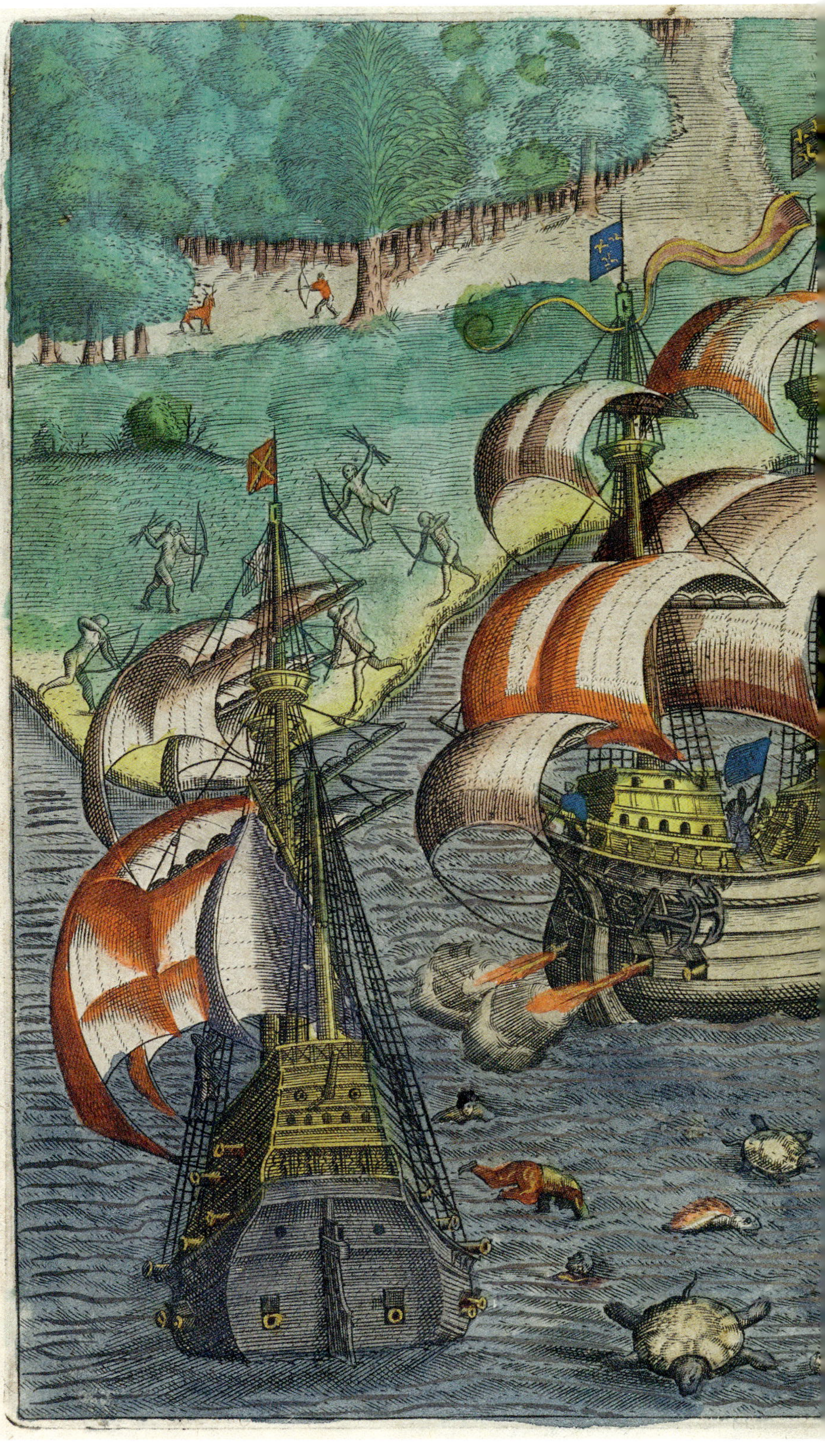

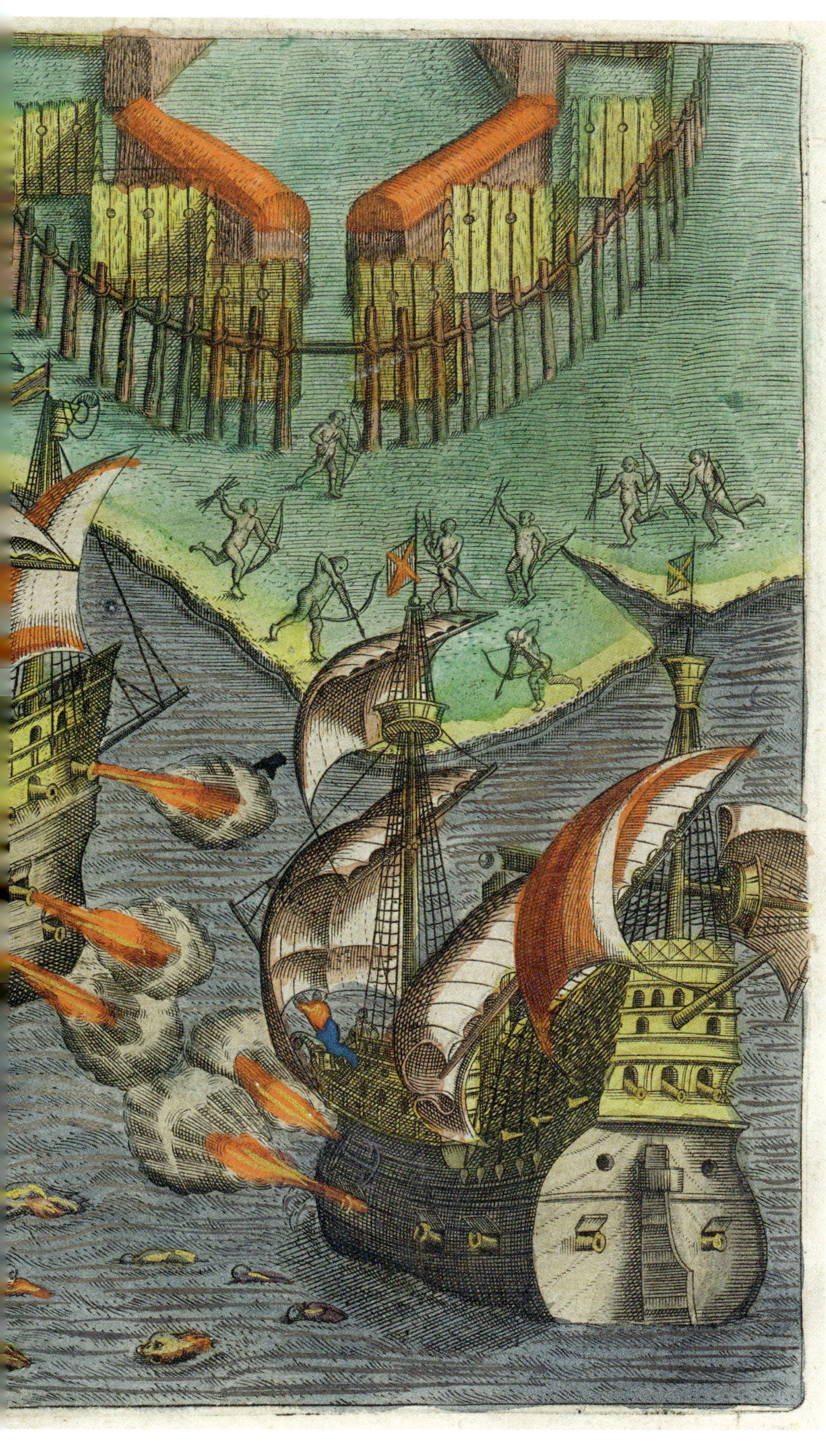

PLATE 4, PAGES 194/195

How we left Pernambuco for Buttugaris, where we fought a French ship

We sailed 40 miles from Pernambuco to the harbour called Buttugaris with the intention of loading our ships with brazilwood, as well as to take more victuals from the savages. When we arrived, we saw a French ship that was also loading wood and we decided to take it from them. They destroyed one of our masts with a cannon, however. Our sails were torn to shreds. Some of our ships were shot full of holes and some of us were wounded. Afterwards, we considered sailing back to Portugal since we could not get into this harbour and collect victuals. The wind was against us and we returned to Portugal with little food, suffering from hunger. Some of us ate rams' testicles that happened to be on the ship. Each day we were rationed a little fresh water and some Brazilian root flour. We were at sea for 108 days. We arrived at some islands on 12 August that were territories of the Portuguese king. We dropped anchor and fished. We saw another ship and learned it was full of pirates. They attacked us, but we gained the upper hand and took their ship. The pirates escaped by boat to the islands. The ship had a lot of bread and wine, which restored us. Afterwards, we encountered five Portuguese ships that were waiting for a ship out of India, which they were supposed to accompany back to Portugal. We stayed here and accompanied the Indian ship to the island of Terceira, where we remained. There were many other ships there, some of which were headed for Spain, others for Portugal. We left Terceira with 100 other ships and arrived in Lisbon on 8 October, 1548. It was the 16th month of our voyage.

PLATE 5

How we came to America via the 28th degree, could not identify the harbour, were separated, and how a great storm arose

On 18 November, our helmsman steered us up to the 28th degree, where we sought the countries out west. We had been at sea for six months and had encountered great danger. Once we got to land though, we did not recognise the harbour, nor the signal that the lead helmsman gave us. We did not want to risk docking in an unfamiliar harbour, so we rowed around near land for a long time without dropping anchor. The wind began to blow and we set about manoeuvring our ships around the cliffs of the island. We tried waiting out the wind with the intention of sailing away from the island once it passed, but it blew us into some rocks that were hidden under the water four fathoms deep. God delivered us safely to the harbour, however. In the evening, there came a boat full of savages who wanted to talk to us, but none of us spoke the language. We gave them some knives and fishing lures and they continued on their way. That same night there came another boat, this time with two Portuguese on board. We said that we had come from Spain, to which they replied that we must have had a very clever helmsman to have safely entered the harbour. We told them that the winds truly should have smashed our ship to pieces and that we had expected to die. We had come safely to harbour quite unexpectedly and had only God to thank for our deliverance. They listened to us in wonder, gave thanks to God, and then informed us that the harbour was called Suprawai. They told us furthermore that we were 18 miles away from an island called St Vincent, where they lived, which belonged to the king of Portugal.

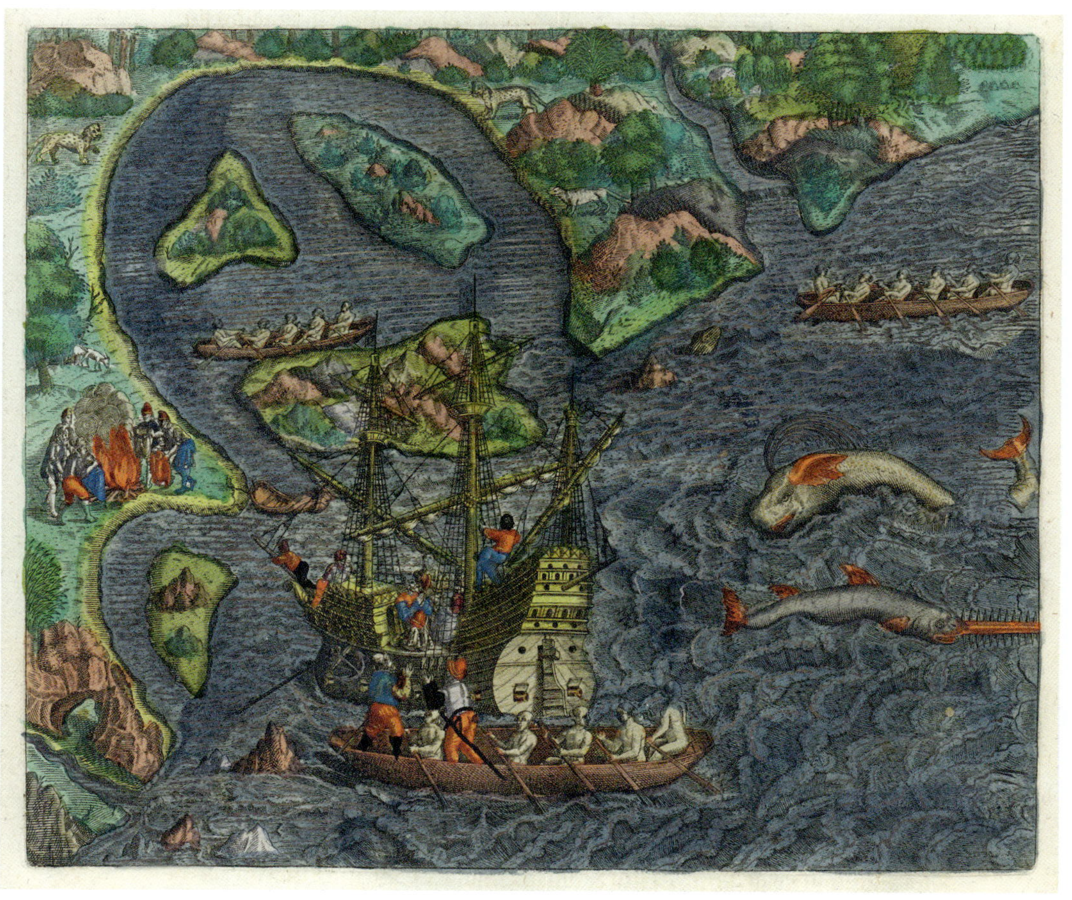

PLATE 6

How some of us went out to survey the harbour and came across a crucifix on a stone

We dropped anchor on St Catherine's Day 1549, armed ourselves and went about surveying the harbour in a boat. We crept along until we saw some huts before a dense forest and went towards them. They were old huts and we found nobody living in them. We found a little island, around the time it became evening, to rest overnight. In the morning we ventured deeper into the island to see if there were any people there, because we had become convinced that there must be people living in the area. As we walked around, we saw from a distance a piece of wood stuck between some rocks. We approached and found a wooden cross held up by rocks. It had a small pedestal attached, which had an illegible inscription. We wondered what people had decided to erect it here. We did not know if this was indeed the harbour where we were supposed to be. We continued, leaving the cross behind, but taking the pedestal. One of us sat down with it and it said, in Spanish: If one of his majesty's ships finds this peradventure, fire a cannon to learn more. We returned to the cross, fired a falconet cannon, and resumed our exploration. At this point, five boats quickly approached us. We readied our cannon. Once they were close, however, we saw that one of them wore clothes and had a beard. We could see he was a Christian, and asked him where we were. He said we were in the Schimerein harbour, as it is called in the language of the savages, named Santa Catarina by its discoverers. We were pleased to hear this, because this was the harbour we had been searching for and we had arrived there on St Catherine's Day. Know then, that God helps those who sincerely ask for it in times of need.

PLATE 7, PAGES 200/201

How we decided to sail to Portuguese-controlled St Vincent, and how we intended to load another ship and end our voyage but were caught in a great storm, shipwrecked and disoriented

Once we had eaten, a wind began to rise up from the south that was so strong we could barely keep our anchor in place. It was evening and we hoped to get to Caninee harbour. It was night before long, however, and we could not find it. Rather, we sailed dangerously close to land. We truly thought the wind would smash us to pieces, for we were at a promontory where the wind gusts harder than out in the middle of the ocean. We were blown so far out to sea that we could not see land any more by the morning. After a long while, we saw land again. One of us who had been there before said this was St Vincent, and so we sailed towards it. The country was covered in clouds and fog so that it could not be properly recognised. We approached the country, which we thought was held by the Portuguese, but were in error. The clouds broke and Roman said he thought the harbour was just ahead of us, behind some rocks we were steering towards. We sailed in this direction and ran aground hard. Death seemed near. This was not the harbour. The wind pushed us ahead towards land and we were shipwrecked. The waves crashed horribly against the land and we begged God to save our souls. As we approached the shore where the waves broke, we were carried high up on the waves, and the ship broke apart as soon as it hit the ground. A few crew members jumped out and swam for shore. A few others floated over on pieces of wreckage. God helped us all come to shore alive. It rained and the wind blew so hard that we all nearly froze to death.

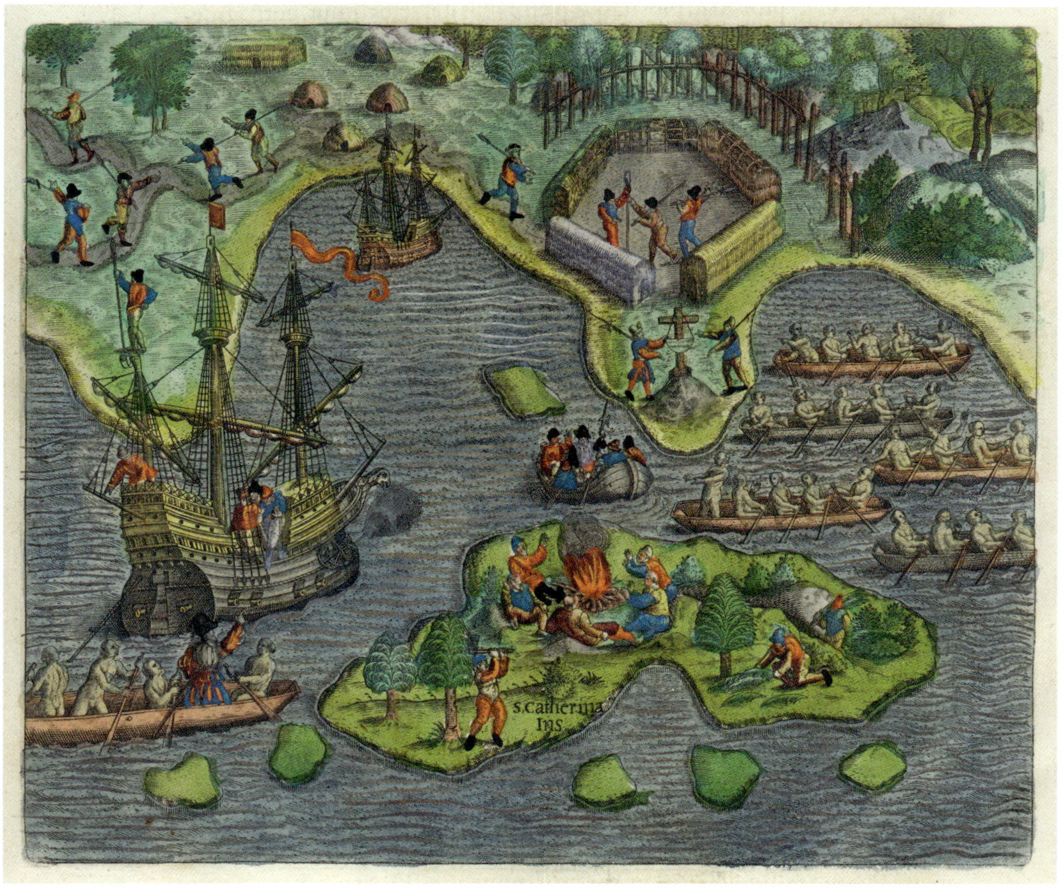
s.catherina
Ins

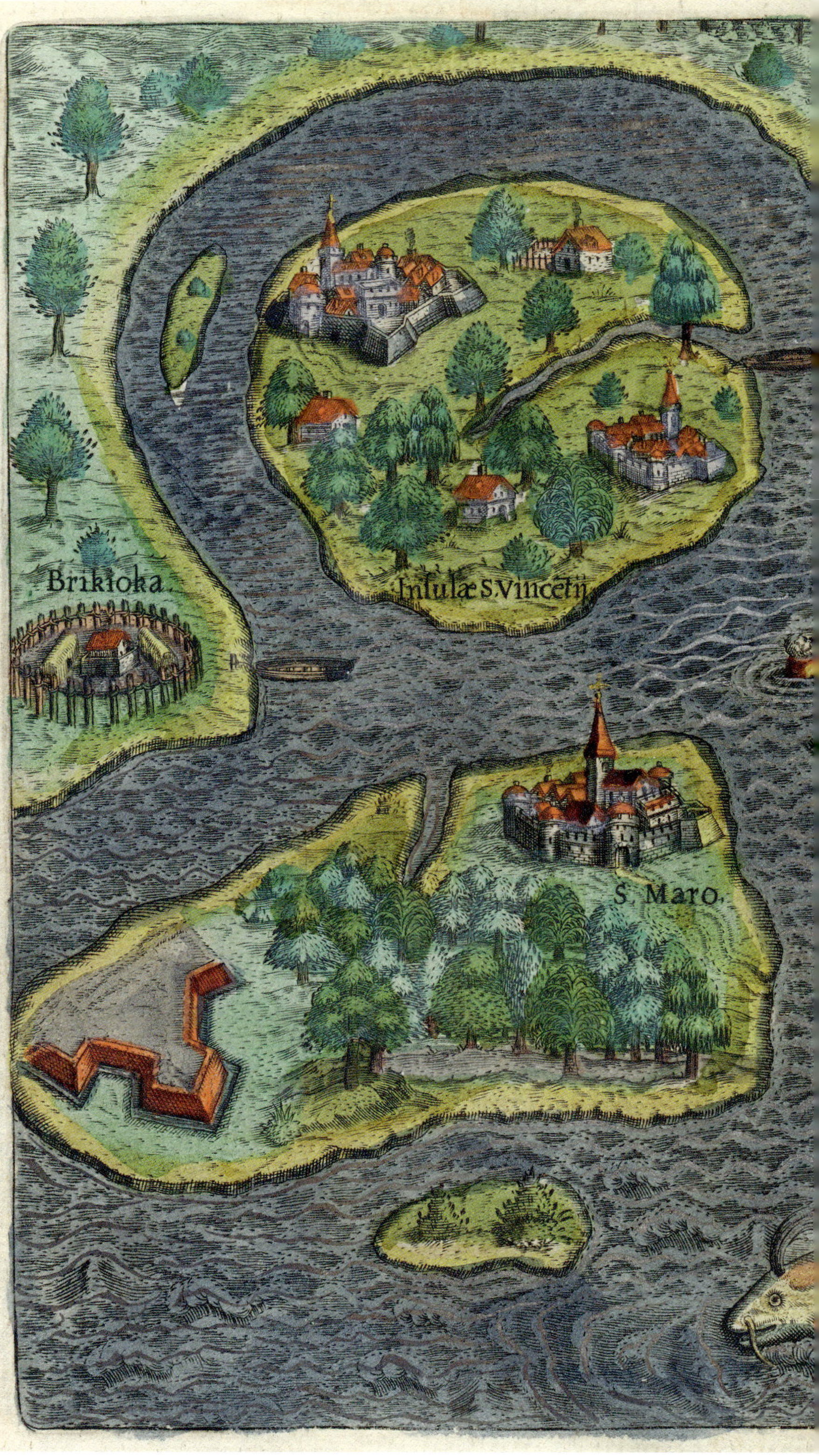
Brikioka
Insulæ S.Vincetij
S. Maro.

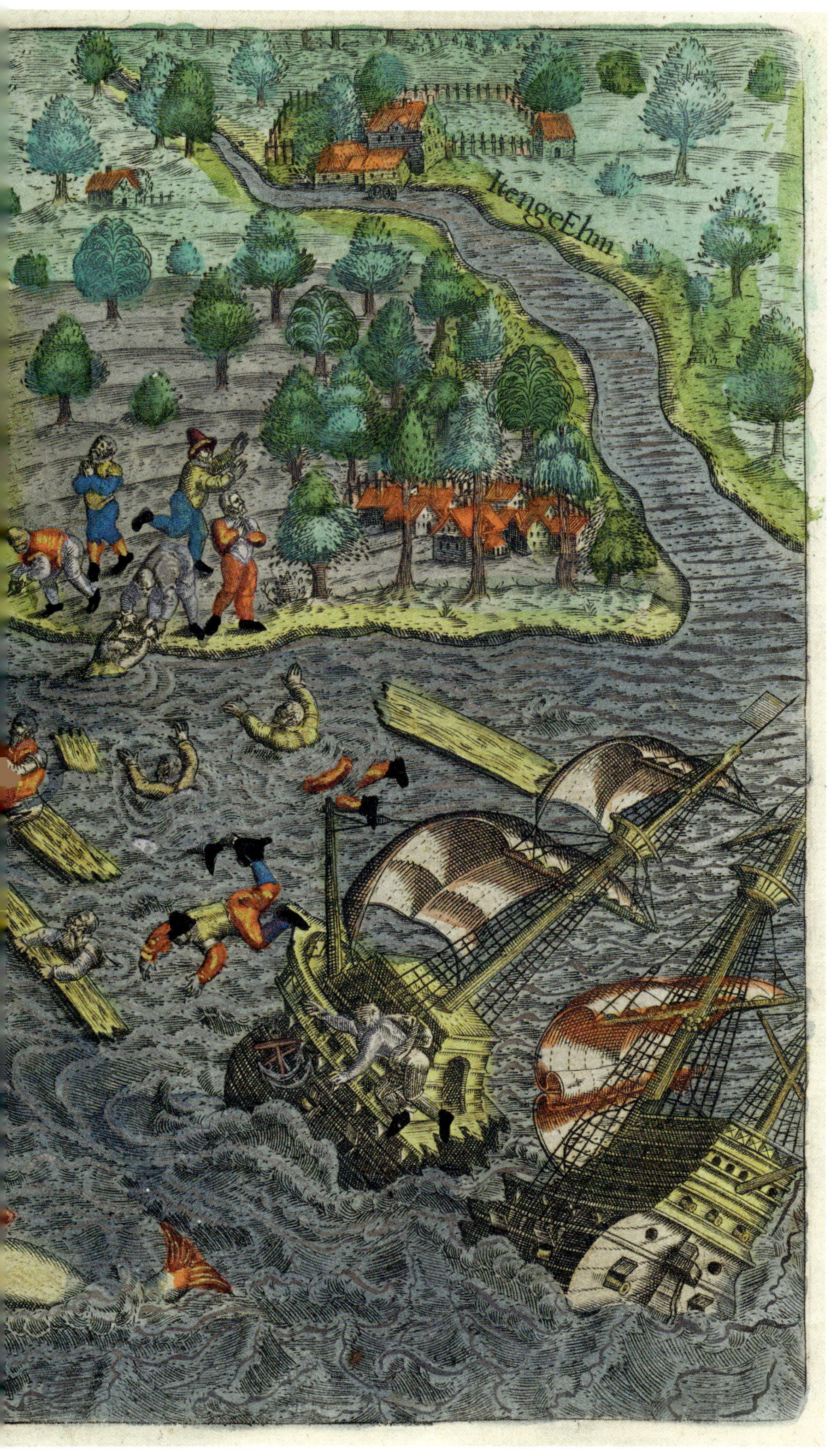
ItengeEhn

PLATE 8

How I was taken captive by savages

As I was walking through the forest, a loud cry arose that I recognised as the call of savages. They quickly came and surrounded me. They shot their arrows at me. I cried out, "Oh God, save my soul!" before they struck me to the ground. They shot and stabbed me, but they only wounded my legs and tore my clothes, praise God. All the while, the others beat me with clubs. Finally, two of them lifted my naked body from the ground. A few other savages stood behind and in front of me. They led me quickly to the sea, where their boats were moored. A large group of savages waited near them. When these others saw me, they all came up biting into their own arms and threatening to eat me too. A king approached with the wooden club they would use to strike me dead. He gave a speech and said they had captured a slave from the Portuguese. Now, he continued, they would avenge the deaths of their friends on me. They brought me to the boats and beat me with their fists. Before they got the boats on the water, they tied my hands together. They were not all from the same village, and some of them began to argue with each other, claiming that they had been just as close to me as the others when they attacked and should therefore also receive a piece. They wanted to kill me right there and then. I stood there praying and looking around frantically until the king ordered me to be kept alive so that their women could see me during the big festival. They would kill me "Kawewi pepicke": they would brew drinks and gather together to eat me as a group. Four ropes were then tied around my neck to lead me into a boat, which was shoved out into the water to take me to their home.

PLATE 9, PAGES 204/205

How our people arrived while the savages were taking me away and tried to take me back, resulting in a skirmish

There is another, smaller island near the one where I was taken. The Uwara bird nests there, which has red feathers. They highly prize the bird's feathers, with which they decorate themselves. When the Uwaras are young, their feathers are greyish white. When they are fully fledged, though, they become a blackish grey. They fly with these feathers for about a year, and then they become as red as red paint. The savages returned to the island to find these birds. As they approached, there were two rifle shots from the area. They looked around and saw that it was the Tupinambá as well as some Portuguese. A slave had escaped the savages when they captured me and had informed this other group, who had now come to release me. They called out to my captors that if they were brave they would come over and fight them. They turned back with their boats to those on land and shot blow darts and arrows at us. They untied my hands but the ropes around my neck remained tied. The king, who was with me in the boat, had a gun and some powder, and made me fire this gun at my rescuers. After they had fought like this a while, they worried that the others might have reinforcements that would follow them. They sailed away after three of them had been shot. They went about the distance of a falconet shot past the bulwark of Brikioka. As we passed, I stood up in the boat so that my companions might see me. They did, and they fired two shots at us, but they fell short. At the same time, a few boats came towards us from Brikioka, but the savages paddled away too quickly for them. When my friends saw there was no chance, they turned back for Brikioka.

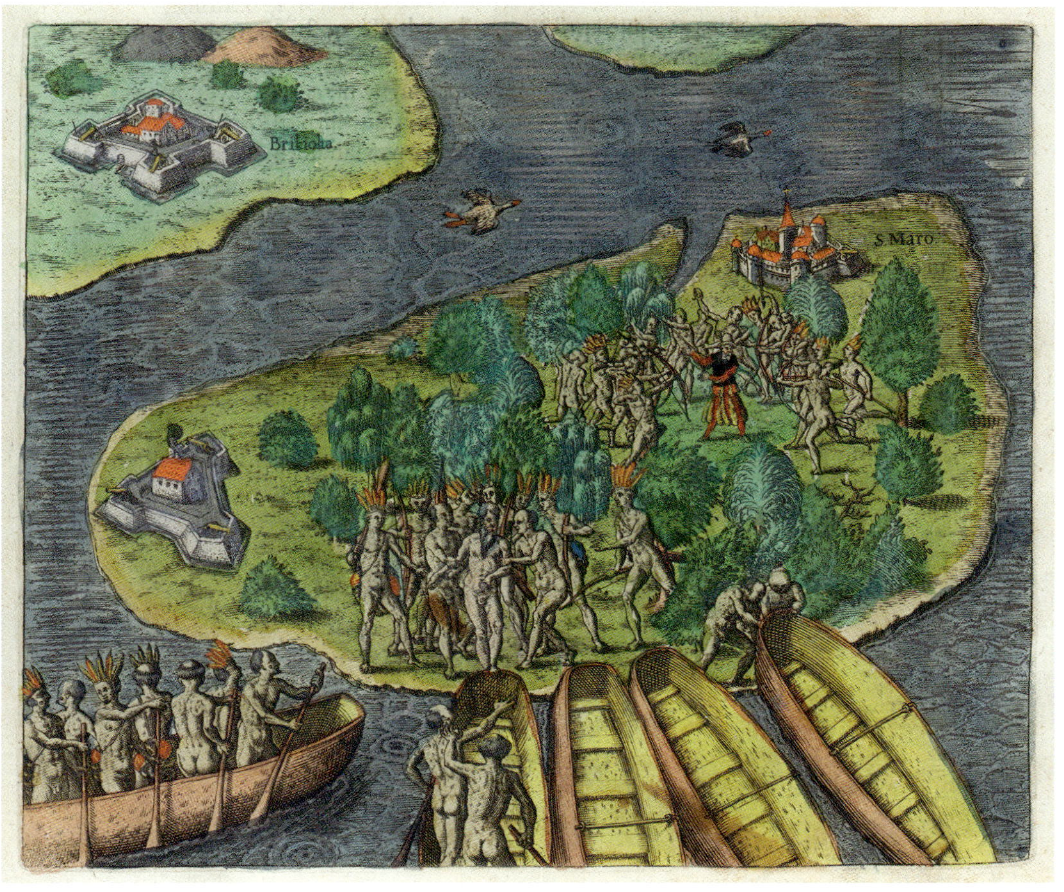
Brikioka
S. Maro

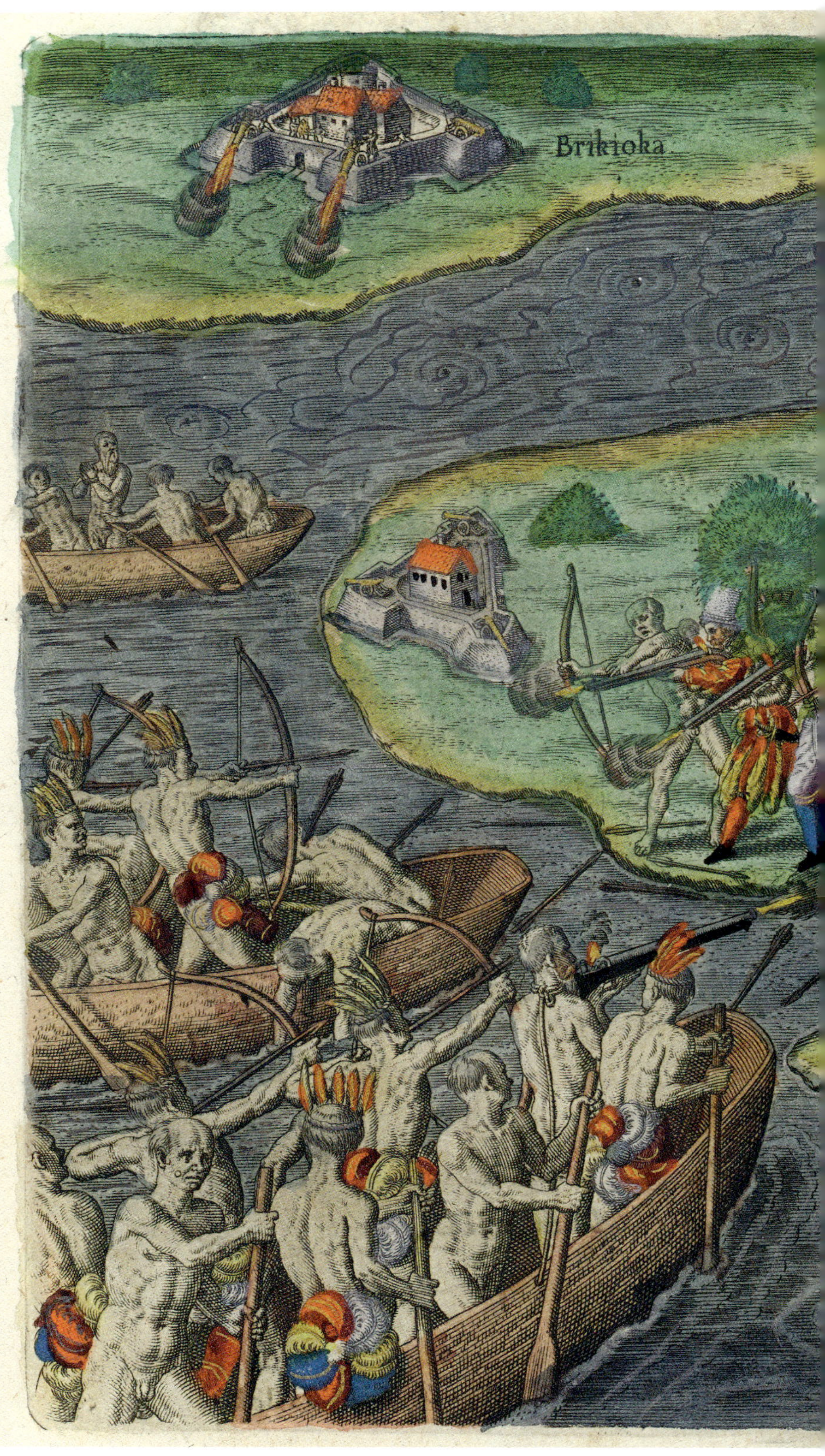
Brikioka

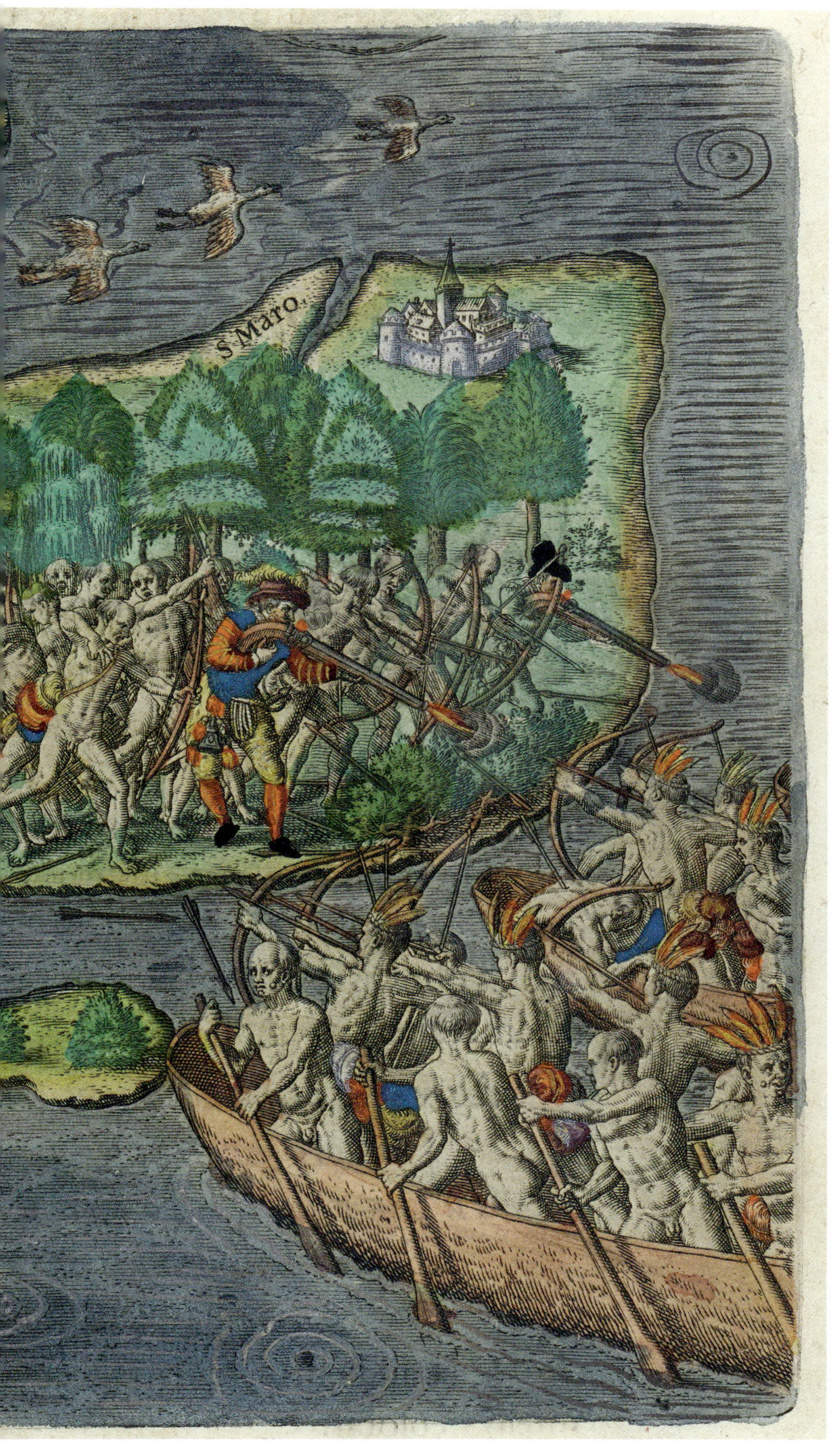
S. Maro

PLATE 10

What they did with me when they brought me to their dwellings

We came to where they lived, which was a small village of seven huts that they called Uwattibi. We were on the shore and nearby the women of the tribe were tending to a root that they called Mandioka. The women went through the rows where they planted this root and pulled some of them up. They made me call out in their language: "A Iunesche been ermi vramme". This translates as: "I, your food, have arrived". Once we were on land, everyone, young and old, came out of their huts to see me. The men took their bows and arrows to the huts and left me under the command of their women, who took me through the village, some walking behind me and some walking before me. They sang and danced, and the songs were the ones they sang to their own people when they planned to eat them. They took me to their Iwara huts, which are a kind of fortification surrounded by a barrier resembling a garden fence to keep enemies out. When I entered, the women beat me with their fists and pulled my beard. They said to me in their language, "Sche innamme pepicke a e", which means, "I herewith avenge my friend, who was killed by those you were with". Then they led me into a hut where they made me lie down. The women came in and out, hitting me and grabbing at me. They taunted me by telling me how they would soon eat me. The men were sitting together in a hut drinking what they call Kawi. They had their gods with them, whom they call Tammerka. They sang songs praising their gods, who had predicted how they would successfully capture me. I heard the song, and for half an hour I saw only the women and children.

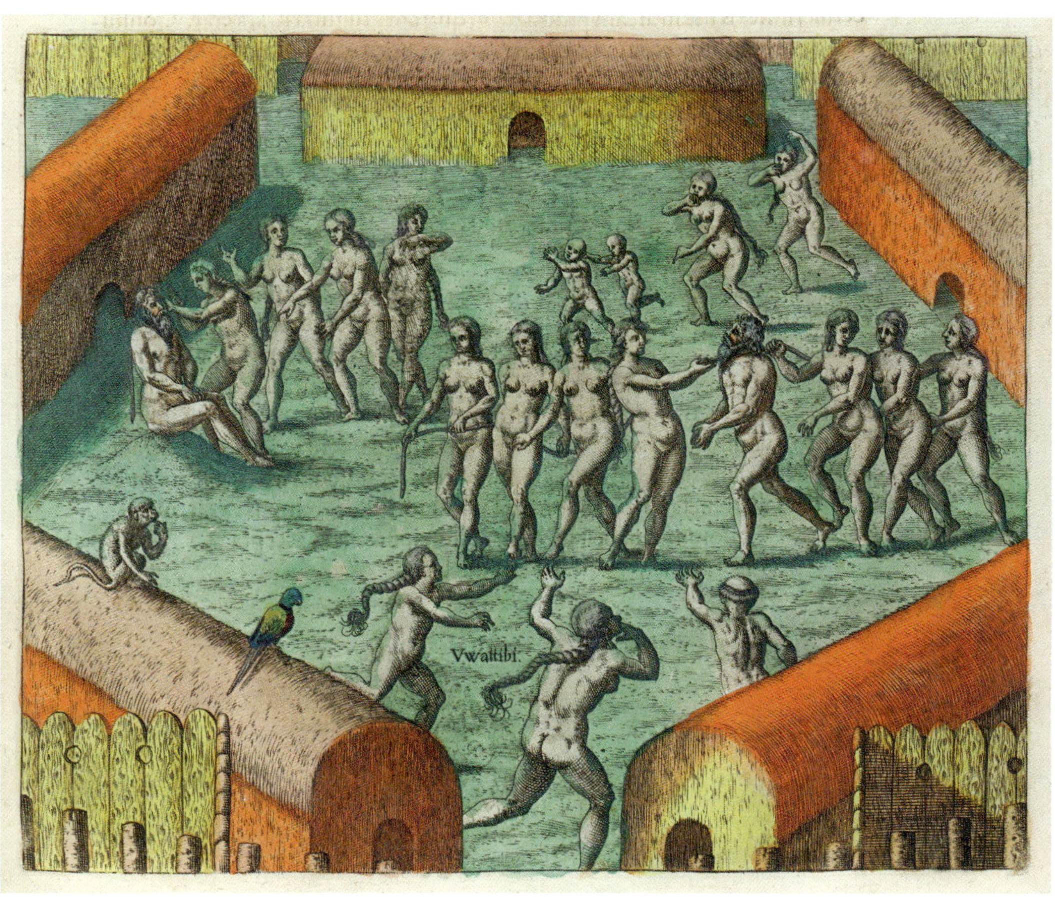
Vwaltibi.

PLATE 11

How they danced with me before the hut where they had their idols, called Tammerka

Afterwards they led me from the place where they had shaved off my eyebrows. They brought me before the hut where their idols were. They made a circle around me with me standing in the middle. Two women were with me and they bound certain rattling objects to my leg with a length of string. They also fastened a square yoke around my neck that was made using the tail-feathers of birds. It is called Arasona in their language. Then the women began to sing and I had to stamp my feet to make the rattles sound along with their song. My injured leg hurt me greatly as it had not been bandaged.

PLATE 12, PAGE 210/211

How the 25 boats of the Tupinambá, about which I had told the king, arrived and attacked the hut where I was

In the meantime, the 25 boats of savages who were friendly with the Portuguese arrived. As I have already said, they had been prepared to go to war before I had been taken captive. And so they arrived one morning at the village. When the Tupinambá attacked the huts and began to shoot arrows at them, it caused turmoil in the huts and the women made as if to flee. I said to them then: "You think I am Portuguese, your enemy. Give me a bow and arrows and release me. I will help defend your huts." They gave me a bow and arrows. I made loud noises, fired my arrows and did everything as closely as I could to their way of fighting. I told them that if they were brave and bold then they would not long have cause for distress. My idea was to get through the stockade that surrounded the huts and run to the other group, because they knew me. They also knew that I was in the village, but I was too quickly detained again. When the Tupinambá saw that they could do nothing for me, they returned to their boats and went away. As they rowed off I was brought back to the hut.

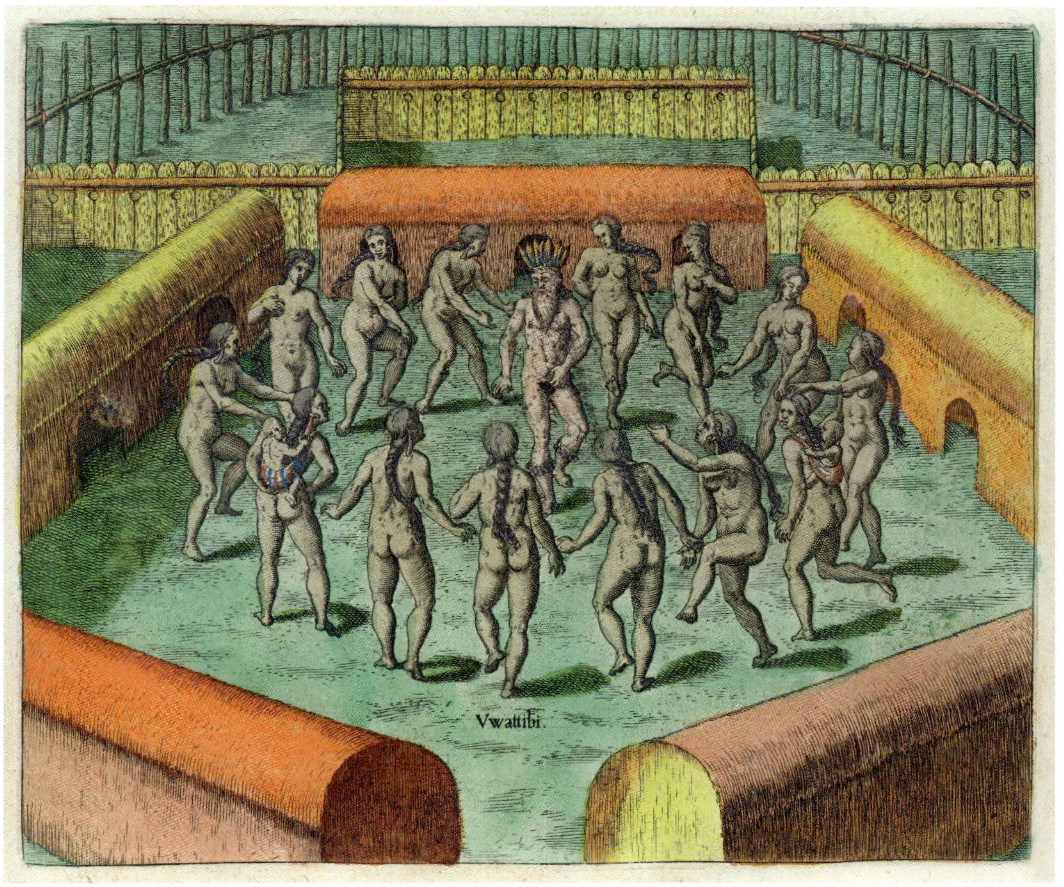
Vwattibi.

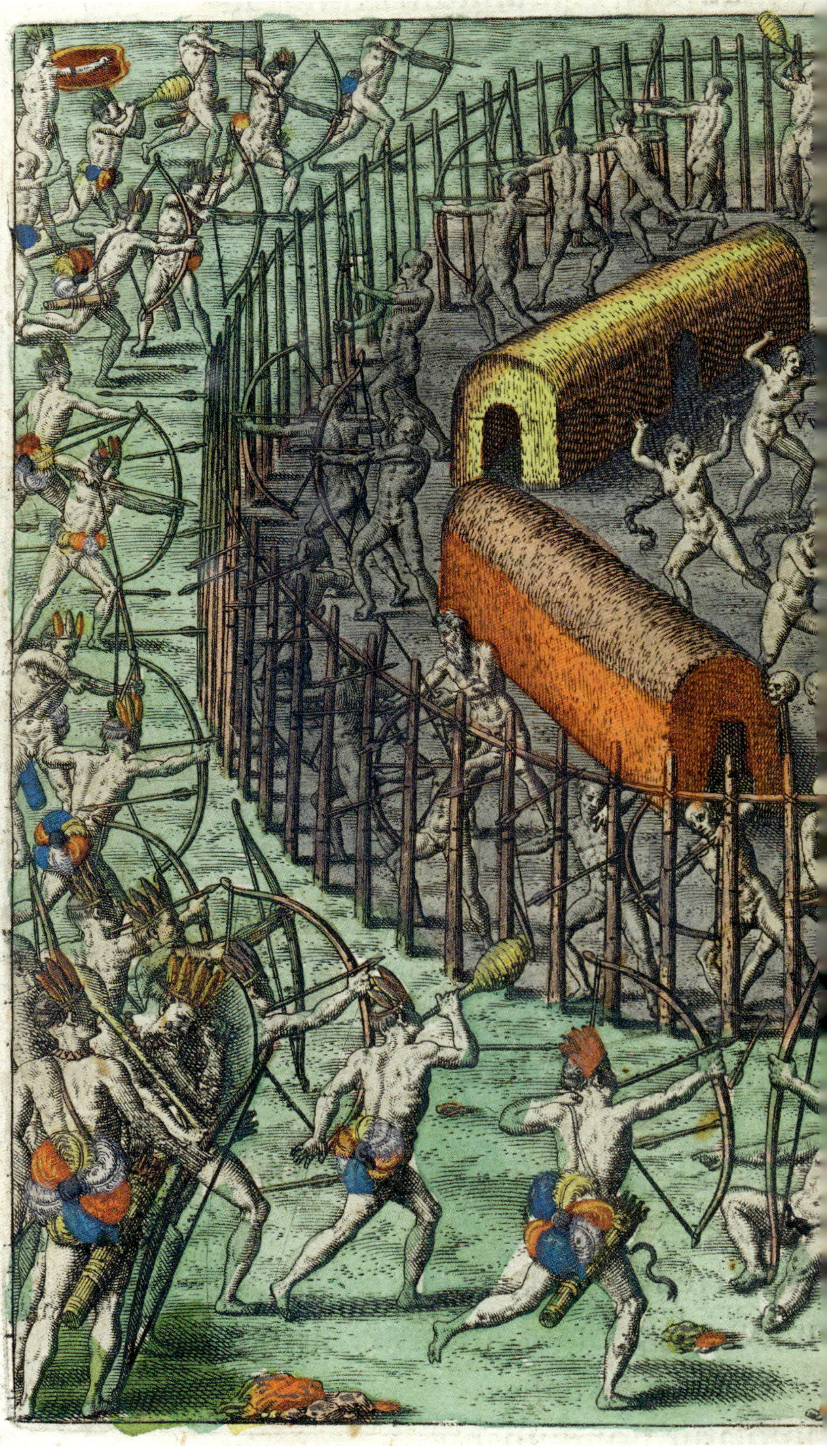

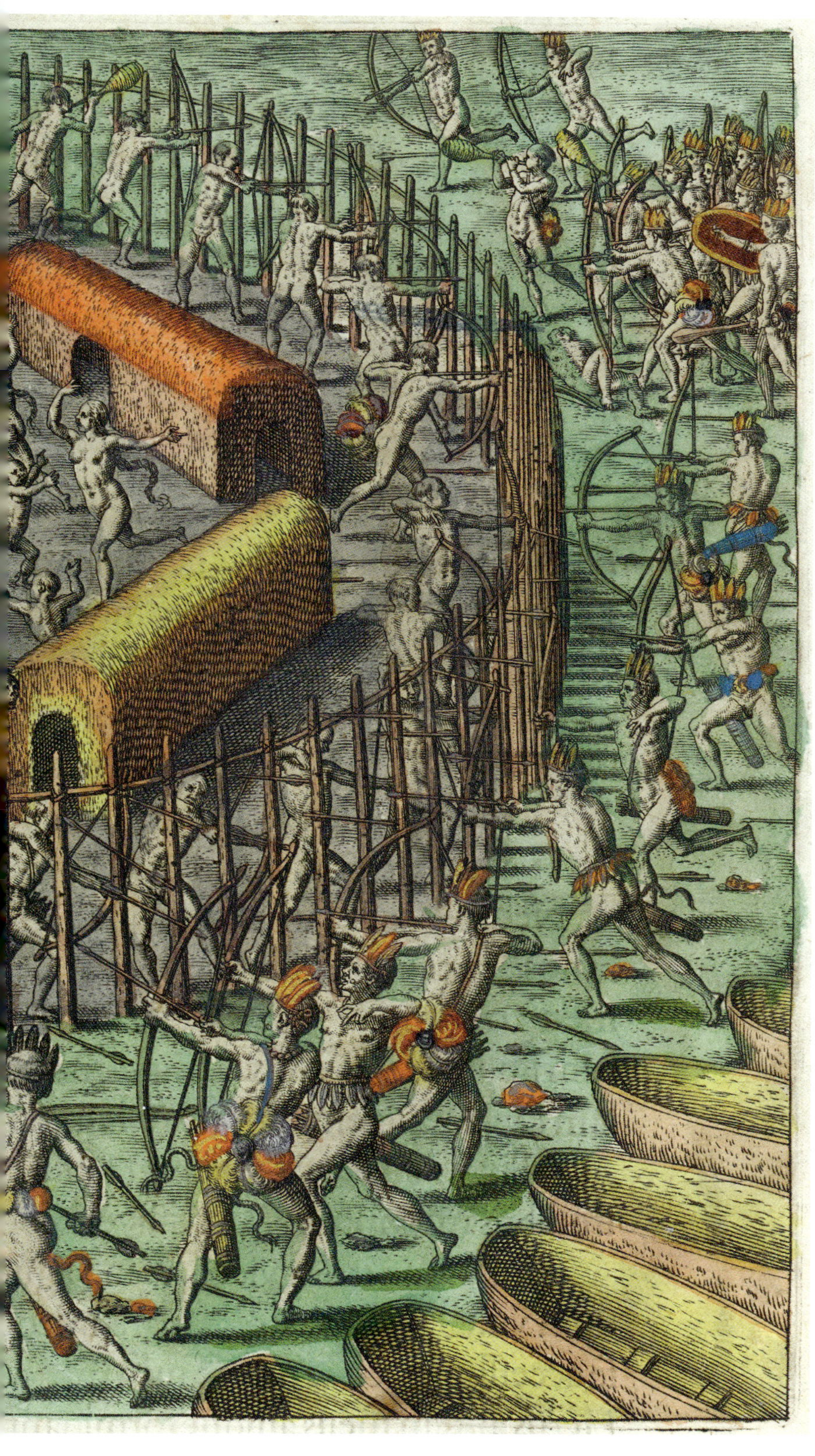

PLATE 13

How two ships were sent by the Portuguese to enquire about me and ask me questions

Meanwhile, a Portuguese ship came from Brikioka and anchored not far from where I was being held. It fired a cannon so that the savages would be alerted and come to speak with them. When they became aware of this, they told me that my friends, the Portuguese, were here and that they would perhaps like to know if I was still alive. Perhaps they would want to buy me. I said: "It is my brother." I supposed that the Portuguese ship would ask about me, and as I did not want the savages to think that I was Portuguese, I told them that I had a brother among the Portuguese who was French. Yet even when I told them that my French brother was on the Portuguese ship they would not have it otherwise that I was Portuguese. They went to the ship in order to speak with those on board. The Portuguese asked them how I was. They answered in a manner that did not invite any further questions. The ship sailed on and those on board perhaps assumed that I was dead. God knows what I thought as I saw the ship leaving. They said to one another: "We have the right man. They are sending ships after him."

While I was in my fifth month of captivity, another Portuguese ship came from the island of St Vincent. The ship that arrived this time fired a shot so that the savages were alerted and came to them. They asked if I was still alive. It was confirmed and the Portuguese asked if they could see me. They had a case full of wares and my brother was on board. This was a Frenchman, Claudio Mirando, who had formerly been my companion and whom I called my brother. He asked if I could perhaps come to the ship so they could ask me questions. They returned from the ship and told me that my brother had come with a chest of wares and wanted to see me. I assured them that the Portuguese did not understand our language. So they took me to the ship until I was about a stone's throw away, and naked, as I always was among them. I spoke to the people on board the ship, saying: "God the Lord be with you dear brothers. One of you should come to speak with me alone while the rest of you do not listen", for I was supposed to appear to be French. One named Johann Senches came forward. He said to me, "My dear brother, we have come here looking for you, not knowing if you were alive or dead. Recently, the captain Brascupas at Sanctus demanded that we find out if you are still alive. If we should learn that you are alive, we are then to learn if we can buy you. If not, we are to capture some of those who are detaining you." To this I said, "May God forever reward you, for I am here in great fear and danger. I do not know what they will do. They would have eaten me had God not prevented it." Since I saw that the savages would not allow us to speak any longer I said to the Portuguese, "Be aware that they are planning a war against Brikioka again." They told me that their savages were also preparing intensively for war and would soon attack the village where I was being held, and that I should be sure that God would let only the best come to pass. I commended them to God the Lord and they wanted to speak with me longer, but the savages took me back to the huts.

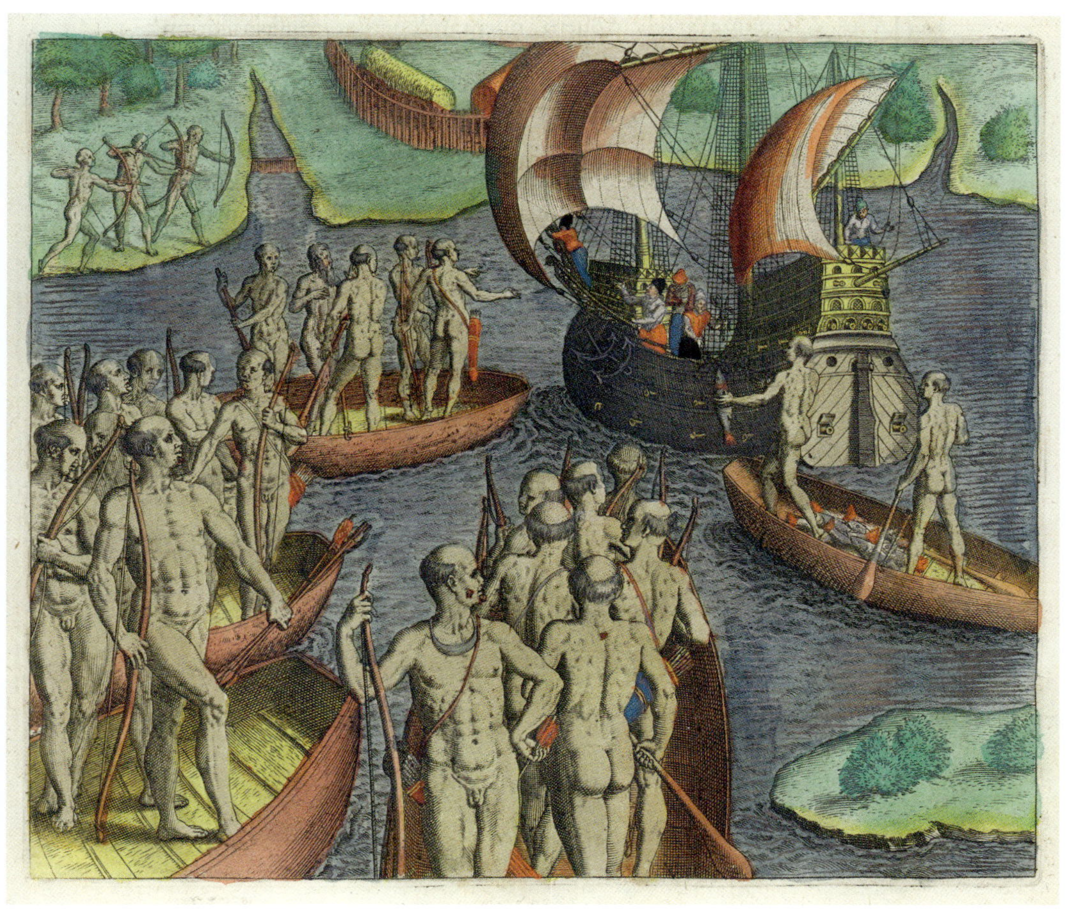

PLATE 14

How the sick king, Jeppipo Wasuwider, came home, and how illness is treated

After a few days, they all came home sick together. I was led into the king's hut and he told me how they had all become sick. I should have known already, he said, for I had told him that the Mon was angry. As I listened to him I thought to myself: "This must have happened by God's grace that I spoke of the Mon." I told him then that it was true. Misfortune had befallen him because he had wanted to eat me even though I was not his enemy. He told me that nothing would happen to me if he were to get better. I thought that if they recovered their health they would kill me anyway. As they began to talk, God made everything come to pass. The king told me most emphatically that they wanted to become healthy again. I went among them and laid my hands upon their heads, which they begged me to do. God did not wish it, however, and they began to die. First a child died, and then his mother. After a few days, a brother of the king died, then another child, then another brother who had told me earlier that they would become sick.

It hurt him to witness his children, mother, brothers, wife and himself dying. I consoled him and told him that he would have no trouble, except that God believed that if he got better, he would kill me. At this he said no and commanded everyone in his hut to do me no harm and not to eat me. He remained sick a little while longer, but then recovered, although his wife was still sick. About eight of his friends died, which also made me grieve. Now the elders who were deeper inside the hut, who had beaten me and threatened to eat me, began to call me Scheraeire, which means "my son". The king said they would not kill me. Then they let me go for a while. They did not know if I was French or Portuguese. After this terrible time, my master regained his health and no one mentioned anything about me being eaten. They continued to keep me captive, however, and did not let me go out on my own.

They give the sick nothing to eat. The sick person then demands food but is left to languish. When it is a painful illness, the healthy ones sing, jump about and carouse incessantly, as is their practice; the poor sick person often dies from the commotion. The afflicted do not complain as they know that it will achieve nothing. If one of them dies and is a house father, the song turns into a kind of howling and a great scream is let out, such that if someone arrives in the village that night to rest, he must either carry on to the next village, or else spend the night without sleep. A person would marvel at their women, whose screams are like those of dogs or wolves.

This is the lament they utter with a quavering voice: "He is now dead, the bravest hero who slew so many enemies for us." Then the others start up: "Oh, the powerful hunter. Oh, the glorious fisherman. Oh, the valiant butcher of the Portuguese and Makayas." In summary, each time one of them begins to lament, they join arms, as seen in the accompanying image, and all lament without end until the deceased is carried out of the hut.

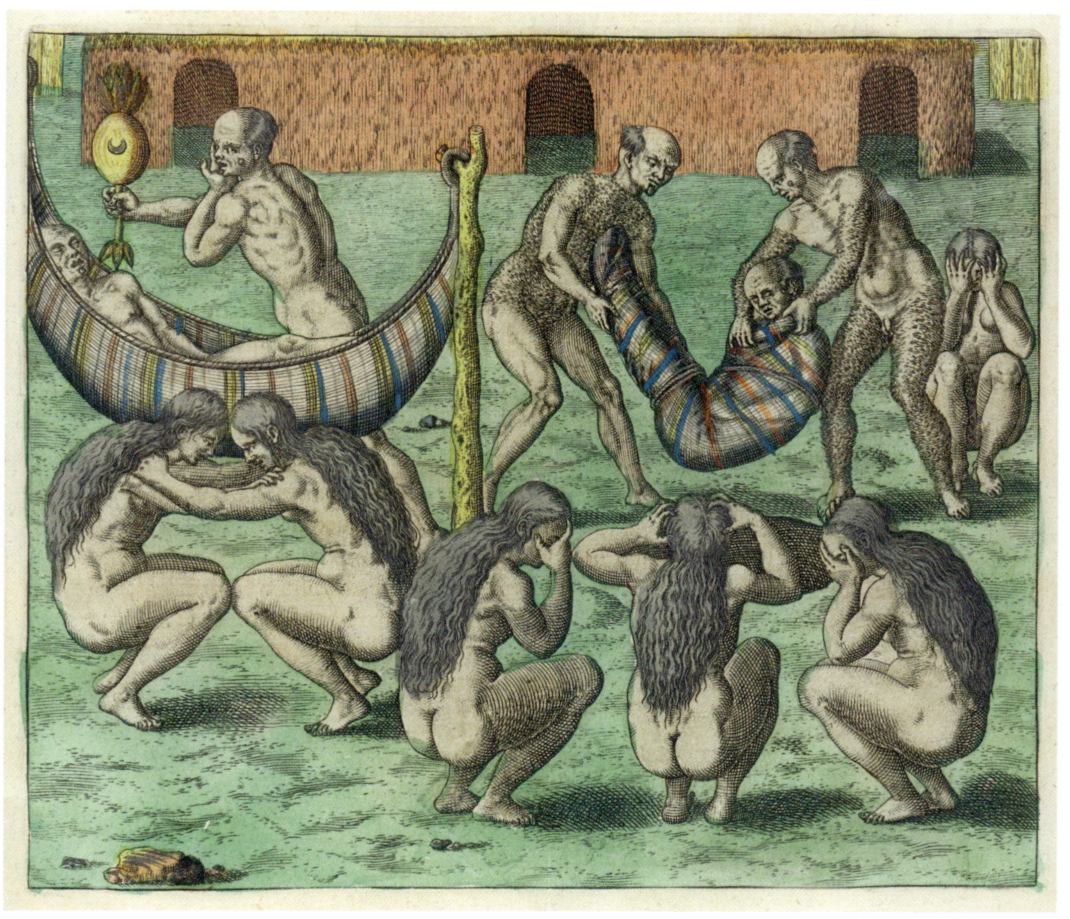

PLATE 15

How the savages went to war, took me with them, and what happened along the way

In four days, some boats were gathered for the purpose of going to war. The commander, Konyan Bebe, was there with his men. My master said to me that he wanted to take me along. I requested to be allowed to stay at home, and he would have done this for me, but Konyan Bebe insisted that I be brought along, and so I was. I let them think that I went unwillingly. That way they would observe me with less suspicion that I would try to run away in the country of their enemy. If they had left me in the village, I would have tried to get to the French ships. They brought me along, however, and we were 38 boats strong, with each boat carrying 18 people. Some had foreseen victory in dreams, through their idols, and other savage foolishness, so that they were all quite confident about the offensive. They made for Brikioka, where they had captured me, and to surround the town. They would capture whoever fell into their hands there. This was on 14 August, 1554. In this month can be seen the fish known in Portuguese as "Doynges", in Spanish as "Liesses" and as "Bratti" in the local language. They come from the sea to fresh water in order to spawn. The savages call this time of year "Pirakaen". The tribes go to war around this time in order to catch the fish and to eat them on their journey. They proceed slowly on the voyage out, but they travel quickly on the return trip.

PLATE 16, PAGES 218/219

How they had a slave who always lied about me and who would have enjoyed to see me killed, but who was killed and eaten himself in my presence

They dragged him in front of King Uratinge's huts, where two men held him. He was so sick that he could not tell what was going on. The one who was to kill him arrived and hit him over the head so that his brains spilled out. Then they let his body lie there in front of the huts and they intended to eat him. I told them not to do this, however, since he had been sick and they did not want to get infected. They were not sure what to do then. At this point, one of them came out of the hut where I was and called to the women to start a fire near the dead body. Then he cut off the head, which had only one eye and was ugly from its disease. He threw the head away and burned the skin off the body at the fire. He then divided up the flesh among the others, in accordance with their customs, and they ate all of him except for his head and intestines, which were afflicted with disease.

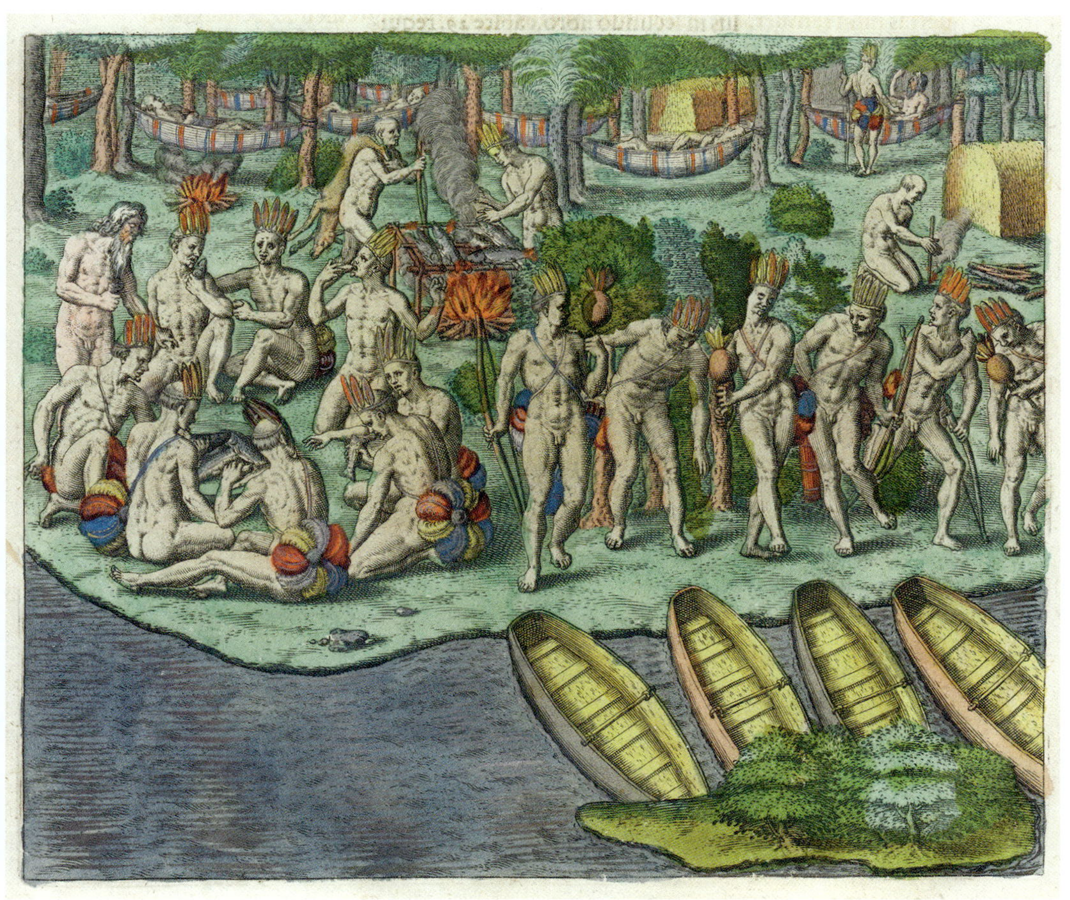

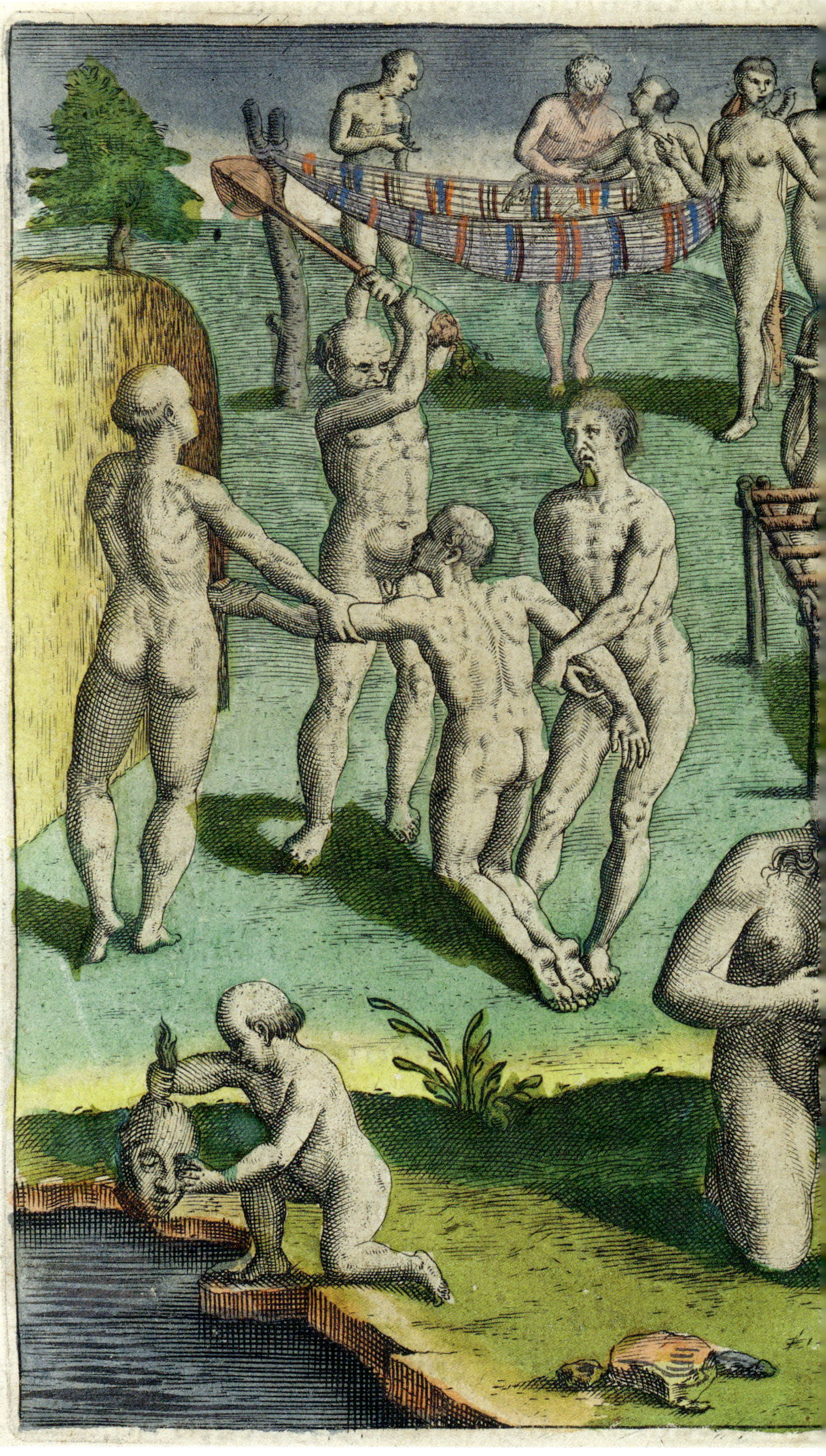

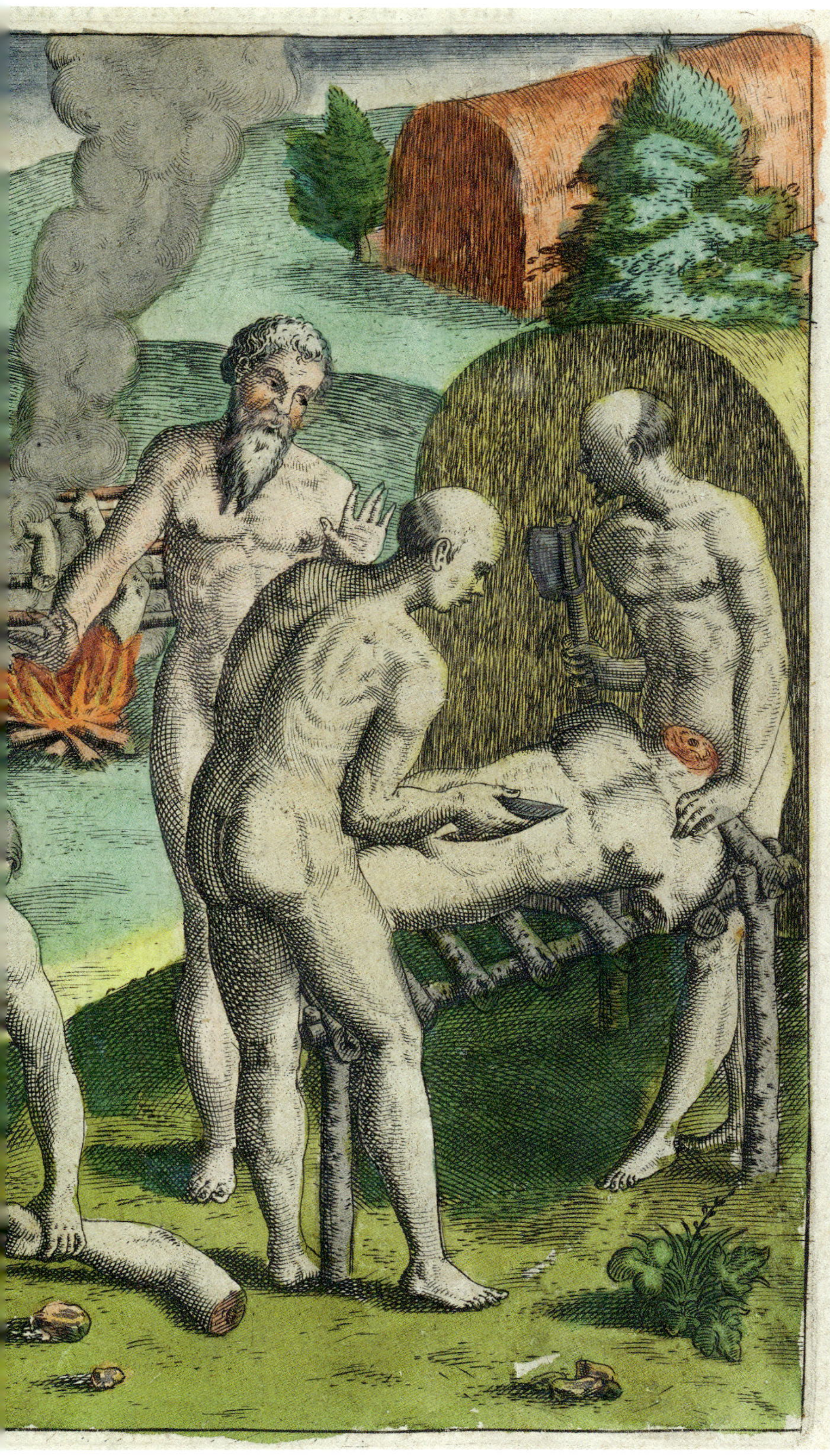

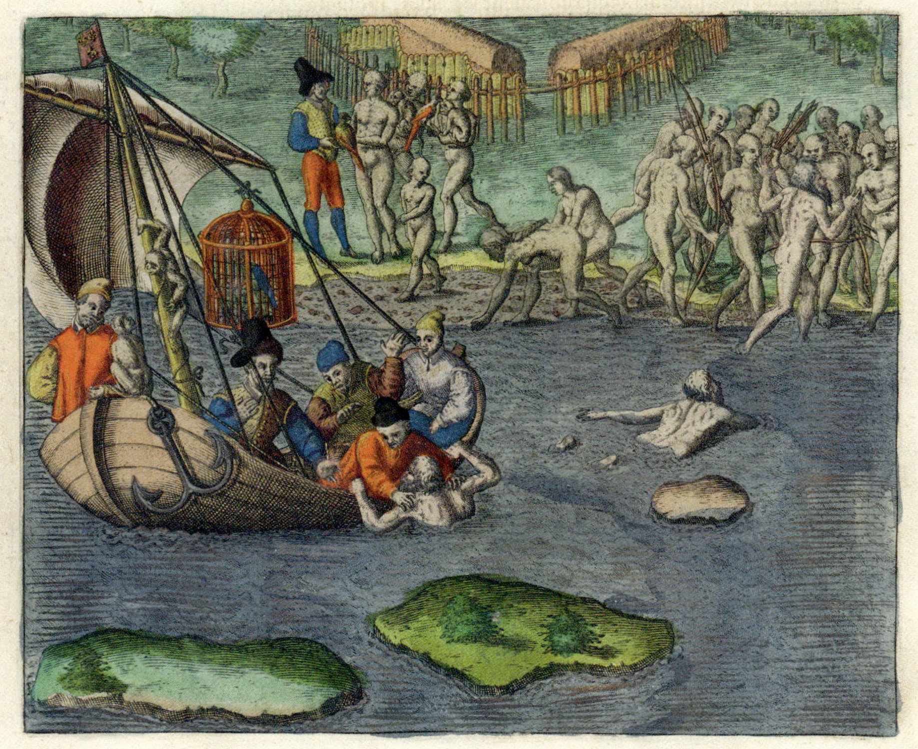

PLATE 17

How a French ship arrived to trade for cotton and Brazilian wood with the savages; I longed to board that ship, but it was not in God's plan

When I saw that the boat was leaving again, I thought, "Oh, gracious God! If that boat leaves without me, I will die here among the savages, who cannot at all be trusted!" I ran out of the hut and towards the water. The savages saw me and some ran after me. I ran ahead, and some tried to grab me. The first of them I was able beat back. The whole village pursued me, but I eluded their grasp and was able to swim to the boat. When I tried to board, however, the French sailors pushed me back and said that if they took me against the will of the savages, they would rise up and become their enemies. At this, I swam back to shore in a gloomy mood. Now I see that it was God's will for me to suffer longer. If I had not tried running away, I would have thought it was my fault. When I returned to shore, the savages were elated. They said, "Look, he's come back!" I told them, "Did you think I would run away?" I explained that I had been to the boat to tell my countrymen to prepare for when the savages returned from war. They should have many wares ready to give to them. This pleased them well.

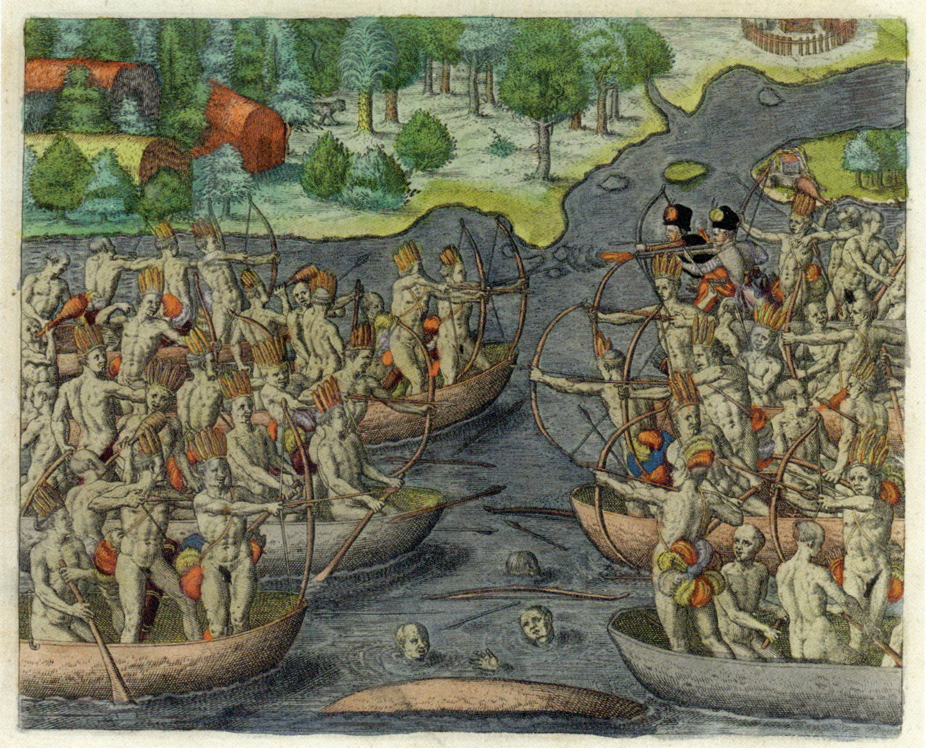

PLATE 18

How they fight against other savages

We continued along the coast and saw boats approaching us from behind the island. They cried out, "Here come our enemies, the Tupinambá!" They wanted to hide behind part of a cliff with their boats so as not to be seen. They noticed us, however, and immediately turned to flee back to their home. We rowed after them as hard as we could for over four hours. We reached them and they had five full boats. All of them were from Brikioka. I knew them all. There were six Mammelucks in one of the boats who had been baptised. There were also two brothers, Diego de Praga and Domingo de Praga. They fought hard against us, one with blow darts and the other with a bow. These two held off our 30 boats for more than two hours. When they ran out of arrows, however, the Tupinambá fell upon them and took them captive. A few were killed on the spot. The brothers were uninjured. Two of the Mammelucks were badly wounded, as well as some of the Tupinambá, including a woman.

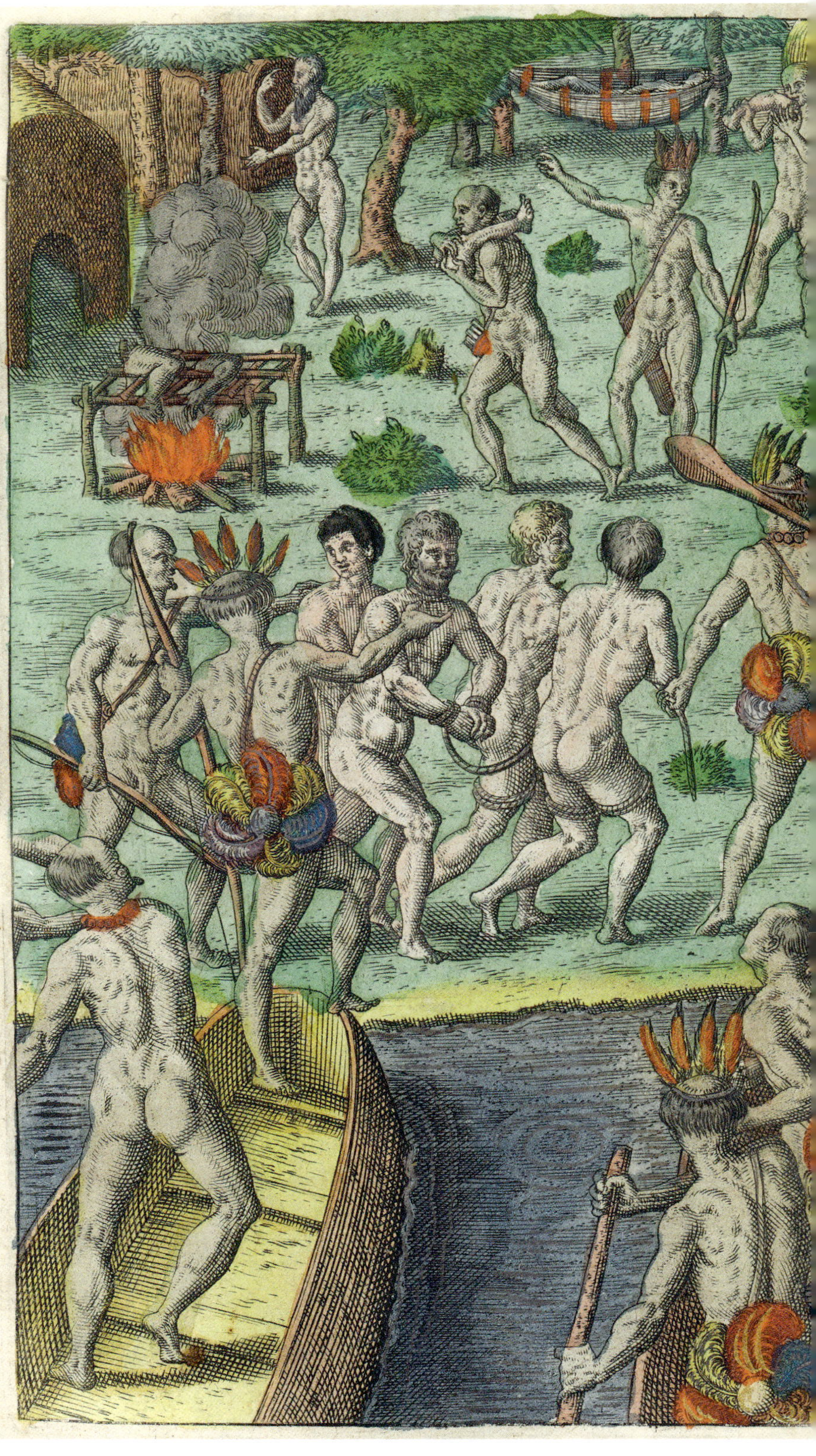

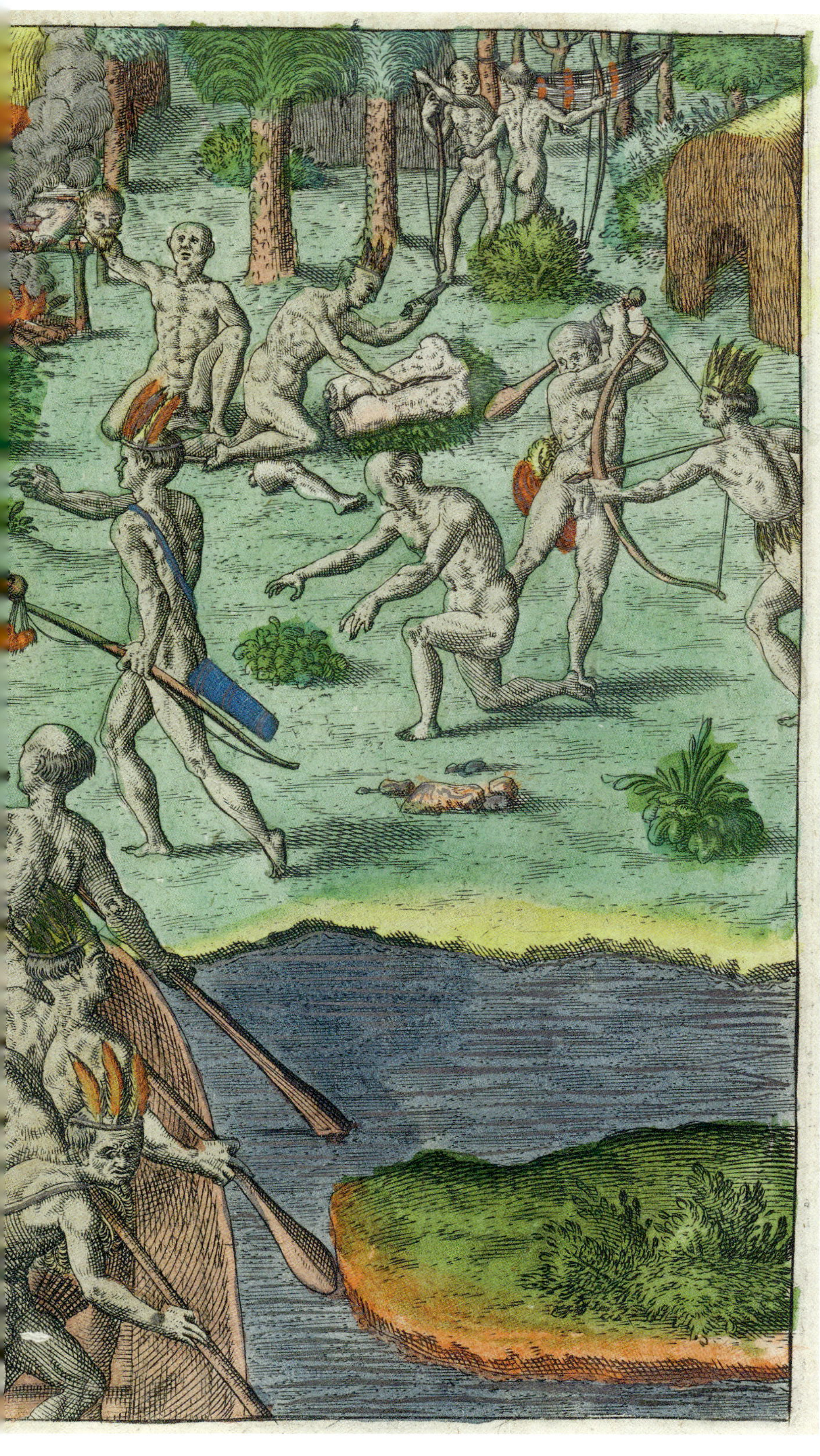

PLATE 19, PAGE 222/223

What they did with the prisoners on the return voyage

When we arrived in Meyen, it was sunset and the savages led each prisoner to his own hut. Those who were badly injured, however, were simply brought on to land and struck dead. They were then cut into pieces, as is their custom, and their flesh was cooked. Among those who were killed and eaten that night were two Christian Mammelucks. One was a Portuguese named George Herrero, whose father was a captain and whose mother was a savage. Another was named Hieronymus, who had been caught by a savage named Parwaa who lived in my hut. Parwaa cooked the body of Hieronymus a few steps from where I lay. Hieronymus had been a blood relative of Diego de Praga.

PLATE 20

How the savages, whose prisoner I was, keep their dwellings

They have their dwellings before the aforementioned large mountain, right by the sea, and stretching back 60 miles behind the mountain. There is a river that flows down from the mountain to the sea, along which they have dwellings for about 28 miles. They have enemies on all sides. They share their northern border with the Weittaka savages. Their southern border is next to the Tupinambá, who are also their enemies. The Wayganna live in the mountain towards the shore. The Markaya, who live between them and the Wayganna, give them the most trouble. These races regularly make war with each other, and whoever wins eats the other. They have their dwellings in places where water, wood, fish and game are readily available. A commander organises 40 or more couples to live there as friends and family. They build houses that are about 14 feet wide and 150 feet long, depending on how many live there. The hut is open inside without room divisions. Each couple has a space of about 12 feet inside the hut, and each couple has their own fire. The leader of the hut also has lodging there. Few villages have more than seven huts. They leave space between the buildings where they kill their prisoners. They also tend to build fortifications around their huts as follows: they build a stockade around the huts out of the trunks of palm trees. The stockade is about one fathom high. It is made thick, so that arrows cannot penetrate it. They have small holes for shooting arrows out. Around that stockade they build another with very tall staves. Sometimes the skulls of those who have been eaten are set on the posts before the entrance to the huts.

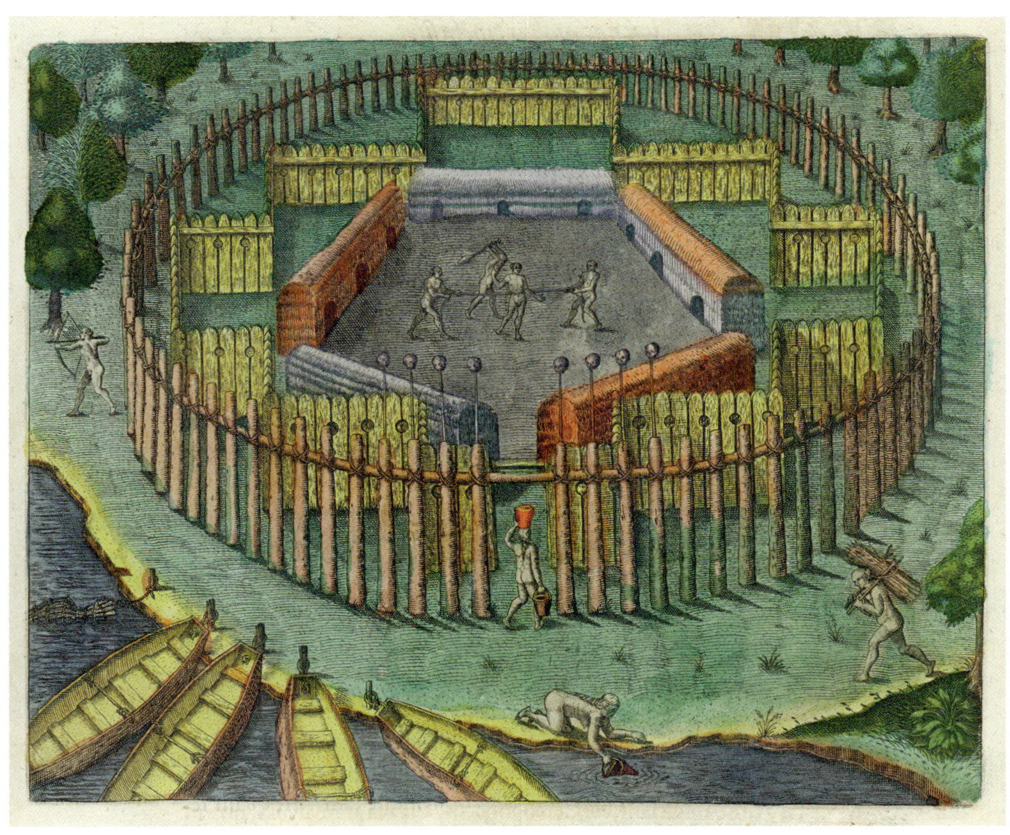

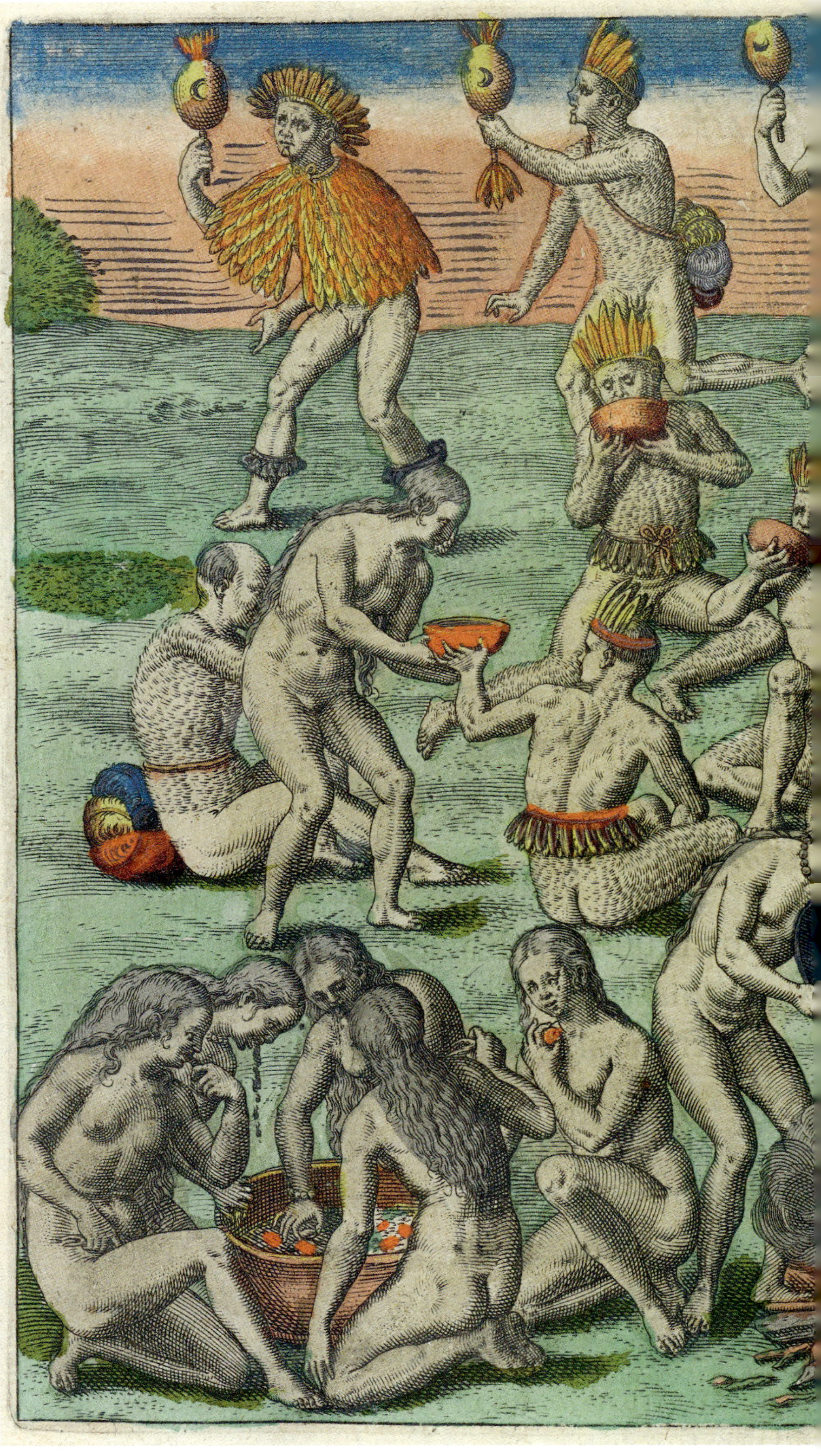

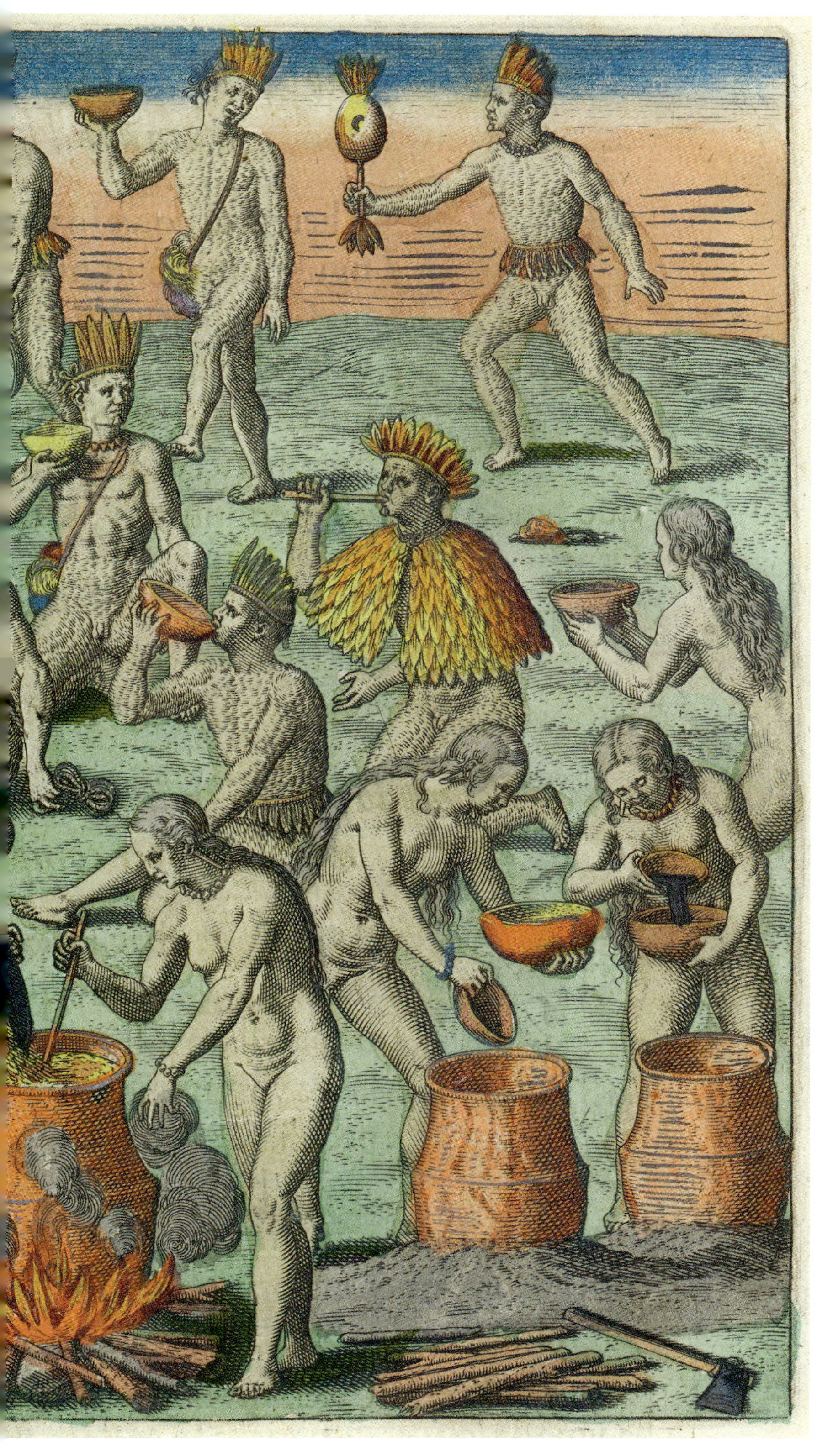

PLATE 21, PAGES 226/227

How they make their drink, which they drink until they are drunk, and how they drink it

The women make the drinks. They take Mandioka root and boil big vats full of it. Once it has boiled, they take it out of the vats and transfer it to other vessels to cool. Young girls are then made to sit next to it and chew it in their mouths. The chewed parts go into yet other vessels. When the boiled roots are all chewed, they put them back into the vats. The vats are once again filled with water and brought to a boil. They have special vessels that are half buried in the ground, which they use similarly to the way we use casks for wine and beer. They pour the concoction into these and seal them up tightly. It ferments there and becomes strong. They let it sit there for two days, then they drink it and get drunk. It is thick and tastes good. Each hut makes its own drink. When a village wants to celebrate with drinking, which they tend to do once a month, they all go into one of the huts and drink. Then they move down the line of houses until all of the drinks brewed in the different huts are gone. They sit all around the vessel and drink there. The women serve the drinks in a particular order. Some stand, drink and dance around the vessel. They also urinate there in the spot where they drink. They drink all night and dance between the fires. They cry out and blow trumpets, making terrible noises the drunker they get. They rarely fight in these situations. They are very generous with each other. If one has more food than another, he always shares.

PLATE 22

Their ceremonies for killing and eating their enemies

When they bring enemies to their village, they are first beaten by the women and children. They paint their enemy with a grey feather, shave off his eyebrows and dance around him. They give him a woman, who looks after him and has intercourse with him. When she becomes pregnant, the child is raised until it is full-grown. They kill and eat the child when it occurs to them to do so. They take care of him a long while. They give him food to eat and furnish him with everything he needs. They prepare drinks in the special vessels they use for keeping the pigments with which they paint him. They make feather tassels and tie them to the club they use to kill him. They prepare a long cord, called a "Mussurana", and tie it to him when he is to die. They decide the time to kill him after they have prepared all of this. They invite savages from other villages to come along. They pour a vessel full of drink. One or two days before the women prepare the drink, the enemy is led to the place where he will die and everyone dances around him. When all the people who have travelled from beyond the village are gathered together, the chief gives a speech welcoming them. He says, "Now come and help to eat your enemy!" The day before they start drinking, they tie the Mussurana cord around the throat of the captive. They paint the club – the "Iwera Pemme" – on the same day, which is smeared with a sticky substance. Then they take grey eggshells that come from a bird called a Mackukawa. They grind this up very finely and spread it on the club. Then a woman sits with it and draws in the powdered eggshells. Once the Iwera Pemme is ready, they hang it on a pole and sing around it all night long.

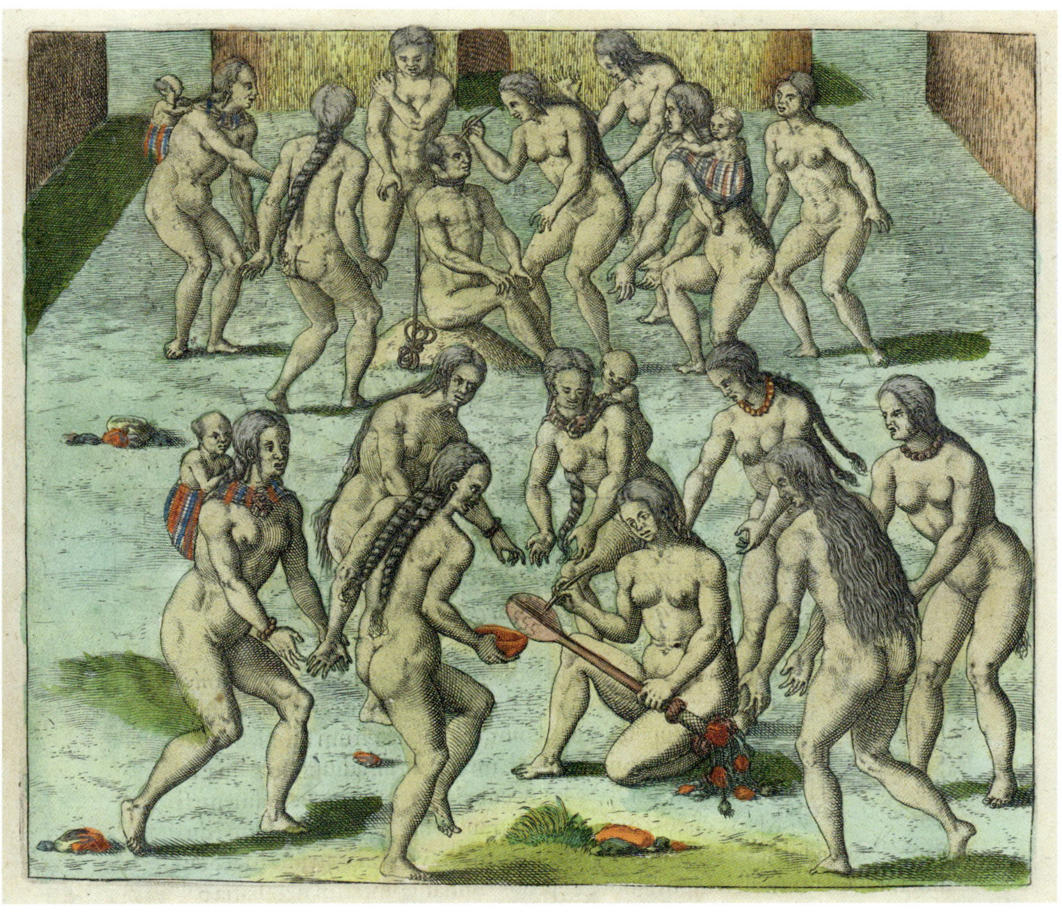

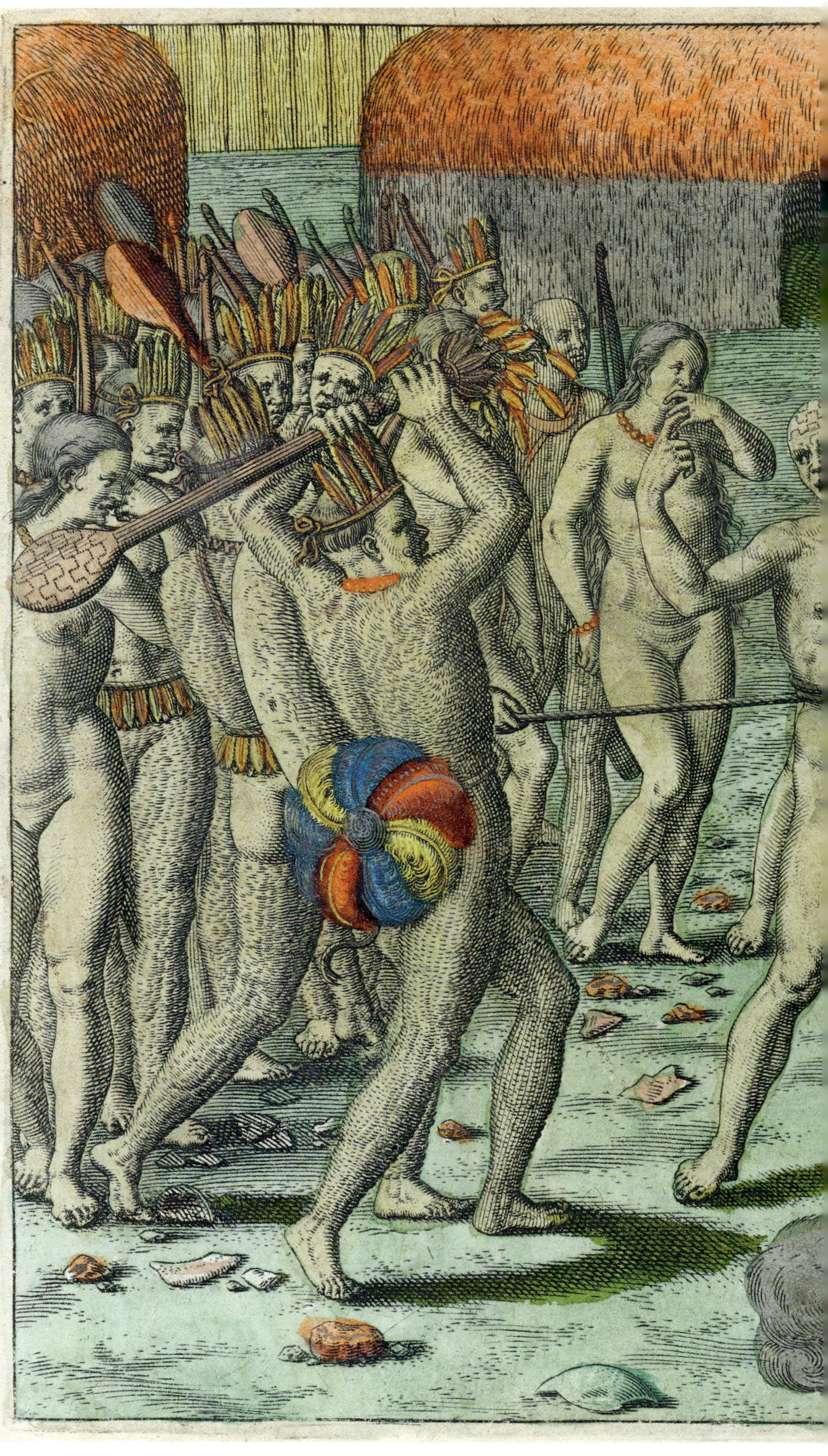

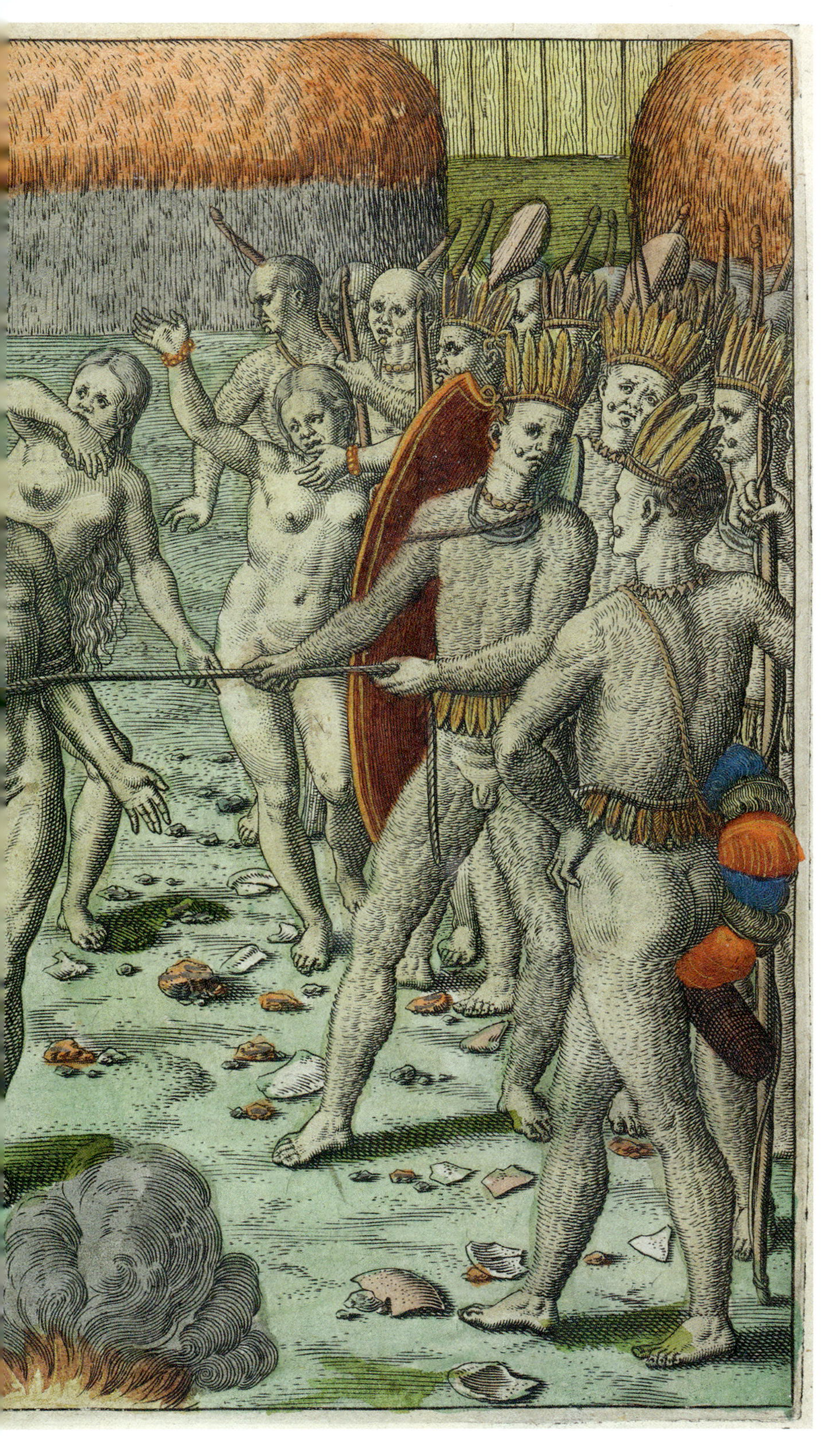

PLATE 23, PAGES 230/231

Their ceremonies for killing and eating their enemies (continued)

They paint the prisoner's face in the same way. While one woman paints his face, the others sing. When they begin to drink, they include the prisoner in drinking and conversation. They make the prisoner a little hut where he will be killed and he lies there guarded throughout the night. A little while before sunrise the next morning, they dance and sing around the club. Then they bring the prisoner out of the little hut, untie the Mussurana from around his neck, tie it around his torso and pull both ends of the cord taut. He stands tied up in the middle of them, and many of them hold the ends of the cord. They let him stand like this a while and place stones beside him for him to throw at the women, who during this time run around threatening to eat him. Then they make a fire about two steps from the prisoner. A woman comes with the Iwera Pemme club, turning the feathers uppermost and shrieking with joy. After this, a man takes the club and steps in front of the prisoner. In the meantime, the man who is supposed to kill him goes with 14 or 15 others to make their bodies grey with ashes. Then he returns with these men to the place of execution, where the club is passed to him. Then the king of the huts takes the club. He puts it between the legs of the executioner, takes the club again and says, "Yes, here I am, I who will kill you. Your people have killed and eaten many of my friends." The prisoner responds, "Once I am dead, I will still have many friends, who will come and avenge me." At this, the executioner strikes him over the back of the head with his club, so hard that his brains spill out. The women immediately seize his body and drag it into the fire. Everyone tears at his skin, which makes him totally white, and they plug his rear with some wood so that nothing escapes out of him.

PLATE 24

Their ceremonies for killing and eating their enemies (continued)

Once his skin has been removed, a man comes and cuts off the legs from above the knee and the arms from against the torso. The women take these pieces and go to the different huts with them, screaming with joy. Then they cut his back and rear and separate them from his front, all of which they divide amongst themselves.

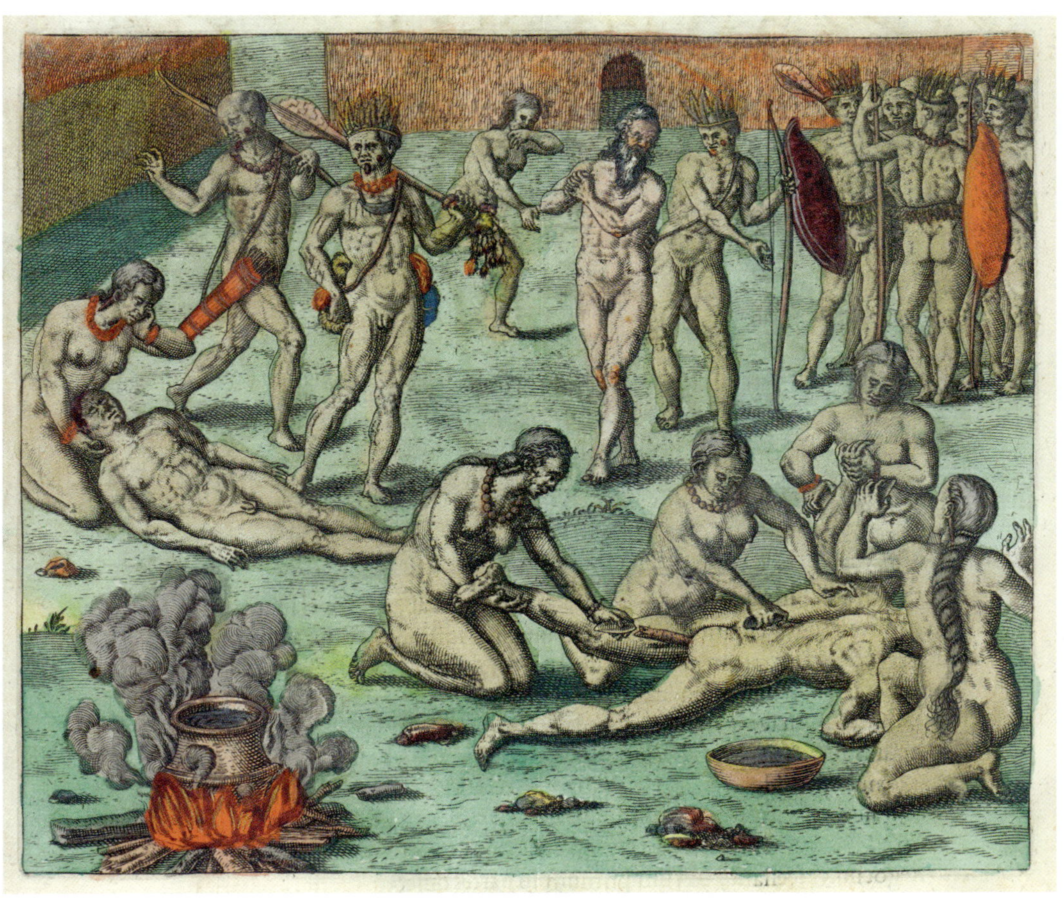

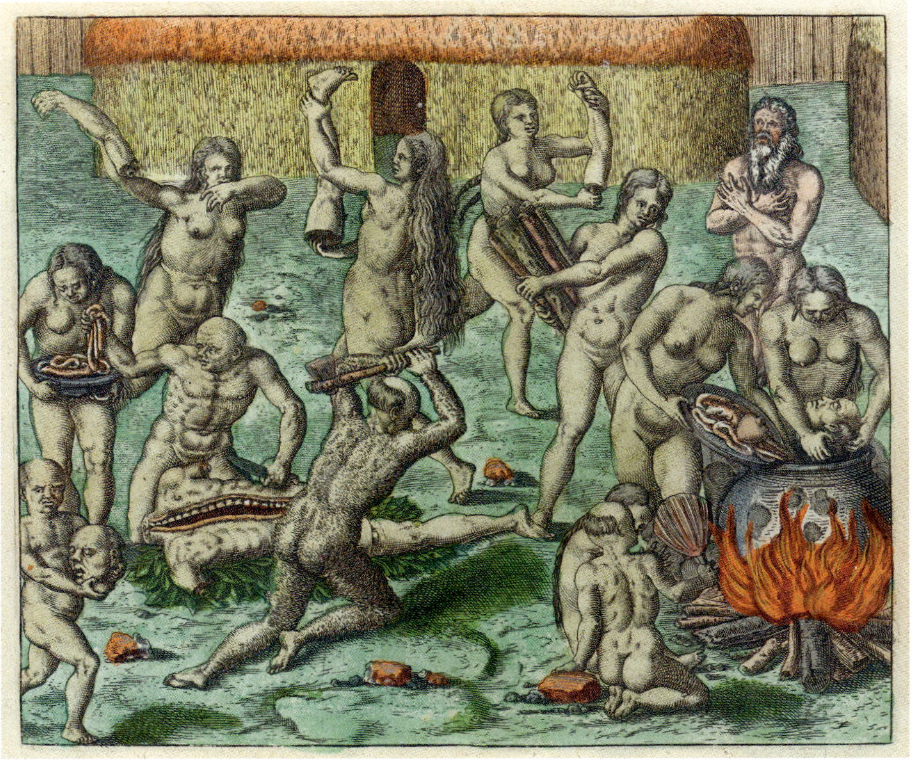

PLATE 25

Their ceremonies for killing and eating their enemies (continued)

Once the prisoner has been slaughtered, his wife cries over his body for a while (as was mentioned before, the prisoners are given wives). This is not so terrible, however. They cry over the body before they eat it, as has also been attributed to the crocodile. Although she is crying over the body of her husband, she is also the first to eat of his flesh, and when she does, he is for her a very different person. Then the old women come with boiling water to rub the dead body. They wash it so thoroughly that it becomes as white as a suckling pig that would be just right for skewering. The young men, who keep hold of the rope tied around the prisoner, regularly have to drive the old women away since they are so hungry for the flesh they are preparing and try to rush ahead of the ceremony.

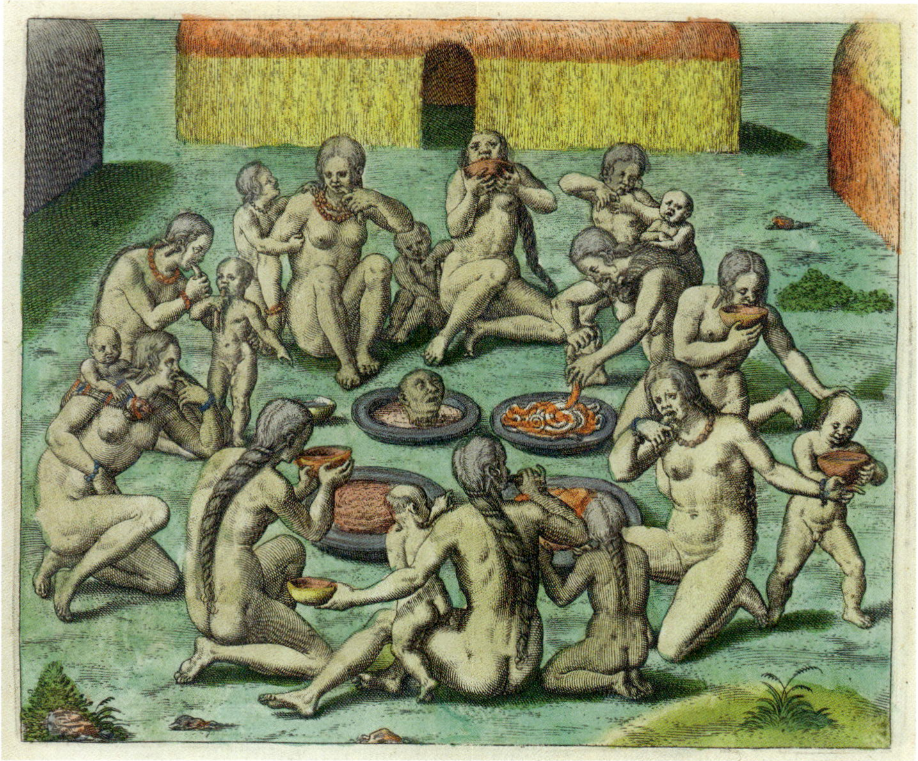

PLATE 26

Their ceremonies for killing and eating their enemies (continued)

The intestines, however, are for the women. They are boiled and the resultant broth is made into a paste, which they call "Mingau". They drink this with their children. They eat the bowels, skin and head with the brain and tongue. Whatever is left that is edible is given to the children. After this, everyone goes home, taking their share with them. The executioner gives himself an extra name and the king scratches the upper part of his arm with an animal tooth. The scar remains visible once this has healed, and this is an honour. The king must lie quietly in a hammock the rest of the day. He takes a bow and arrow to pass the time by shooting wax. This is done so that his arm does not become unsure from the terrible death blow. I witnessed all of this myself.

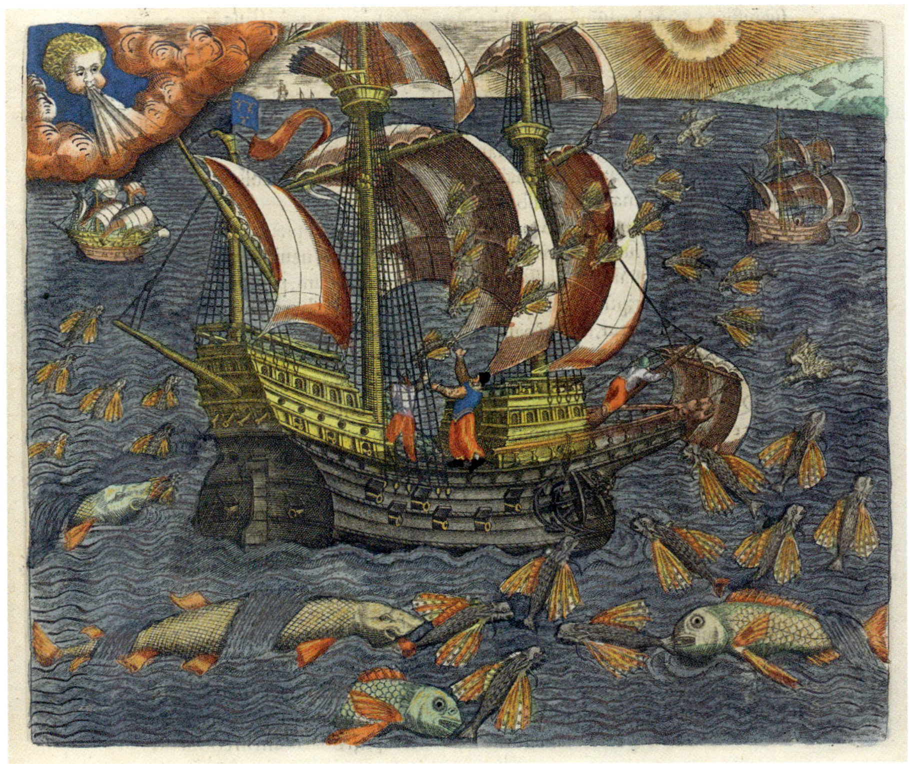

PLATE 27

Of the bonet fish, albacore, auratus, porpoises, and of flying fish with wings that we not only saw in the light of day, but actually caught

Along the third equatorial degree we saw very large numbers of porpoises and auratus fish. We also caught many albacore and bonet fish. There were also flying fish. When my fellow sailors first told me about these, I thought they were making fun of me. Then I saw them with my own eyes. They lift themselves into the air in large groups, go as high as a long spear and as far as 100 feet across the water. They often bump into the masts midflight, fall down, and are then easily caught with the hands. They are similar to a herring, although this one is a bit longer and rounder. It has a downy feather under its throat, and wings like a bat's, which extend outwards. Since I had never seen one of these in the Tropic of Cancer, I at first assumed that they stayed in the tropics for the warmth and would therefore not be found near the poles. I have since read, however, that terns have been seen in the Strait of Magellan and in the South Sea. I believe that these two are the same creature. I also observed that these flying fish were pursued by predators wherever they went. Under water, they were hunted by the albacores, but then if they took flight they were caught and eaten by various seabirds.

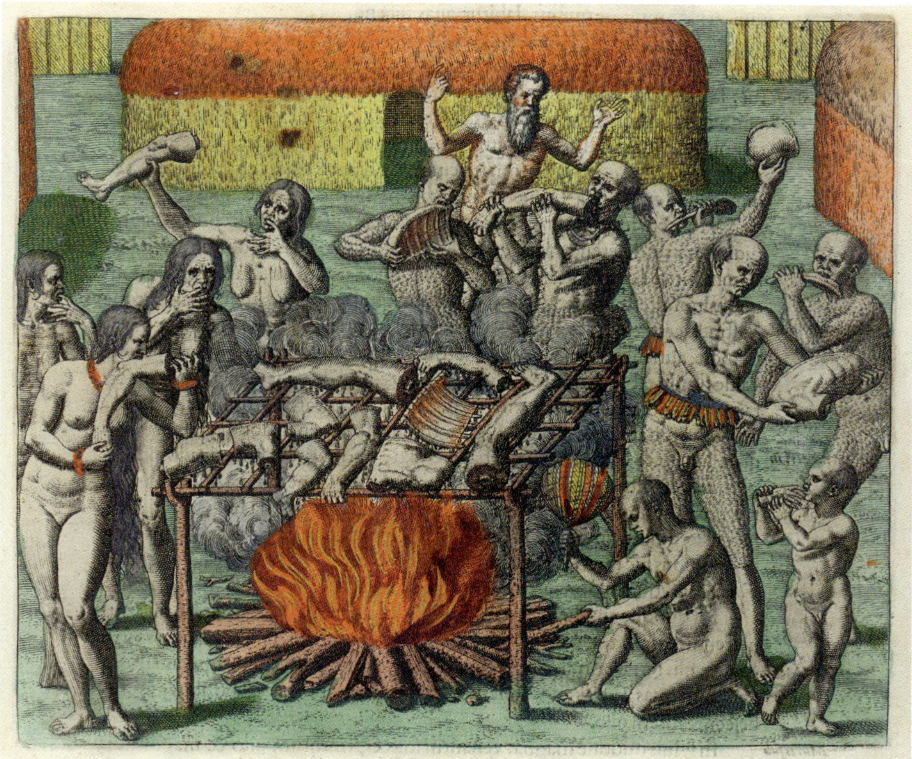

PLATE 28

The "Bucan", and how they preserve their meat

The savages set four posts in the ground that are about as thick as a human arm. These are set at four points, forming a square where each post is about three feet from the others. Then they lay sticks over these, with each stick separated from the other by about two feet. These form a wooden grill, which they call a "Bucan" in their language. There are many such grills in the individual huts. They cook their meat on it, which they cut into pieces. They set dry wood underneath and make a gentle fire that produces almost no excess smoke. A cook tends to the meat, cooking it there for as long as he feels is right, flipping it twice over two hours. They do not salt their food, as is common in our country, but they have other methods of preserving meat. If they catch 30 animals on the hunt, they cut them into pieces and put them on the grill, layering them as much as they can. The meat is often cooked there for 24 hours until it is thoroughly cooked inside and out. The meat will keep after this for a long time.

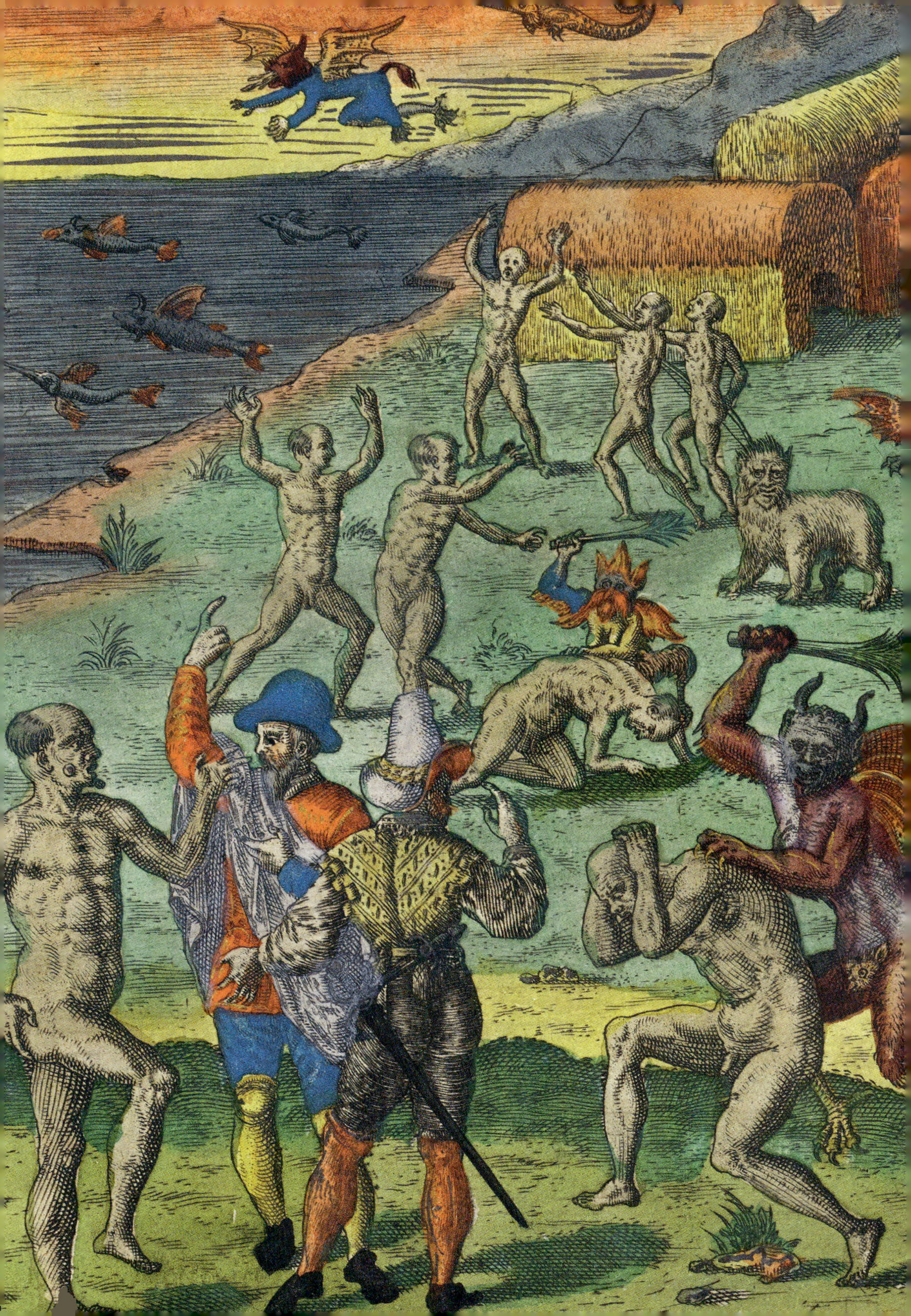

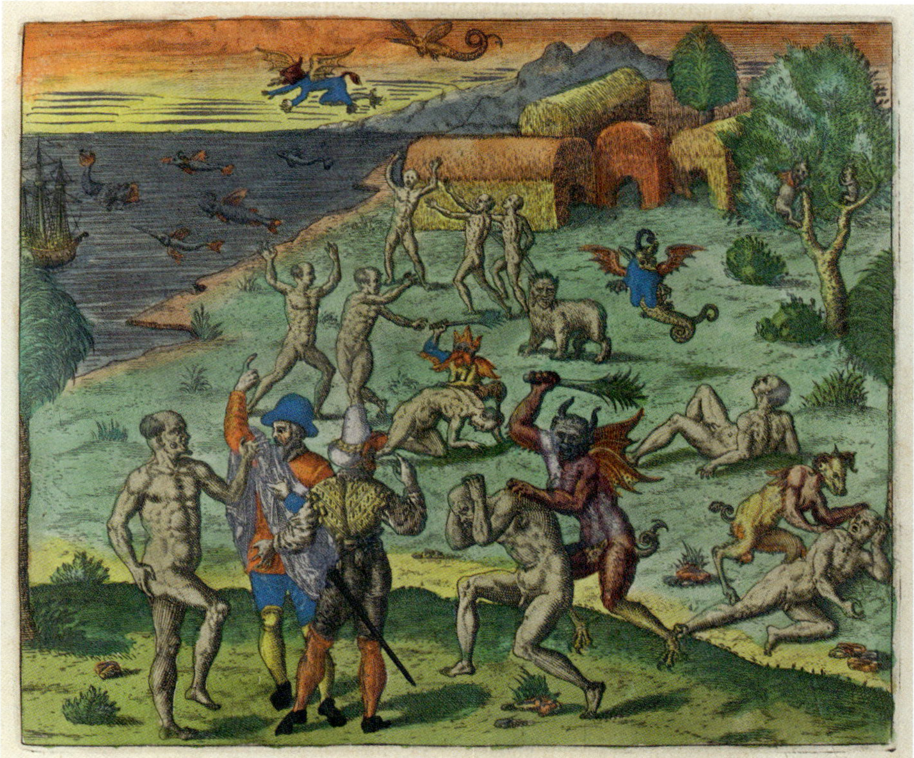

PLATE 29

How they deal with Aygnan, the Devil

Now the savages are also afflicted in this life by the Devil, whom they refer to as "Kaagerre" and I have seen him and his activities with my own eyes. When we were talking with them, they began in the middle of the conversation to scream and cry out. They were frantic, calling out, "Hey, hey, help us! Aygnan is beating us!" They say that they see the Devil in the form of an animal, usually a bird. Sometimes they see him in other terrible forms. It amazes them that this evil spirit does no harm to us. We tell them that the God we are always praying to protects us from afflictions that are even greater than Aygnan, and because of this we do not worry about him at all. However, I will attest to having seen the sweat of anxiety breaking out on them and to have seen their legs collapse beneath them. They cry out in desperation: "Maier, Atouraflap, Aceque i cy Aygnan Atoupaué", which translates as, "Oh, you dear fool, oh, my good companion, I am far more afraid of the Devil than of any other evil." One of us said to them then, "Nacequeie Aygnan", or, "But I did not ask about the Devil". They cried miserably at this and said, "Oh, we would be such blissful people if we were as sure as you." We told them that they should have faith in Him who is more powerful than Aygnan. Even if they promise to do this in the throes of agony, however, they revert to their old ways as soon as it has passed.

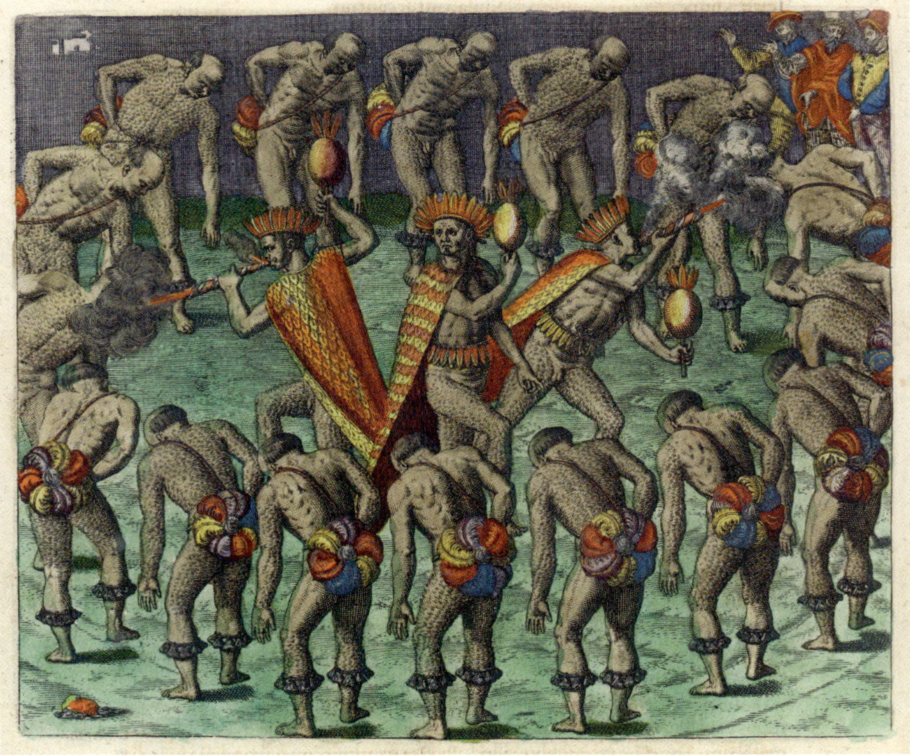

PLATE 30

How they reach out to the spirits

They stand in a circle, with each one hanging on to the other. They do not link together by the hand, however, but rather bend over slightly and tap their right foot with their right hand resting on their buttock. The left hand hangs straight down. They do this when they sing and dance. The savages form this circle, and in the middle of the circle are three or four Caribs. They wear hats, clothes and armbands decorated with feathers. Each holds two maracas, which are the rattles I described earlier. They are made from a fruit that is similar in form, but a little bigger than an ostrich egg. They use it to bring the spirits into conversation with them. In the following picture I have illustrated how the dancers and Caribs move in the circle. The Caribs go behind and in front of each other while they dance. They do not stand in one place, as the others do. I also observed them regularly going around with a long pipe in which they burned tobacco. They went around to the dancers and blew smoke in their faces with the following words, "Bring unto yourself the spirit of power so that you may conquer your enemies." This happened often. The ceremonies lasted two hours and the men all sang and leaped about. Their voices and harmonies went together so delightfully, that someone who has never heard it would scarcely believe it could be possible. It is all the more remarkable in so far as the savages comprehend nothing of music.

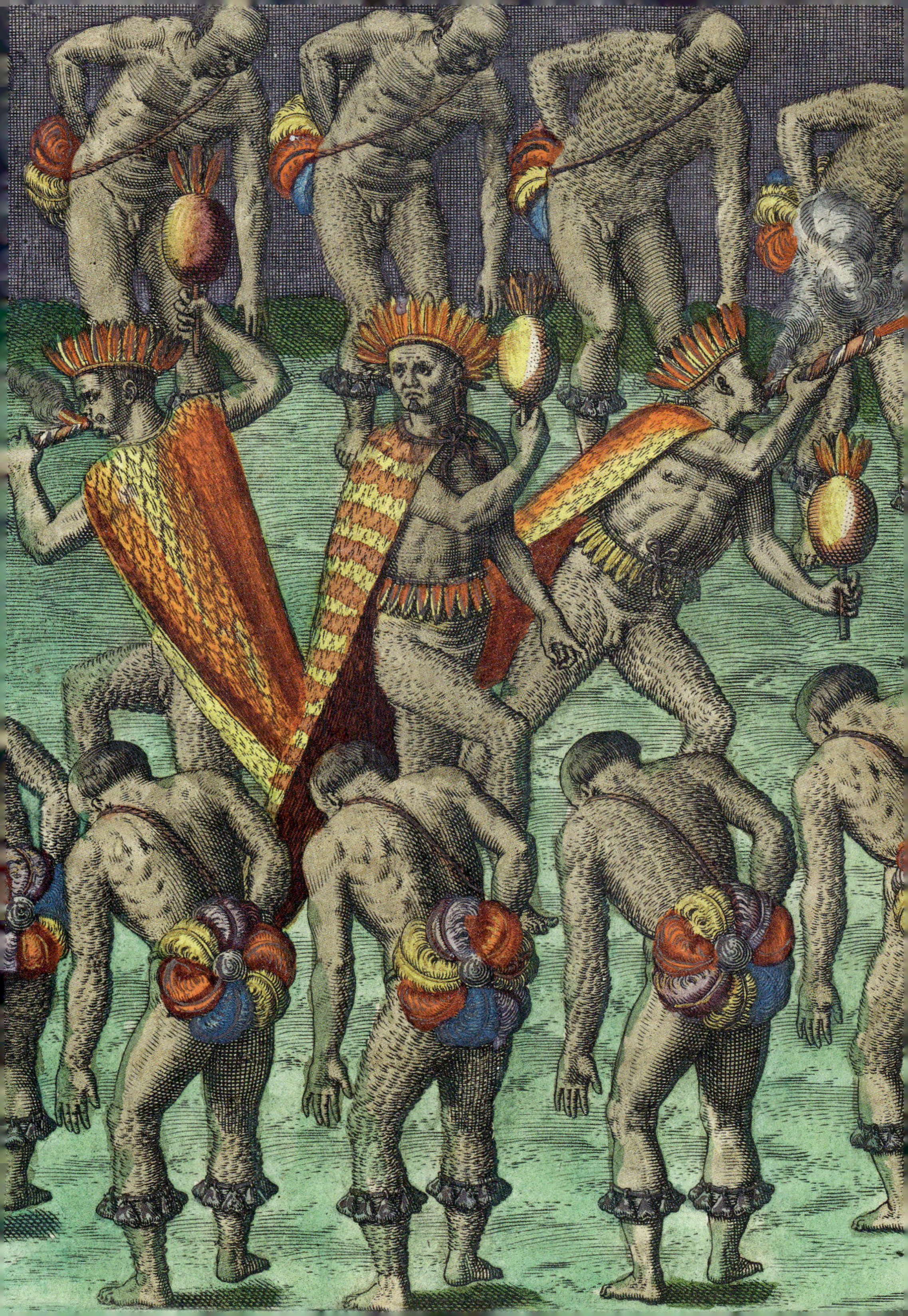

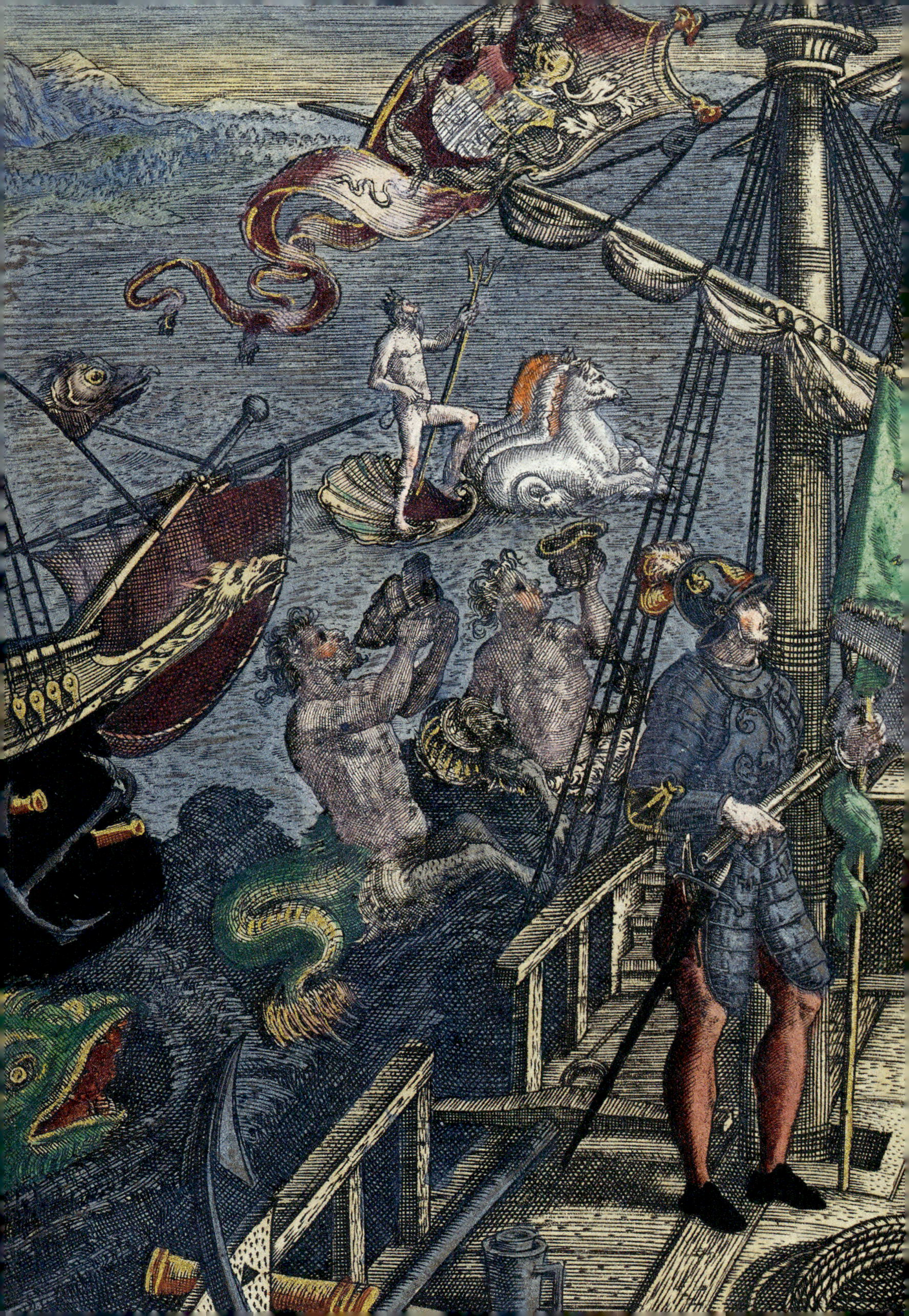

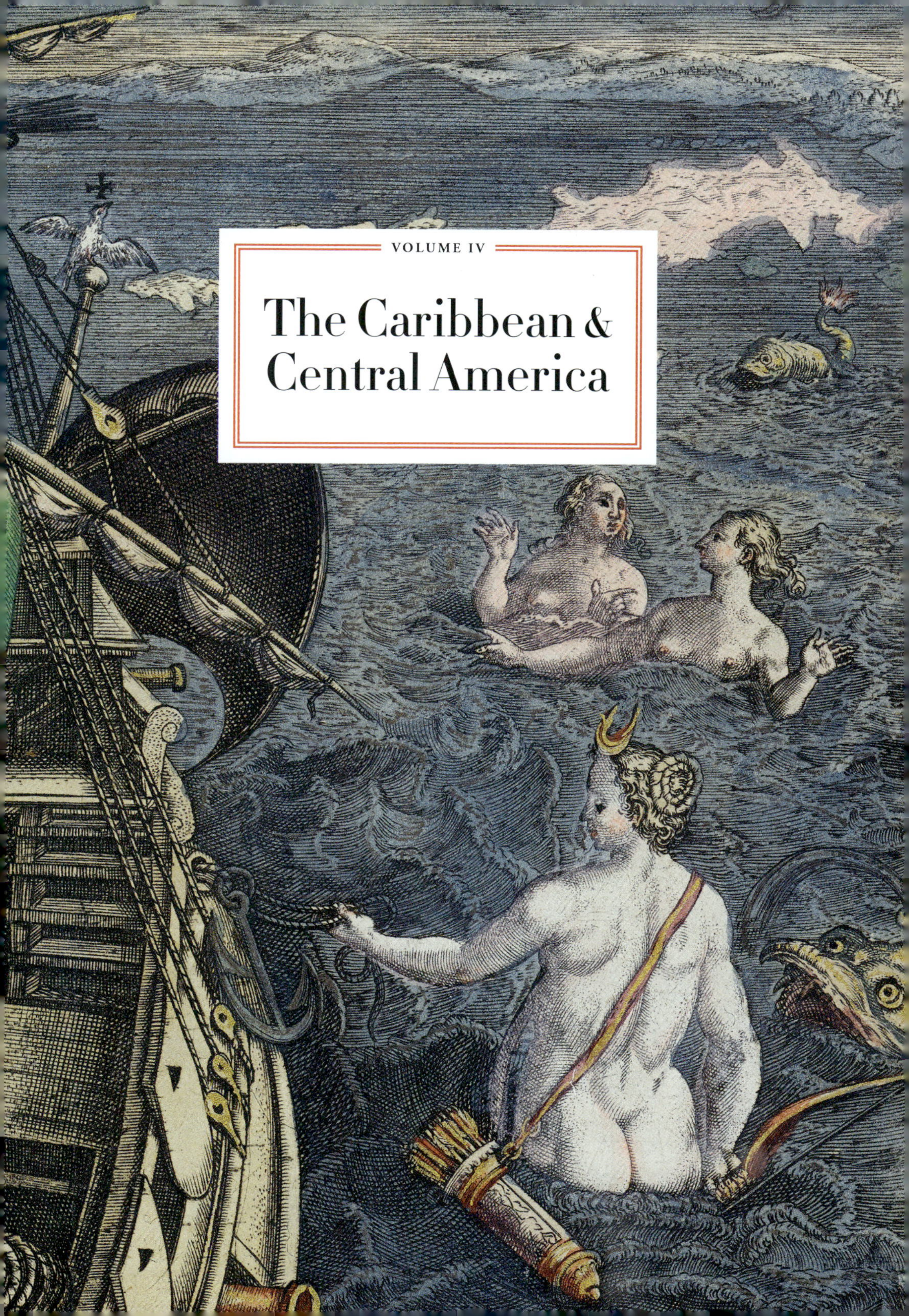
VOLUME IV
The Caribbean & Central America

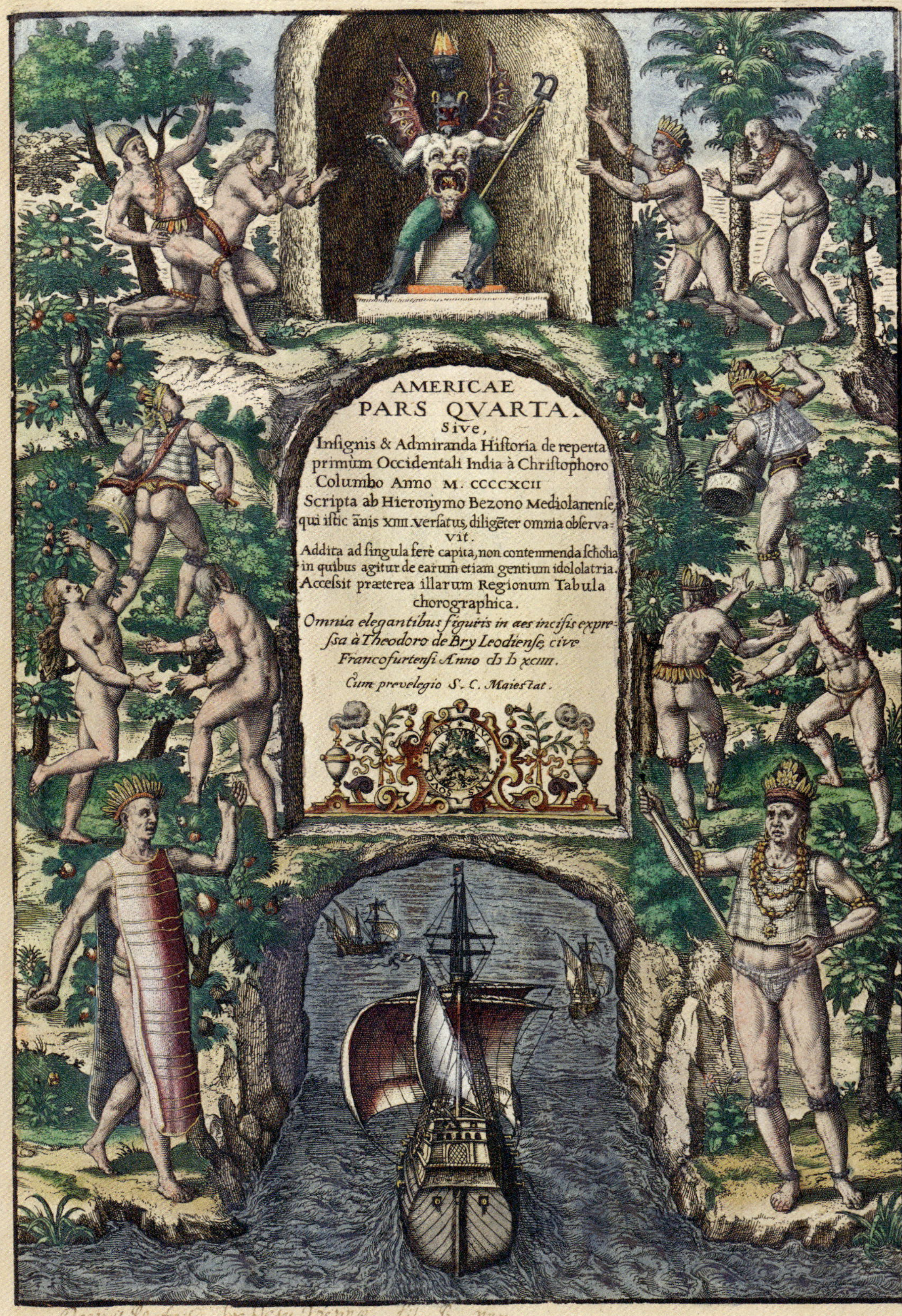

AMERICAE
PARS QVARTA.
Sive,
Insignis & Admiranda Historia de reperta
primùm Occidentali India à Christophoro
Columbo Anno M. CCCCXCII
Scripta ab Hieronymo Bezono Mediolanense,
qui istic ãnis XIIII. versatus, diligẽter omnia observa-
vit.
Addita ad singula ferè capita, non contemnenda scholia
in quibus agitur de earum etiam gentium idololatria.
Accessit præterea illarum Regionum Tabula
chorographica.
Omnia elegantibus figuris in aes incisis expre-
ssa à Theodoro de Bry Leodiense, cive
Francofurtensi Anno cIↃ IↃ XCIII.

Cum prevelegio S. C. Maiestat.

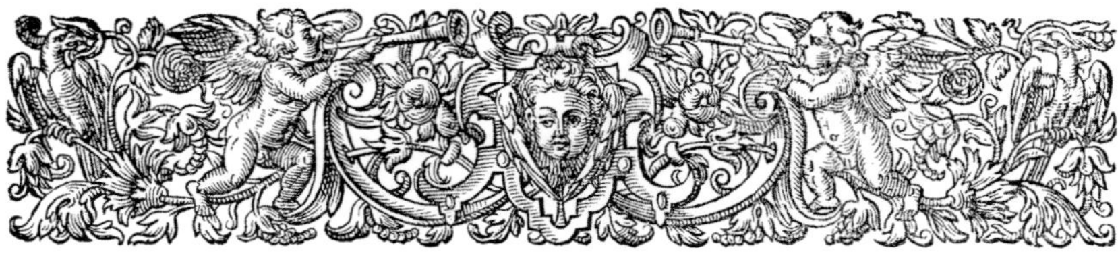

Volume IV

Based on: Girolamo Benzoni, *Historia del Mondo Nuovo* (Milan, 1565), subsequently published in several editions

Girolamo Benzoni was a Milanese traveller who left his hometown for Spain in 1541, and then sailed to the Americas where he spent 15 years in several regions under Spanish rule. Unlike all the other travellers whose accounts the De Brys incorporated in the *America* series, Benzoni visited many different provinces of the New World, from the Greater Antilles in the north to Peru in the south. His observations throughout are mainly characterised by his criticism of the Spanish noblemen whose conduct he witnessed first-hand. Even so, Benzoni was not a very systematic and reliable observer, while he also copied earlier writers uncritically, such as Peter Martyr d'Anghiera and Francisco López de Gómara, and more than once in his extensive account he contradicts himself. For the De Brys, this presented a further challenge, and their sequence of illustrations and captions reveals that they struggled to put all of Benzoni's observations in the right order and context.

Benzoni's critical assessment of the behaviour of the conquistadors emerged at a politically explosive moment in Europe, at a time when the treatment of Native Americans was being hotly debated by various theologians in Spain. The most famous account of greed and misconduct in the West Indies, written by the Dominican friar (and former bishop of Chiapas in Mexico) Bartolomé de Las Casas, contained vehement criticism of the Spanish crown and the lower Spanish nobility who exploited the natural riches and the people of the New World for their own personal benefit. Benzoni almost certainly copied some of his observations from Las Casas's *Brevísima relación*, which appeared in Seville in 1552 and was eagerly translated throughout early modern Europe, especially in Protestant areas where booksellers and readers alike saw in Las Casas's account objective proof of the 'tyrannical' and corrupt behaviour of the Spanish elite.

Frontispiece of volume IV

Pages 242/243
Detail of volume IV, plate 6

Benzoni's account thus came to stand alongside the *Brevísima relación* as one of the key pillars of the so-called Black Legend – a term for historical writing that took a line in anti-Spanish propaganda.

That Benzoni's account provided a watered-down version of Las Casas's biting criticism was probably one of the reasons the Italian text appealed to the De Brys. By the time they began work on their collection of voyages, graphically illustrated editions of Las Casas's account were being circulated in Protestant Europe, and the De Brys added to this by publishing their own version, with the famous illustrations of murder and bloodshed by Jodocus van Winghe, in 1598 – in both German and Latin as they were accustomed to doing for the voyages. But crucially the De Bry version of Las Casas was never made part of the collection, and remained a separate publication. In this way the potential controversy the book might have caused in the Habsburg monarchies in Spain and Portugal would be reserved for a single work from the De Bry firm, but would not automatically be extended to their lucrative collection of voyages.

The De Brys separated Benzoni's account into three parts, which were issued as volumes IV (1594), V (1595) and VI (1596) of the *America* series. Volume IV in particular contains several striking images of European colonialism in the Americas, many of which were in fact invented by the De Brys themselves (Benzoni's second Italian edition of 1572 contained only a handful of crude woodcuts). The mythical story of Columbus's egg – with the captain explaining to his crew that finding America was nothing more than a creative mind solving an old puzzle – was first printed by Benzoni but first illustrated by the De Brys. The depiction of Columbus's arrival on a beach on Hispaniola in 1492, being immediately approached by natives presenting him with their gold, has been used and adapted so often for book covers and posters that it is easy to forget it was invented by the De Brys only a full century after Columbus's encounter first took place. The dreamlike engraving of Ferdinand Magellan circumnavigating the world in 1522 was inspired by allegorical images by the Antwerp artist Johannes Stradanus, but attained its wider popularity after being included in *America* IV. Of course, none of these events had been witnessed by Benzoni in person, who merely alluded to them in his account in order to summarise events in the New World before he arrived there in the early 1540s. Selecting these episodes for depiction was therefore another significant aspect of the De Brys' editorial strategy. They were keen to use Benzoni's narrative of the emergence of Spanish America after their first three volumes had focused on later developments in Virginia, Florida and Brazil. Volume IV then set the tone for the next three *America* volumes by emphasising Spanish atrocities, which, by the time the De Bry edition appeared in 1594, had been experienced directly by many Europeans. But the general message of the De Brys was not exclusively anti-Spanish in nature. Some of the early images, as well as the very last engraving in this volume's sequence of illustrations, strongly emphasise the uncivilised and un-Christian behaviour of the Native Americans, just as Thomas Harriot, René de Laudonnière and Hans Staden had done in their respective accounts. By choosing to highlight not the innocence but instead the savage nature of the Indians, the De Brys in this volume laid the groundwork for what would become the main theme in their entire collection. Portrayals of heathendom and a general lack of native sophistication would henceforth take centre stage, often presented in sharp contrast to the level of civilised behaviour the Europeans had achieved over the centuries. This message became particularly evident in the years after the death of Theodore de Bry, when Johan Theodore and Johan Israel took control of the collection's illustrations.

Detail of volume IV, plate 21

Pages 248/249
Map of the West Indies showing Native American settlements

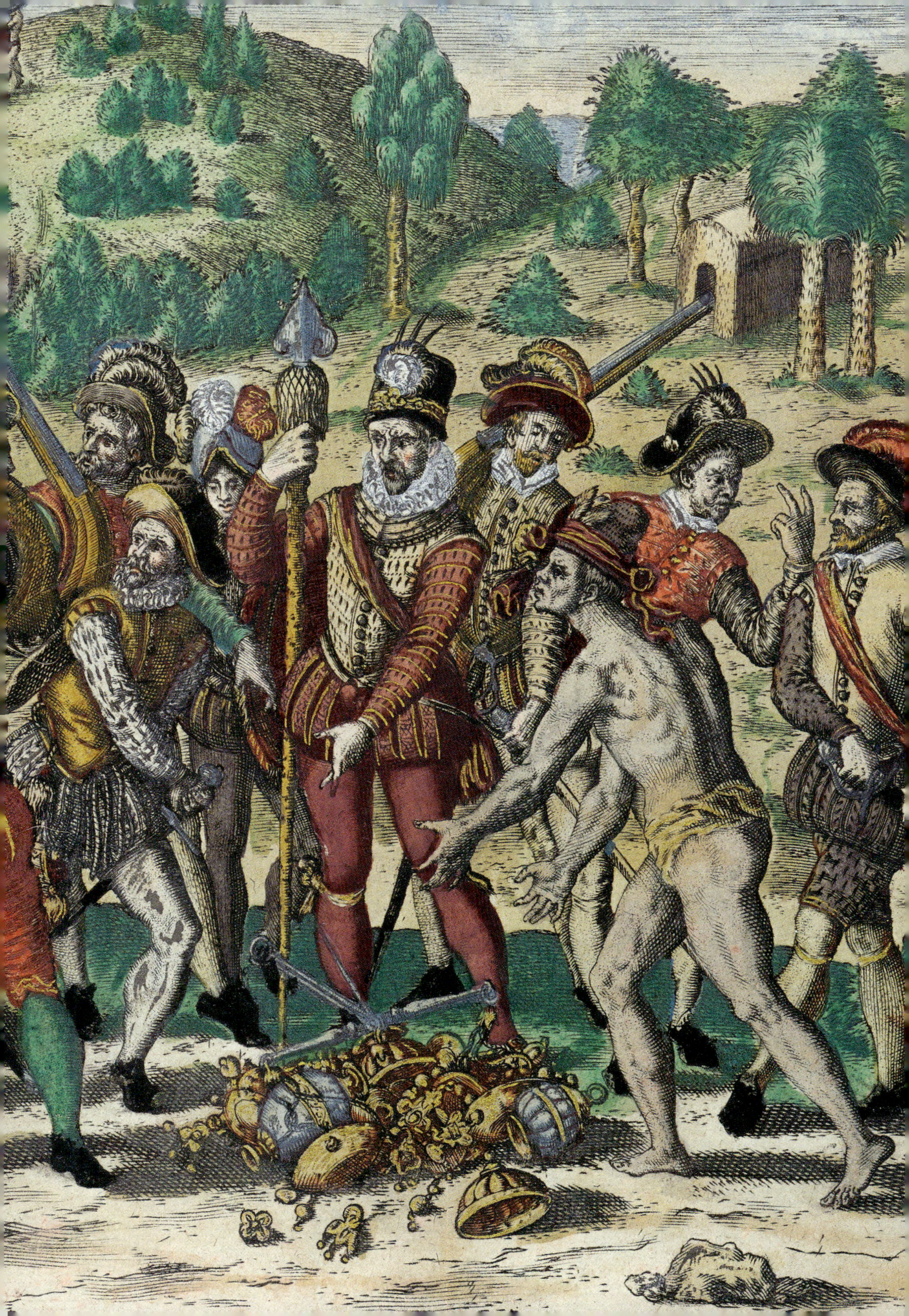

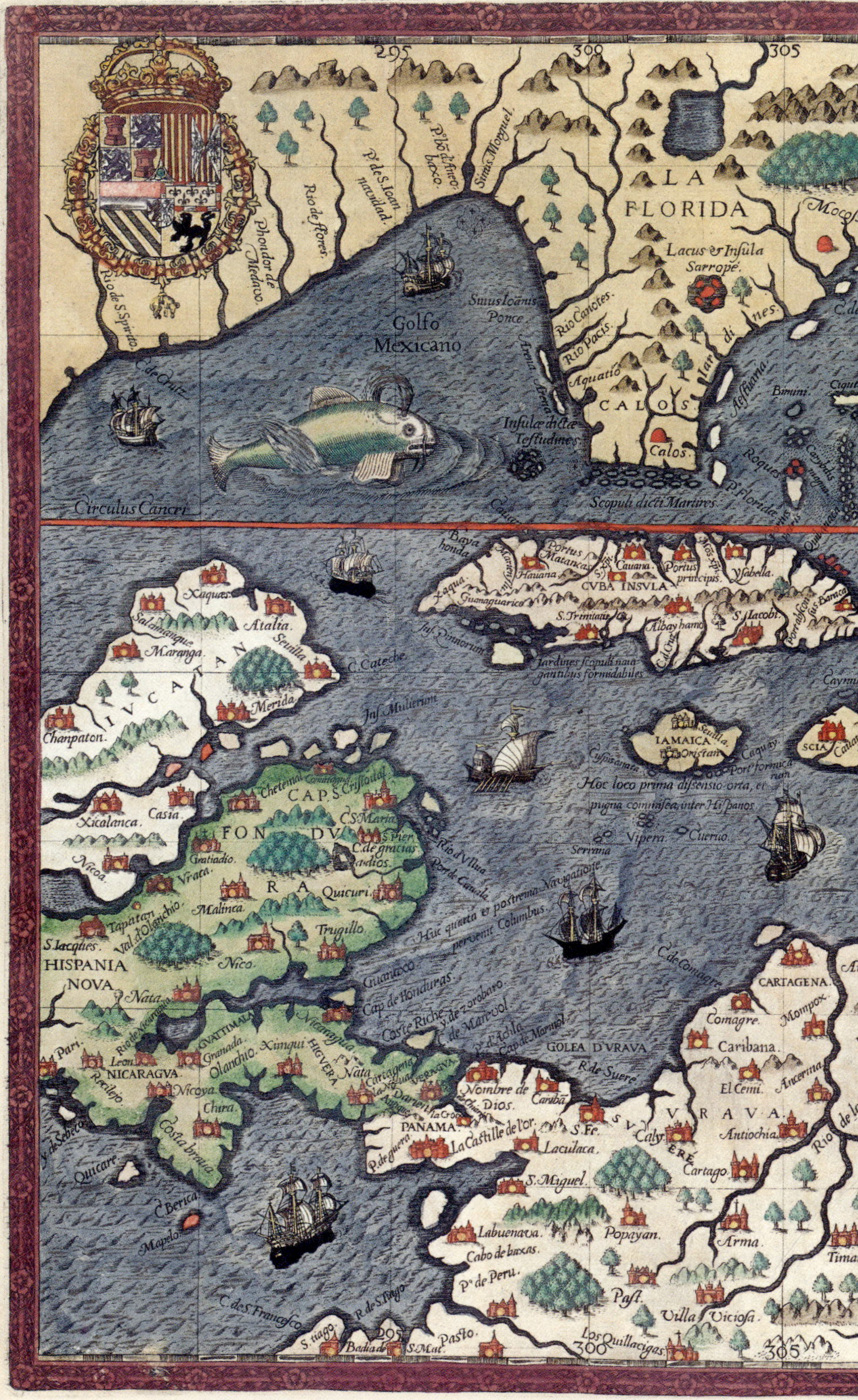
295
300
305
LA FLORIDA
Lacus & Insula Sarropé.
Golfo Mexicano
Rio de flores.
Pª de S. Ioan nacidad.
Sinus Morguel.
Sinus Ioanis Ponce.
Rio Canotes.
Rio Pacis.
Aquatio
CALOS.
Calos.
Bimini.
Insulæ dictæ Testudines.
Scopuli dicti Martires.
Circulus Cancri
C. de Cruz.
Rio de S. Spirito.
Baya honda.
Portus Matanca.
Hauana.
CVBA INSVLA
Cauana.
Portus principis.
Ysabella.
Guanaguarico.
S. Trinitatis.
S. Iacobi.
Albay hamo.
Jardines scopuli nauigantibus formidabiles.
C. Catoche
Xaquas.
Salamanque.
Atalia.
Maranga.
Seuilla.
IVCATAN
Merida.
Champaton.
Ins. Mulierum
IAMAICA
Seuilla.
Oristan.
SCIA
Hoc loco prima dissensio orta, et pugna commissa inter Hispanos
Vipera.
Cueruo.
Serrana
Xicalanca.
Casia.
Nicoa.
CAP. S.
C.S. Maria
FON DV RA
C. de gracias a dios.
Gratiadio.
Vraca.
Malinca.
Quicuri.
Trugillo.
Tapatan
Val d'Olanchio.
Rio d Vlua
Port de Canala
Huc quarta & postrema nauigatione peruenit Columbus.
S. Iacques.
HISPANIA NOVA
Nata.
Nico.
Guanaxo
Cap. de Honduras.
C. de Comagre
CARTAGENA.
Comagre.
Mompox.
Caribana.
GOLFA D'VRAVA
R. de Suere
El Cemi.
Ancerina.
VRAVA.
Antiochia.
Pari.
Leon.
NICARAGVA.
GVATTIMALA
Granada.
Olanchio.
Xinqui.
HIGVERA
Nata
Nicoya.
Chira.
Costa brava
Realejo
Quicare
C. Berica
Mapelo.
Nombre de Dios.
Caribá
PANAMA.
La Castille de l'or.
S. Fe.
Laculaca.
Caly.
Cartago.
S. Miguel.
Labuenaua.
Popayan.
Arma.
Cabo de baxas.
Pº de Peru.
Past.
Villa Viciosa.
Timana
C. de S. Francesco
R. de S. Iago
S. Iago
Badia
S. Mat.
Pasto.
Los Quillacigas
295
300
305

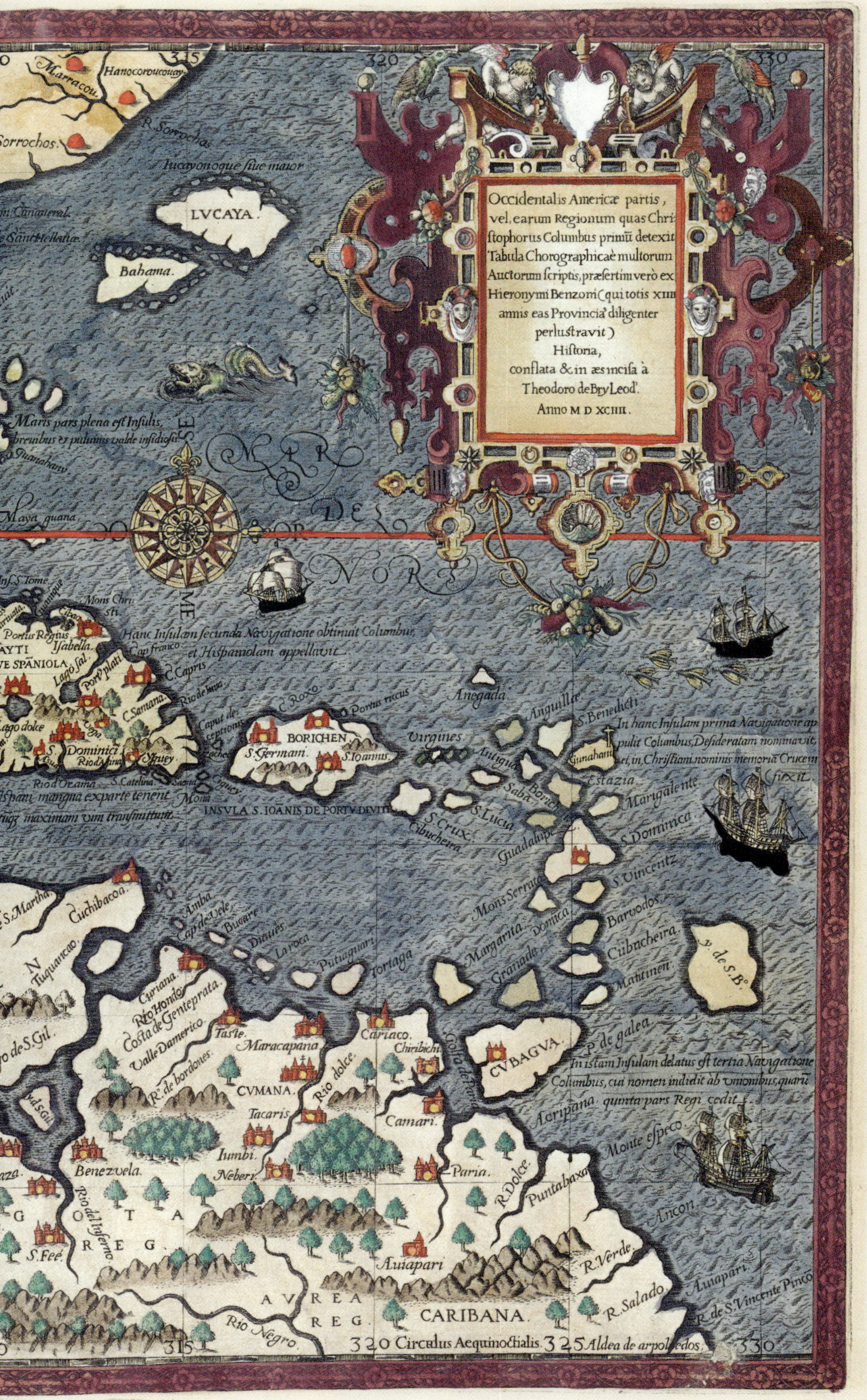
Occidentalis Americæ partis, vel, earum Regionum quas Christophorus Columbus primũ detexit Tabula Chorographicæ multorum Auctorum scriptis, præsertim verò ex Hieronymi Benzoni (qui totis XIIII annis eas Provincia diligenter perlustravit) Historia, conflata & in æs incisa à Theodoro de Bry Leod. Anno M D XCIIII.
Marracou
Hanocoroucouay
Sorrochos
R. Sorrochas
Iucayonoque siue maior
LVCAYA
Bahama
Maris pars plena est Insulis, brevibus & pulvinis valde insidiosis
MAR DEL NORT
Hanc Insulam secunda Navigatione obtinuit Columbus, et Hispaniolam appellavit
HAYTI
VE SPANIOLA
Portus Regius
Ysabella
Lago sal.
Lago dolce
S. Dominici
C. Samana
C. Capris
BORICHEN
S. Germani
S. Ioannis
C. Roxo
Portus riccus
INSVLA S. IOANIS DE PORTV DIVITE
Anegada
Anguilla
S. Benedicti
Virgines
In hanc Insulam prima Navigatione appulit Columbus, Desideratam nominavit, ei, in Christiani nominis memoriã Crucem fixit.
Estazia
Margalente
S. Crux
S. Lucia
Saba
Cibucheira
Guadalupe
S. Dominica
S. Vincentz
Mons Serrat
Barvodos
Margarita
Granada
Dominica
Cubucheira
Matinen
y. de S. B.
Tortuga
Cuchibacoa
Tuquarcao
Curiana
Rio Hondo
Costa de Genteprata
Valle Damerico
Taste
Maracapana
Cariaco
Chiribichi
CVMANA
Rio dolce
Tacaris
Camari
CVBAGVA
P. de galea
In istam Insulam delatus est tertia Navigatione Columbus, cui nomen indidit ab unionibus, quarũ quinta pars Regi cedit.
Acripana
Monte especo
Iumbi
Nebery
Paria
Benezuela
R. Dolce
Puntabaxa
Ancon
Rio del Inferno
S. Fee
Auiapari
R. Verde
R. Salado
AVREA REG.
CARIBANA
Rio Negro
R. de S. Vincente Pinco
Circulus Aequinoctialis
Aldea de arpolledos
315
320
325
330

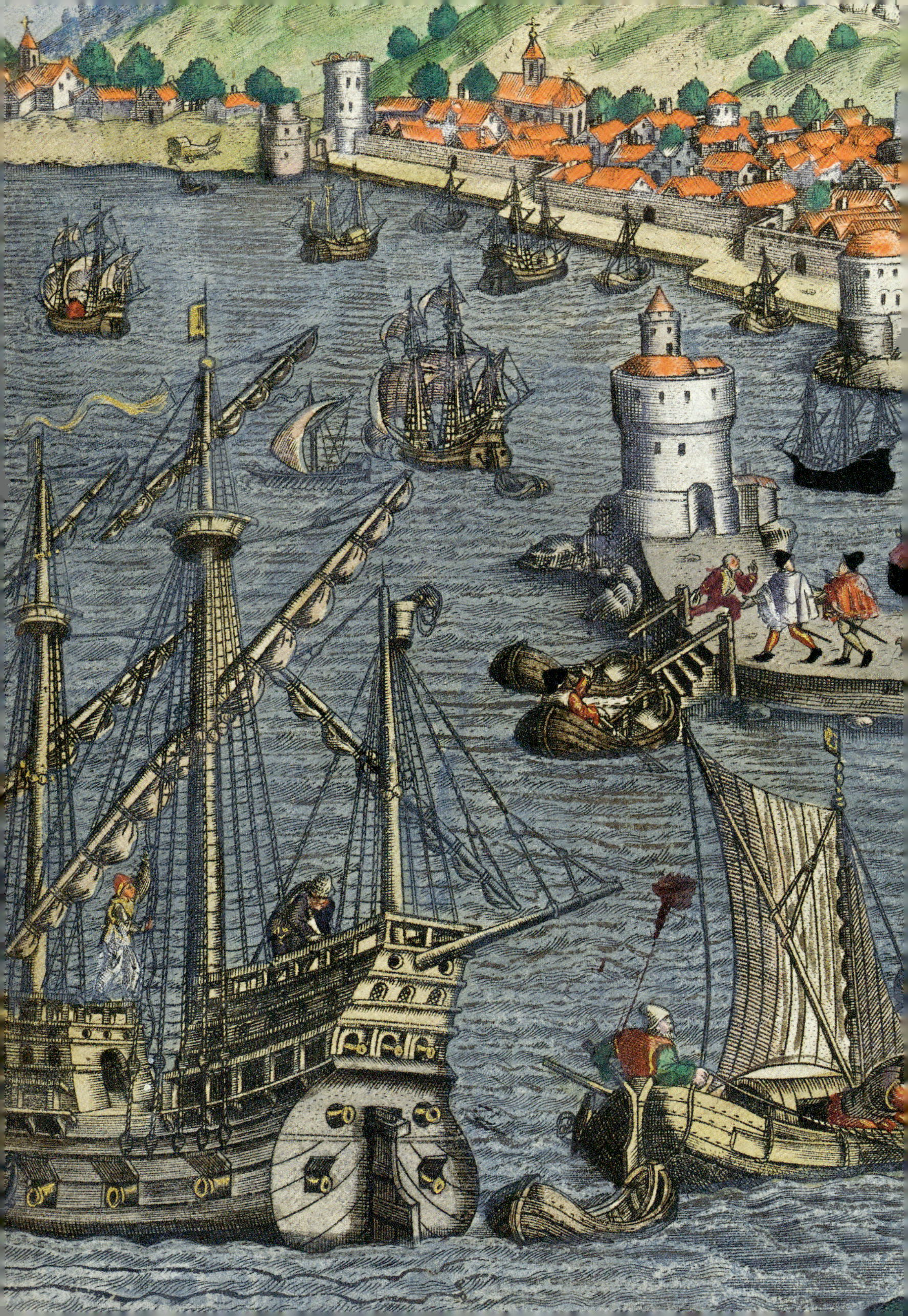

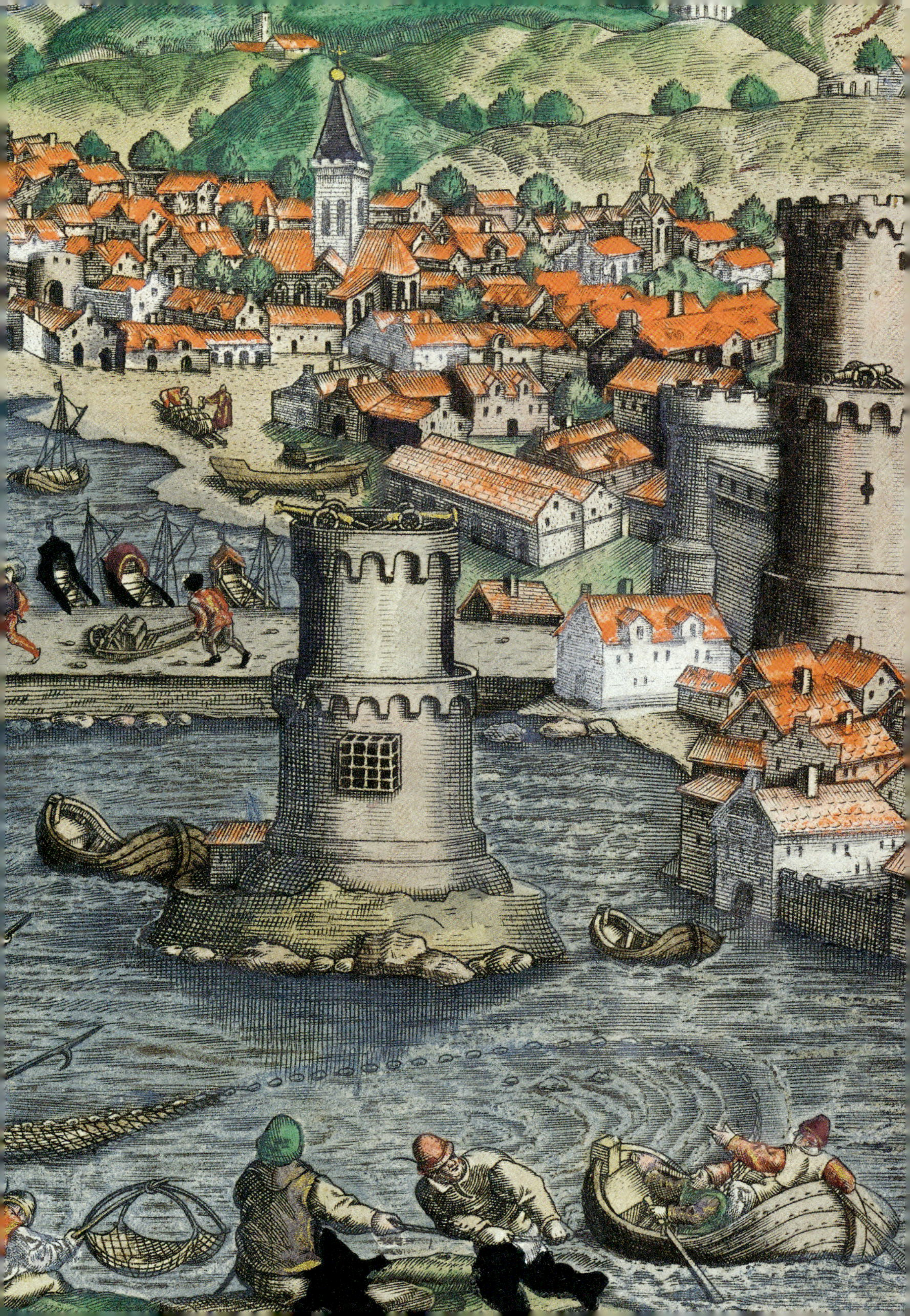

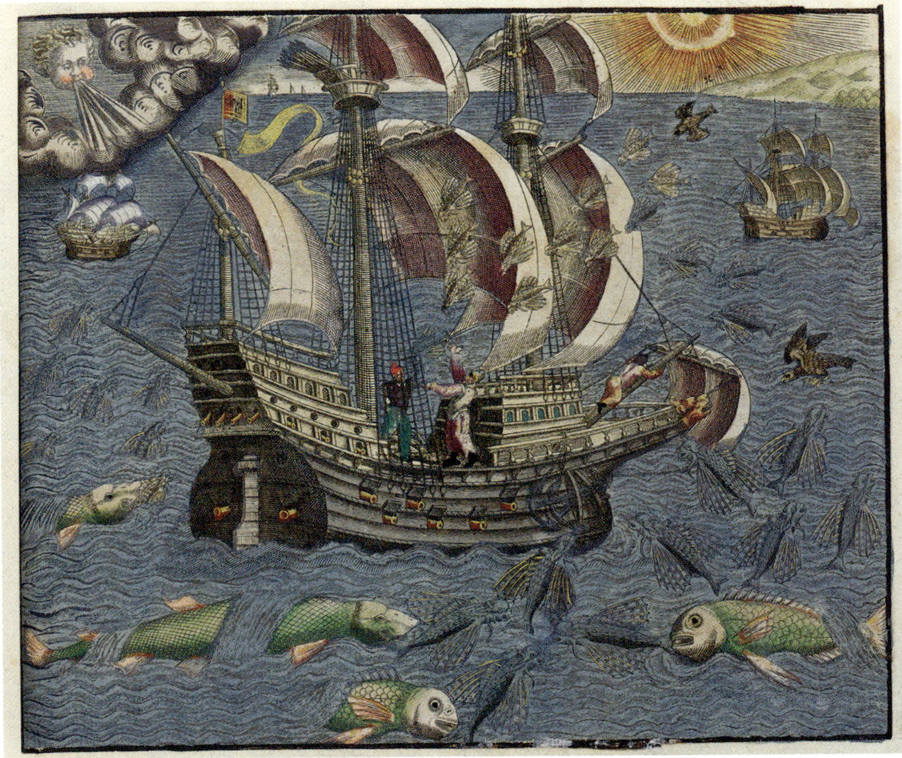

PLATE 2

Flying fish at sea

After having sailed for 14 days with a steady wind, some flying fish which were as long as a human hand fell on the deck. They have wings almost like those of bats, and when they unfold them they fly for a hundred feet or more above the ocean's surface, escaping from other fish who pursue them. Then they dive, in turn hiding from the danger of seabirds.

PLATE 1, PAGES 250/251

The beginning of Girolamo Benzoni's voyage to the West Indies

Girolamo Benzoni was eager to visit the so-called West Indies. He departed from Seville, the most famous main city of southern Spain, and arrived with a small boat in San Lucar de Barrameda. After having found a suitable vessel, he sailed to Gran Canaria, and from there to the island Palma where he had learned he could board a fast ship loaded with wine. Soon he was on course for the Indies.

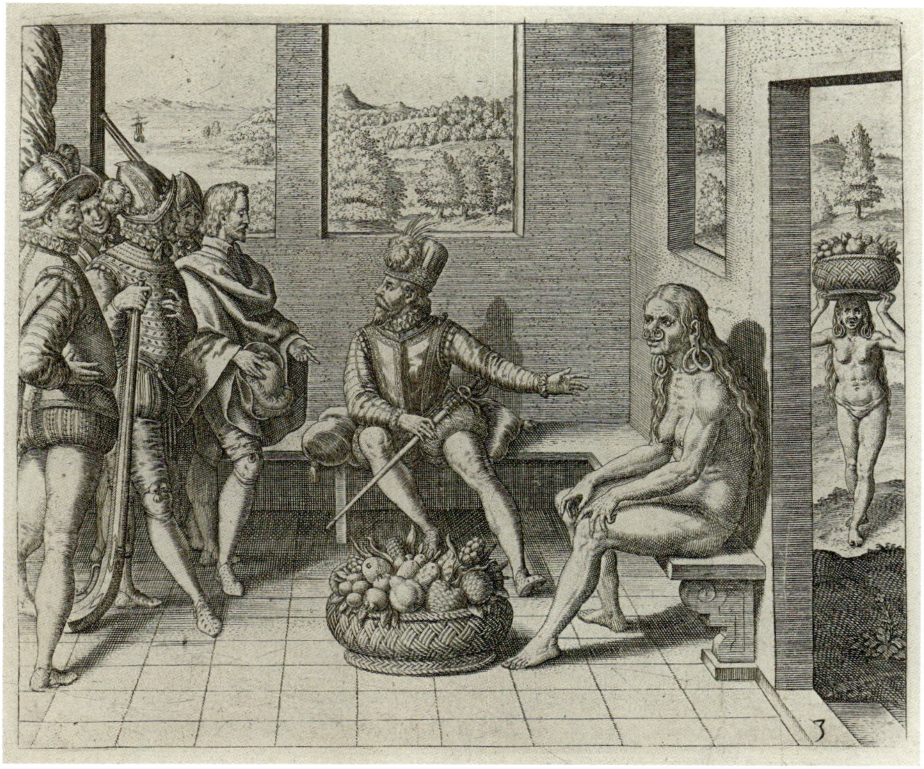

PLATE 3

The wife of the king in the province of Cumana brings gifts to Viceroy Herrera

When Viceroy Herrera anchored for several days at the island of Cumana, the wife of the king of this province came to him carrying a large woven basket full of fruits that grow on the island. Her face and her body looked so horrid that Benzoni, who was struck by her new and wondrous appearance, could not bear to look at her. She looked more like a marvellous animal than a human being.

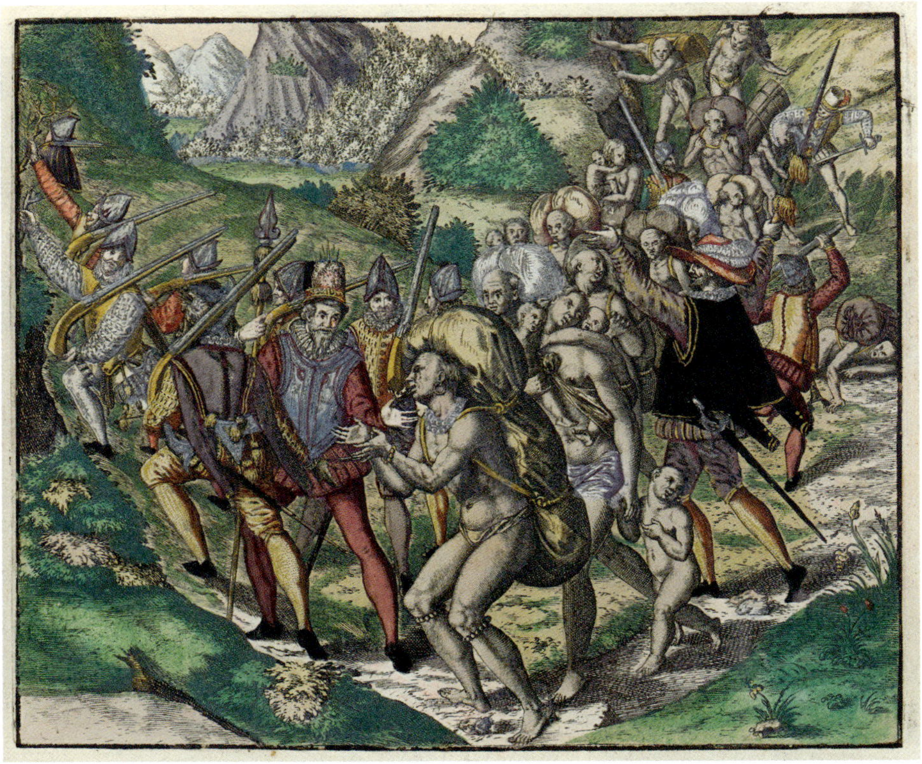

PLATE 4

The cruelty of Pedro de Calice against the Indians

When Benzoni was in Amaracapana, Pedro de Calice, a military commander, arrived with 4,000 Indian slaves. He would have brought more, had they not died from fatigue and sorrow, or sometimes because of the stab wounds in heart and lungs inflicted on them by the Spaniards if they could no longer carry the heavy luggage of the conquistadors.

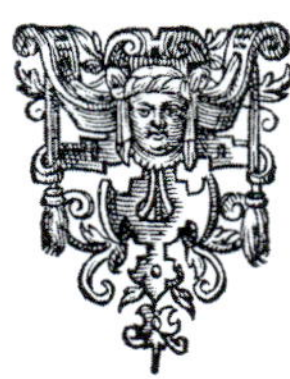

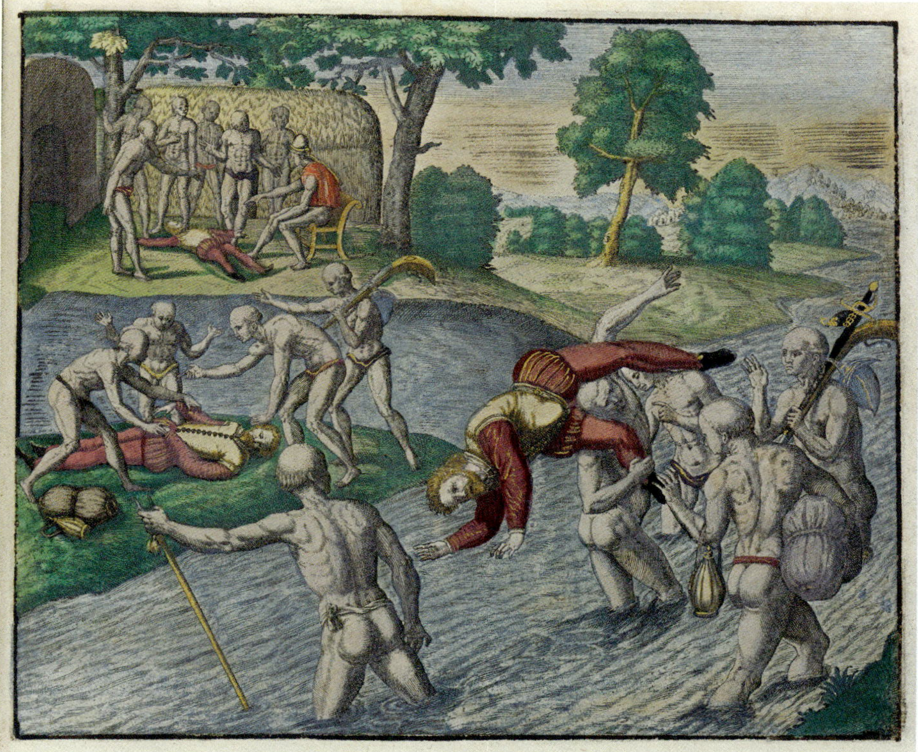

PLATE 5

The Indians, in order to test the immortality of the Spaniards, drown the Spaniard Salcedo

The inhabitants of Puerto Rico believed the Spaniards who wanted to rule the island to be immortal. One of the most important men on the island, by the name of Vraioan, head of the province of Iaguaca, wanted to test this. He courteously received the Spaniard Salcedo who visited his province, and when he left he sent some of his men with him to carry his luggage, ordering them to drown him in the river they had to cross. They did as they had been told, and then returned the drowned Salcedo to their ruler. From this, the islanders realised that the Spaniards were mortal just like other people.

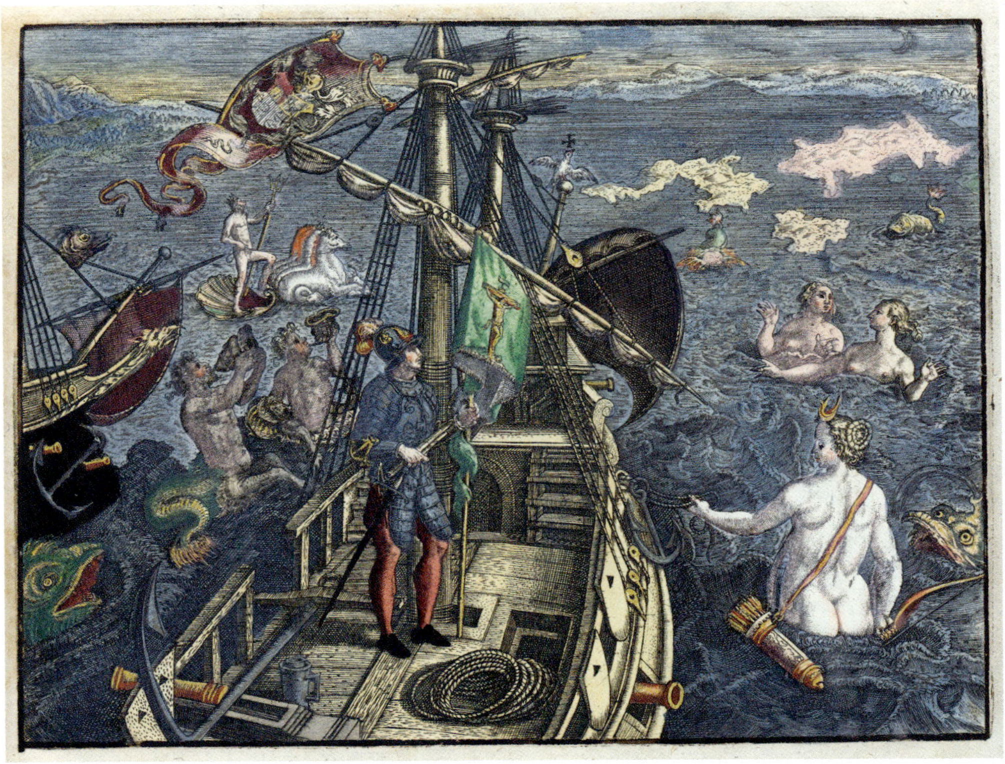

PLATE 6

Columbus, the first discoverer of the West Indies

When sailing past Cádiz to Portugal and onwards to the ocean, Columbus often observed that certain winds blow every year at the same time from the west, steadily and for many days. He estimated that they might blow from an overseas coast. For some time he had been thinking about this, and then he wanted to have confirmation. For this reason he presented his plan to look for this other coast to the Republic of Genoa and to other princes. Neglected by all of them, he then turned to Ferdinand and Isabella of Spain, who supported his mission.

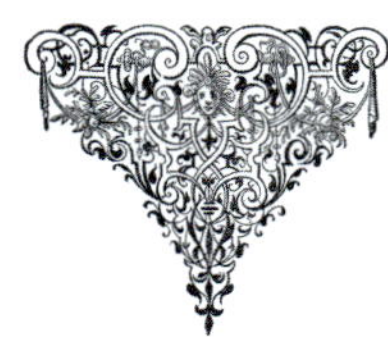

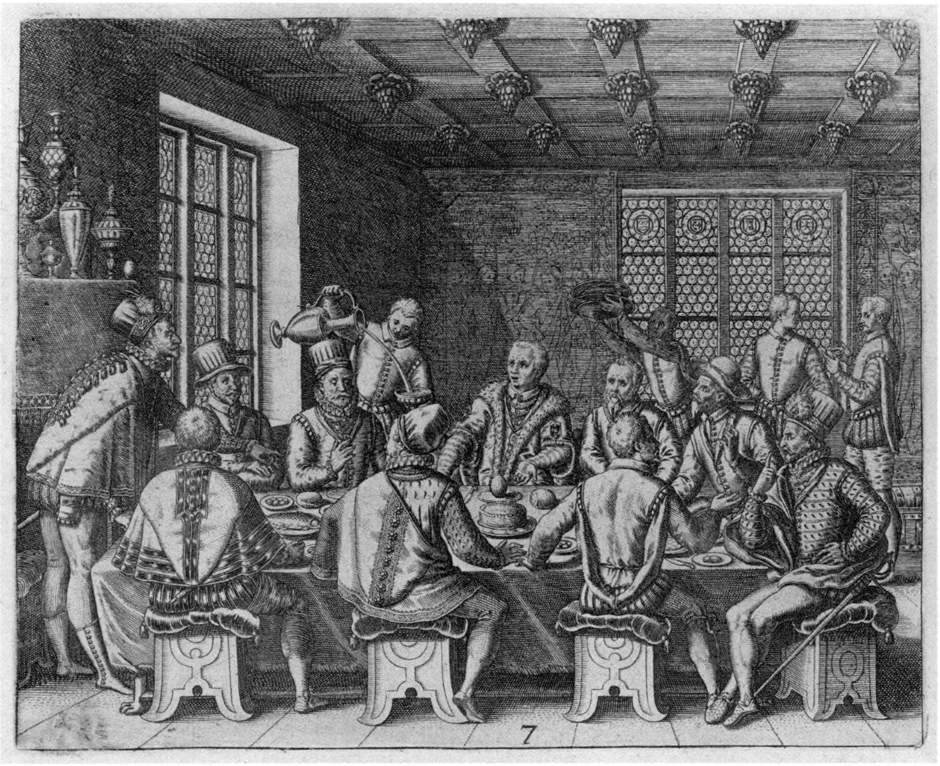

PLATE 7

Columbus, during a banquet, mocks those who have ridiculed him

After Columbus had discovered the New World, he was invited to a dinner with many Spanish noblemen to talk about the Indies. One of them turned to Columbus and said: "If you had not found the Indies, there would not have been a lack of men here in Spain who could have tried the same thing. After all, there are many great and ingenious men here." Columbus said nothing in response, but had an egg brought to him, and asked all the others to make it stand upright on the table. When none of them succeeded, he demonstrated how it could be done.

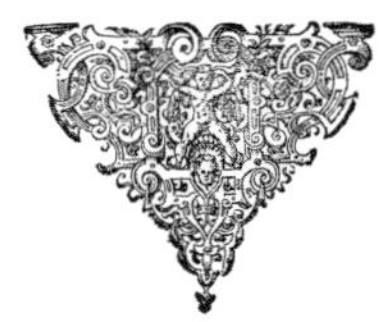

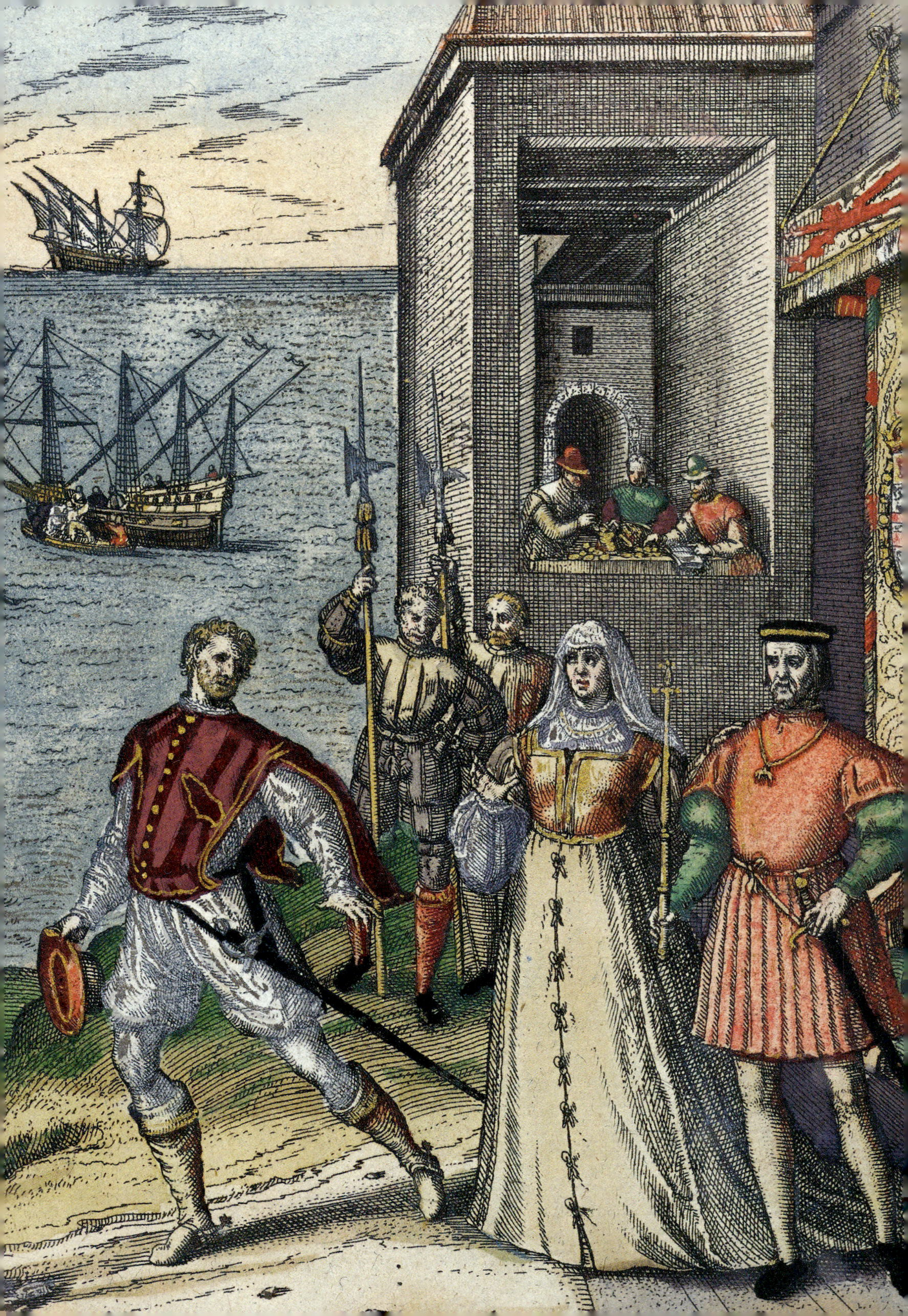

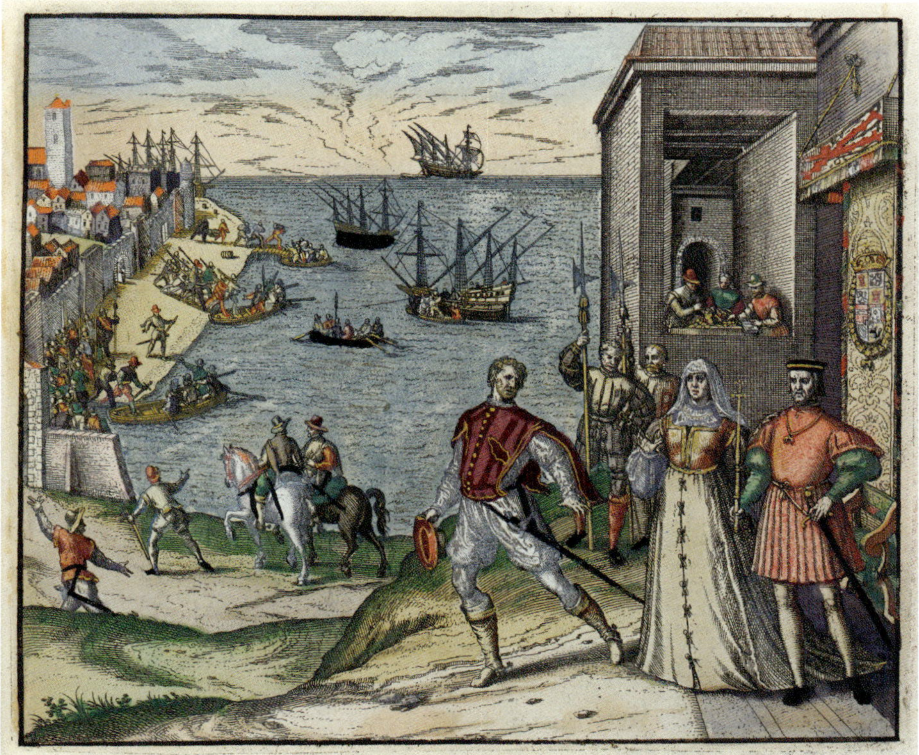

PLATE 8

The first voyage of Columbus to the Indies in the year 1492

After having been given three vessels by King Ferdinand, Columbus sailed with his brother Bartolomeo to the Canarian island of La Gomera. Here he took in water and other things he needed, and then he began his expedition by turning west to follow the setting sun. After several days, with no land in sight, sailors began to criticise Columbus. He reassured them as well as he could by saying that within days, with God's help, they would encounter new land, and continued his voyage. Yet after another few days, and still no sight of land, their criticism resurfaced, and they threatened to throw him overboard if he would persist in his venture. The next day, Columbus then ordered for the sails to be taken down. It is to be believed that Columbus already realised from looking at the sky, the wind and the clouds which appeared around the rising sun that they were close to land.

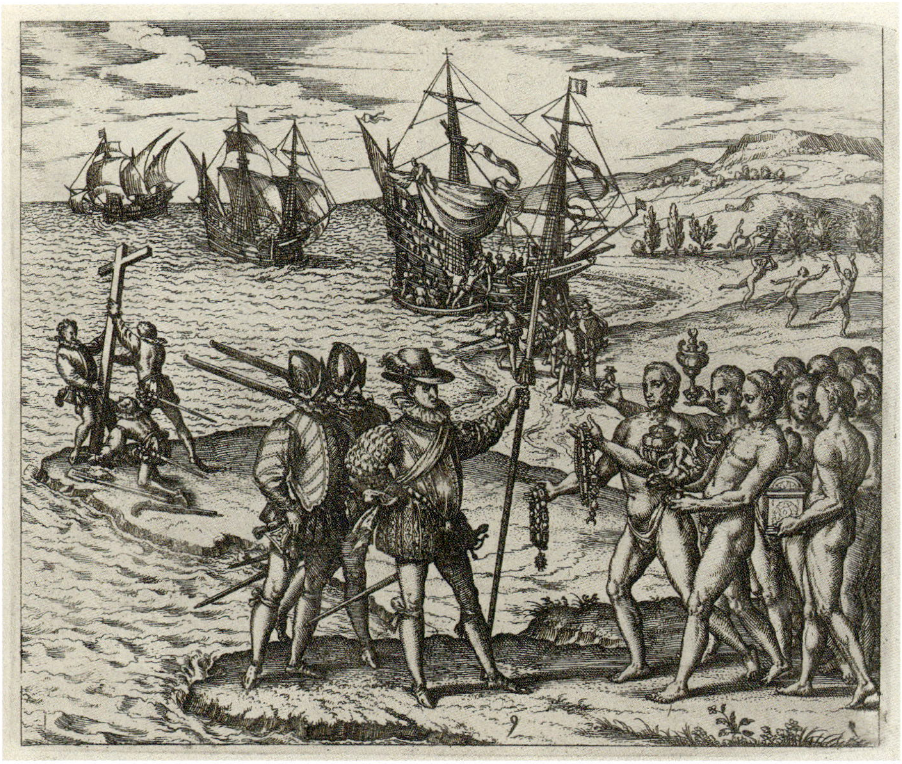

PLATE 9

On his first arrival in the Indies, Columbus is received by the locals with great gifts

When Columbus reached land on his first voyage, he planted a wooden cross on the shore. Subsequently he proceeded towards the island of Haiti, which he called Hispaniola, and he went ashore with many Spaniards. Here he was received with great honour by the cacique of that place (which is what they call a king) by the name of Guacanarillo. They exchanged gifts, and pledged to each other their future friendship. Columbus gave them shirts, hats, knives, mirrors and the like. The cacique in turn gave Columbus a large quantity of gold.

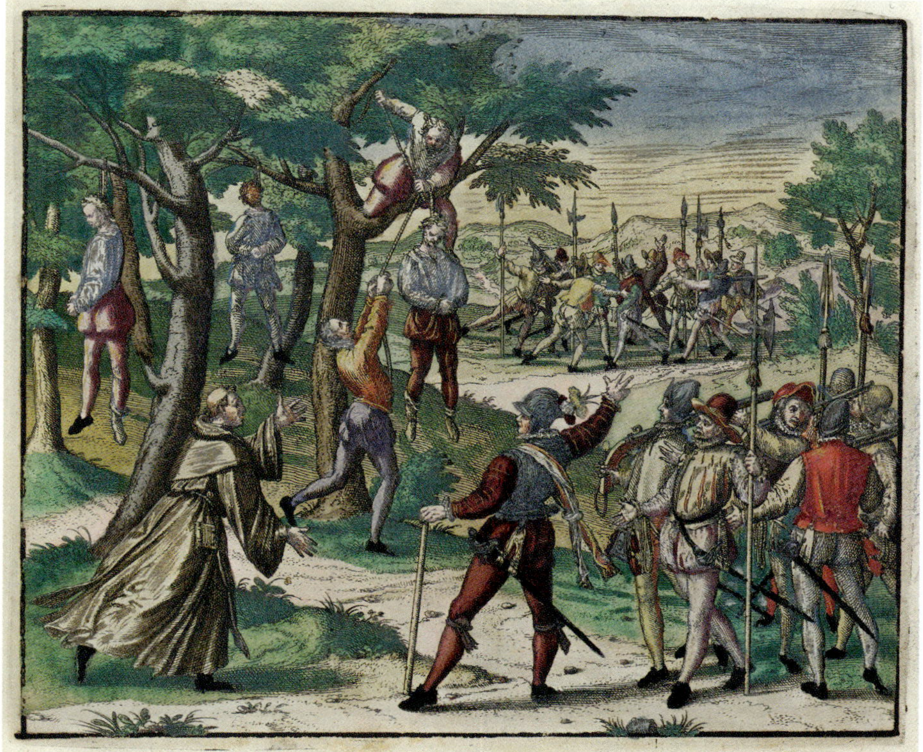

PLATE 10

Columbus orders rebellious Spaniards to be executed

Because of his bad health, Columbus returned to Hispaniola after undertaking an expedition against the Caribs. Here he found great disorder because several Spaniards had committed robberies and crimes when he had been away. He prudently put an end to these evil practices, and sentenced to death all Spaniards who had instigated rebellion, and who were found guilty of committing crimes. He himself tried to appease the cacique as best he could. For this strict policy, many Spaniards hated Columbus to the extent that they could not even mention his name without getting angry. A Benedictine friar even denied Columbus the sacrament. In turn, Columbus ordered that none of the provisions should be given to the monks. For this reason, many people wrote very negatively about Columbus and his brother to the king of Spain. When he had regained his strength, Columbus felt obliged to return to Spain.

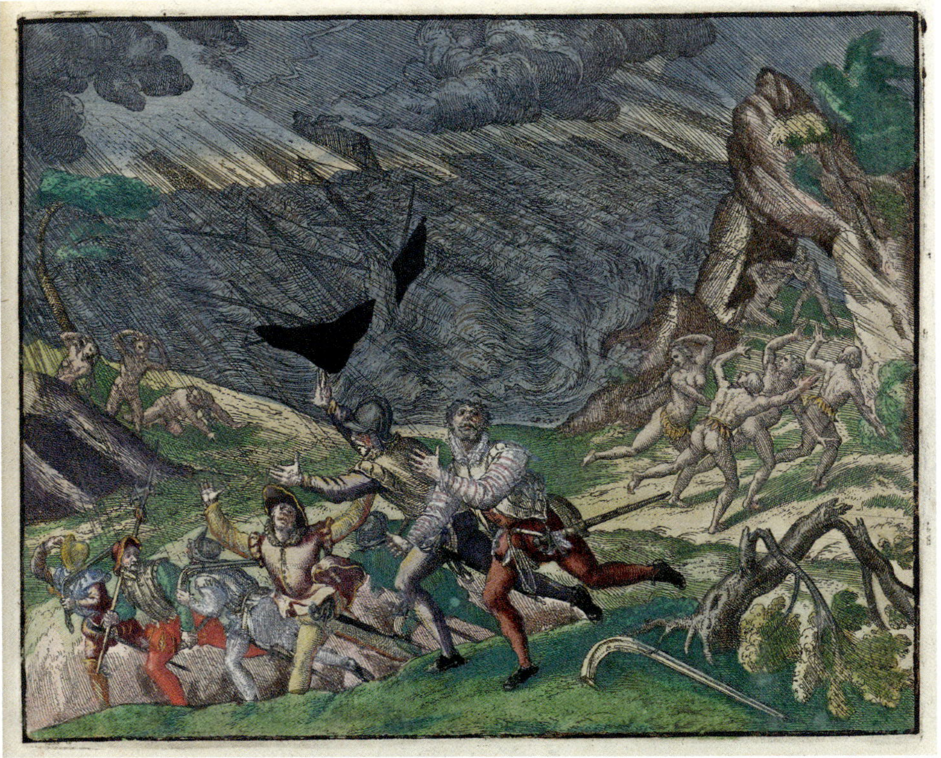

PLATE 11

A horrible and unprecedented storm

At the same time, something miraculous and extraordinary happened in that region. From the east, such a raging storm set up that none of the islanders could remember ever to have experienced the like. First an extremely strong typhoon (the Spaniards call it Huracan) arrived that seemed to be intent on converging heaven and earth. Everybody was stunned by the unforeseen terror, and believed that they were staring death in the face, and that the end of time was about to arrive. Then the heavens were torn apart by an awful sound, and in the midst of the terrible thunder a light flashed, and the sky was set on fire by lightning. The day turned into a night that was more black and more dark than ever before, so that those who ran towards each other could not see each other. People were running around, filled with fear, in all directions. Meanwhile the force of the storm was such that amidst the howling winds trees were uprooted and large rocks fell on to the plain, ruining farms and huts and killing many people. The raging storms even lifted up and destroyed entire houses and their families. Within a few hours enormous damage was caused: even three ships that were believed to be safely anchored in the harbour were not spared this disaster. Once even the most solid anchors had been broken, these ships and their crews perished. Many Indians, who had sheltered in caves, survived.

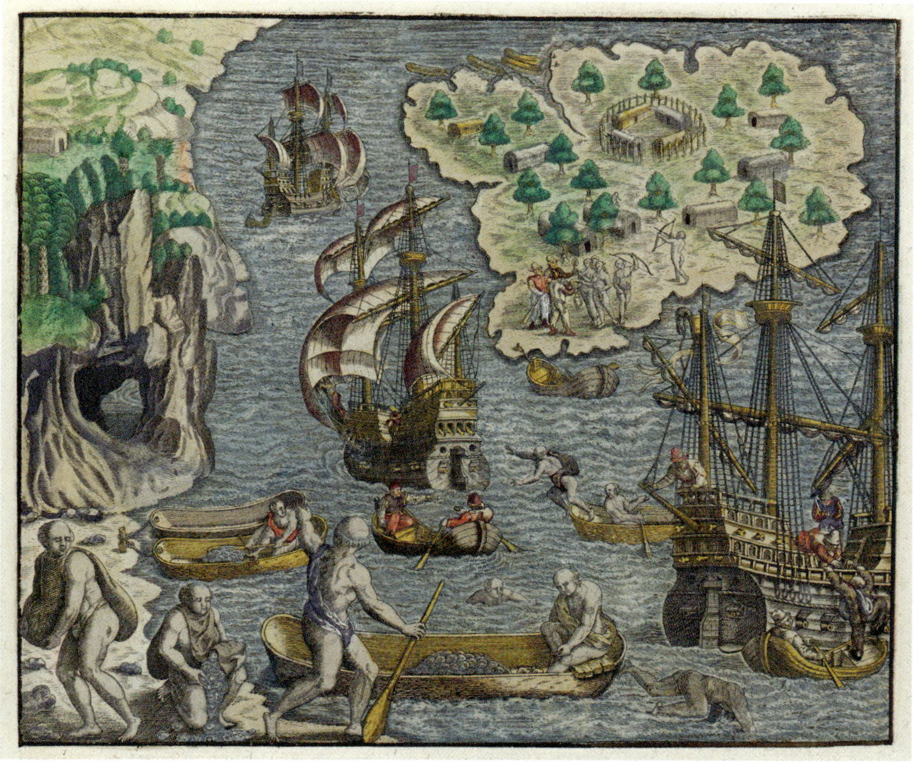

PLATE 12

Pearl Island, named as such because of the multitude of pearls that are found there

As Columbus sailed to the Indies for the third time, he ended up on the island of Cubagua which he renamed Pearl Island for the following reason: as he passed by this inlet, he had seen several Indians in small boats catching sea snails, which the Spaniards thought they caught as food. However, when they opened their shells, they were full of pearls. When they disembarked, they saw Indian women wearing extremely beautiful pearls around their arms and necks. The Spaniards obtained these pearls from them in exchange for worthless goods.

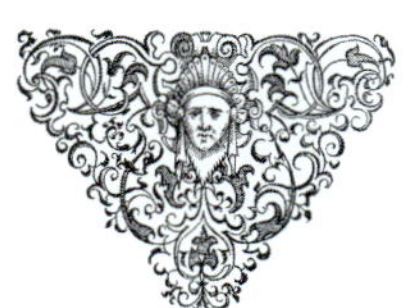

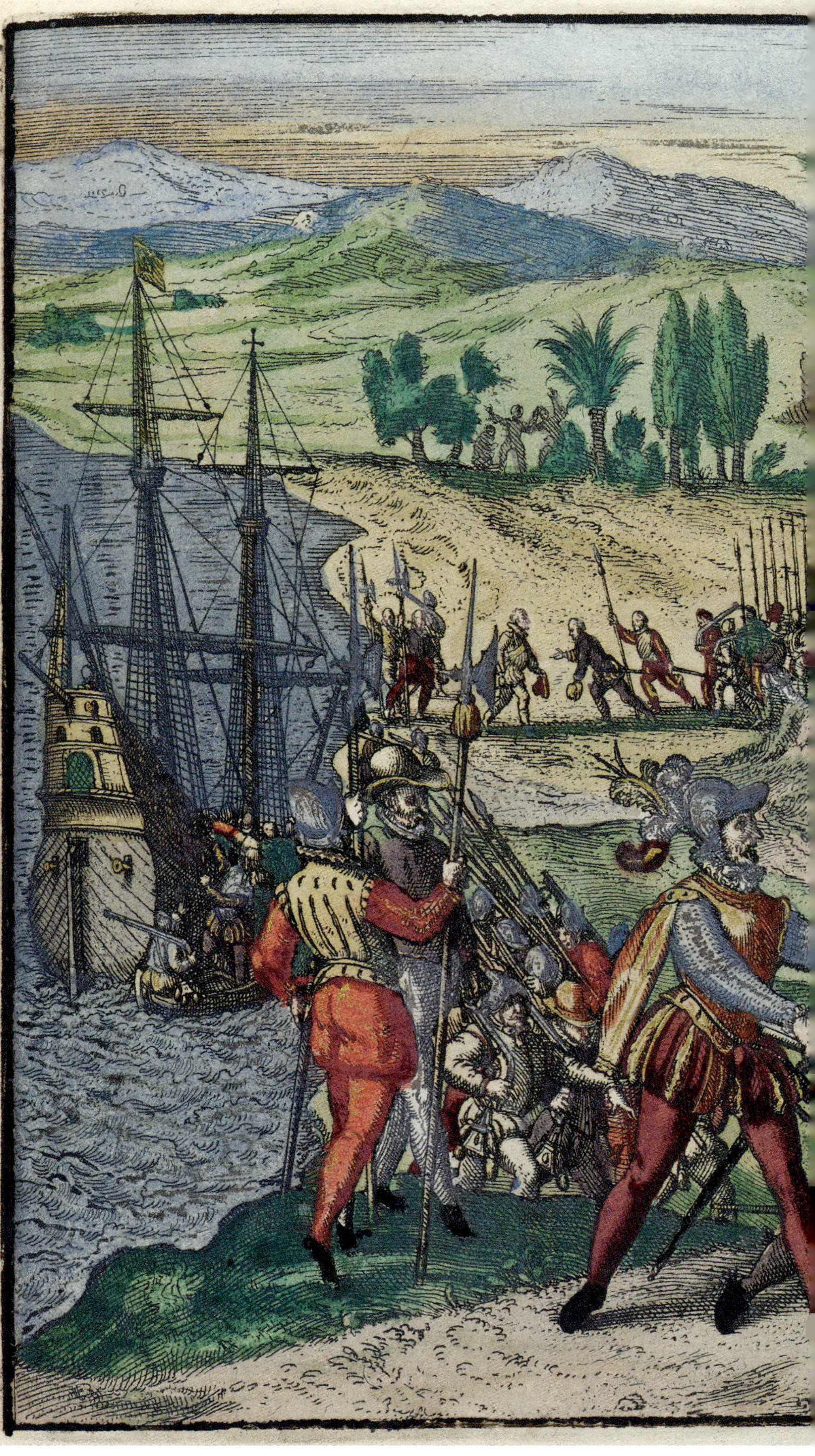

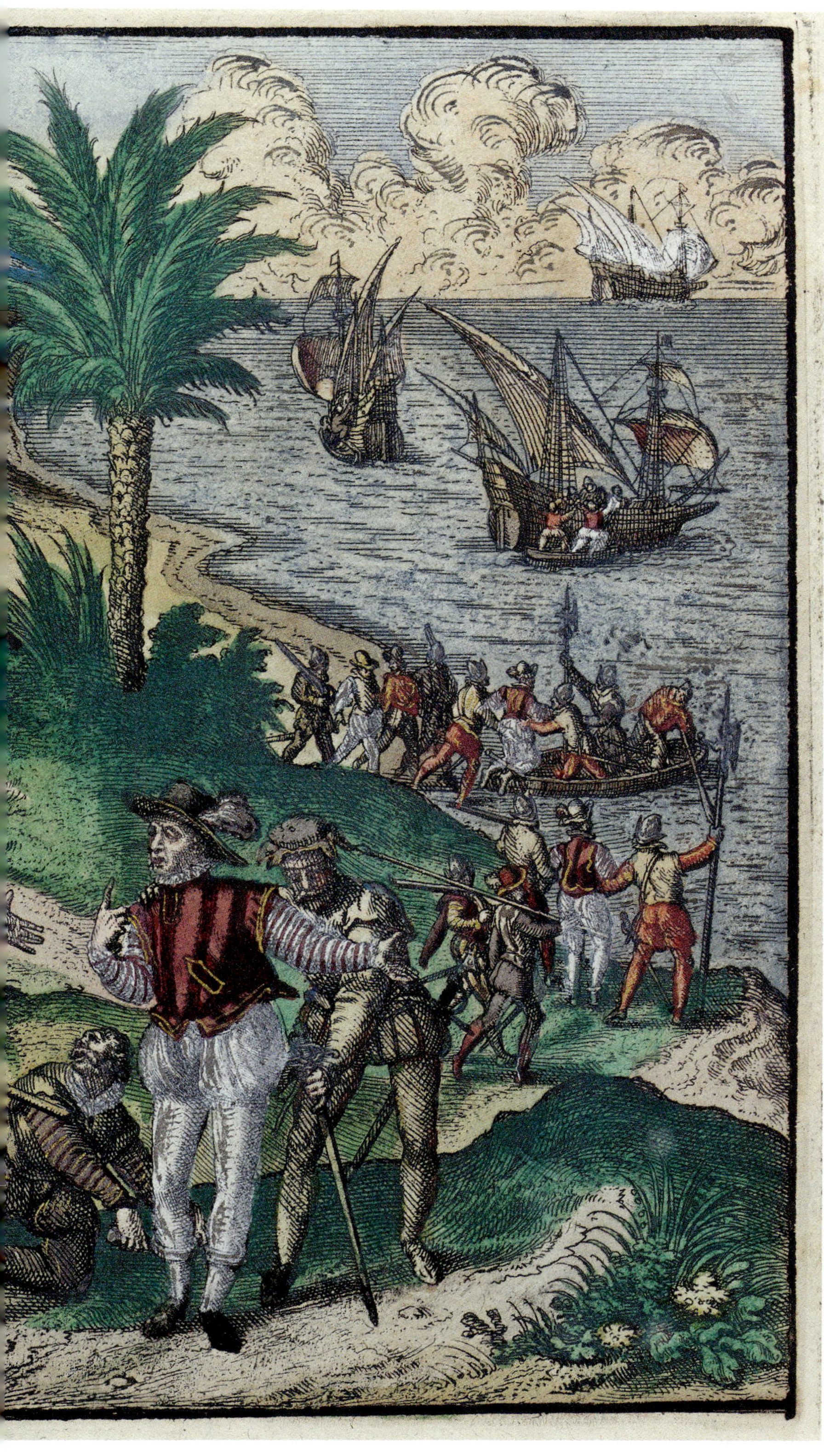

PLATE 13, PAGES 264/265

Columbus and his brother Bartolomeo are taken captive and returned to Spain

When King Ferdinand had learned about the discord which had arisen between Columbus and Roland Ximenes, he appointed Francisco de Bobadilla as governor of Hispaniola, sending him there with full powers and ordering him to set up an inquiry into the causes of the rift between Columbus and Roland. In 1499 he set sail with this brief from the port of Cádiz, crossing over to Hispaniola with four vessels. Having heard about the landing of the new commander, the admiral and his brother Bartolomeo went to meet the royal messenger, and receive him in an honourable way. When they came to the port, thinking that others too had good intentions, the brothers by way of greeting and embracing were taken captive. Soon the two, in chains, were separated, by which they suffered even more, and were sent back to Spain in two ships. But as soon as they arrived in Spain, and the king was informed that such famous men were brought here with shackled feet, and in such an awful state, he pitied them. He sent a courier to Cádiz with an order to release them from custody, and also that they were to come to him personally with a wonderful procession worthy of such men. When they came to court, the king listened to them in a friendly manner.

PLATE 14

A battle between Columbus and Francisco Poresio

When on his fourth voyage to Hispaniola Columbus was denied access to the port by Bobadilla, he set sail for the island of Jamaica. There Francisco Poresio, captain of a caravel, together with his brother and a great number of soldiers, mutinied against Columbus, and tried to escape to Hispaniola with a number of Indian vessels tied together. But when he was frustrated in his attempt to cross the sea with such small boats, he came back. When Columbus heard about his return, he marched towards Poresio with his brother. It came to a battle, in which several were killed and many wounded on both sides. Francisco Poresio and his brother were captured.

PLATE 15, PAGES 268/269

The discovery of the Sea of Magellan

Ferdinand Magellan, offended by the king of Portugal, went to Emperor Charles V. He stated that Castile had a claim to the Moluccas, and he hoped that he, intent on sailing to the west, would be able to find a strait that would lead him to the South Sea and from there directly to the Moluccas. Also that by this route, with fewer costs and fewer difficulties, oriental spices and other commodities could be imported. Charles, after consulting the leading figures in the Council of the Indies, provided him with ships and gave him the supreme command. Magellan set sail from Seville, and after a long voyage finally discovered a strait which was 110 miles in length, and two, sometimes several miles in breadth. This strait has been named the Strait of Magellan.

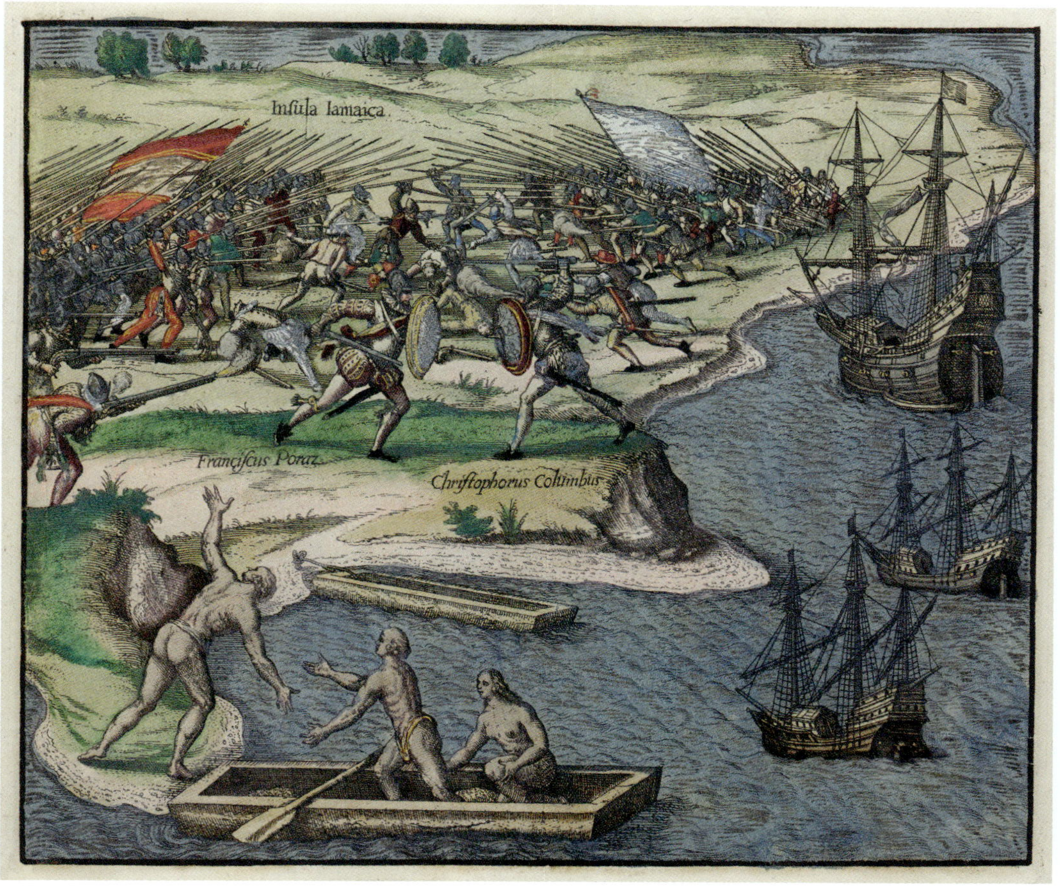
Insula Iamaica
Franciscus Poraz
Christophorus Columbus

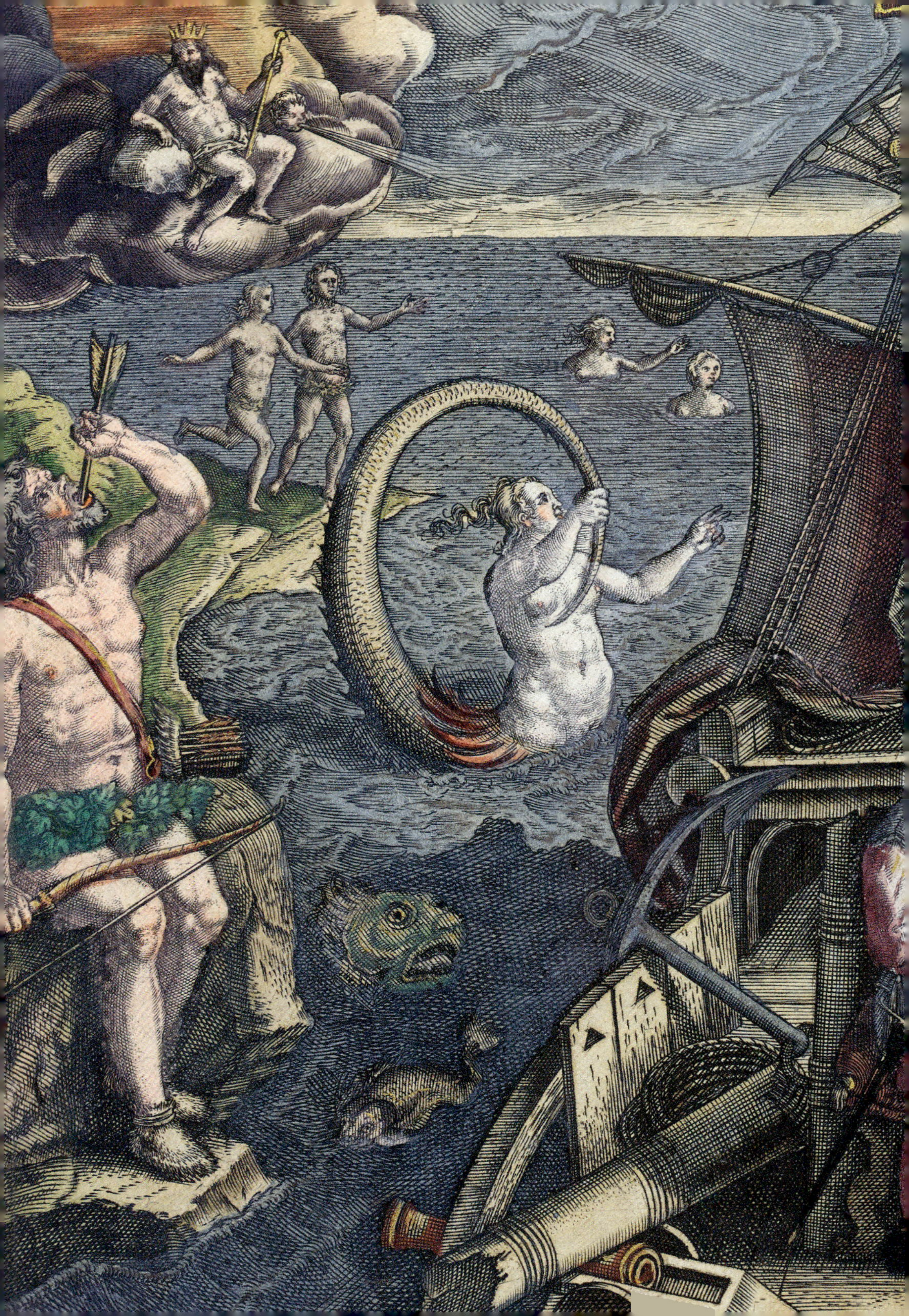

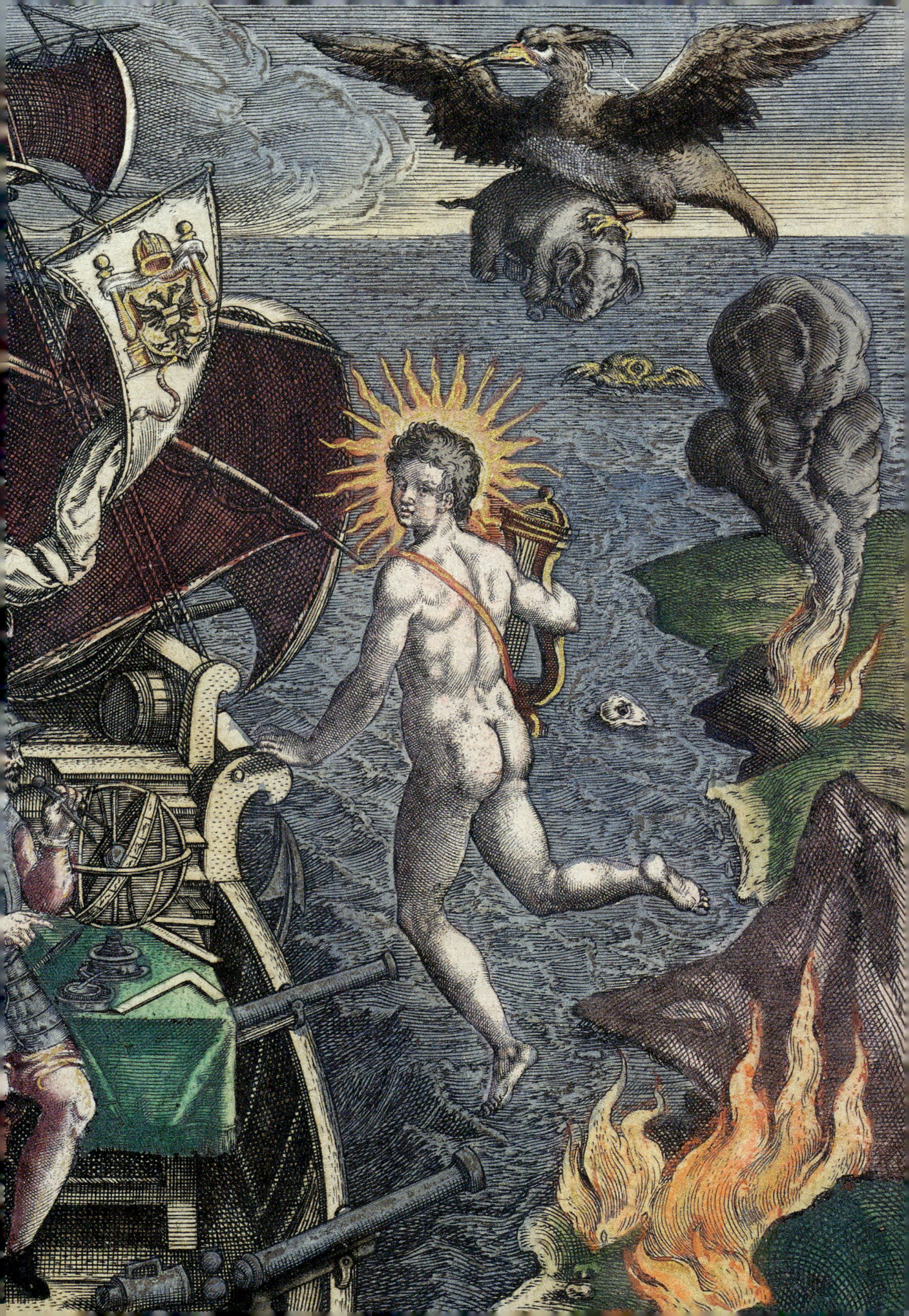

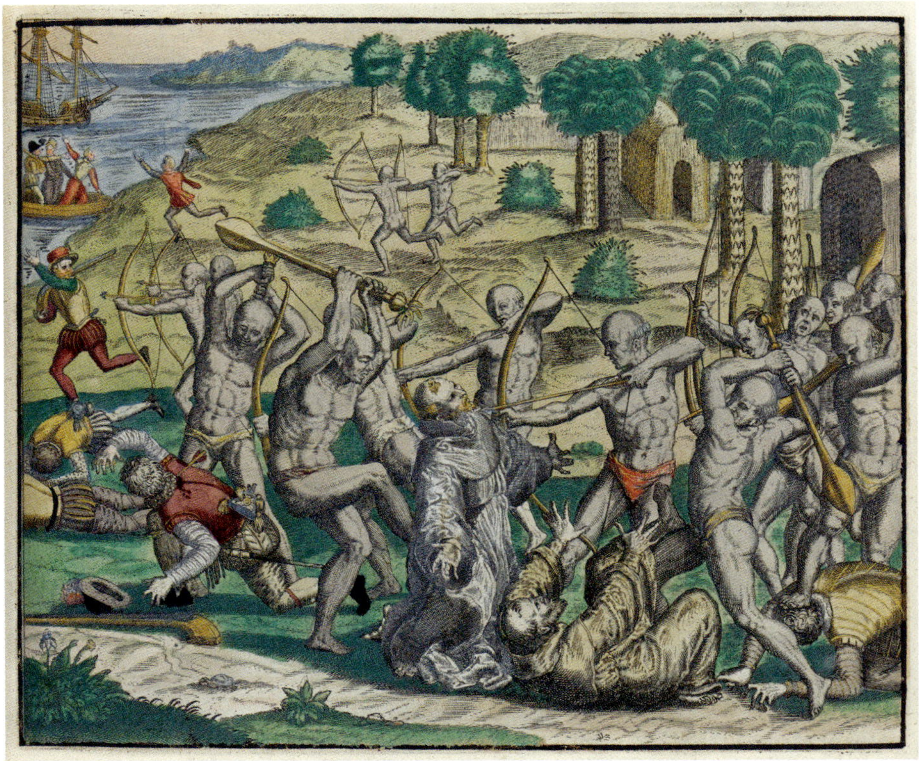

PLATE 16

Some Spaniards and monks are murdered by the Indians

At the time when pearl fishing flourished, a number of monks crossed the ocean to the Indian continent to initiate the Indians into the Christian faith. Many Spaniards crossed the ocean too to trade. By then already, the Indians refused to carry on business and detested the harsh government of the Spaniards. One day at sunrise, the Indians ran up to them and cruelly murdered them. Some of them, however, managed to escape in a vessel which was anchored on the bank of the river Cumana, and reached Dominica. They reported the rebellion of the inhabitants of Cumana to Bartolomeo, the governor of the island.

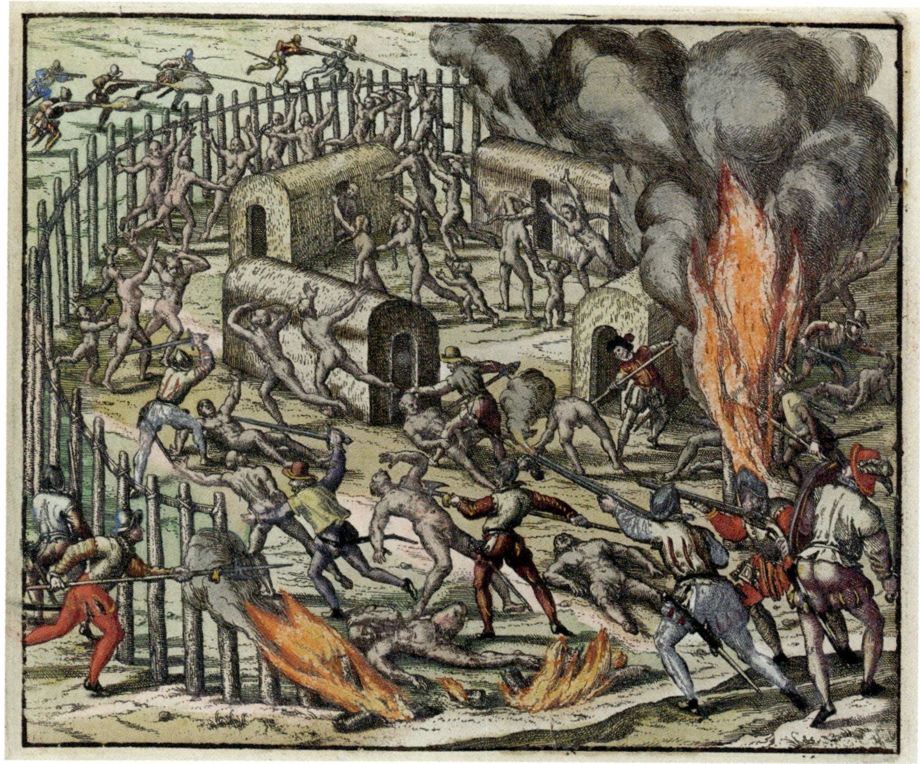

PLATE 18

Some Indians are killed, others perish in a fire

Hoieda marched from Cartagena 12 miles inland, lured by the hope and desire of a large booty. He aimed an attack at a certain tribe because he believed that he would find a great treasure of gold in that location, as the Indians had assured him. But on this expedition he only harvested wounds and damage, because the barbarians assaulted him so violently that he was forced to retreat to the coast, with a loss of 75 soldiers. When Niquesa arrived with a large number of soldiers, they contrived to attack the same tribe together, and to avenge the death of their men. Towards the evening, most soldiers secretly set out from their encampment. After having marched quietly and fairly slowly, they overwhelmed the careless and sleepy Indians at daybreak. Shocked by their wounds and by the burning of their huts, the Indians tried to escape. But the roads were blocked by Spanish soldiers. Some Indians perished because they encountered these soldiers, others threw themselves in the fire which they preferred to falling prey to the Spaniards. So all died with the exception of a few who escaped at dawn. Only six were taken prisoner and presented as slaves to Hoieda. Among the cooling ashes the victors looked for gold, but found hardly anything. Without having discovered the large booty, they returned to Cartagena in an ill temper.

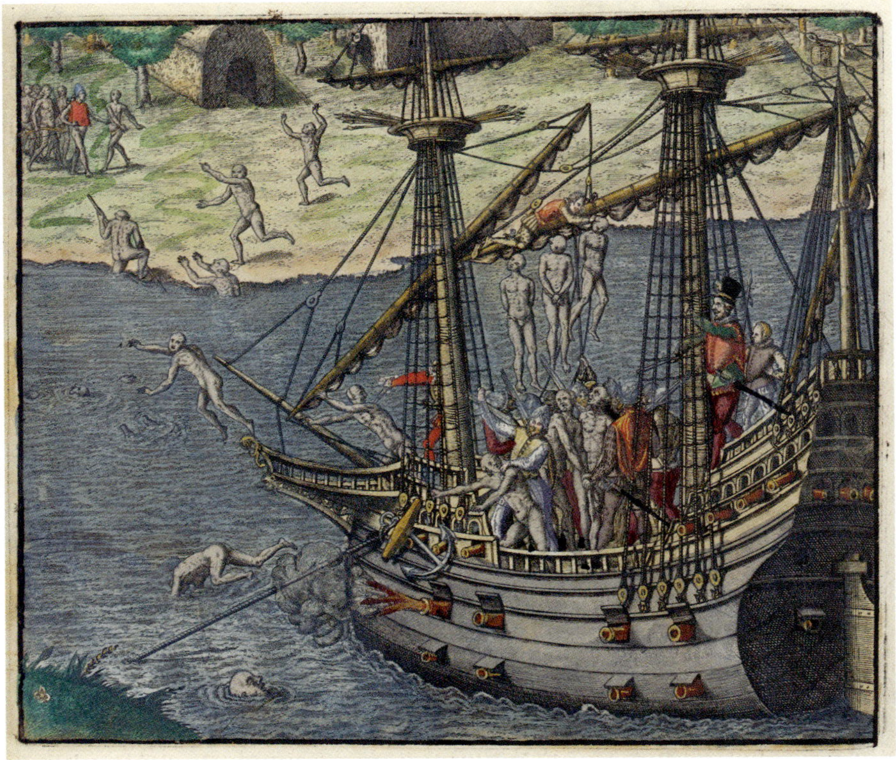

PLATE 17

Didaco Ocampo punishes the rebellion of the Indians

Didaco Ocampo set out from the port of Dominica with 300 soldiers, and quickly reached Cumana. To draw the barbarians to his ships, he ordered all his men, with the exception of his sailors, to hide in the hull of the ship. The Indians, thinking that there were only a few Spaniards, would be more willing to come on board thinking they had come from Spain. Some Indians boarded the ship, pretending to trade by carrying pearls. Having noticed the very limited number of Christians, they went back to shore and reported to the cacique that there were only a few men on board. He then ordered many more Indians to go on board. The Spanish commander gave his soldiers the signal to come out of hiding. Some of the Indians, who had not anticipated this unexpected appearance, were captured, others were killed. All those who were captured by Ocampo were hanged.

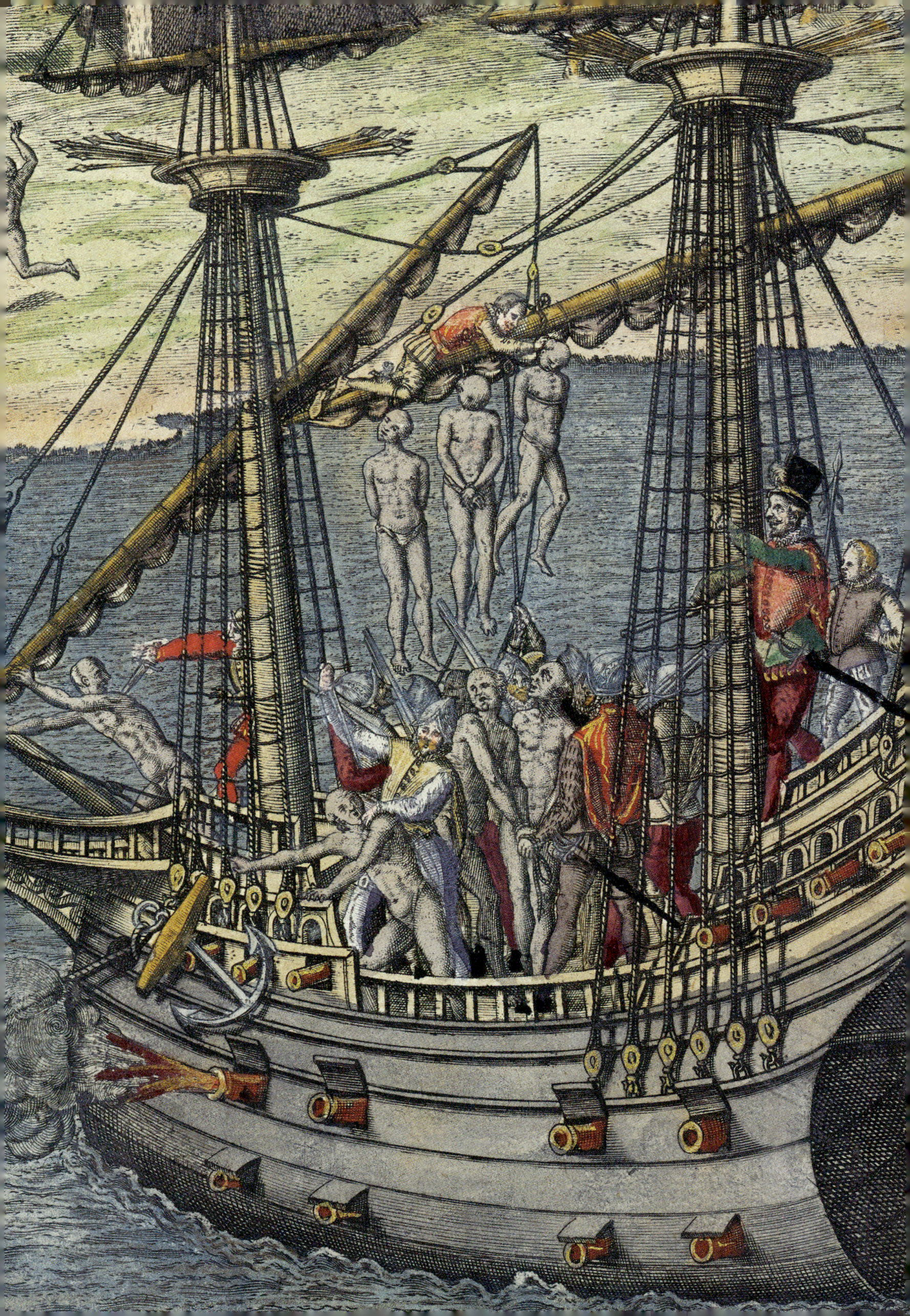

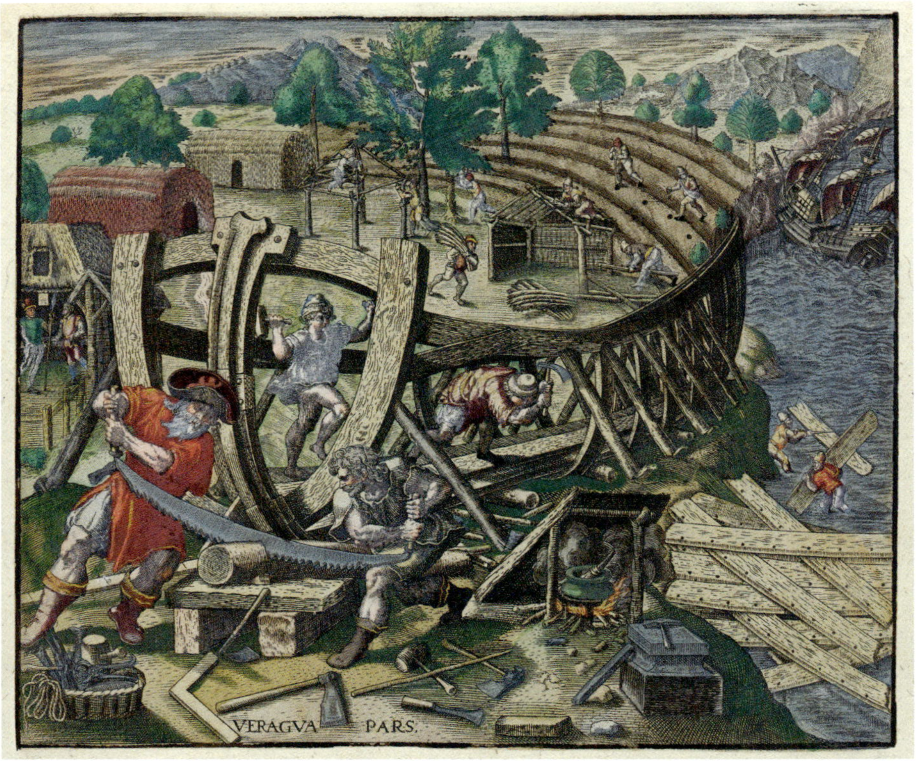

PLATE 19

Olando orders a ship and houses to be built

When a storm came up at night, Niquesa was drifted off, away from his men. They travelled hundreds of miles to find him but to no avail, and they named Olando as their commander until the return of Niquesa. Olando allowed the ships to be wrecked on the shore, to deprive his companions of their hope to escape. When the mistake, made in haste, had been punished, he ordered a caravel to be built from the planks of the wrecks in case of sudden need. Subsequently they began to build houses and sow corn.

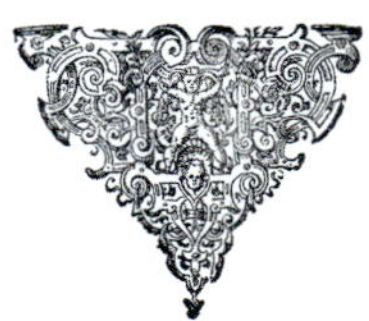

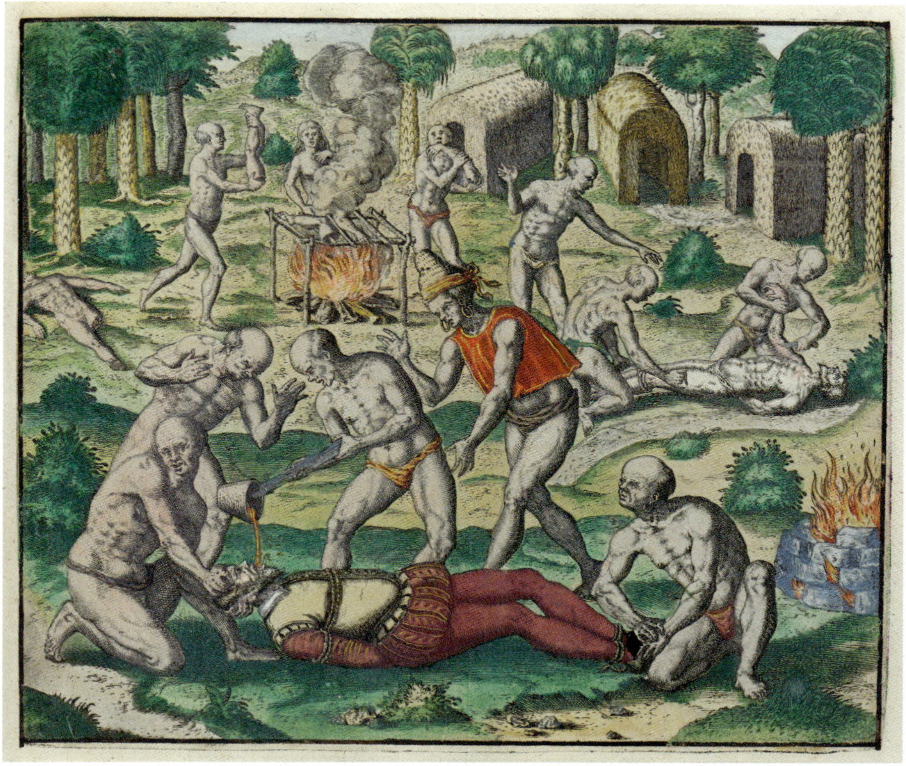

PLATE 20

The Indians pour liquid gold into the mouths of the Spaniards who are thirsty for it

Offended by the Spaniards because of their tyranny, cruelty and avarice, the Indians captured as many Spaniards as they could, especially military commanders, tied their hands and feet, and laid them on the ground. Then they poured liquid gold into their mouths, to answer their avarice, and exclaimed: “Eat, eat gold, Christian!” In order to torture them, they used stones to cut off a Spanish arm here, a shoulder there, and a leg of yet another, put them on coals, and then roasted and ate them.

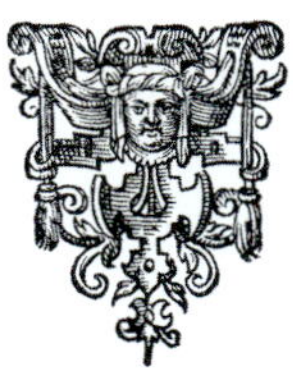

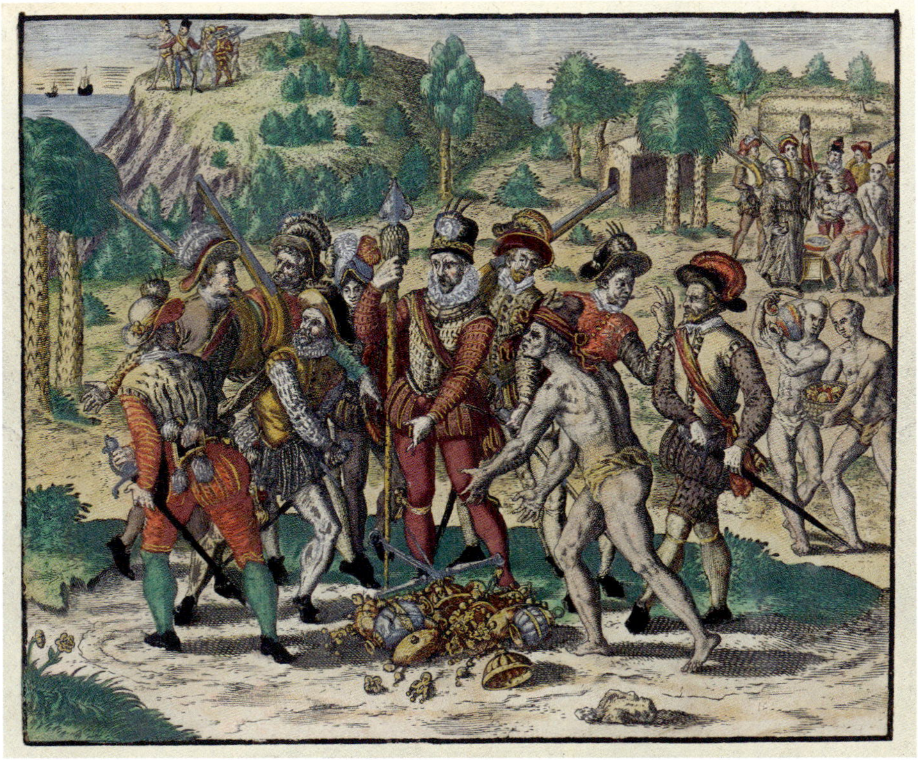

PLATE 21

A strong pronouncement by an Indian on the greed of the Christians

The ruler Panchiaco, who maintained friendly relations with Núñez de Balboa, gave him a great hoard of gold which had been manufactured into plates, dishes and necklaces. Seeing that the Spaniards quarrelled with each other and threatened to kill each other while the gold was being prepared, he took away the gold with the scales, and sharply criticised their greed. If their thirst for gold was really so great, he said, he would point them to regions where it could be found in abundance. Then he led Balboa along difficult roads to the highest mountain ridges, and showed him the Pacific Ocean. On his return Balboa had Panchiaco baptised, and christened him Carolus.

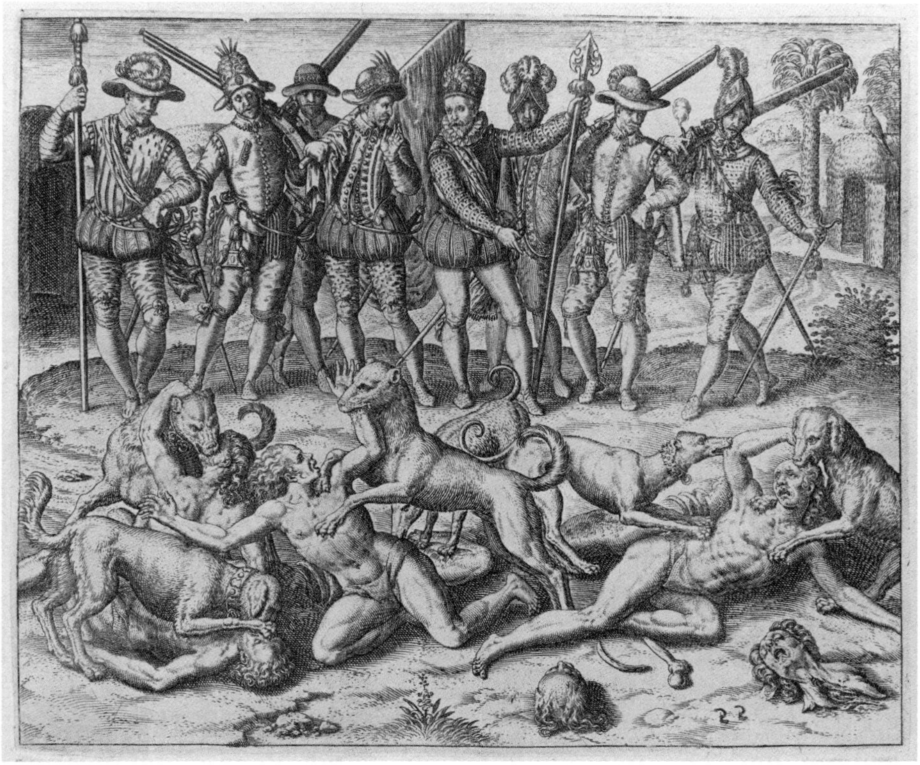

PLATE 22

Balboa has Indians who committed the sinful act of sodomy thrown before the dogs to be torn to pieces

During the trip to the mountains, Balboa triumphed over a prince in Esquaragua and killed him along with many Indians. When he marched into the village, he saw that the prince's brother and a number of others were dressed in women's clothes. Greatly surprised, Balboa asked for the reason. He was told that the murdered prince and all those belonging to his court were tainted with that godless sin against nature. Balboa, astounded that such a detestable crime had reached these barbarians, had all of them (around 40) taken prisoner, and thrown to the dogs which he had taken along on his journey, to let them be devoured.

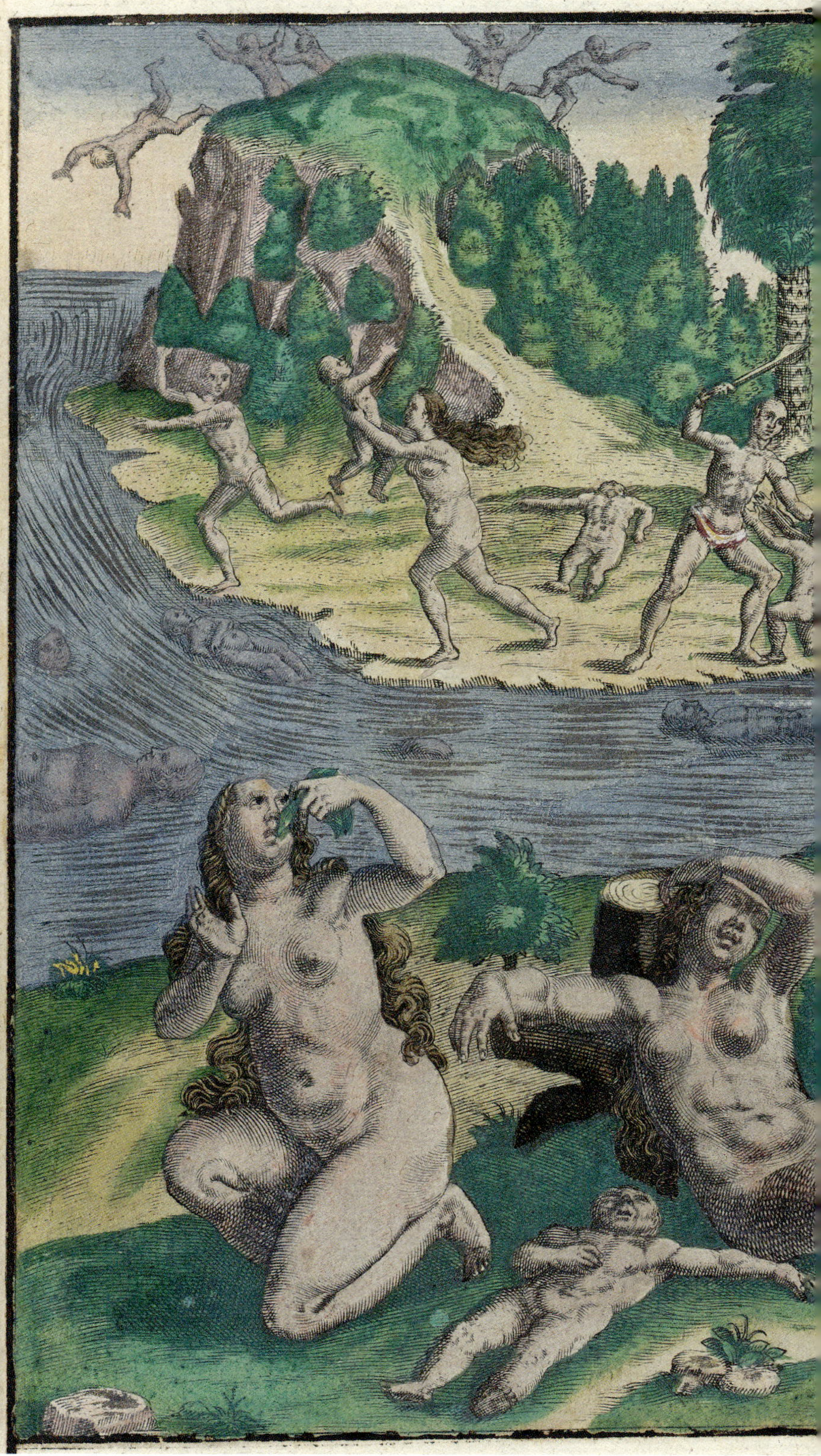

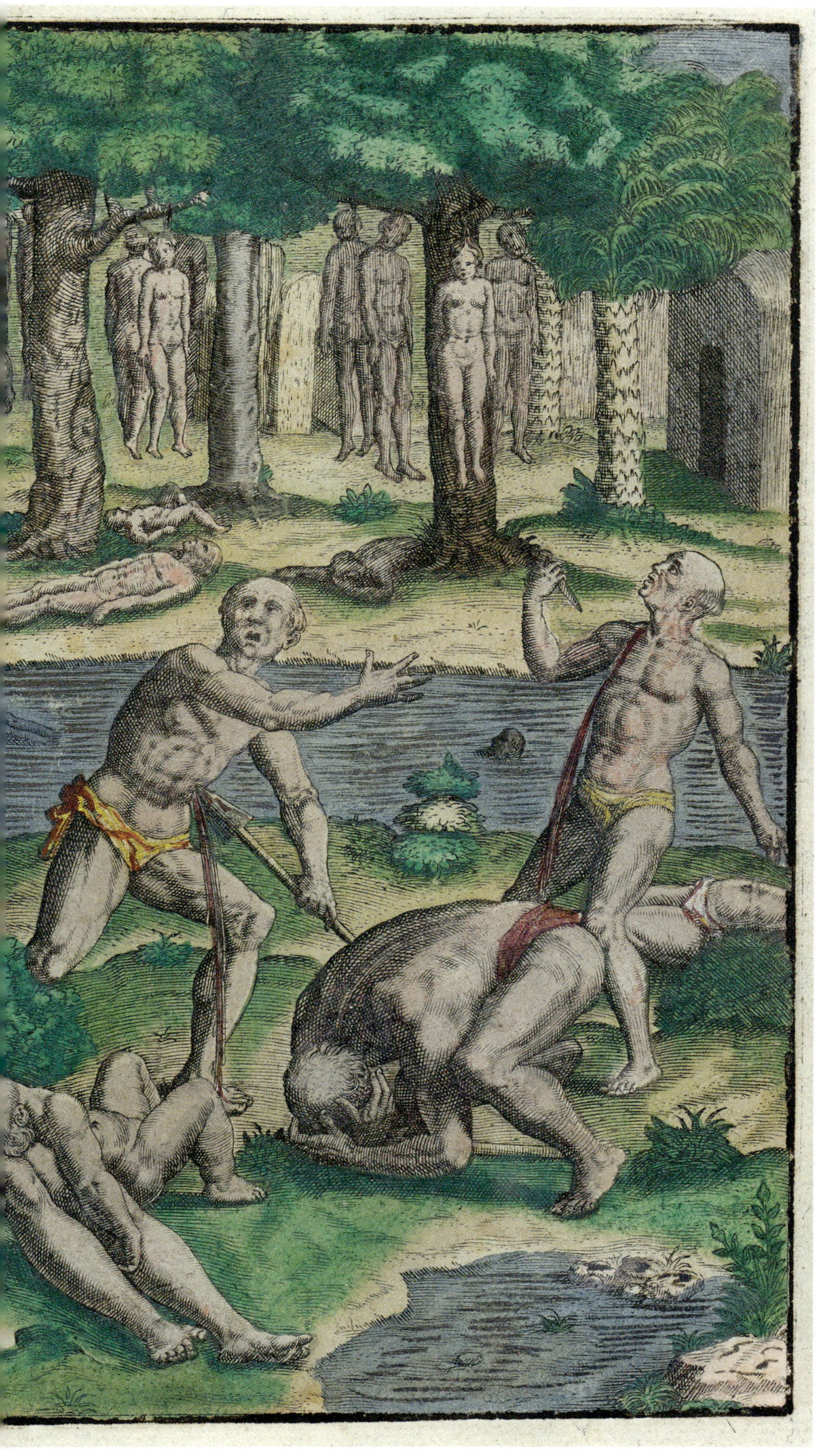

PLATE 23, PAGES 278/279

The Indians who cannot bear the ruthlessness of the Spaniards lay their hands upon themselves

The inhabitants of Hispaniola felt desperate by their unbearable misery and believed that there would be no end to the catastrophes. After having lamented their situation, they chose death following much prayer. Many of them, having given up all hope, went into the woods and hanged themselves from the trees, after having first killed their children. The women followed in the men's footsteps by making an end to their lives by rope, having first killed their unborn children by eating some poisonous plant. Some drowned themselves by jumping off the cliffs into the sea, and others by throwing themselves into the river. Several voluntarily starved themselves. There were even some who, with very sharp flint knives or with pikes, pierced their chests or sides.

PLATE 24

The religion of the Indians

Oviedo says in his treatise about the religion of the Americans that he had not seen among them a painting or sculpture that was worshipped in public more intensely than the horrible, repelling effigy of Cacodaemon. They acknowledge him as their God and ask of him what they desire. When one of the caciques of Hispaniola instituted a veneration for his god, he organised for all his subjects a day on which they should assemble. When they had come together for this ceremony, they drew up in an orderly line. The cacique himself led the procession and entered the temple first, where priests were worshipping the idol. As soon as he had sat down, he began beating the drum. The whole crowd followed, led by the men who had decorated their bodies, which had alternately black, red and yellow marks, but also mixed colours, along with the feathers of parrots and other birds. Their necks, arms and legs had been wrapped in bracelets made of pieces of seashells. The women had not painted and adorned their bodies. The virgins were completely naked, with only their private parts concealed. Thus attired, they entered the temple dancing and singing certain traditional songs in praise of the idol. Then they worked up their vomit by putting a small staff into their throats, to demonstrate to the idol that they were not carrying evil in their chests. Suddenly another row of women appeared, carrying baskets full of roses and other flowers, sprinkled with scents, and encircled the singers. When the songs had finished, they sang a hymn of praise together for their prince. Finally, the idol was given bread.

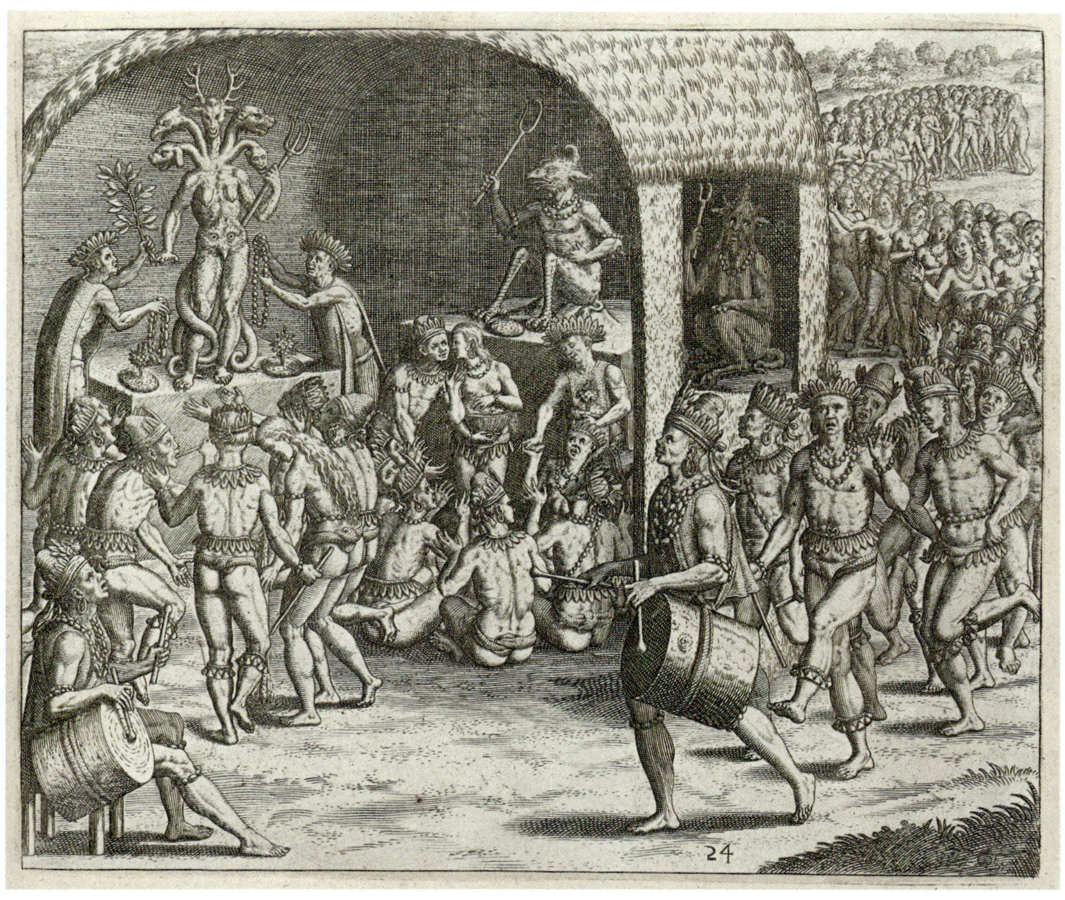
24

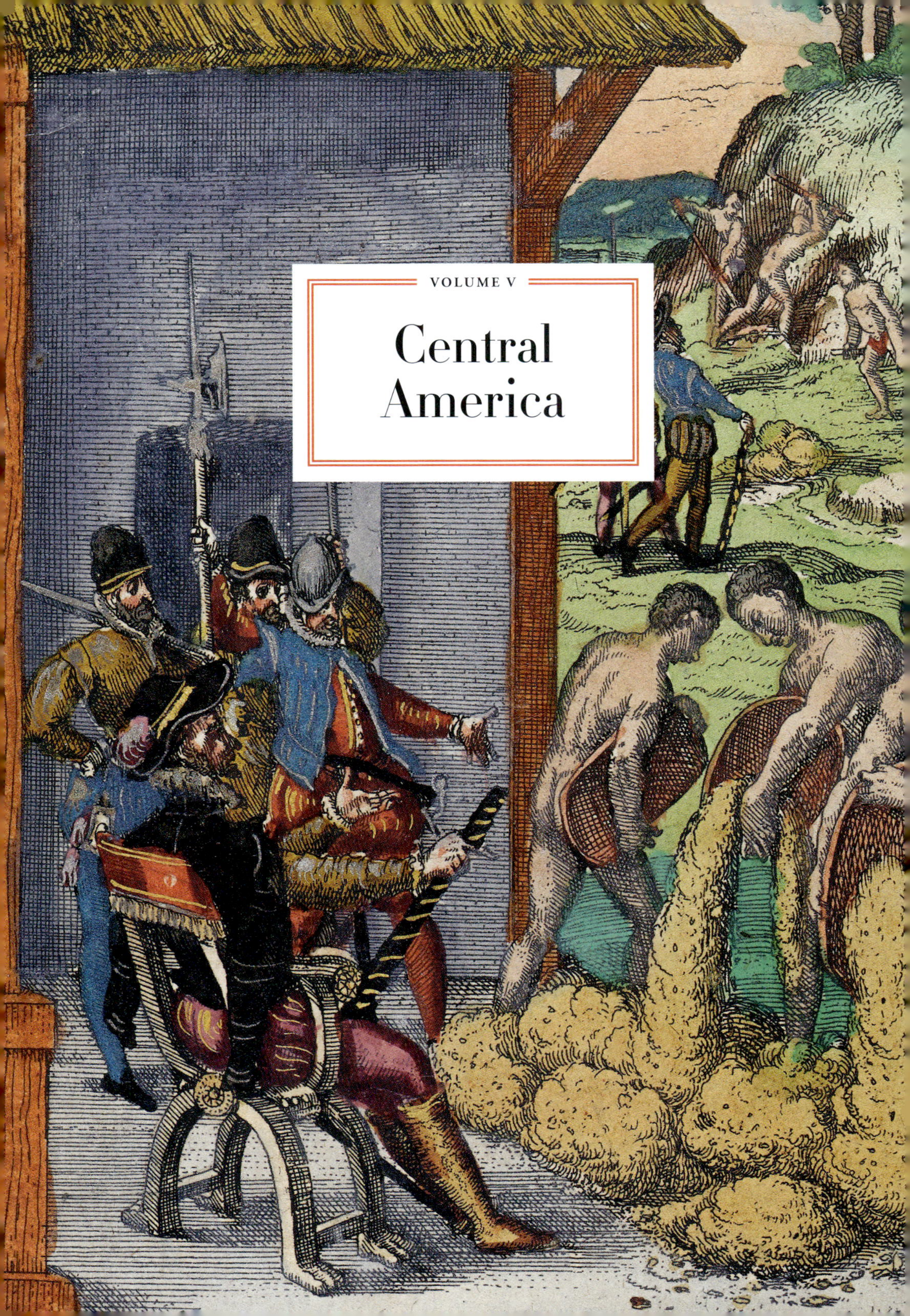
VOLUME V
Central America

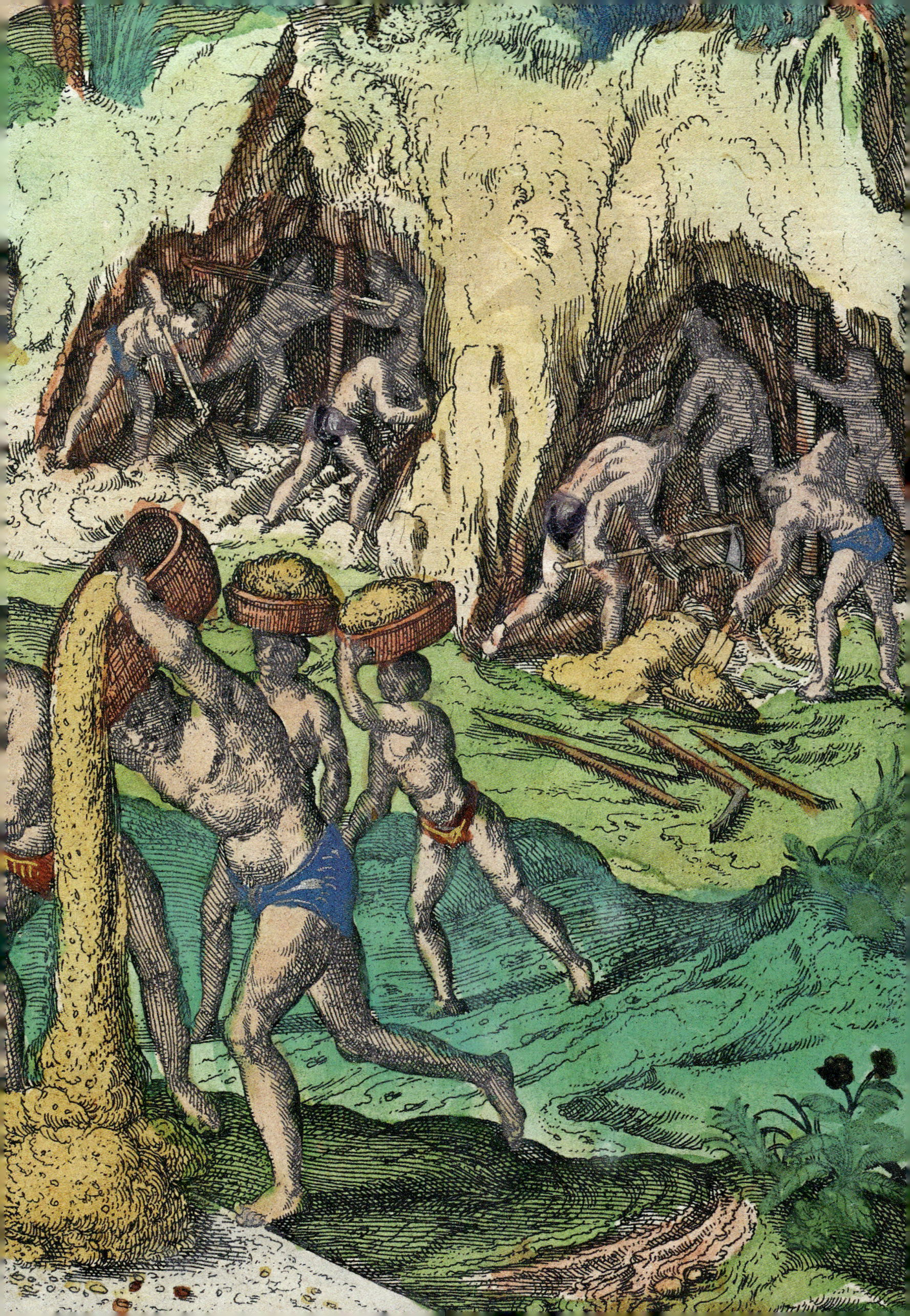

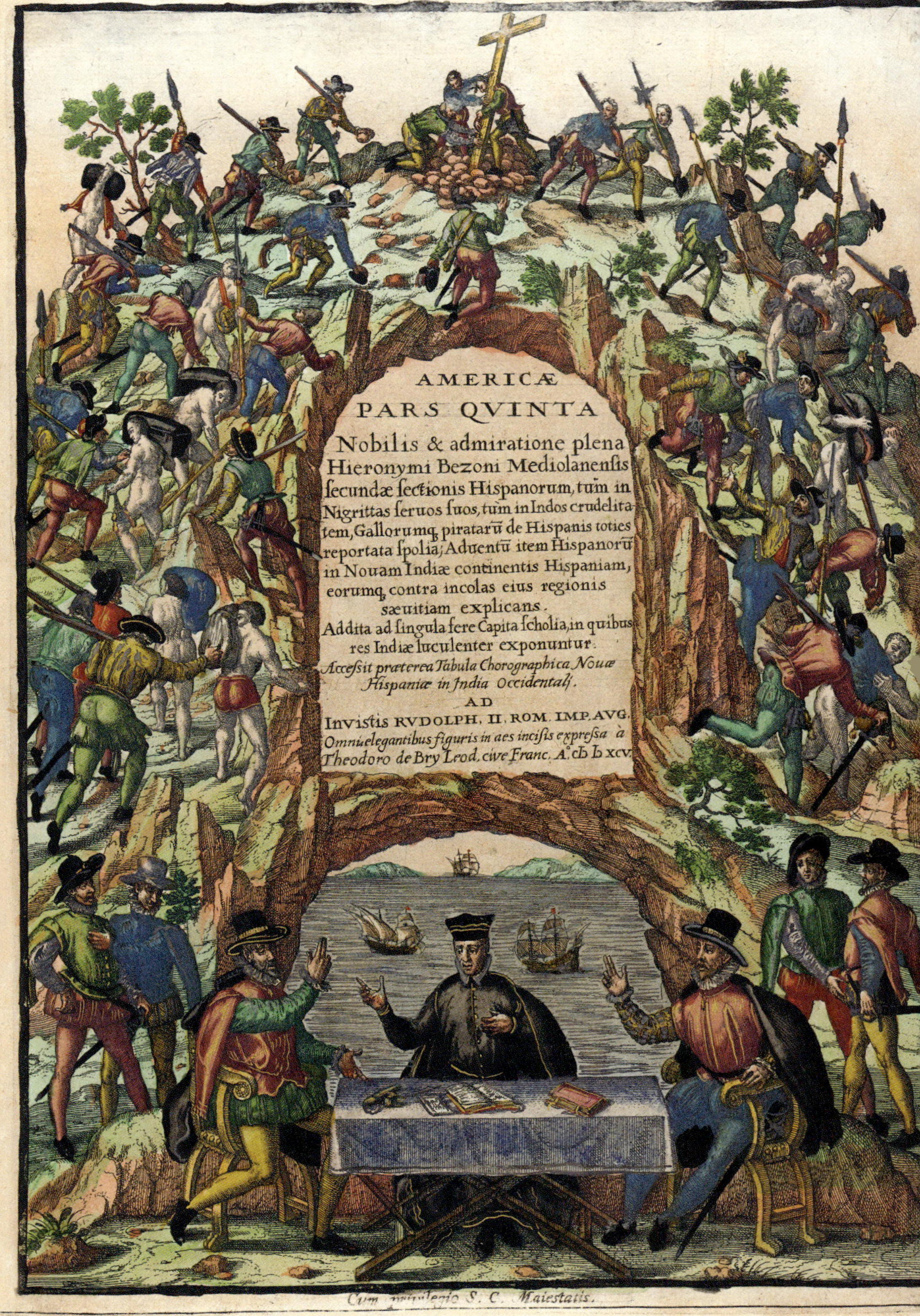

AMERICÆ
PARS QVINTA
Nobilis & admiratione plena
Hieronymi Bezoni Mediolanensis
secundæ sectionis Hispanorum, tum in
Nigrittas seruos suos, tum in Indos crudelitatem, Gallorumq; piratarũ de Hispanis toties
reportata spolia; Aduentũ item Hispanorũ
in Nouam Indiæ continentis Hispaniam,
eorumq; contra incolas eius regionis
sæuitiam explicans.
Addita ad singula fere Capita scholia, in quibus
res Indiæ luculenter exponuntur.
Accessit præterea Tabula Chorographica Nouæ
Hispaniæ in India Occidentali.
AD
Invistis RVDOLPH. II. ROM. IMP. AVG.
Omniu elegantibus figuris in aes incisis expressa à
Theodoro de Bry Leod. cive Franc. A°. cIↄ Iↄ xcv.
Cum privilegio S. C. Maiestatis.

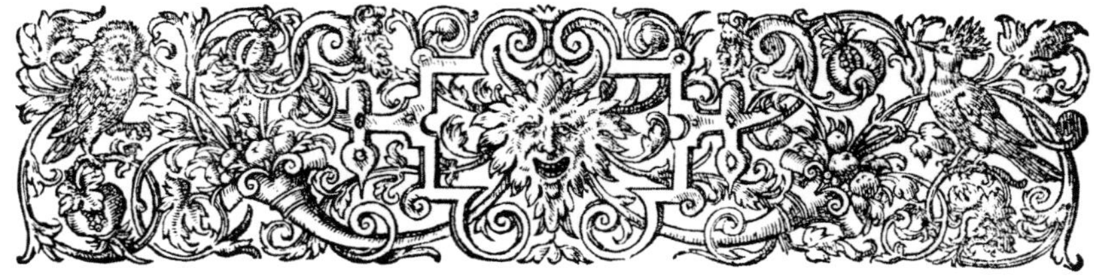

Volume V

Based on: Girolamo Benzoni, *Historia del Mondo Nuovo* (Milan, 1565), subsequently published in several editions

The second part of Benzoni's work appeared as volume V of the *America* series, and continued the narrative begun in volume IV by focusing in the main on the Spanish conquest of the Caribbean. While the frontispiece of the previous volume had positioned a pagan idol at the top of the composition, this volume's frontispiece reflected European progress by depicting a cross being raised up. The sequence of illustrations, all invented or heavily adapted by the De Brys, begins with four scenes showing slave labour on the plantations of Hispaniola, a rare reference to a practice that would become a mainstay of the colonial economy in the 17th and 18th centuries. Because Benzoni described slave labour as part of a catalogue of Spanish misconduct, the illustrations of slavery in the De Bry collection from 1595 are some of the earliest (and for a long time were some of the only) critical representations of forced labour in the Americas. Interestingly enough, the colourist depicted the enslaved labourers as white, depriving the image of some of its ethnic meaning in the process. The following images depicted some of the elements which had already been presented in the earlier volumes, namely the Franco-Spanish conflict, aspects of native culture, the increasing greed of the Spanish conquistadors and Native American reactions to European violence. Here too, as in volume IV, the sequence of illustrations ran through a series of unrelated New World territories – Florida, Mexico, Nicaragua – which corresponded to Benzoni's amalgamated and generally quite superficial account.

While Benzoni himself had dedicated the original edition of his book to Pope Pius IV – right at the time when the humanity of the Native Americans (and thus their capacity to be converted to Christianity) was the subject of intense debate in Europe – the De Brys dedicated all three Benzoni volumes (in the German edition) to the Calvinist Landgrave Maurice of Hesse-Kassel,

Frontispiece of volume V

Pages 282/283
Detail of volume V, plate 1

one of their most loyal and consistent benefactors over the years. In return for his unwavering support, the De Brys presented him with a luxurious edition of the first six volumes of the *America* series, bound in red morocco, for which they again received a considerable sum of money. Many of the nobility, especially in the Holy Roman Empire, began to see the collection as a desirable and prestigious item. The other side of the coin, however, was that by the time volume V appeared, the accumulation of volumes had already become too much for ordinary readers. Each volume was a separate publication, and there are several known individual customers who returned to their local bookshop every year to buy the latest volume in the collection. By the mid-1590s though fewer and fewer customers were doing this, and it was probably around this time that the assemblage of volumes came to be viewed by readers as a collection.

A wealthy readership also meant that the quality of the volumes, in every respect, was of great importance for the publishers. For each and every volume in their collection of voyages the De Brys relied on a local printer to produce the books (they did not possess their own printing press). The name of the printer invariably appeared on each volume's title-page, but for the Latin edition of *America* V the printer's name is unknown. The reason for this can be found in a letter Theodore de Bry wrote in 1595 to Carolus Clusius, who no longer translated for the De Brys but continued to write captions to accompany the set of engravings at the end of every volume. De Bry complained to Clusius that the printer had done a bad job on volume V, printing some of the copper engravings over and across the texts. The inclusion of copper engravings in printed books was a relatively new technique in Frankfurt in the 1590s, and clearly not every printer could accomplish it at the level the De Brys required, but this was a form of artisanal sloppiness the De Brys could ill afford for their flagship publication. As Johan Theodore and Johan Israel de Bry took on more and more responsibility for the collection from their ailing father, they increasingly abandoned the circle of Sigismund Feyerabend's associates upon whom Theodore had relied in favour of their own associates with whom they continued to work for a number of years.

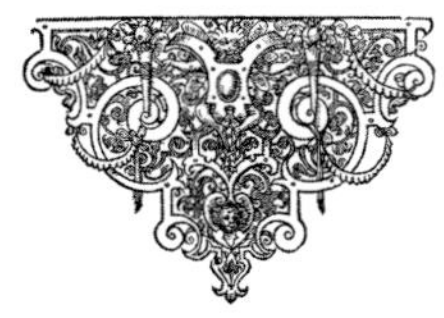

Detail of volume V, plate 10

Pages 288/289
Map of New Spain showing Native American settlements

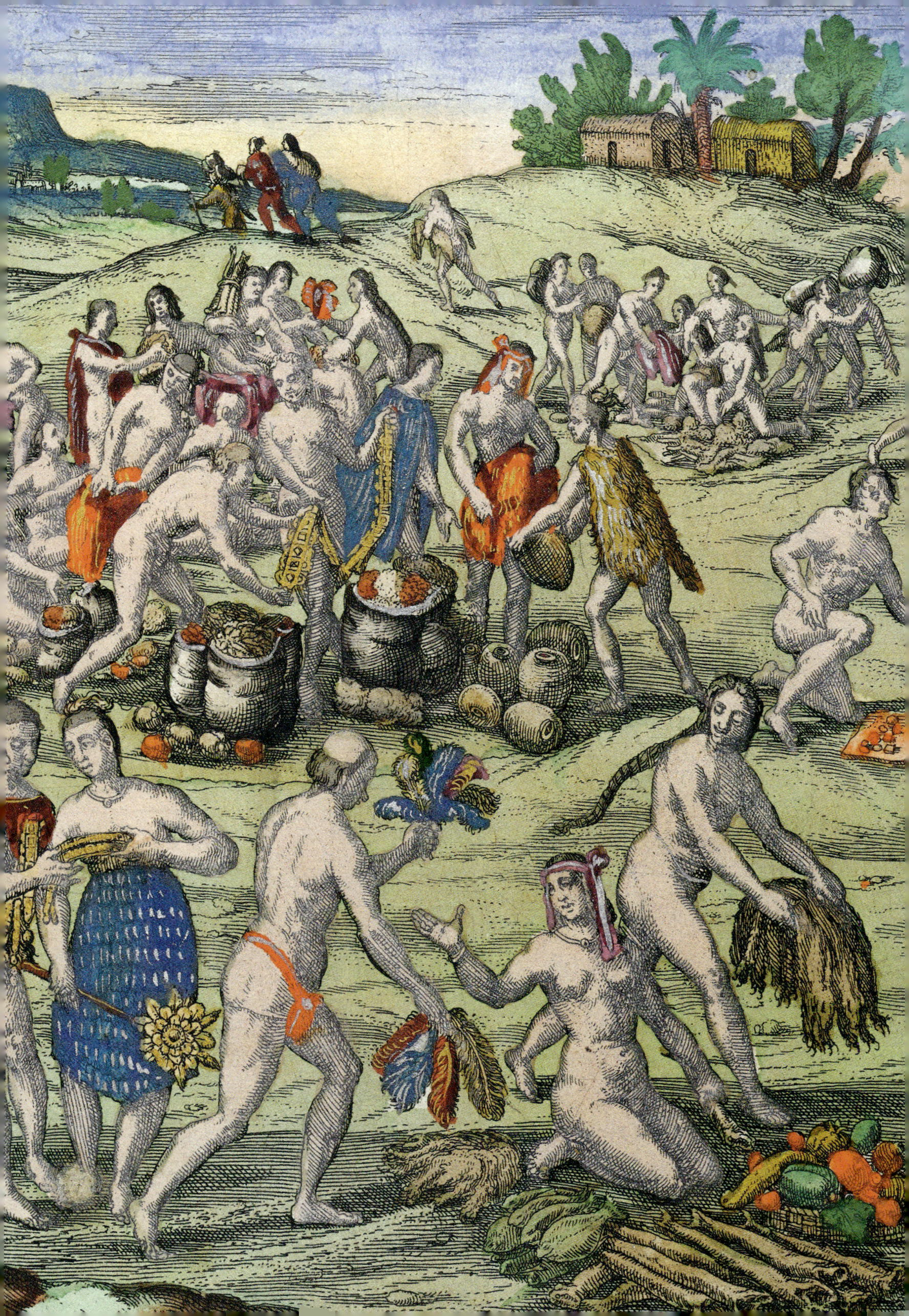

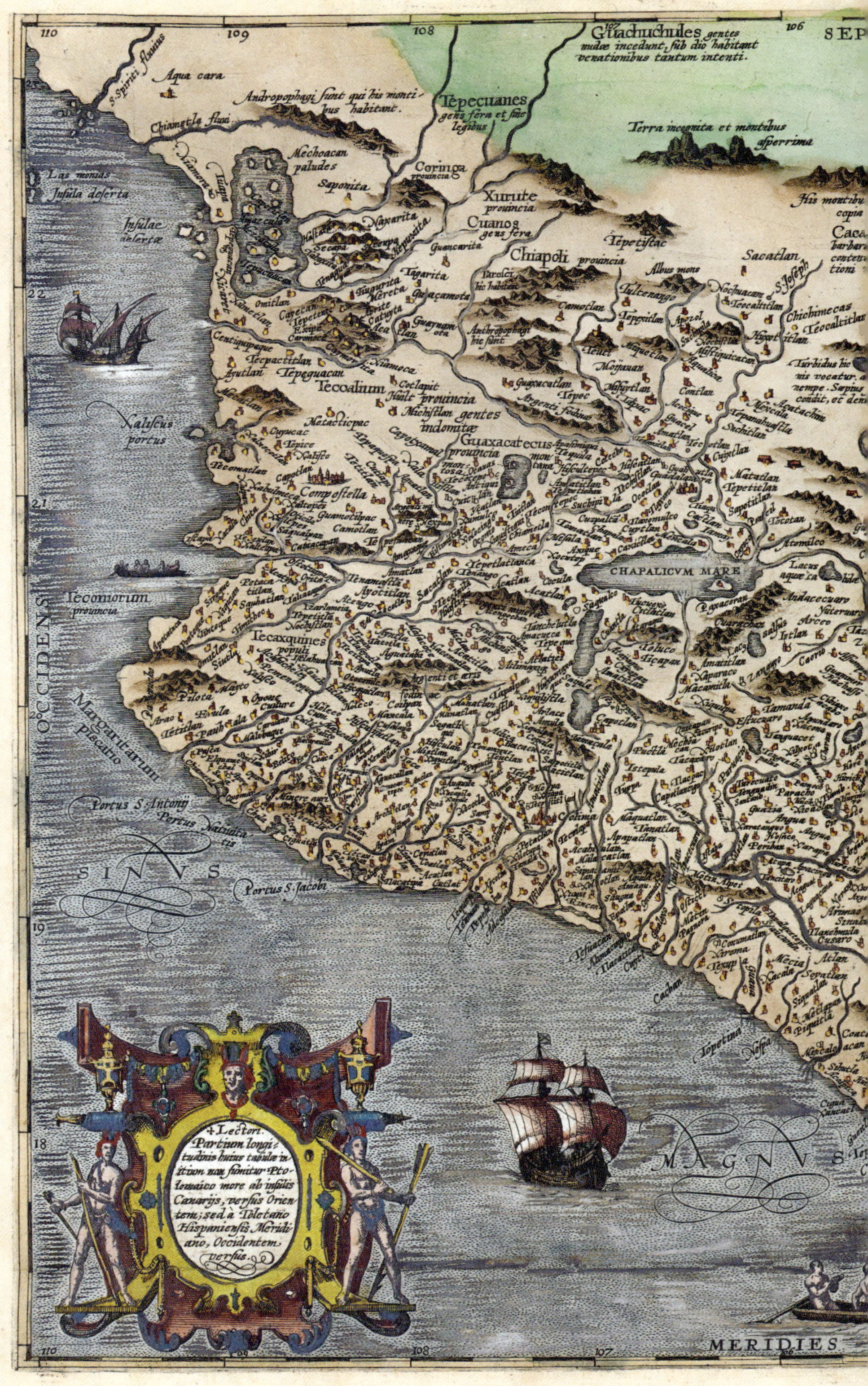
Guachuchules gentes nudae incedunt, sub dio habitant venationibus tantum intenti.
Tepecuanes gens fera et sine legibus
Terra incognita et montibus asperrima
Andropophagi sunt qui his montibus habitant.
Aqua cara
Mechoacan paludes
Coringa prouincia
Xurute prouincia
Cuanos gens fera
Chiapoli prouincia
Tepetistac
Sacatlan
Albus mons
Chichimecas
Teocalcitlan
Tecoalium
Michistlan gentes indomitae
Guaxacatecus prouincia
Xalliscus portus
Compostella
CHAPALICVM MARE
Tecoaniorum prouincia
Tecaxquines populi
Margaritarum piscatio
Portus S. Antonij
Portus Natiuitatis
Portus S. Jacobi
SINVS
OCCIDENS
MAGNVS
MERIDIES
Lectori.
Partium longitudinis huius tabulae initium non sumitur Ptolemaico more ab insulis Canarijs, versus Orientem; sed à Toletano Hispaniensis Meridiano, Occidentem versus.

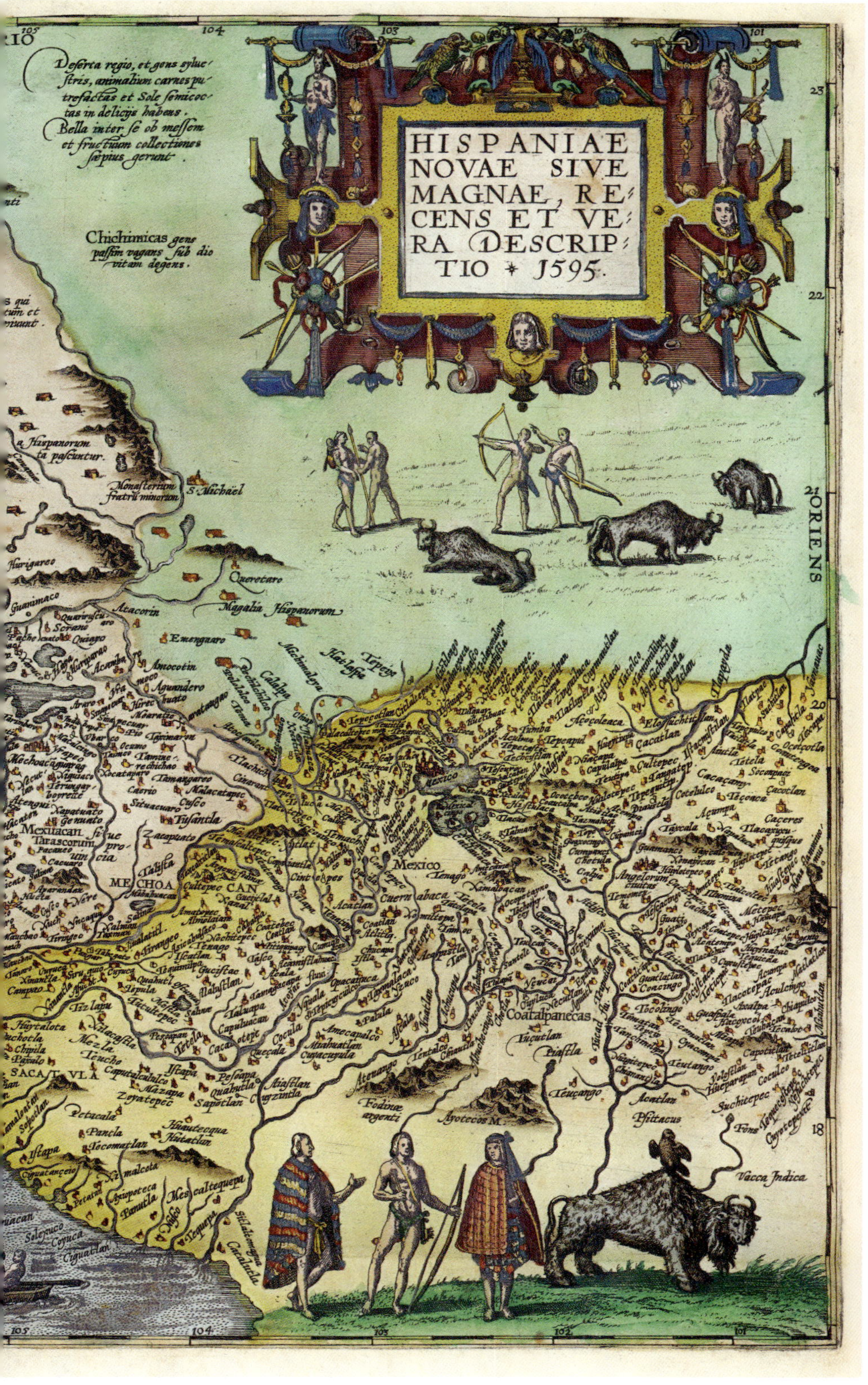
HISPANIAE NOVAE SIVE MAGNAE, RECENS ET VERA DESCRIPTIO 1595.
Deserta regio, et gens sylue- stris, animalium carnes pu- trefactas et Sole semicoc- tas in delicijs habens. Bella inter se ob messem et fructuum collectiones sæpius gerunt.
Chichimicas gens passim vagans sub dio vitam degens.
Monasterium fratrũ minorum
S. Michaël
Queretaro
Magalia Hispanorum
ORIENS
Mexico
MECHOA CAN
Coatalpanecas
Fodinæ argenti
Acatlan
Pſittacus
Vacca Indica

PLATE 1

African slaves are sent to the islands by the Spaniards to search for gold

When the inhabitants of Hispaniola were exhausted, and almost died from persistent labouring, the Spaniards began to assemble slaves from elsewhere to dig tunnels and search for mineral riches with their help. With their money they purchased Ethiopians, or black slaves, and imported them from Guinea, a province in West Africa. From then on they would make use of their services until over time they had extracted every precious metal that could be found on the island. When the Portuguese had conquered Guinea (their inhabitants call it Genni or Genna) they sold hundreds of natives to foreign regions within several years to make up for shortages of slaves there.

PLATE 2, PAGES 292/293

After exhausting the mineral riches, the African slaves have to dedicate themselves to the production of sugar

And so the Spaniards have made use of slave labour to search for mineral riches. When these were exhausted, they applied the services of the slaves to operate treadmills to crush the sugar-cane for cooking and thickening, and they have continued to do that until today. Since Hispaniola is humid and warm, the sugar-cane grows excessively well. It is crushed and thrown into kettles, boiled, purified one more time, and then congealed into sugar, and then tends to yield great profit. In addition, the services of the African slaves are used to tend the cattle and look after other things which are necessary for their practices.

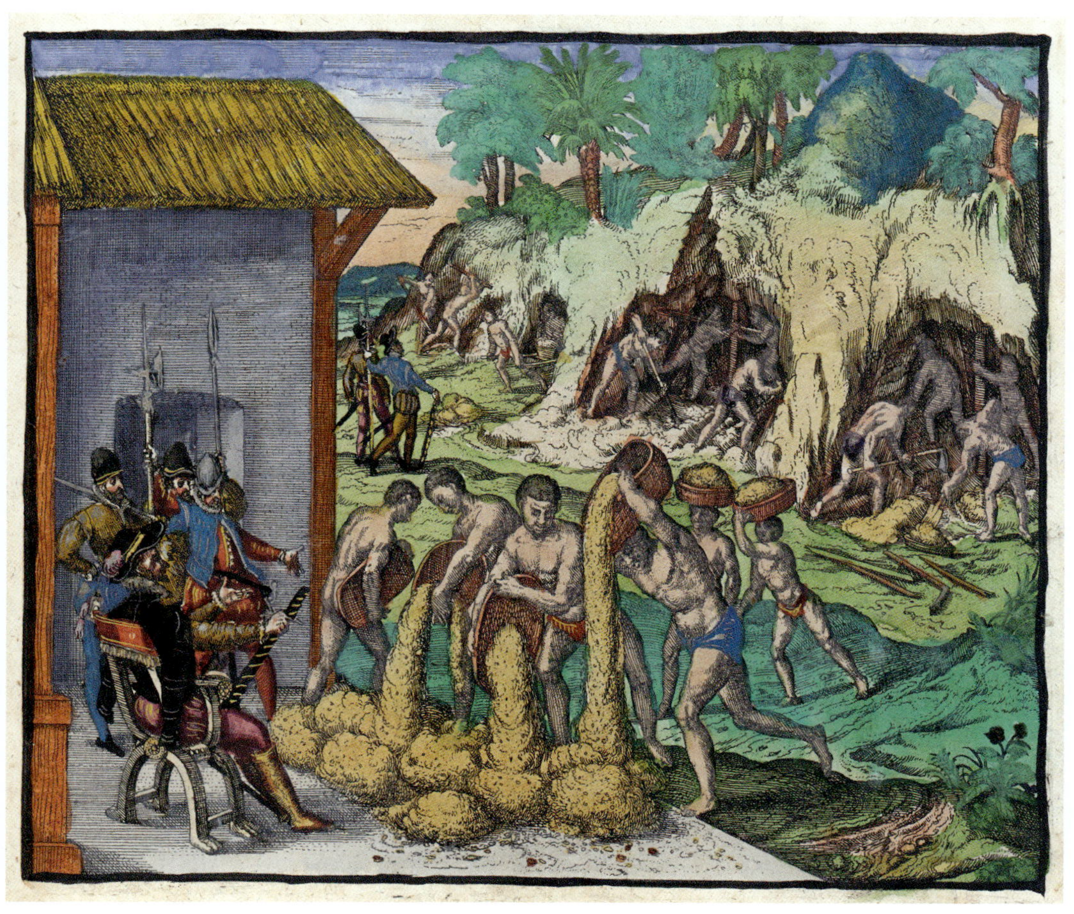

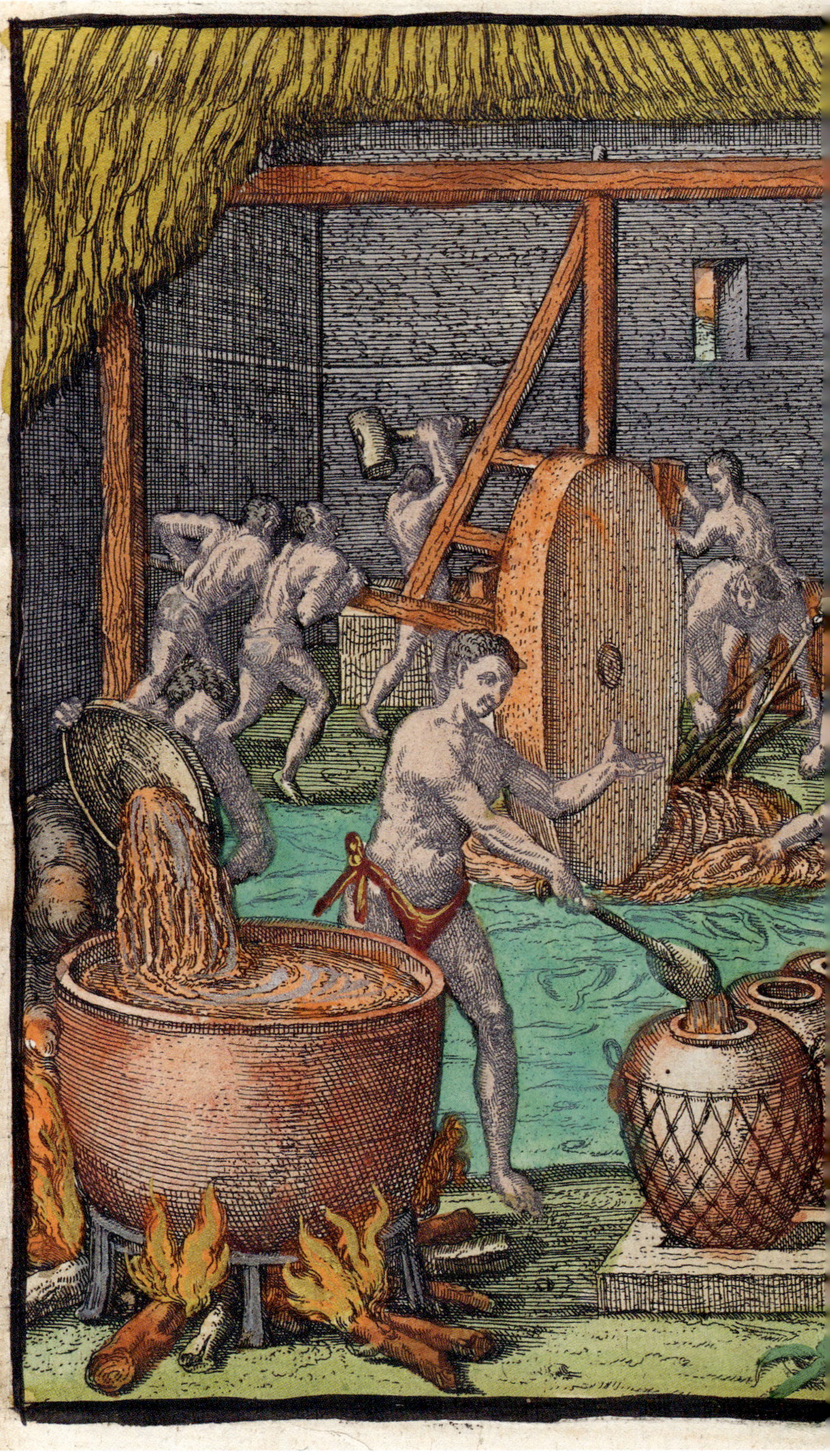

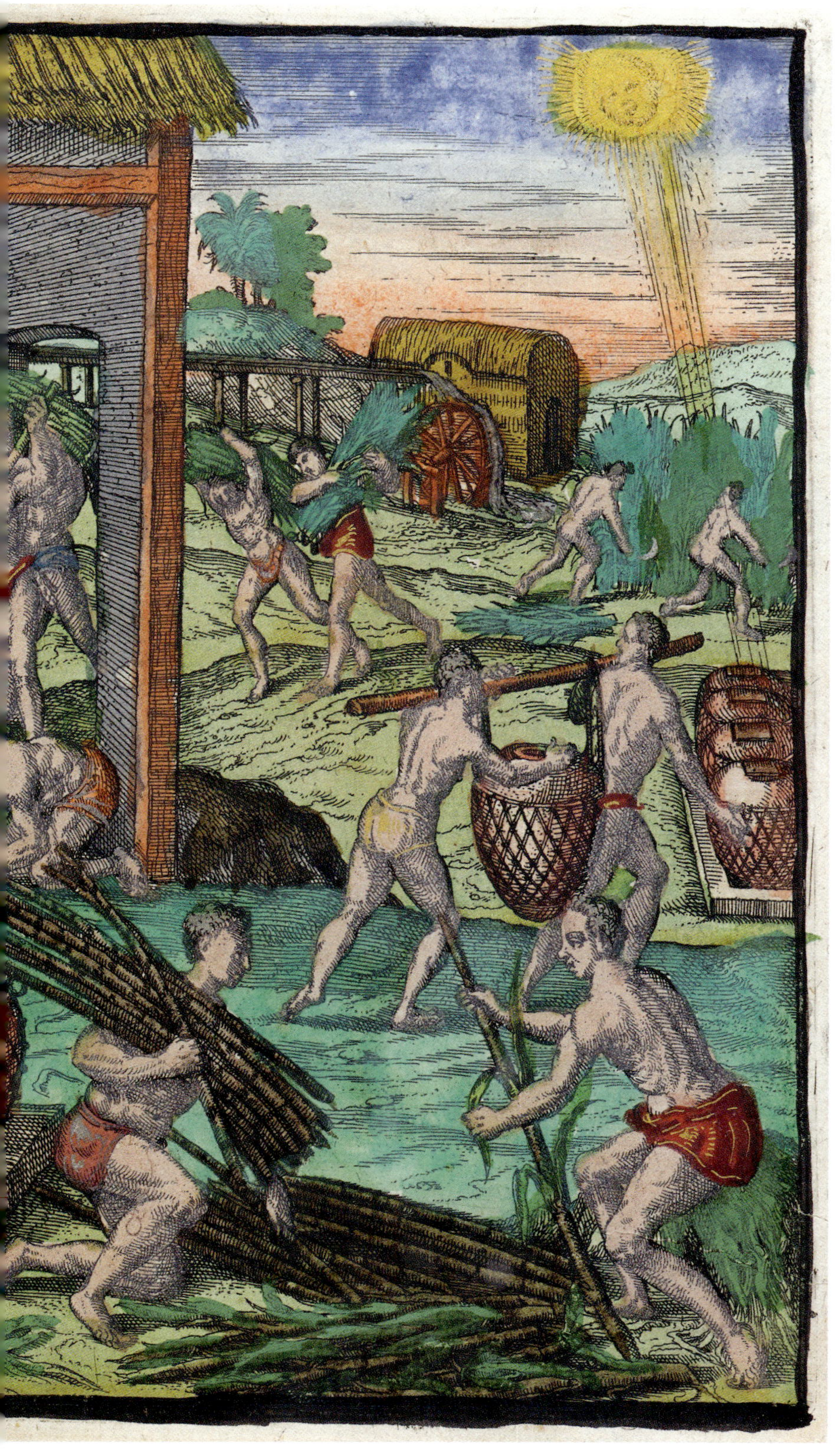

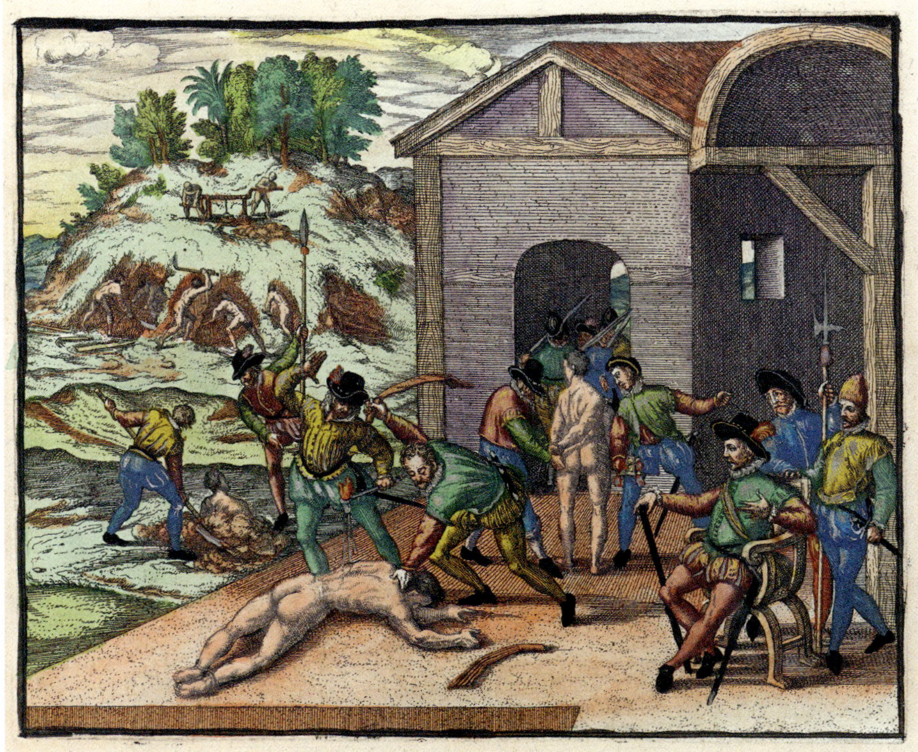

PLATE 3

African slaves who have not performed their daily duties are treated cruelly by the Spaniards

Although only a few Spaniards are cruel by nature, they influence others around them if they want to punish those who are negligent during daily duties or who commit a crime. When the slaves came home in the evening, they received no food, but their clothes were torn from their bodies (if they had any). They were pushed to the ground, naked and chained, and beaten with whips or ropes until blood dripped from their bodies. Then the Spaniards slowly dripped boiling tar or olive oil into their open wounds. Finally they rubbed in some ground Brazilian pepper, mixed with water. They laid the slaves down full length on a table or plank, covered them with a blanket, and left them there until their master thought they would be ready to work again. There are some Spaniards who punish their slaves in a different way. After flogging them, they dig a hole in the ground and bury them until only their head sticks out. They claim to do this as a favour to the slaves, for the earth dissolves the running and clotted blood, and keeps their bodies intact. If one of them dies, which often happens because of the unbearable pain, the owner cannot be blamed, as long as he provides the king with another slave as a replacement.

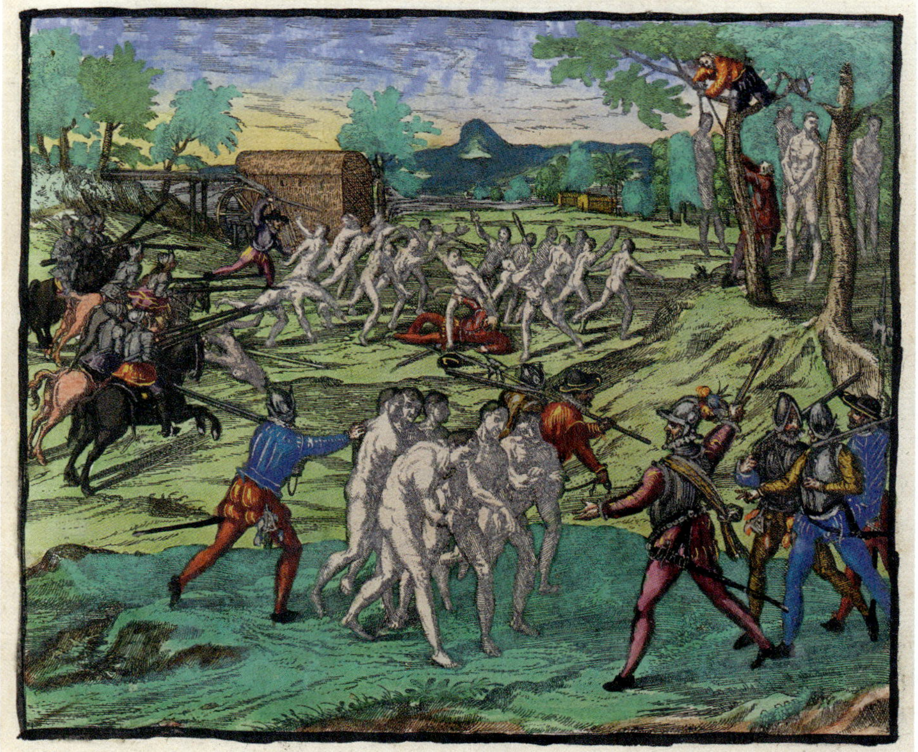

PLATE 4

The African slaves run from the Spaniards, kill a few of them, but are finally put to death by the Spaniards in different ways

Several slaves, embittered by these Spanish cruelties, ran away from their masters. They roamed across the island, bursting into the quarters of other slaves, rounded them up, and killed as many Spaniards as they could. Their numbers increased so quickly that they presented the Spaniards with grave problems. Admiral Ludovico Columbus discussed the problem with the president and other councillors near Santo Domingo, and then gathered his soldiers to pursue the slaves. He lured some of them to him with false claims of liberty, and then bribed them. Hence he came to know the whereabouts of the others who had run away. One night, he overwhelmed some of them in their sleep, and killed them like sheep. Some were hanged from the branches of trees as an example to others. At first, the Spaniards managed to turn the issue in their favour, but later on the slaves learned from their mistakes and stood guard at night, thus presenting the Spaniards with great difficulties.

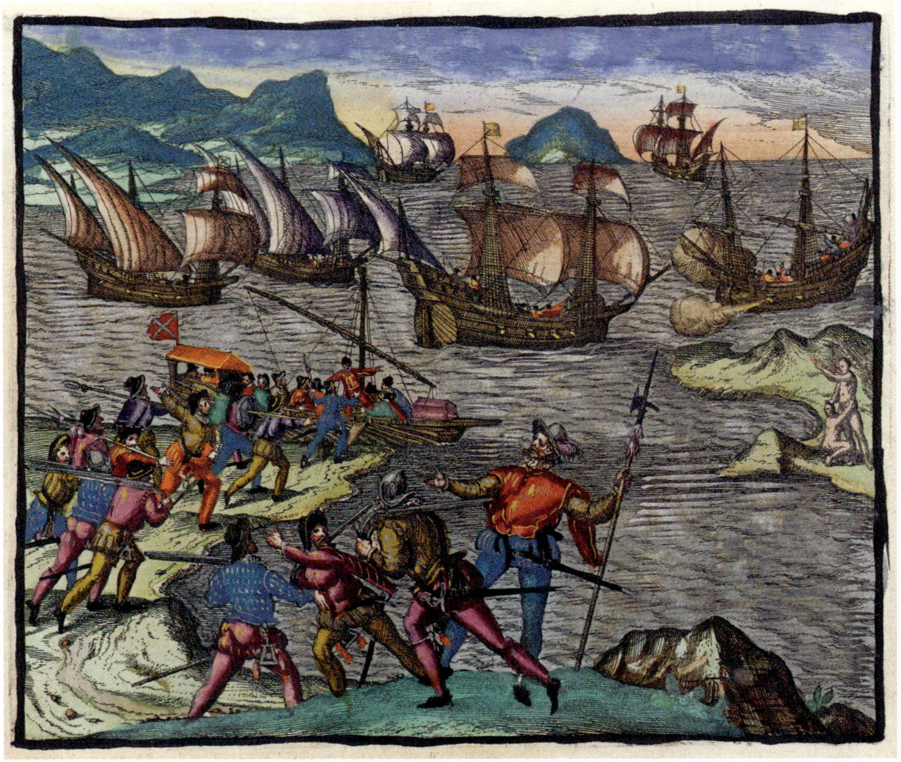

PLATE 5

The Spaniards capture a French vessel because of the lack of courage of the French captain

The directors of the Royal Council in Santo Domingo were informed that two French vessels were close to the town, causing havoc at sea. They sent five vessels, two of which were large, to pursue the French. The Cantabrians, whose home province was contested by France, were afraid when they saw so many Spanish vessels, that they might be taken captive and put to death as traitors, because they were subjects of the king of Spain. The captain of the second French ship did not believe that he could resist the enemy ships on his own, and advised his crew to lay down their weapons and surrender to the Spanish vessels. The majority of the crew protested, particularly the man who fired the guns. He claimed that he would bring down the enemy flagship with four shots. Without further delay, he fired a cannonball towards the Spanish ships, which did great damage to the flagship. When he wanted to fire again, the French captain forbade him to do so, and thus it was only through his cowardice that the French were overtaken and brought to Santo Domingo as captives, where the local inhabitants celebrated as if the whole of France had been taken by Spain. The ship was taken ashore, and burned after the anchors, ropes, sails and other useful equipment had been secured.

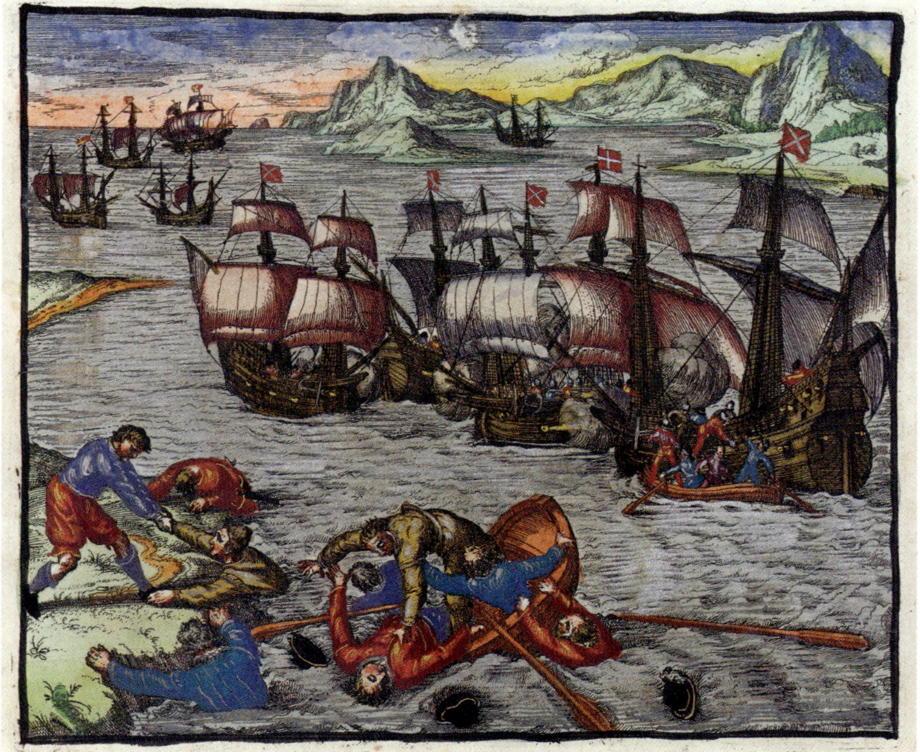

PLATE 6

The Spaniards flee from the French, who fine the town of Havana a large sum of money

In 1536, a French ship arrived in the port of Havana, and the French who were on board captured the town. The Spaniards paid a ransom of 700 ducats to save the town from being burned, which the French accepted and then left. But the Spaniards were angry that a single French ship had caused them to pay up, and the following day the governor ordered three ships full of gold, silver and other merchandise to unload their cargo and pursue the French vessel. The ships set sail, each taking along a small boat. The flagship tracked the French vessel, but did not dare to attack it on its own, and decided to wait for the other two. When the French noticed the hesitation in the Spanish ranks, they fired their guns first, leading the Spaniards to such confusion that they failed to defend themselves, jumped into the boat that was tied to their ship, and fled. The boat was pushed under the waterline by the weight of all the crew, and the Spaniards were forced to swim to the coast. Those who sailed on the second Spanish vessel saw that the flagship had been abandoned, and subsequently also fled, just like the soldiers of the third ship. The French, who were initially afraid of the three ships, rejoiced, took possession of the three vessels, sailed back to Havana and took as much gold as they could from the local inhabitants. Then they left.

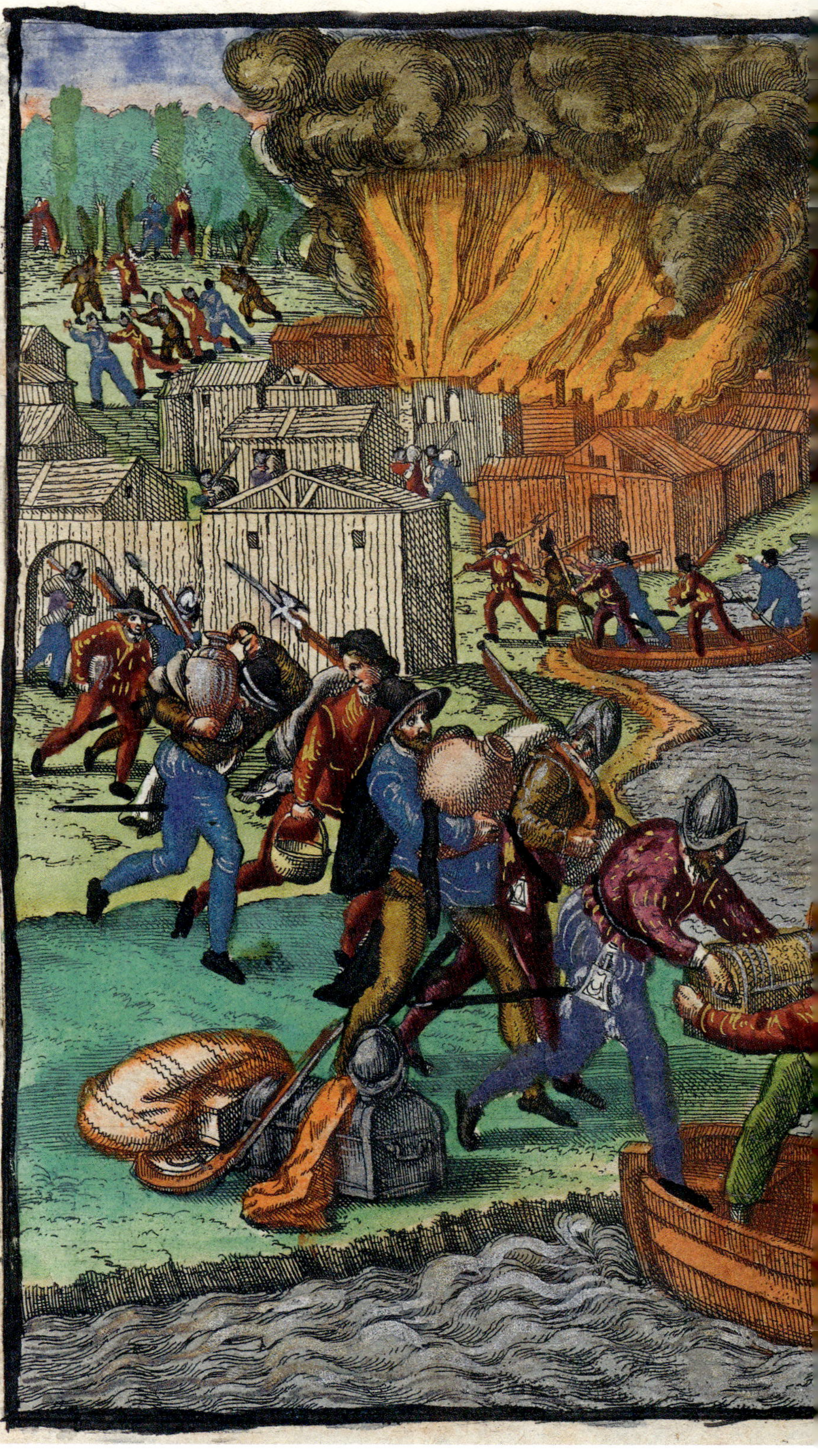

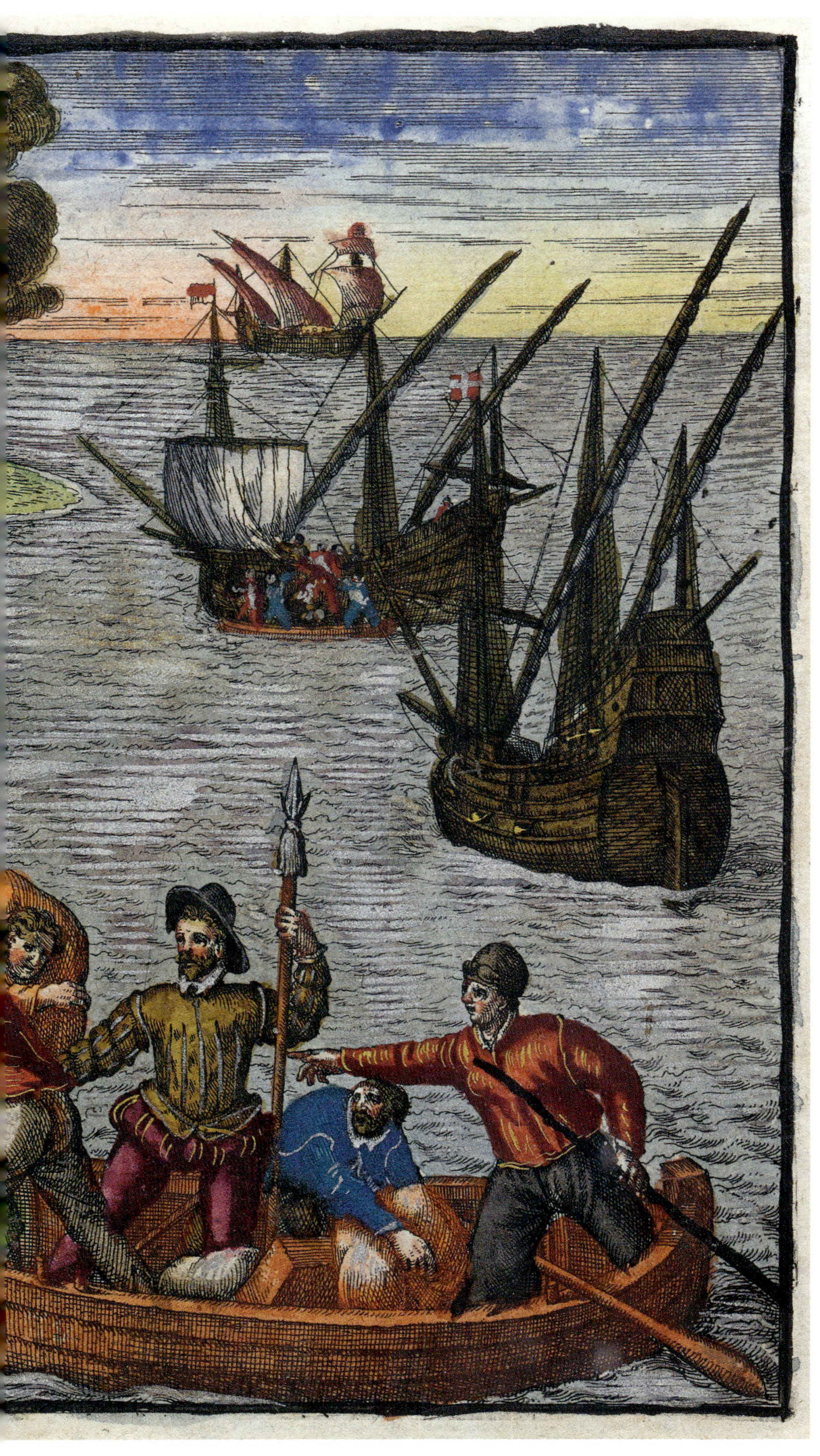

PLATE 7, PAGES 298/299

The French occupy the town of Chiorera, sack it and set it on fire because of the inhabitants' perfidy

Chiorera, a town on the island of Cuba, was taken by the French who found an enormous booty there, because the Spaniards, who had taken these riches from the French in the first place, kept it on their estates. When the French were collecting the booty, however, two Spaniards were sent to observe how numerous the French were under the pretext of negotiating a treaty with them about prisoners of war and the taxation of the town. The French officer demanded 600 ducats. The Spaniards excused themselves for their poverty, and claimed that they could not pay the amount even if they collected all the money from the local population. Instead, they would inform the Council and would return with an answer the following day. Meanwhile, the Spaniards started preparing for battle, choosing not to listen to the warnings of others who were more experienced. Assisted by their African slaves, they attacked the French at night in the hope of overwhelming them in their sleep. Yet the French were not surprised by the attack, and took up arms. The commander had ordered tar to be smeared on all the doors and rafters which were then set on fire. While the fire razed the town, the commander personally set fire to the church. A Spaniard who had observed all this said: "Please, officer, have you not sufficiently satisfied your wrath by burning the town, without also setting fire to the House of God?" The officer replied: "You, criminal, do you not realise that people who know no faith do not need a church?" He then took his ship into the harbour, loaded it with riches, and left.

PLATE 8

The French occupy Cartagena led by a Spanish sailor, who stabs a local judge who had sentenced him

Around the same period, a Spanish judge in Cartagena, a city on the American continent, had a sailor flogged for a minor offence and then set him free. After returning, the sailor defected to France. From there he led five ships to the Indies where they dropped their anchors before the entrances to the bay of Cartagena. He put a hundred men into small boats and sent them ashore. With these men, he marched to the city and one hour before sunrise, he attacked the Spaniards in their sleep. They violently opened the doors and took possession of the houses, the majority of which were made of wood or sugar-cane, and covered with palm leaves. The Spanish sailor, with some French troops, broke into the house of the judge who had punished him, and stabbed him several times with a knife. The other Frenchmen sacked and pillaged the city. The Spanish colonists fled looking for safety, meaning that the city was taken by the French and ultimately consumed by fire. They say that each of the persons who sacked and burned the city took more than 150,000 ducats as booty from the prisoners.

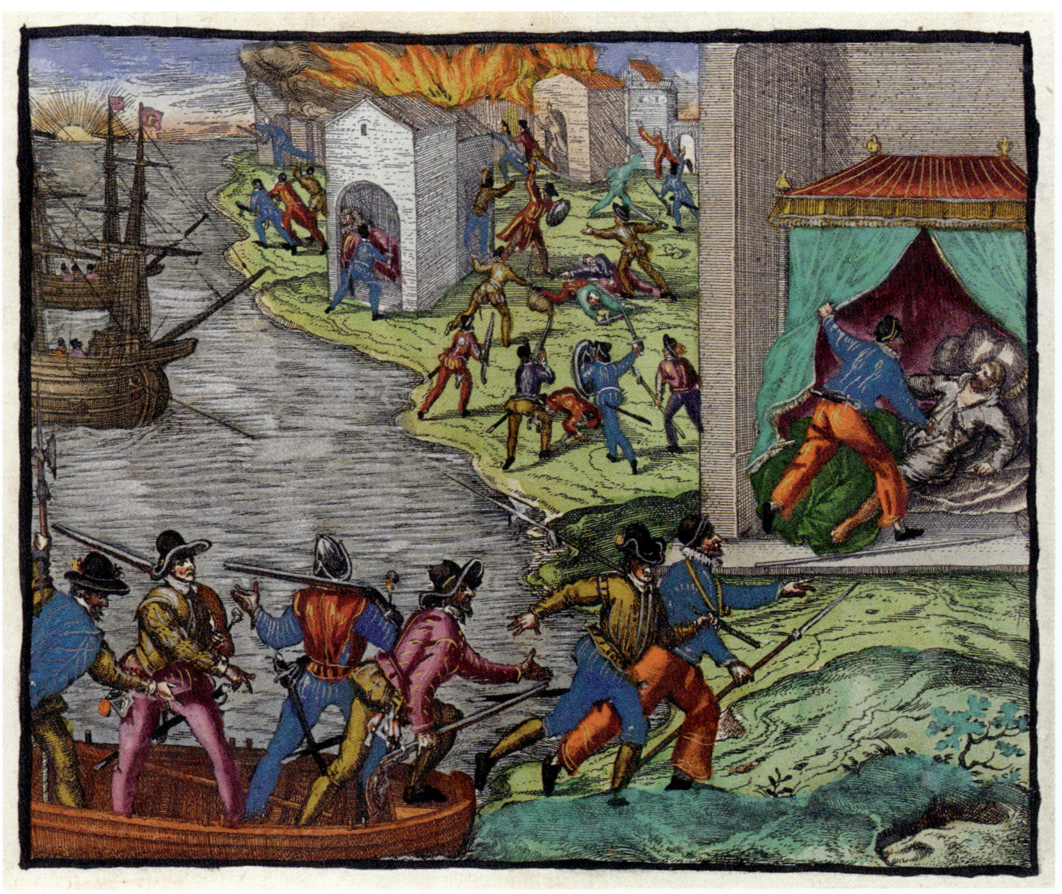

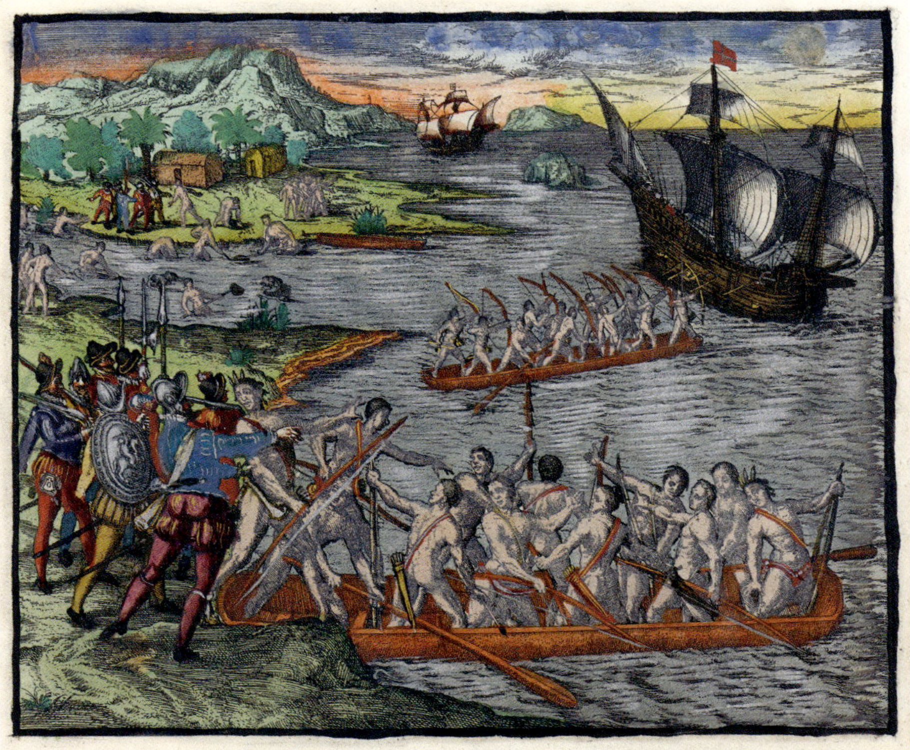

PLATE 9

The Spaniards incite the Indians on the island of Cubagua to rise against the French

To finish my stories about the booty the French have taken from the Spaniards, I will add one last example. When they were fishing for pearls on the island of Cubagua, a French vessel arrived there. The Spaniards immediately filled two native boats with men who were armed with bows and arrows, and sent them to the French ship. They convinced them that the French sailors were impure sodomites who, if they did not kill them, would come ashore and abuse the men and women of the island. The Indians rowed to the ship without further ado. When the French saw them coming and saw that they were naked, they thought that the Indians were only curious or perhaps willing to exchange pearls for other commodities. But when the Indians came closer, they attacked the French with their bows and arrows, injuring several of them. The French realised that the wounds were lethal because the tips of the arrows had been coated with poison. Without delay, they departed. Subsequently no other French vessels have ever approached the island. The Spaniards, who had been alarmed, had managed to keep the French at a distance by using this strategy.

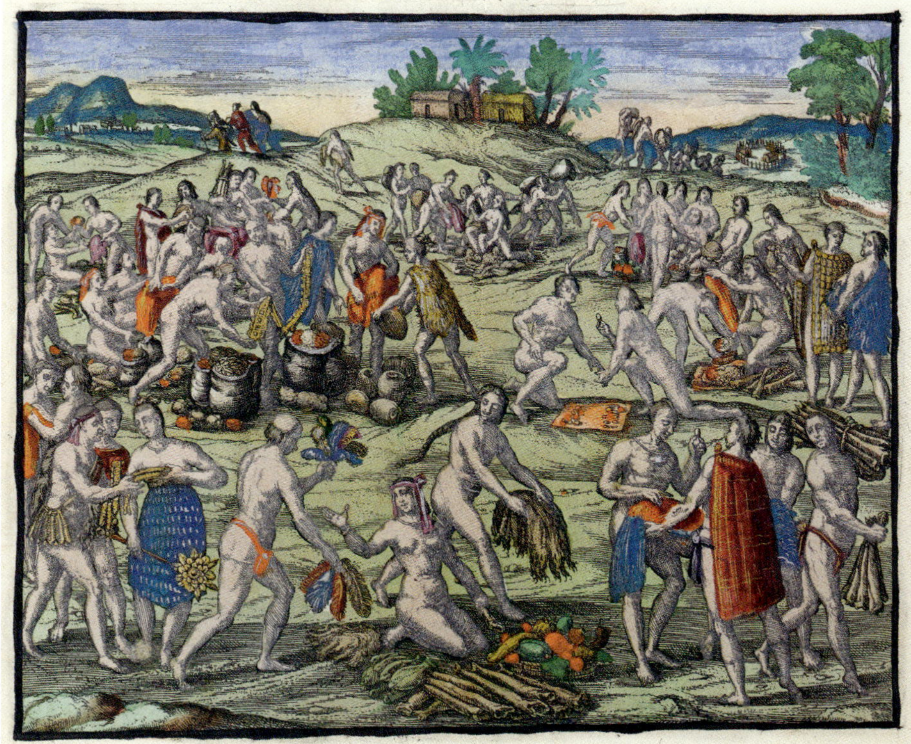

PLATE 10

How the Indians carry on their commerce and negotiations

The inhabitants of the province of Cartagena have an abundance of fruits, fish and other things which are vital for their subsistence. Their weapons are arrows coated in poison. The commodities they usually exchange for other items are salt, fish and pepper, which they bring to other provinces of the continent where such things are in demand. Some time ago, when there was peace in the region, there were large markets of grain, fruits, cotton, feathers, cloaks made of feathers, necklaces of gold, various minerals, emeralds, slaves and other things from the region. And this trade was conducted on an exchange basis, everyone taking only what he needed without any avarice or greed, saying to each other: "You take this, and then give me that". Nothing is valued more by them than food and drink. It is true that many of these tribes, introduced to our practices, have started to increase their riches, but mostly this desire has subsequently cooled down.

PLATE 11

How the Indians go to war

The inhabitants of the Tunia valley and the adjacent regions consider the sun to be their highest God, and worship it. When they wage war, they hang the skeletons of famous and strong men who used to live among them from roofs or poles and carry them around as military standards. When engaging with the enemy, they are spurred on by the sight of them. Their weapons are palm-wood spears and swords made of stone. It was their custom to bury their leaders with gold necklaces, emeralds, bread and wine. The Spaniards have discovered rich grave-sites. Those who live on the sea arm which flows between Cartagena and Santa Marta – and also the inhabitants of Santa Marta – are all Caribs. They coat the points of their arrows with deadly poison. They are strong, confident and devoted to their freedom. When they go to war, they bring their idol Chiappa, who brings them victories and to whom they make sacrifice before going to battle of slaves' children or captured enemies. They smear the idol with the blood of those they have sacrificed. The warriors themselves eat the human remains after having roasted the flesh. If they have achieved military victory, they return very happy and indulge in a drinking feast while they smear their idol with the blood of their defeated enemies. If they have lost, however, they try to please their idol with new sacrifices to demand a renewed victory.

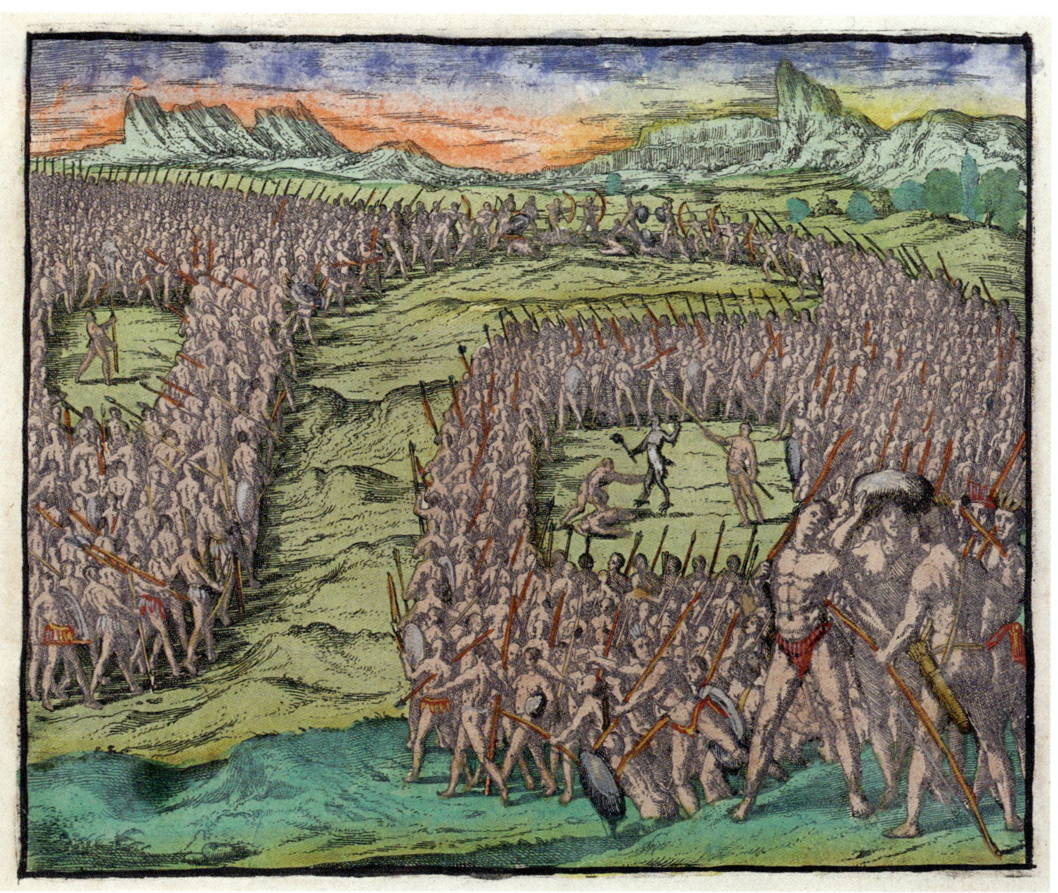

PLATE 12

At night some merchants go to the houses of the Indians when there is no food in the area

Girolamo Benzoni departed overland from the small town of Achla, situated on Uraba Bay, with some merchants and many mules to Panama, accompanied by a guide and slaves to take care of the mules and as many provisions as they thought were needed for such a long journey. When it took longer than anticipated because of the bad roads, and they still had a long way to go after having eaten all the food, and they did not find anything to eat in the desolated region only occasionally dotted with small towns, the merchants decided to kill a mule to feed themselves for the rest of the journey. Then, from a mountain top, they noticed smoke in a valley which was surrounded by mountains on all sides. It can be imagined how relieved they were. When they realised they would not reach the huts before the middle of the night, they feared that the Indians had noticed them and would run away in fear of being captured as slaves. Thus they descended halfway and spent part of the night there. Only then did they proceed to the huts. The Indians were alarmed by the noise and began to scream "Guacci, Guacci" (which is a four-legged beast that roams in the night looking for prey). This name they gave to the Christians, and they filled the rest of the night with loud cries and lamentations. The Christians tried to calm them down, and explained to them that it was now forbidden by royal decree to enslave Indians. And so they obtained bread, fish, fruit, meat and wild boars to cover the rest of their journey.

PLATE 13, PAGES 308/309

Benzoni and his companions, racked with hunger, hunt for turtles which are unusually big

Emperor Charles V appointed Diego Gutierrez governor of the very rich province of Cartagena. To this place Gutierrez invited the caciques, who brought an estimated 700 gold objects. Then they left, sending some of their subjects to the Spanish governor with venison, fish and fruit. But this happened only very rarely, and the Spaniards ran out of provisions and left, leaving behind only Gutierrez, his nephew, four servants and a sailor. Just when the governor had little hope left, the officer Bariento arrived with a ship full of soldiers and provisions. He received them gratefully, but sent the ship back to Nombre de Dios under the command of his nephew Alfonso of Pisa to get more support and supplies. When Alfonso brought more men, including Benzoni, he was caught in heavy storms and was forced to land on a coast where they found Indians and some provisions. They then left again, and after having travelled for eight days seeing nothing but thick forests and very rough mountains, they were forced to retrace their route overland along the coast, where they did not find any food except for some crops and snails. Finally they reached governor Gutierrez, and their ship did not arrive until three weeks later. The governor once again sent them back to get more soldiers. While they were waiting, they found and hunted turtles which were unusually big. For four months a year, these turtles are found ashore because they lay their eggs in the sand. Parts of the turtles they ate immediately, and parts they conserved in salt, though they went bad after a short time. They then liquefied the fat and preserved it in earthen pots.

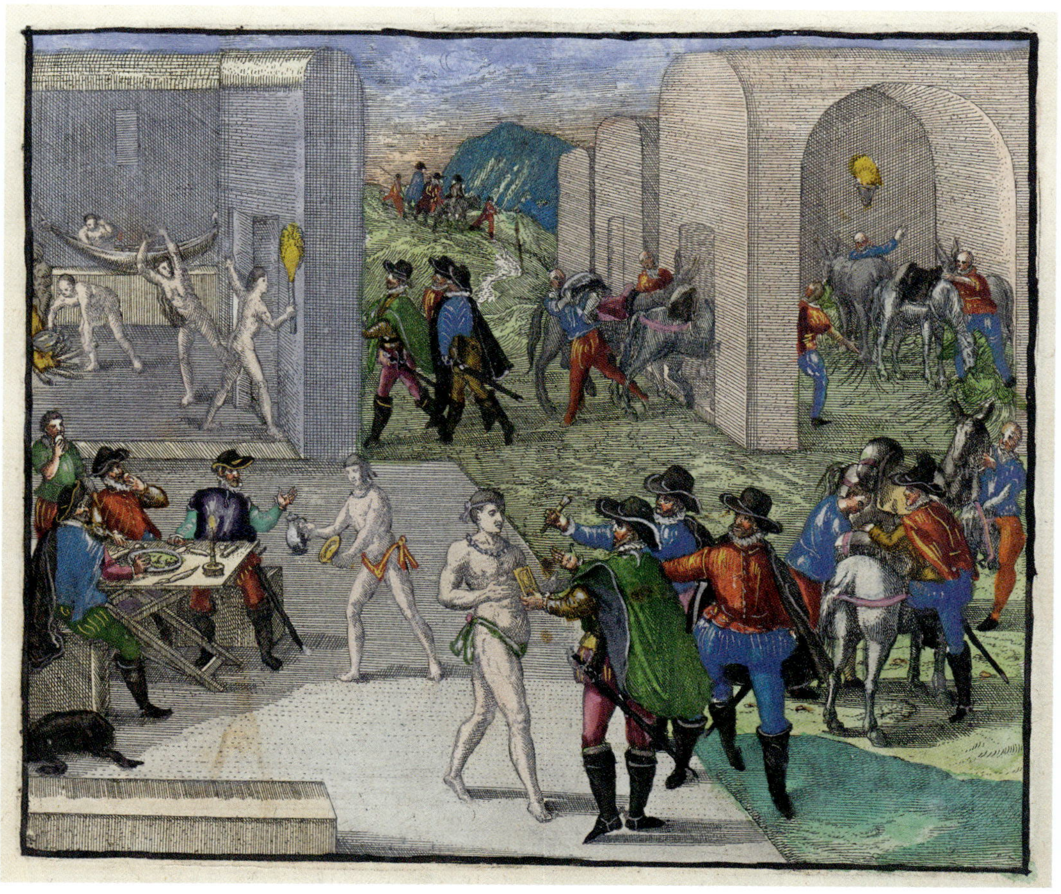

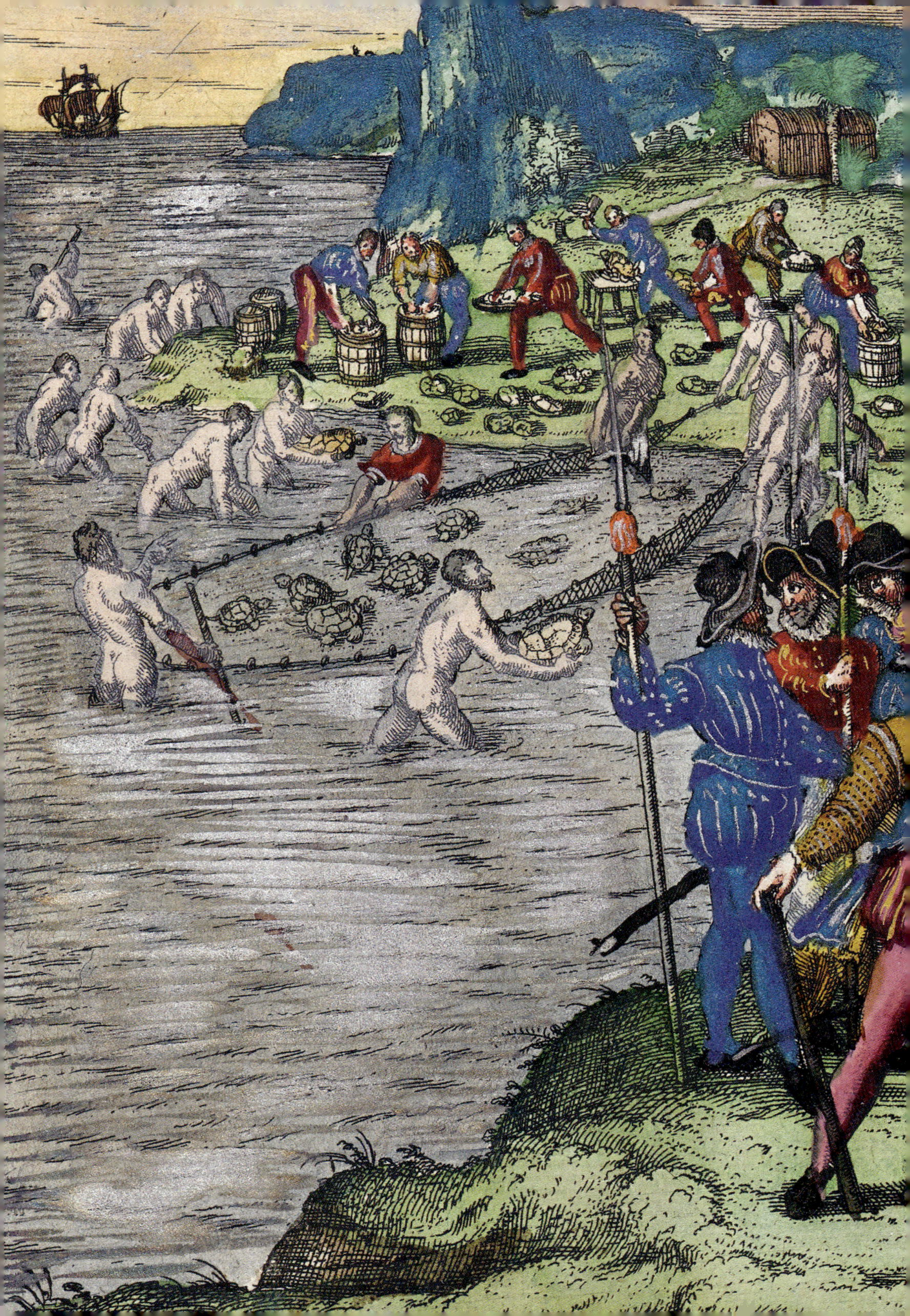

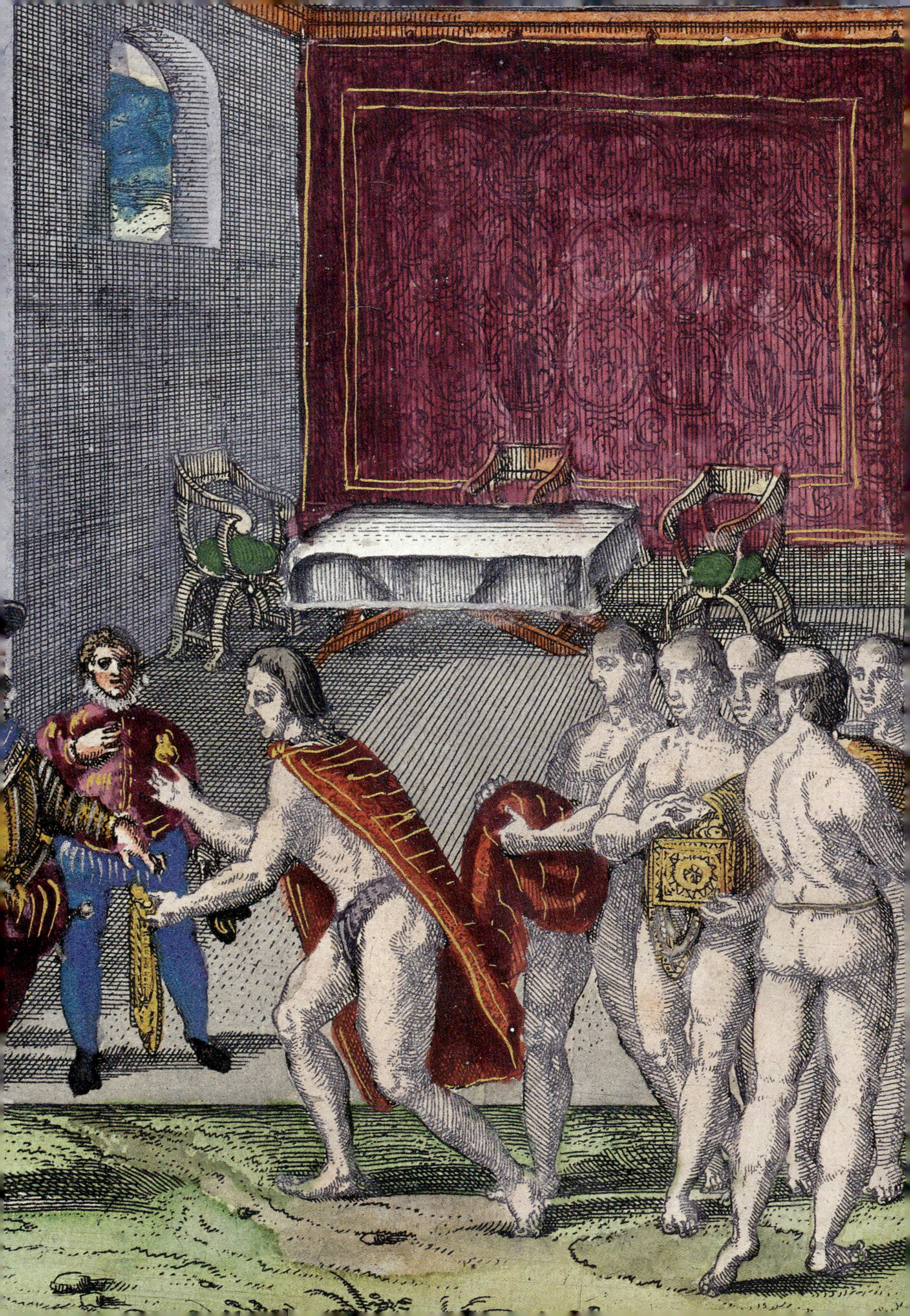

PLATE 14

Diego Gutierrez, the Spanish governor, invites the caciques of Suere, Chiuppa and others who had welcomed him to his table

Governor Gutierrez sailed with all his soldiers about 30 miles upstream and arrived in the territory of the Suerenses. After surveying the property, he immediately went to the house of its ruler, which extended 45 steps in length and around 10 steps in breadth, fenced in with palm leaves which had been plaited ingeniously. While he was there, the rulers of Suere and Chiuppa and other caciques came to greet him and presented him with fruit. He was surprised that they had not brought any gold, and explained through his Spanish interpreter that he had come to the region to discuss matters of great importance which would encourage them very much. He forced them to have dinner with him, and he brought to the table a priest and the interpreter. During dinner, the Indians did not have any appetite, because only chicken and salted pork were served – food they did not know. They gave it to their servants who were sitting on the ground. They in turn laughed and threw it to the dogs. Having finished their meal, the governor said: "I have come to these regions, my dearest friends, to abolish the idolatry which Satan had unleashed, and introduce you to the true faith to salvage your souls. For Jesus Christ, son of God and our Redeemer, descended from heaven to rescue the human race, as you can understand from this priest who has come from Spain for no other reason than to instruct you in the faith of Christ. Prepare your hearts to receive the Divine Law, and to subjugate yourself to Emperor Charles V of Spain, ruler of the world." The Indians listened attentively, with bowed heads, as if consenting. Then they went home.

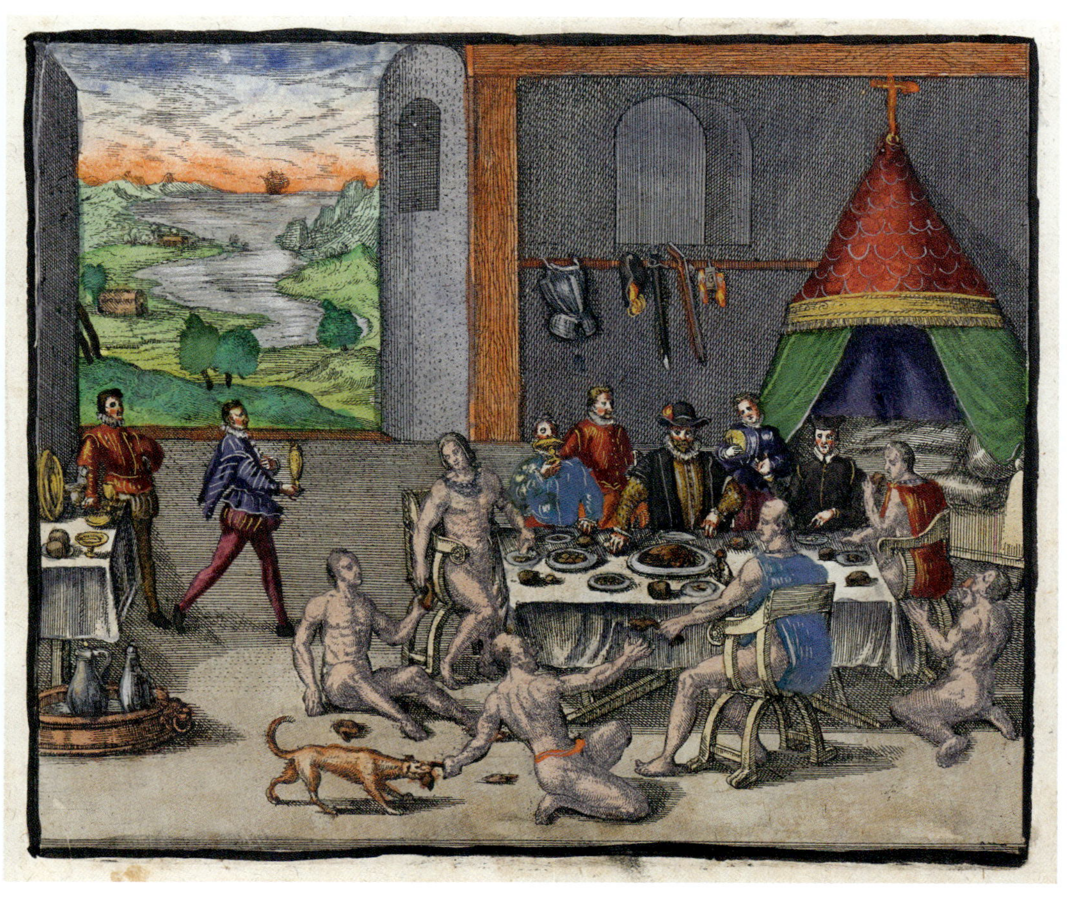

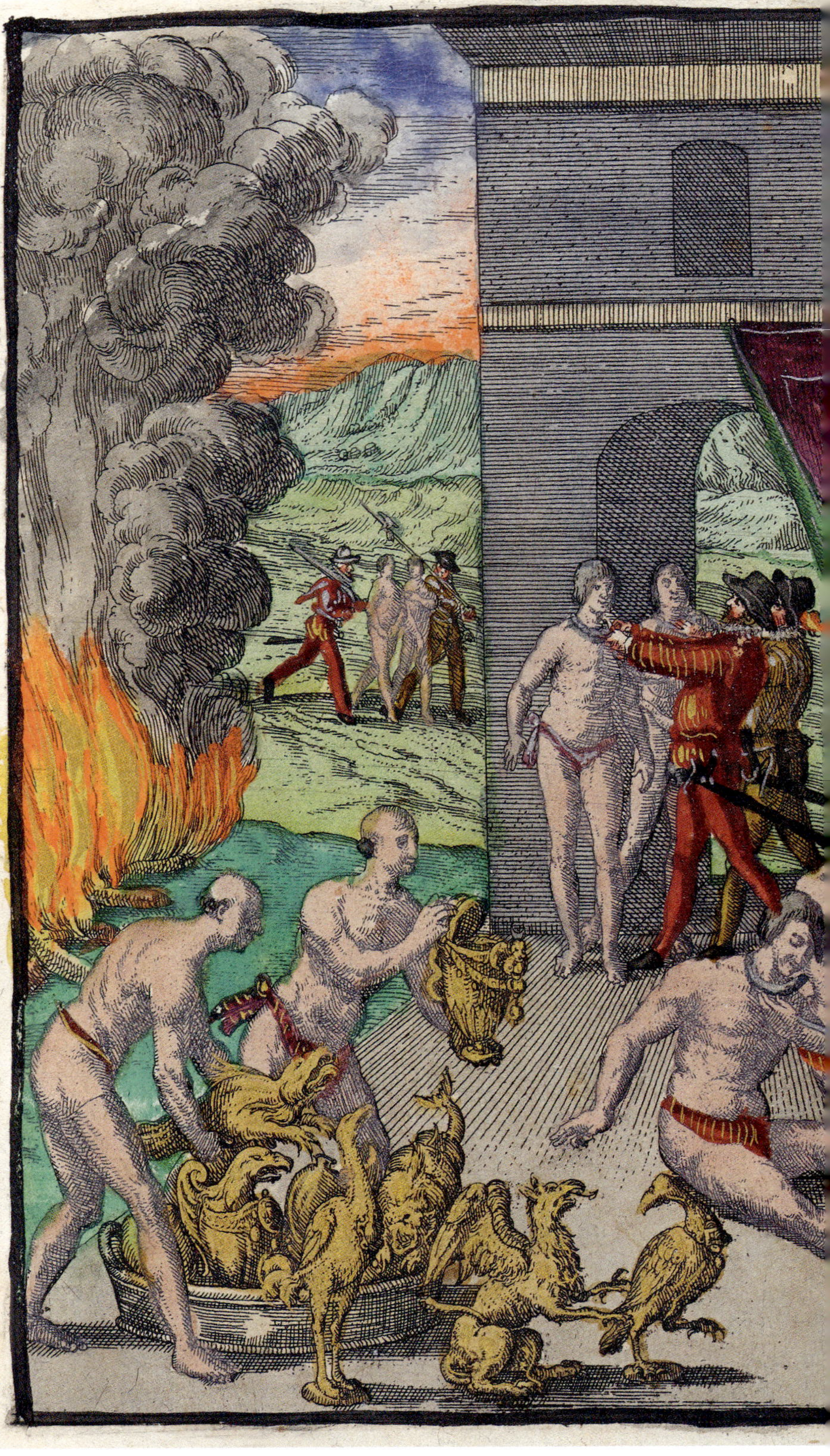

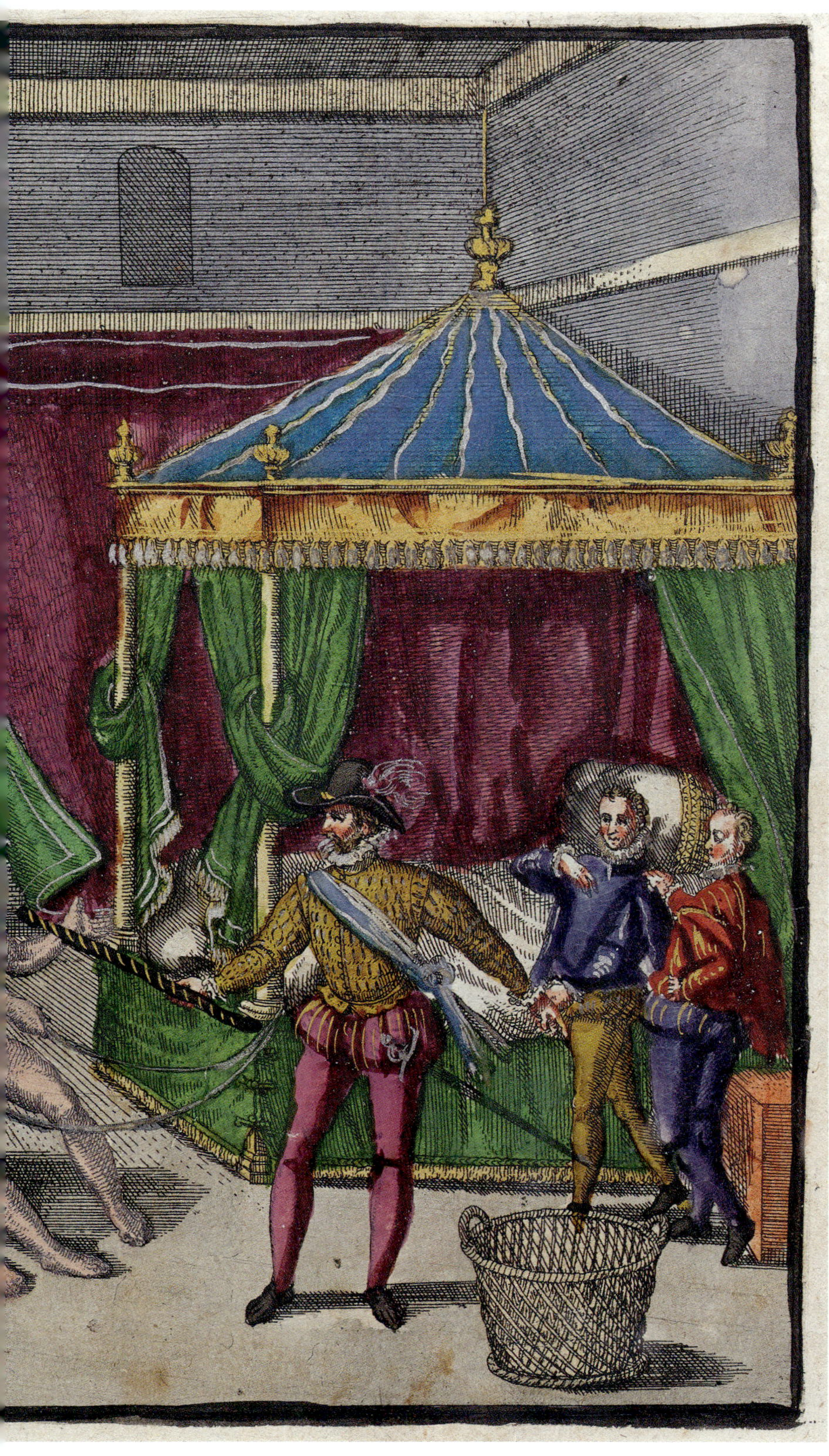

PLATE 15, PAGES 312/313

The Spanish governor puts some caciques in chains, and threatens to set fire to them if they do not fill a basket with gold six times

The next day the Spanish governor sent a soldier with two Indians to two caciques who lived elsewhere along the river, and made them come to him from there, promising them that no harm would be done to them. They obeyed, albeit against their will (they had, after all, presented the governor with 700 gold objects when he had just arrived in the region). The governor then had them carried off and tied to his bed. He asked them what had happened to the salt and honey which he had buried close by, but they told him they did not know. The governor grew angry, and threatened that he wanted them returned to him. The younger of the two, Camachire, was frightened to death and gave him gold vases which weighed more than 2,000 gold coins. But this was less than the governor desired. So he ordered a great pile of wood to be set on fire, had a big basket brought in and threatened that, if Camachire would not fill it with gold six times within four days, he would be thrown into the flames alive. The cacique agreed to do what he had been told. But one night he broke free and escaped, and because of this the governor was so disappointed that he became ill. Having recovered he ordered another cacique, Corori, to be called to him, and he threatened to slaughter him if he did not bring the demanded gold. With the cacique firmly denying that he owned any gold, the governor became angry again: "You are fooling me", he said, "if you do not bring me the gold I desire, I will feed you to the dogs." But the cacique said: "No, you are fooling me, and you are a liar because you have told me many times I would be killed, and yet you do not do it. I cannot understand what kind of people the Christians are who commit crimes wherever they go", and he said that he was surprised that the earth tolerated such terrible creatures.

PLATE 16

They attack the Spaniards and kill their commander, but they do not run away. They are then conquered when they are driven to the coast by other Indians. Having received help, however, those who survived escape

When the Spaniards proceeded through a desolate region and were short of provisions, the Indians attacked them from the forest. They killed the commander and several other Spaniards. When they had been fighting for almost a quarter of an hour, in which many Indians were killed, the others fled to safety. When Indian reinforcements arrived, however, the tired Spaniards were either killed or forced to flee, escaping danger until they encountered Alfonso of Pisa, who with a party of 24 Spaniards was looking for the commander. Together they made their way to the coast to run away from danger. The entire group of enemies armed with swords and shields taken from the Spaniards they had killed, blocked the way. They danced, calling out in Spanish which some of them had learned: "Take the gold, Christians, take the gold". The Christians reached the sea only with great difficulty. In these skirmishes 34 Spaniards and two African slaves were killed and only six escaped. Of the estimated 4,000 Indians, however, many more were killed.

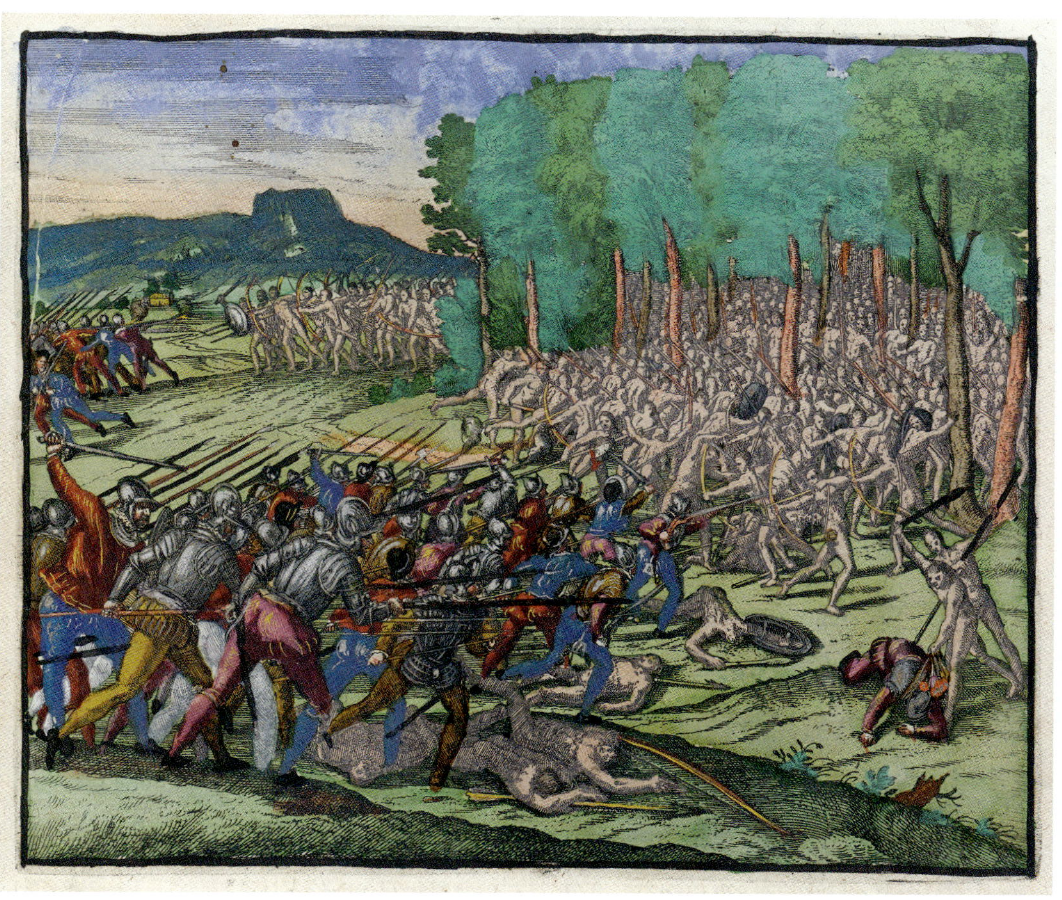

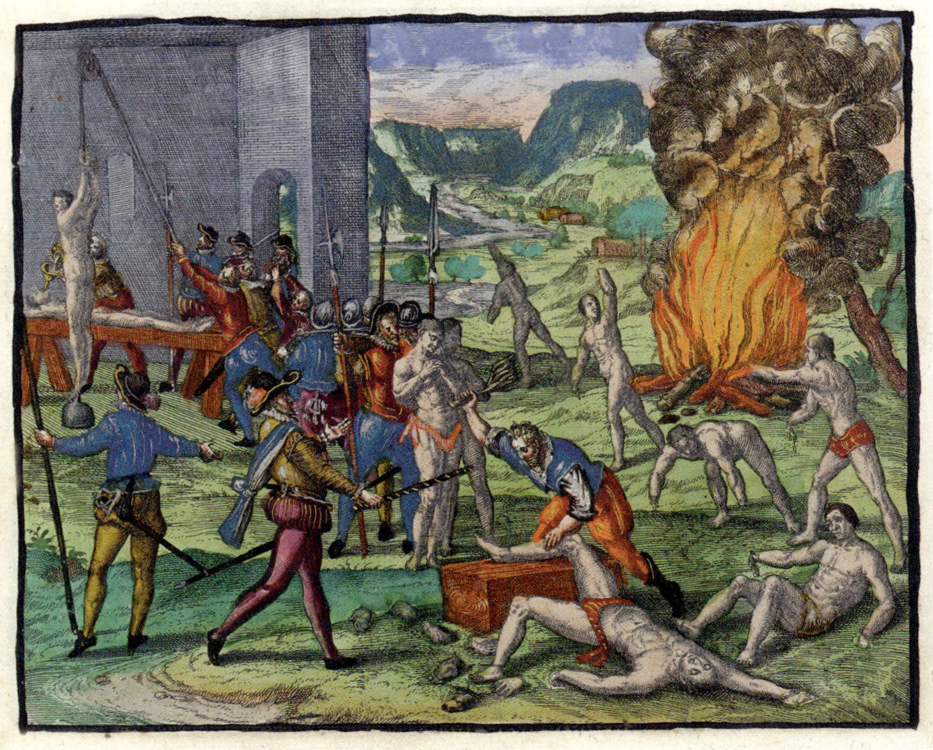

PLATE 17

Hernando de Soto reigns cruelly in Florida and even cuts off the hands of the caciques

Hernando de Soto became governor of Florida. Upon arrival, he travelled around to various parts of the province, all the while dreaming of great riches. Wandering about in this way, he encountered some Indians who were wearing necklaces and other valuables. When asked where they obtained this gold, they replied: in other regions which are far away. De Soto thought that the Indians had given this answer to make sure he would leave the province (because he knew that the Indians understood very well what the Spaniards wanted), and ordered some of them to be taken and tortured, so that they would tell where they got the gold. But among the cruel things he committed on these poor people, I privately consider this one the least incriminating. He ordered the 15 caciques to be captured and threatened to burn them alive if they did not tell him where they obtained the gold they were wearing. Frightened to death by this cruel sentence, they promised that within eight days they would take him to a place where he could take as much as he desired, but they did not know what they said or promised. Soto followed them, looking for the veins of gold. When, after a journey of 12 days, no trace of gold had been found, Soto, disillusioned, became so angry towards the caciques that he ordered their hands to be cut off, and then he chased them away.

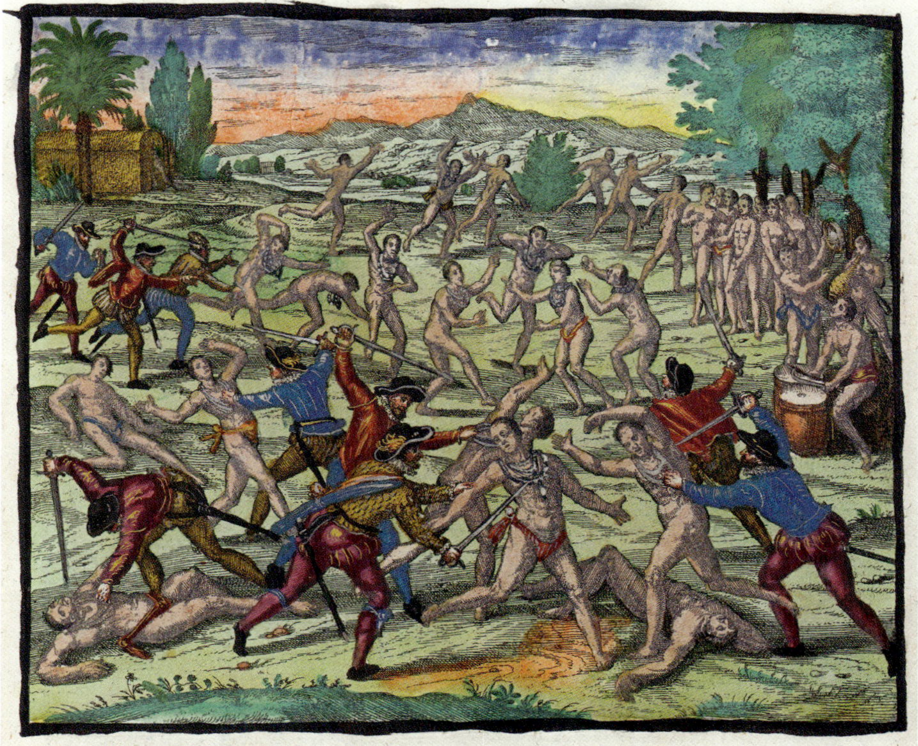

PLATE 18

When Cortés was away, Pedro de Alvarado put to the sword numerous Mexicans who attended their feasts, and took away the rings they wore in decoration

When Hernán Cortés had been admitted into Mexico by King Montezuma, he heard that Pánfilo de Narváez had been sent with 900 Spaniards to chase him away. But he marched against Narváez, leaving Pedro de Alvarado, his lieutenant, with 250 soldiers in Mexico. After Cortés had left, it happened that a great number of Indian noblemen, with some of the common people, celebrated a religious festival where they ran through the city dancing and singing. The Spanish soldiers observed this spectacle, and saw the Indians wonderfully adorned with necklaces and other precious metals. They were taken by a detestable greed, and very indecently Alvarado and most of the Spaniards attacked the dancers with swords. They did not expect anything like it, and they were killed and robbed of their ornaments. The Mexicans, however, took up their own arms and killed many Spaniards.

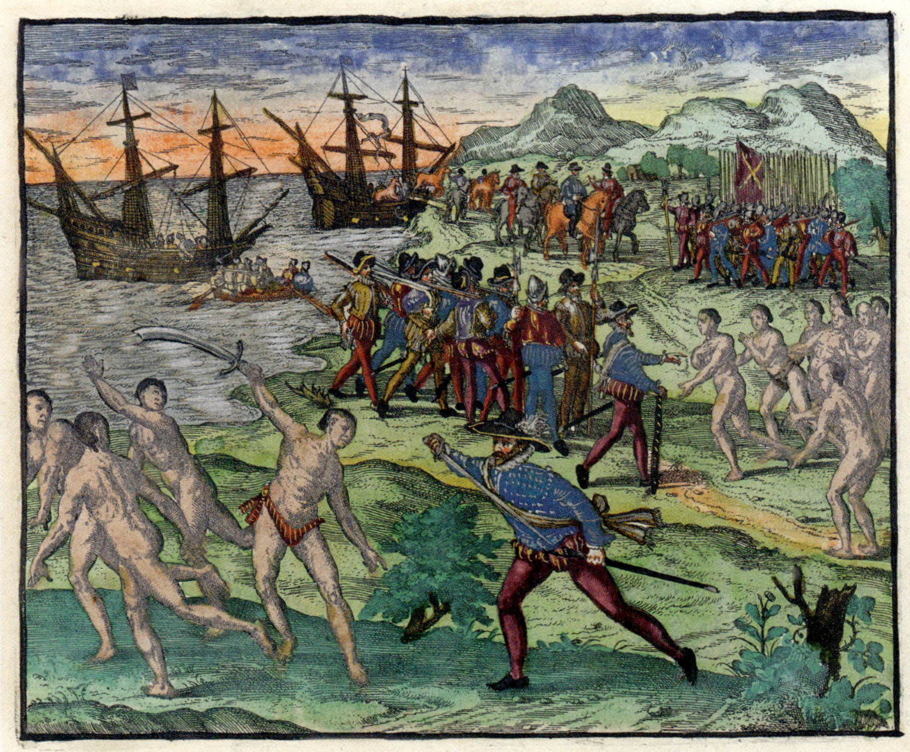

PLATE 19

Francisco de Montejo becomes governor of Yucatan. One cacique who claims to desire an alliance with him tries to kill him with a sword

In 1527, a Spanish officer by the name of Francisco de Montejo heard that the province of Yucatan was very rich, and left for New Spain, adorned with the title of governor of this province. He went there with 500 Spanish soldiers, a great number of horses and the necessary provisions. Upon arriving, several caciques of the region came to greet him, as if they wanted to strike an alliance. To convince him, they stayed in his company for a while until one seized the opportunity and tried to kill the governor with a curved sword, which he had taken from an African slave. But the governor had read his intention and defended himself. When the Indians saw that their plan had failed, they fled without causing further problems for the Spaniards. But the governor ordered his soldiers in formation and invaded the region from different places, filling the area with murder and fire. The Indians, however, did not lose heart and resisted the Spaniards. But weakened by nine years of war, and having lost almost all of their leadership, they were eventually subjugated by the Spaniards.

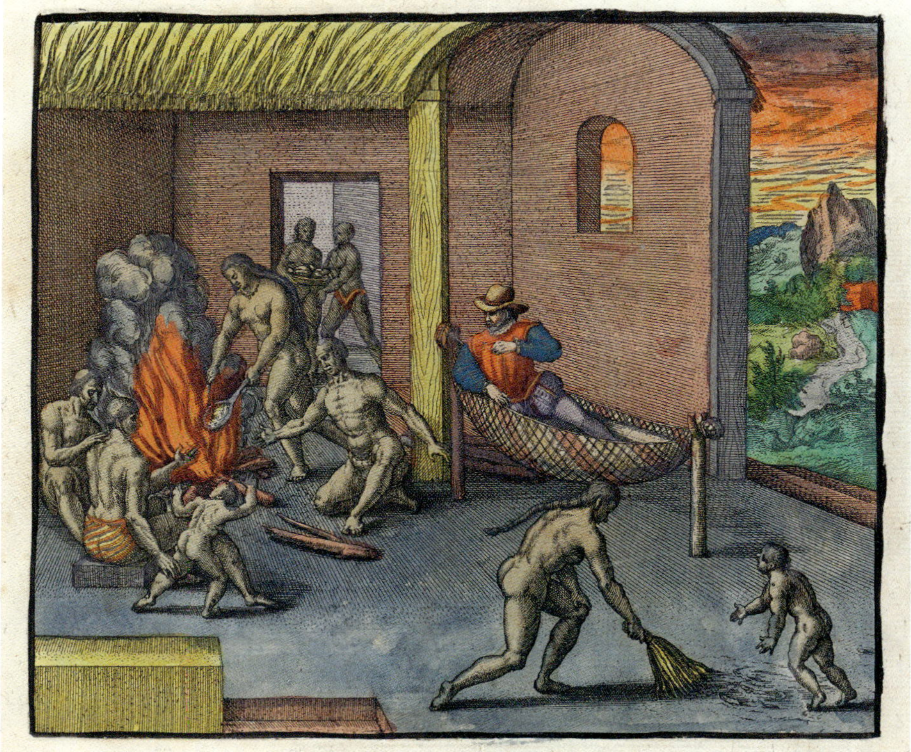

PLATE 20

The conversation between Benzoni and a Nicaraguan cacique about Christian morals

When Benzoni went to the province of Nicaragua, he was hospitably received by a prominent 70-year-old cacique of this province, who was well versed in Spanish and whose name was Gonsalvus. The next morning he looked at Benzoni, fixing his eyes upon him, and said to him: "Christian, what kind of people are Christians? As soon as they arrived here they demanded maize, honey, cotton, a blanket and an Indian woman to sleep with. They want gold and silver, they avoid labour, they lie, are addicted to gambling, are cruel and blasphemous. If they enter the church to hear mass, they keep talking and belittle those who are absent. They fight each other with swords. In short, they are criminals." Benzoni replied that criminals did these things, but not those who are honest. But the cacique then asked: "Where are the honest men, then? So far I have seen only bad people." I changed the topic and asked him why they had so amicably received the Spaniards in their region. He said: "We have resisted them as much as we could. But when we were time and again defeated by their horses, we ultimately decided it would be better to be subjugated than for our people to be become extinct."

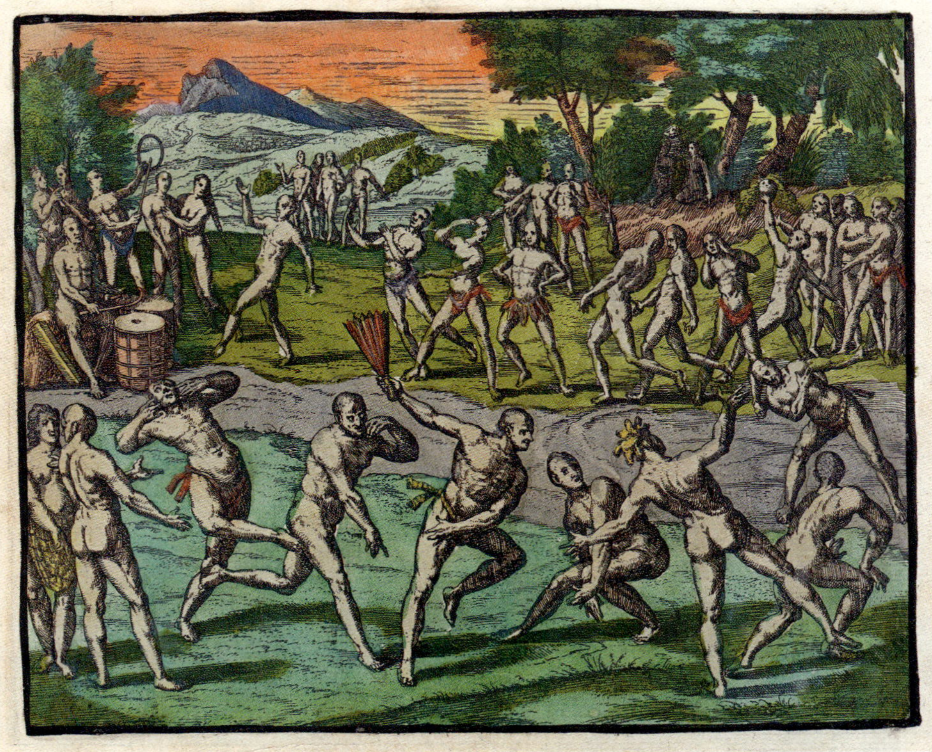

PLATE 21

The religious dancing ceremonies of the Nicaraguans

The people of Nicaragua practise the following custom in their dancing: 200, 300, sometimes as many as 4,000 people gather in one place, depending on the size of the region's population. When the place where they are going to dance has been cleaned, one of them leads the others out, the upper half of his body reclining and swerving at the same time. Three or four at a time follow him, observing a strict order. A tambourine-player meanwhile beats the rhythm of a song. The dance leader reacts first to the drum, and then others repeat his words, making more strange gestures. One holds a fan in his hand, another a squash which rattles because small stones have been put inside, a third has feathered headgear, a fourth has bells made of shells tied to his arms and legs. Some swerve this way, some the other. Some lift their legs, others spread their arms. Some pretend that they only have one eye, some pretend to be deaf, some wail and some laugh. In short, they make thousands of strange gestures. During the dance they receive cavacate, a common drink. They tell each other to drink, and thus continue dancing through the day and often through the night.

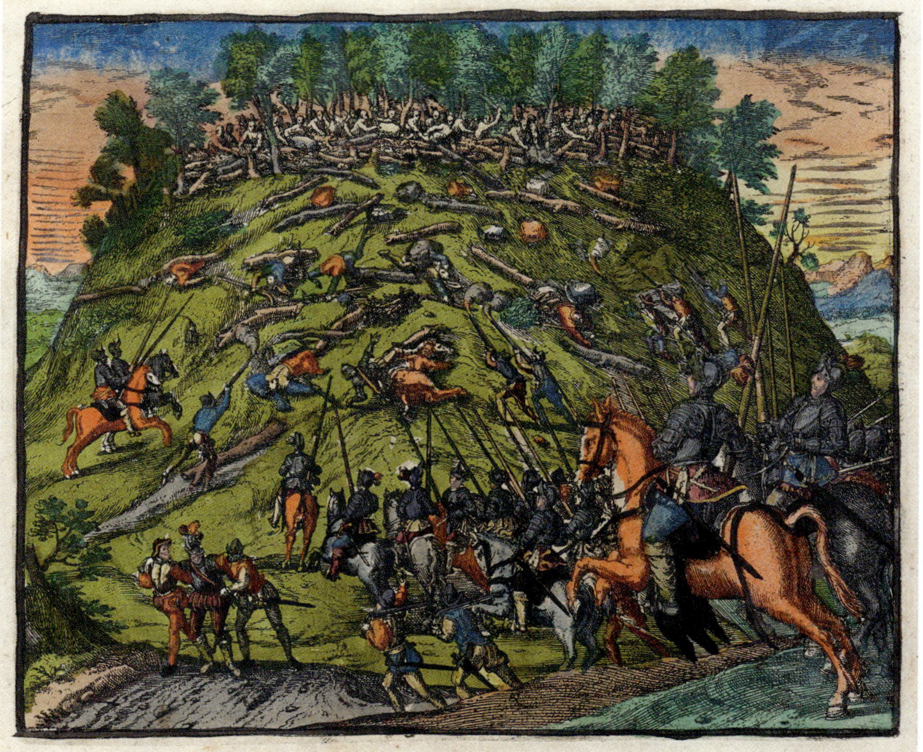

PLATE 22

Pedro de Alvarado is sent to Sibolla by Antonio de Mendoza. He is killed with most of his men by the Xaliscans

Antonio de Mendoza, viceroy of New Spain, sent Pedro de Alvarado with 700 soldiers to the province of Sibolla, which he had heard was very rich. After having assembled horses and other necessary provisions he set sail, and while on his way heard that the inhabitants of Xalisco had rebelled against the Spaniards. He set out with the majority of his soldiers to help them. On his way there he met Pedro de Zuniga who was aggrieved by the Indian murder of many Spaniards. He took Zuniga under his protection and together they went to the Xaliscans. They besieged a hill to which the Indians had fled and where they had entrenched. They had put large tree trunks on the ground, with big stones in between them, and hid behind this structure. In similar fashion they had piled up other stones. Upon arrival, the Spaniards rode their horses towards the barriers in a frontal attack. The Indians screamed, and cut the rope which had held the tree trunks together. They rolled the trees from the hill, as well as the stones, towards the Spaniards who galloped uphill. The stones and the trees knocked all the Spaniards down, and crushed them. Alvarado himself had been thrown off his horse, just like the others, and died after two days. When asked where it hurt the most he said: “In my soul”.

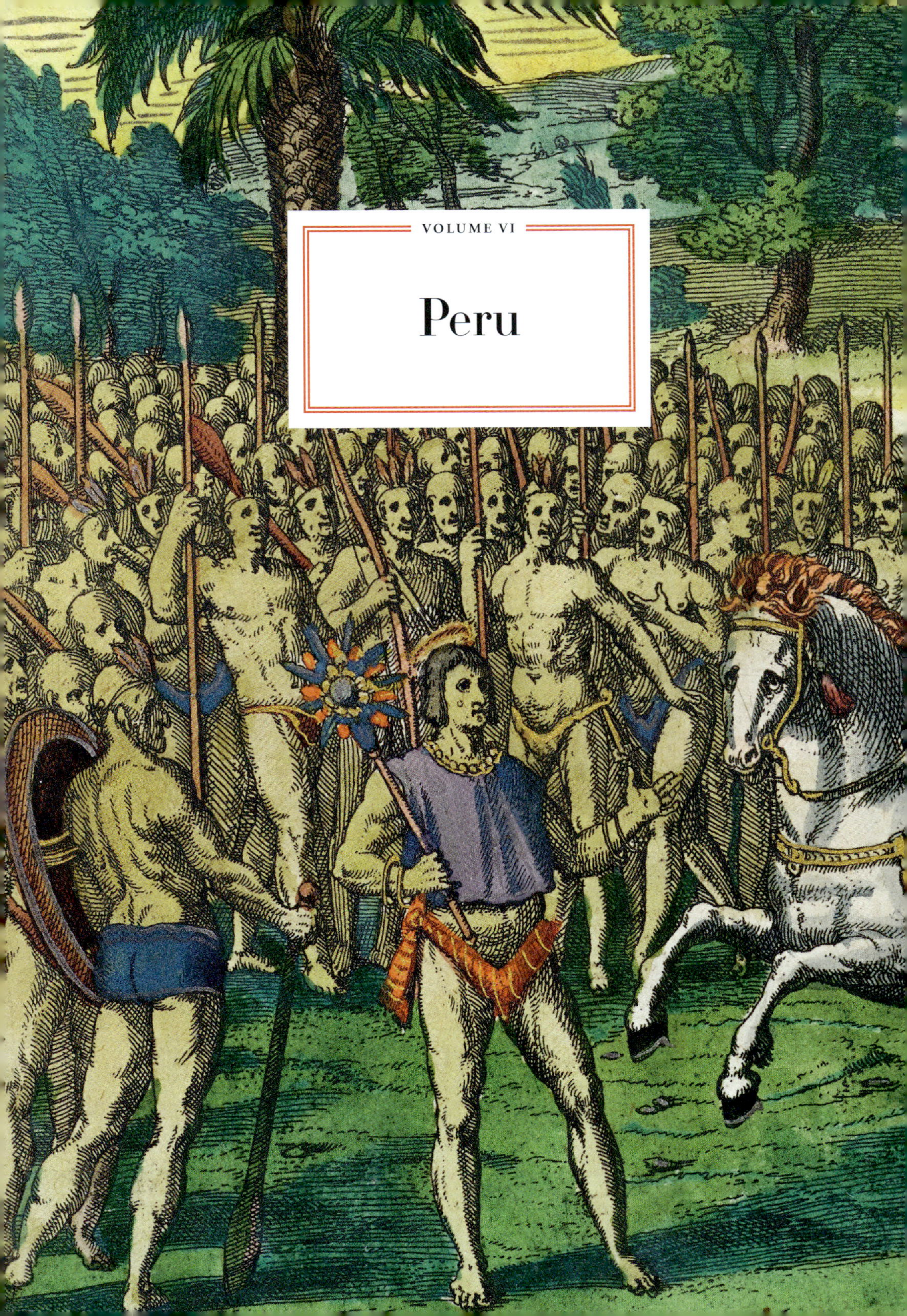
VOLUME VI
Peru

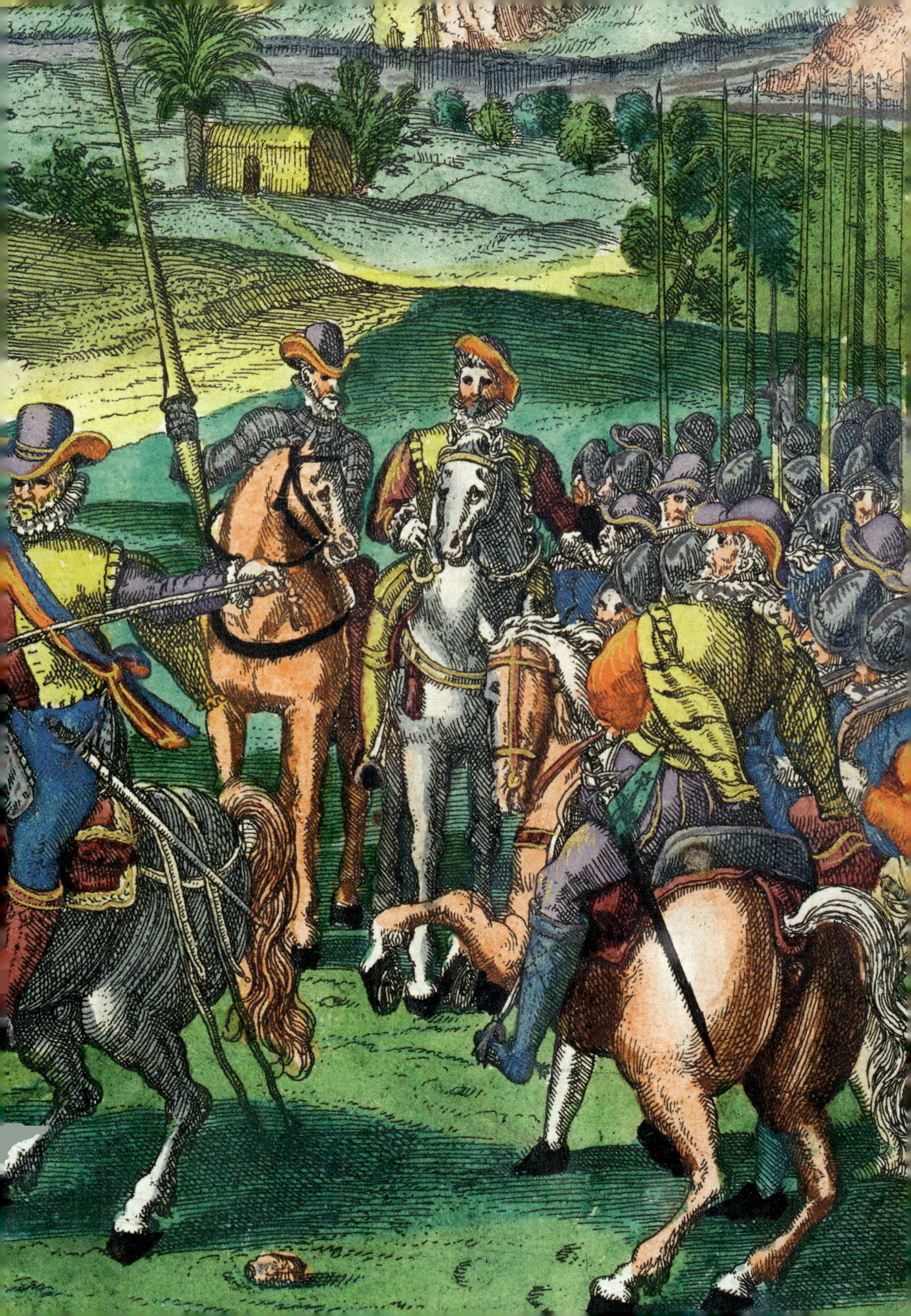

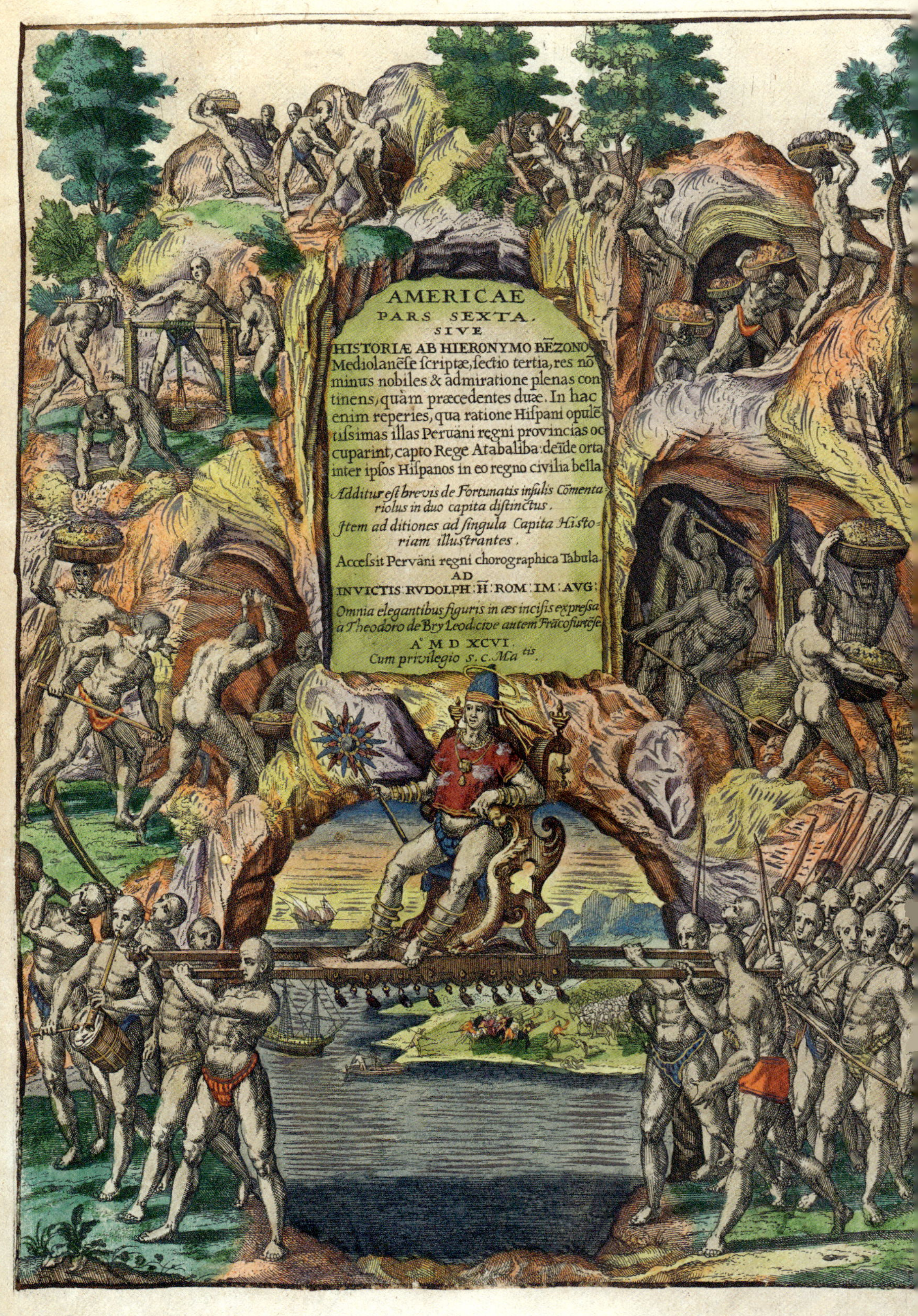
AMERICAE
PARS SEXTA.
SIVE
HISTORIÆ AB HIERONYMO BĒZONO
Mediolanēſe ſcriptæ, ſectio tertia, res nō
minus nobiles & admiratione plenas con
tinens, quàm præcedentes duæ. In hac
enim reperies, qua ratione Hiſpani opulē
tiſsimas illas Peruäni regni provincias oc
cuparint, capto Rege Atabaliba: deīde orta
inter ipſos Hiſpanos in eo regno civilia bella.
Additur eſt brevis de Fortunatis inſulis Cōmenta-
riolus in duo capita diſtinctus.
Jtem additiones ad ſingula Capita Histo-
riam illustrantes.
Acceſsit Pervāni regni chorographica Tabula.
AD
INVICTIS: RVDOLPH: II: ROM: IM: AVG:
Omnia elegantibus figuris in æs inciſis expreſsa
à Theodoro de Bry Leod: cive autem Frācofurtēſe.
Aº M D XCVI.
Cum privilegio S. C. Matis.

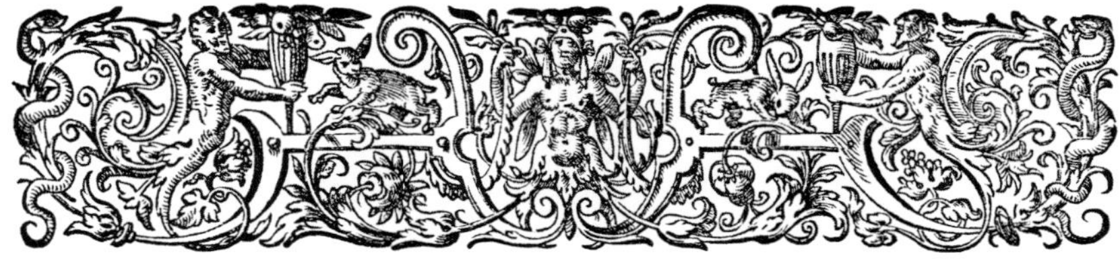

Volume VI

Based on: Girolamo Benzoni, *Historia del Mondo Nuovo* (Milan, 1565), subsequently published in several editions

The third instalment of Benzoni's account of his experiences in the New World shifted attention to South America. This volume's title-page reflected European progress by representing Native American labourers digging in the mountains for, presumably, precious metals. The hilltop, here presented to readers for a third time, had evolved from a beacon of heathendom into a site of Christian conquest, and now into a location where new riches could be discovered. Volume VI continued where the two previous volumes had left off, with their three main themes: first, the tale of the internal Spanish struggles for leadership in the Americas, and the resulting tensions between some of the leading noblemen; second – set within the margins of the first story – the collapse of the Inca Empire, and its leader Atabalipa (Atahualpa), at the hands of the Spanish invaders; and third, the sequence of illustrations which ended with some of the more marvellous 'highlights' of Native American culture. One particularly interesting engraving in this respect, and quite likely for the De Brys personally, was the illustration showing Native American goldsmiths. The images produced by these Peruvian workers looked remarkably similar to the sort of images Theodore de Bry must have produced during his time as a goldsmith in Liège and Strasbourg, decades before he became a publisher in Frankfurt.

Volume VI also contains a unique piece of archival information about the process of making the collection, more specifically the task of writing the captions which accompanied the engravings in the final segment of each of the volumes. In September 1595 Theodore de Bry sent a letter to Carolus Clusius, who had provided the Latin translations for some of the early *America* volumes. Together with his letter, he sent him: "… 28 pieces of the third and final part of the account of the Indies mentioned before, on the back of which you will find the chapter for each, so that you may

Frontispiece of volume VI

Pages 322/323
Detail of volume VI, plate 5

much more easily find the discourse associated with the 'portraits' that are mentioned. I request you most kindly to make the descriptions for each history, in the manner in which you have done for the earlier one(s)." The exact reason why the De Brys decided to outsource this task is unclear. The name of Clusius was well-known in intellectual circles across early modern Europe, but his name was not mentioned anywhere in volume VI where these 28 captions appeared.

Perhaps in order to mitigate Benzoni's account, which was brimming with anti-Spanish sentiments, the De Brys decided to add another travel account to the Latin edition, something they had also done for the Latin edition of volume III where Jean de Léry's account was overtly critical of French Catholics. They chose the Frenchman Nicolas Le Challeux's *Discours de l'histoire de la Floride*, another account of the French misfortunes in Florida which had formed the subject of volume II of the *America* series. Exactly why the De Brys chose to add this account to the Latin edition of volume VI is unknown, and the same account does not appear anywhere in the German collection. Moreover, even in the Latin edition, Le Challeux's account could not alleviate the overall impression of Spanish malpractice. Francisco Pizarro was the obvious villain of volume VI, and came to embody everything Europeans in the 16th and 17th centuries thought was wrong with Spanish policy in the Americas. Pizarro's expeditions into South America had started in 1524 and culminated in the execution of Atahualpa and the overthrow of the Inca Empire in 1532, duly sealed by the capture of Cusco and the founding of Lima. Even before Benzoni arrived in the New World, then, these expeditions had already acquired mythical status, although by the time the De Brys produced volume VI only Hernán Cortés – the conquistador *par excellence* who had subjugated the Aztecs (but who is largely absent from the De Bry collection) – had a reputation that was on a par with Pizarro's. Benzoni, and in turn the De Brys, decided to follow the story of Pizarro until after the conquest of Peru, when mutual distrust and power struggles developed among the Spanish noblemen. It was with this catalogue of rather bleak afterthoughts that the De Brys finished their reworking of Benzoni's account.

Detail of volume VI, plate 23

Pages 328/329
World map showing Terra Australis

Pages 330/331
View of Cusco

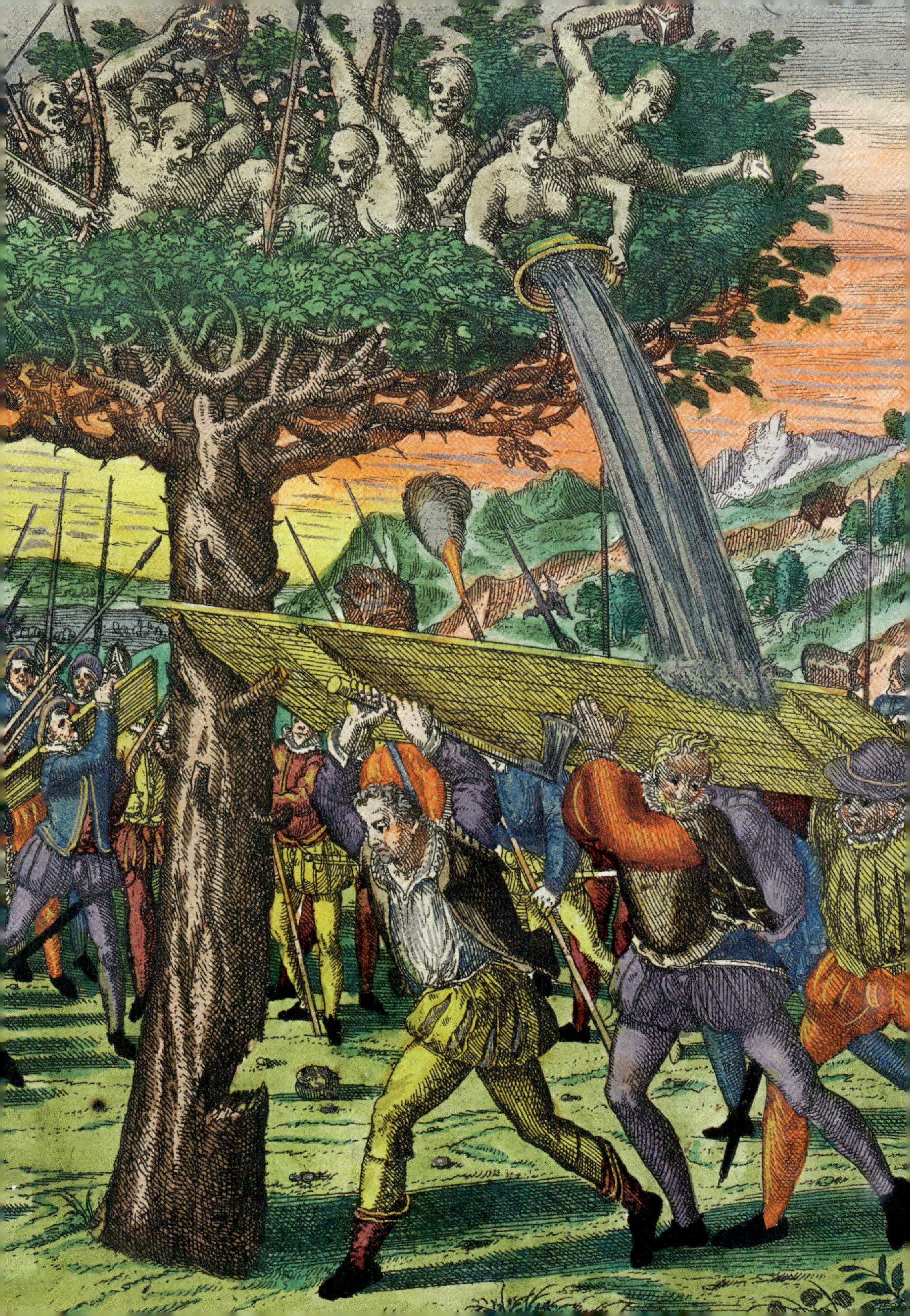

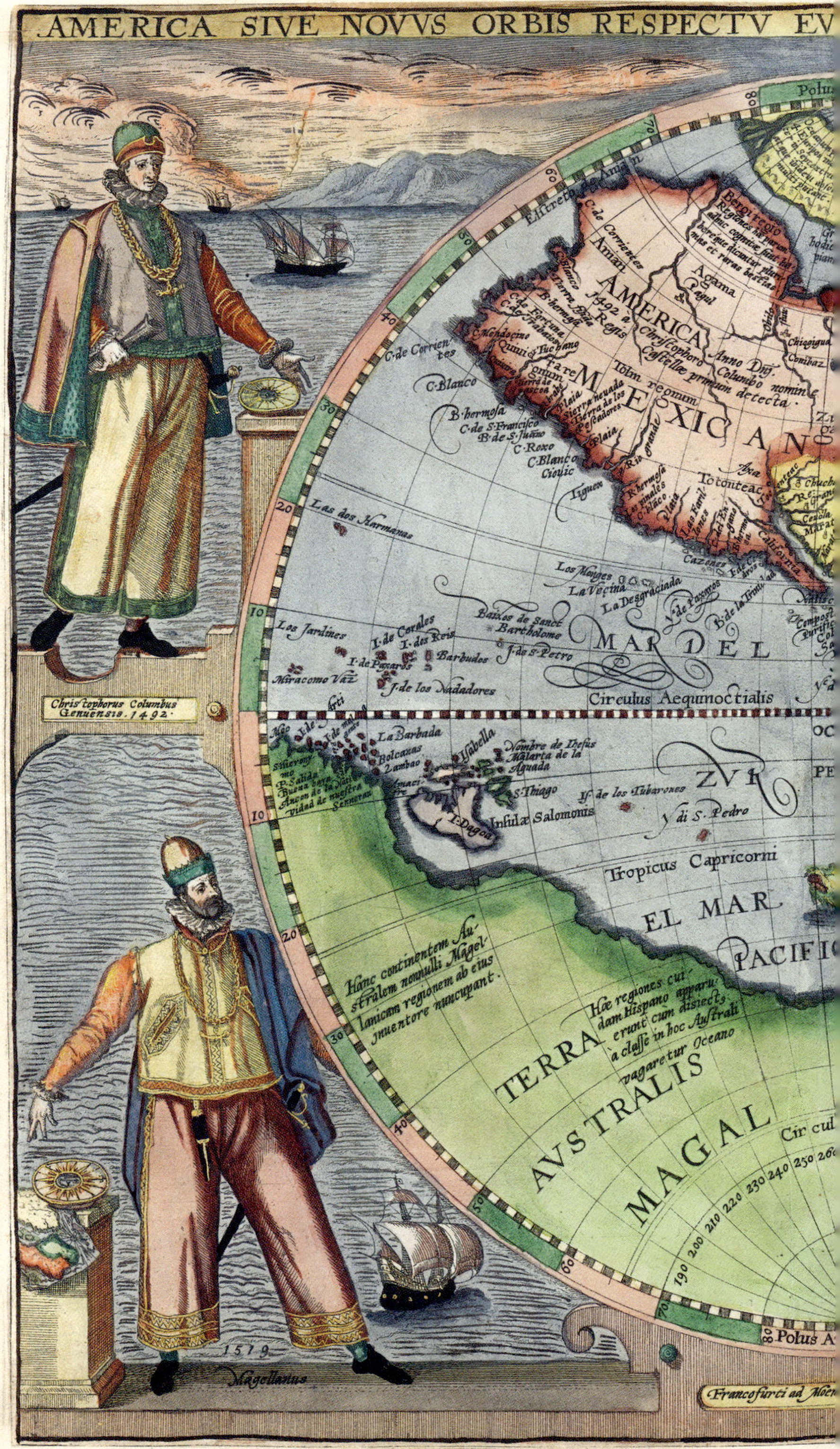
AMERICA SIVE NOVVS ORBIS RESPECTV EV
Chris tophorus Columbus Genuensis. 1492.
1519
Magellanus
Francofurti ad Moen
AMERICA
MEXICANA
MAR DEL
ZVR
EL MAR PACIFIC
TERRA AVSTRALIS MAGAL
Circulus Aequinoctialis
Tropicus Capricorni
Hanc continentem Australem nonnulli Magellanicam regionem ab eius inuentore nuncupant.
Hæ regiones cuidam Hispano apparuerunt cum disiectis a classe in hoc Australi vagaretur Oceano
Los Jardines
Las des Hermanas
I. de Corales
Infulæ Salomonis
Polus A

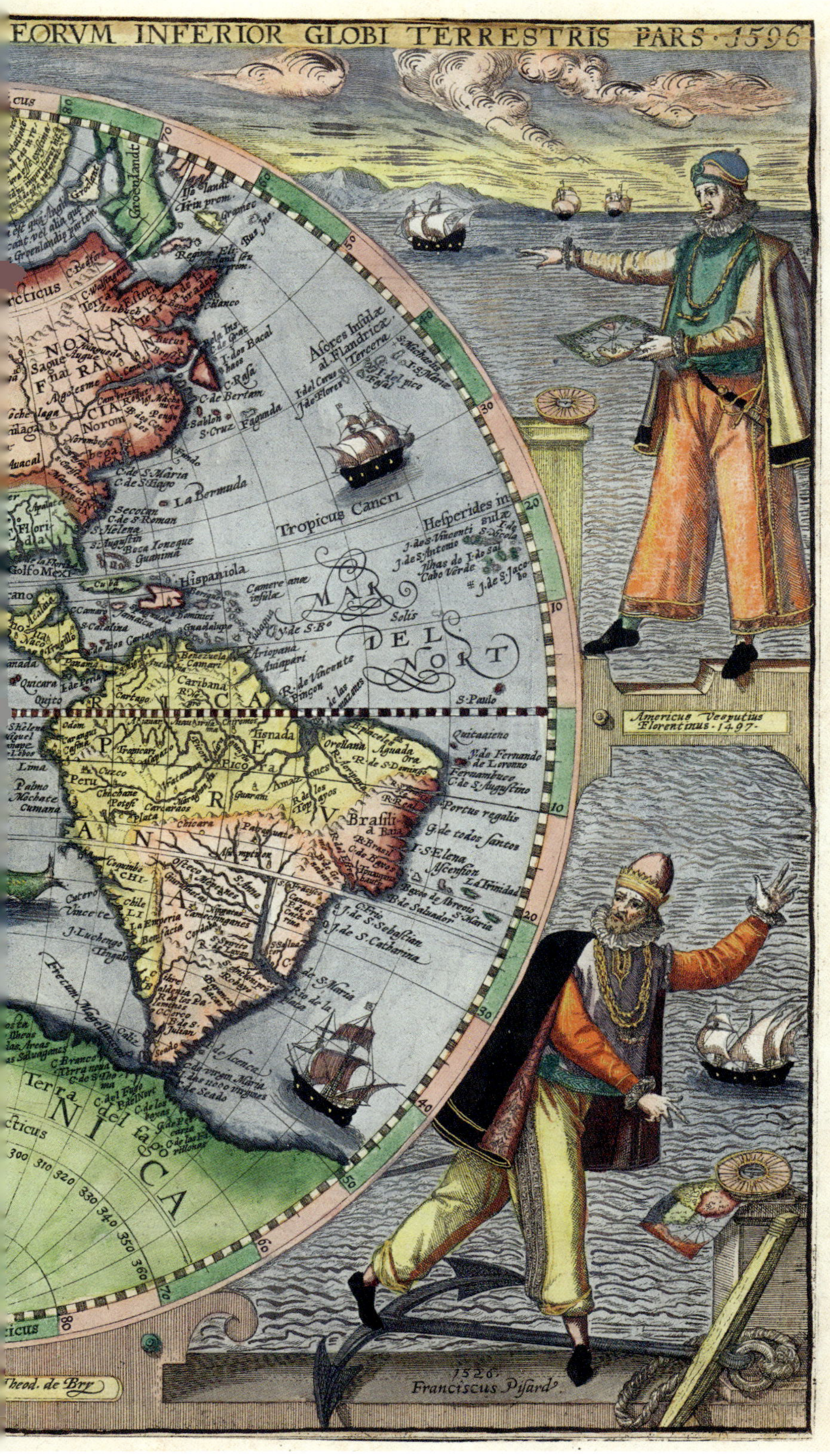

EORVM INFERIOR GLOBI TERRESTRIS PARS · 1596
Americus Vesputius
Florentinus · 1497 ·
1526.
Franciscus Pisard
Theod. de Bry
Tropicus Cancri
MAR DEL NORT
Hispaniola
La Bermuda
Hesperides insulæ
Azores Insulæ al. Flandricæ
Tercera
Brasili
Portus regalis
Terra del fogo
Golfo Mexi
S. Paulo
Cabo Verde

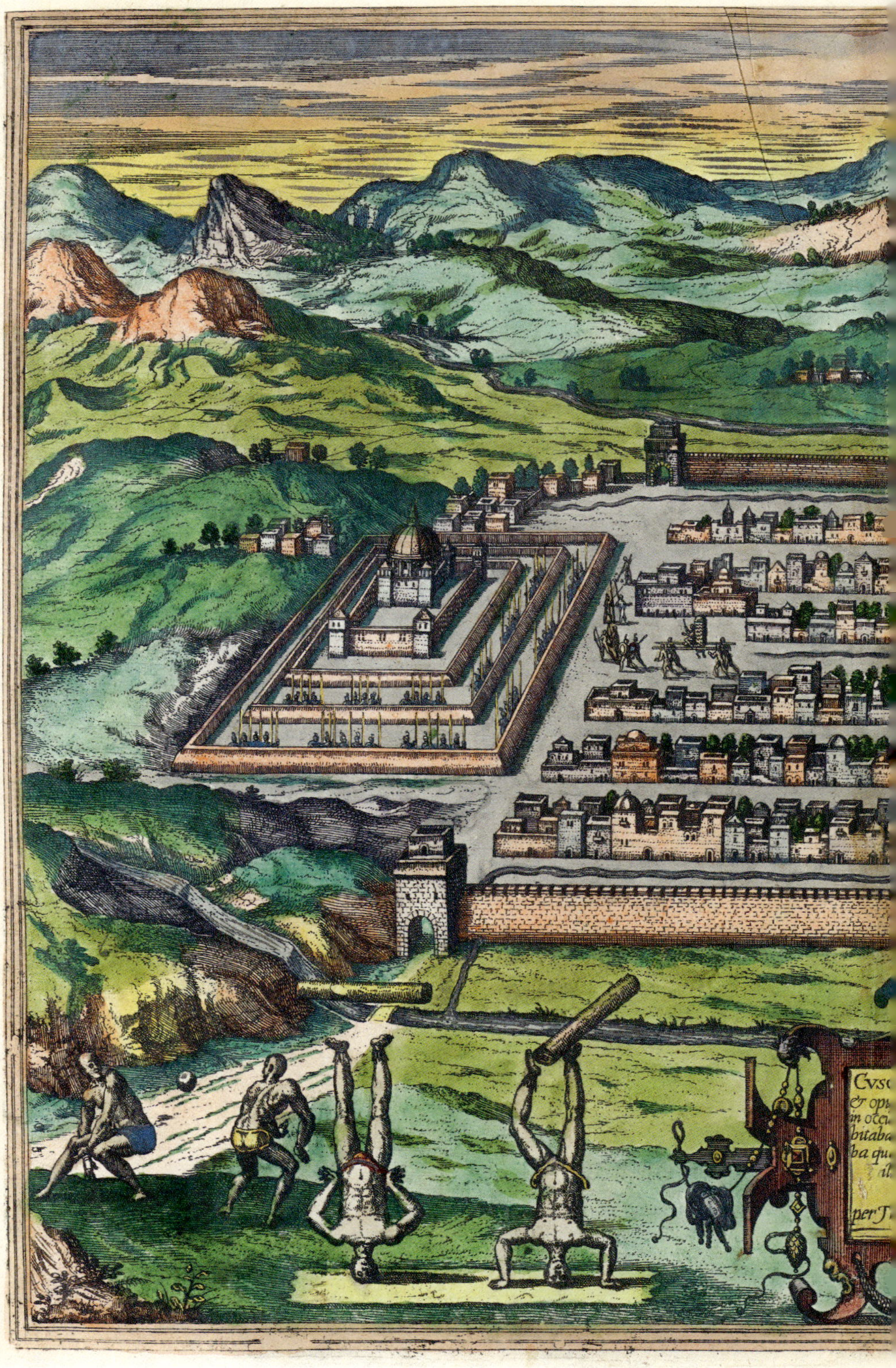

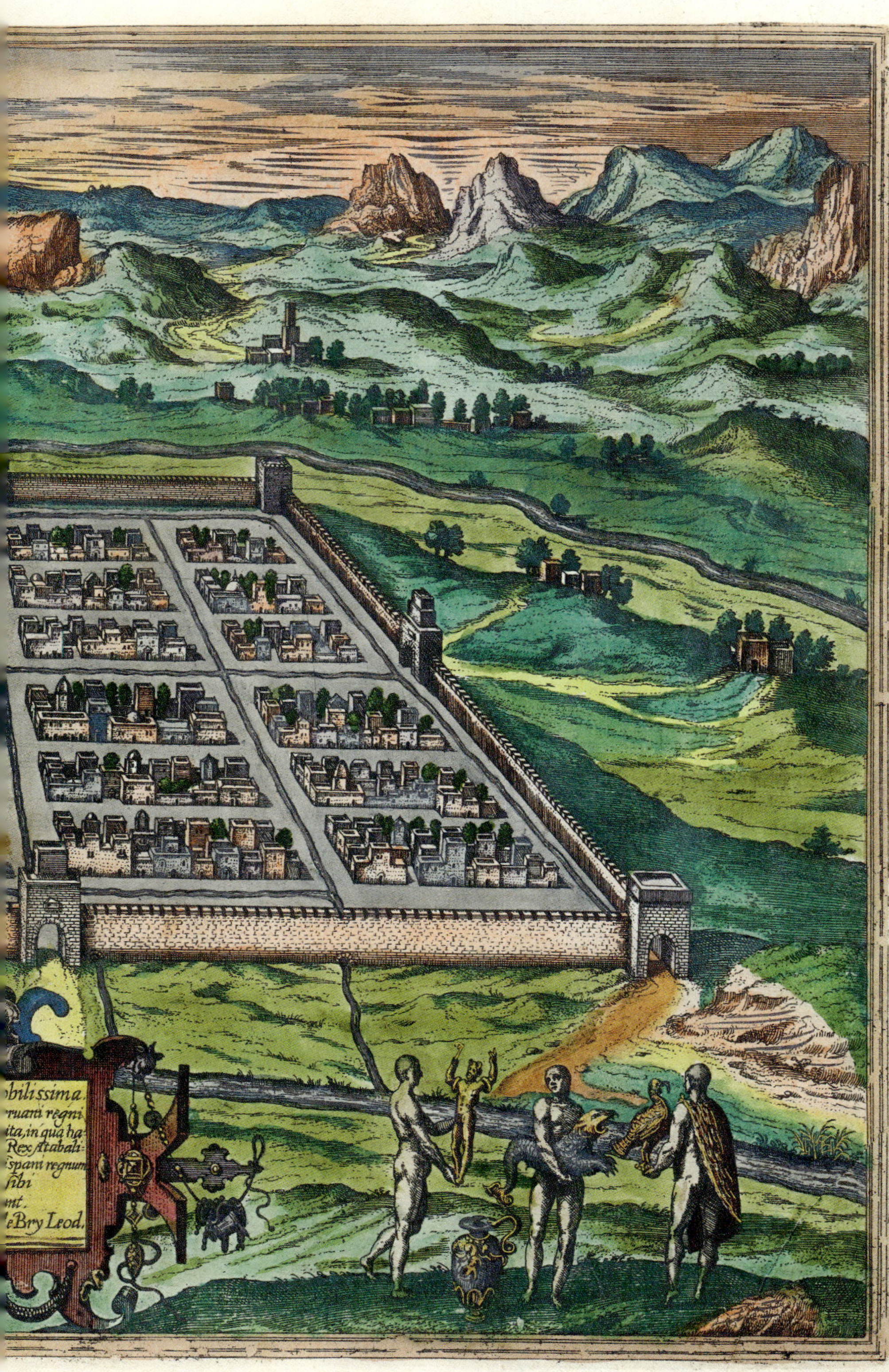
obilissima.
ruani regni
ita, in qua ha-
Rex Atabali-
spani regnum
sibi
nt.
e Bry Leod.

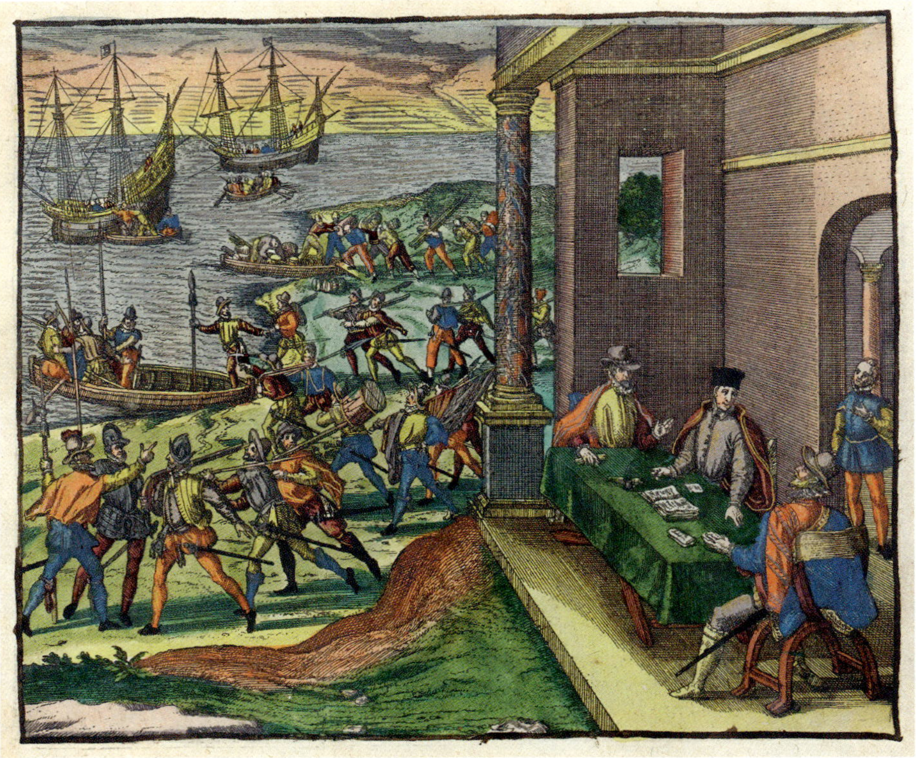

PLATE 1

Francisco Pizarro, Diego Almagro and Hernando Luque form a company together

Having heard stories about the riches along the Pacific coast, three prominent inhabitants of Panama, Francisco Pizarro, Diego Almagro and a priest called Hernando Luque, together formed a company to exploit this land, rich in gold, silver and precious metals. They did so jointly, promising each other to share the spoils and the honour they would acquire together without deceit. They purchased two ships and equipped them with soldiers and necessities. Pizarro and Almagro departed from Panama, leaving Luque behind to provide all that might be useful. But the first expedition was not successful, and they returned to Panama and dismissed many soldiers.

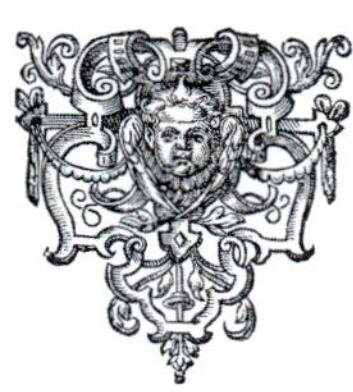

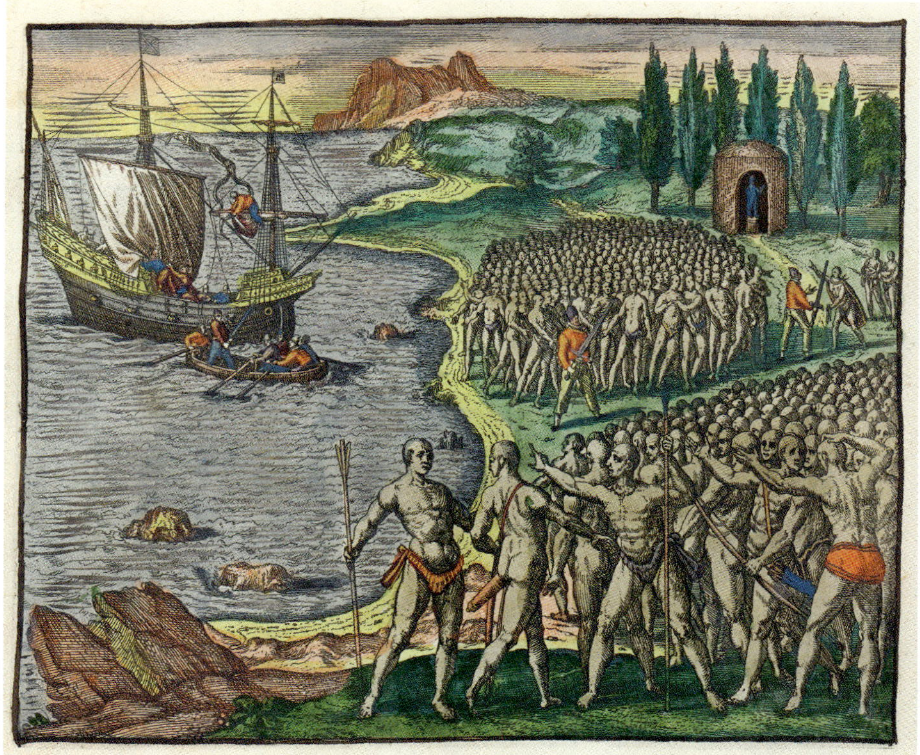

PLATE 2

A fearless Cretan soldier of Pizarro's army forces his way through a crowd of Indians

After having recovered from the losses, Pizarro and Almagro fitted out a fleet with new soldiers and necessities to try their hand once again. Having lost many soldiers again, they were forced to retreat to an island called Sangayan. Here Pizarro ordered his partner to return to Panama to get new supplies. From the island, many soldiers deserted Pizarro and returned to Panama as well, except 13 or 14 men, mostly sailors, who remained. He expressed his thanks to them, and promised them many riches if they stayed loyal to him and waited for Almagro's return. Finally Almagro sent a ship with provisions, but without further auxiliary troops. Then Pizarro, feeling that he should not stay on the island too long, set sail for the coast of Peru until he reached Tumbes, which the Indians had told him was a very rich area. None of the men dared to go ashore, however, because they had seen a multitude of Indians there. A Cretan soldier, Pedro, offered his services. He took a big sword and boarded a small vessel. Unconcerned, he jumped out of the vessel on the beach, and forced his way through the crowd of Indians, who were astounded by the appearance of this bearded man. The local governor received him kindly and showed him the temple dedicated to the sun. When he returned to Pizarro and the others, he told them about the wealth of the land.

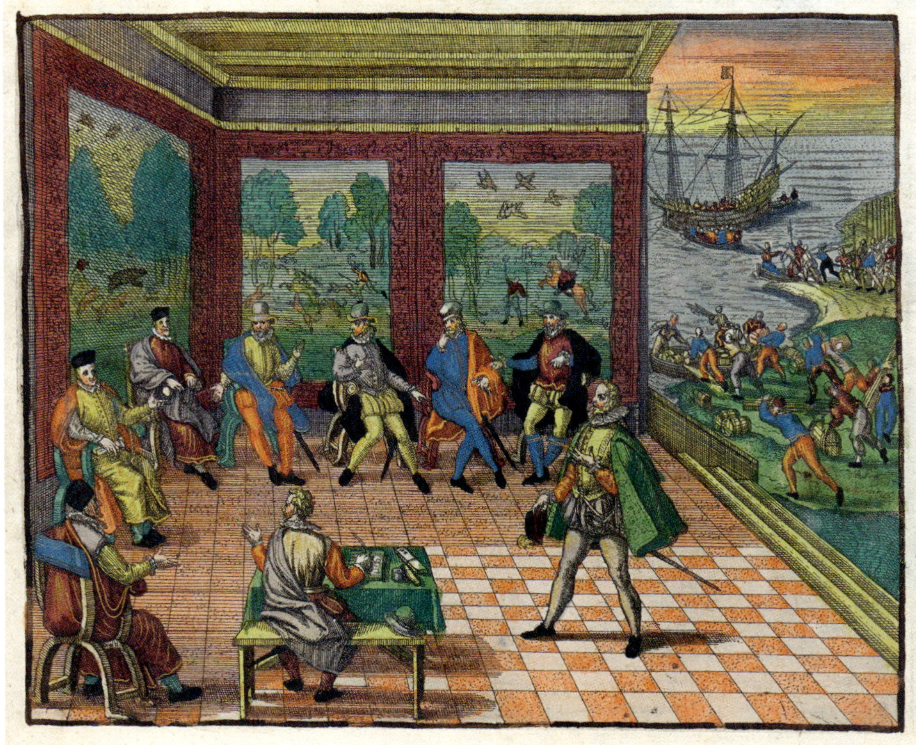

PLATE 3

Pizarro returns to Spain and is named prefect of the region he discovered

Francisco Pizarro, having heard these stories, then returned to Panama, telling his partners about the fertility of the Chira region and speaking highly of the wealth in Tumbes. Almagro and Luque delegated Pizarro to Spain to ask the emperor for permission to take possession of Tumbes and be appointed its governors. Once in Spain, Pizarro reported to the Council of the Indies about his discovery, and explained how much he had spent to achieve this and how much trouble he had encountered. Then he requested to be named prefect, predicting the additional wealth of the Kingdom of Spain – but without making any mention of his two partners. His request was granted, and he received a patent with the imperial seal. When this was settled, he prepared for the return voyage to Panama, taking along Hernando, Gonsalvo and Juan Pizarro, as well as Martino de Alcantara. But his two partners learned that he was appointed prefect by himself, and Almagro in particular found this difficult to deal with, because he had spent so much money on this expedition, more than Pizarro himself.

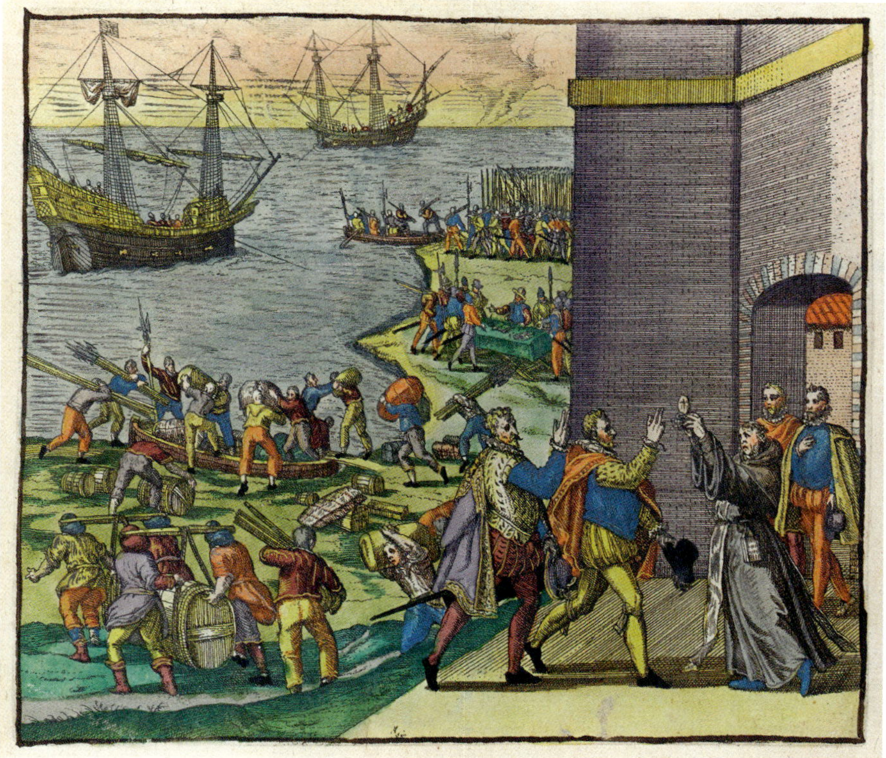

PLATE 4

Pizarro and Almagro bury their differences and each swears to keep his promise

One doctor Gama then reconciled Almagro and Pizarro, and devised the conditions of a new partnership. Almagro supported Pizarro with weapons, horses, money and whatever else he needed, for Pizarro needed somebody's help as he could not do it alone. Almagro, then, would equally share in the honours, the position and the dignity which the emperor had bestowed on Pizarro. Together they sealed this new partnership, from which Luque was excluded, with an oath on consecrated sacramental bread which they had jointly received, and promised to keep their pledge to each other until the death of one of them. When this had been settled, Pizarro left with 150 soldiers and many ships and horses from Panama, leaving behind Almagro with instructions to follow him with further provisions and as many reinforcements as he could muster. At last, Pizarro reached the coast of Peru and dropped anchor around Colonche, and from there he continued to the island of Puna, where he was kindly received by the local governor. When the governor became aware of the Spaniards' insolence, he sent in his army to drive them from the island.

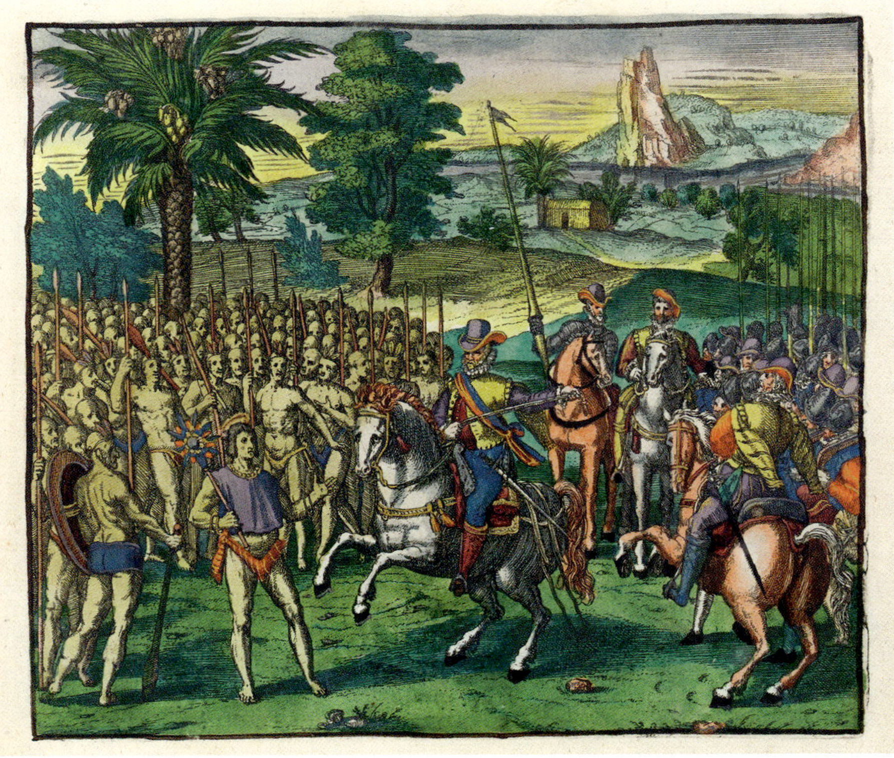

PLATE 5

Hernando de Soto is sent with several others by Pizarro to King Atahualpa

Pizarro and his army arrived in Caxamalca and encountered an Indian nobleman who did not allow them to go anywhere until Atahualpa arrived. Pizarro did not reply, retreated to a house with his men, and hastily ordered the officer Hernando de Soto with some others to Atahualpa to greet him on his behalf, and to ask him whether it would be allowed for him to meet him himself. De Soto made his horse prance right in front of Atahualpa, so close in fact that foam from the horse's mouth was blown into his face by the wind. Atahualpa, however, was not impressed, and ordered many of his own men who had fled in fear of the horses to be killed, because he did not want them to acknowledge that the bearded men did not recognise his dignity. Then Hernando Pizarro arrived, and introduced himself as the brother of the Spanish commander, and that he had come straight from Spain with an order given to him by the pope and the emperor to strike an alliance with them. He urgently asked them to come with him to Caxamalca to discuss in private matters of great importance.

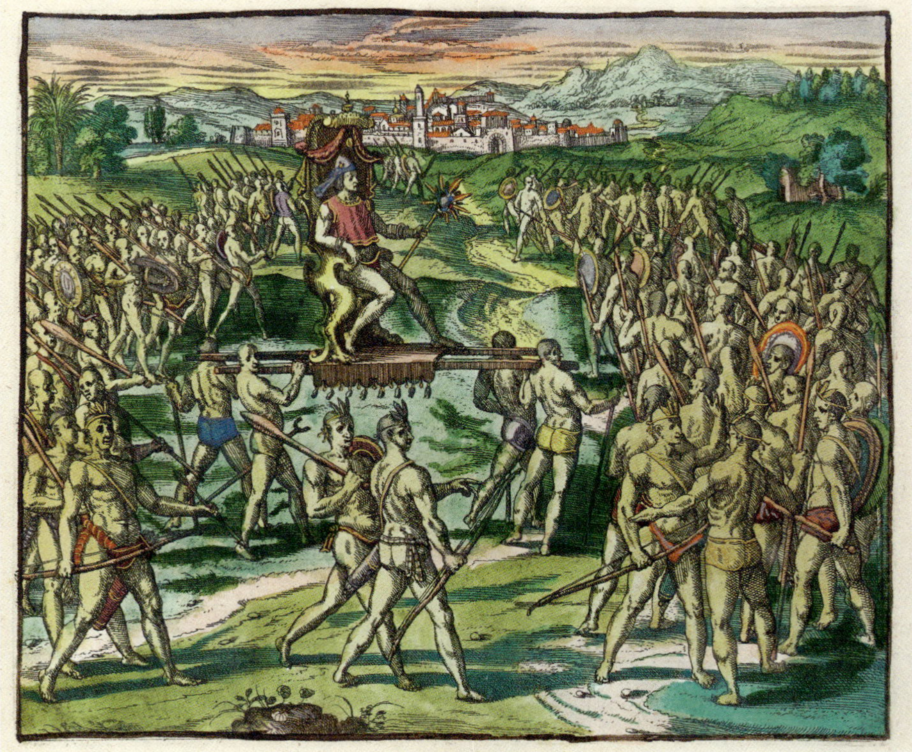

PLATE 6

Atahualpa enters Caxamalca with pomp and splendour

When Hernando Pizarro was convinced that Atahualpa would be prepared to do this, he returned to his own people to tell them about the riches of the king. Then he disclosed what he expected would happen: King Atahualpa would by no means allow them to remain in his province, but he would not spurn the friendship of the emperor, providing that the commander returned the gold and silver which he had already taken from his subjects, and also that he would come to Atahualpa in Caxamalca the next day. Meanwhile he instructed his men to prepare for battle if things turned sour, and had artillery installed in the house where he had taken his domicile. The following day, Atahualpa arrived with more than 25,000 Indians. Carried around by some of his subjects, he was taken into Caxamalca with great pomp and splendour, until he reached the palace where he was supposed to receive the embassy of bearded men. He was carried there in a seat made of gold plates with multi-coloured feathers, and sitting on a woollen cushion embellished with many precious stones. From a distance, he noticed a number of Christians whom Pizarro had put in a tower, with orders to have them expelled or killed.

PLATE 7

Atahualpa, King of Peru, is taken captive by Francisco Pizarro

A Dominican friar, Vicente de Valverde, pushed his way through a crowd of natives, and faced King Atahualpa, cross and Bible in hand. Through an interpreter, he indicated that he had been sent by the emperor, on the authority of the bishop of Rome, the representative on earth of Jesus Christ, who bestowed these territories on the emperor on the condition that he would send educated men there to teach and spread the Holy Gospel, and root out their sins. Then he held out his Bible before him, and declared it to be the divine law. God has created everything from nothing, and after beginning with the story of Adam and Eve, he then talked about the creation of man and his fall, the coming of Christ from heaven, being born of a virgin, and finally being crucified before he was resurrected to redeem all mankind. When he returned to heaven, he left the church to St Peter and his successors, the popes. Atahualpa then asked the friar how he knew all this, and he responded that these stories were written in the book he was holding in his hands. Atahualpa took the book, glanced at it, and said, "It contains no meaning to me", and then threw it away. The friar picked up the book and called for Pizarro at the top of his voice, urging him to correct this behaviour. Pizarro instantly ordered his brother Hernando to fire his guns and attack the Indians who, shaken by the artillery fire and the jingling bells of the horses, fled in every direction. Pizarro himself attacked Atahualpa with his foot soldiers, and when many Indians had been killed, he pulled him from his seat and took him away.

PLATE 8, PAGES 340/341

After having defeated Atahualpa, the Spaniards fulfil their desires with the women they encounter bathing in his camp

After having imprisoned Atahualpa, Pizarro, who did not lose any of his soldiers, had gained a memorable victory over the Indians. The Spaniards enjoyed having so much booty, as well as having defeated such a powerful king. They caroused for part of the night, and rested the other part, because they had not eaten for an entire day. The next day they raided the province around the town of Caxamalca, and seized the women they found in the natural baths a mile outside the town. These and others they captured at Atahualpa's camp, they raped. Authors who have written about the West Indies even tell us that there were more than 5,000 women in the baths and in Atahualpa's camp.

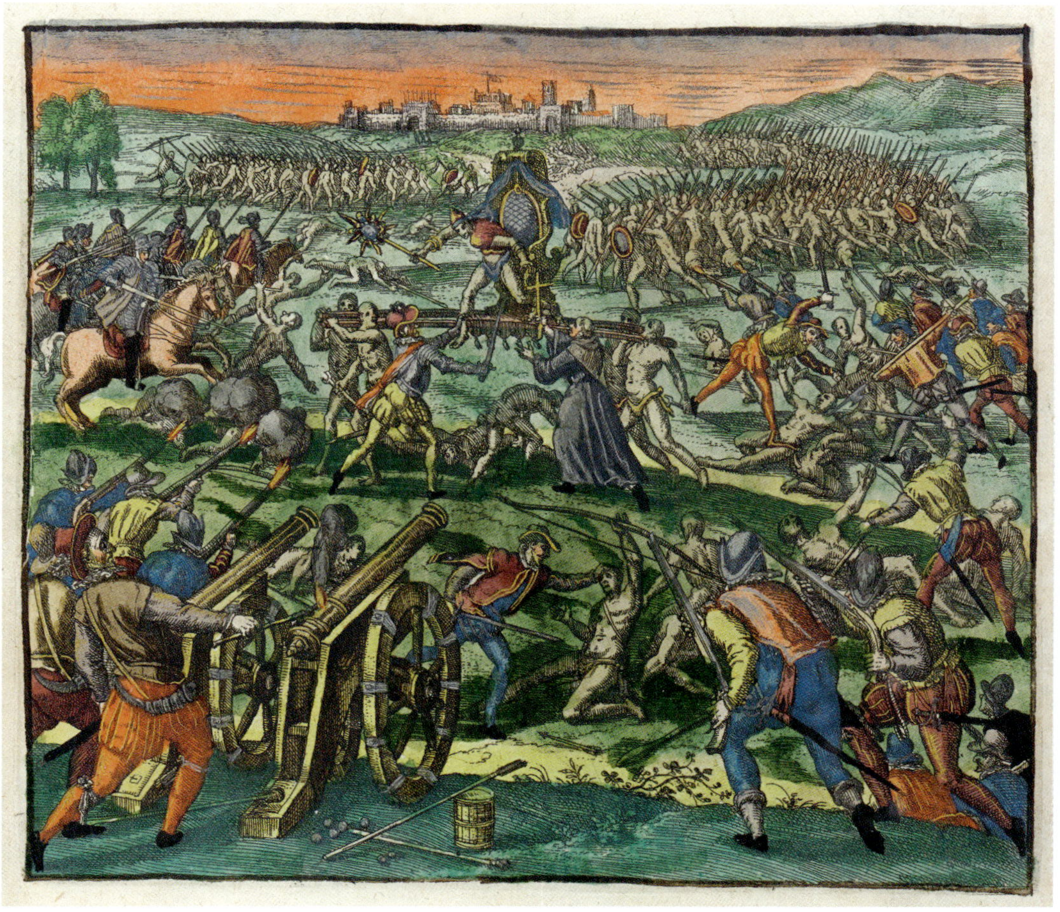

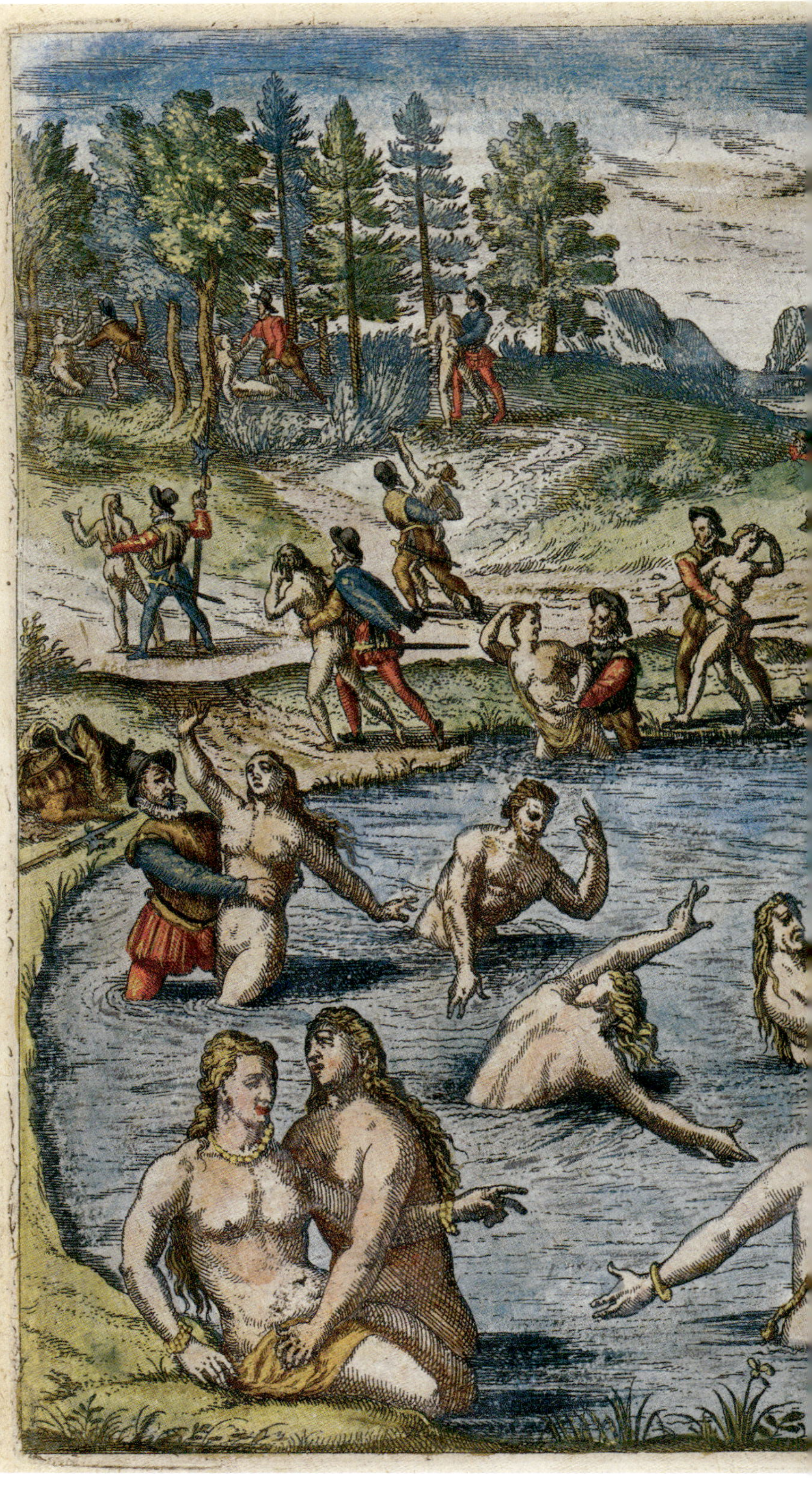

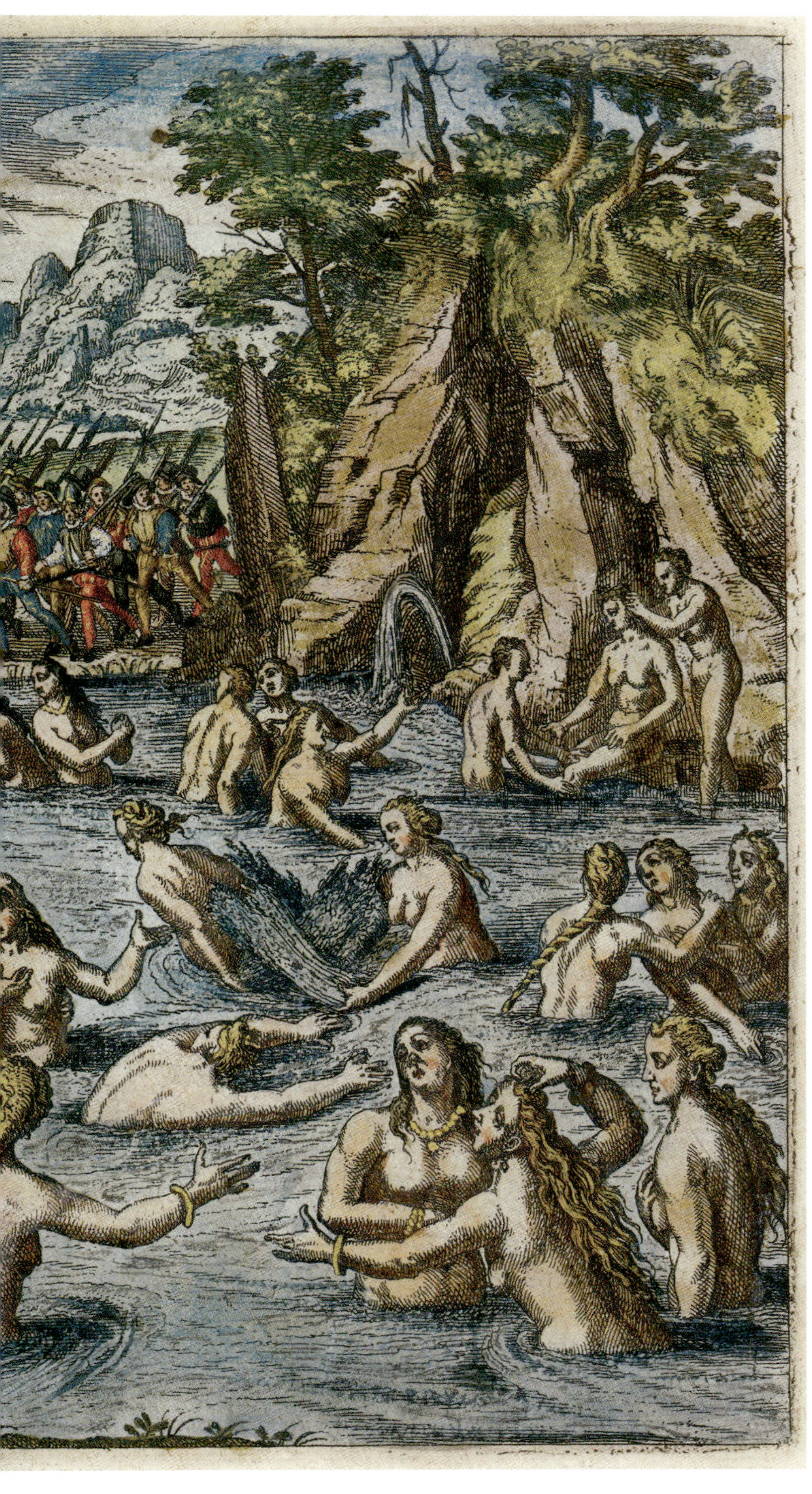

PLATE 9

Atahualpa concludes a treaty with Francisco Pizarro about the amount of money he has to pay

The Spaniards found many riches in Atahualpa's camp, including a jar weighing 200 pounds of pure gold. The utensils and tableware of gold and silver had an estimated value of 100,000 ducats. The following day, Pizarro went to Atahualpa to talk to him, because the latter had complained that he had been locked up. But Pizarro could not help him, and Atahualpa asked him if he could be treated well. Aware of the Spanish greed, however, he promised that if they would take off his chains and release him, he would bring them enough gold to be made into vases that would completely surround the room where he was being held captive, from the floor up to a red line that he had drawn for this purpose. He added that the vases could not be melted or broken. Pizarro promised to treat him well, and gave his word that he would release him in time on the condition that he would pay the amount he had promised.

PLATE 10, PAGE 344/345

Atahualpa sends his men to various places to collect gold and silver after it is promised that he will be released

Atahualpa chose to believe Pizarro's promises and ordered his men to bring him gold and silver vases, and precious metals in whatever shape or form, and required them to return as quickly as possible if his freedom meant anything to them. Shortly after, his men returned with lots of gold and silver. But since the hall was very large, and the loads carried by the Indians whilst of great size were yet light, they filled the eyes of the onlookers less than they did the room. The Spaniards were impatient, waiting to divide the gold and silver among them. In this way most of them claimed that Atahualpa was deliberately delaying the process, and had secretly ordered his men to kill the Christians. A majority of them said that he must be removed, but as Hernando Pizarro resisted the idea it did not happen. Atahualpa suspected these plans were being discussed, and told Pizarro their fear was unfounded, because he was in chains, and he could not order the gold and silver vases to be brought to them any faster, considering the distances to the places from which they had to be carried. Because Quito, Pachacama and Cusco were a long way from Caxamalca. If they wanted to make sure that he did not plot their downfall (and instead behaved correctly), they should delegate some from their midst to check if there was anything going on. Hernando de Soto set out for Cusco, 200 miles from Caxamalca, and Hernando Pizarro for Pachacama, some 100 miles from Caxamalca, and they did not witness any soldiers being recruited, but only the bringing of various vases to Caxamalca.

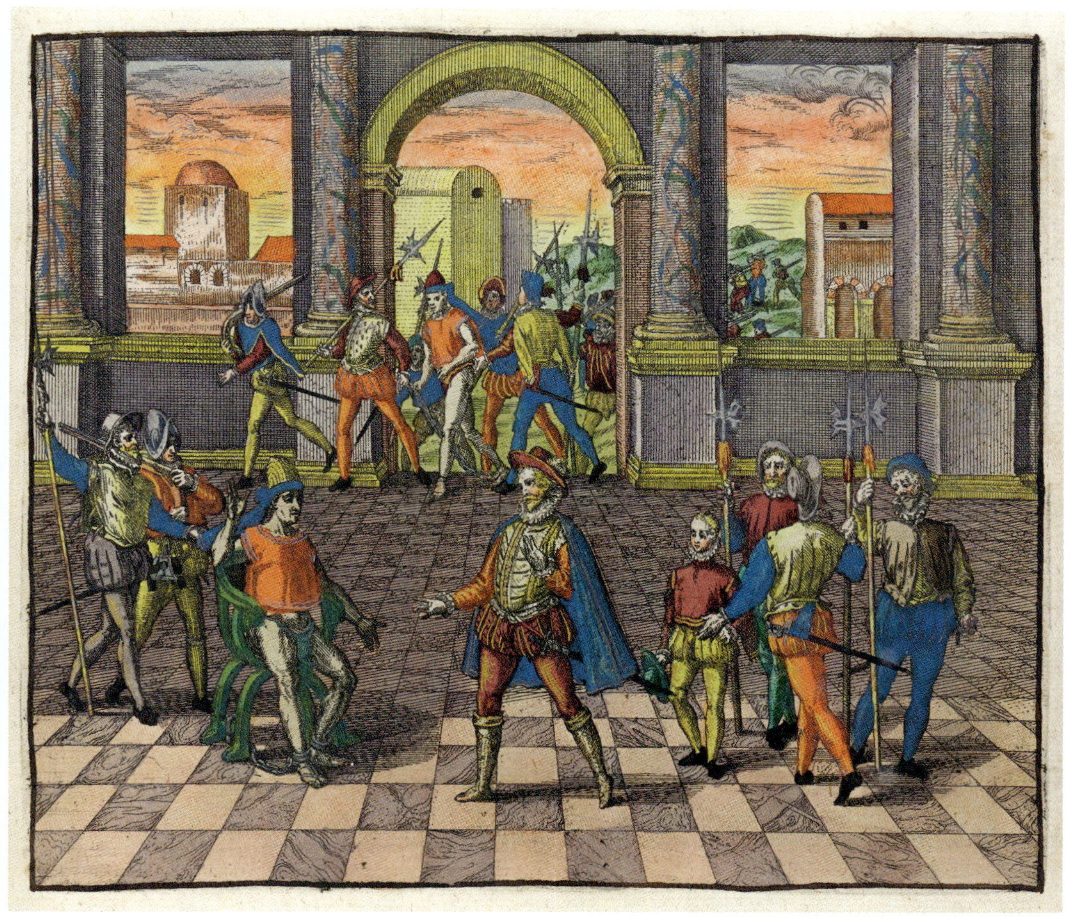

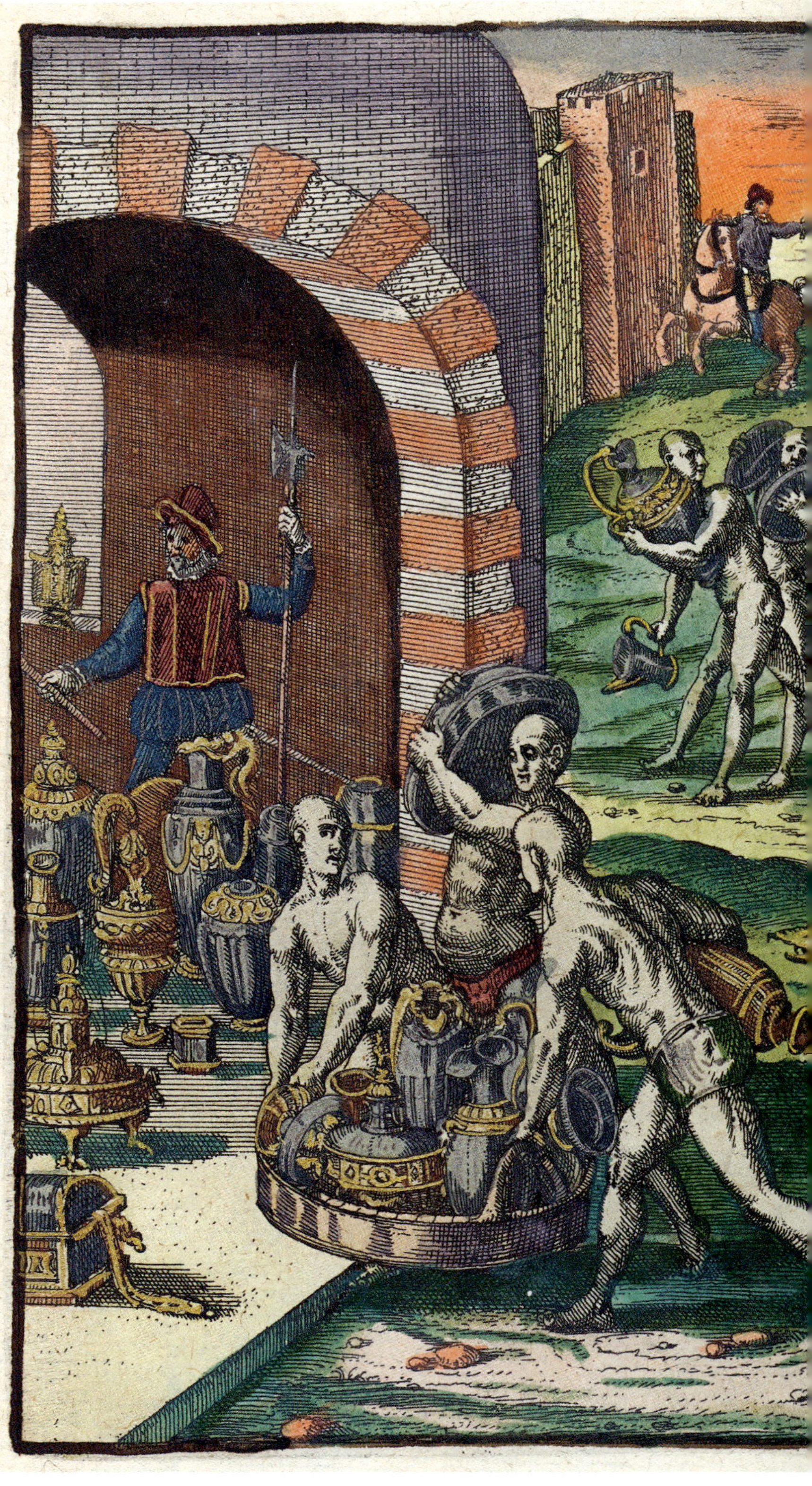

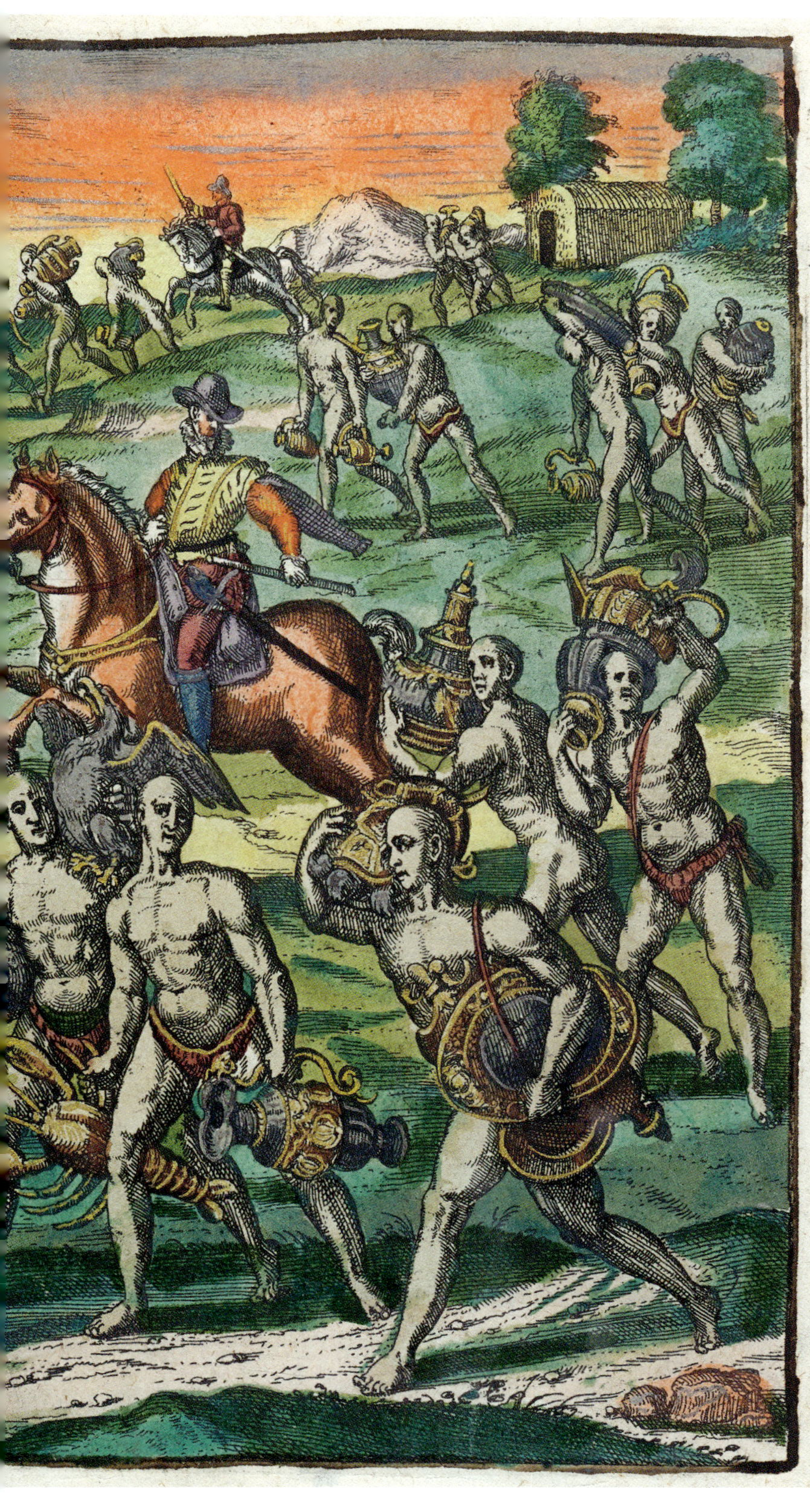

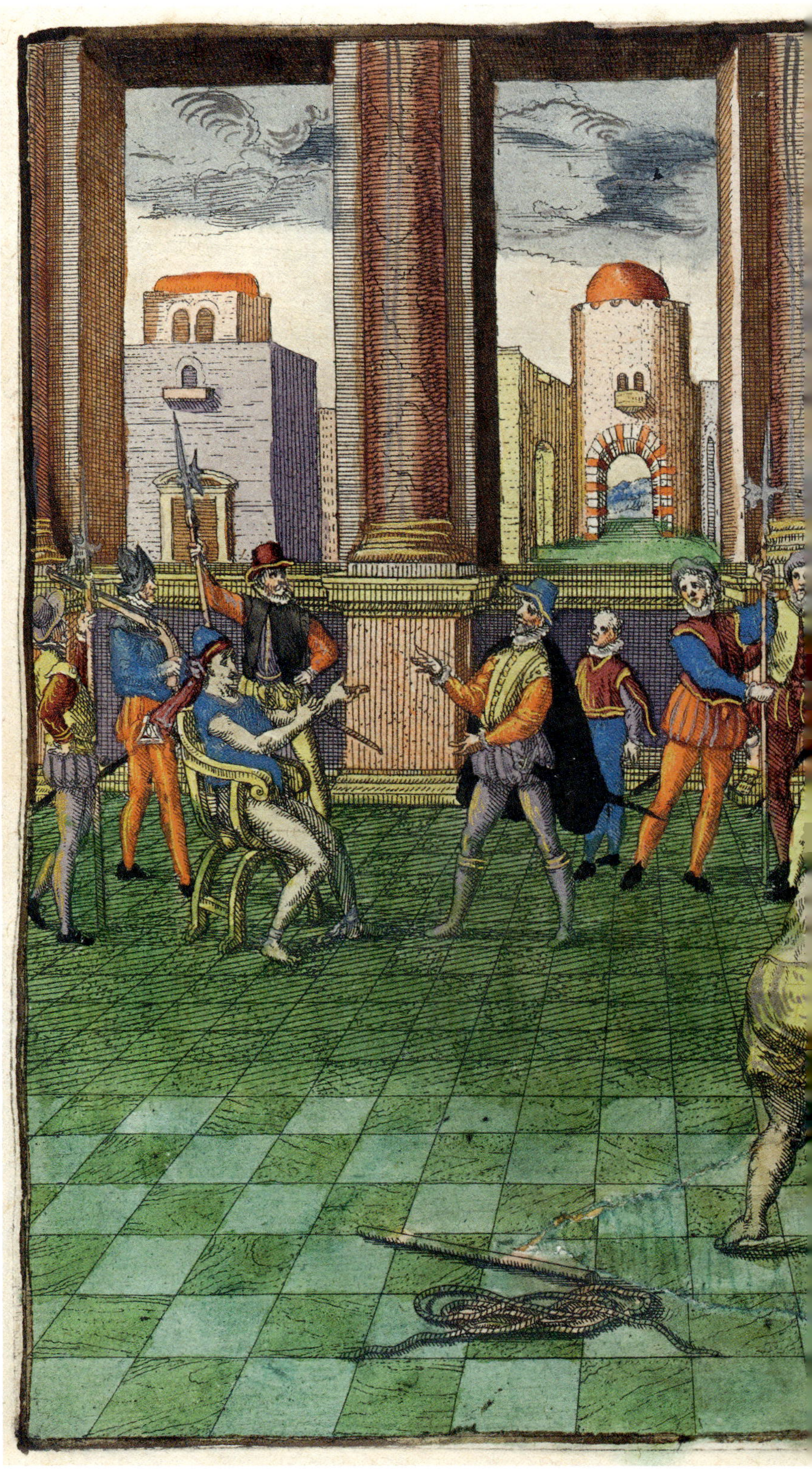

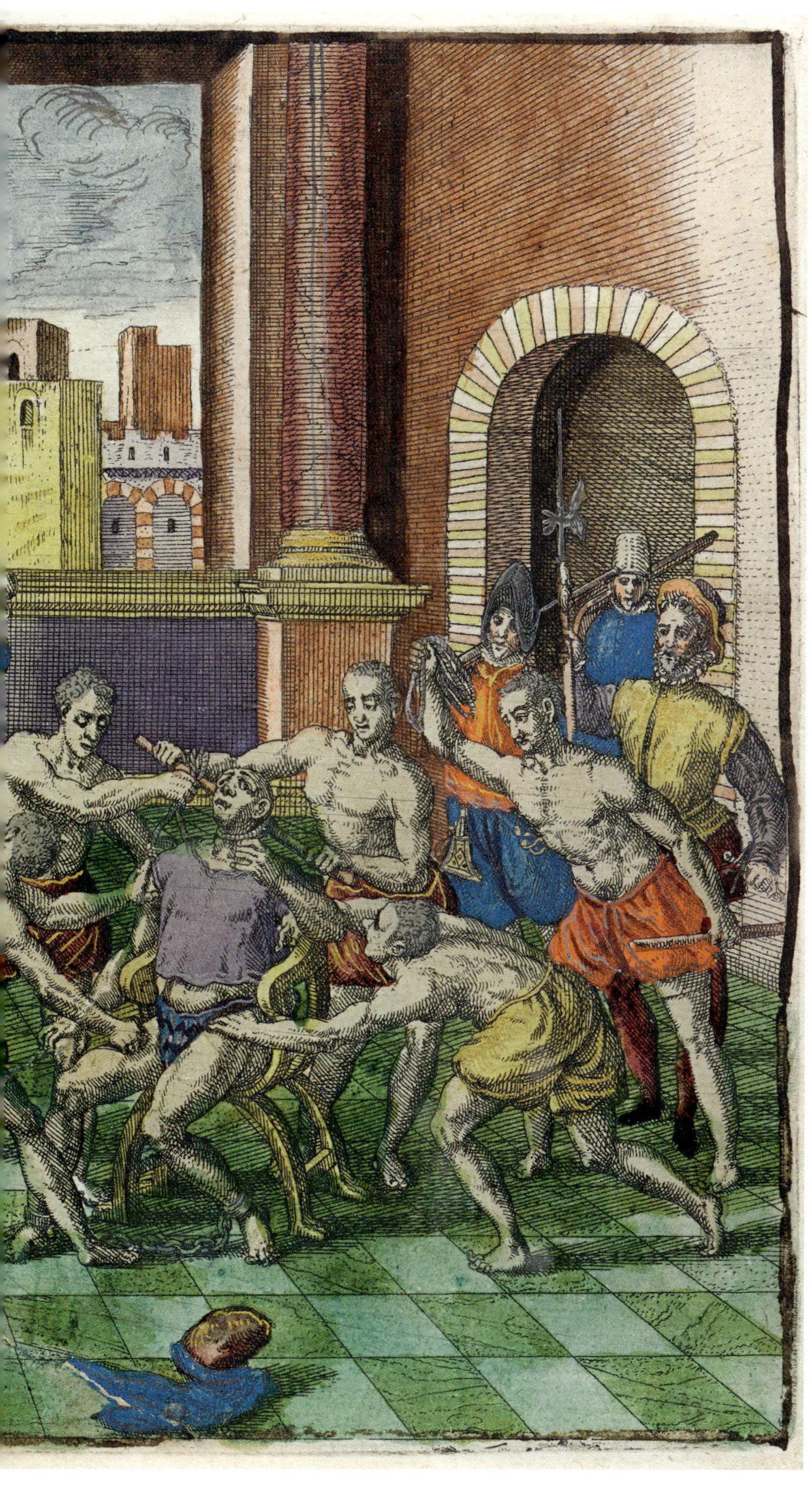

PLATE 11, PAGES 346/347

Pizarro has Atahualpa murdered, breaking his promise

Several days after the capture of Atahualpa, the Spaniards began to urge Pizarro to divide the booty they had obtained, and that which had been brought to them for Atahualpa's release. The total amount was 120,000 pounds of pure silver, and in gold many hundreds of thousands of Spanish pesos. Of this total amount one-fifth was for the emperor, in total 400,000 pesos, while the soldiers each received 8,900 gold pesos and 90 pounds of silver – a little more for the officers, and a little less for the foot soldiers. Never before have soldiers become so rich in such a short time, and without danger. Having divided the booty, Francisco Pizarro sent his brother Hernando to Spain with the emperor's share. After his departure they began to plot to kill Atahualpa. Most of them wanted him to be murdered, for their own safety and that of the province. Others thought that he should be sent to the emperor in Spain, and that such a great ruler should not be killed, even if guilty. But the former opinion prevailed. They created the pretext that Atahualpa's brother Guascares had been taken prisoner and put to death, because he had secretly planned the downfall of the Spaniards. Having been informed of this cruel verdict, Atahualpa complained about Pizarro's promise to set him free after he had paid the ransom, and begged to be sent to Spain. But Pizarro did not listen, and had him strangled by his African slaves. The murder of the prince would not remain unpunished, however. Later on, all those who had conspired to kill him perished. Pizarro put on a black gown after Atahualpa's death, and provided him with an honourable funeral.

PLATE 12

Cusco, the richest town in Peru, is occupied by the Spaniards

When Francisco Pizarro learned how powerful and rich in resources the Incan capital Cusco was, he left Caxamalca and journeyed to Cusco. He had to be careful on the way though, because a captain named Quizquiz, one of Atahualpa's most decorated officers, was crossing that same territory with a mighty army. Quizquiz had initiated a number of skirmishes and fought with Soto, and later with Almagro. Pizarro travelled this way with the rest of his army. The nearer they came to Cusco, however, the more they heard about a bright fire burning there. They sent half of the army to extinguish the fire, for they were sure that the residents of the town had started the fire in order that they would not end up in the hands of the Christians. It turned out not to be a fire intended to do great damage, however, rather to signal to the town's residents, as well as those in the neighbouring town, to assemble there. Indeed, such a large number fell upon the party of Spaniards outside the town that they succeeded in driving the armoured soldiers away with just rocks. When Pizarro came to this town, however, he killed many of these people and drove the rest violently into the town. The following night, those who had started the fight packed their belongings and fled. The Spaniards were able to enter Cusco the next day without resistance, where they plundered the temple to the sun and the castle of Huayna Capac. It will be taken as an obvious truth that this town had great riches and exploits, as when King Atahualpa was earlier captured and conquered.

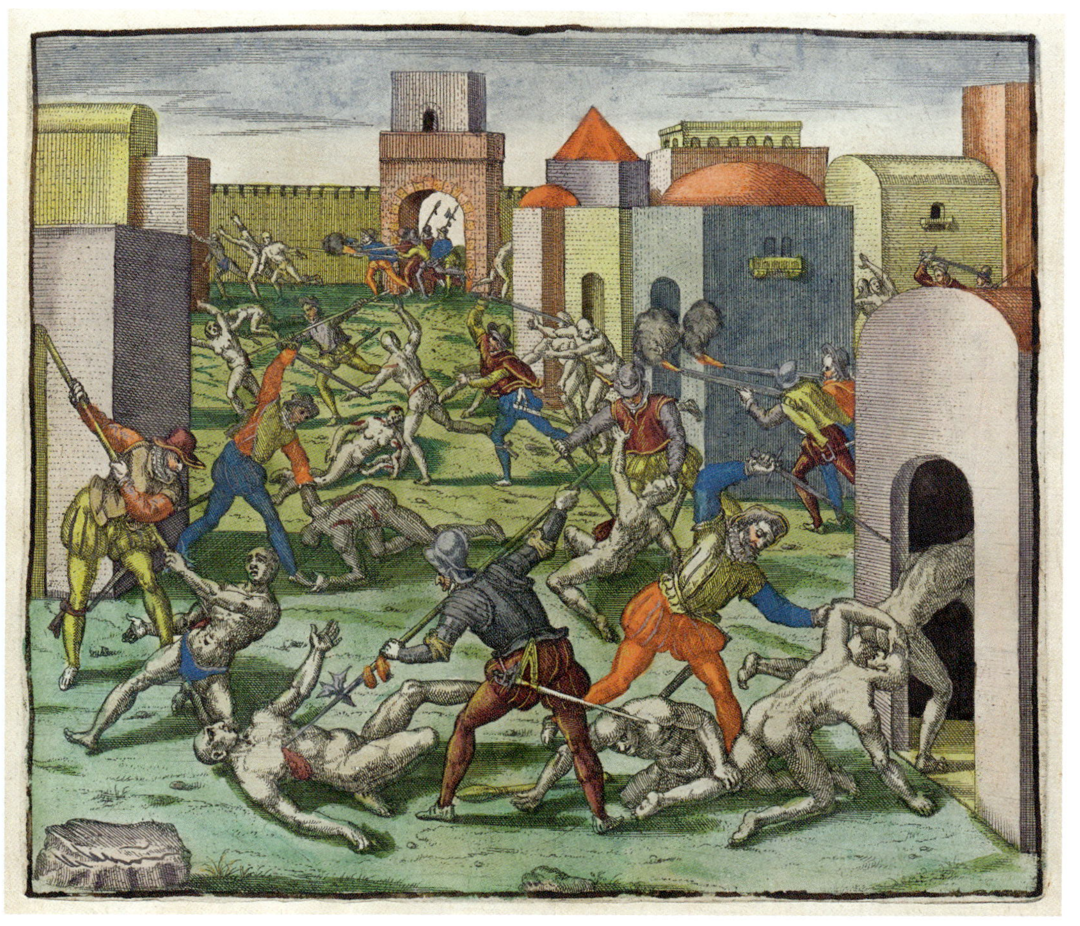

PLATE 13

A battle between the Spaniards and the Indians for the town of Cusco

Mango, the son of Huayna Capac and brother of Atahualpa, secretly sowed unrest among his subjects and created a strong position against the Spaniards. For this he had been taken into custody. Some time after this he became the best friend of Hernando and Juan Pizarro. As soon as he was alone, however, he urged his vassals to a rebellion against the Spaniards. He had the majority of the Spaniards as well as the Indians working for them in the mines killed on the spot. He sent his commander along with a considerable army to seize Cusco. When the commander arrived, he took the castle from the Spaniards and held it for six or seven days. The Spaniards were forced to remain on the defence, and some of them, notably Juan Pizarro, perished before they could retake the castle. Mango subsequently laid siege to the town. Francisco Pizarro sent several of his captains to assess the situation, but they were each captured by the Indians and killed. Pizarro became all the more distressed since none of the officers he dispatched had returned, and so he sent his captain Francisco Godoy. Godoy, however, was surrounded by the Indians and only escaped because his horse was very fast and returned straight away to Pizarro. On the way, he met several Spaniards who had gone along with the previous captains and who had managed to run away. These revealed to him all the ways into Cusco, and with this information he headed towards Lima. Pizarro called upon his entire army to assemble. Alfonso Alvarado, Pizarro's right-hand man, was put in charge of 300 armed men, and ordered not to relent until the Indians had been beaten back and the siege of Cusco ended. The Indians attacked them when they got near Cusco, but after holding their ground a long time, they fled.

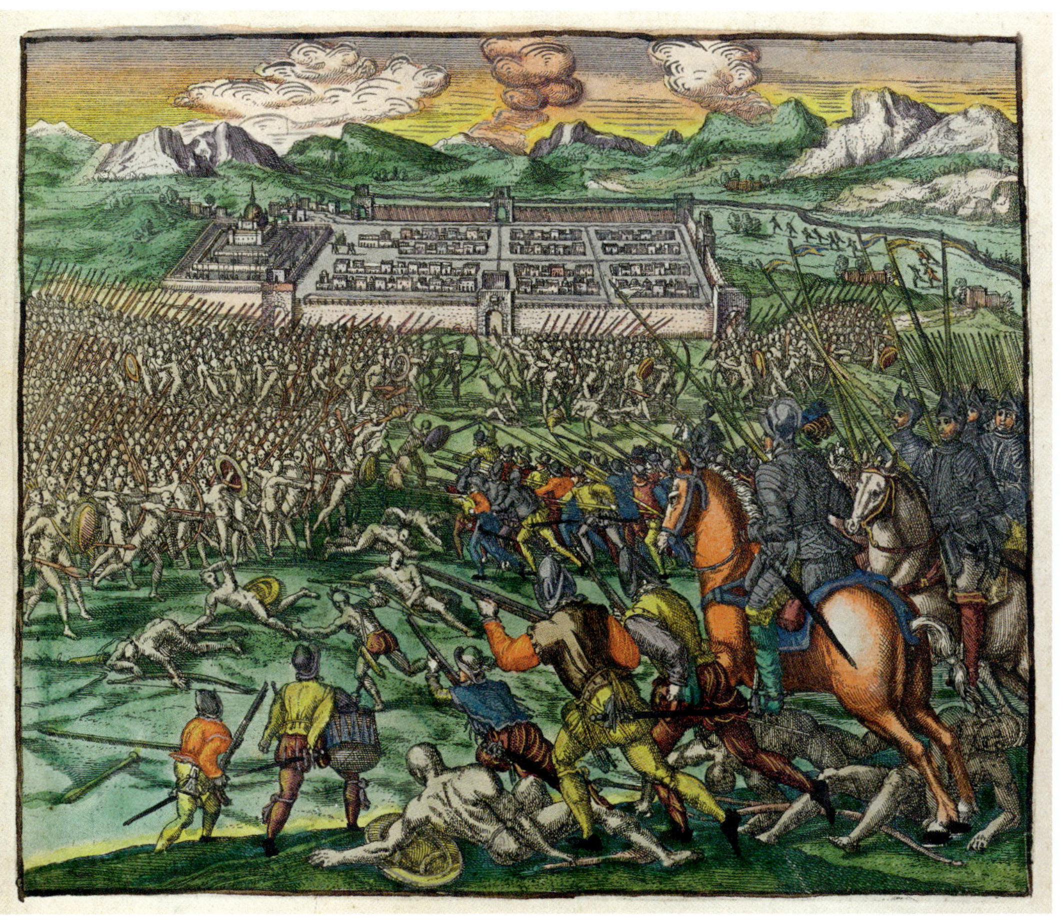

PLATE 14

Almagro is put in chains by Hernando Pizarro, strangled, and then publicly decapitated

When Almagro left the Chilean trail again, he took the town of Cusco by night. Hernando Pizarro violently defended Cusco against Almagro. It was reported to the viceroy Francisco Pizarro that his brother Gonsalvo had been taken into custody, and so he raised an army against Almagro. However, it was decided the situation would be tolerated according to the following points. Both sides should disband their armies, Almagro should release Hernando (Gonsalvo had already escaped custody). They should also both send a legation to his majesty the emperor in Rome so that he could graciously make a decree of their joint governance, and ride to Mula with only 10 horses each in order to confirm the truce. When Almagro made his way to Mula, Gonsalvo began to chase him. Almagro turned back towards Cusco when he realised this. He took soldiers to guard him and complained about Pizarro's perjury, as well as that of the monks who had recommended these conditions. The viceroy feared that Almagro would kill those who were still being held in custody. He therefore sent his captain, Jacob Alvarado, to Almagro in order to ensure him that the viceroy had had no knowledge of what his brother had done. Although Almagro trusted the viceroy's word very little, he nevertheless allowed himself to be persuaded by Alvarado, once again accepted the terms of the truce, and set Hernando free. After the viceroy had secured his brother's freedom, he once more became disloyal. He sent a message to Almagro that he should leave Cusco peacefully or else he would remove him by force. At this they both declared war on each other. Hernando met with Almagro, who was there overpowered and taken into custody by Hernando, sentenced, and strangled in prison. His body was then publicly decapitated. No one knew that Almagro's father had lived without a wife, but had had a son with an Indian woman in Panama who shared his name.

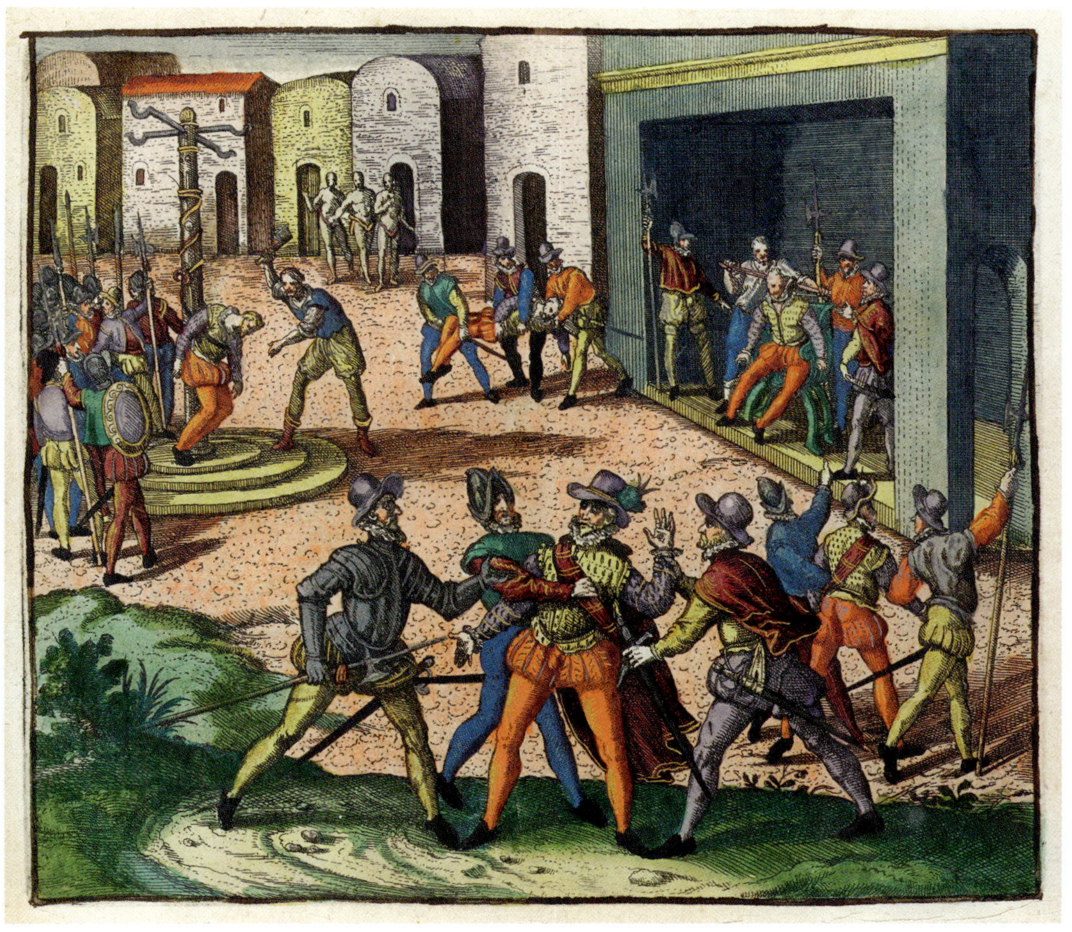

PLATE 15

Pizarro is killed in his own house by the younger Almagro and his allies

When Francisco Pizarro returned to the town of Regum, he thought to ensnare Almagro's son, but it did not work out. Rather, the younger Almagro resolved to avenge his father's death. Pizarro became angry at this and removed all the Indians from his care and that of his followers so that they would be driven by extreme hunger to come back to him. Almagro's followers became embittered, secretly collected weapons together and brought these to Almagro's dwelling. The viceroy Pizarro learned of this, but did nothing. Meanwhile a cry went out that Pizarro was after their lives. Pizarro was again warned to be careful, but rode out happily, so that the followers of Almagro would see him in the fullness of life, and took no bodyguards with him. The conspirators resolved to kill him in the church on St John's Eve. One of them revealed the plot to a priest of the church. This was related to Pizarro, who did not attend church on the designated day. The conspirators saw from this that it was all over, unless they wanted to rush to the viceroy and kill him. Thenceforth, Juan de Rada brought together his allies and went at midday to Pizarro's palace. His people stood outside brandishing their weapons and cried loudly that the tyrant must die. De Rada had nothing but a sword that was smeared with the blood of a ram he had killed shortly before. He cried out "Pizarro dies now!" to stir up the 200 followers of Almagro who were in the city to aid de Rada. Francisco Chavez thought he could drive these people away with his reputation and authority. He was immediately stabbed, however, and his body thrown down the stairs. The followers of Almagro stormed in after this. Seven of them surrounded Pizarro, who fought back for a long time until he took a sword to the throat, fell down and lay dead. Pizarro was a strong, courageous, reputable man, but he cared little to protect his own body.

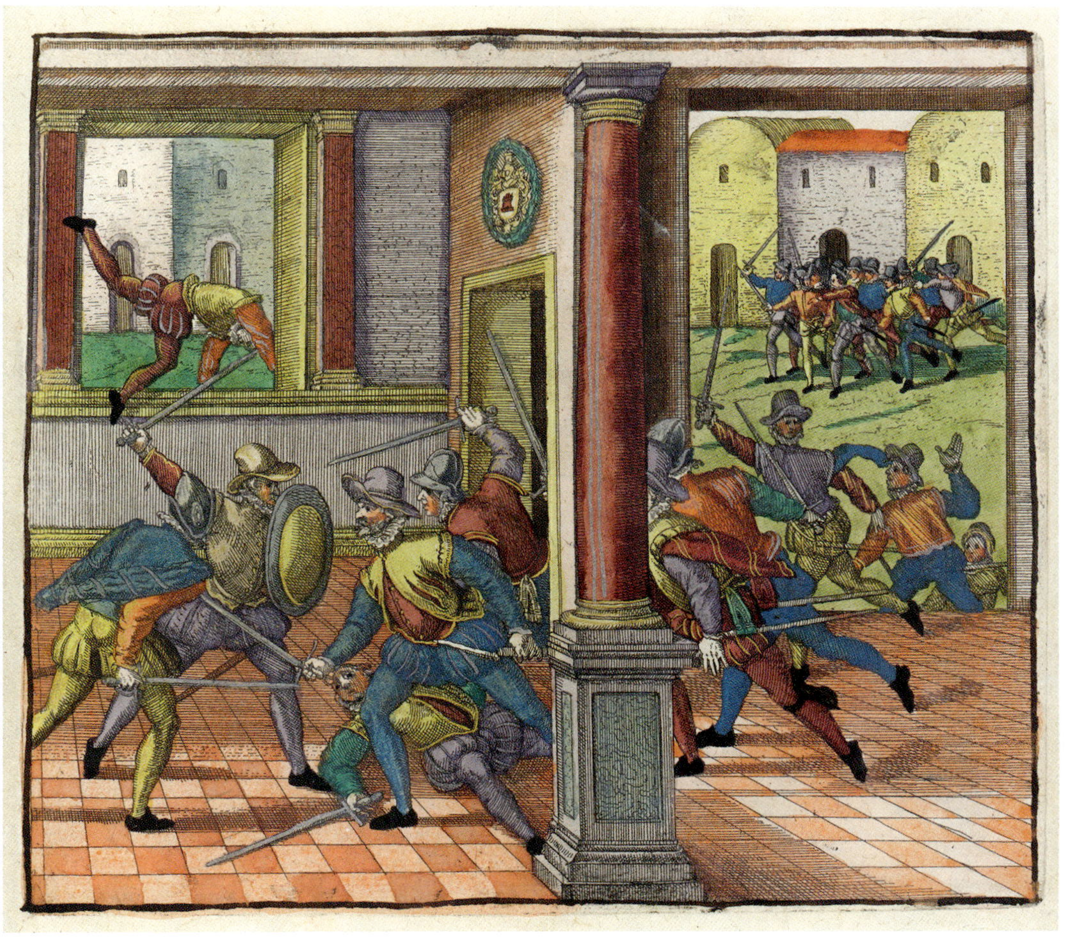

PLATE 16

A battle between Vaca de Castro and the younger Jacopo Almagro

After Almagro had slain the viceroy, his followers cried throughout the city, "Long live the king!" Jacopo Almagro plundered the dwelling of Pizarro as well as of other rich friends of the Pizarros. The younger Jacopo Almagro was appointed by his followers the governor of Peru, while Juan de Rada was made the highest general in charge of the army. When Vaca de Castro of Quito learned what Almagro had done, he travelled to Lima and wrote to Almagro, who had already left Cusco. He urged him to lay down his arms and come into his service. Almagro answered him that he wanted to continue with governance, like his father. He also wanted a contractual letter, certified with his majesty the emperor's seal. Otherwise he could not consent to any of Vaca de Castro's terms. He offered to fight a battle, for which he counted on his army of 700 Spaniards. He foresaw a good outcome and promised them the wives of the soldiers they killed in battle. They moved straight away to encamp on a hill two miles from Guamanga. When Vaca de Castro learned of these plans, he left Guamanga. He knew the rugged landscape better than Almagro and camped on a high plain called Chupas. He emboldened his men and let word travel to Almagro via a public edict that he had promulgated. Both sides approached each other and began to fight, and for a long time it was not possible to say who had the upper hand. Finally Vaca de Castro was victorious, although he suffered many losses to his own army. Almagro fled towards Cusco and was apprehended there and signed over to Vaca de Castro, who had him beheaded. After his death there was once again peace in the land.

PLATE 17, PAGES 358/359

Viceroy Blasco Núñez Vela stabs Guillermo Xuarez, the royal procurator

After the emperor received word about the insurrections in Peru, he called on several learned, honourable men to write new statutes that would bring peace back in a Christian manner. Many of these laws, however, were quite harsh and not appropriate to the situation there. This was brought to his majesty's attention, and as a man of great esteem, he decided which of the statutes should actually be issued. All the Spaniards became riotous over this. His majesty gave Blasco Núñez Vela the esteemed position of governor. Vela had the new laws promulgated as soon as he arrived, even though he had been advised to wait for a new decree from his royal majesty. A few Spaniards were to be dispatched to his majesty to persuade him to ease the severity of the new laws. They did not want to lose the freedoms that they had enjoyed as subjects of his royal highness. However, Vela threatened to hang all who would break the new law. This severity and unbending discipline was much to the chagrin of all. Before he arrived in Lima, the inhabitants would not allow him to enter the city. The royal procurator Guillermo Xuarez wanted to ensure that the privileges were maintained. Vela promised that he would abide faithfully by all that had been established by the emperor and to serve this land. As soon as he entered the city, however, he enacted his new law and judged all matters according to it. He then had Vaca de Castro incarcerated. There was a great uproar, mostly associated with Gonsalvo Pizarro, the procurator's brother-in-law. This caused the governor great anxiety, and he therefore had Alfonso de Monte Majore gather together 50 horses which he could join when he fled. The procurator was captured on the way. The governor stabbed him twice and called for him to be killed. He then had the dead body thrown out and dragged through the street by the feet.

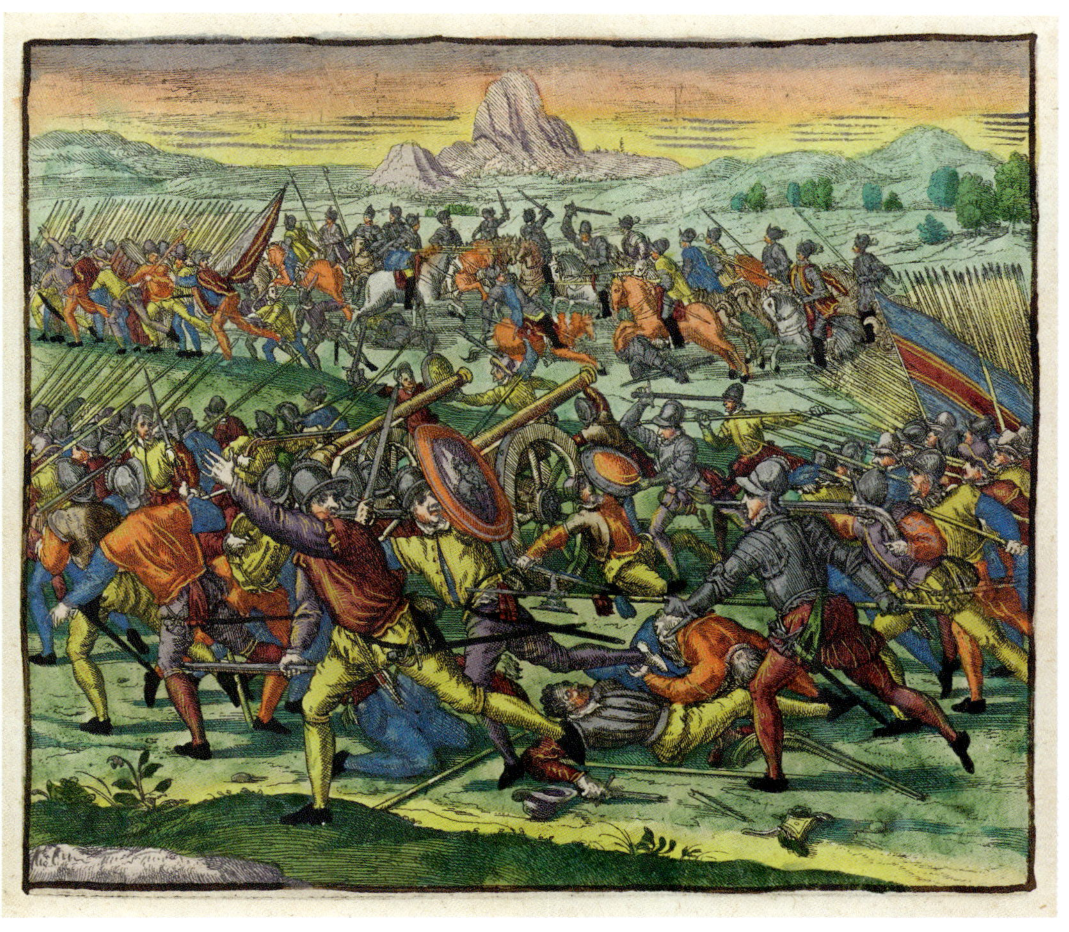

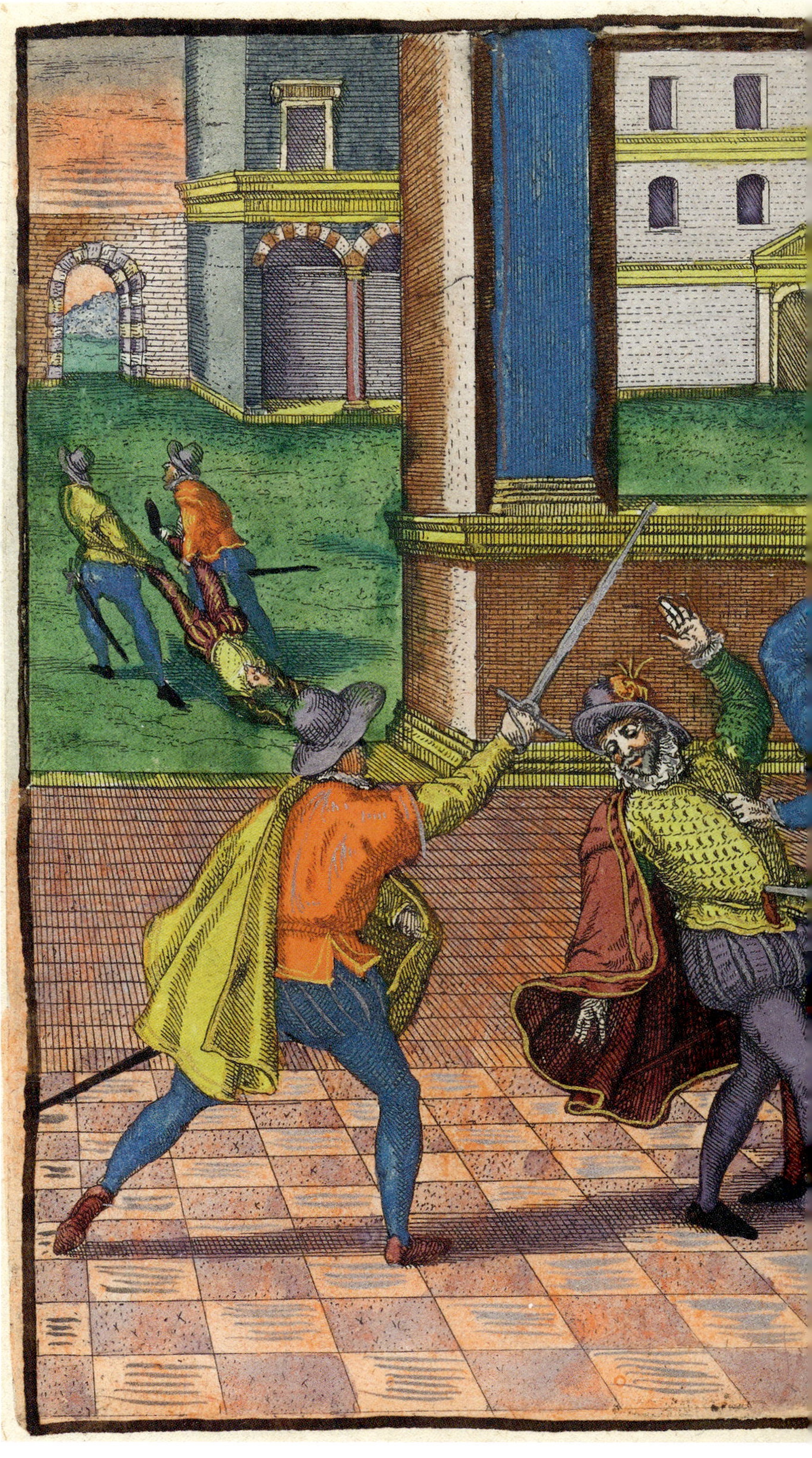

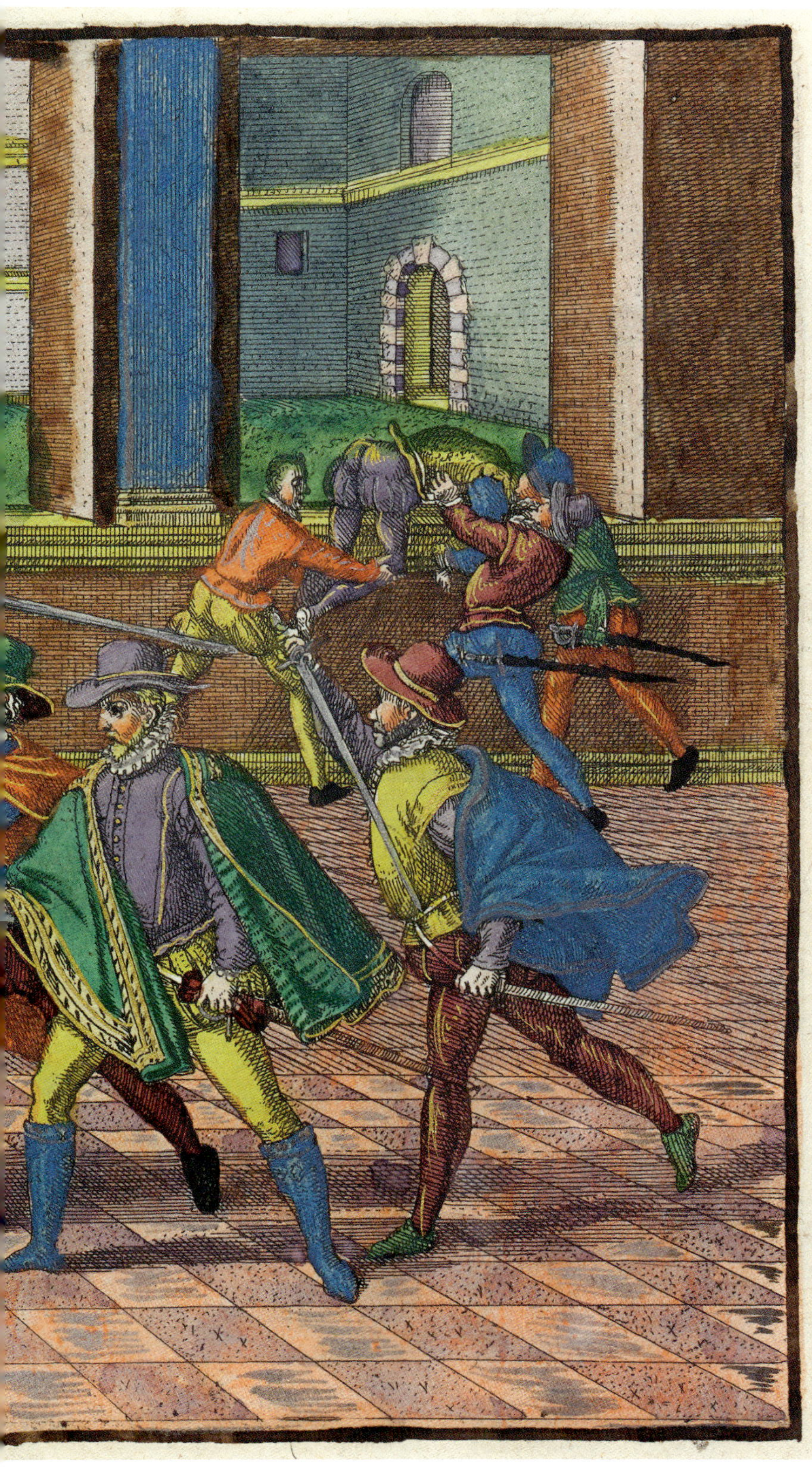

PLATE 18

Viceroy Blasco Núñez Vela is incarcerated

A great outcry went through Lima when people learned that the procurator was dead. It was said that the viceroy would thenceforth take the law into his own hands and kill anyone he wanted to. The arrival of Pizarro was therefore much anticipated. This made the viceroy very anxious. He took the contents of the chancellery and coffers for himself to transfer to Trujillo, telling his advisers they would leave Lima to travel with gold, silver and women to Trujillo. They opposed this order, however. His imperial majesty, they said, had ordered that they work in one place as privy counsellors. When he heard their answer, Vela promised to stay in Lima. As soon as they had left the council chamber of his palace, however, he called on his captains and commanders, informed them why he wanted to leave Lima for Trujillo, and ordered them to arm themselves the next day. Then he decided to move in person with the women and plunder in the ship and had his brother Vela Núñez accompany them with an army. When his advisers found out about this they resolved not to back down from their objections, but also not to allow the people to follow the viceroy. They requested that the viceroy stay, ordered that the people not allow their women to go to the boats, even if the viceroy were moving ahead with his plan. The same night, the licentiate Capada brought weapons into his house. The advisers met together the next day. The viceroy also prepared arms against them, but 400 honourable Spaniards came quickly upon him and advised him to stay put. Once the advisers separated from the licentiate Capada, many people came to them. The viceroy's commanders were forced to flee, and his palace was stormed and plundered. He himself was held captive by Martino de Robles.

PLATE 19, PAGES 362/363

Many people avenge personal issues in the name of the emperor

His imperial majesty sent Pedro de Hinojosa to the kingdom of Peru to ease the tensions there and to assure forgiveness for all those who bowed down to the emperor. When he had arrived in Panama he urged Gonsalvo Pizarro in writing to lay down his weapons and renounce the governorship. The emperor was prepared to forgive him for his misdeeds as well as to nullify the recent orders, and to permit the use of his goods as before. Pizarro was further advised not to speak about this arrangement to those around him; if they learned he was in the graces of his imperial majesty they might become disloyal. At this Pizarro gave him his word that he would give him the governorship, but that he must dedicate himself to this with his body and life. Meanwhile, Pedro de Hinojosa, the leader of the imperial armada, independently sent Aldanam with three ships to Lima in order to distribute copies of the emperor's decree as well as to make known that Hinojosa was blocking the governor's path with his fleet. This promulgation led to big changes in Peru, for many towns and commands shifted their allegiance from Pizarro to the emperor. There were many among these who nurtured under a guise of obedience their private hatred and desire for revenge. Rodrigo de Salazar stabbed Pedro de Puelles in Quito while he lay in bed. Francisco de Olmos killed Emanuel Statum. Jacob Mendez had Captain Morales strangled with a cord. The many murders among the Pizarro camp were deeply upsetting for President Hinojosa. He punished the offenders with the harsh words: "You must obey his majesty the emperor. Your private jealousy and vindictiveness have no place in your obedience to him. You cannot behave this way as his subjects."

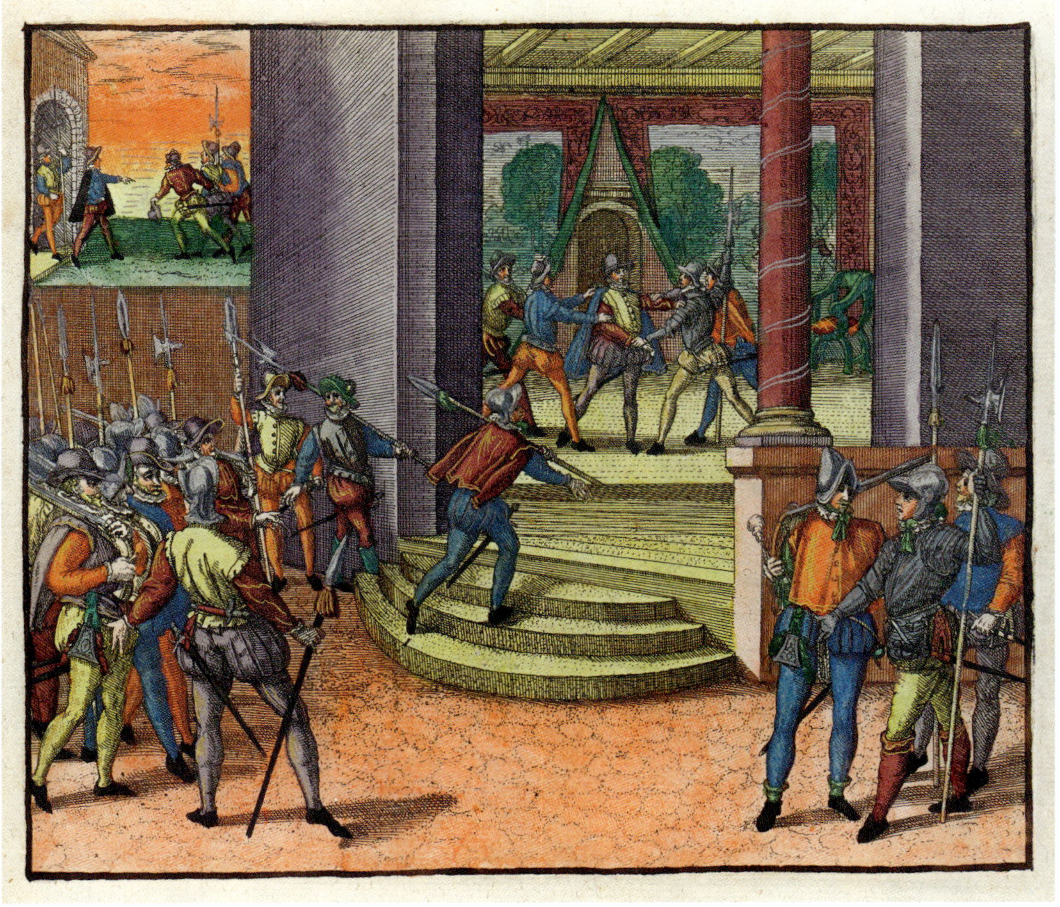

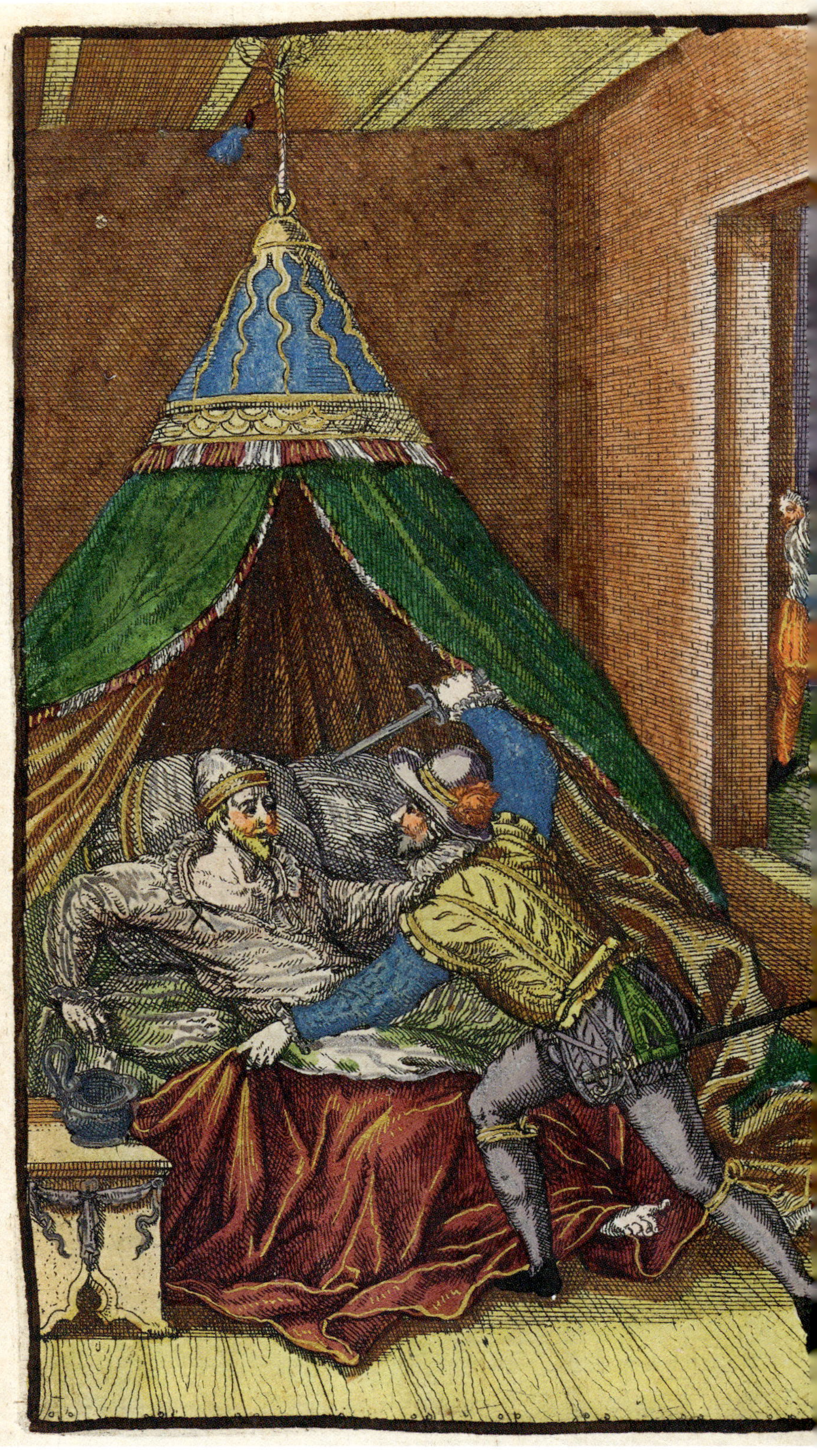

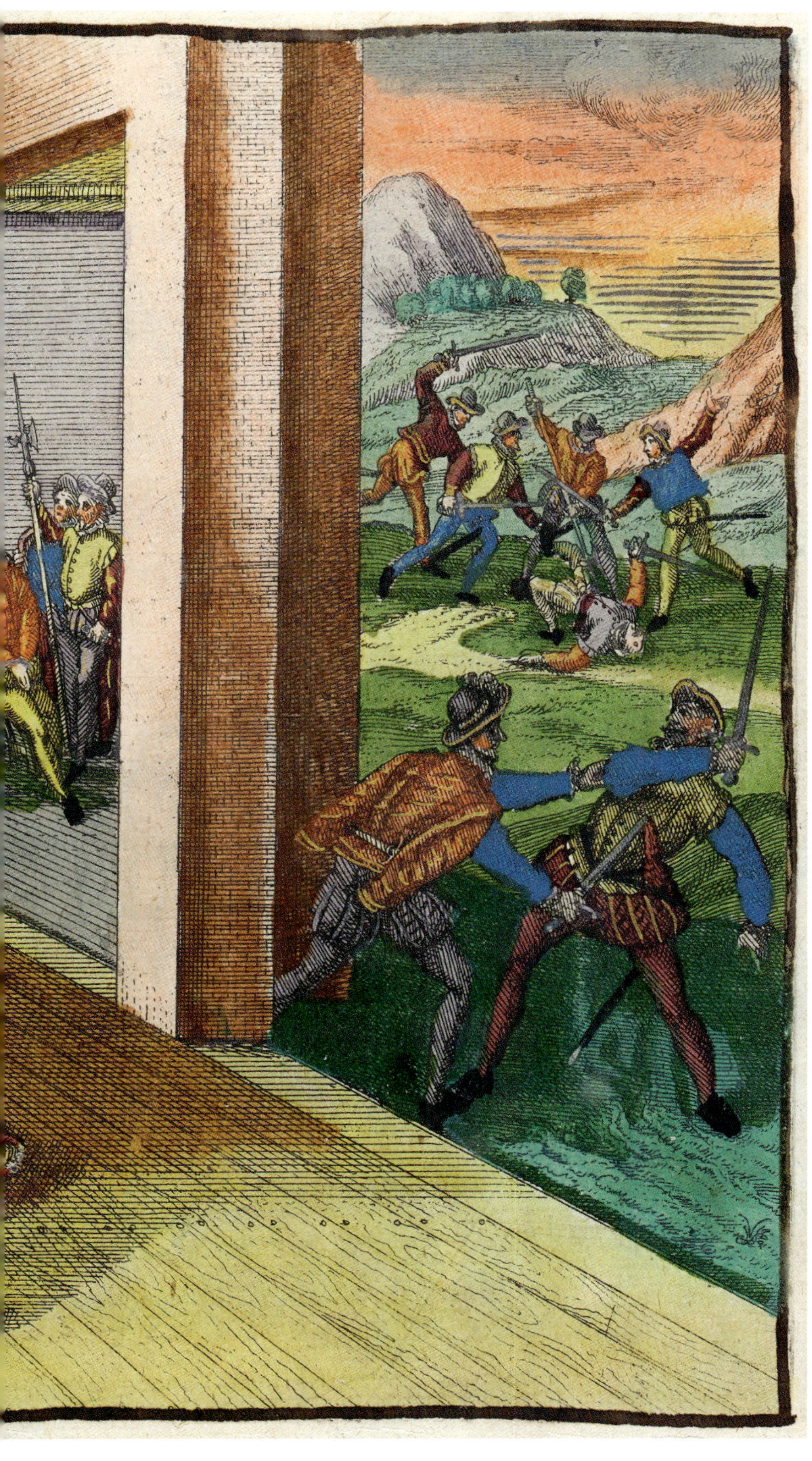

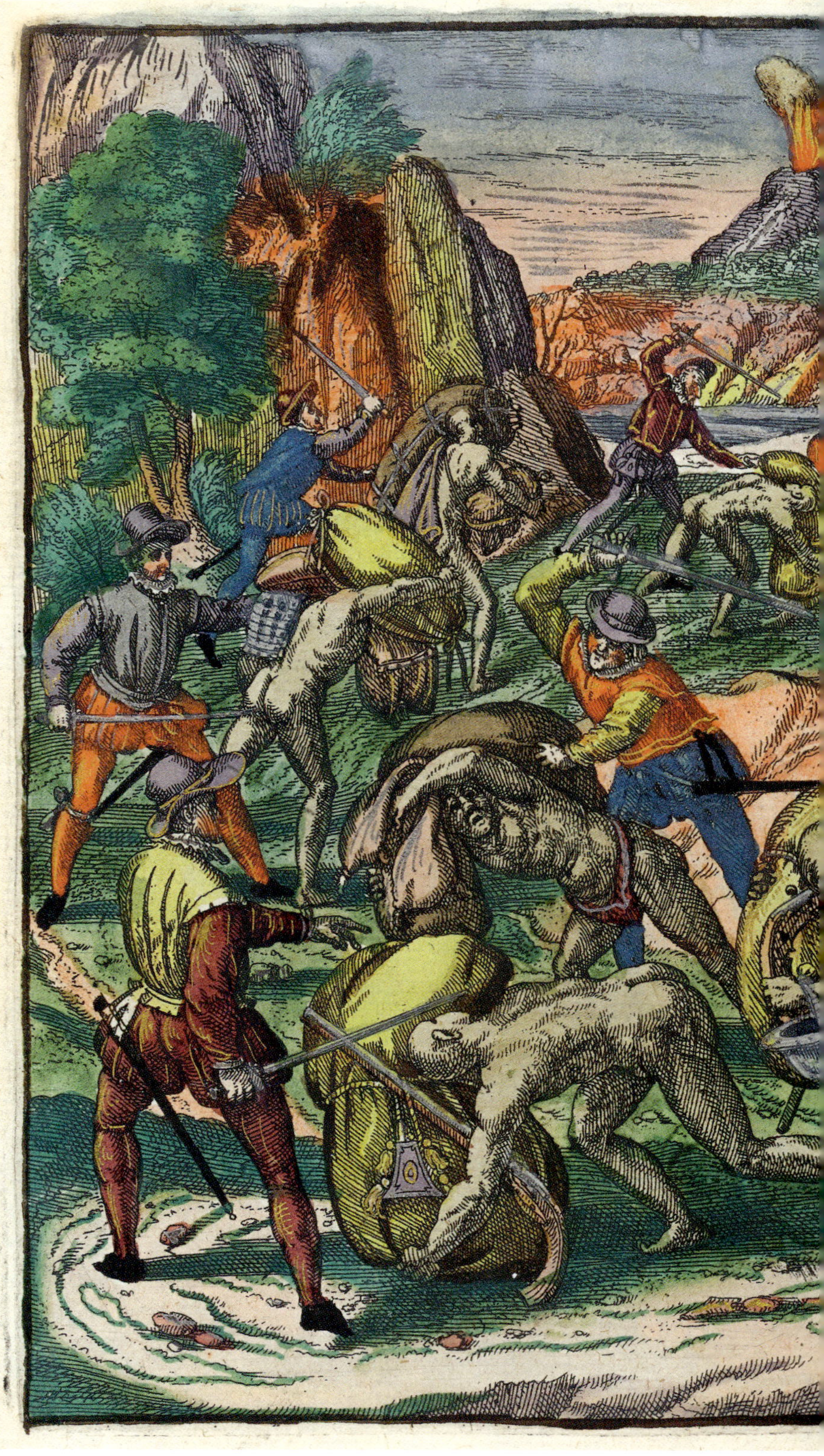

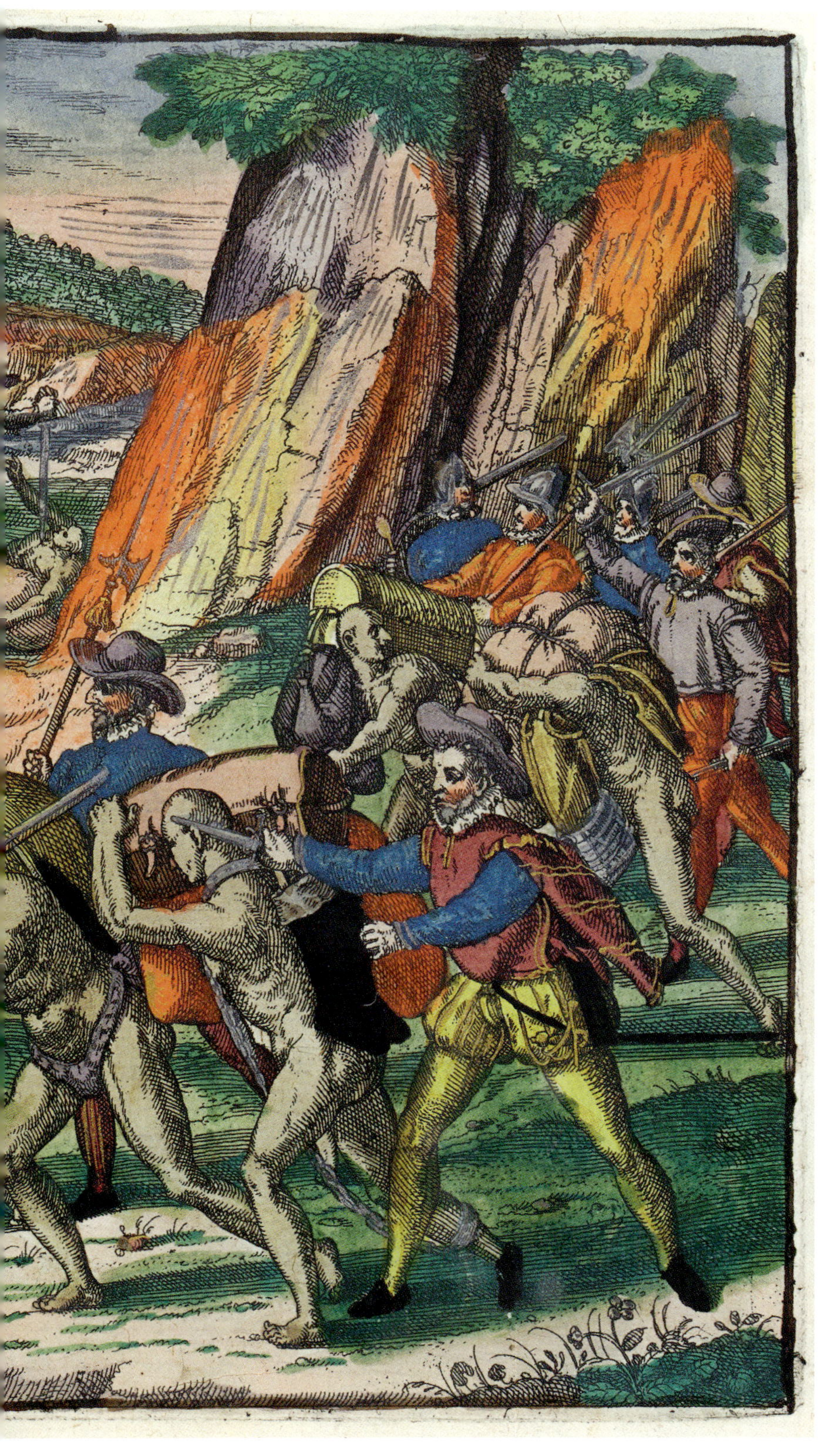

PLATE 20, PAGES 364/365

The Spaniards cruelly abuse the Indians who collapse under their workload

When the president Hinojosa settled down in Trujillo, many captains and reputable soldiers came to him such that in a short while he had over 500 choice men gathered around him. He was all loaded for travel so he and all his people began to move away from Trujillo. He had with him a large number of Indians to carry his property. The Indians were all connected together with chains to prevent them from running away. Many of them died on the way from thirst and fatigue. The Spaniards reacted to this with cruelty, whipping them, even though they could have easily lightened their load. The Spaniards did not even take the time to undo the chains around the necks of those who died, but rather cut off their heads. This they would do to Indians chained up alone. Those chained together were stabbed with a rapier all at once. They then cut the noses, ears, arms and legs from the bodies and left them lying on the ground in pieces. The Spaniards treated the poor Indians with such mercilessness and cruelty until they arrived in Guamanga.

PLATE 21

Gonsalvo Pizarro is defeated, captured and sentenced to death

After the president had seen his armies across the Apurimac River with great difficulty, he began to plan in earnest an attack on Pizarro. Pizarro left Cusco and crossed him on his way, quickly attacking his camp. The next day the trumpets were sounded and the majority of Pizarro's troops fell on the battlefield, especially those led by the auditor Capada. These losses wounded Pizarro deeply and made his remaining troops lose heart. Then a massive cannon assault caused a large part of Pizarro's army to abandon their weapons and flee to the other side. At this point, Pizarro's army was completely lost. Pizarro stood unarmed and stuck in this situation along with certain captains who had neither effective weapons nor wanted to flee. Pizarro saw Villavicencio running by and asked him who he was, whereupon he answered he was the lieutenant-colonel of the imperial army. Pizarro replied, "And I am the unhappy Gonsalvo Pizarro." At this, Villavicencio drew his sword and gleefully led his captive to President Hinojosa. Hinojosa then had him delivered to Jacopo Centeno to be watched over by him. The next day, the licentiate Cianca and quartermaster Alvarado were ordered to question the prisoners and to determine sentences for them. Pizarro was beheaded. His head was brought to Lima and set on a marble column. Above it was written: "This is the head of the traitor and reviled fiend Gonsalvo Pizarro, who tried to raise an army against his imperial majesty in the Xaquixaguana Valley." President Hinojosa moved to Cusco after Pizarro's execution. There he destroyed the houses of the Pizarros and other reviled fiends. He likewise had a stone column erected with this inscription: "This is where the house of Gonsalvo Pizarro once stood."

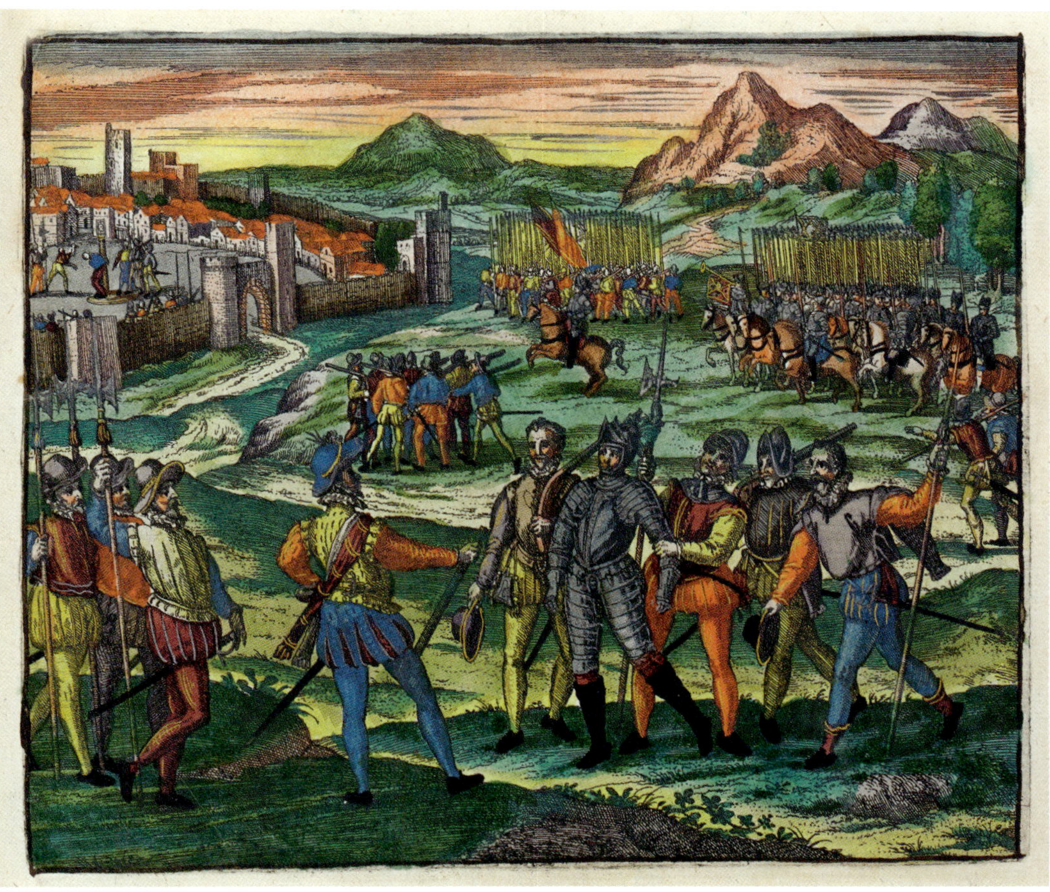

PLATE 22

The soldiers incarcerated by Ferdinand and Pedro de Contreras are stabbed to death in Panama by order of the governor

Now that there was once again peace in Peru, the president prepared to return to Spain. On the way, he travelled towards Panama. He sent his traveller's tax ahead of him to the town called Nomen-Dei, followed quickly on, and left behind him silver worth as much as 600,000 crowns that he could not carry with him. Meanwhile, the majority of his army rode together, after they had been passed over in the distribution of the booty, and joined the brothers Ferdinand and Pedro de Contreras, the sons of Roderigo Contreras, who were angry because their father had lost his position. They had received word that the president was travelling with the emperor's money. When they realised he had gone to Nomen-Dei, however, they fell violently upon the quarters of the royal sheriff Martin Ruiz. They took all the money that was there, along with gold and other goods they found in the town, and had it put in their ships. They then decided to head to Nomen-Dei and attack the president before he could learn about what they had done in Panama. When Martin Ruiz and Juan de Laiez saw that the brothers had split up, they called for the citizens to arm themselves and led them to meet Juan de Bermeo, and brought along two people and sent them on two separate ways to inform the president and the citizens of Nomen-Dei of what had happened in Panama and to warn them about Ferdinand. They stormed Bermeo's camp, capturing many of his people, and he fled. Martin Ruiz was now on Ferdinand's trail and hoped to catch him before he reached Nomen-Dei. When Pedro learned of his brother's and of Bermeo's predicament, he got in a rowing-boat and abandoned the ship with the booty. Upon interrogation, those who had been captured informed the interrogators about a tower the brothers used. They were stabbed to death there by the Spanish police.

PLATE 23, PAGES 370/371

The Spaniards fight with the Indians who live in trees

The Indians of the Southern regions who live next to standing water build their dwellings in trees. The ground there is wet and musty. Because of this, the Spaniards have not yet been able to subjugate them, since they cannot be approached with horses. Balboa was the first to have come to this Southern sea and seen these tree-houses, which surely appeared quite foolish to him and his men. It was so strange to them, that they could think of no other explanation than that these were the nests of some kind of stork or magpie. The trees were so tall that a stone could hardly be thrown over them. In places their leaves were so dense that it would take eight people working at it to clear them. There are similar houses found in other damp areas of the country. The people who live there are bellicose and rich in silver and gold. They have always defended their territories against the Spanish, and have triumphed most times. Pedro Cieza de León also remarks upon these houses in the first part of his *Peruvian Chronicle*, chapters 12, 26 and 29. He writes that their interiors are so spacious that they can house multiple families.

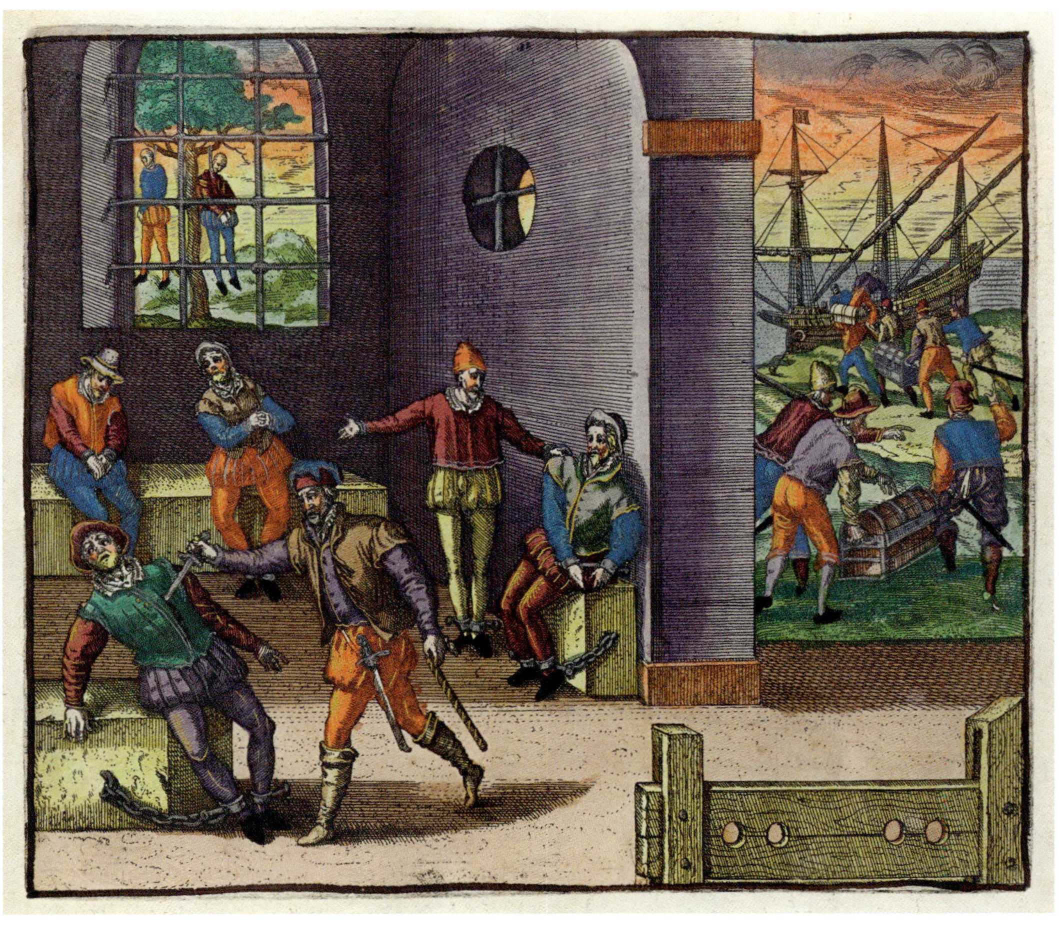

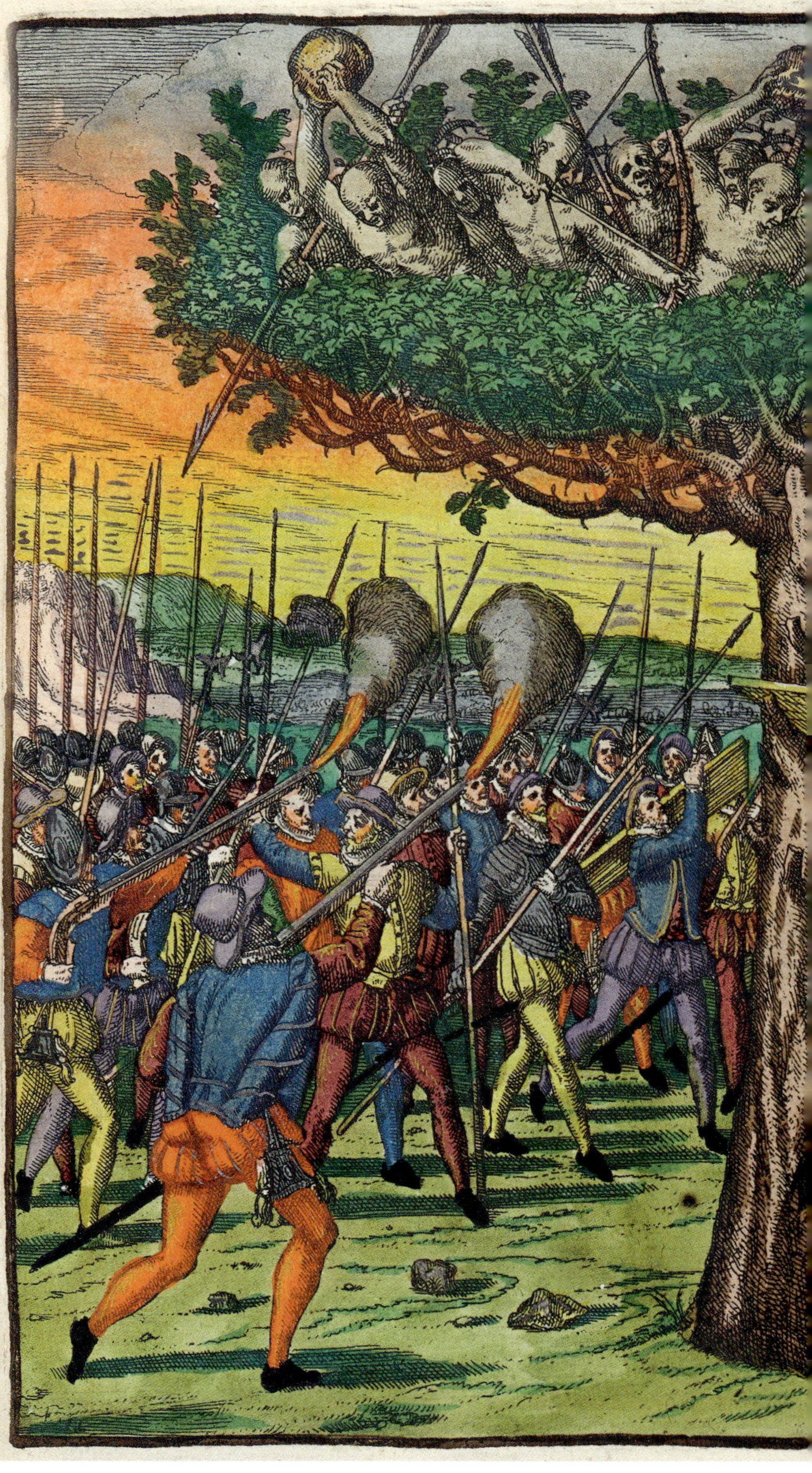

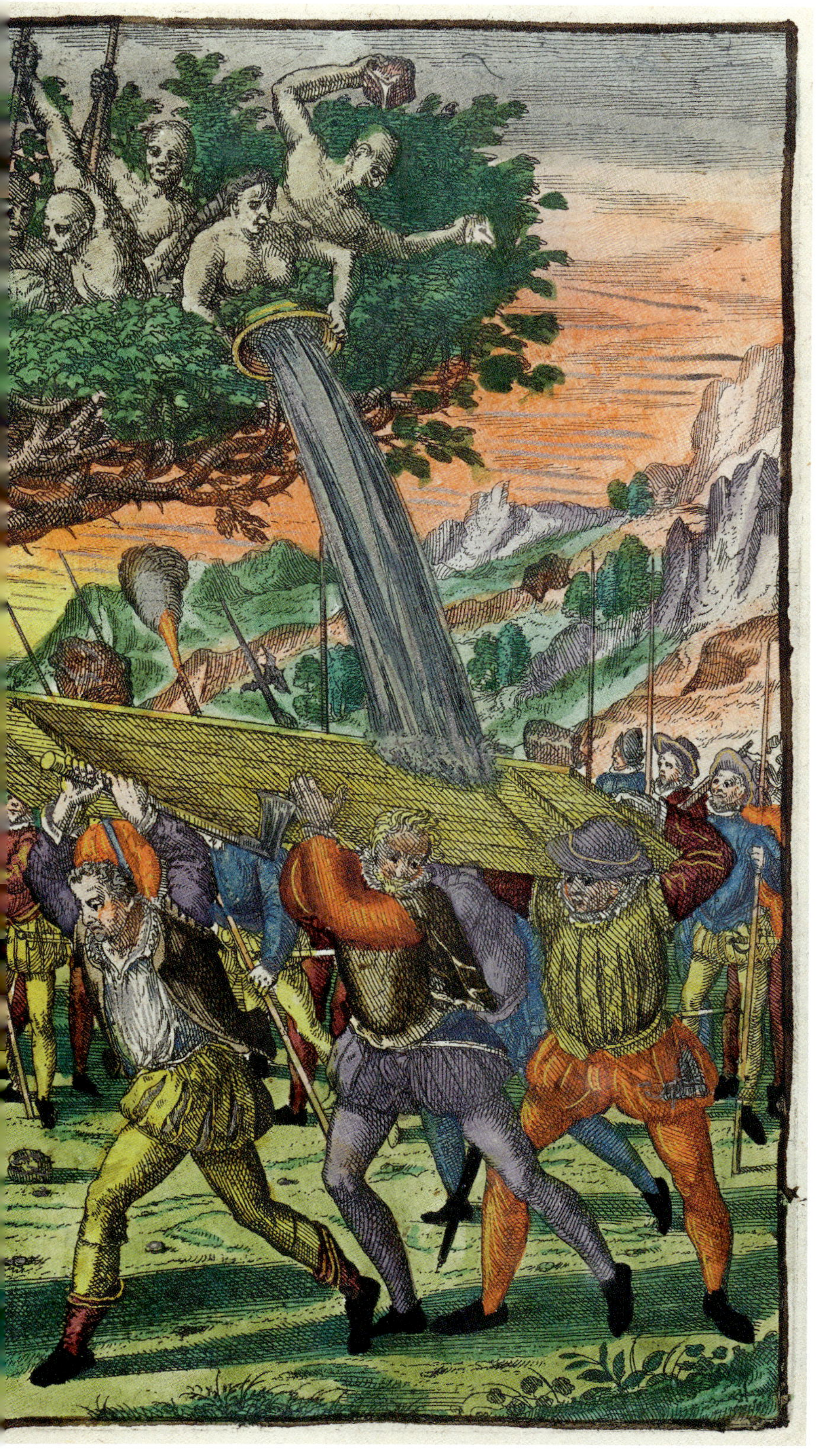

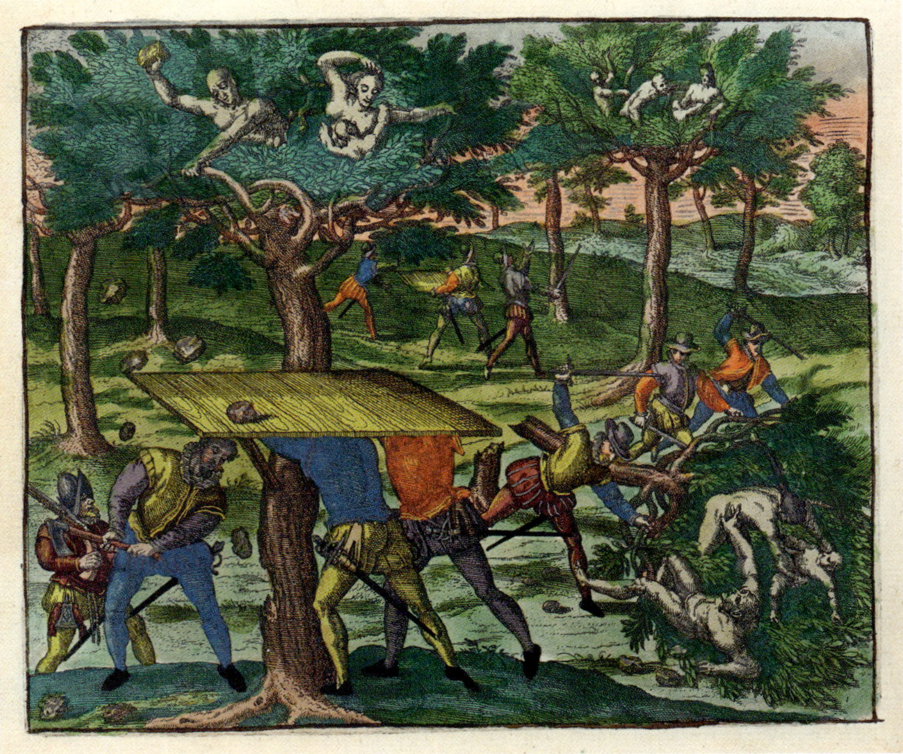

PLATE 24

The Spaniards cut down the trees where the Indians live

Benzoni writes that the Spanish captain Caspar de Andagoya, who was in charge of Matthew's Bay, passed through this area with 100 soldiers one summer. His men carried long wooden planks and boards to defend themselves against the stones and arrows of the Indians. When the Indians learned of the Spaniards' arrival, they armed themselves with stones, spears and boiling water to rain down upon their enemy. The Spaniards, however, were kept safe beneath their protective planks. They sawed at the trees until they fell down along with the Indians and their houses. The Indians went about pathetically afterwards until they were dead. The Indians avenged themselves against the Spaniards, however. Indeed, several Spaniards were killed by the falling trees, or wounded very badly, which was very fortunate for the Indians. The area was undeveloped and harsh, and could only support a small number of people living there, so finally Andagoya left, bringing along the great amount of gold he had managed to scrape together there.

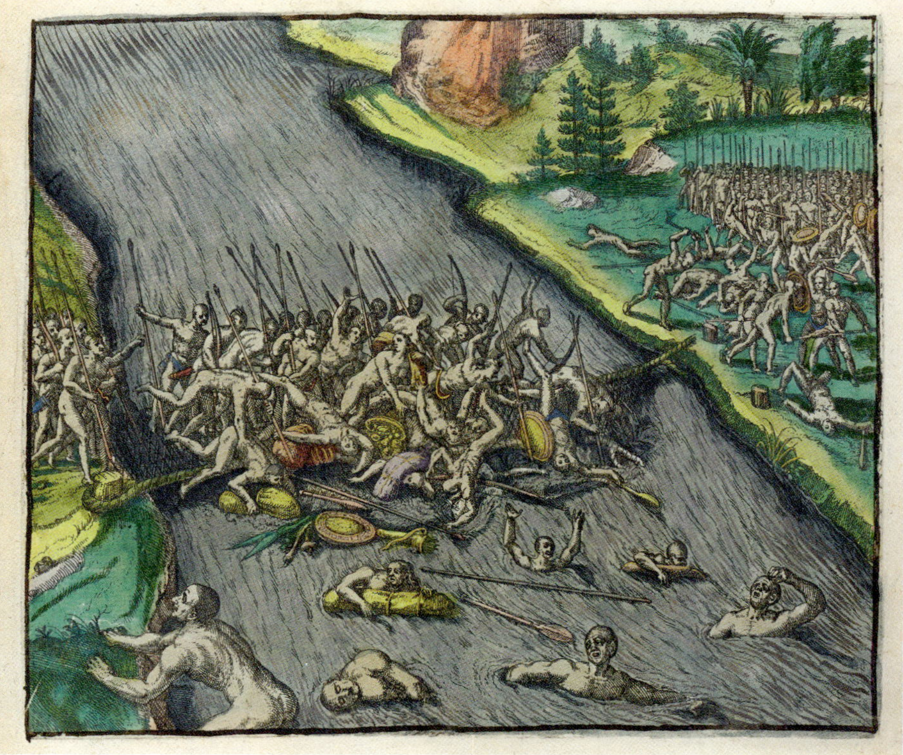

PLATE 25

How the Indians made a bridge of rope, and concerning the Huayna Capac Pass

There is a rope bridge that crosses the Chiovo river. It is secured from a hill, which is called the Huayna Capac Pass. The name derives from that of the king Huayna Capac who once sent an army to claim the area. When they came to the river, the people there were ordered to build a bridge across it so that the army could cross. They built a bridge as the people do in that area, namely they stretched strong ropes on either side of the river and pulled them taut. These were then crossed transversely with other ropes. When it was announced that the bridge was finished, the army proceeded to cross the river on it. As soon as they were on the bridge, however, the fiends who had constructed it cut the ropes at both ends. All the soldiers who were on it – some just beginning to cross, some nearly at the other side – plunged into the river, and with that nearly the entire army was gone. When King Huayna Capac learned of this, he left Quito with a much larger army than the one he had sent the first time and destroyed with fire and sword everything that crossed his path throughout the whole land. In order that people could more comfortably cross over the river, however, he had a stone bridge built. This ended up being a futile task, for the current of the river was much too strong. Francisco López de Gómara mentions such a bridge as well in chapters 90 and 105 of his *General History of the Indians*. Pedro Cieza de León does so too in chapters 10 and 85 of his *Peruvian Chronicle*.

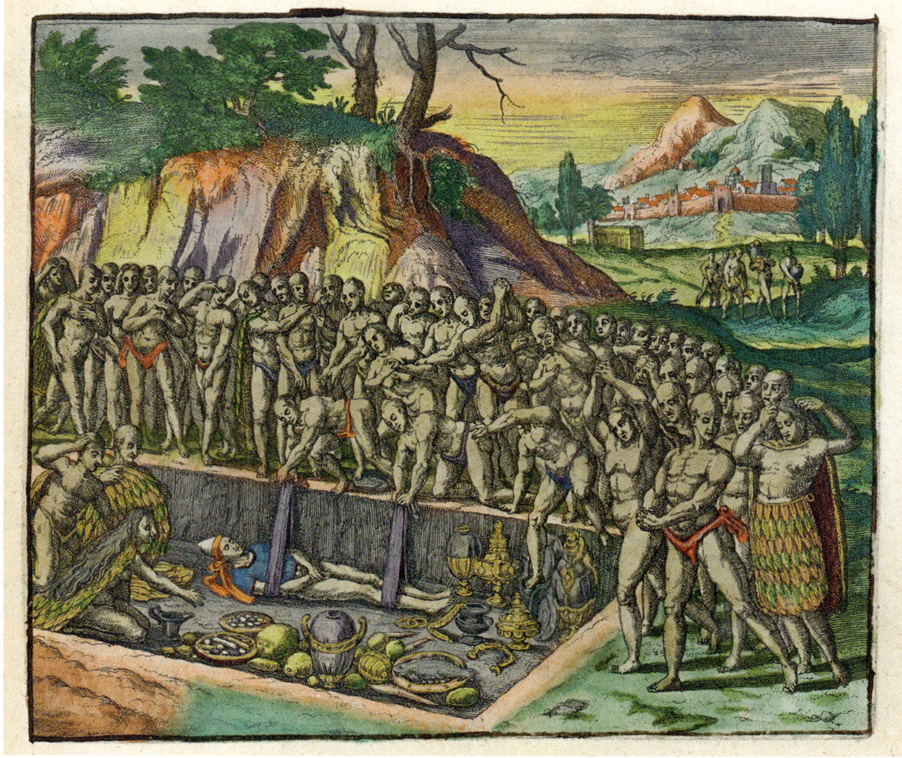

PLATE 26

Of the care with which kings and royal servants are buried in the West Indies

They tend to their dead kings with special solemnity and bury them with magnificent honours. First, they dig a large grave into which they lower the dead king. Then they place inside it gold and silver vessels, along with other precious objects the king had prepared for his burial. Finally, his wives are placed inside, either the most beautiful or the ones he loved the best, as well as some of his most loyal servants. His favourite clothes and food are included with his wives and servants so they may have something to eat along the way in death and so that they all may share in the enjoyment of the same things with their king. It is clear from this that they believe in the immortality of the soul. They are, however, blinded by the Devil in so far as they believe they will experience good things in this other place in the same way as they did in life. The Devil appears to them from time to time (according to God's design) in the form of a dead king in order to tell them about how he now lives in a kingdom of great pleasures where he receives all that he desires. Such visitations are the reason why the poor, blind Indians put far more effort into their burials than into any other thing. Now, most of the kings in Peru have been shown other methods of burial. When the Spaniards first arrived, they found many treasures in the royal sepulchres, but most of these have remained buried.

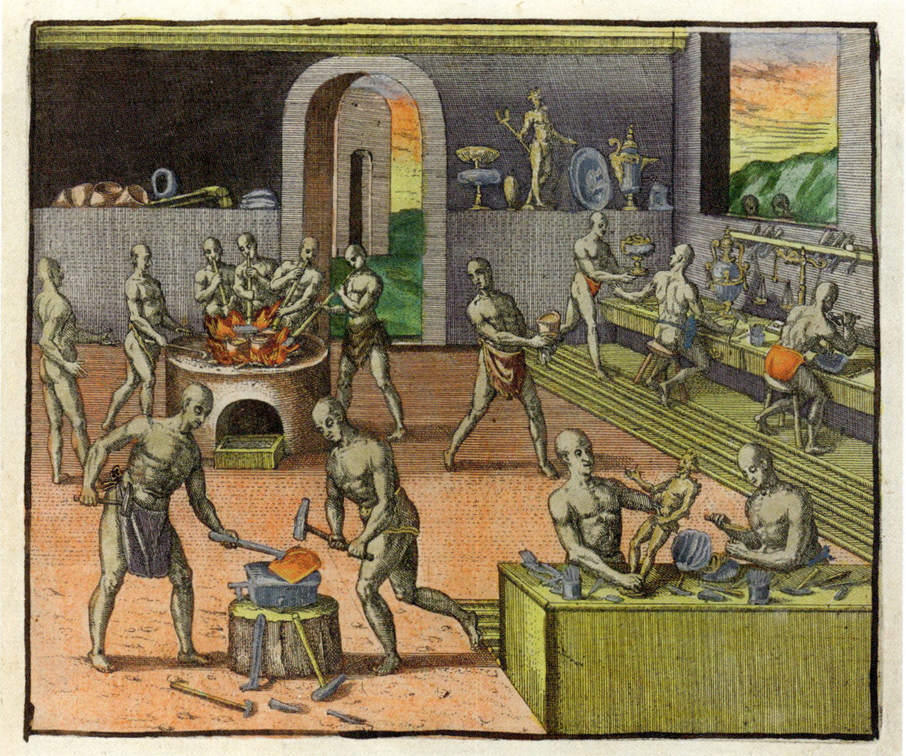

PLATE 27

The ingenious goldsmiths that are found in Peru

Based on what they have told us, the Peruvians did not live in nearly as much splendour nor were they as accomplished in the arts before the reign of the Incas. Under the grand prince, however, they began to pursue the arts, as he was very interested in ornamentation for his house, monuments, columns and decorated vessels. Smithies were established across the kingdom, which produced vessels and jewellery out of silver and gold. Indeed, the objects they produced were so masterfully made that all who saw them were in awe. Pedro Cieza de León is reticent about writing of them in the *Peruvian Chronicles* because he had not seen them for himself. What he does say, however, is that the vessels, fountains, candelabras etc., which the Indians could produce with just two pieces of ore and three black stones, rivalled the products of our best goldsmiths. All they needed for smelting was a clay oven, into which a few men shovel coal. It has been written that King Huayna Capac kept golden sculptures as big as giants in his treasure vaults, which were completely hollow. Every golden animal, as well as every fish, was done after a kind that could be found in that kingdom or on the waters that it bordered. We also read of the Incas' pleasure garden, where the grand princes desired to hold a banquet and enjoy themselves. They had various plants, trees and flowers made out of gold for the occasion. It is certain that the goldsmiths made these things just as they would have made columns, statues, vessels, jewellery and clothes, all out of a sense of worship and desire to decorate their temple.

PLATE 28

There is no other fresh water on the Island of Ferri, part of the Canary Islands, other than that produced by one tree, which it secretes daily

Ferri Island is one of the Canary Islands, which are also known as the Fortunata Islands. On this island there is a natural marvel; a single tree that every day secretes enough fresh water to satisfy the needs of all the people as well as the animals there. There are no other rivers, ponds or springs on the island, and no springs or cisterns to yield drinkable water. This tree bears nuts and dense foliage and is quite tall. It is surrounded by a wall which functions like a kind of trough to collect the water. Every day, the whole tree is enshrouded in mist two hours before sunrise. During this time, it sweats and drips the water for which it has become famous into the trough below. When the Spanish first arrived, they asked the residents of the island where they could find drinkable water, at which they were told to try collecting rainwater in vessels left outside. They had covered the pipes and trough and kept their natural wonder a secret though, in the hope that this would force the Spanish to leave the island. A woman, however, who kept company with one of the Spaniards, informed him of their device and explained how it worked. When the Indian leaders learned that the woman had betrayed their secret to the Spanish, however, they had her secretly killed. Some believe that this tree is the one referred to by Pliny in the 32nd chapter of his *Natural History*. Others believe it is another tree, also discussed by Pliny, which is like the ferula flower. This flower also excretes water, which in its case is somewhat black and bitter. Part of it is also white, however, and this makes for good, fresh drinking water.

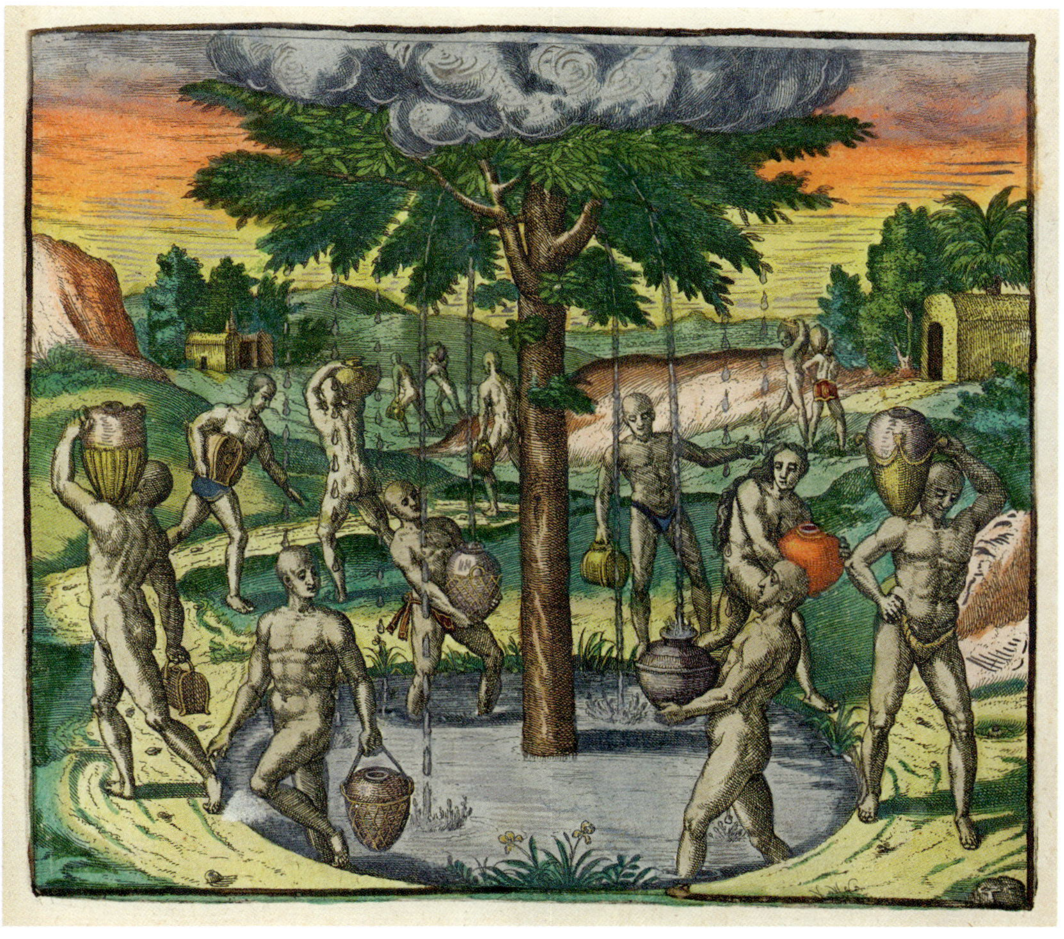

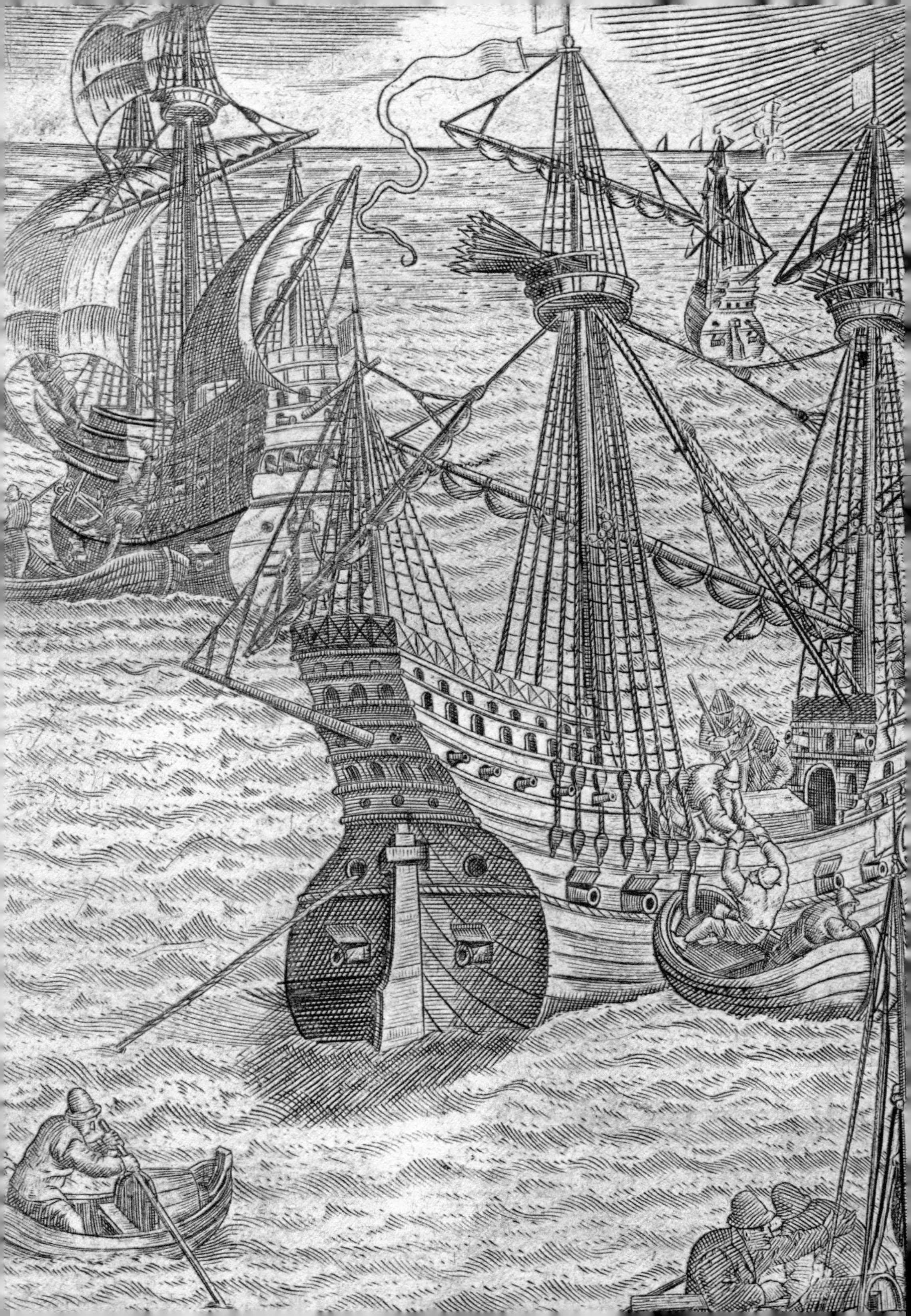

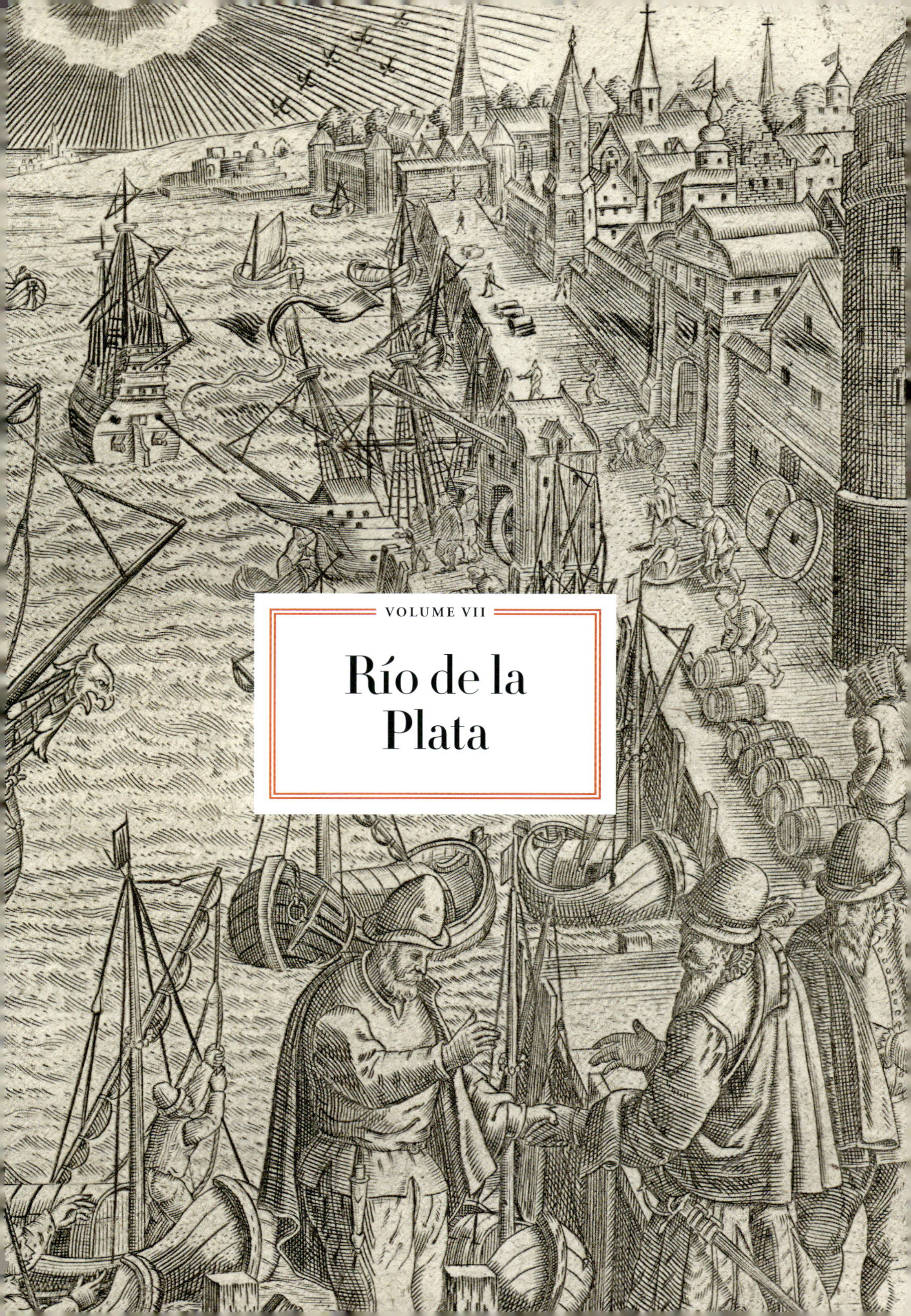

VOLUME VII

Río de la Plata

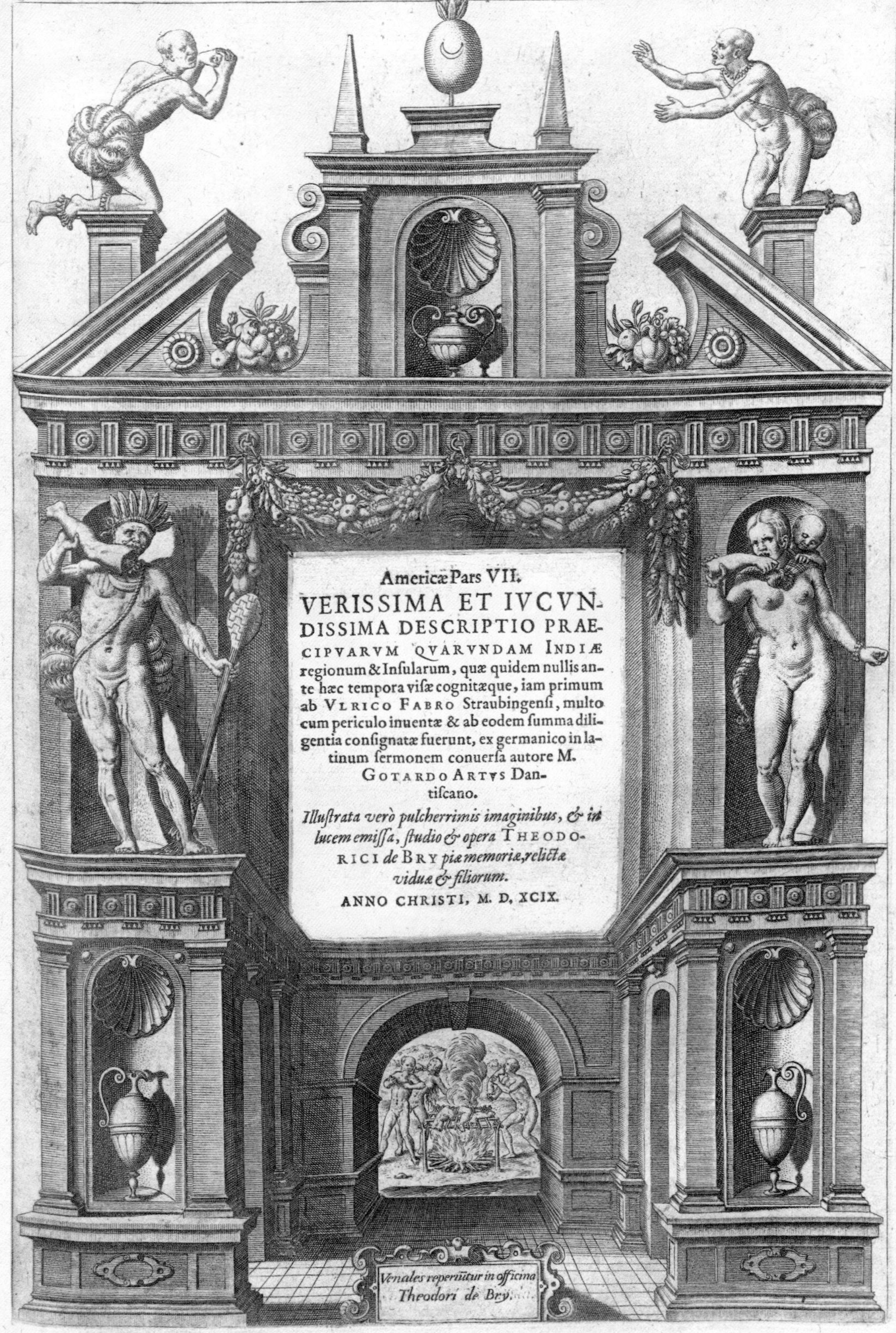
Americæ Pars VII.
VERISSIMA ET IVCVN-
DISSIMA DESCRIPTIO PRAE-
CIPVARVM QVARVNDAM INDIÆ
regionum & Insularum, quæ quidem nullis an-
te hæc tempora visæ cognitæque, iam primum
ab VLRICO FABRO Straubingensi, multo
cum periculo inuentæ & ab eodem summa dili-
gentia consignatæ fuerunt, ex germanico in la-
tinum sermonem conuersa autore M.
GOTARDO ARTVS Dan-
tiscano.
Illustrata verò pulcherrimis imaginibus, & in
lucem emissa, studio & opera THEODO-
RICI de BRY piæ memoriæ, relictæ
viduæ & filiorum.
ANNO CHRISTI, M. D. XCIX.
Venales reperiũtur in officina
Theodori de Bry.

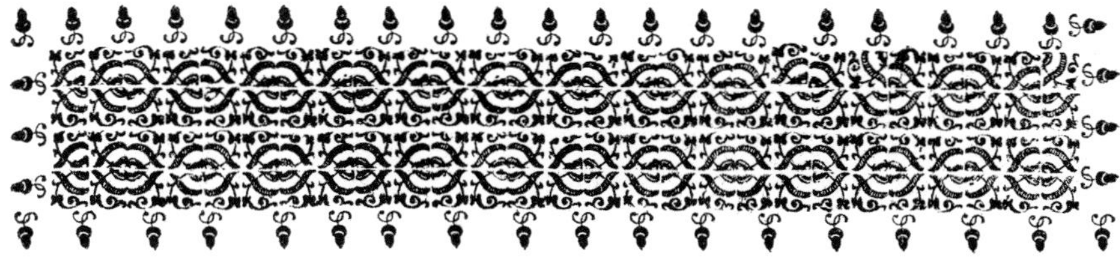

Volume VII

Based on: Ulrich Schmidel, *Wahre Geschichte einer merckwürdigen Reise* (Frankfurt, 1557)

Just like Hans Staden, one of the two main sources for volume III of the *America* series, Ulrich Schmidel travelled to South America as a soldier in the service of an Iberian ruler, in this case the Spanish king. Schmidel embarked on his journey some 15 years before Staden did, leaving behind his native Bavaria in 1534. At first he joined the ranks of Pedro de Mendoza, who led an expedition to Río de la Plata (present-day Buenos Aires). He remained in South America for more than 19 years, accompanying Spanish troops on their exploration of the continent along the inland waterways towards Paraguay and Peru. After returning to his hometown of Straubing in 1554, he wrote a narrative based on the diary notes he had kept for many years, but although he had served in the company of various Spanish noblemen, his perspective was quite different from that found in Spanish accounts of the same expeditions. One of the most striking stories Schmidel told (and which Spanish observers did not) was that the Spanish and Portuguese resorted to eating their own comrades because they were starving in the harsh landscape of the vast and unknown South American interior.

It is remarkable that the De Brys did not select these episodes for their engravings. Part of the reason for this may be to do with the chaotic process of making volume VII, if we can assume that from the fact that it included only a single illustration (the previous six volumes had included 28, 42, 30, 24, 22 and 28 copper engravings respectively). In 1599, just before the German edition of volume VII appeared, the same account was published in German in Nuremberg by Levinus Hulsius, who from 1598 had also been issuing a collection of voyages. For his version, moreover, Hulsius used a more detailed original text than the version the De Brys had. In the long term, however, this proved to be the exception to the rule, and usually Hulsius selected travel accounts

Frontispiece of volume VII

Pages 378/379
Detail of volume VII, plate 1

which had already been published by the De Brys, thus sparing him extensive translation costs while at the same time providing a cheaper version of the De Bry edition for a less affluent German readership. After 1606, the De Brys incorporated the Hulsius collection of voyages into their own editorial strategy, as discussed at greater length in the introduction. The one-time reversal of roles may help to explain why the De Brys rushed their version to press, which in turn might explain the inclusion of only a single copper engraving. Three more illustrations to Schmidel's voyage were later added to *America* VIII – yet still on other topics than Spanish cannibalism.

For the Latin edition of volume VII, the translation from German was made by the Lutheran school-teacher Gotthard Artus von Dantzig – his first contribution to the collection of voyages. In the beginning, Artus was something of a controversial figure who had published the semi-annual periodical *Mercurius Gallobelgicus*, which was banned by various European ruling bodies for spreading sensitive (political) information, but over the years he became one of the De Brys' most reliable employees. Apart from working for the De Bry workshop as a translator, Artus also served as the censor of newly printed books on behalf of the (Lutheran) magistrates in the Imperial Free City of Frankfurt. On multiple occasions over the next 20 years, Artus would first translate a travel account for the De Bry collection, and subsequently approve his own translation in his capacity as local censor – a very convenient convergence of responsibilities. Artus continued to work for the De Brys as a translator at least until 1620, and during this period the De Brys never again clashed with the authorities over the projected publication of a book as they had done at least once before 1597.

PLATE 1

An accurate description of some Indian countries and islands, which were first explored at great risk and described by Ulrich Schmidel von Straubingen

We left Spain and came to three islands that are very close to each other. The first is called Tenerife, the second is La Gomera and the third is La Palma. The islands belong to the emperor and many Spaniards live there with their women and children. We also docked at La Palma for four weeks and restocked our provisions there. After our commander Pedro Manchossa travelled eight or nine miles away, however, his cousin Jorge Manchossa fell in love with the daughter of a local. Since we were planning to leave soon, Jorge Manchossa went ashore one night at midnight with 12 loyal companions and gathered the woman along with her attendant and all of her possessions to bring back to our ship. When we tried to leave the next morning, however, a storm wind forced us to turn around in the harbour and stay longer. Once we had dropped anchor, Captain Heinrich Paine wanted to go ashore in a little ship called a *pat* or *podell.* When he reached the shore, however, he was met by 30 armed men who had the intention of taking him captive. He was warned by his own crew to turn the boat around. He could not heed this advice though, because he was already on land, and the men were too close for him to board his own boat again. So he boarded another boat that was nearby. When the armed men saw that he was getting away, they stormed La Palma and loaded their cannons. They fired four shots at Paine's little ship, since it was still close to shore. The first shot landed just behind the ship in the harbour, where four barrels of fresh water were being stored. These splintered everywhere. The third shot put a big hole in the middle of the ship and a man was killed by it. There was another captain nearby, who helped us to make a truce with the people from the town. The condition was that Jorge Manchossa, the local's daughter and her attendant all be handed over.

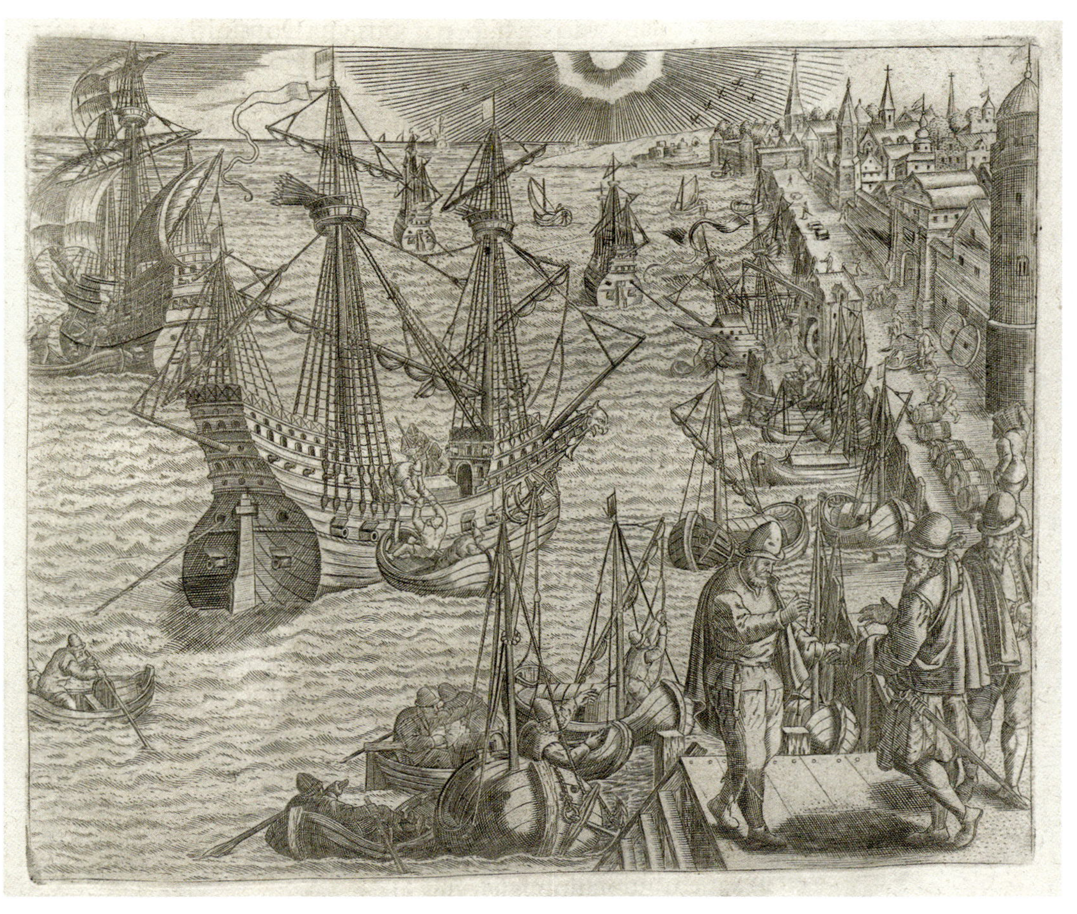

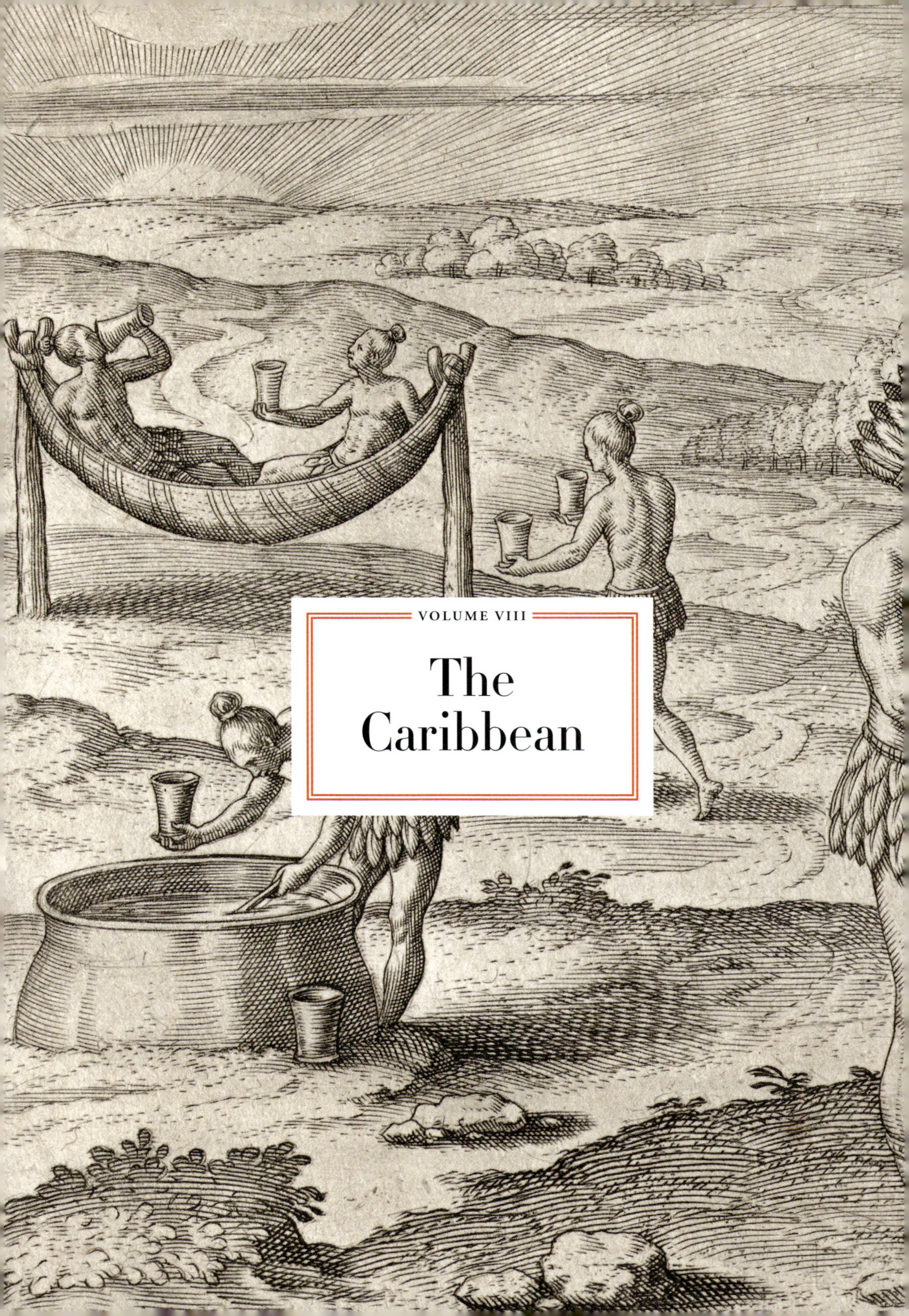

VOLUME VIII

The Caribbean

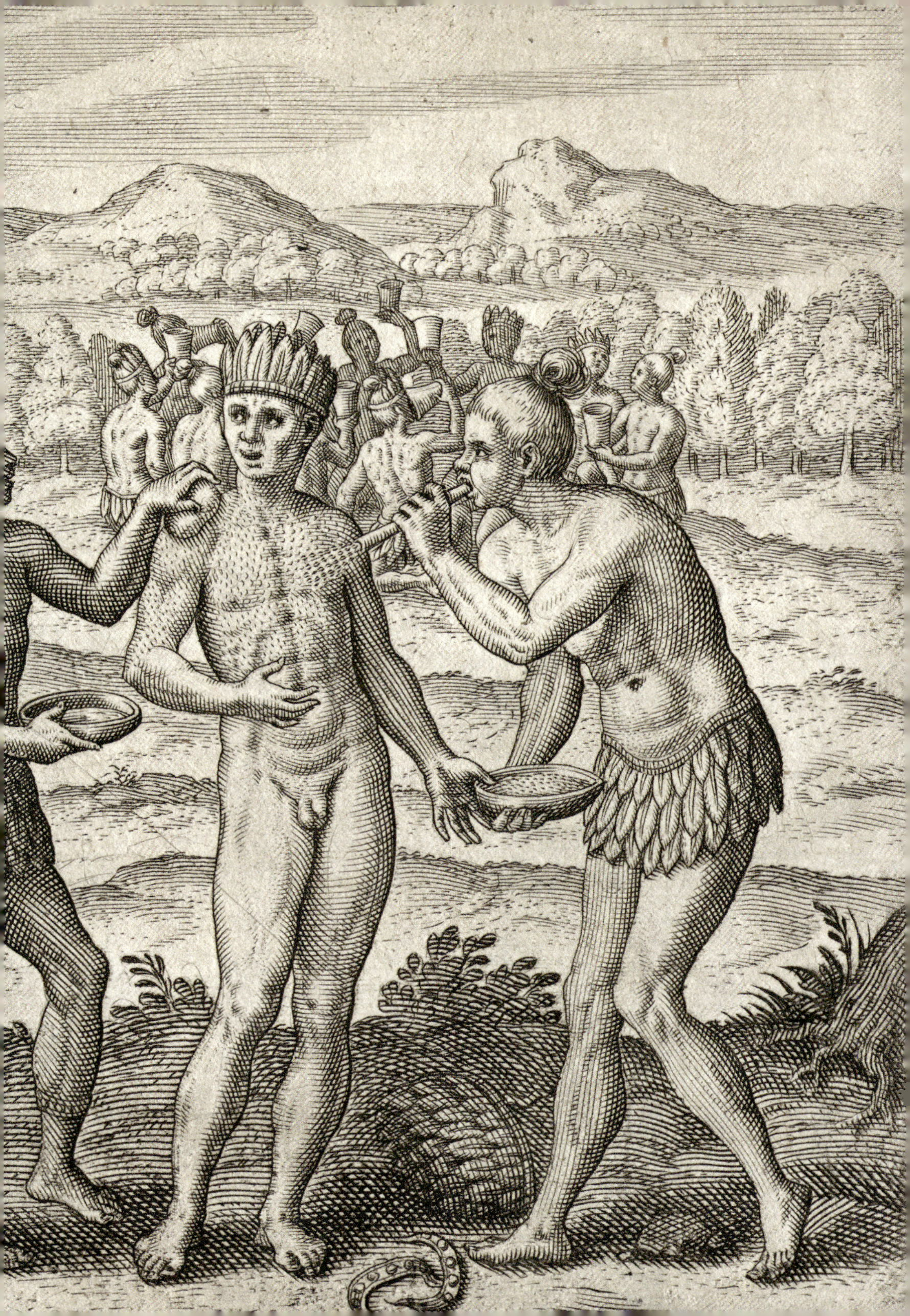

AMERICÆ PARS VIII.

Continens

PRIMO, DESCRIPTIONEM TRIVM ITINERVM NOBILISSIMI ET FORTISSIMI EQVITIS FRANCISCI DRAKEN, QVI PERAGRATO PRIMVM VNIVERSO TERRARVM ORBE; postea cum nobilissimo Equite IOHANNE HAVCKENS, ad expugnandum ciuitatem PANAMA, in Indiam nauigauit, vbi vitam suam ambo finierunt.

SECVNDO, *iter nobilissimi Equitis* THOMÆ CANDISCH, *qui duorum ferè annorum spacio, 13000. Anglicana miliaria in mari confecit, vbi describuntur quoque omnia quæ in hoc itinere ipsi acciderunt & visa sunt.*

TERTIO, *duo itinera, nobilissimi & fortissimi Domini* GVALTHERI RALEGH *Equitis & designati gubernatoris Regij in Anglia præsidij, nec non fortissimi Capitanei* LAVRENTII KEYMS.

QVIBVS ITINERIBVS DESCRIBITVR AVRIFERVM ET POTENTISSIMVM Regnum GVIAÑA, ad Septentrionem fluminis ORENOQVE, aliàs ORELIANA dicti, situm, cum metropoli eius MANOA & MACVIEGVARAI, aliisq; finitimis regionibus & fluuiis, mercibus item præstantissimis, & mercatura, quæ in regno hoc exercetur.

PRIMO QVIDEM ANGLICANA LINGVA PARTIM AB EQVITIBVS IPSIS, PARTIM ab aliis, qui hisce itineribus interfuerunt, sparsim consignata: Iam verò in vnum Corpus redacta, & in Latinum Sermonem conuersa, auctore

M. GOTARDO ARTVS DANTISCANO.

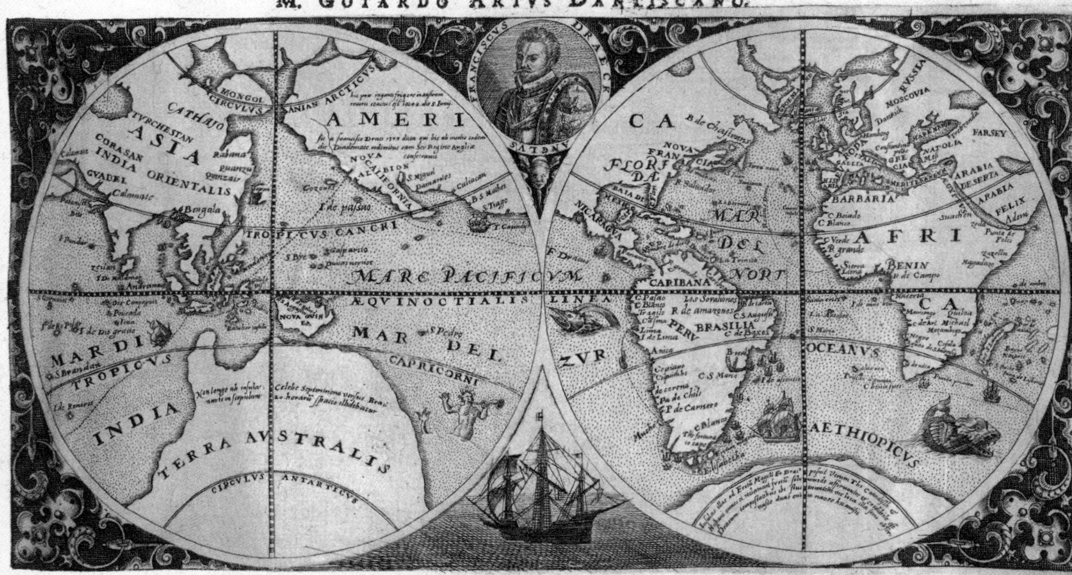

Figuris & imaginibus artificiosè illustrata & in lucem emissa, opera & sumptibus THEODORICI de BRY P. M. relictæ Viduæ & filiorum.

ANNO M. D. XCIX.

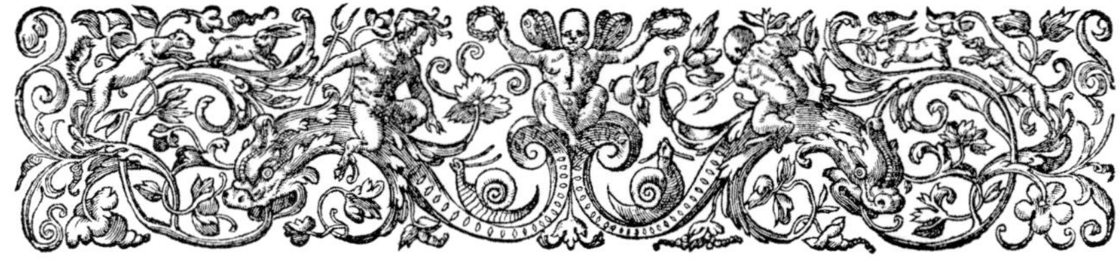

Volume VIII

Based on as many as six English travel accounts, written by authors including Walter Bigges, Thomas Cates, Walter Raleigh, Lawrence Keymis and Francis Pretty, dealing with English adventures in the Caribbean, and with Francis Drake's and Thomas Cavendish's circumnavigations

In volume VIII, the De Brys returned to the American adventures of Elizabethan England which had been the subject of volume I. The pirate raids of Francis Drake and Thomas Cavendish against Spanish interests in the Caribbean in the 1570s and 1580s arguably had more appeal for European readers than the attempts to colonise North Carolina, so it was not surprising that the De Bry brothers collected these accounts. Drake's attack on Cartagena de Indias, one of the major strongholds of Spanish America on the Colombian coast, his subsequent circumnavigation of the globe and his exploration of the area he christened Nova Albion (present-day California) represented the highlights of these expeditions, and the De Brys selected precisely these episodes as the subject matter for their illustrations. The third expedition which received disproportionate attention in Frankfurt was the search for El Dorado, led by Sir Walter Raleigh himself. The De Brys did not represent mountains of gold as they had done in depicting Spanish America in volume IV (in any case, Raleigh did not find any), but they did invent several engravings which showed Raleigh's encounter with the native population of the Amazon region and the Wild Coast (present-day Guyana, Brazil, French Guiana, Suriname and Venezuela).

The choice for at least some of the accounts the De Brys selected for this volume was conditioned by the increasing dominance in the European book market of publishers from Holland, most notably from Amsterdam. Cornelis Claesz was one such, who published a considerable number of best-selling books on voyages overseas, some of which formed the basis for the De Brys' *India Orientalis* series, which had begun in 1597 and relied heavily on Dutch tales of adventure. In previous years Claesz had also translated (into Dutch) the accounts of Raleigh, Keymis, Pretty and Drake, and the De Brys eagerly included these published reports in their own collection,

Title-page of volume VIII

Pages 384/385
Detail of volume VIII, plate 15

translated by Gotthard Artus von Dantzig (Latin) and August Cassiodorus Reyna (German). Volume VIII, as the sequence of illustrations shows, also included several images taken from Ulrich Schmidel's account but which had apparently somehow not been ready when volume VII appeared. Perhaps the sudden accumulation of volumes, not just for the *America* series but also for the *India Orientalis* series, was a little too much for Johan Theodore and Johan Israel to manage. The collection's volumes always appeared right on time for the Frankfurt book fair, held twice a year (Lent and September), where many international booksellers gathered to purchase the newest titles. Given their collection's pan-European readership, publishing the books on time was probably crucial for the De Bry firm, and perhaps in the late 1590s the pressure proved too much. The problem was not entirely solved by the time volume VIII appeared, because for the German edition an 'Additamentum' was published the following year, which included a further three illustrations that were never included in the Latin edition.

Of the illustrations the De Brys made for volume VIII, the encounters between Drake and the inhabitants of Nova Albion have acquired canonical status. Once again, pagan native rituals are on display, as in so many other volumes in the De Bry collections, but it is the encounter between Drake and the Californians which really catches the eye. The engraving of Drake stepping ashore on the American west coast, and planting the royal standard with the portrait of Elizabeth I, can be favourably compared to the image the De Brys created several years earlier of Columbus's arrival in Hispaniola. However, whereas Columbus was received by Native Americans bringing him their gold objects, a foreshadowing of the Spanish avarice which according to so many other Europeans characterised their conduct in the New World, Drake's arrival in Nova Albion gave rise to celebrations among the local population. A key illustration is the one showing the leader of the Native Americans performing a coronation ceremony along European lines (and therefore very recognisable to readers throughout the Old World), thus emphasising the hierarchical yet amicable relationship between the English visitors and the Native Americans. In the wake of the three Benzoni volumes, which represented the establishment of Spanish control in the Americas as an extremely violent process, the reception Drake received boded well for Elizabethan England. His territorial claim on American soil, made in 1579, also preceded the claims on Virginia that had been represented in the first volume of the *America* series. Speculation persists about the exact location where Drake made landfall, since the description of the bay where his ship *Golden Hind* anchored is too vague to identify precisely. Possible sites that have been suggested include an inlet just north of San Francisco Bay – the location officially recognised by the US government as a National Historical Landmark – but also as far north as Whale Cove (Oregon) and even Vancouver Island in British Columbia, Canada.

Detail of volume VIII, plate 10

Pages 390/391
Coastal map of Guyana and the Amazon River

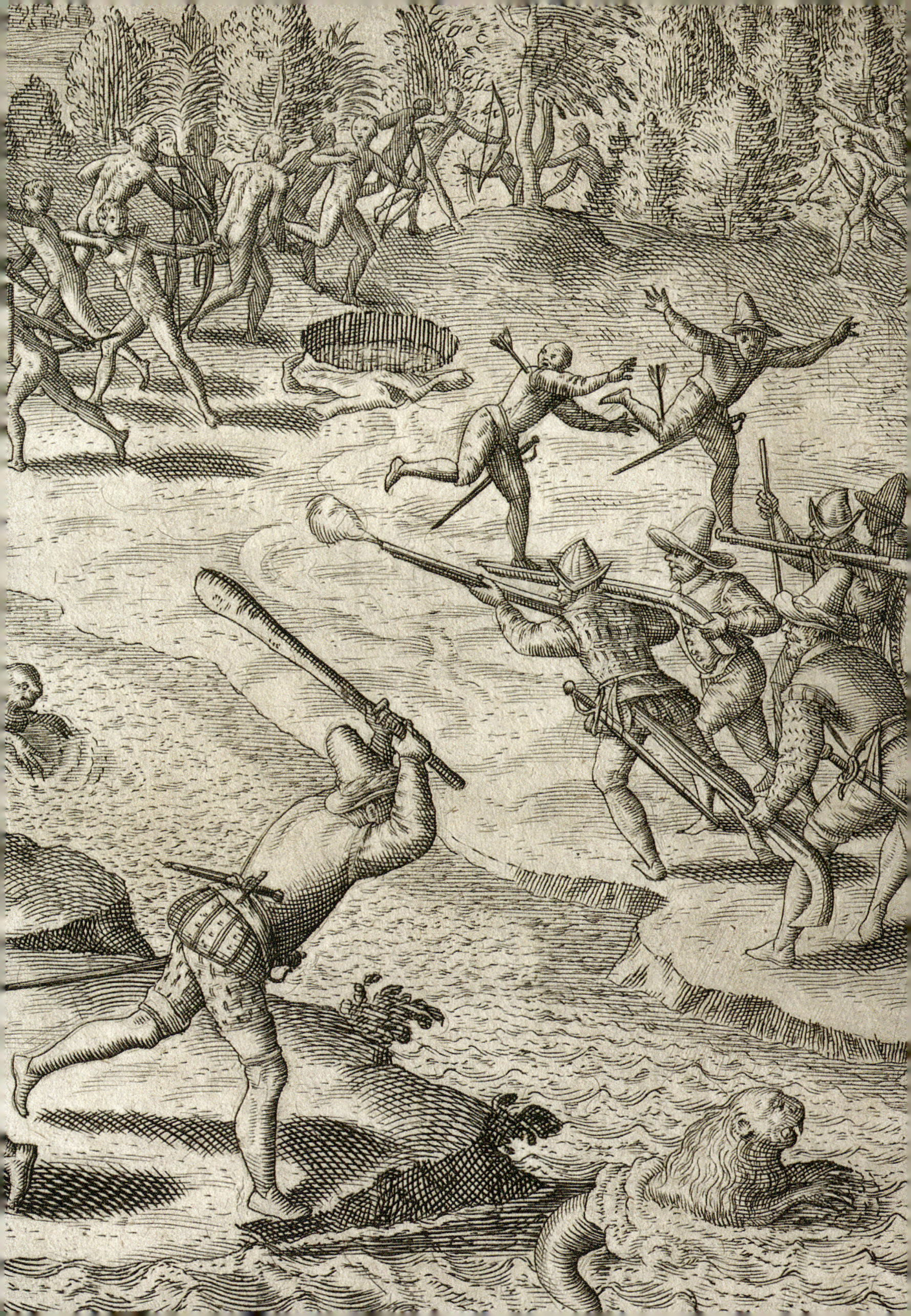

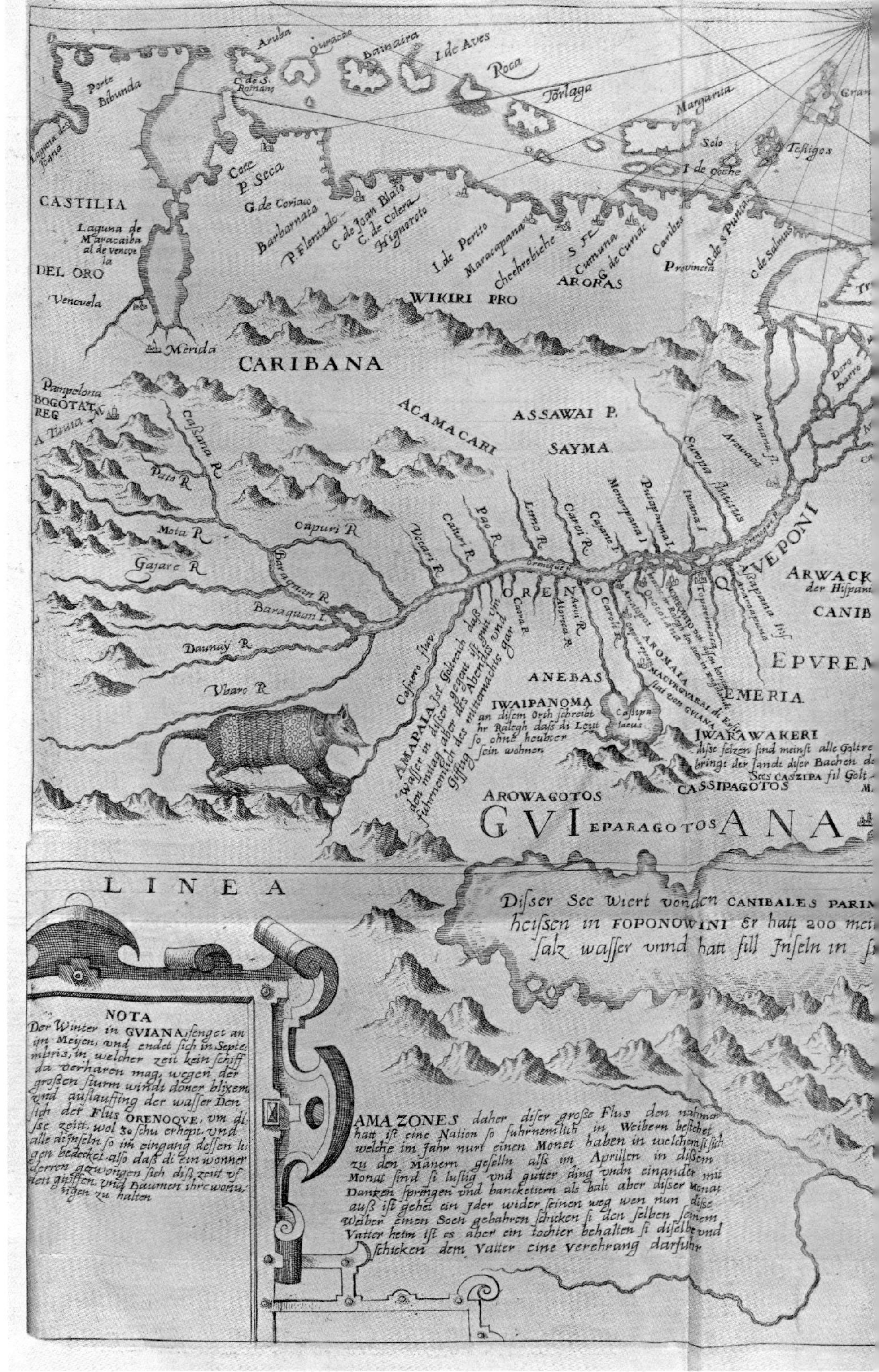
Aruba
Quracao
Bainaira
I. de Aves
Roca
Torlaga
Margarita
Solo
Testigos
I. de Coche
Porte Bibunda
Laguna de S. Joana
C. de S. Roman
Cote
P. Seca
G. de Coriaco
CASTILIA
Laguna de Maracaiba al de Venevela
DEL ORO
Venevela
Barbarnata
P. Flentado
C. de Joan Blaco
C. de Colera
Hignoroto
I. de Pertto
Maracapana
Cheehrebiche
S. Fe
Cumuna
G. de Curiat
AROFAS
Caribes
Provincia
C. de S. Punto
C. de Salmas
WIKIRI PRO
Merida
CARIBANA
Pampolona
BOGOTAT REG
A. Tiuisa
Cassana R.
ACAMACARI
ASSAWAI P.
SAYMA
Pato R.
Mota R.
Gajare R.
Capuri R.
Baraguan R.
Baraguan I.
Daunay R.
Vbaro R.
Vocari R.
Caturi R.
Pao R.
Limo R.
Carvi R.
Cajani I.
Menoripana I.
Putapumal I.
Iwana I.
Europa fluvius
Arowaca
Amana fl.
AVEPONI
O R E N O Q V E
Orenoque R.
Cassanar R.
Arui R.
Atoreca R.
Caroli R.
Assapana flu.
ARWACK der Hispanier
CANIB
EPVREM
EMERIA
AROMAIA
ANEBAS
IWAIPANOMA
an disem Orth schreibt hr Ralegh dass di Leut so ohne heubter sein wohnen
Cassipa lacus
IWARAWAKERI
dise selzen sind meinst alle Goltre bringt der sandt dyser Bachen d
Sees CASZIPA fil Golt
Cassiore flu.
AMAPAIA ist Goltreich dass wasser in diser gegent ist gifft um den mittag, aber des Abendts und fuhrnemlich des mittnachts gar Giffig
AROWAGOTOS
CASSIPAGOTOS
GVI EPARAGOTOS ANA
L I N E A
Disser See wiert von den CANIBALES PARIM heissen in FOPONOWINI Er hatt 200 mei salz wasser vnnd hatt fill Inseln in
NOTA
Der Winter in GVIANA, fenget an im Meijen, und endet sich in Septembris, in welcher zeit kein schiff da verharen mag, wegen der großen sturm windt doner blixem, und auslauffing der wasser Den sich der Flus ORENOQVE, um dise zeitt, wol 30 schu erhept, und alle di Inseln so im eingang dessen ligen bedecket, also daß di ein wonner derren gezwongen sich diß zeitt uf den gipffen, und Baumen ihre wonungen zu halten
AMAZONES daher diser große Flus den nahmen hatt ist eine Nation so fuhrnemlich in Weibern bestehet welche im Jahr nurt einen Monet haben in welchem si sich zu den Mänern geselln alss im Aprillen in dißem Monat sind si lustig vnd gutter ding vndn einander mit Danken springen vnd bancketiern als balt aber dißer Monat auß ist gehet ein Jder wider seinen weg wen nun dise Weiber einen Soen gebahren schicken si den selben seinem Vatter heim ist es aber ein tochter behalten si diselbe und schicken dem Vatter eine Verehrung darfuhr

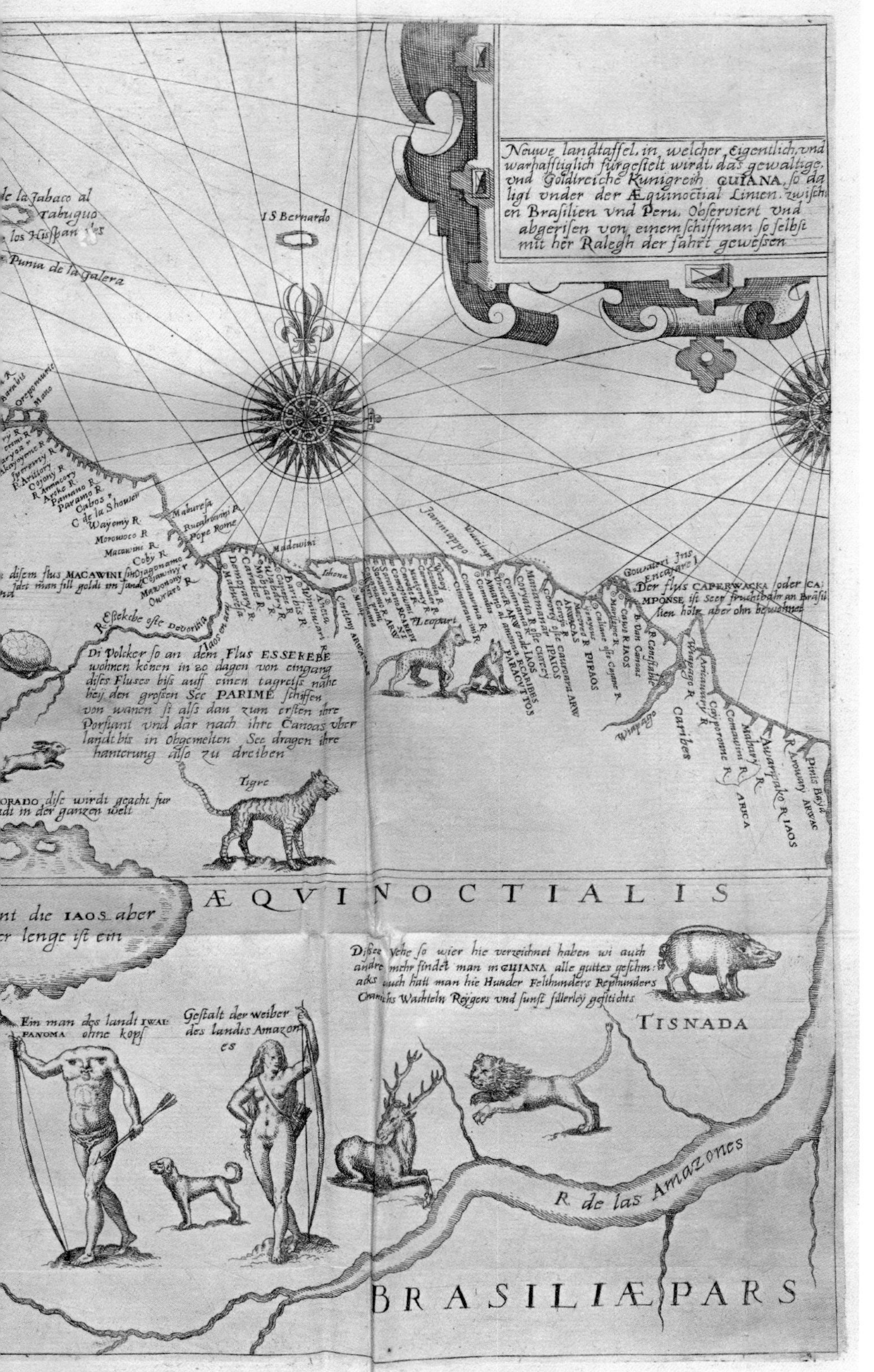

Nouwe landtaffel, in welcher eigentlich, und
warhafftiglich furgestelt wirdt, das gewaltige,
und Goldreiche Kunigreich GUIANA, so da
ligt under der Æquinoctial Linien, zwisch
en Brasilien und Peru, Observiert und
abgerisen von einem schiffman so selbst
mit her Ralegh der fahrt gewesen
I S Bernardo
Punta de la galera
Di Volcker so an dem Flus ESSEREBE
wohnen konen in 20 dagen von eingang
dises Fluses biss auff einen tagreiss nahe
bey den grossen See PARIME schiffen
von wanen si alss dan zum ersten ihre
Porsiant und dar nach ihre Canoas uber
landt bis in obgemelten See dragen ihre
hanterung also zu dreiben
Der flus CAPERWACKA oder CA
MPONSE ist seer fruchtbar an Brasi
lien holtz aber ohn bewohnet
Leopart
Tigre
Caribes
ÆQVINOCTIALIS
Dise Vehe so wier hie verzeichnet haben wi auch
andre mehr findet man in GUIANA alle guttes geschm:
aks auch hatt man hie Hunder Felthunders Rephunders
Cranichs Wachteln Reygers und sunst allerley gestichts
TISNADA
Ein man des landt IWAIPANOMA ohne kopf
Gestalt der weiber des landts Amazones
R. de las Amazones
BRASILIÆ PARS

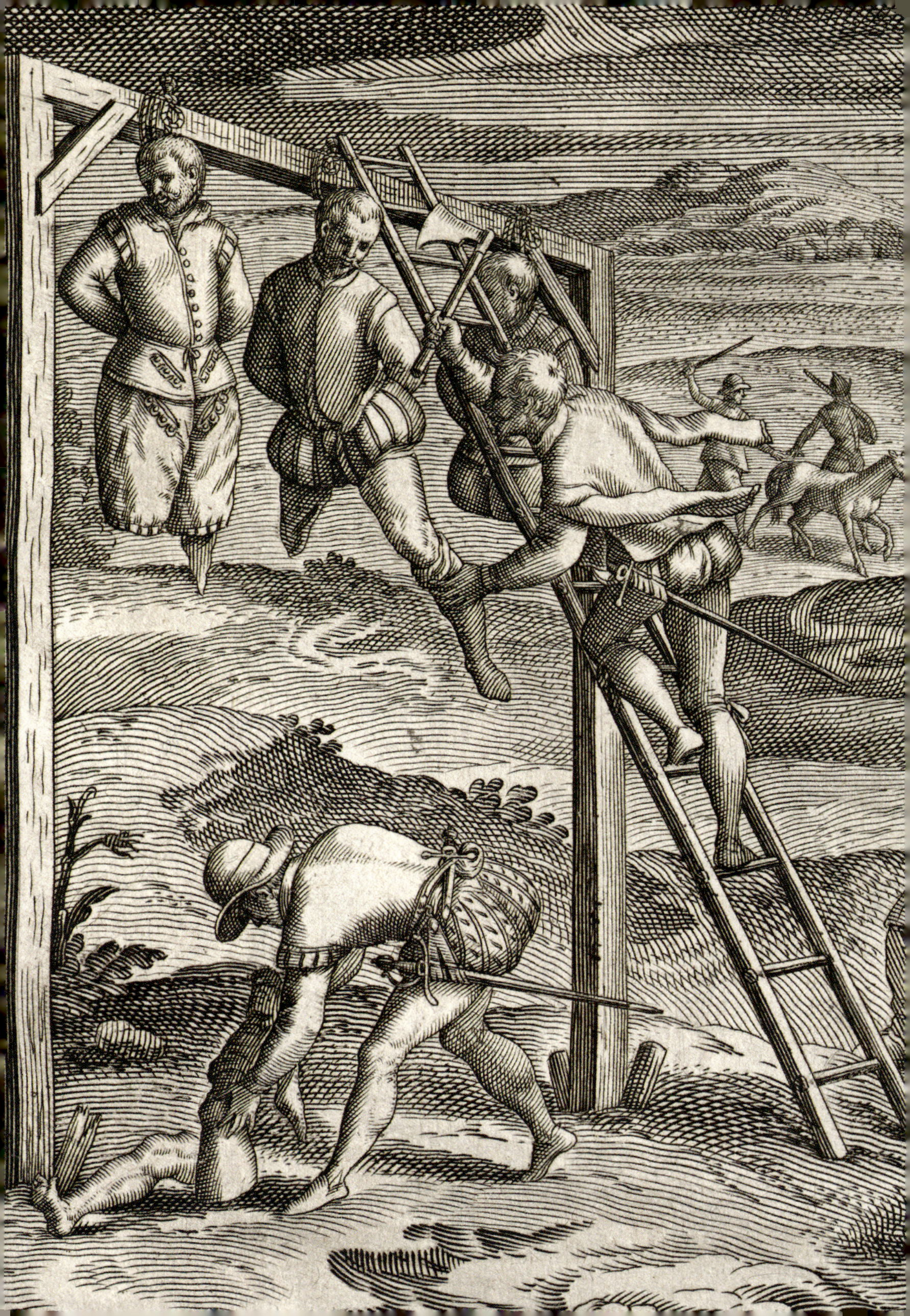

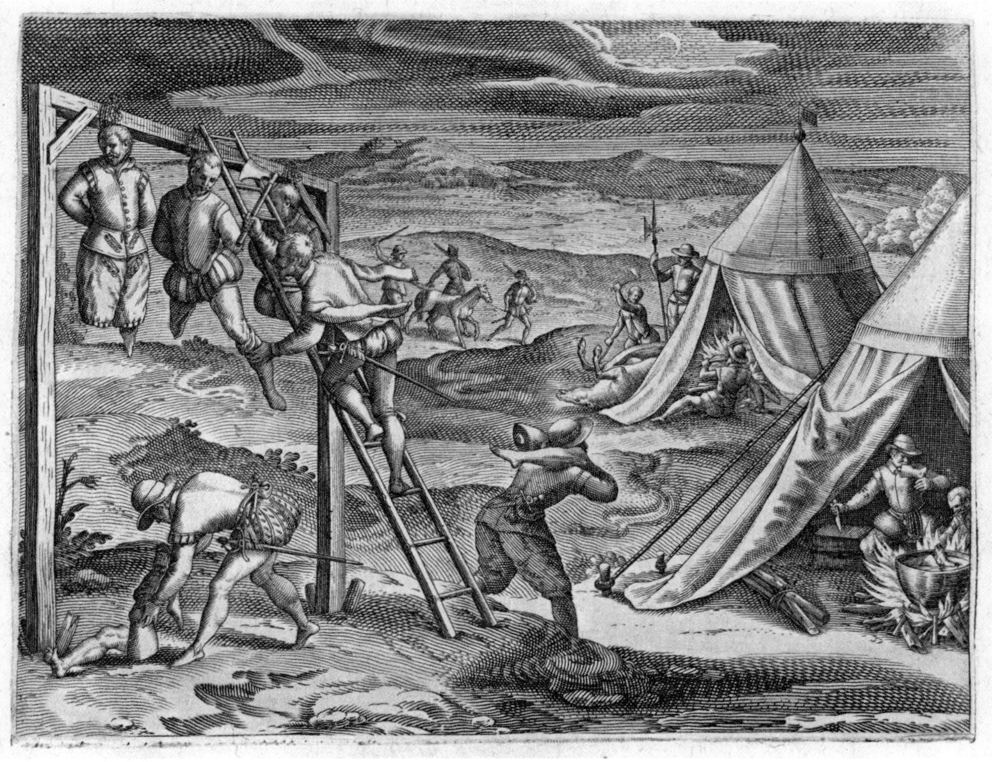

PLATE 1

Pedro de Mendoza administers justice in the case of three thieves

During a period of great hunger in Pedro de Mendoza's camp, his soldiers ate not only clean but unclean animals, and even vermin, in order to suppress their hunger. Even shoe leather and other such things were not spared. Once, three Spaniards tried in secret to lead away a horse to kill and eat it, but it made a noise and a commander had all three of the men hanged. This greatly pleased certain others at the camp. During the night, three others came and removed the legs, arms and whatever else they could from these bodies which they then cooked and ate with much pleasure. It may be seen from this that there is no greater tyrant than hunger. There is another horrifying example of this in the fourth chapter of this history where a man kills and eats his brother.

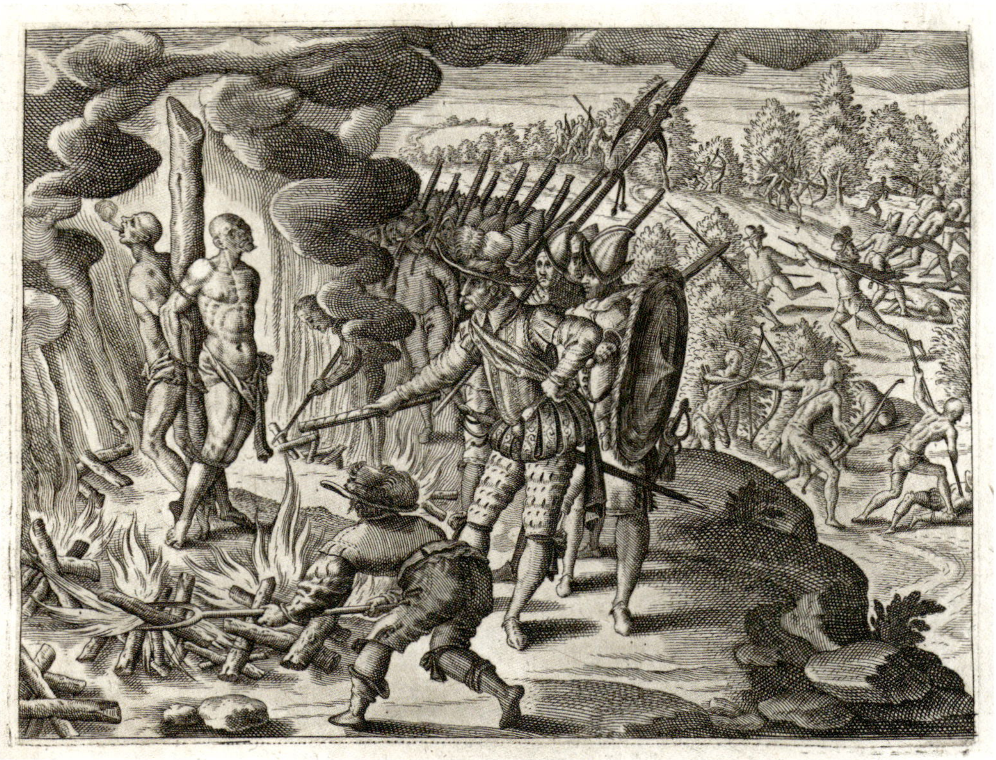

PLATE 2

The Spanish are treacherously killed by the Indians

When Juan Eijollas travelled through the foreign country, he arrived at the border of two nations. They were Naperij and Peijembas. They gave him signs of friendship, but they had secretly entered into an agreement with each other to kill the Christians at an appointed time, which they then acted upon. Then, on a day when Juan Eijollas wanted to go from the Naperij to the Peijembas, these Indians waited for him in a forest through which he had to pass. They fell upon him with great violence with the intention to kill him and all his men. When Captain Martino Domingo Eijollas learned of this, he captured two Peijembas and had them burned at the stake until they died of the pain.

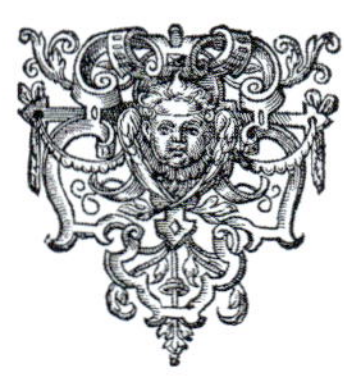

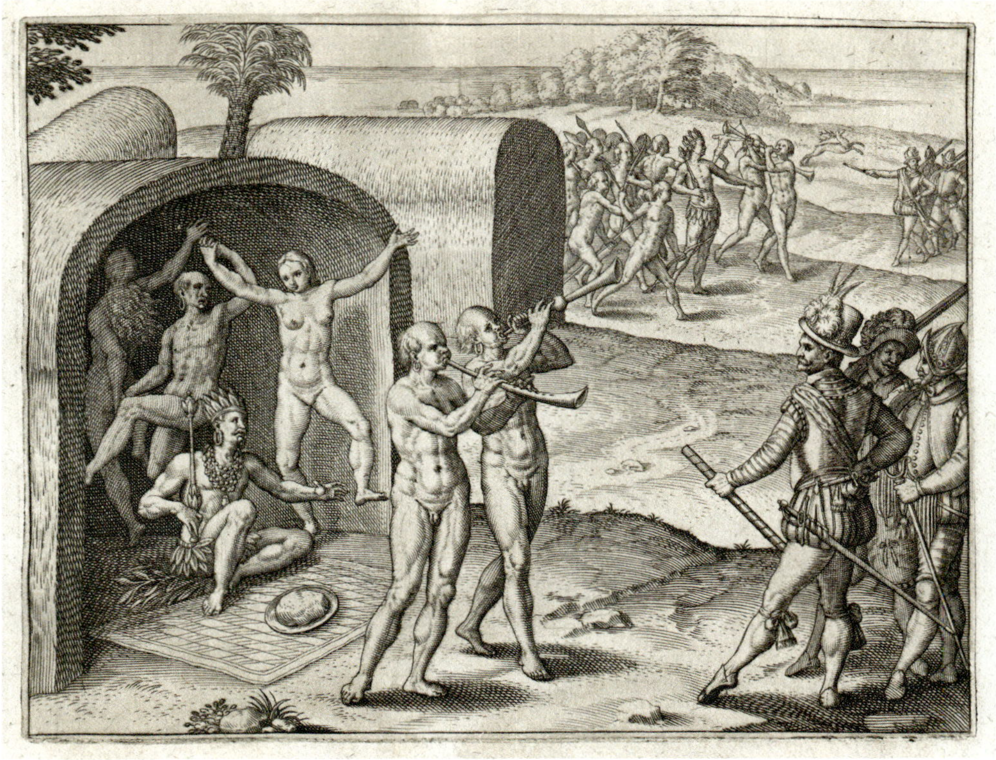

PLATE 3

How the Christians came to the Shervos and what they saw there

Once we came upon a nation called Shervos, whose king travelled a long way and with great majesty and warmth in order to meet us. His musicians preceded him, and behind him followed a great crowd of people too numerous to count who were all naked. The king received us in a dignified manner and offered us all houses in which to stay. The captain, however, was given a castle. The king had deer and other game prepared for us. His musicians made music for him every day at the table, and their pipes are not unlike our shawms. Likewise, he had the most beautiful women and men of the nation dance before him while he ate. This was a great pleasure and pastime of his.

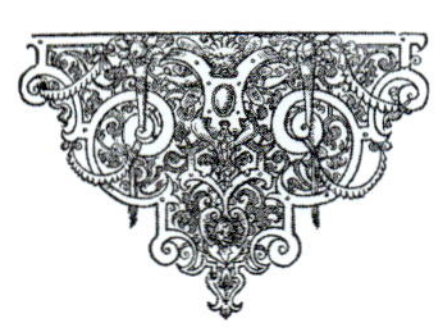

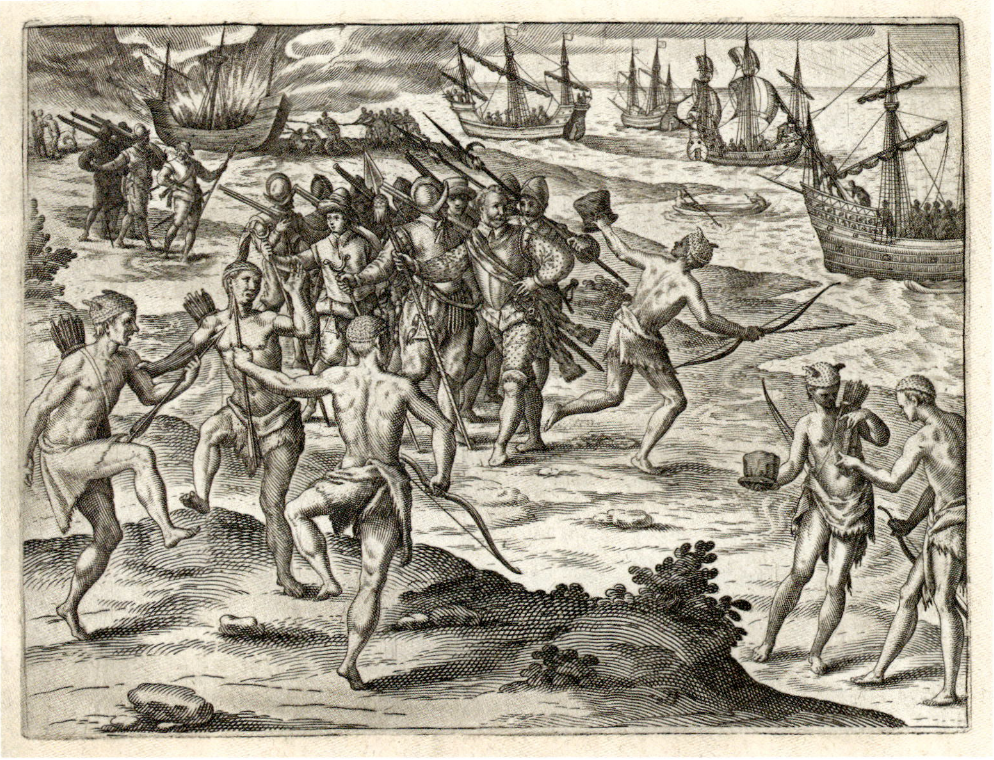

PLATE 4

What happened to Francis Drake not far from the island of Río de la Plata

During his first voyage sailing around the world, Francis Drake came upon a river called Río de la Plata. His ship could not follow the others here. It crashed into land and burned. At this point, natives of the island approached him and began to dance with each other. Drake and his men looked on with amusement at their strange movements. When Drake turned around for a moment to speak with his men, however, one of the Indians leapt away from the dance and stole Francis Drake's hat, which had gold lace. He took it from right off his head and returned to his people, whereupon he gave another the lace but kept the hat for himself. The Indians then all began to leave in a hurry. Later, not far from this place, Captain Drake put one of these people who had forfeited his life on trial in the English manner. His head was cut off with an axe.

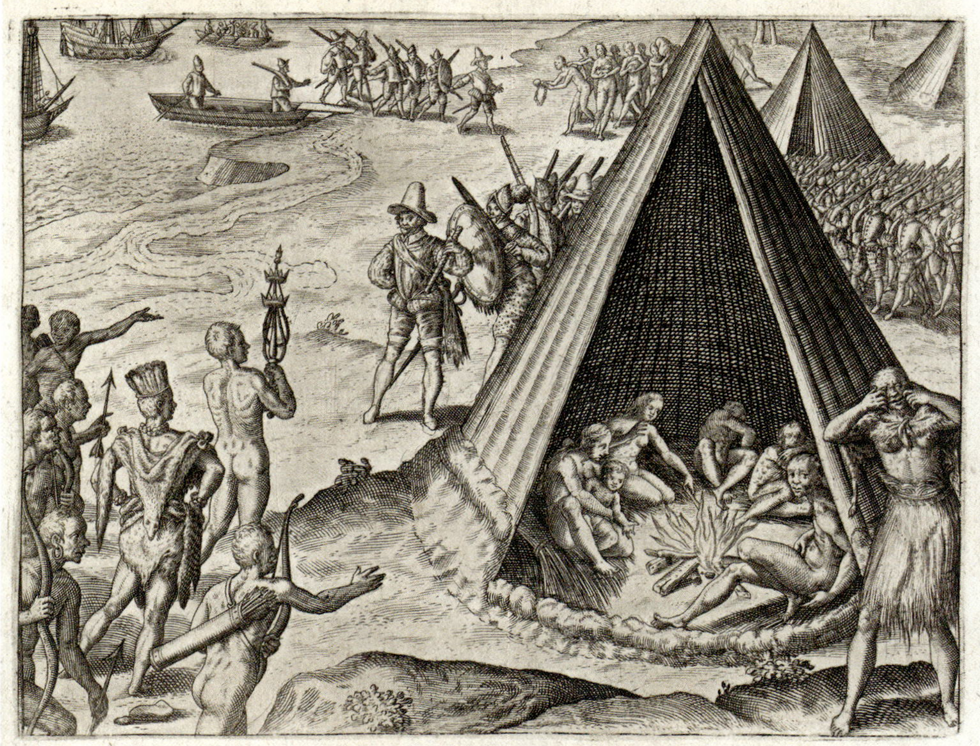

PLATE 5

How Francis Drake arrives at a place where the king meets him

When Francis Drake journeyed on, he eventually came to a place where he saw some huts built on the shore made of poles and masts, pointed on top and rounder at the bottom. Outwardly they were quite high and secured in the ground, but inside the poor people – mother, father and child – sat in a circle on straw, for they had no other bed. A fire burned in the centre of the house. These people honoured the visiting Englishmen with gifts, as is told about in the account. The king also appeared, which was uncommon. He heard that the Christians had arrived and he called together 12,000 men to accompany him in great magnificence. Although his subjects were all naked, the king wore robes of rabbit fur and other animals. A herald preceded him carrying his sceptre. When Francis Drake first saw these people approaching, he ordered his men into a battle formation. The king, however, gave him signs of peace and held a long speech via his herald. When the speech was over, he had two crowns placed on Francis Drake's head, and three wonderfully crafted ivory necklaces hung around his neck. The king intended to make his entire kingdom subject to Francis Drake and his regiment through this ceremony. Furthermore, there were women who scratched their faces for joy until they were bloody. They also went naked, but they had aprons made of rushes and other such things that they hung on their bodies, as well as deerskin over their shoulders.

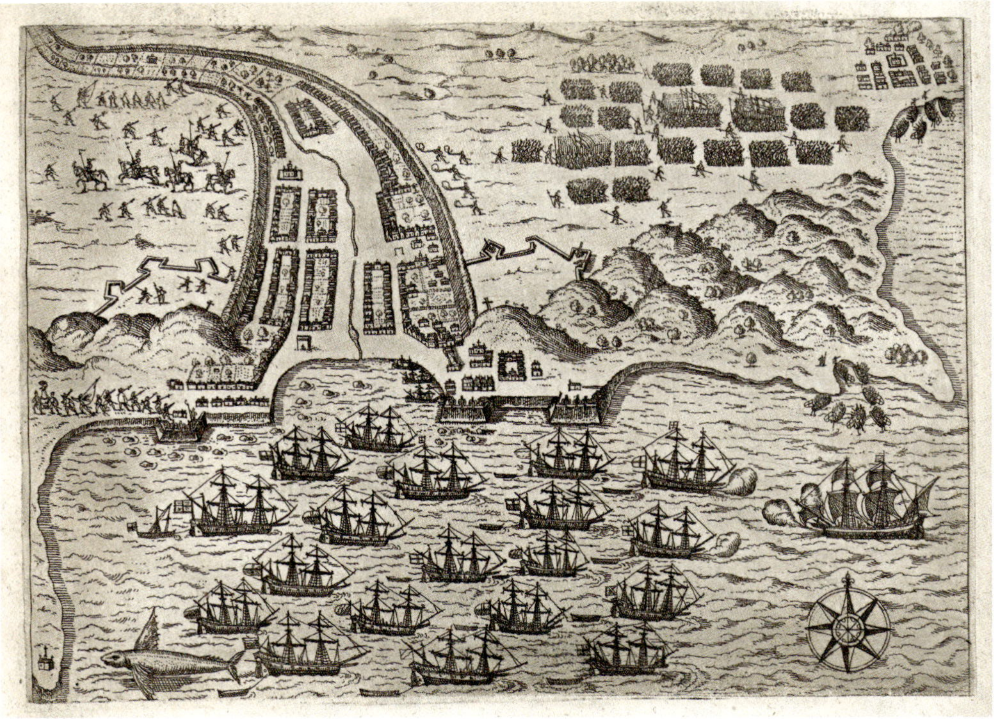

PLATE 6

How Francis Drake occupied the town and Island of St Iago

St Iago is the most famous of the islands off the coast of Africa. It lies just across from Cape Verde, forming a kind of strait. The other islands in the area, even though some are over a mile away, are also named after this saint. The town of St Iago also shares the name. It has much commerce with Guinea and other lands nearby in Africa, by which they also provide many wares to the traders there from Portugal and Lusitania.

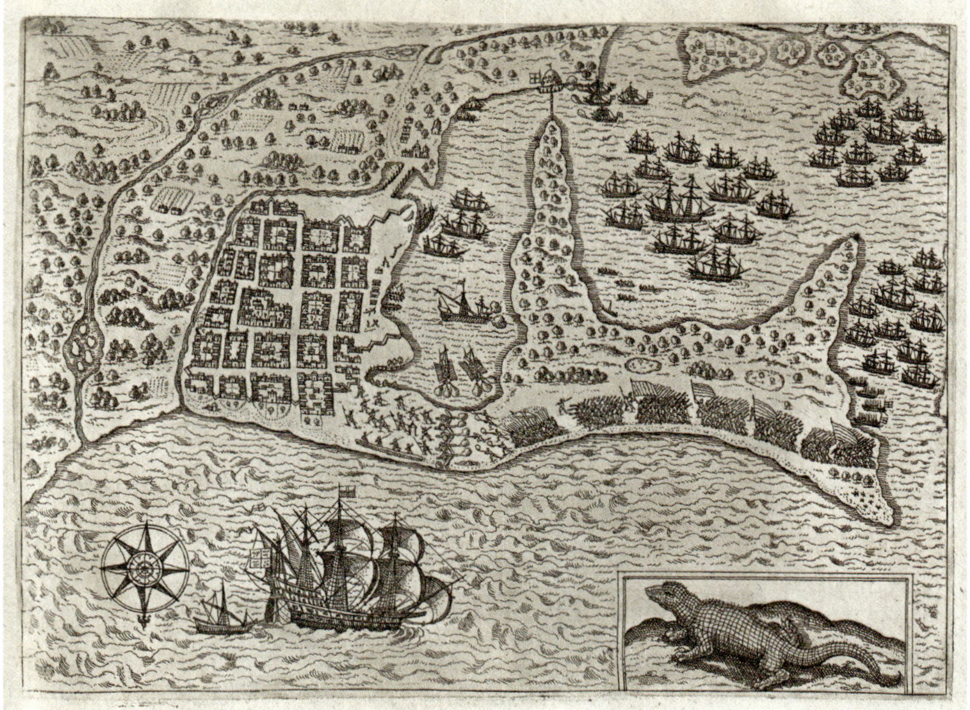

PLATE 8

The town of Cartagena is won by Francis Drake

The city of Cartagena lies where the sun sets and has a commodious harbour that supports trade between Spain and Peru.

PLATE 7, PAGES 400/401

How Captain Francis Drake conquered the town of Santo Domingo on the island of Hispaniola

Santo Domingo is in the Indies on the island of Hispaniola, which is almost comparable with England in size. The city was built lovingly by the Spanish, but it menaces all of the neighbouring lands.

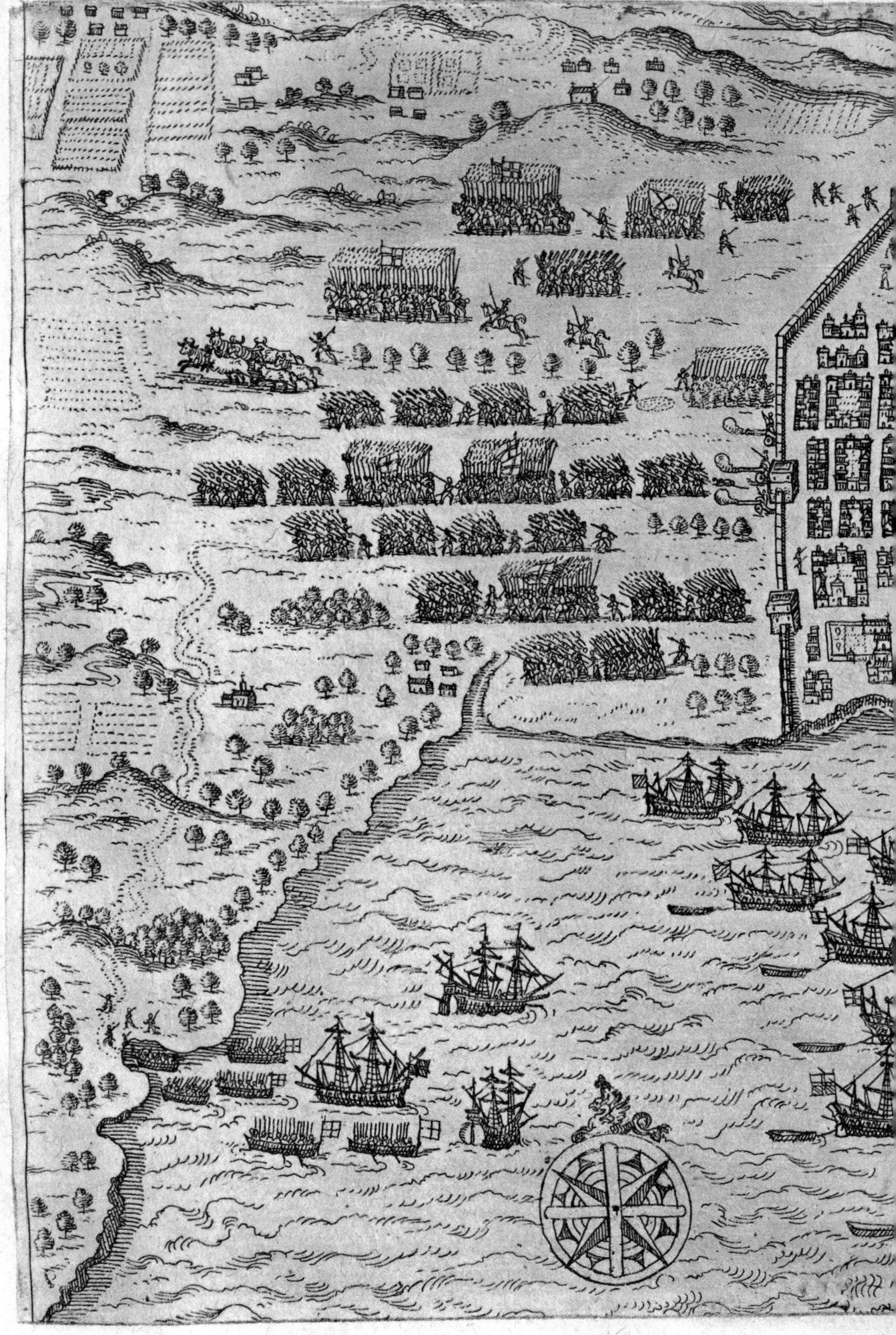

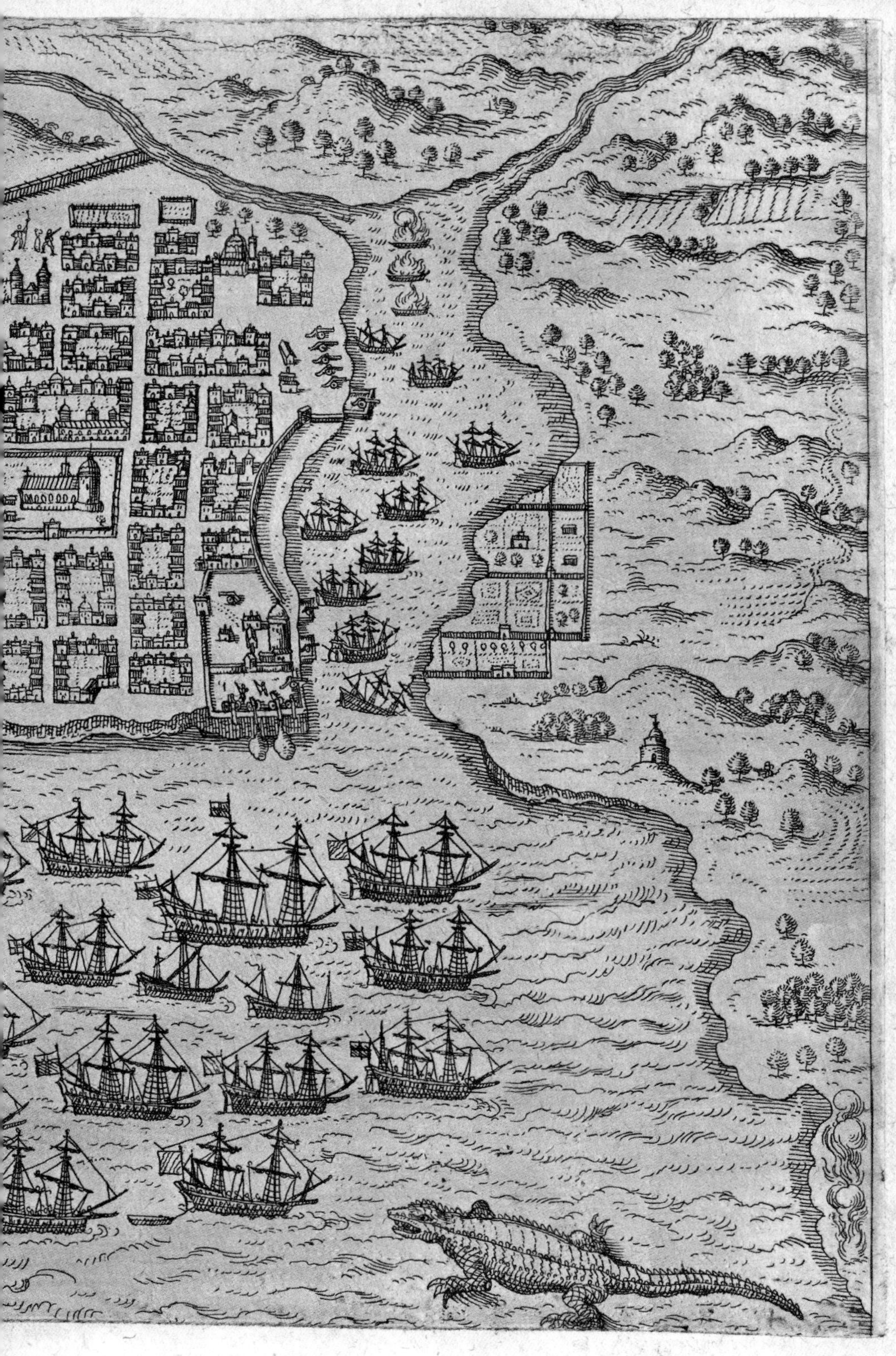

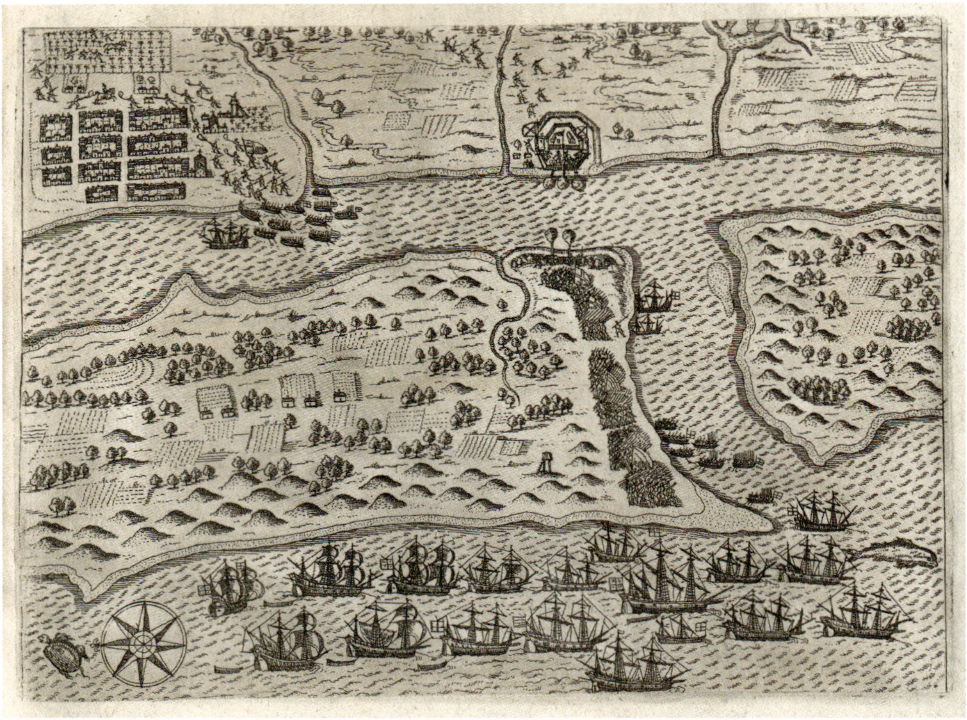

PLATE 9

The conquest of St Augustine in America

St Augustine is constructed out of wood. It has beautiful, pleasing gardens and very fertile soil. Upon leaving this place, however, we burned it all to the ground. There are 150 men stationed here as part of the occupation, in the same way as 12 miles west the Spanish stationed men at St Helena to make sure the English and French could not pass through and seize the land around the town that had not yet been developed.

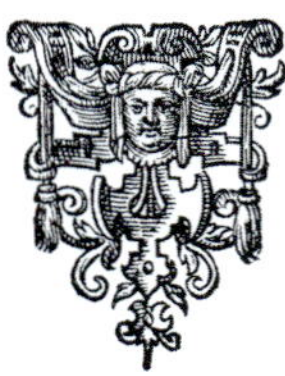

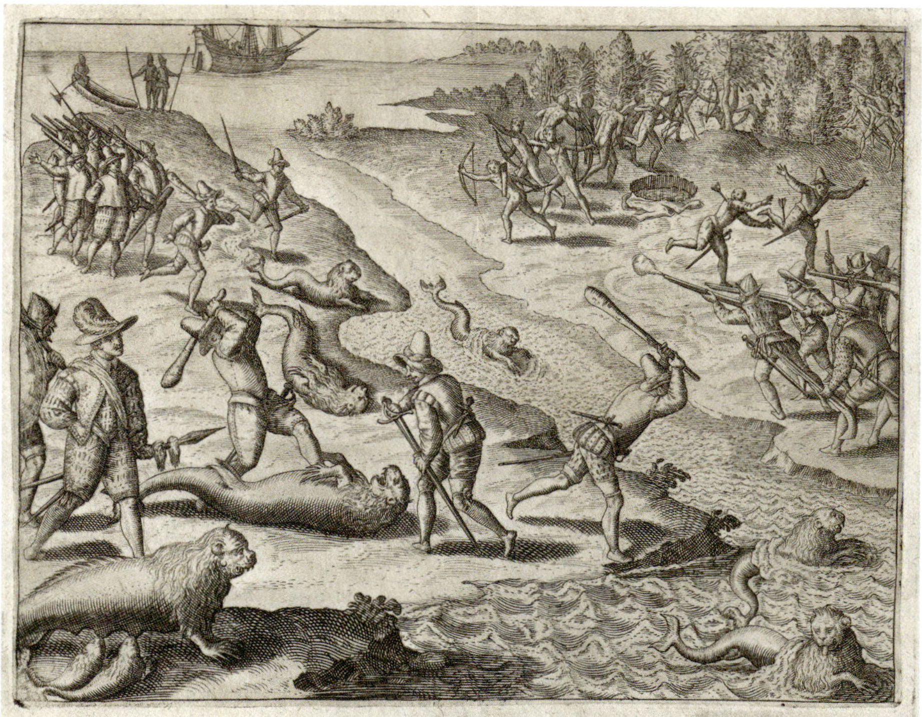

PLATE 10

How Thomas Cavendish comes to an island where there are many strange seals

While Thomas Cavendish was on his way to circumnavigate the globe, he came to an island populated by seals of an outrageous size. Half of their body, including the head, which had long curly hair, resembled that of a lion. They gave birth to their young all months of the year and suckled them with their milk. We could not kill them except with clubs, with which we beat them over the head. It took three or four men to subdue and kill one. They make good food, and their meat tastes almost like mutton or veal. Once a man of ours went out with a boy to a well we had dug in order to wash shirts, but he was suddenly fallen upon by a group of Indians. The man and boy were both hit with arrows, one in the shoulder and the other in the knee. As soon as the rest of the English saw these two wounded, they quickly came to their help, and the Indians did not hesitate in running away.

PLATE 11

How Thomas Cavendish came to an island where the Indians gave him wood and fresh water

When Thomas Cavendish arrived in Maramouena, the Indians there descended from the mountains and cliffs to give him kindling and fresh water as a sign of their humility. They led him to where they lived. They were made as one sees in the above picture. They stick several staves in the ground, then lay more across these and cover it all with straw or something similar. They live in these structures with their wives and children and sit on animal hides on the floor. They eat almost exclusively what they catch from fishing, of which they are masters. Their boats are made of two animal skins stitched together. They have artfully attached bladders to both ends of the boats, which they can inflate whenever they want to use the boat. The skin of the boat is extended whenever the bladders are full of air. They tie up the bladders and go wherever they wish.

PLATE 12, PAGES 406/407

What was delivered to Cavendish on his voyage by a number of Indians

When Thomas Cavendish in the course of his Indian voyage reached the Ladrones Islands, more than 60 canoes and other boats came out to greet him, laden with all sorts of provisions and vegetables which the Indians had brought to the Englishmen to trade. When the English had taken as much from them as they needed, in exchange for some old iron, and wished to continue on their way, the Indians followed them with so much noise and uproar that the English, in order to get rid of them, were forced to fire several bullets at them. The Indians then jumped into the sea so quickly, or else fled in their boats, that the English in the end did not know if some of them had died.

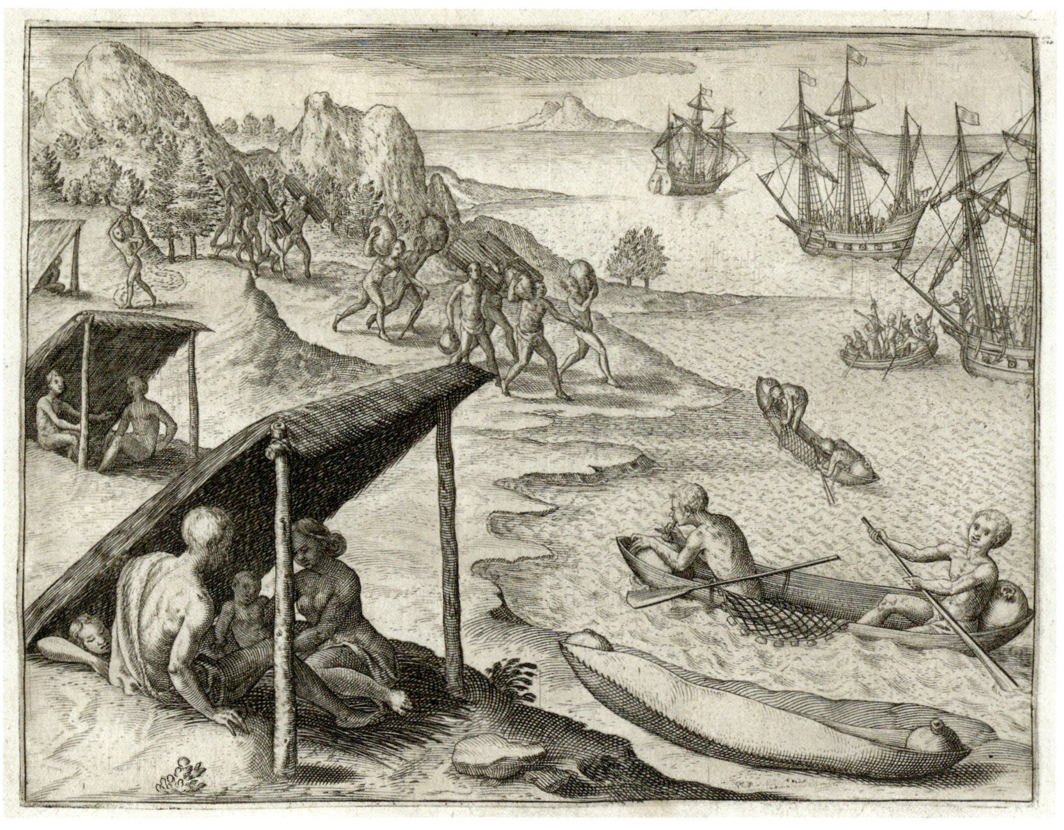

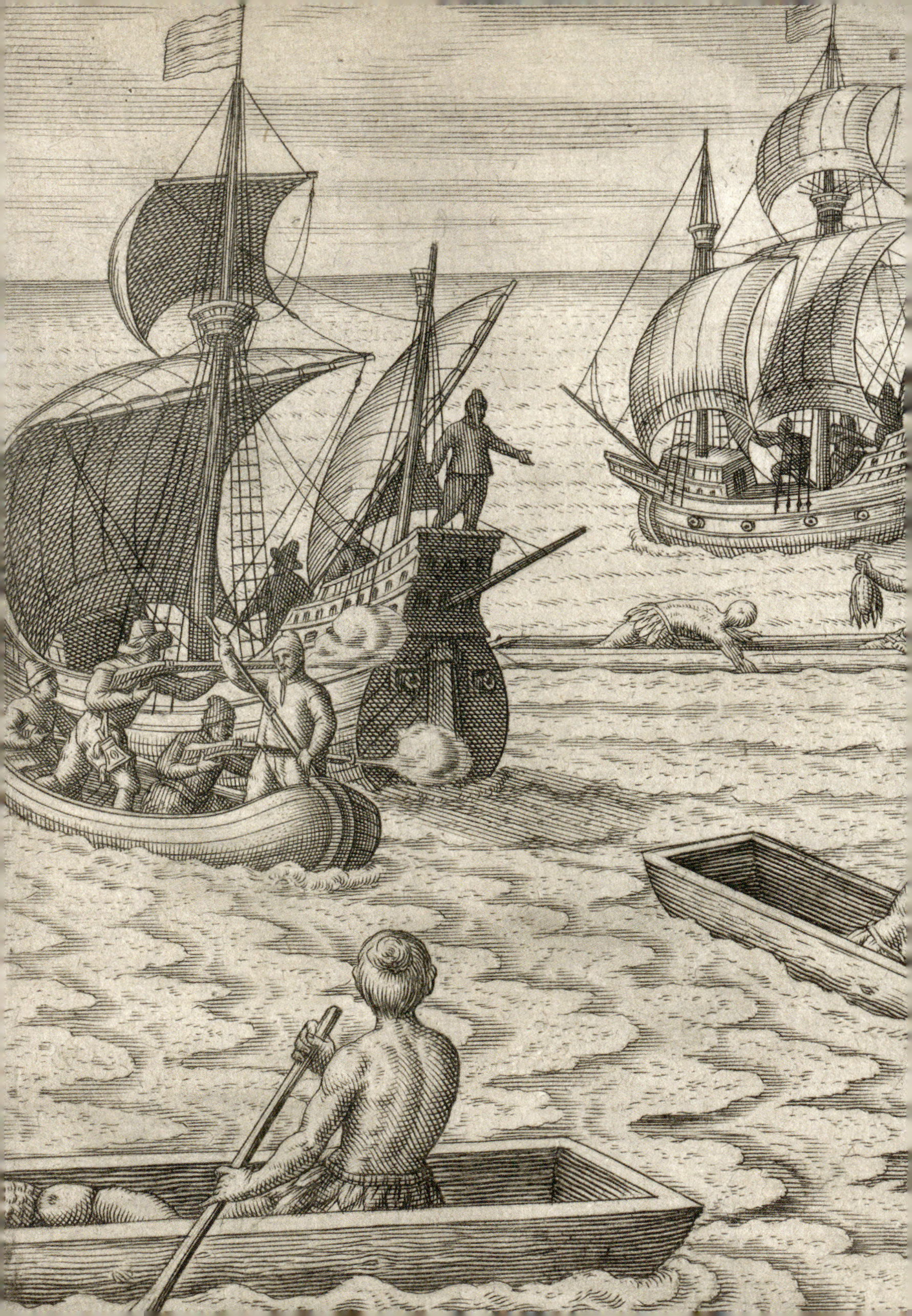

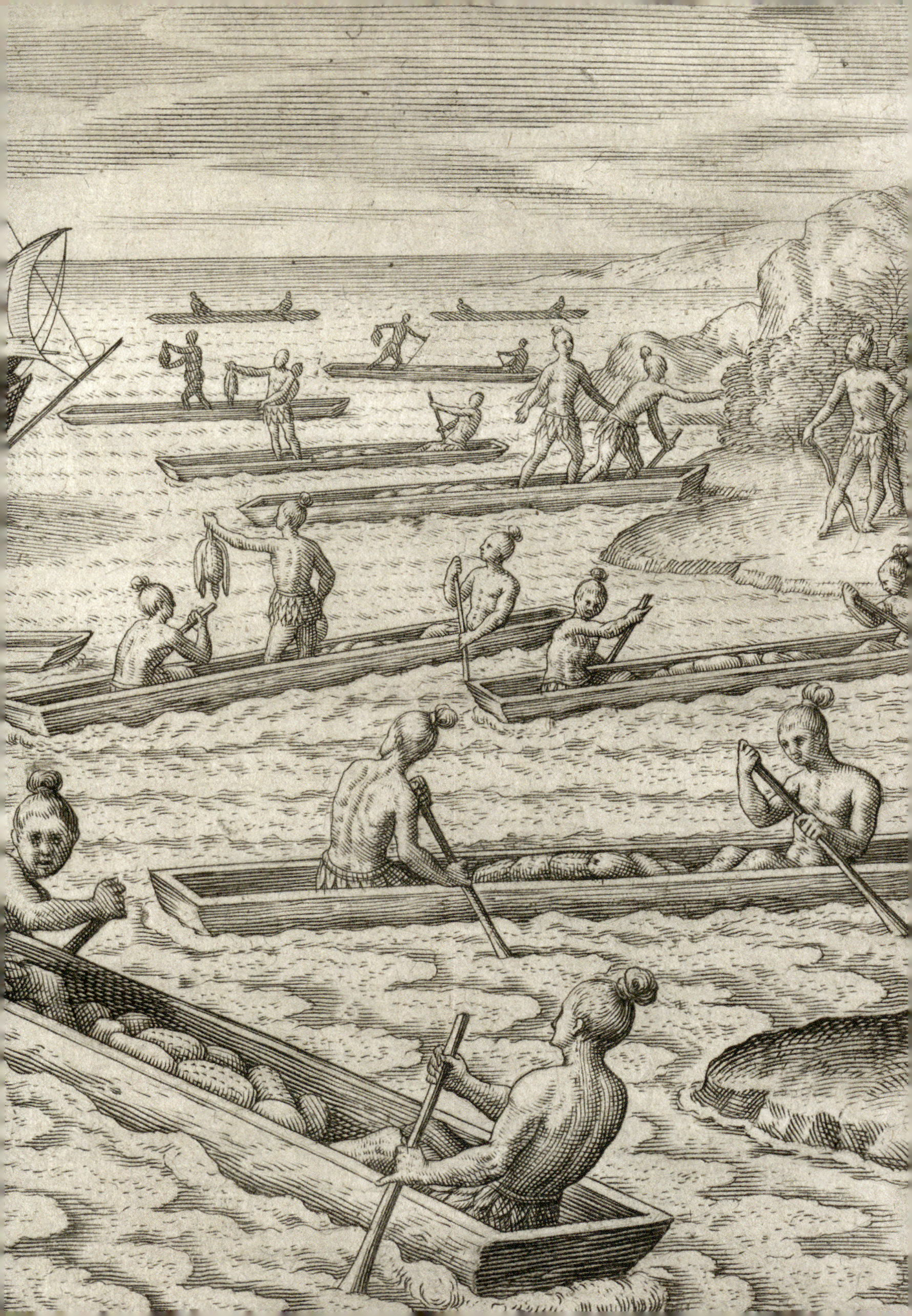

PLATE 13

How Walter Raleigh conquered a city, and captured the Spanish governor

When Walter Raleigh reached the island of Trinidad with his ships, he tricked the Spaniards at Puerto de los Españoles into coming to meet him with pleasant words and friendly gestures, and then inquired about the general situation of the island and the strength of the Spanish forces until he had heard enough. Then he ordered commander Caulfield and 100 soldiers to come to him, and these then fired cannonballs at the city of San José, where the Spanish governor and viceroy Don Antonio de Berrío resided. Those in the city defended themselves courageously, but were ultimately forced to surrender. Raleigh let the soldiers go, but Berrío and his companions he captured and imprisoned on his ship.

PLATE 14, PAGES 410/411

How some peoples live in trees or high cliffs during the winter, with remarks on the ceremonies they hold for their dead

Tinitiuas is a nation of Indians in America. In the wintertime, they have to make their dwellings in high cliffs and in trees because of the river Orinoco. Between May and September, the Orinoco rises 30 feet higher than normal, bringing it up 20 feet past its usual banks and making the grounds around it inhospitable. This is a good time for fishing, however, and for catching other things in the water to eat. Their neighbours the Capuri and Macuri have ceremonies for honouring their dead where, if their leader dies and is buried, they greatly mourn him. When they think that the flesh has rotted and fallen away from his bones, they dig his corpse up again. His body remains together because of the nerves and sinews. They hang these remains up in their homes in memory of the leader, decorating his head with all manner of beautiful feathers. They hang golden plates and other ornaments from his arms and legs, such as he had in life, and let him hang there like that.

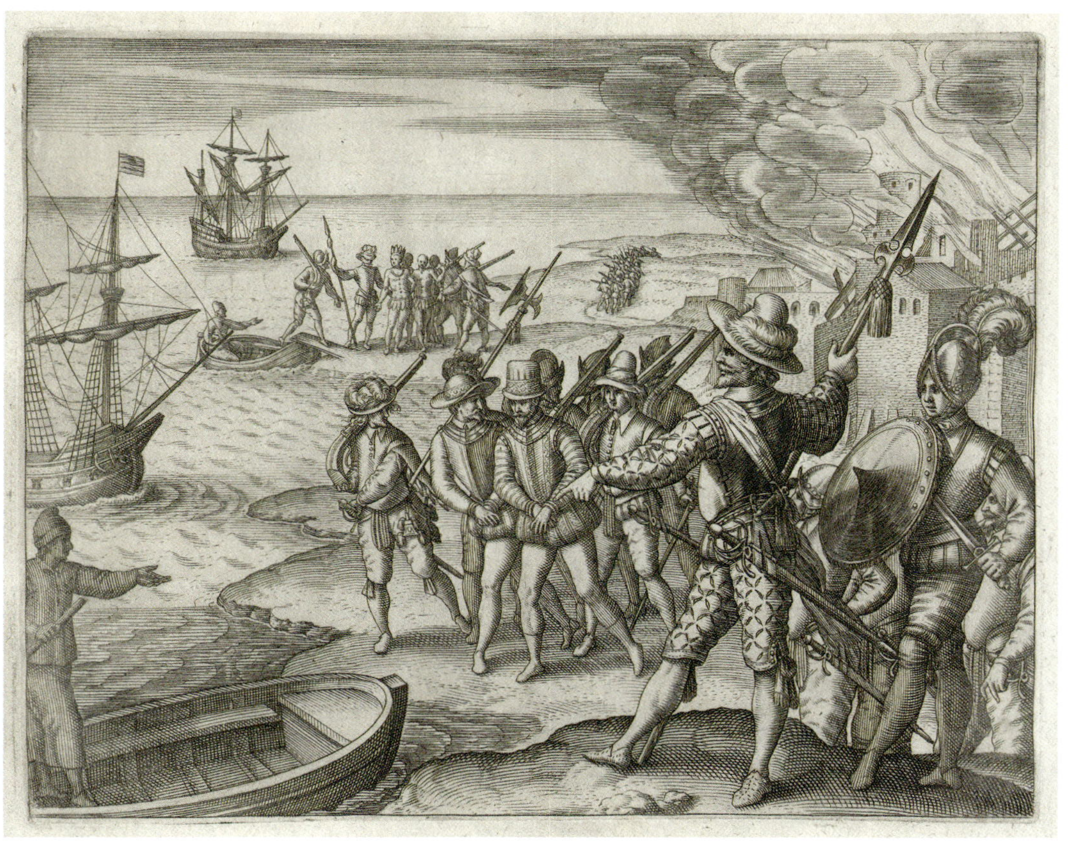

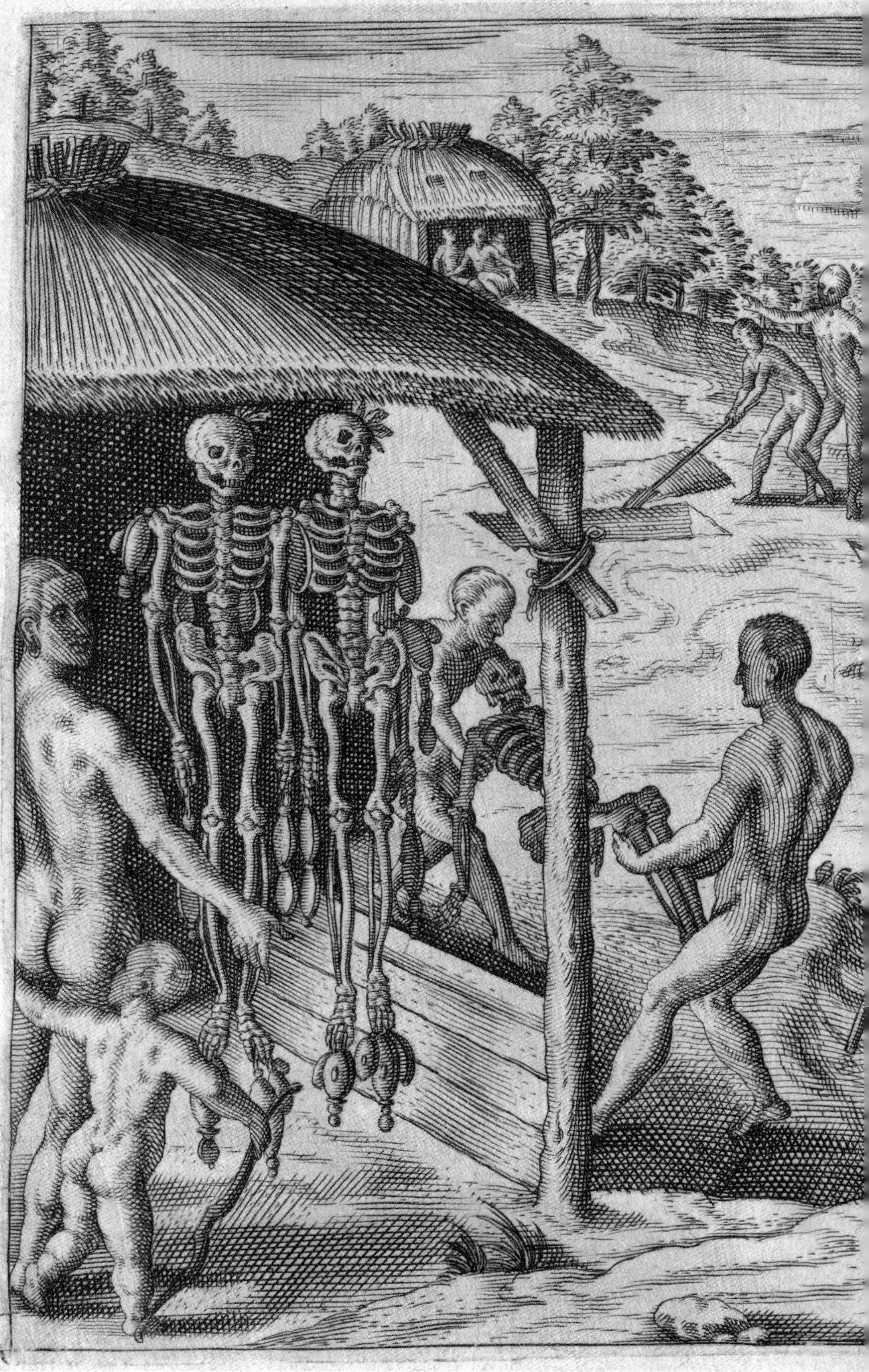

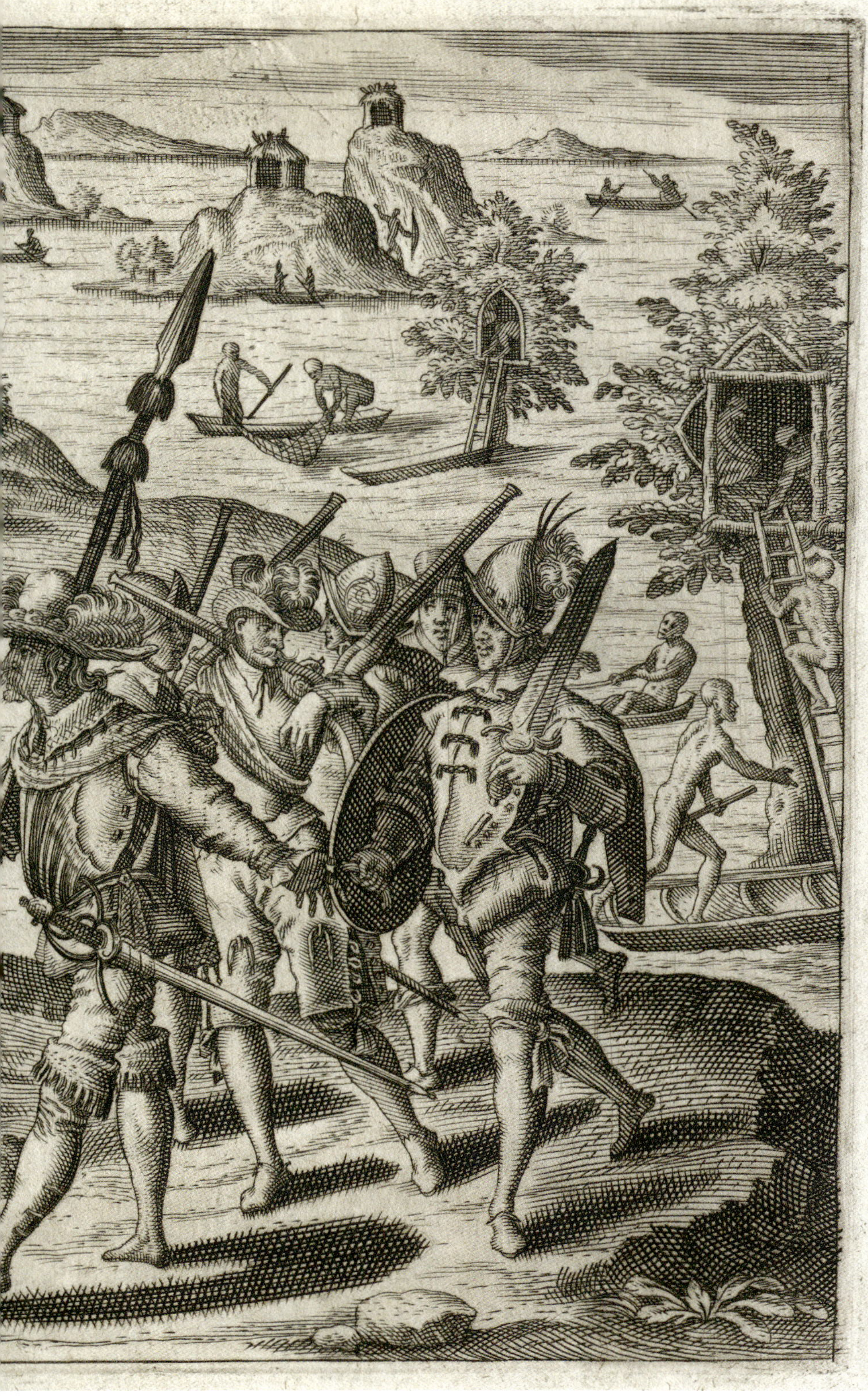

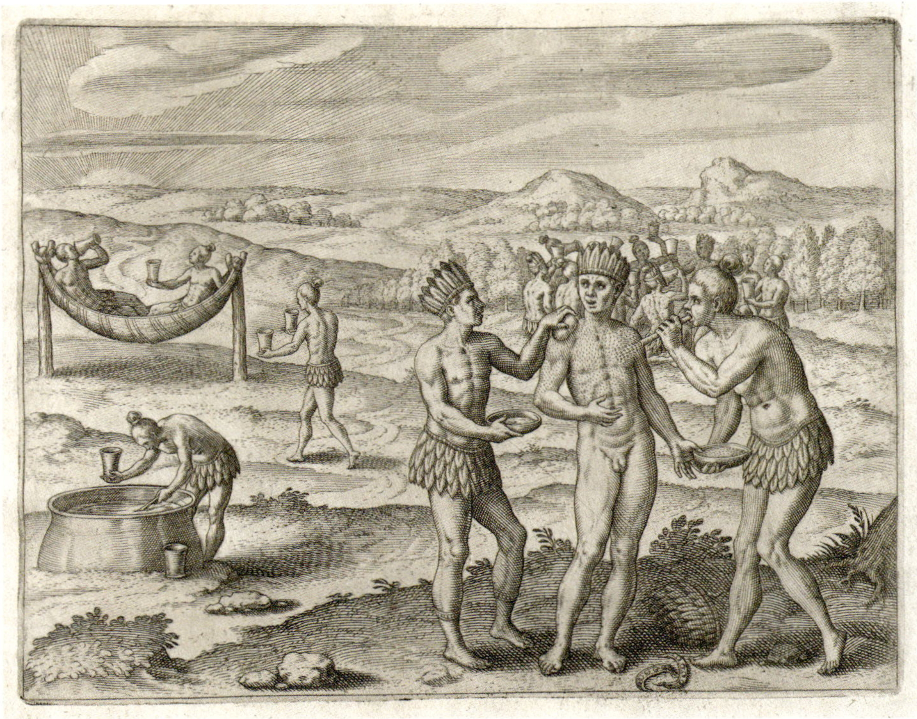

PLATE 15

How the emperor of Guyana treats his noblemen, when they come to visit him

Just like all of their neighbours, the inhabitants of the province of Guyana enjoy getting drunk, and in fact exceed all others in drinking alcohol. When the emperor organises a banquet for his administrators and noblemen, all of the invited guests are undressed by his servants and then covered in a white balm from head to toe, after which grains of gold dust are blown on to their bodies through a straw so that they stick to the balm as if it were a glue, making them all look as if they themselves were made of gold. In this way they gather together, as many as 50 or 100 men for seven or eight days, until they are all sated. The English also arrived in a village before a cacique called Toparimaca, who had another strange cacique in his company, and both of them sat together in a Brazilian hammock while two women poured drinks for them. Their drinks are made from the juice of certain herbs to which all kinds of roots and spices are added, and they store it in very large earthenware kettles.

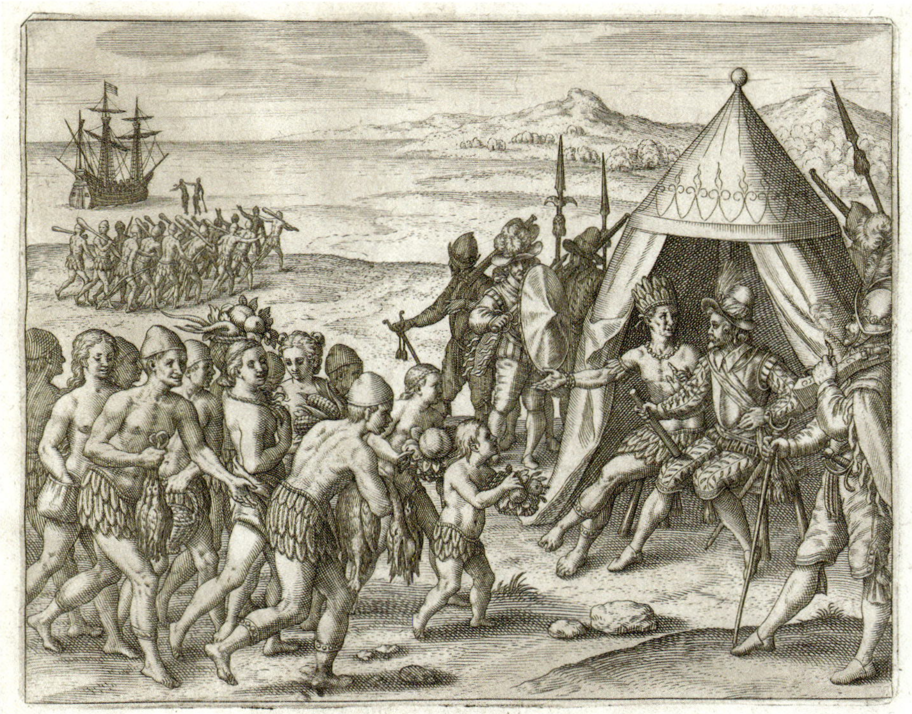

PLATE 16

How Raleigh established friendly relations with the king of Arromaia

After the English had managed to continue on their way with considerable good fortune, they proceeded without trouble and ended up in a province called Arromaia. Here the king instantly sought an opportunity to establish friendly relations with the English, for when he learned of their arrival he did not hesitate to travel to them, even though it was some 14 English miles to the coast, and he was a man of 110 years. He was accompanied by many men, women and children, who brought all sorts of provisions along to honour the English. The king was received warmly by Raleigh, and after he had heard the king's reports from the province of Guyana, he was allowed to go home in peace. That means this 110-year-old king travelled 28 English miles altogether.

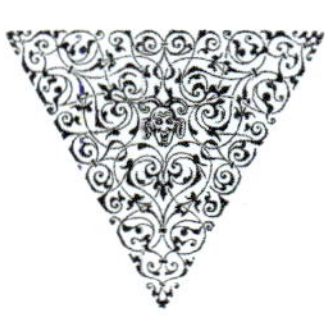

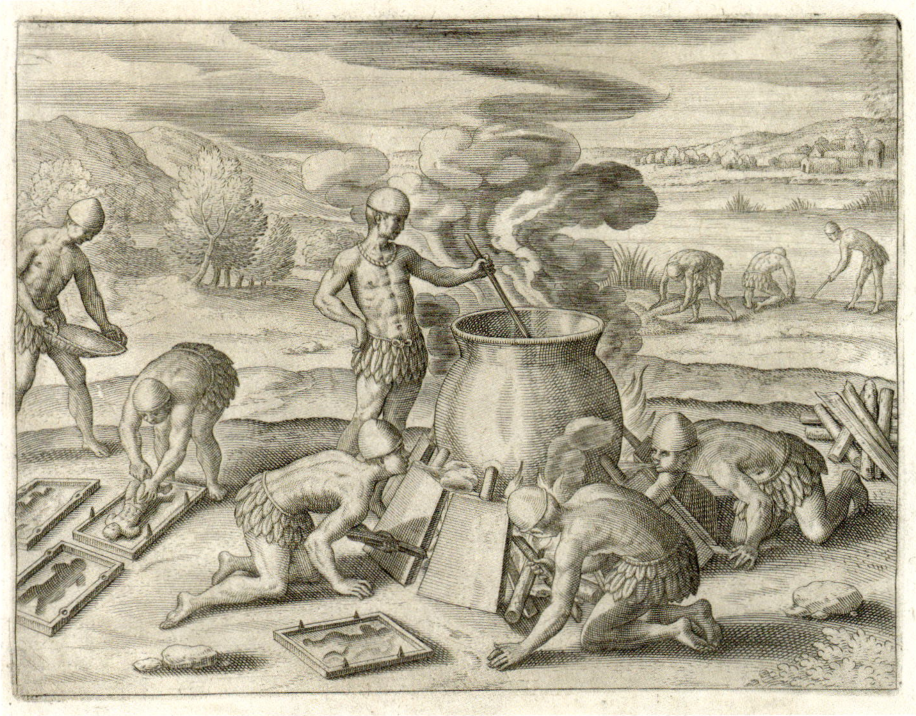

PLATE 17

How the Guyanese make their golden statues

The inhabitants of Guyana make their idols and images mainly from grains of gold, which they collect from a large lake close to the great capital of Manoa, and from the rivers that flow into this lake. And what they do with it is as follows: they put the gold, after adding a little copper to it so that it becomes smooth, into a large kettle with several holes in it. In these holes they place small wooden straws, which are attached at the other end to moulds in the shape of their idols. Some of them blow upon the fire for a very long time until the gold melts and flows into the moulds.

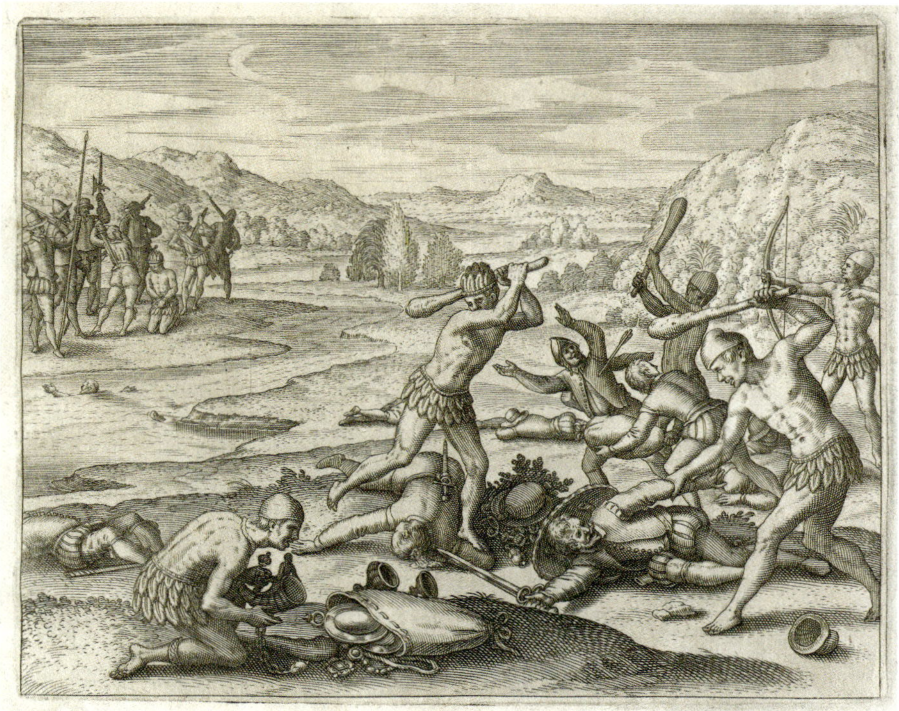

PLATE 18

Concerning the 10 Spaniards who were attacked, beaten and robbed by the Indians

The account mentions how the Spanish governor Don Antonio de Berrío sent out 10 of his men on a reconnaissance mission to the gold-rich capital of Manoa and the surrounding area. These Spaniards were accompanied by Morequito to Mercureguarai, and from there on to Manoa. When they reckoned they had done what they had been instructed to do, and had also acquired for themselves all manner of riches from that country, they decided to return, having no longer any concern for possible dangers. It was then that Morequito told his people to overwhelm them most treacherously, and take possession of all the riches they had collected, amounting in value to some 40,000 pounds sterling. The Spaniards, one of whom was a monk, were all beaten and one of them jumped into the river and was killed with arrows. When Berrío heard of this, he sent all his forces to burn and plunder Morequito's country, and to pursue him all the way to Cumana, where he had fled, and there they found him and beheaded him.

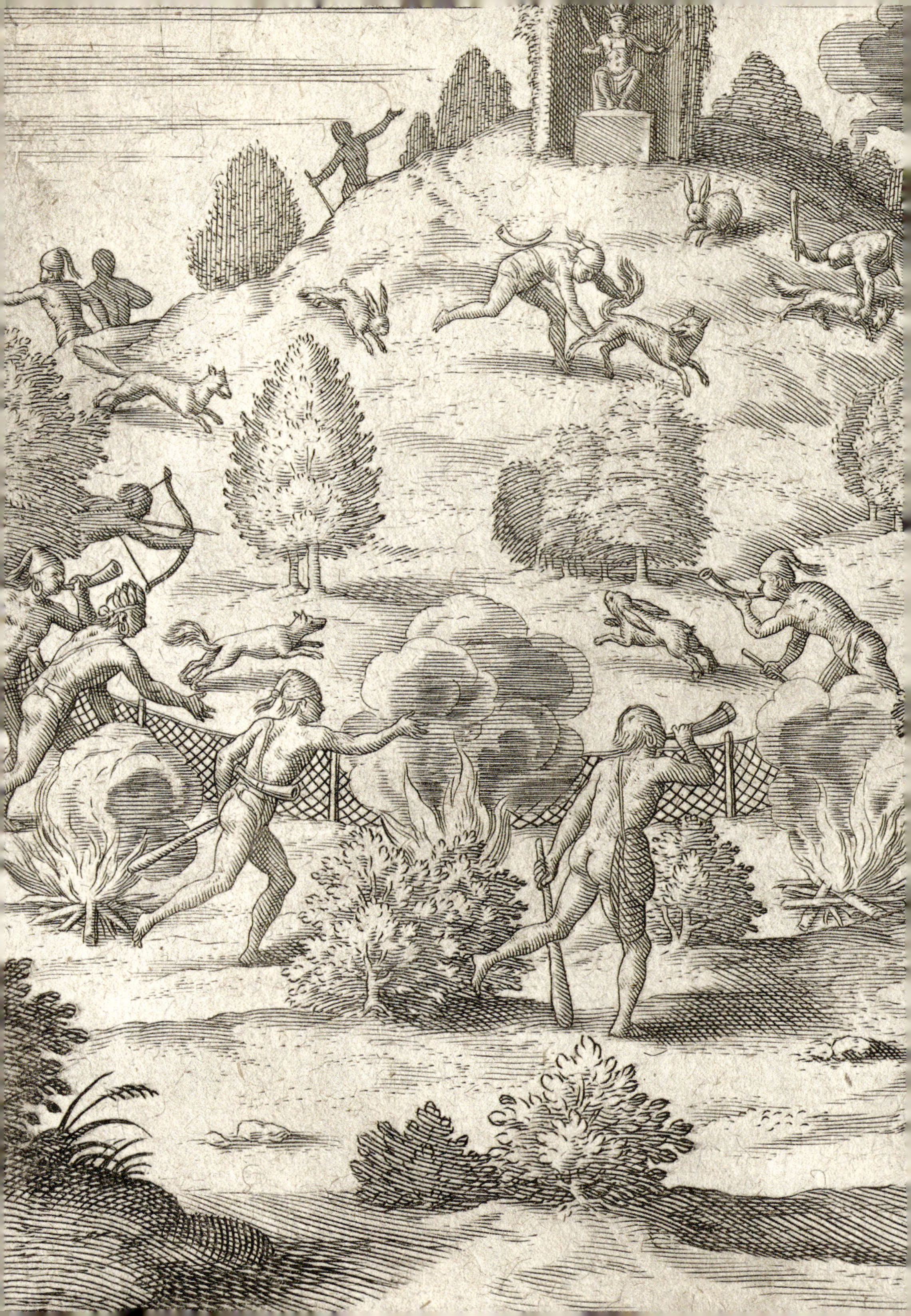

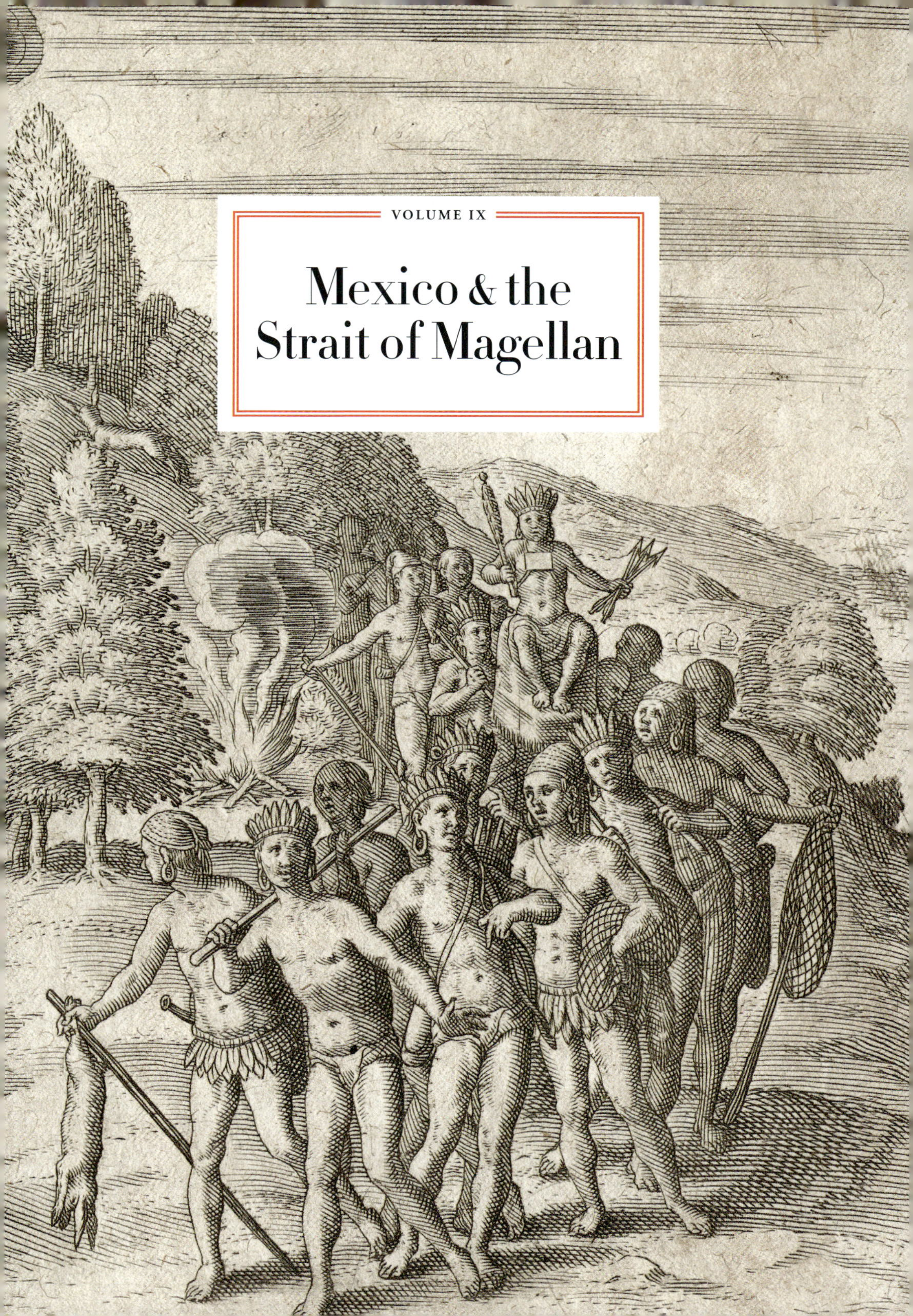
VOLUME IX
Mexico & the
Strait of Magellan

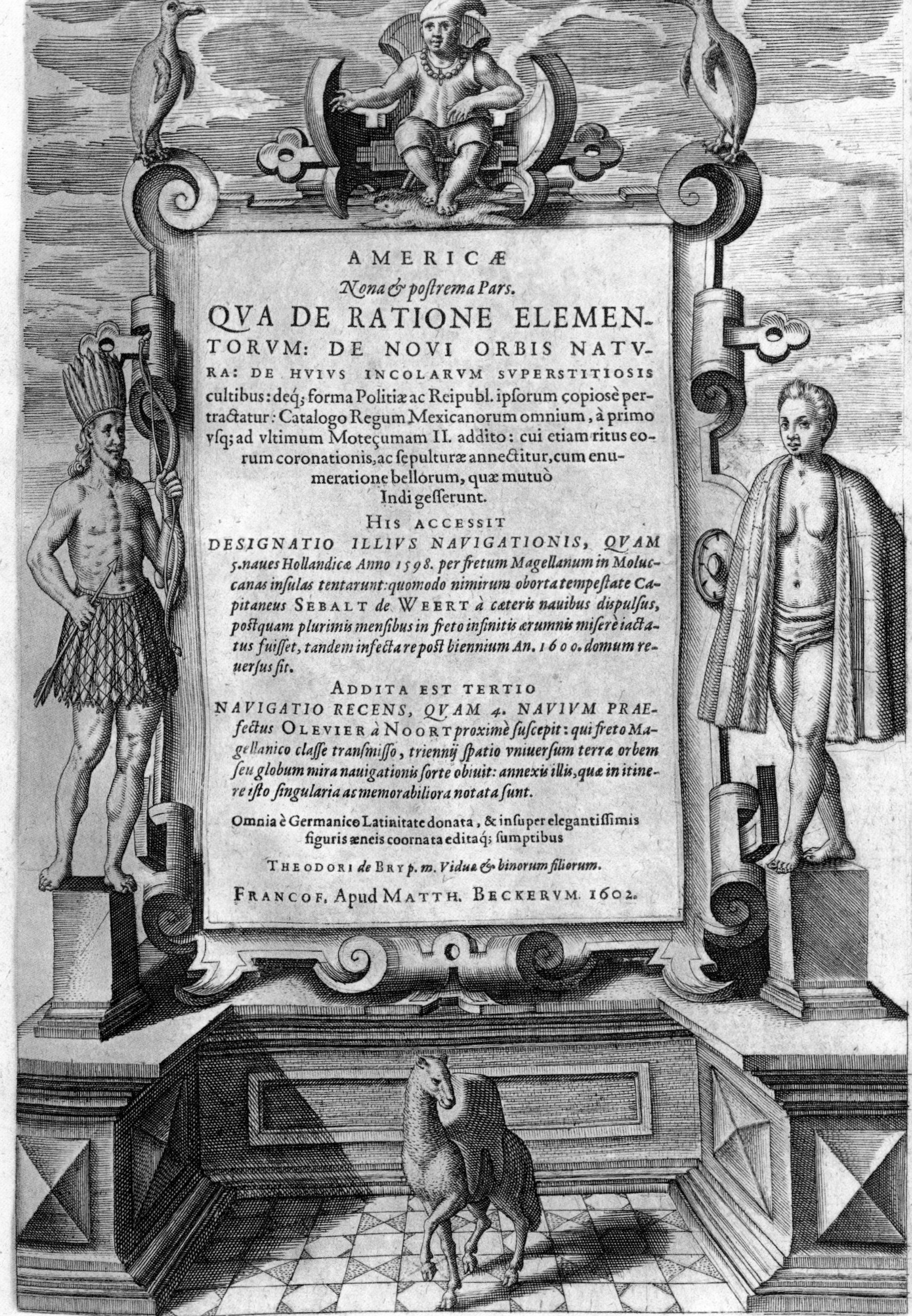

AMERICÆ

Nona & postrema Pars.

QVA DE RATIONE ELEMENTORVM: DE NOVI ORBIS NATVRA: DE HVIVS INCOLARVM SVPERSTITIOSIS cultibus: deq; forma Politiæ ac Reipubl. ipsorum çopiosè pertractatur: Catalogo Regum Mexicanorum omnium, à primo vsq; ad vltimum Moteçumam II. addito: cui etiam ritus eorum coronationis, ac sepulturæ annectitur, cum enumeratione bellorum, quæ mutuò Indi gesserunt.

HIS ACCESSIT

DESIGNATIO ILLIVS NAVIGATIONIS, QVAM 5. naues Hollandicæ Anno 1598. per fretum Magellanum in Moluccanas insulas tentarunt: quomodo nimirum oborta tempestate Capitaneus SEBALT *de* WEERT *à cæteris nauibus dispulsus, postquam plurimis mensibus in freto infinitis ærumnis miserè iactatus fuisset, tandem infecta re post biennium An. 1600. domum reuersus sit.*

ADDITA EST TERTIO

NAVIGATIO RECENS, QVAM 4. NAVIVM PRAEfectus OLEVIER *à* NOORT *proximè suscepit: qui freto Magellanico classe transmisso, triennij spatio vniuersum terræ orbem seu globum mira nauigationis sorte obiuit: annexis illis, quæ in itinere isto singularia as memorabiliora notata sunt.*

Omnia è Germanico Latinitate donata, & insuper elegantissimis figuris æneis coornata editaq; sumptibus

THEODORI *de* BRY *p. m. Viduæ & binorum filiorum.*

FRANCOF. Apud MATTH. BECKERVM. 1602.

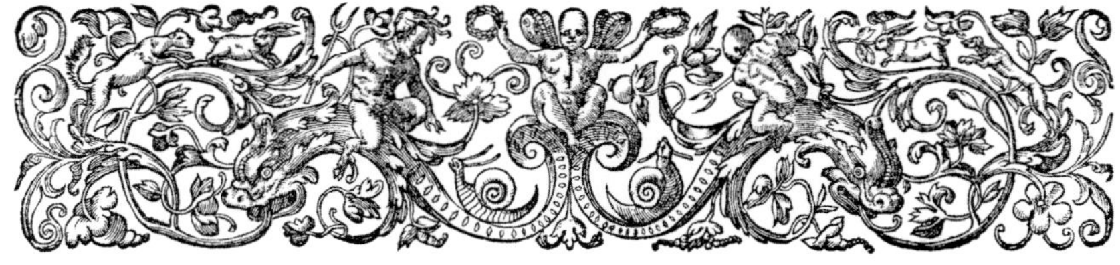

Volume IX

Based on: José de Acosta, *Historia natural y moral de las Indias* (Seville, 1590), and Barent Jansz, *Wijdtloopigh Verhael* (Amsterdam, 1600)

Volume IX of the *America* series features two radically different travel accounts, and it is unclear why the De Brys decided to combine them, other than for practical reasons. The Spanish Jesuit father José de Acosta's canonical treatise on the natural world of the Americas, which brought the author great fame for his so-called "land bridge theory" where he posited that the New World's inhabitants had arrived many thousands of years ago via an overland route from the eastern tip of Asia (thus legitimating the Biblical division of humanity into three groups), was an extremely learned text. The De Brys used the Dutch translation from 1598 by the famous traveller Jan Huyghen van Linschoten, whose own work *Itinerario* had filled the pages of three new *India Orientalis* volumes they published between 1598 and 1600. For the second account, the De Brys used another narrative which had recently been published in Amsterdam, written by the ship's surgeon Barent Jansz, who was part of the first Dutch attempt to circumnavigate the world but which failed to get beyond the Strait of Magellan. In contrast to Acosta's intellectual discussion, Jansz provided readers with mythical tales of Patagonian giants living in Tierra del Fuego.

One obvious similarity between the two accounts was that they both lent themselves very well to graphic illustrations, which is doubtless part of the reason they appealed to the De Brys. Acosta described in great detail the practice of human sacrifice among the Aztecs in Tenochtitlán, present-day Mexico City, and although the De Brys significantly shortened his text, they left these spectacular passages intact, and gratefully used the Jesuit's observations to create 14 completely new designs. None of the previous editions of the *Historia natural y moral de las Indias* had contained images, so the accompanying illustrations in *America* IX were clearly all invented in Frankfurt. The Native Americans the De Brys represented looked similar throughout the series of 14 illustrations,

Frontispiece of volume IX

Pages 416/417
Detail of volume IX, plate 6

despite being associated with completely different provinces in the New World. During the 16 years he spent in the Americas, Acosta travelled extensively from Cartagena de Indias to Peru, and then back north to Mexico. Perhaps it was because he began his travels in the region around Nombre de Dios (Panama) that the Indians in volume IX closely resembled those in volume VIII, which had focused on Drake's raids in the same locale. Indeed the De Brys, in illustrating Acosta's work, even went so far as to depict Incas from Peru alongside Aztecs from Mexico, and all the same in appearance. This practice of conflating various native identities and constructing a homogeneous appearance for the New World without regard for regional differences came to characterise the De Bry collection.

Something similar can be observed when looking at the engravings the De Brys made for the other text in volume IX, Jansz's *Wijdtloopigh Verhael.* In this case, the original account published in 1600 contained several large woodcuts, which the De Brys were very happy to use. But the visual adaptations to this second account in volume IX provide arguably the best example of the meticulous representational strategy of the Frankfurt engravers. Whereas Jansz, or his unnamed illustrator, had represented the Patagonian giants as fearsome creatures, the De Brys turned the power balance upside-down by emphasising the fear the giants experienced when they encountered Dutch sailors carrying firearms. The impression thus given in the De Bry collection was an altogether more reassuring one for European readers than the brutal imagery on display in the original Dutch edition. For this account too the De Brys created several new designs, taking their inspiration from the woodcuts in the Dutch edition. However, as in the case of Acosta's account, they did so without any regard for the diversity of the people across the Atlantic. The De Brys transplanted one of the women from Patagonia to Gabon, where the Dutch had made landfall before crossing the Atlantic. As a result readers could be forgiven for thinking that similar people inhabited the entire world beyond their own European horizon.

America IX constituted the final volume of the series, or at least that is what the De Brys decided since they opted to focus instead on their *India Orientalis* series, which rapidly expanded in the years that followed thanks to the large number of Dutch travel accounts which were published. Their decision to stop producing new volumes for the *America* series was at least partly down to commercial reasons. For every volume in the series established by their father (who had died in March 1598), the De Bry brothers had to share the revenues with their stepmother Katharina Rölinger, with whom they had a difficult relationship. Only after her death in 1610, and the death of her second husband Paul Raab in 1616, did Johan Theodore resume the *America* series, for which he then produced another four volumes. But the selection of sources he and his son-in-law Matthaeus Merian made for volumes X to XIII, published between 1618 and 1634, also reveals that new and interesting travel accounts were not available in the same numbers as they were for Asia. Despite the inclusion of voyages by Amerigo Vespucci and the Englishmen Ralph Hamor and John Smith, the final four volumes did not match the quality of the first series of nine. According to the inventories of private libraries in the 17th century, it is clear that many readers of the time possessed only the first nine volumes.

Detail of volume IX, plate 8

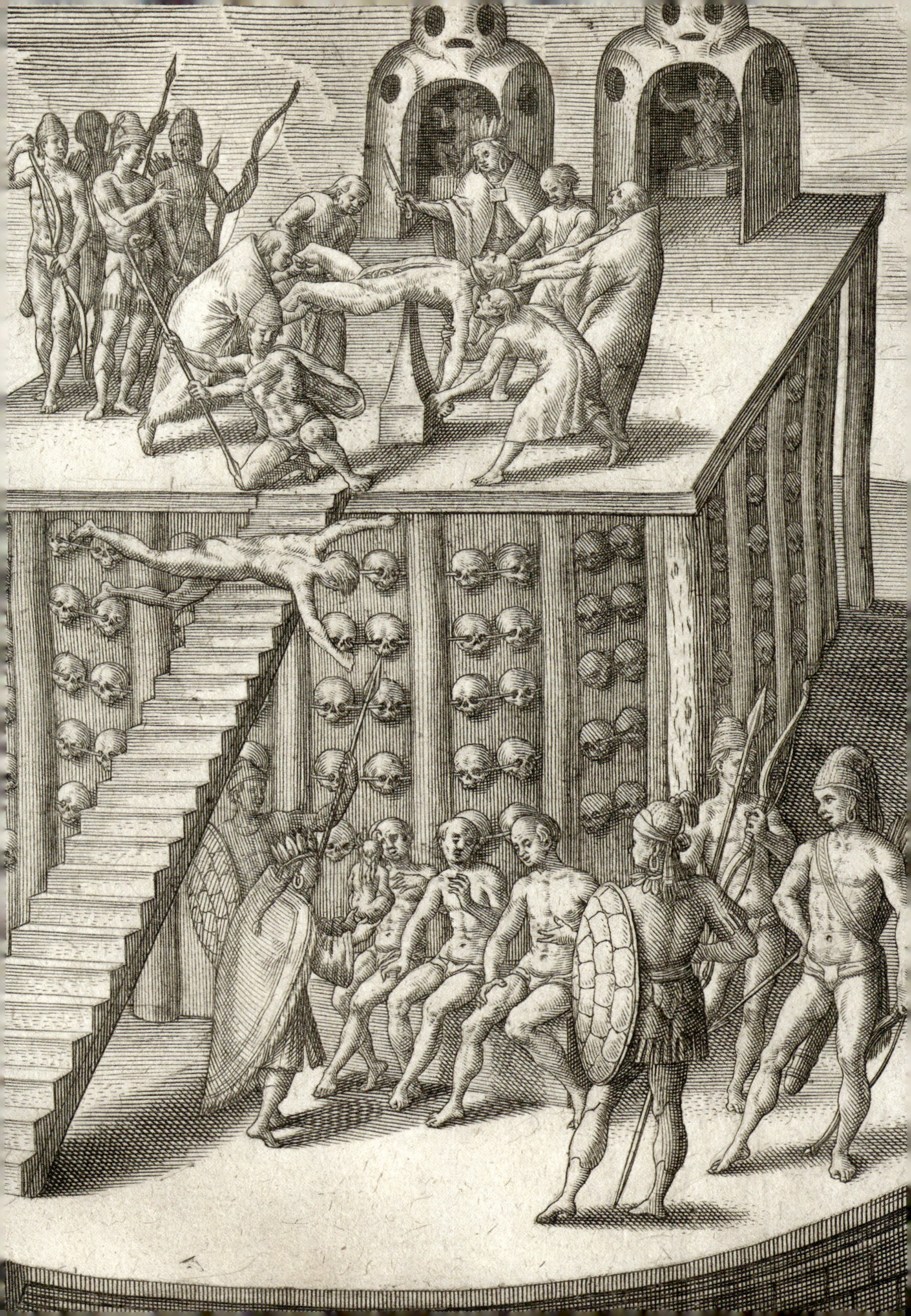

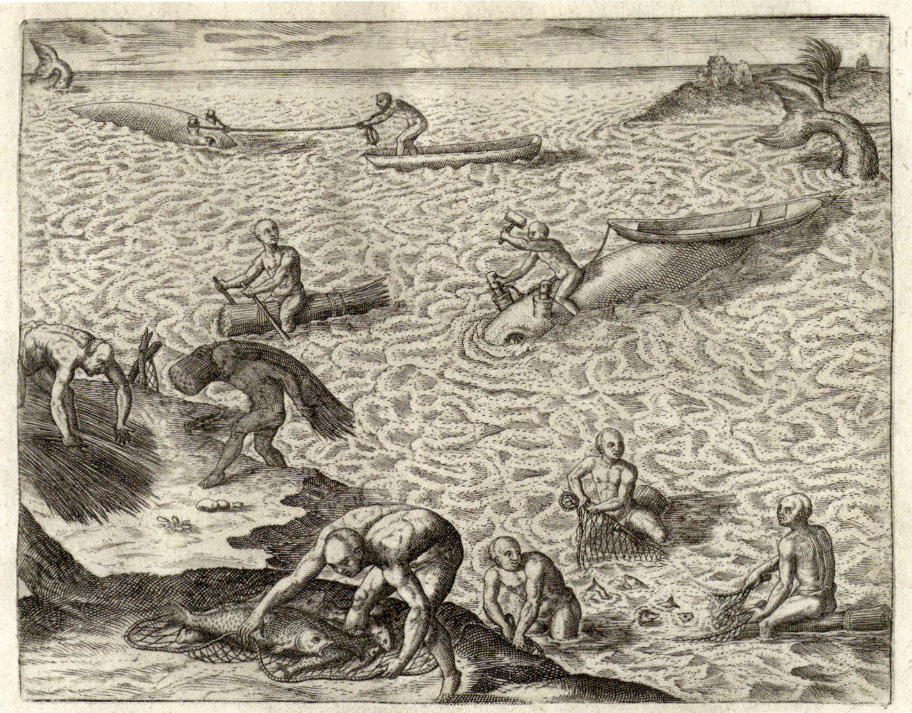

PLATE 1

Concerning the marvellous way in which the Indians catch fish

When the Indians go fishing, they usually do it in the following way: intending to attack large whales, they row to sea, each of them having taken a seat in his own boat. If an Indian spots a big fish coming into view, he rapidly approaches it in his boat, jumps on its back, and lets down two wooden poles which have been readied for this reason into the whale's nostrils, or rather its ears, from which the fish occasionally spouts water it has imbibed. Although the fish disappears under the water's surface every so often and then re-emerges, the fisherman, undaunted, remains on its back, pushing the poles further into these holes. Then he returns to his boat, and tows the fish by means of a rope which earlier he has tied to one of the poles. When the fish is tired and weakened for lack of fresh air, which it sucks into its nostrils, the fisherman drags it from the water on to the shore. Then they cut the fish into pieces and divide it equally. Yet they also practise a method of fishing which is more straightforward, simply by casting nets. They tie together many rushes and then sit on them as if on horseback, rowing everywhere they want by using wooden oars. Unaware of good fishing spots, they keep casting their nets until they catch enough fish. Having caught them they return to land, take their boats out of the water or spread out the rushes to dry.

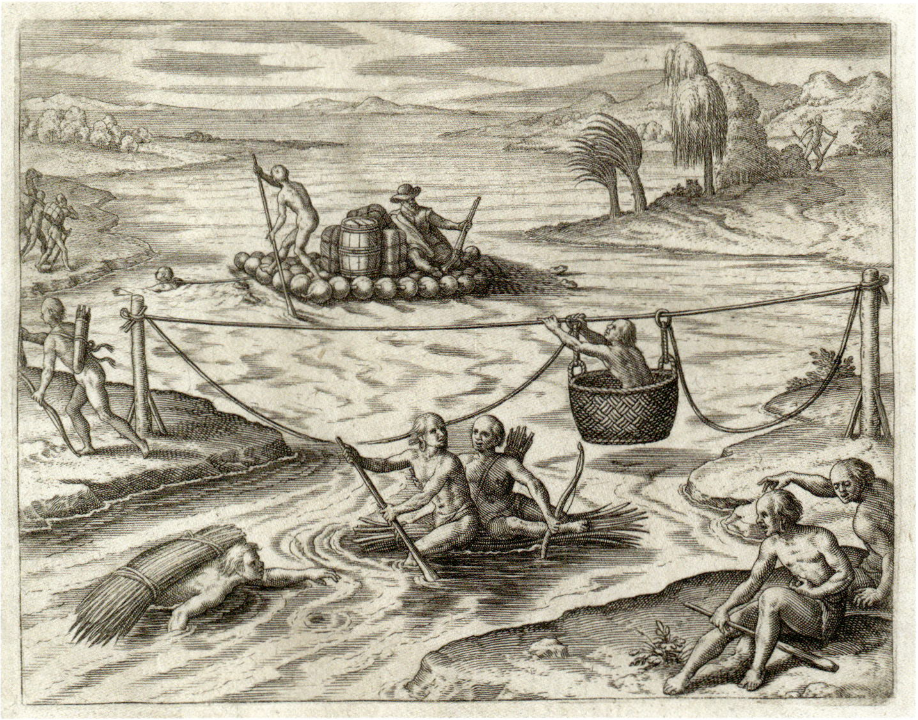

PLATE 2

The way the Indians cross the river without boats or bridges

In the Indies there are a large number of rivers or streams that are much wider than those in Europe. They lack bridges, however, and do not know how to make boats, and use the following constructions in different places. They fasten a rope to two poles on either side of the stream, and attach it to a basket in which the person who desires to cross the river takes their place. He pulls himself to the other side. People who have difficulty crossing the river this way are put on a raft of plaited rushes, rowing it with wooden poles. Still others make a structure of dried squashes which have been tied together. Thus they transport both people and goods across the stream, as is clearly described in the account.

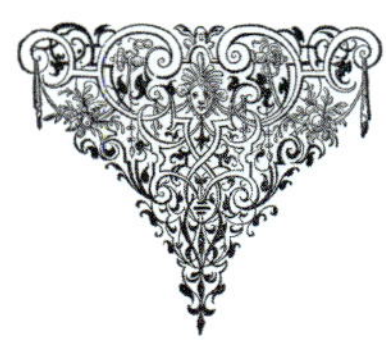

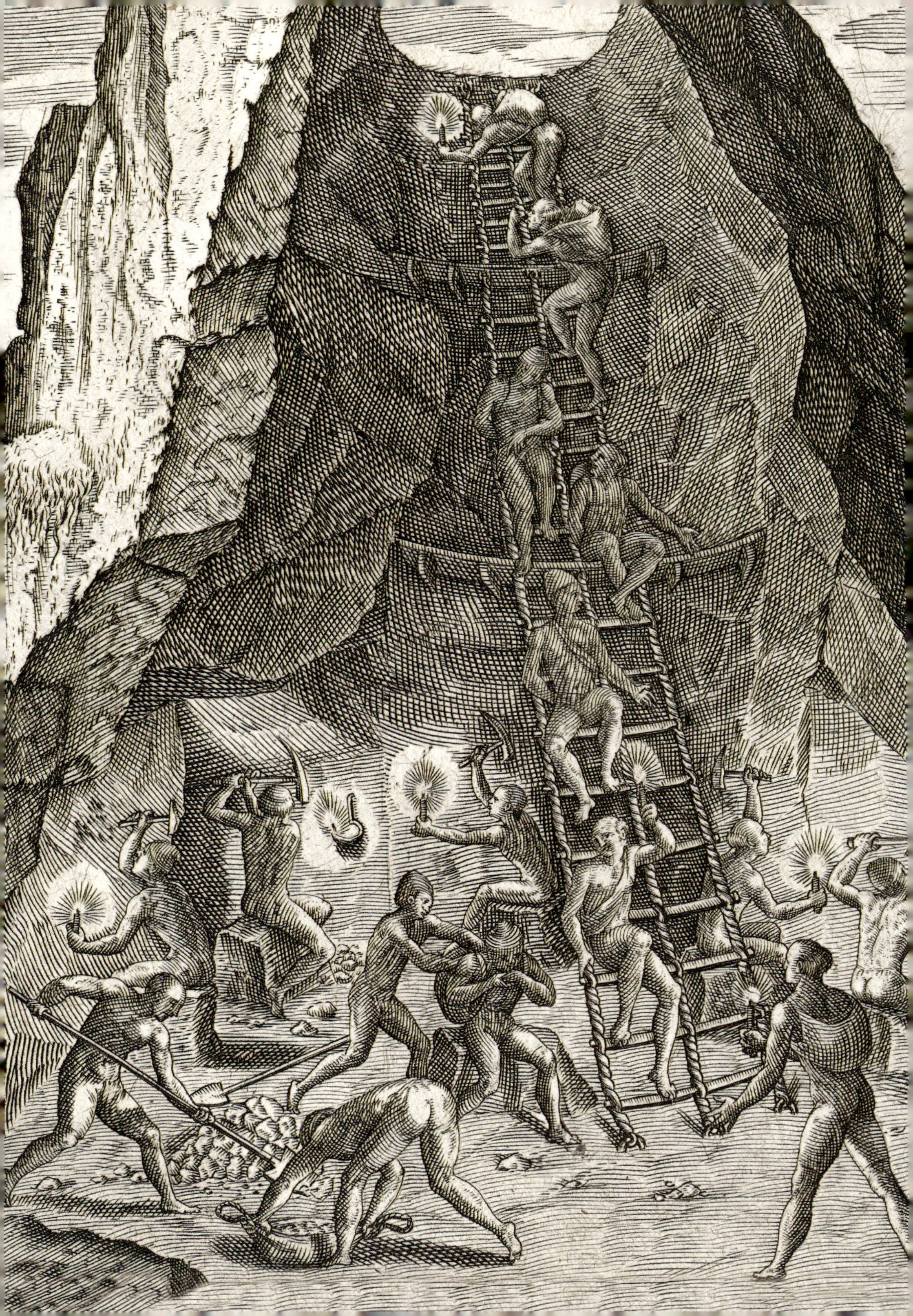

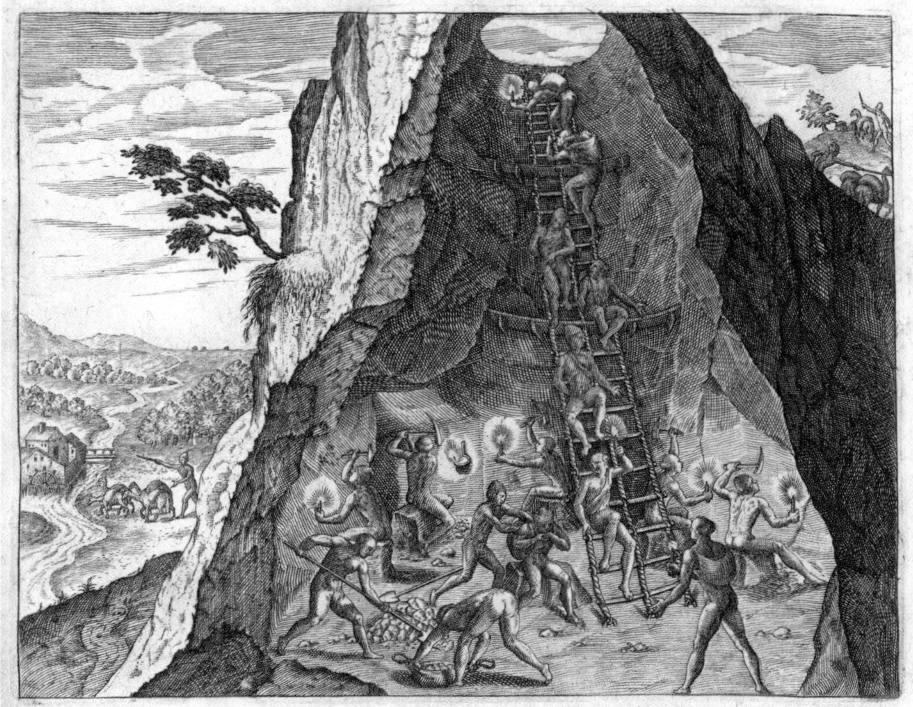

PLATE 3

The way in which the Indians extract gold from the mountains

The Indians dig gold from the mountains of Potosí, which are the richest in the entire Indies, in very much the same way as we do in our regions. They divide the labourers into two groups, those who work during the day and those who work at night. The latter group rests during the daytime. They do not see daylight while working and generally need to light candles, working more than 150 fathoms below the earth's surface. Yet despite the enormous depth of the mines, they are still required to carry the gold which they have dug up to the surface on their back. They use ladders and two are always tied together for this purpose. The ladders are made of leather strips, which are twisted and then strengthened by wooden poles which are placed horizontally, so that three men can ascend on one side, while three descend on the other side. As the challenge of climbing forces them to hold on to the ladders with both hands, the first climber has a candle attached to his thumb. In addition benches have been constructed halfway because the climb is too long to complete at once. Here they can put down their loads for a while.

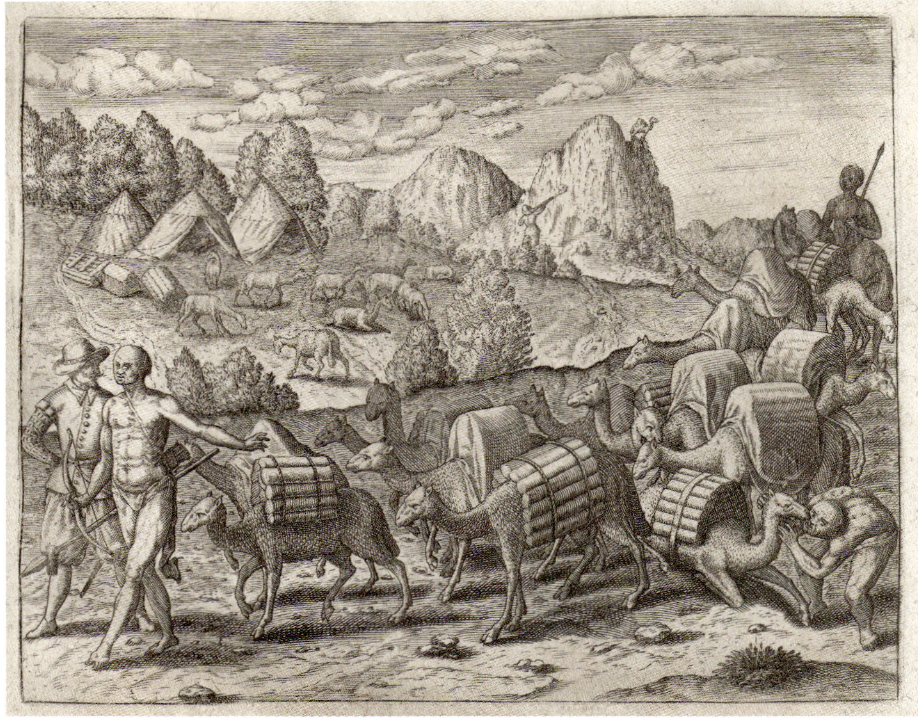

PLATE 4

About the Indians' sheep which carry precious metals from the mountains

The region of Peru has a special kind of sheep, which the Indians call llamas. Their meat serves as food, and their wool is good for making cloth, but their utility is particularly striking in carrying big loads just like horses or donkeys. The Indians load everything on to these sheep which they want to transport outside of their region. They carry silver from the mines of Potosí to Arica, 70 miles away. They go in herds, 300 or 400 having been driven together into a single group, which requires only a few humans to herd them. In one day, they usually walk four miles. These animals are very cheap for their owners, because they do not require saddles, horseshoes or other equipment, and feed themselves with what they find along the road. But those who accompany them need to make sure they do not offend them, because if one of them refuses to go on and lies on the ground, nothing can make it move along again unless one of the attendants lies down too, and coaxes it back into action with nice words for two or even three hours before the animal rises and continues the journey. If one of them accidentally wanders off in the mountains, there is no other way to make them return than to fire a shot which bewilders the animals and makes them want to return to the herd.

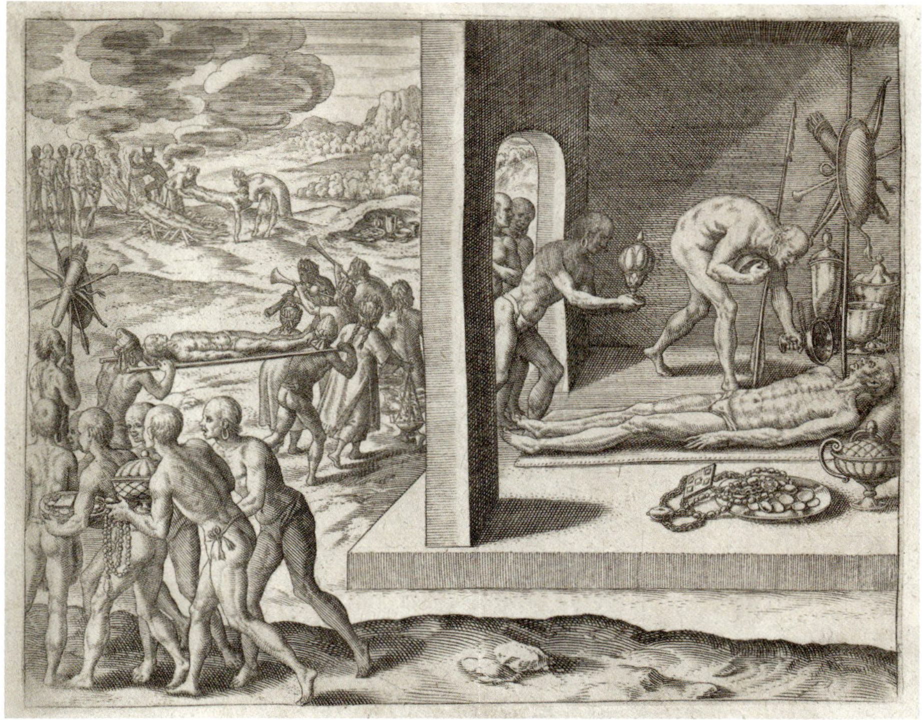

PLATE 5

Concerning a peculiar habit of the Mexicans when they bury their dead

In the account a peculiar superstition of the Mexicans when they bury their dead is described as follows: when one of their leaders has died, his body is put down flat on his back on the bedroom floor. All his friends and relatives are invited to say their goodbyes. They enter the house in a long line, and bring many important gifts. If he has been a brave and strong man during his lifetime, all his weapons are put on display around him. When he has been lying in this position for some time, and the time of the funeral has arrived, priests carry him in a solemn procession to his grave. The first group is comprised of a number of men who make a sad sound with their flutes and other instruments. Behind them follow priests carrying incense, and then the body is carried to the grave. Then come the weapons of the deceased, and finally, one by one, the gifts, carried by slaves, to be burned with the body because they were of value to the deceased and may be of use to him in the next world. Having arrived at the designated funeral place, the body is laid down solemnly on a pile of wood which is then set on fire, as are all the things that have been given to him. A priest carefully tends the fire, dressed in a garment which is decorated with a hideous depiction of the Devil, while everything goes up in flames. Then they carefully collect the ashes in a vase, and inter it together with the remaining gifts and weapons of the dead man. This concludes the funeral.

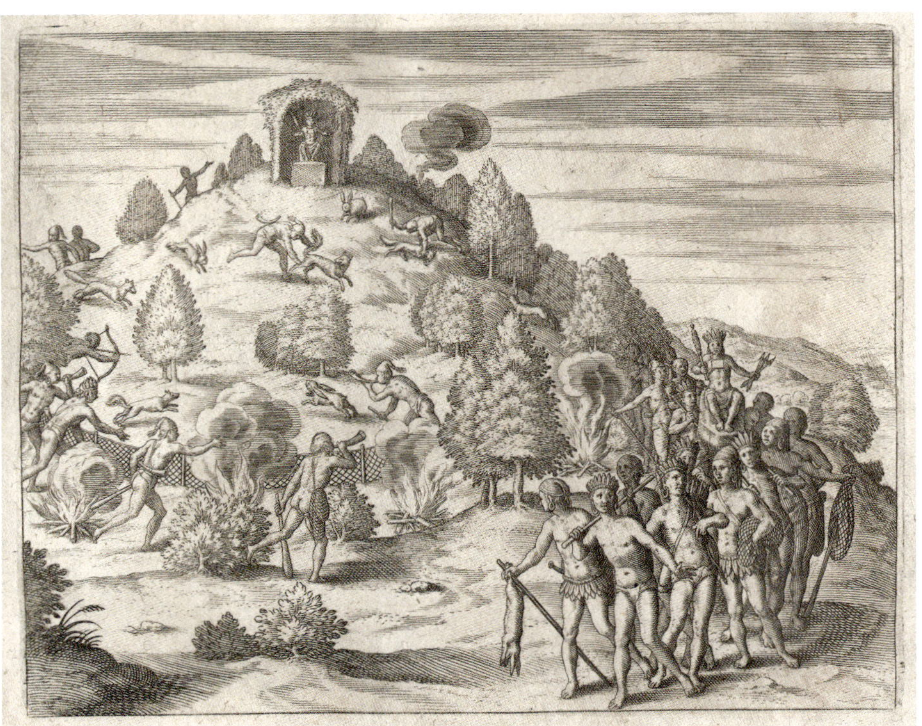

PLATE 6

The way in which the Indians hunt

The Mexicans use the following strategy for catching game: at daybreak, they go around the community playing the flute or the trumpet. When the hunters hear this, they gather with their bows, arrows, nets and everything else they need for hunting. They then take their idol and quickly, spurred on by the loud music, climb the mountain which has been marked as their hunting ground. At the top they have built a small temple, and in it an altar on which they place their idol with great care. Then they descend and close off the foot of the mountain by spreading nets, and they drive the game from the shrubs and bushes by lighting fires and chasing them out. When the animals have come to the top of the mountain, they beat or pierce them to death, whatever they prefer. Having done this, they carry their idol back on their shoulders and return home in a group with the hares, rabbits, foxes and so on they have caught. After the idol has been placed back in its former temple, they sacrifice the hearts of the most important animals. This is the way they conclude the hunt.

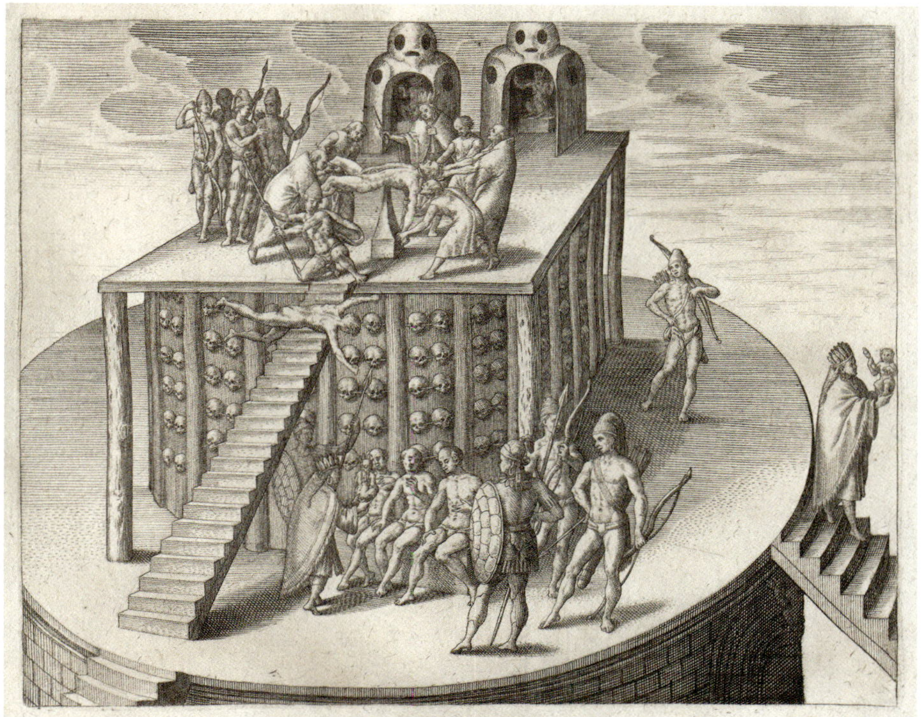

PLATE 8

How the Mexican Indians sacrifice men

A Mexican sacrificial temple as described in the account is depicted here. During a special annual ceremony they bring together all their enemies whom they have captured in war, and lead them to a round temple furnished with heads that have been cut off and placed in rows. Then a priest emerges from the right of the hill, dressed in a chasuble, with the idol in his hands. After having performed some rituals, he goes and looks at the condemned men, and holds the idol before each and every one of them, saying: "Look, this god is yours!" Having done that, he goes down the stairs again. Then the condemned men are led up another flight of stairs, closely following each other. There the priests who are going to make the sacrifices emerge, six of them in a row. When the accused have performed the ritual with the idol, with weak knees, each of them is grabbed by their arms and feet with great swiftness by four priests. A fifth priest places a wooden shackle around their neck. Then they lift up the unfortunate man and break his back by crushing him on a stone lying on the ground. Finally the high priest jumps at him and rips open his chest, tearing out the still beating heart. He shows the heart to the sun, and throws it in the idol's face. They then let the body roll down the stairs, and the man who killed the condemned runs towards it and carries the corpse home, roasts it, and eats it with friends who have been invited to the ceremony, and is merry. The others await the same fate.

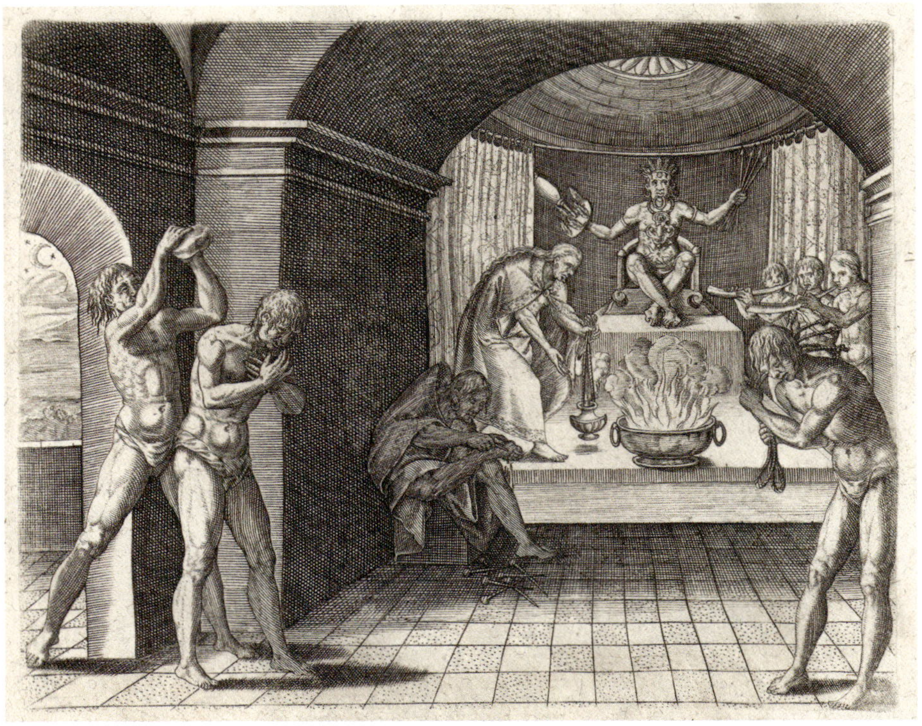

PLATE 7

How the Indian priests do penance for the sins of their people

On certain fixed and special days, Mexican priests make sacrifices to their idol Vitzliputzli. When one of these days is coming up, they go to the idol in a group and play for him on their trumpets, flutes and other instruments. Immediately thereafter the high priest enters with a thurible containing incense. From a vase which stands in front of the idol and where a flame is eternally burning, he takes some fire, lights the incense and covers the idol with smoke. Then he retires to a special room in the temple, takes a spear (of which several have been fastened to the various walls of the chapel) and pierces his leg. He catches the blood to smear it on his forehead. The spear, which he dips in the blood, he hangs in a special place for all to see, so that everyone realises the severe penance he has done for their sins. There are also times during the year when the people flog themselves, and wound their bodies either with ropes or with stones, as can be seen in this image and in the account more generally.

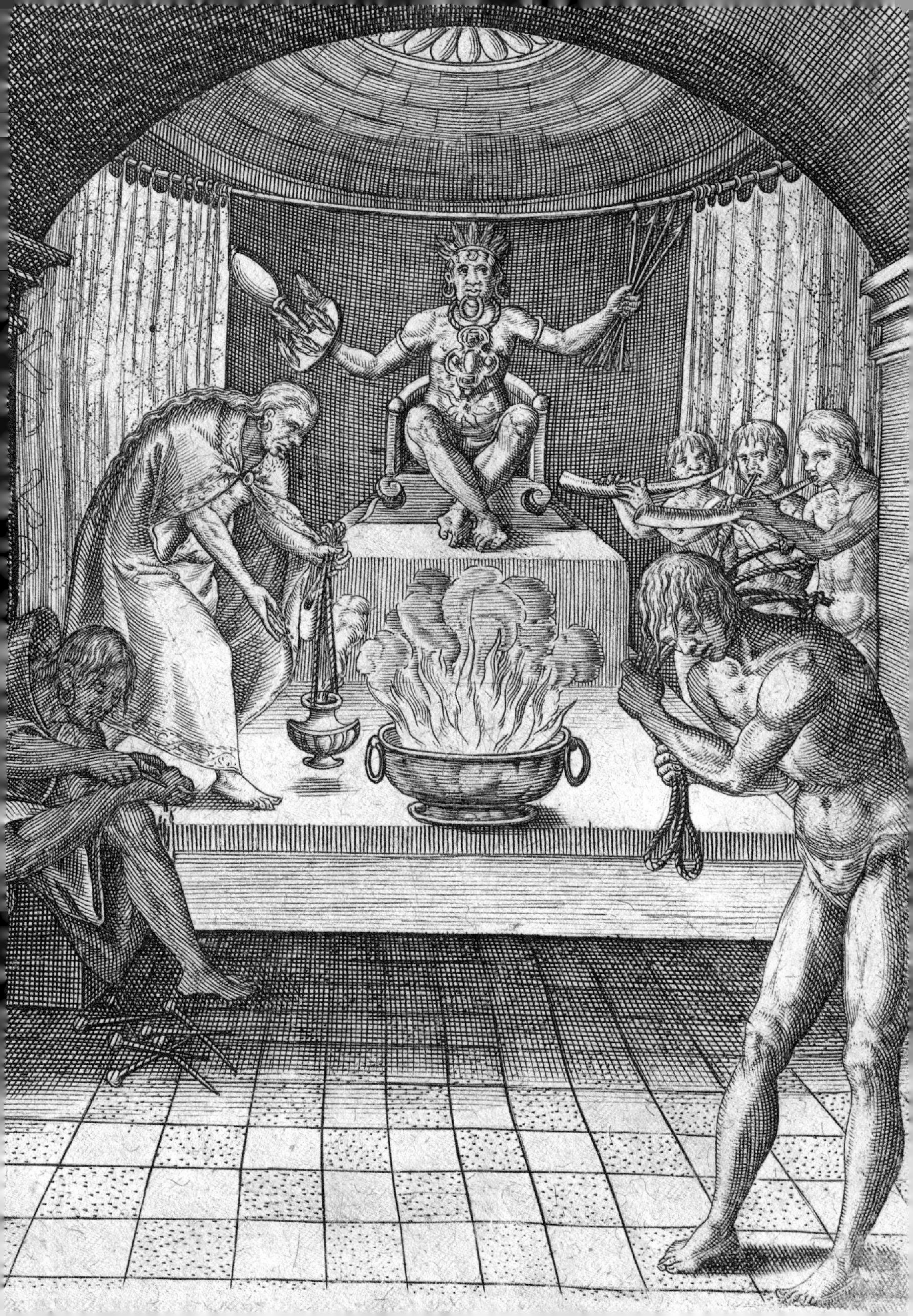

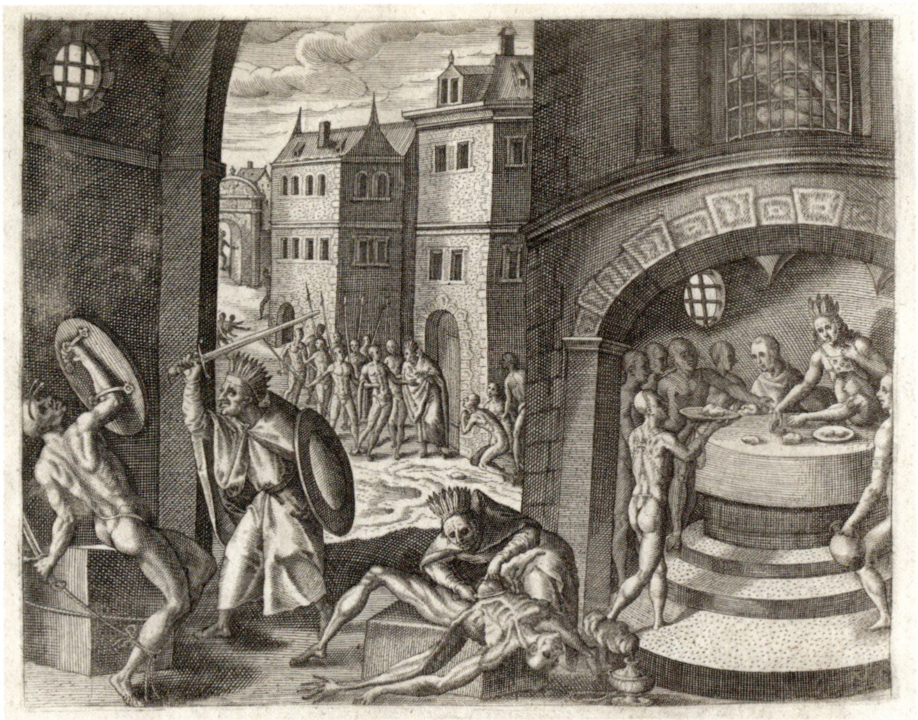

PLATE 9

Another ritual of sacrifice of the Indians

The Mexicans have yet another annual ceremony of sacrificing or slaughtering men. They choose a prisoner of war or slave and lock him up in one of the most lavish and splendid of all rooms in the temple. They dress him in the most beautiful clothes and attire of their idol, let him enjoy the most delicious food, and have him waited upon by the highest and most revered gentlemen. At night, however, he is locked in a big case to make sure he cannot escape. At daybreak he is released, and free to go where he pleases, but he is heavily guarded by a number of men who follow him closely. When he is walking in the streets, people who encounter him step to one side and worship him by kneeling before him. He holds a piece of reed in his hand to warn those who do not recognise him to get out of the way. For one whole year he is free to do as he likes, but when this period comes to an end, a special feast is organised where he is tied by one foot to a stone, given a sword and shield, and ordered to fight a man who is directed to kill him. Should he win the fight, he is set free, and is celebrated as a leader for the remainder of his years. If he loses to the sacrificial priest, he is skinned alive on a stone. His skin, which is torn off, is carried around from house to house by the priests, in every direction, who collect gifts for the maintenance of their idol.

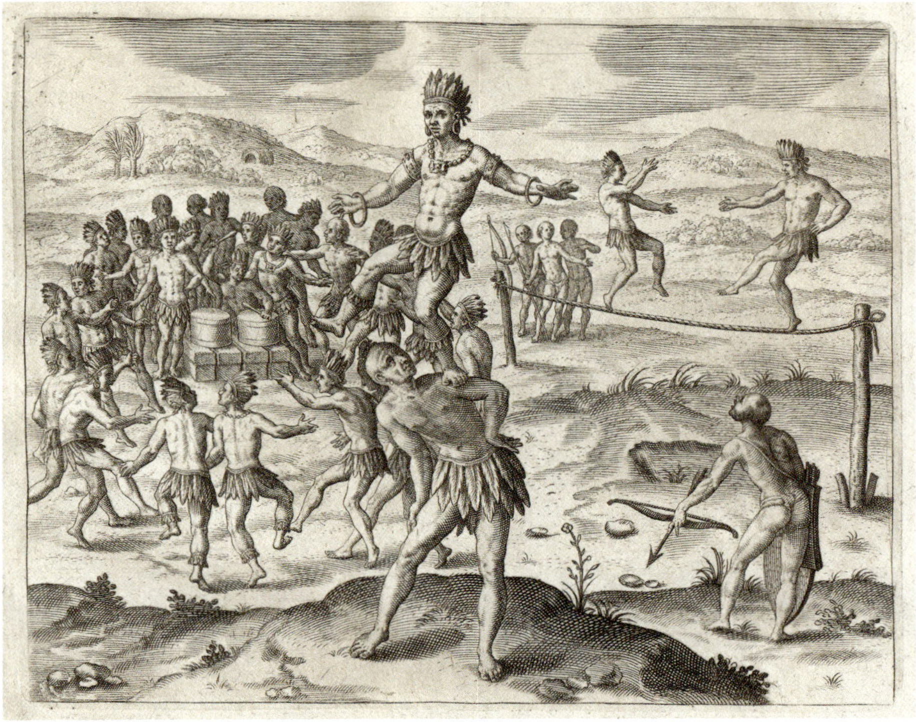

PLATE 11

About the various dances and acrobatics which the Indians do

In New Spain, especially in Mexico, the Indians perform a number of different dances in which they take great joy. Some dance on a rope stretched between two poles. Others dance while standing on each other's shoulders. But they also group together in orderly fashion and perform a dance. The instruments which make the sound they dance to look like our tambourines, and often singers join in. The dancers are continually in tune with the tambourines and the singing, moving their feet to the rhythm. From the account, it may be understood how enjoyable it is to witness this spectacle.

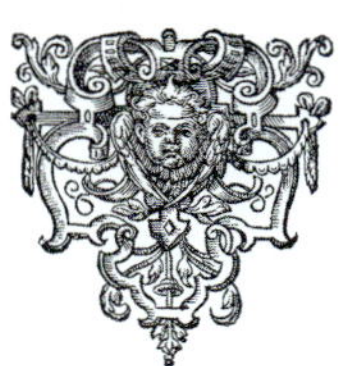

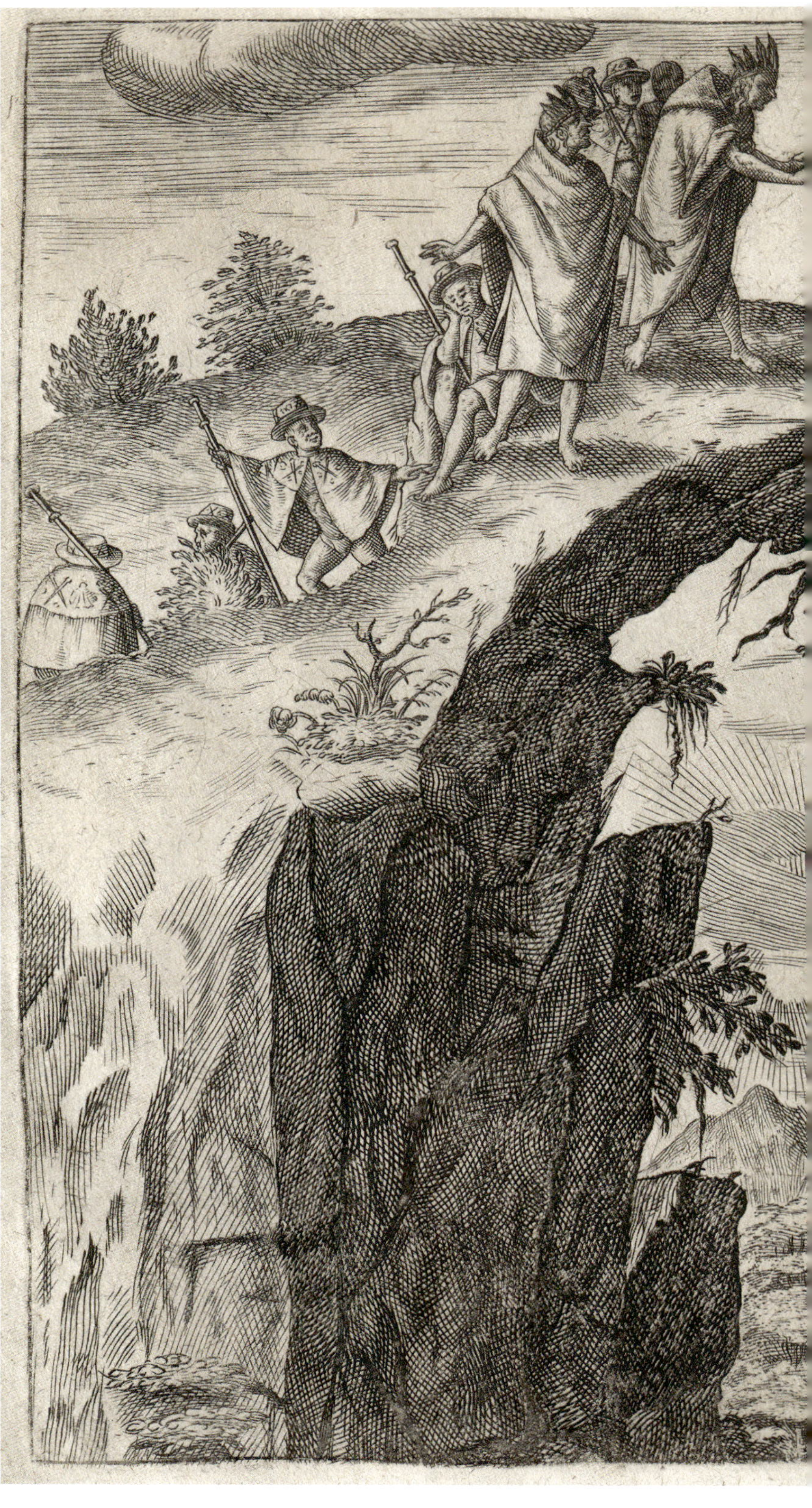

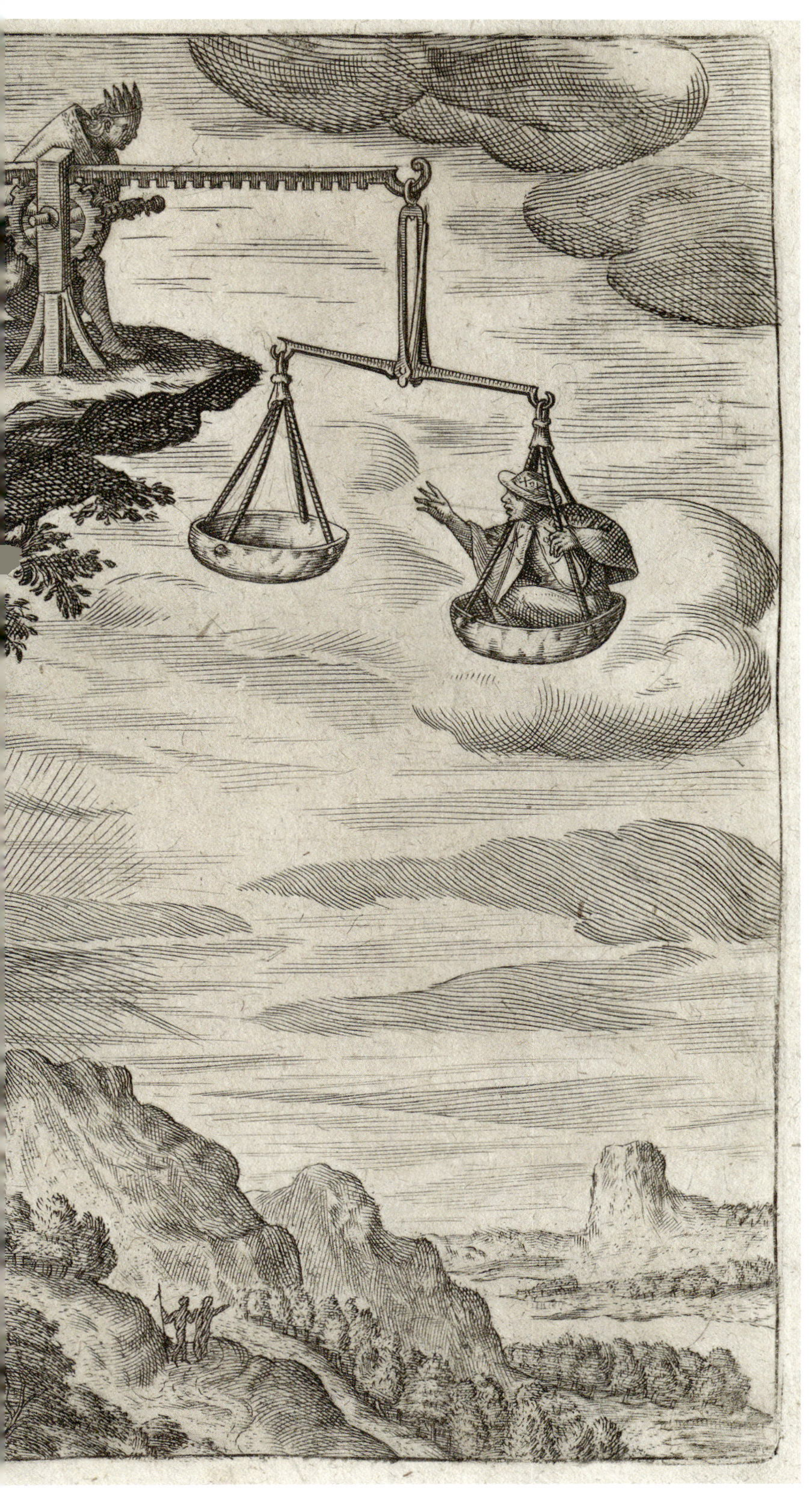

PLATE 10, PAGES 434/435

Concerning the miraculous way in which they confess

Among the other memorable tales in this account is the strange way in which the Japanese confess their sins. The area of Osaka is known for its steep and very high mountains and rocks, some of which rise up 200 fathoms. One of these is a rock which projects very far in comparison to the others. Strangers, whom they call Xamabuxis, become afraid and tremble when they observe it from afar. From the hanging summits of these mountains an iron pole is projected, which has been made in such a way that it can be drawn back and forth with a rope. At the end of the pole is a big scale. When a Xamabuxis sits down in the furthest scale to confess his sins, it is turned into the open air and pushed away from the mountain. The empty scale goes up, while the loaded scale goes down. Meanwhile the sinner is urged by the Goquis (priests who are disguised as devils) to confess, and if he does the empty scale is lowered to the extent that it is on an equal level with the loaded one. When that point has been reached, the pole is pulled back and the penitent is set free while another man is ready to take his place. If one of the sinners happens to conceal his sins, the scale is shaken so vehemently that even before he falls to the bottom of the ravine, he is already inanimate, torn and shattered into many small pieces.

PLATE 12

How the Mexicans were originally charmed by their false god or idol

This image depicts the way in which the Mexicans originally passed through desolate regions until, according to what their idol Vitzliputzli had predicted, they reached the place where the tree Tunal stood, rising from a single rock. An eagle with a very tiny bird in its talons was sitting at the top of this tree when they arrived, which they accepted as a good omen. Catching sight of the bird, they knelt down and worshipped it. Meanwhile they erected a wooden building on that very spot in honour of their idol, which ultimately developed into the city of Mexico. The amount of taxes the Mexicans have to pay to their king Azcapuzalco is specified every year. When a long time ago he considered expelling the Mexicans from the area, he decided to tax them so heavily that they would not be able to pay him. But their idol Vitzliputzli quite easily solved the matter. The taxes consisted of a garden which was filled with maize and also peas. There were also storks who had built nests in the garden, and geese who had settled there with their young. Everything that had been born and bred there, below and above the waterline, was taken to the king.

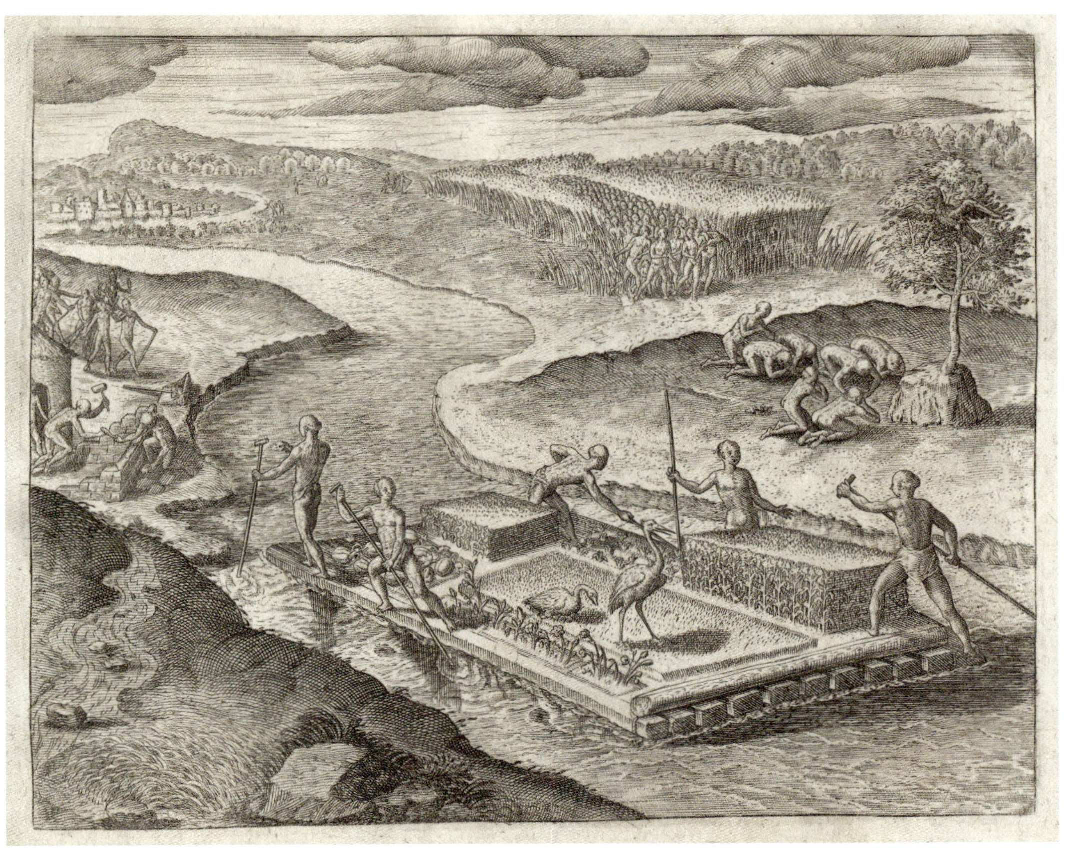

PLATE 13

How the Mexicans, challenged to war, have conquered and coerced the Cuyoacanos

When the other native people in the region saw that the Mexican Indians increased in number and stature, they made plans to expel them by force. They abused the Mexican women, for example, who visited their regions and markets, with insults. The Cuyoacanos had a different strategy when the Mexicans did not let themselves be provoked in this fashion. They invited the most prominent among the Mexicans to some ceremony as guests of honour. When they had entertained them for a considerable time with song and dance, they forced them to wear women's clothes and sent them home in this disgraceful manner (supposedly because they were feminine men who did not have the courage to fight). The Mexicans became very angry at this, swiftly assembled their soldiers and attacked the Cuyoacanos with great force, occupying the town of Cuyoaca and persecuting their enemies for 10 miles around in such a manner that ultimately they were forced to surrender to the Mexicans.

PLATE 14, PAGES 440/441

About the miraculous steadfastness of a Mexican prisoner

Montezuma, the first emperor, waged war against the inhabitants of Chalco when his own brother, together with many others, was captured in a fight. When the inhabitants of Chalco realised that their prisoner was the brother of Montezuma, and moreover a brave fighter, they called him to them and announced him to be their king, because Chalco was not ruled by a king until then. When they disclosed their plan to him, he refused at first. But when they persisted and he understood that they would continue to urge him, and with him being a prisoner, he had to accept their offer. He then ordered a platform to be set up on top of a stout pole, where he would accept his new position and give orders to the entire population of Chalco. They obeyed him because they thought he was preparing to organise a splendid acceptance ceremony. But when he had summoned all the Mexican prisoners, after having ascended to the platform, he announced that the inhabitants of Chalco had chosen him as their king. He would show them loyalty to his own origins by expressing his desire to be torn to pieces rather than be disloyal to his native country. Then he threw himself on the ground, and was cut to pieces by the locals. The inhabitants of Chalco, extremely angry at this, killed all the other Mexican prisoners in a very miserable way.

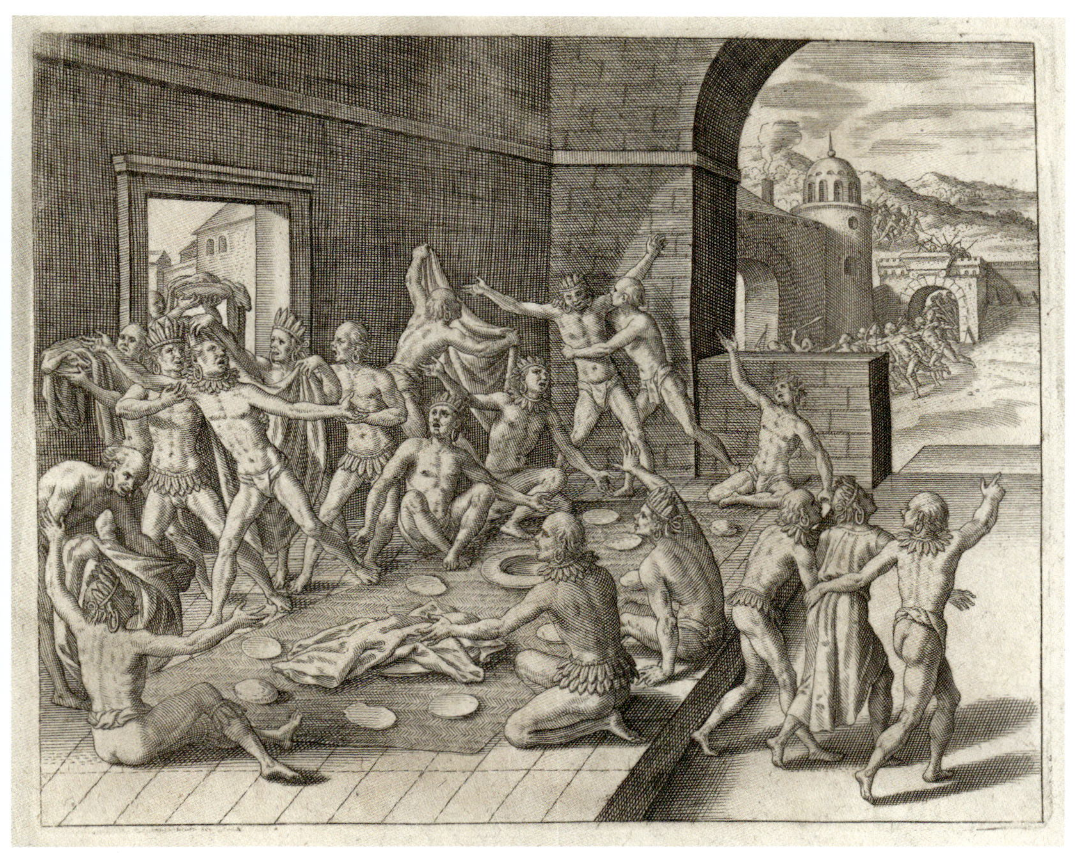

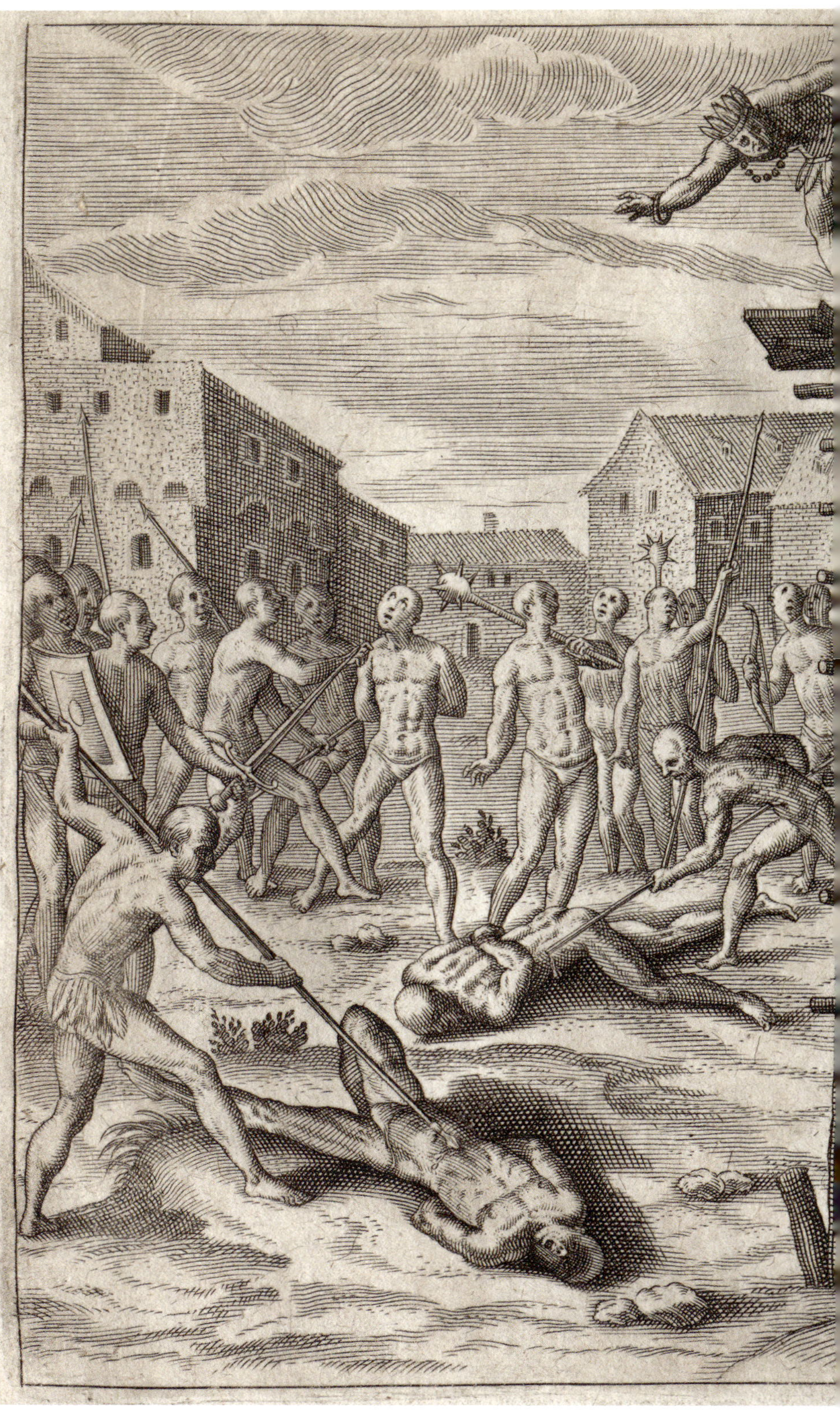

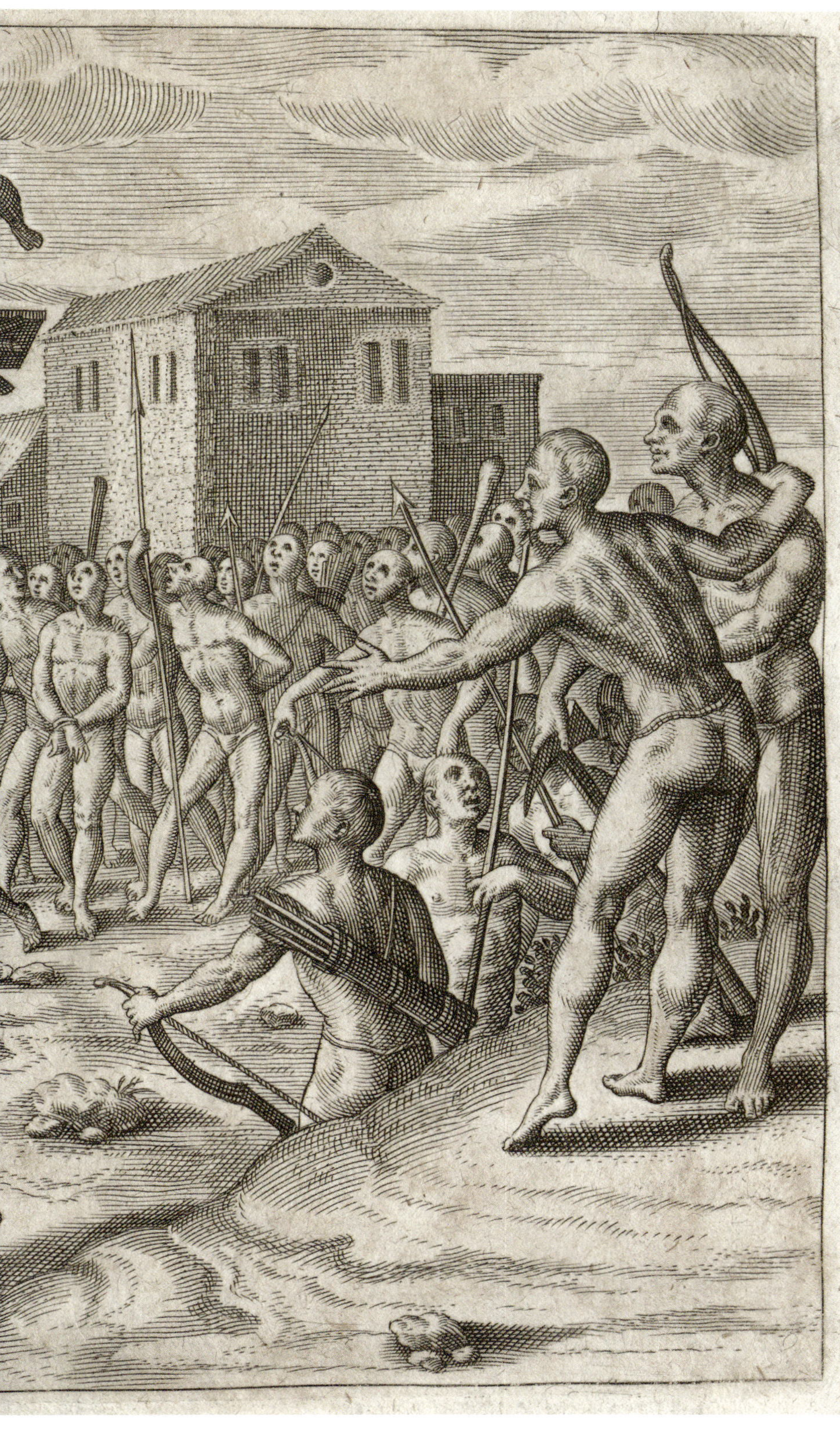

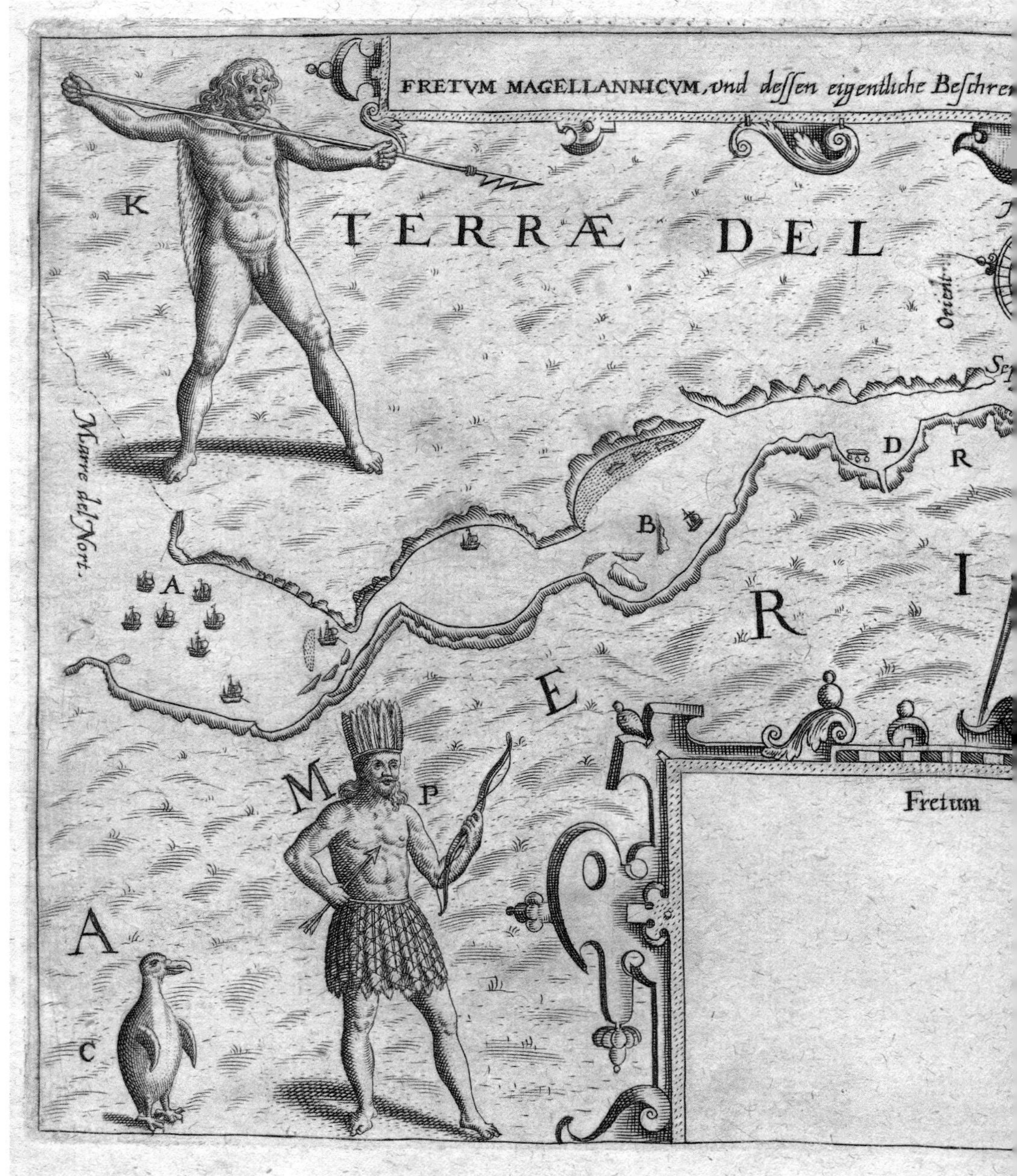
FRETVM MAGELLANNICVM, vnd dessen eigentliche Beschre
TERRÆ DEL
R
I
E
M
A
K
A
B
D
R
P
C
Marre del Nort.
Fretum

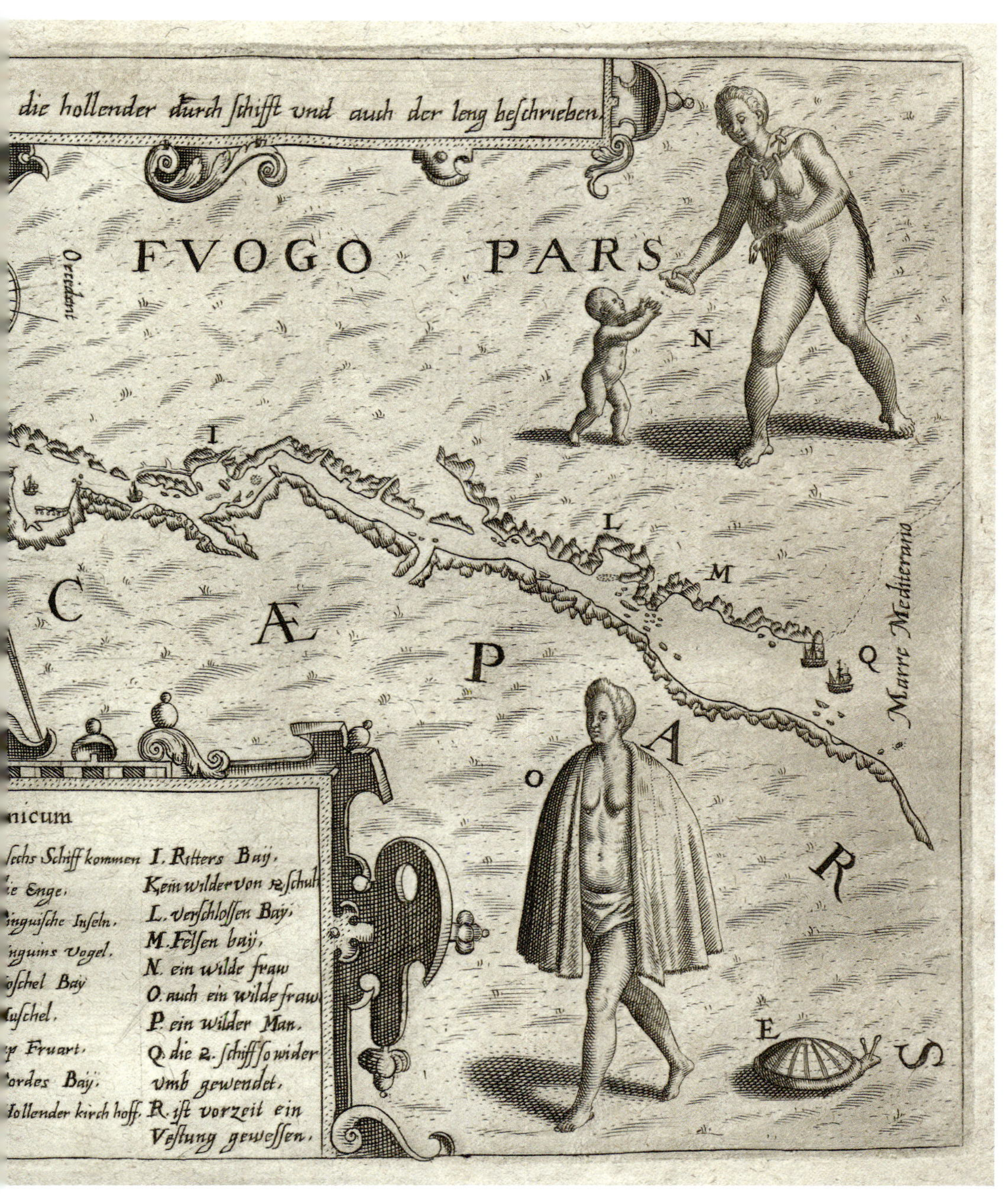

Map depicting the Strait of Magellan, which separates Tierra del Fuego from mainland South America

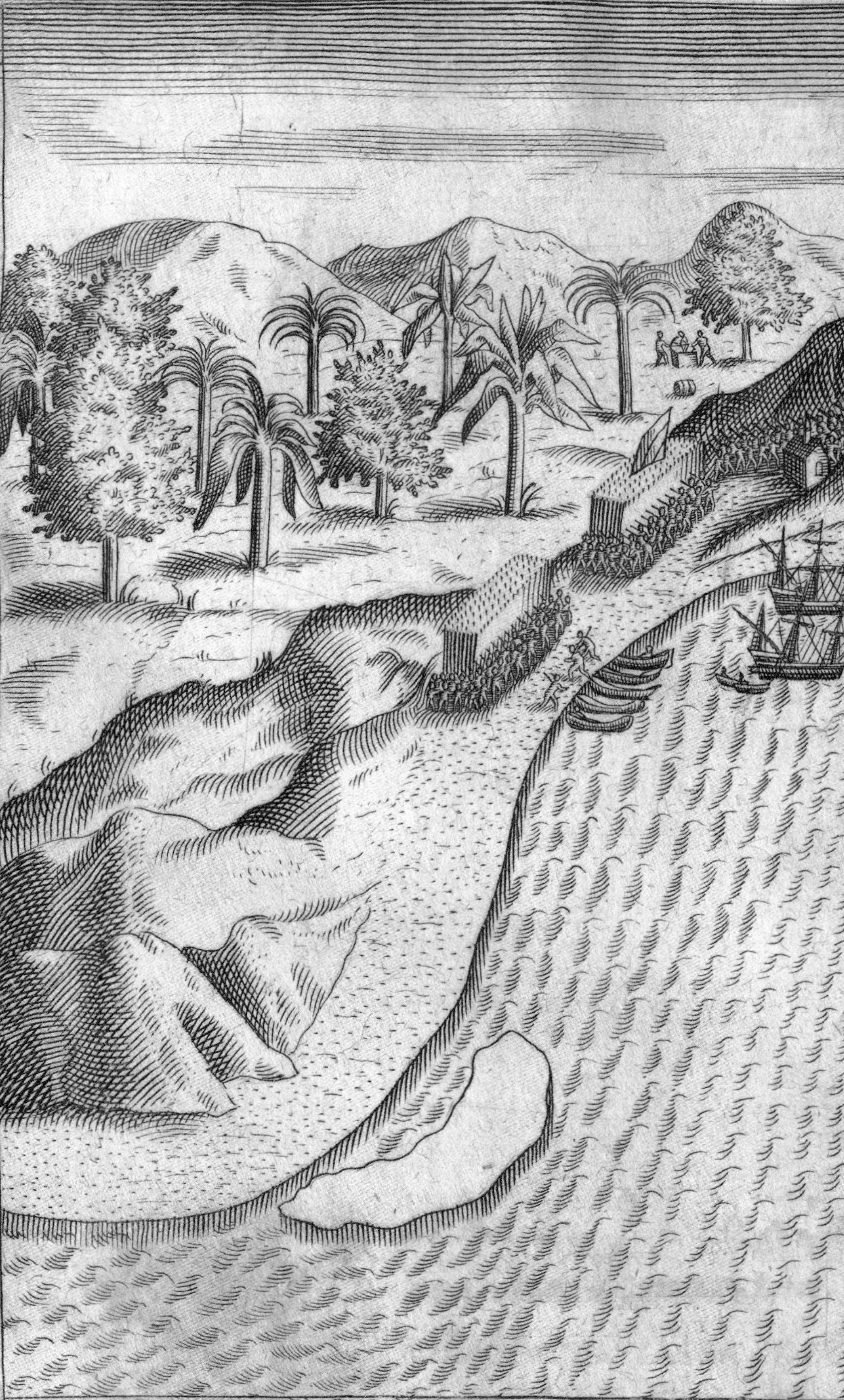

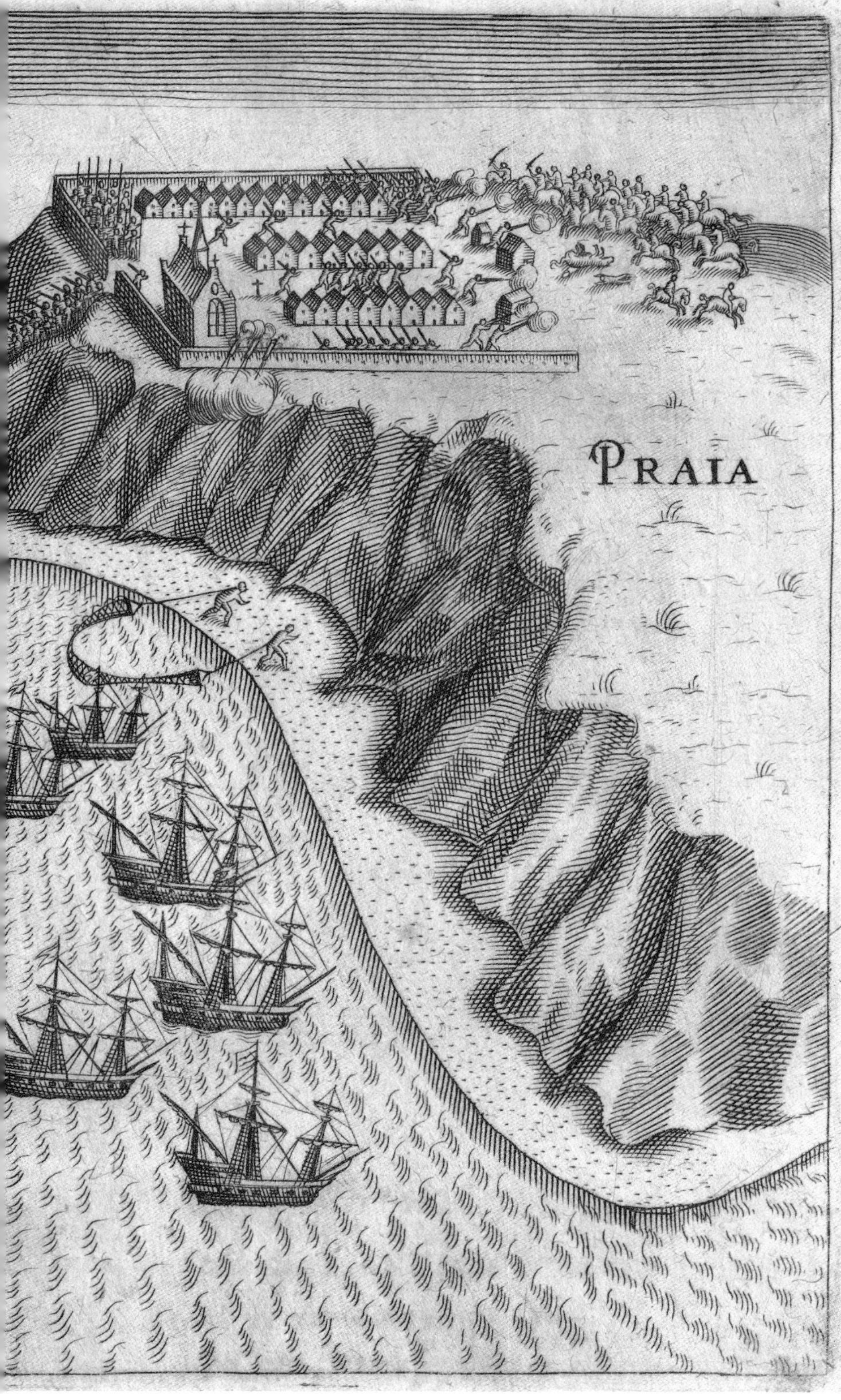
PRAIA

NOW SOME PICTURES AND REPRESENTATIONS OF THE TOWNS, FORTS, STORIES AND PEOPLES ENCOUNTERED BY THE DUTCH WHILE FOLLOWING THE ROUTE OF MAGELLAN BETWEEN 1595 AND 1599

PLATE 15, PAGES 444/445

An accurate depiction of Fort Praia

This is the island St Iago, where Fort Praia is located. It is controlled by the Portuguese and has a Spanish governor. It is built high up on the side of a cliff facing the water, and secured by a protective wall. The way up is very high – 175 steps by foot – and so narrow that six men at the top could fend off 1,000 trying to come up from below. The Dutch, moreover, found three cannons where the Portuguese had hidden them in a field. The Dutch really thought they had found something good here, but the Portuguese had lured them there with empty promises of other spoils. This gave them enough time to flee the fort, which the Dutch then seized without resistance. The Dutch also eventually left.

PLATE 16

A true representation of St Iago

This is an accurate depiction of St Iago, which the Portuguese held with cannons and manpower. It is furnished with good parapets on both the water- and land-facing sides. The town is two miles away from Fort Praia. The Portuguese tried to lure the Dutch away from Praia by appearing as if they would co-operate. The Dutch felt betrayed, however, when they arrived at St Iago with two ships. The Portuguese received them quite insolently: they were not only waiting for the Dutch on the coast fully armed, but they had prepared their cannons as well. When the Dutch saw this, they decided against landing there, since they did not have as much manpower as they would have needed.

PLATE 17, PAGES 448/449

What the Dutch encountered on the island of Brava, and how their admiral died

The Dutch sailed from St Iago to the island of Brava, which is distinguished by a high mountain. When they arrived, they tried to buy provisions from the Portuguese on the island, but they apologised, saying they had nothing for the Dutch, and went on their way. The Dutch continued searching until they came upon some ruined huts that were empty. One, however, had its doorway blocked with stones, which when they cleared it revealed itself to be full of corn or "Turkish grain". The Dutch brought all of this back to their ship. Their highest-ranking admiral, Jacob Mahu, died on this island. His body was placed in a coffin, which was then weighted down with rocks so that it would sink better. The coffin was carried by other men of rank on to the ship and allowed to fall over the side, where it sank. Three hours later Daniel Resteau also died, and he was buried at sea as well.

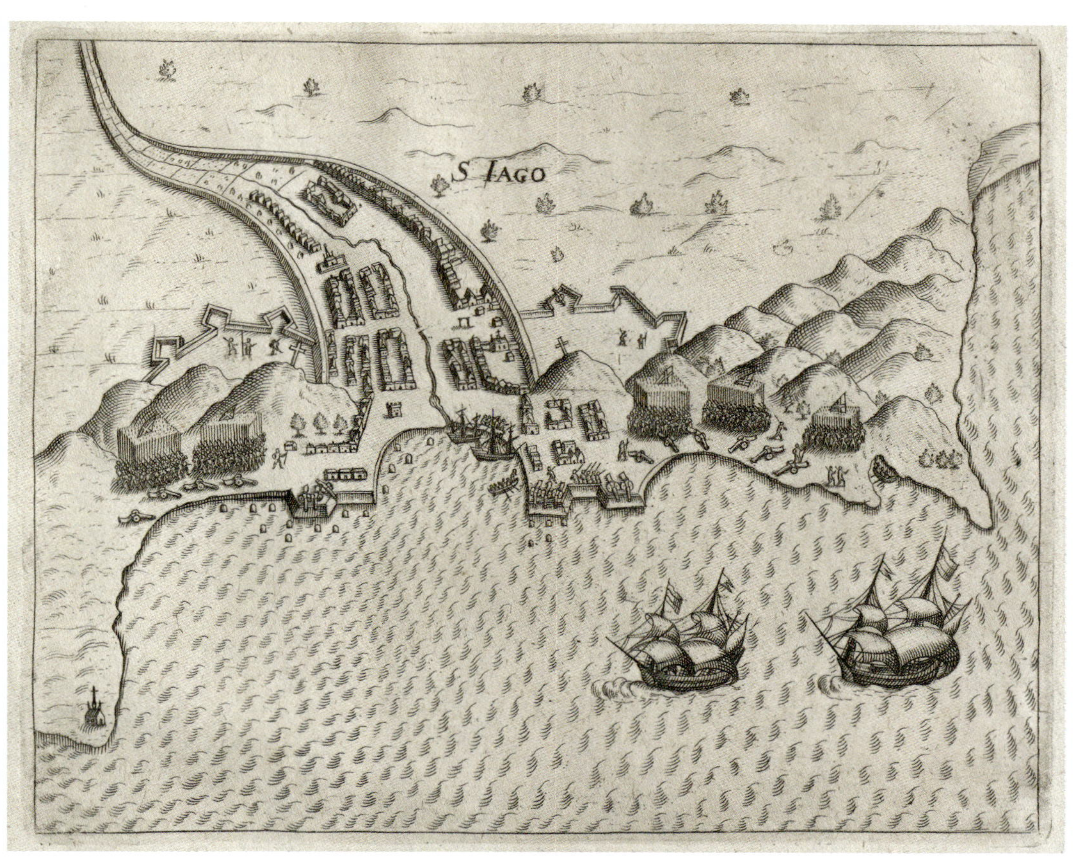
S IAGO

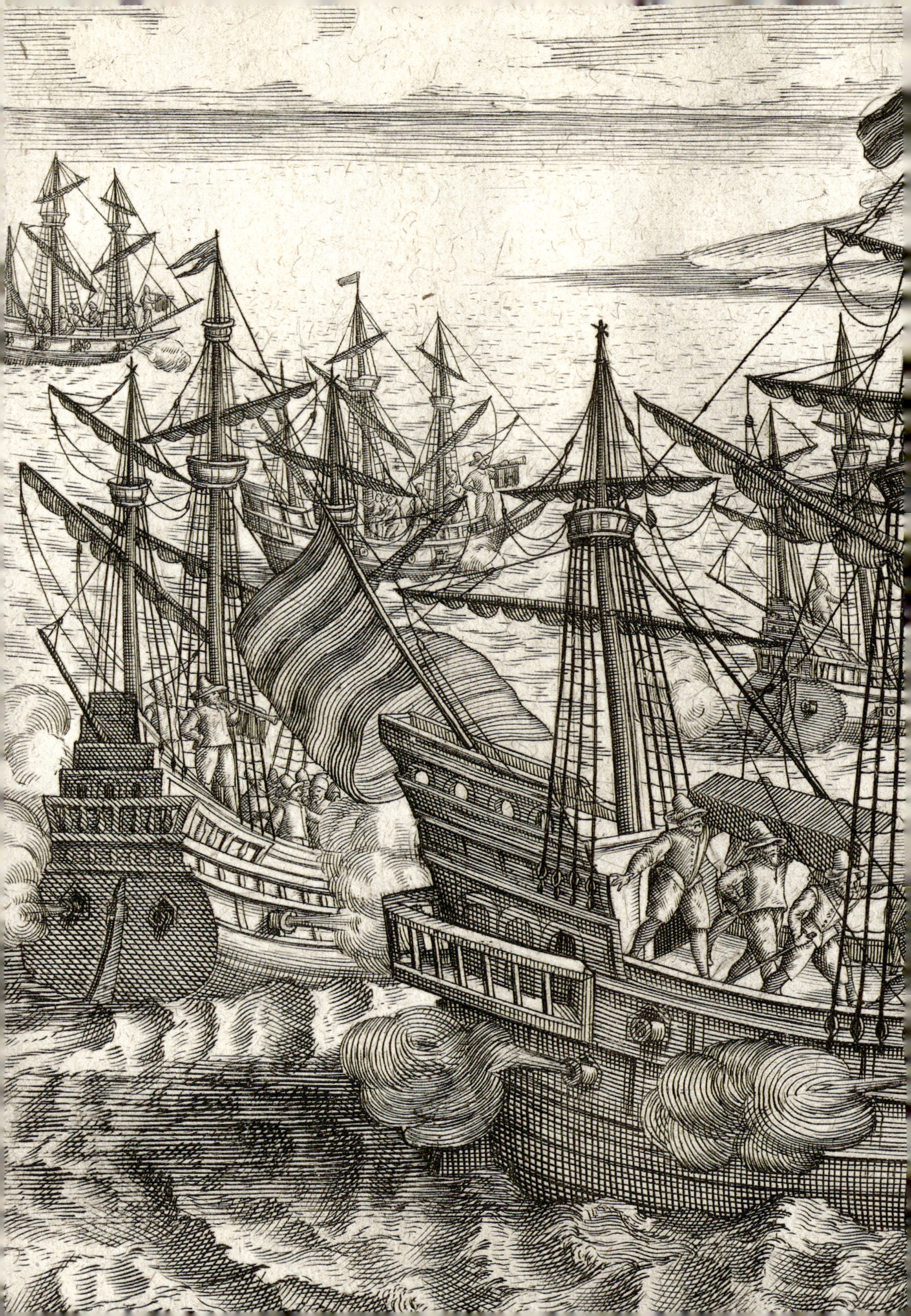

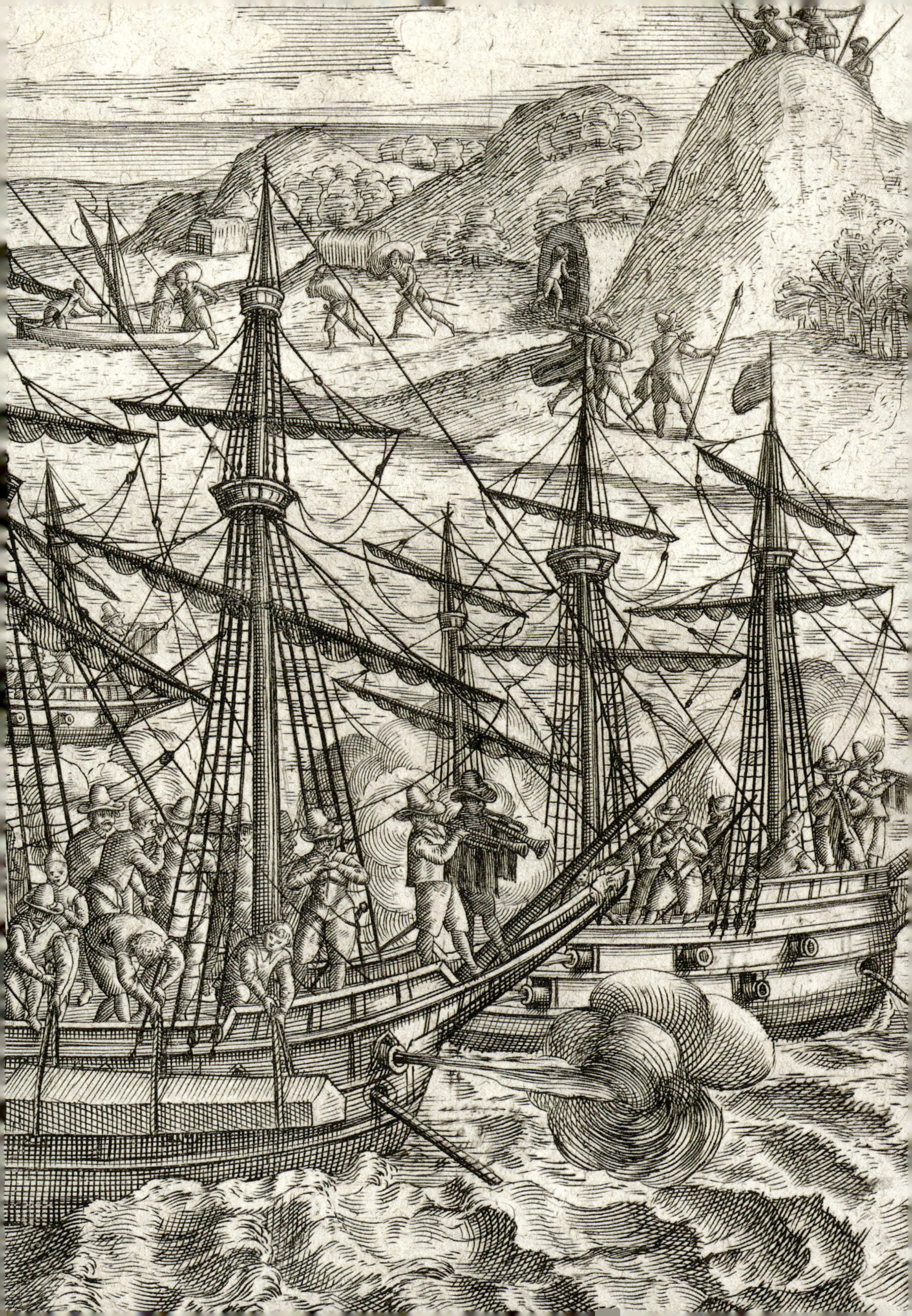

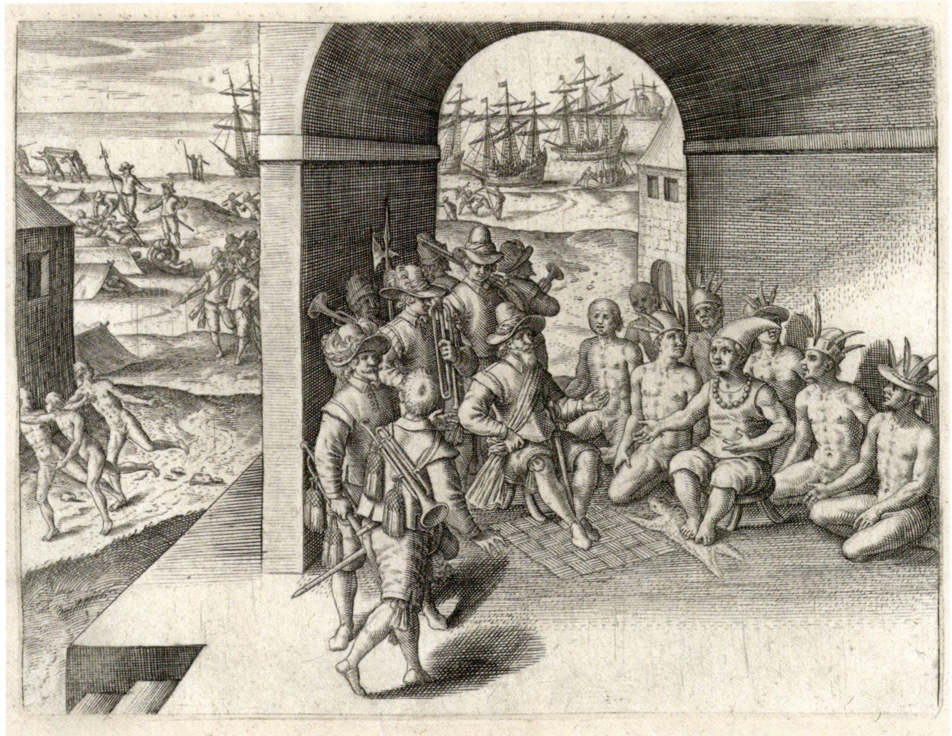

PLATE 18

How the Dutch visited the coast of Guinea

The Dutch were miserable, sick and lacking in fresh water when they arrived on the coast of Guinea. They sent a legation and interpreter to meet the king. The king, upon learning of their arrival, made ready to appear at his most opulent. He dressed in a cassock or tunic and trousers of purple cloth decorated with gold-coloured threads. He wore neither a shirt, stockings nor shoes. He wore a long pointed hood on his head. He sat down on a low chair wearing yellow, red and blue garments as have been described. He had a sheepskin spread out under his feet and his nobles stood naked behind him. When the Dutch captain came in to meet him, the king let him sit on a similar cushioned chair and they had their conversation via the interpreter. At this time, the admiral let all of the sick on board be brought to land, where they waited until they were well again. They died, however, and he had them buried there on the island. The Dutch at first found these savages to be rather timid and scared, but as they got used to them, it became more pleasant to deal with them.

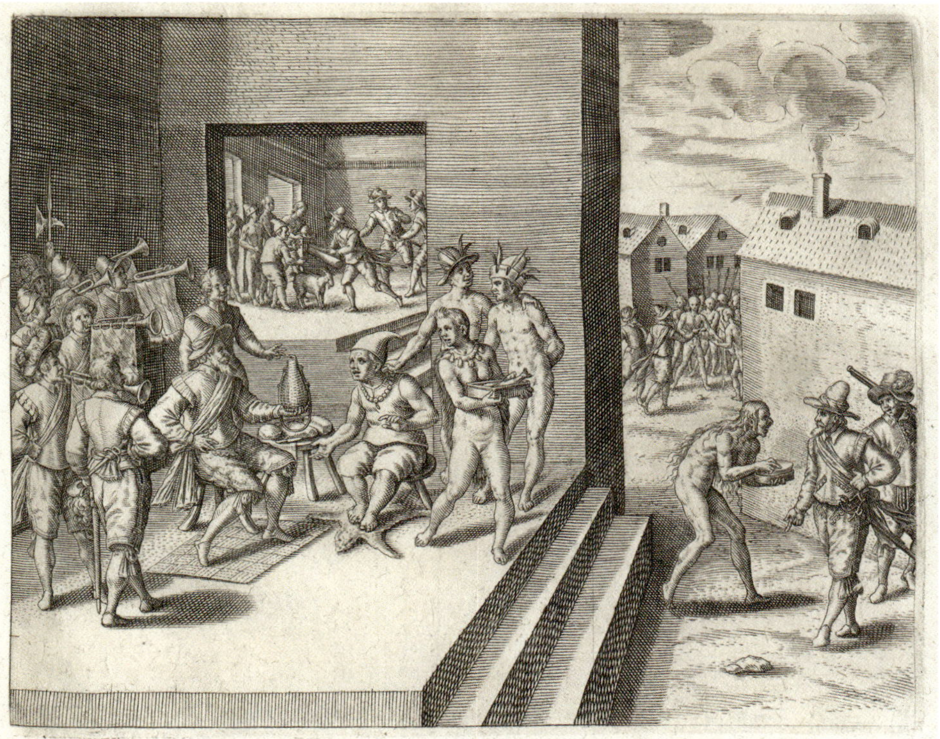

PLATE 19

What the Dutch captain discussed with the king and what happened to him

Now that the captain was in discussions with the king, he was brought food to eat by one of the king's women. It was lightly fried plantain and dried fish served on a wooden tray. He drank palm wine. The captain was hungry, but when he was served this food that he was not used to, he requested the smoked meat, cheese, bread and a bottle of Spanish wine he had brought with him from the ship. These provisions pleased the king better than his own and he drank so much of the Spanish wine that he had to be put to bed in his room. When the captain made to return to his ship with his people and the provisions he had received from the king through trade, the Guineans blocked his way out. Thus, he had to stay the night against his will with the barbarians. When he went to the door the next morning and looked around, an ugly old woman approached him wearing no clothes. She held a box full of ashes. She walked in a circle three times around the captain and gave him a terrifying look. She shook the box so that a thick layer of ash landed all over the captain's clothes. Throughout this, the woman muttered to herself, which was an unsettling sight. After she had circled around the captain three times, she once again was silent and went on her way. The captain took his leave of the king at this point and returned with his people to the ship.

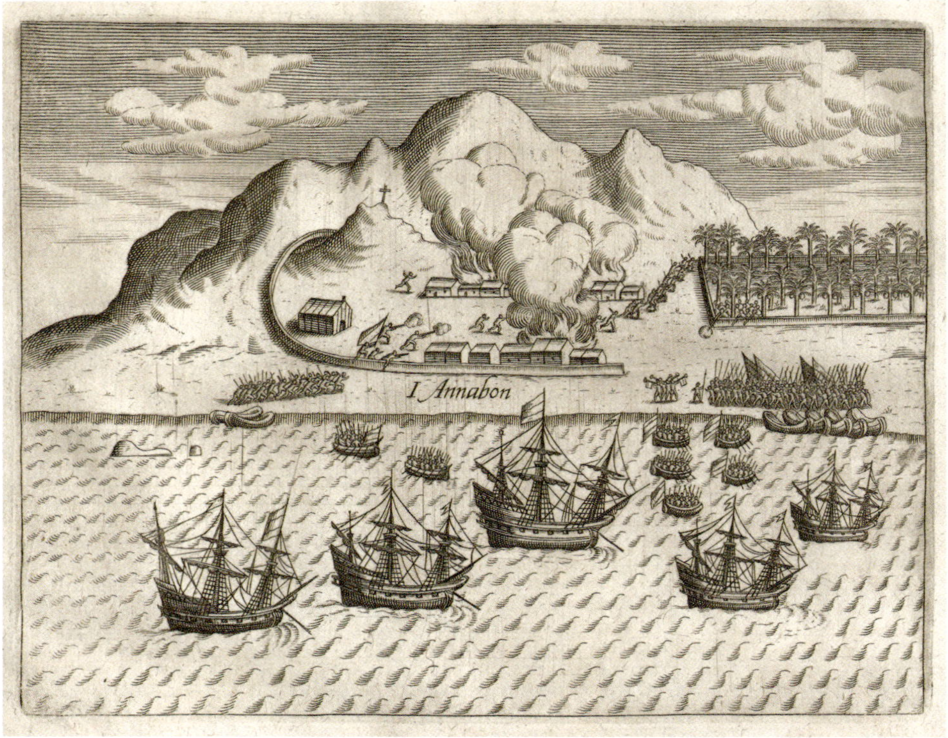

PLATE 20

How the Dutch landed at the island of Annabon and what they encountered there

When the Dutch got back on their way, they arrived at the island called Annabon. There they tried amiably to trade money and gold for provisions from the Portuguese and the Moors who occupied the island. When they were refused, however, they decided to obtain provisions by force. Thus, they headed to the shore in their boats. As soon as the Portuguese noticed the Dutch approaching, however, they fired a few cannon rounds upon them. After their houses caught fire, however, they fled to the mountains. When the Dutch took possession of their camp, they put their sick in the church and undamaged houses so that they could recover.

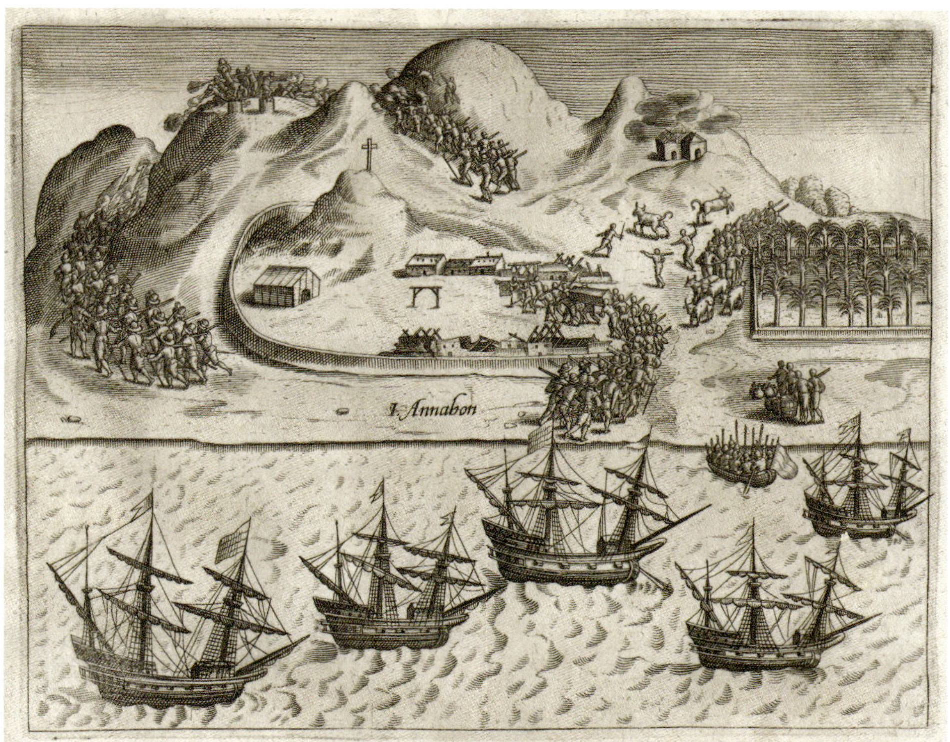

PLATE 21

What else the Dutch accomplished at Annabon

While the Dutch established themselves at Annabon, some of the soldiers ventured deeper into the country looking for spoils. They did not find any, however, since the Portuguese hid in the woods with their muskets. One Dutchman was killed. The captain had to erect gallows to discourage his people from rooting around in the woods for treasure, since warning them did not work. When he sent a well-armed troop of soldiers to see if they could catch some Spaniards, they met no one, but were able to return to the fort with 25 head of cattle. They then realised that the Spanish had fortified themselves on a mountain. Captain de Cordes then went with about 150 well-armed men, divided into two groups, to climb both sides of the mountain. After the Portuguese had thrown stones and fired cannons on the Dutch for a while – and they did some damage to their adversaries indeed – they were ultimately beaten back by the Dutch muskets and forced to abandon their fortifications and retreat. The Dutch seized the mountain and found baked bread, as well as containers of wine and two types of Dutch cheese. They brought these back to the ship with them. Upon leaving the mountain, they set fire to two houses on the way. They also buried a cadet who had died there. Finally, they returned to the ship and continued their voyage.

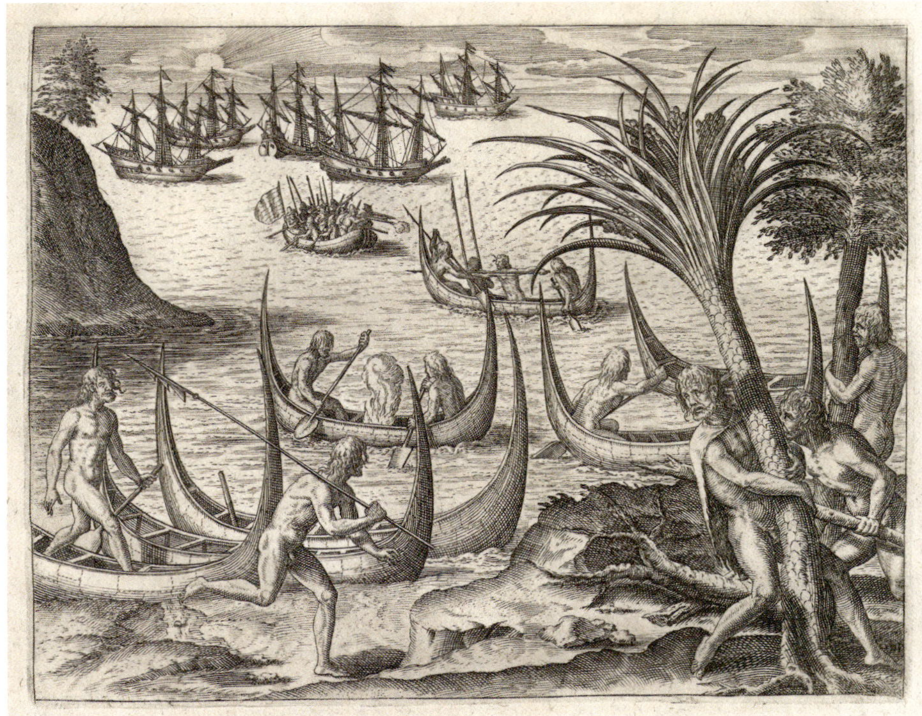

PLATE 22

How the Dutch followed Magellan's route to an island populated by large and horrifying people

While following Magellan's route, the Dutch sent a couple of boats to explore an island, whereupon they became aware of seven boats manned by terrifying and large people. They were between 10 and 11 feet tall and their skin was brownish red. They wore their hair long. These people wanted to attack the Dutch, but the Dutch fired upon them with their muskets as soon as they became aware of their presence. Three of the savages were killed, and the others fled to land upon witnessing this. They pulled trees out of the ground and built a defensive barrier with them. Then they waited for the Dutch with arrows and stones. The Dutch, however, found it unnecessary to pursue these terrible people. When three Dutchmen were later caught by them, however, they slaughtered them in a ghastly manner. Their style of boat is also shown in this picture.

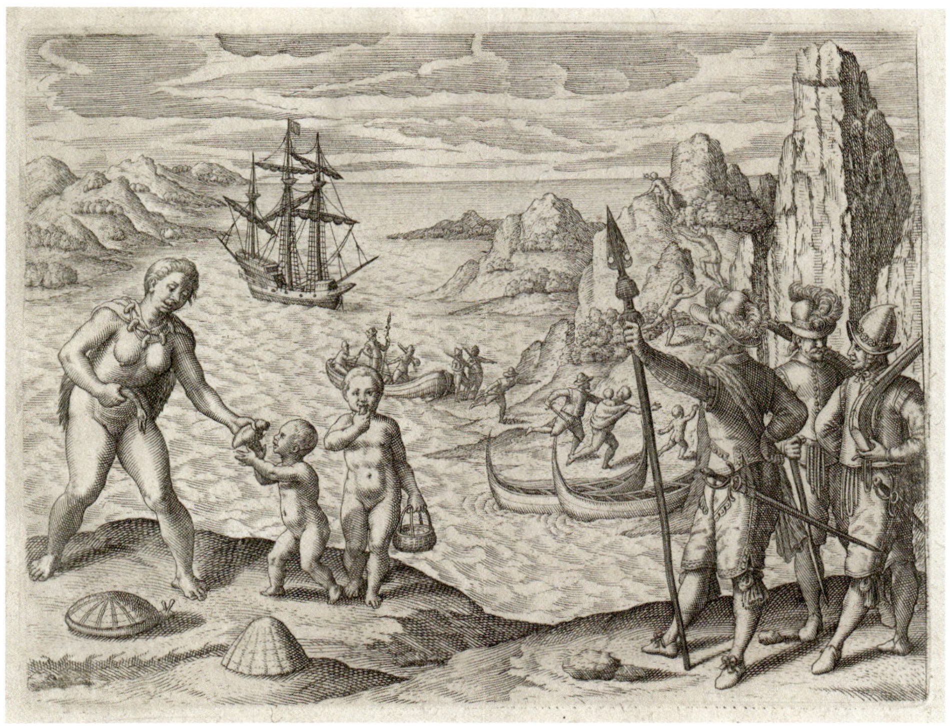

PLATE 23

The Dutch find more canoes, or boats, as well as some Indians. They seize a woman and two children from them

When Captain de Weert set out with a group to go on land, he noticed three Indian boats. After the Indians had seen the Dutch, however, they fled to the mountains, which they climbed as quickly as monkeys. They left behind a woman and two children, however, who were still trying to catch up. The woman was naked except for an animal pelt hanging over her back. She wore a string with a snail shell around her neck. The women of this area wear their hair quite short as opposed to the men, who keep theirs long. This woman refused to eat what was offered to her when the Dutch captured her. Instead, she had a bird that was in her canoe, which she ate raw after plucking its feathers. She barely held it over the fire at all and the bird's blood dripped on to her chest when she took a bite, and more may be read about this in the account.

PLATE 25

The form of the penguin, of which the Dutch caught many

When the Dutch decided not to complete their voyage, but rather to return home, as the account tells, they furnished themselves with as many provisions as they could. They were still on the route set by Ferdinand Magellan, so they returned to the island they referred to as Penguin Island, since there were so many there. Indeed, the island was so overrun with penguins that they could have filled 25 ships with them. Indeed, they caught 900, but they had to work hard for these because the weather was against them. These birds are formed as is shown here in the accompanying picture. They are as big and as plump as a goose. They weigh between 8 and 16 pounds. They have a black back and a white crest. Their feet are also black and they have a form similar to that of a goose. They have no wings, but rather smooth feathers. They are very fast swimmers. They walk upright, as is shown here, and as is further explained in the account.

PLATE 24, PAGES 458/459

How the Dutch went to Penguin Island and what happened to them there

One time when the Dutch went to Penguin Island, as they had several times before, with the hope of catching a lot of penguins, they were caught up in a great storm wind. They had 450 penguins and it looked like their boats were going to be utterly destroyed by the waves. They worried that they would languish back on land, but after gathering together and holding a collective prayer, they mustered the courage to return to the island. It took all their might to get back to land. Once there, they found an Indian woman in a penguin burrow who was wearing a coat made from the skins of wild animals. They found no living men on the island, except one who was dead and whose body had been decorated with feathers.

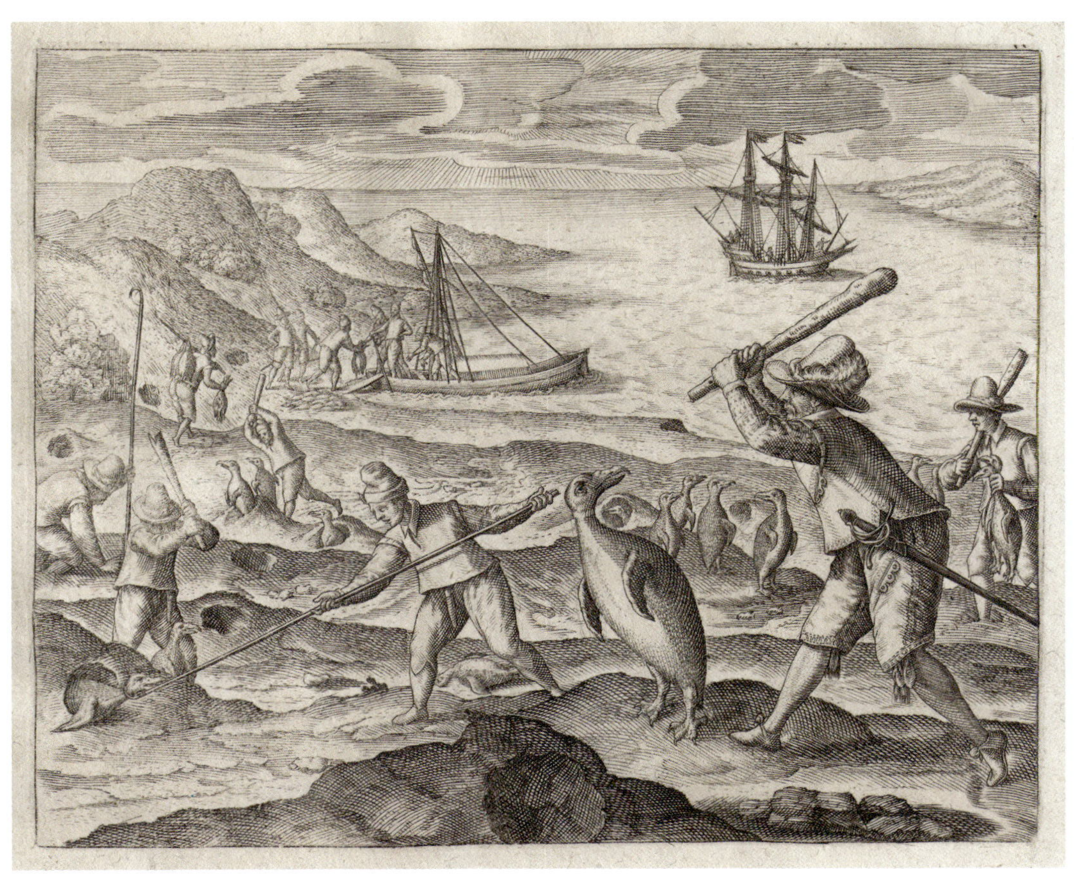

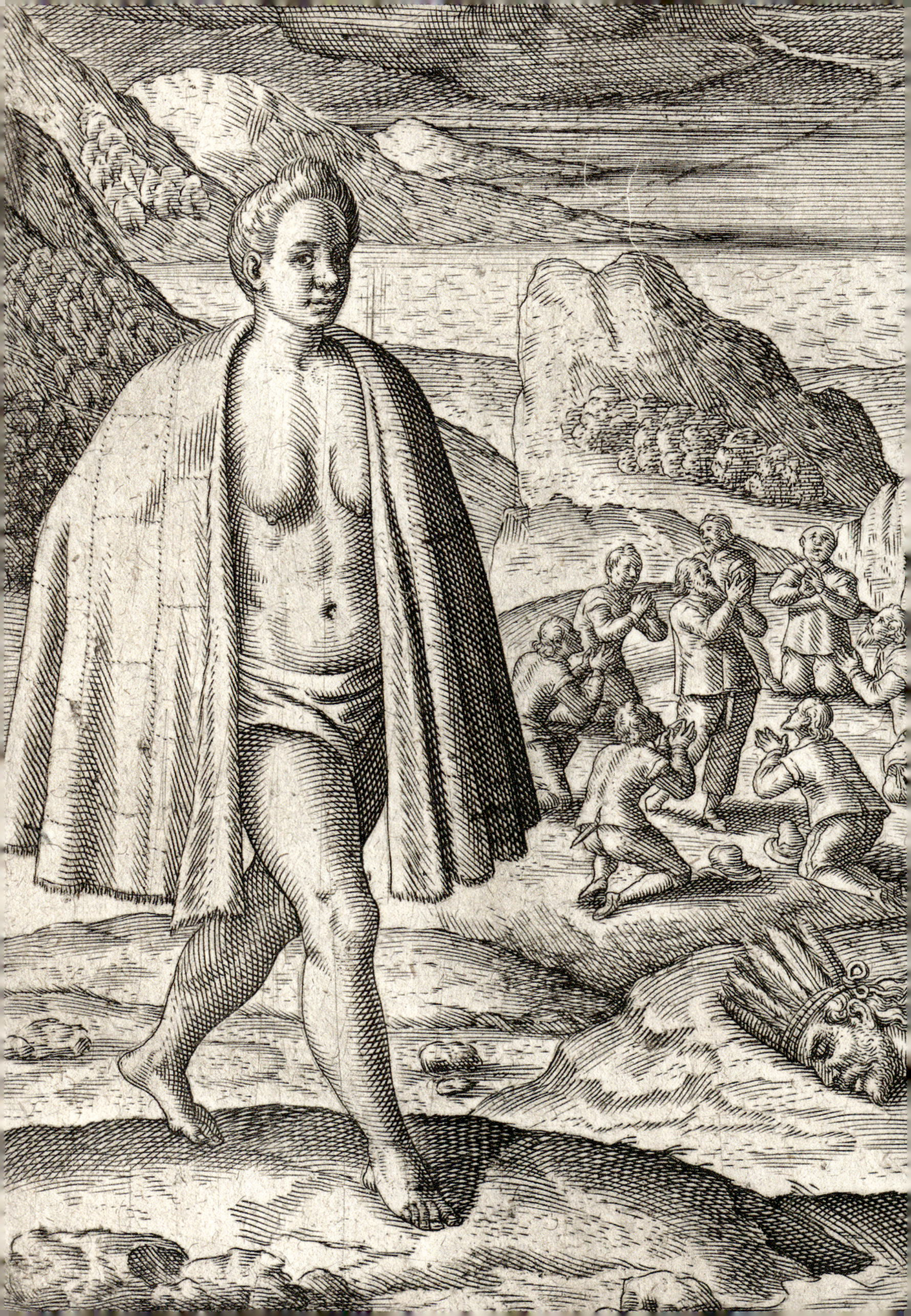

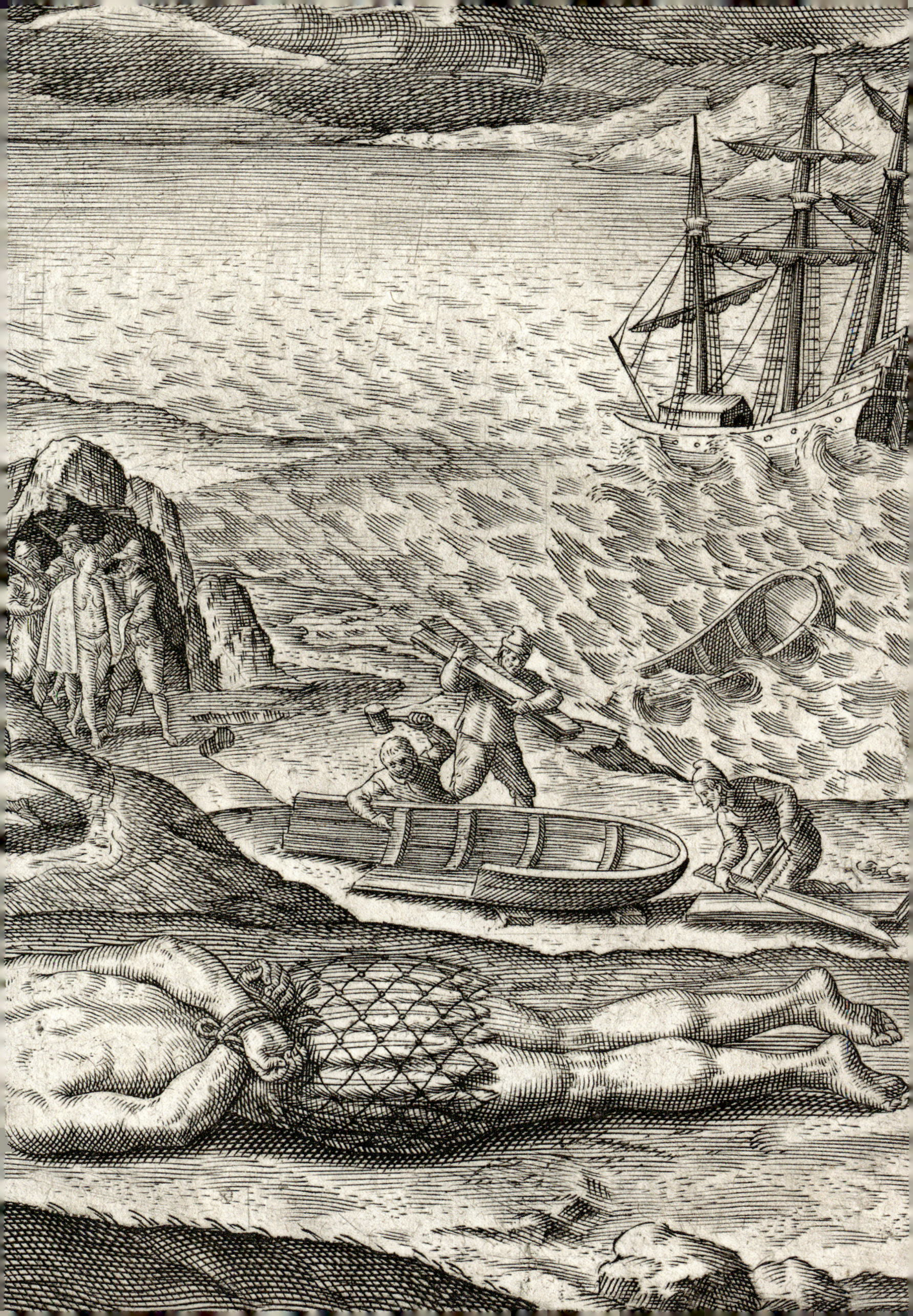

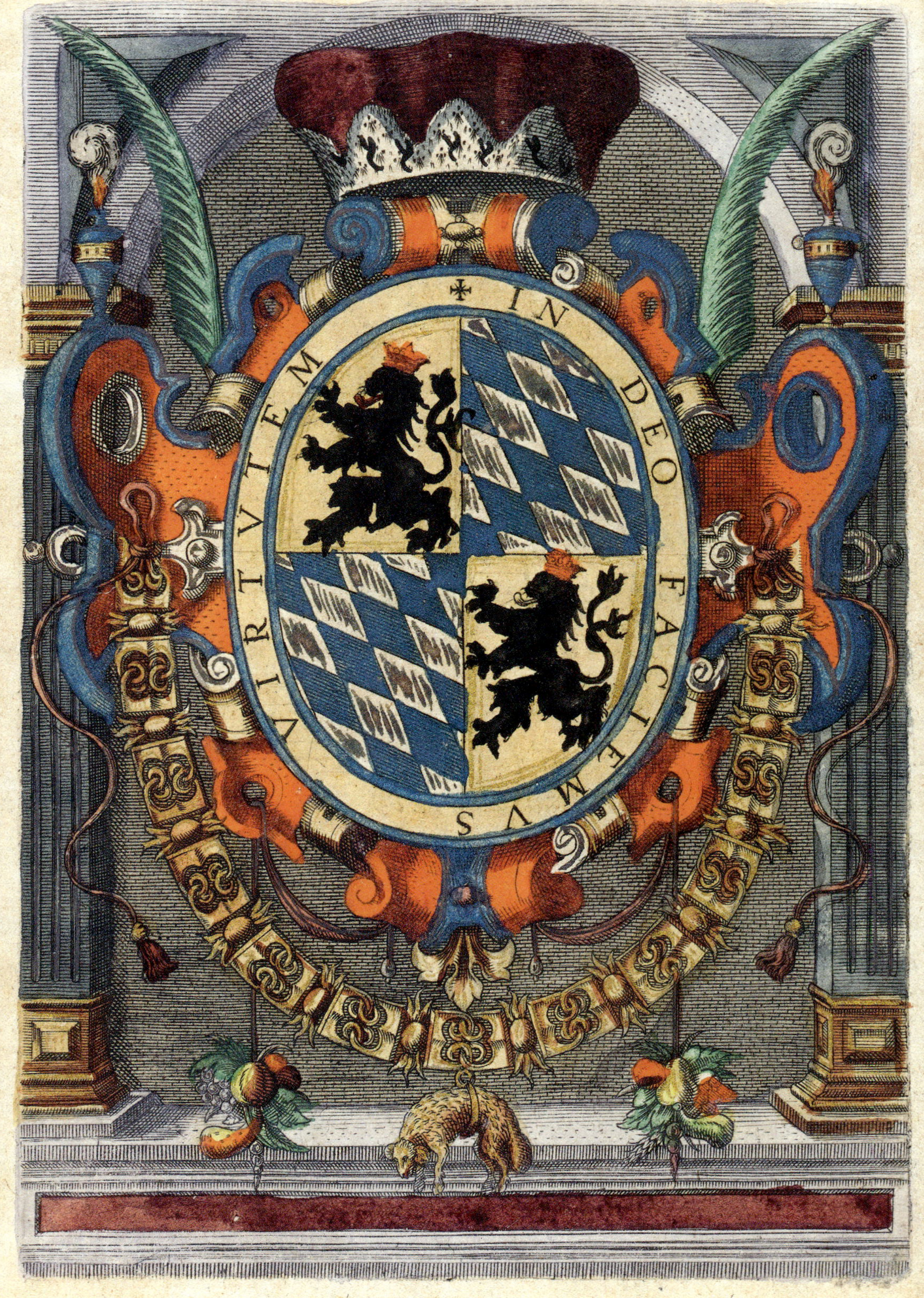
VIRTVTEM IN DEO FACIEMVS

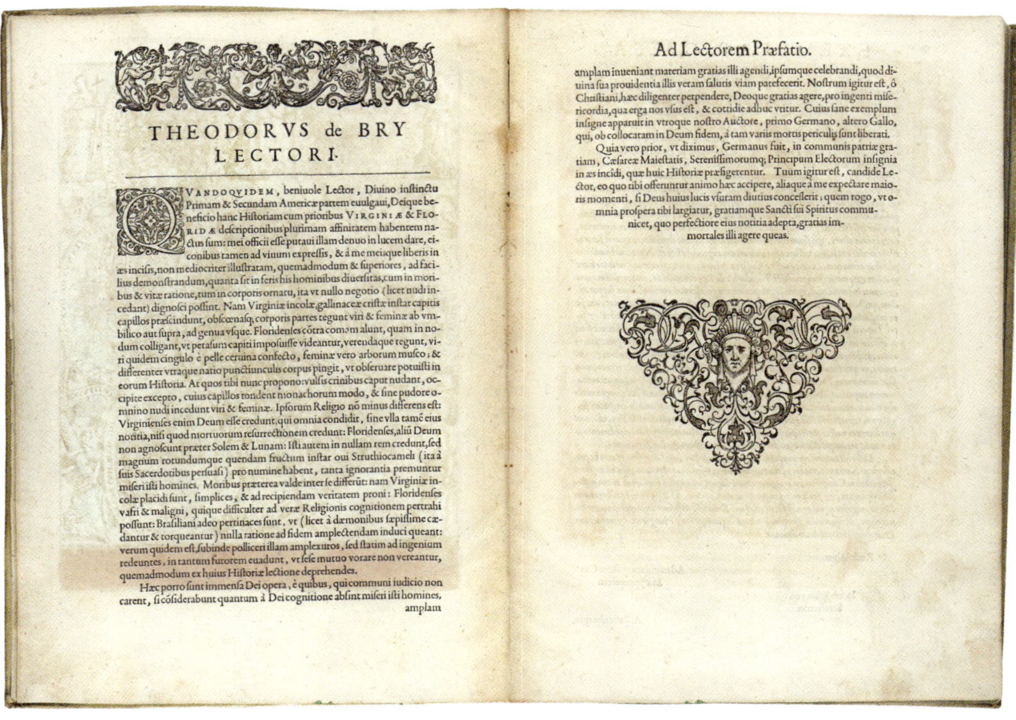

THEODORVS de BRY LECTORI.

QVANDOQVIDEM, beniuole Lector, Diuino instinctu Primam & Secundam Americæ partem euulgaui, Deique beneficio hanc Historiam cum prioribus VIRGINIÆ & FLORIDÆ descriptionibus plurimam affinitatem habentem nactus sum: mei officii esse putaui illam denuo in lucem dare, eiconibus tamen ad viuum expressis, & à me meisque liberis in æs incisis, non mediocriter illustratam, quemadmodum & superiores, ad facilius demonstrandum, quanta sit in feris his hominibus diuersitas, cum in moribus & vitæ ratione, tum in corporis ornatu, ita vt nullo negotio (licet nudi incedant) dignosci possint. Nam Virginiæ incolæ, gallinaceæ cristæ instar capitis capillos præscindunt, obscœnasq; corporis partes tegunt viri & feminæ ab vmbilico aut supra, ad genua vsque. Floridenses cōtra comam alunt, quam in nodum colligant, vt petasum capiti imposuisse videantur, verendaque tegunt, viri quidem cingulo è pelle ceruina confecto, feminæ vero arborum musco; & differenter vtraque natio punctiunculis corpus pingit, vt obseruare potuisti in eorum Historia. At quos tibi nunc propono: vulsis crinibus caput nudant, occipite excepto, cuius capillos tondent monachorum modo, & sine pudore omnino nudi incedunt viri & feminæ. Ipsorum Religio nō minus differens est: Virginienses enim Deum esse credunt, qui omnia condidit, sine vlla tamē eius notitia, nisi quod mortuorum resurrectionem credunt: Floridenses, aliū Deum non agnoscunt præter Solem & Lunam: Isti autem in nullam rem credunt, sed magnum rotundumque quendam fructum instar oui Struthiocameli (ita à suis Sacerdotibus persuasi) pro numine habent, tanta ignorantia premuntur miseri isti homines. Moribus præterea valde inter se differūt: nam Virginiæ incolæ placidi sunt, simplices, & ad recipiendam veritatem proni: Floridenses vafri & maligni, quique difficulter ad veræ Religionis cognitionem pertrahi possunt: Brasiliani adeo pertinaces sunt, vt (licet à dæmonibus sæpissime cædantur & torqueantur) nulla ratione ad fidem amplectendam induci queant: verum quidem est, subinde polliceri illam amplexuros, sed statim ad ingenium redeuntes, in tantum furorem euadunt, vt sese mutuo vorare non vereantur, quemadmodum ex huius Historiæ lectione deprehendes.

Hæc porro sunt immensa Dei opera, è quibus, qui communi iudicio non carent, si cōsiderabunt quantum à Dei cognitione absint miseri isti homines, amplam

Ad Lectorem Præfatio.

amplam inueniant materiam gratias illi agendi, ipsumque celebrandi, quod diuina sua prouidentia illis veram salutis viam patefecerit. Nostrum igitur est, ô Christiani, hæc diligenter perpendere, Deoque gratias agere, pro ingenti misericordia, qua erga nos vsus est, & cottidie adhuc vtitur. Cuius sane exemplum insigne apparuit in vtroque nostro Auctore, primo Germano, altero Gallo, qui, ob collocatam in Deum fidem, à tam variis mortis periculis sunt liberati.

Quia vero prior, vt diximus, Germanus fuit, in communis patriæ gratiam, Cæsareæ Maiestatis, Serenissimorumq; Principum Electorum insignia in æs incîdi, quæ huic Historiæ præfigerentur. Tuum igitur est, candide Lector, eo quo tibi offeruntur animo hæc accipere, aliaque à me expectare maioris momenti, si Deus huius lucis vsuram diutius concesserit; quem rogo, vt omnia prospera tibi largiatur, gratiamque Sancti sui Spiritus communicet, quo perfectiore eius notitia adepta, gratias immortales illi agere queas.

Editorial Note

The *America* series consists of 13 volumes altogether, so why has it been decided to present here only the first nine of them? The fact is that those volumes form a cohesive unit on their own, in which all the important regions of the New World that were known at the time were discussed. The series was started by Theodore de Bry in 1590 and finished by his two sons in 1602 – volume IX was, moreover, also announced as the final volume in the series. While a volume X did appear, it was 16 years later in 1618, at a time when Johan Theodore de Bry was beginning to pass on responsibility for the firm's everyday running to his son-in-law Matthaeus Merian. The images in the last four volumes (X–XIII) are of notably inferior artistic quality, and the written accounts do not display the same clear editorial strategy as the first nine. Within that distinction, only the first six volumes can be found with contemporary colouring, which explains why in this book volumes I–VI are in full colour, and volumes VII–IX are not.

The plate descriptions have been compiled by Michiel van Groesen and are based upon the texts of the original De Bry volumes.

Page 460
Coat of arms, from: *America*, vol. III

Above
A preface from Theodore de Bry to the reader, with decorative element, from: *America*, vol. III

infelicis exercitus tui in Hispaniam ad triumphum & ludibrium deferunt. Quum sibi tantum licere in tuis te sciente ac vidente pulcrum ducunt, possúntne apertius demonstrare quid facturi sint, si teipso potiantur?

QVAMOBREM, vt tuæ Maiestati & Gallico nomini iniustum dedecus meritis paricidarum suppliciis deleas, generosum & dignum te, dignum auis tuis, spiritum indue: Deo beneiuuante, subditorum tuorum causam suscipe, susceptámque qua potes ac debes fide tuere: vt coram toto Christiano orbe tuam in protegendis subditis fortitudinem, tum etiam tuorum innocētiam, testatam facias. Nullo quidem maiore piaculo (ô Rex) tum innoxio nostrorum sanguini, tum iustæ iræ tuę parentare potes, quàm latronum pœna: vt non tantùm cęsorum viduę coniuges, propinqui & liberi desiderium suorum & graues suos dolores eo solatio leniant: sed etiam te omnes verè Regem tanto parem nomini, & Patrem populi tui, agnoscant.

FINIS.

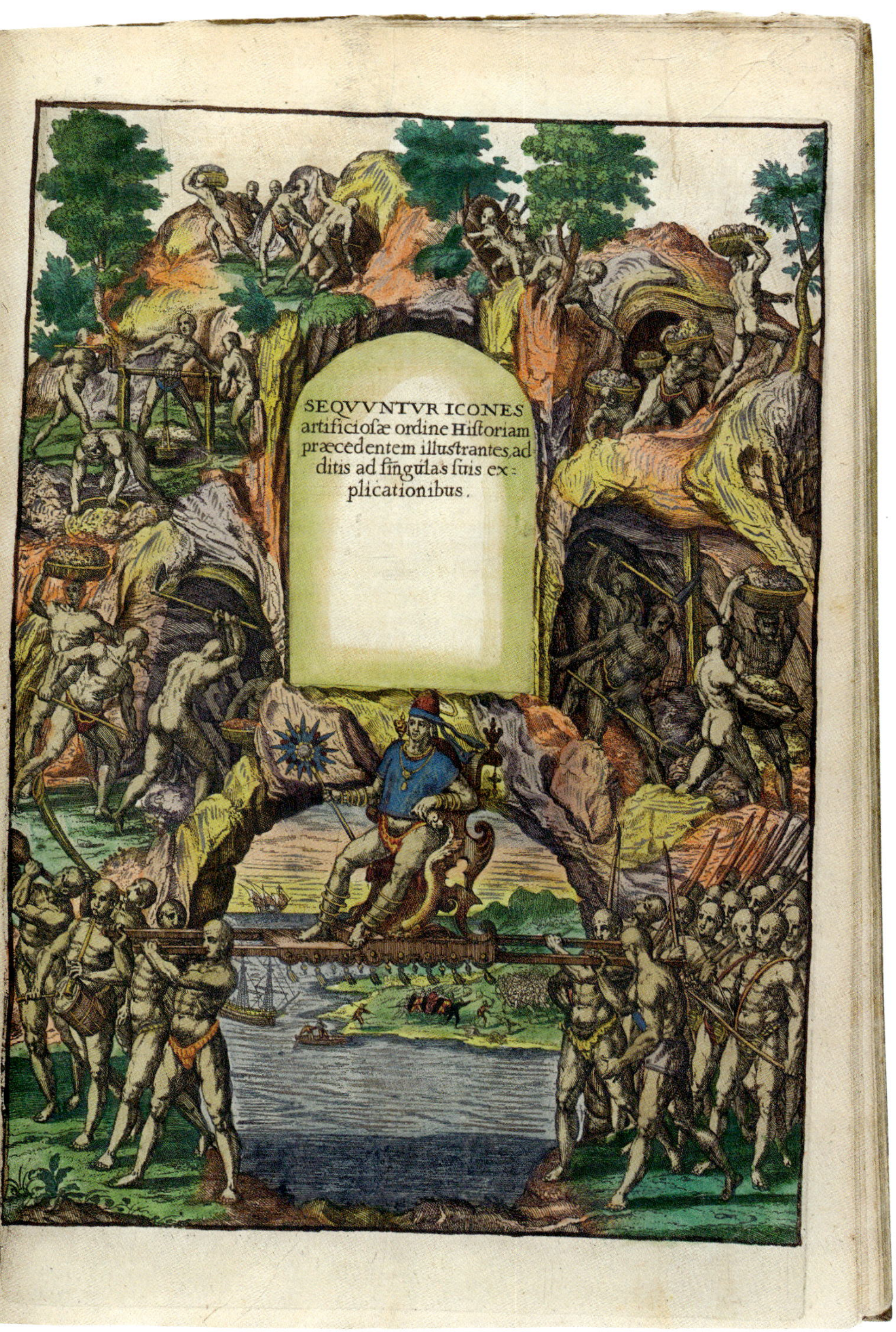
SEQVVNTVR ICONES
artificiosæ ordine Historiam
præcedentem illustrantes, ad
ditis ad singulas suis ex-
plicationibus.

Selected Bibliography

Bucher, Bernadette. *Icon and Conquest: A Structural Analysis of the Illustrations of De Bry's Grand Voyages*. Chicago: University of Chicago Press, 1981.

Burghartz, Susanna (ed.). *Inszenierte Welten: Die west- und ostindischen Reisen der Verleger de Bry, 1590–1630 / Staging New Worlds: De Brys' Illustrated Travel Reports, 1590–1630*. Basel: Schwabe, 2004.

–. "Mehrdeutigkeit und Superioritätsanspruch. Inszenierte Welten im kolonialen Diskurs um 1600", *Zeitenblicke* 7–2 (2008).

–. "Transformation und Polysemie. Zur Dynamik zwischen Bild, Text und Kontext in den *Americae* der de Bry", in: Ulrike Ilg (ed.). *Text und Bild in Reiseberichten des 16. Jahrhunderts. Westliche Zeugnisse über Amerika und das Osmanische Reich*. Venice: Marsilio, 2008. pp. 233–68.

Carey, Daniel and Claire Jowitt (eds.). *Richard Hakluyt and Travel Writing in Early Modern Europe*. Farnham: Ashgate, 2012.

Conley, Tom. "De Bry's Las Casas", in: René Jara and Nicholas Spadaccini (eds.). *Amerindian Images and the Legacy of Columbus*. Minneapolis: University of Minnesota Press, 1992, pp. 103–31.

Davies, Surekha. *Renaissance Ethnography and the Invention of the Human: New Worlds, Maps and Monsters*. Cambridge: Cambridge University Press, 2016.

Duchet, Michele (ed.). *L'Amérique de Théodore de Bry, une collection de voyages protestante du XVI*[e] *siècle: Quatre études d'iconographie*. Paris: C. N. R. S., 1987.

Duviols, Jean-Paul. "Théodore de Bry et ses modèles français", *Caravelle* 58 (1992), pp. 7–16.

Gaudio, Michael. *Engraving the Savage: The New World and Techniques of Civilization*. Minneapolis: University of Minnesota Press, 2008.

Grafton, Anthony. *New Worlds, Ancient Texts: The Power of Tradition and the Shock of Discovery*. Cambridge, MA: Belknap Press, 1992.

Gravatt, Patricia. "Rereading Theodore de Bry's Black Legend", in: Margaret R. Greer, Walter D. Mignolo and Maureen Quilligan (eds.). *Rereading the Black Legend: The Discourses of Religious and Racial Difference in the Renaissance Empires*. Chicago: University of Chicago Press, 2007, pp. 225–43.

Greenblatt, Stephen. *Marvelous Possessions: The Wonder of the New World*. Chicago: University of Chicago Press, 1991.

Greve, Anna. *Die Konstruktion Amerikas: Bilderpolitik in den 'Grands Voyages' aus der Werkstatt de Bry*. Cologne: Böhlau, 2004.

Groesen, Michiel van. *The Representations of the Overseas World in the De Bry Collection of Voyages (1590–1634)*. Leiden: Brill, 2008.

Keazor, Henry. "Theodore de Bry's Images for America", *Print Quarterly* 15 (1998), pp. 131–49.

Kupperman, Karen O. (ed.). *America in European Consciousness 1493–1750*. Chapel Hill: University of North Carolina Press, 1995.

Leitch, Stephanie. *Mapping Ethnography in Early Modern Germany: New Worlds in Print Culture*. New York: Palgrave Macmillan, 2010.

Lestringant, Frank. *Mapping the Renaissance World: The Geographical Imagination in the Age of Discovery*. Berkeley: University of California Press, 1994.

McGrath, John T. *The French in Florida: In the Eye of the Hurricane*. Gainesville: University Press of Florida, 2000.

Pagden, Anthony. *The Fall of Natural Man: The American Indian and the Origins of Comparative Ethnology*. Cambridge: Cambridge University Press, 1986.

Perplies, Helge. *Inventio et repraesentatio Americae: Die 'India Occidentalis'-Sammlung aus der Werkstatt De Bry*. Heidelberg: Winter, 2017.

Quilligan, Maureen (ed.). *Theodore de Bry's Voyages to the New and Old Worlds [Journal of Medieval and Early Modern Studies 41–1]*. Durham: Duke University Press, 2011.

Schmidt, Dorothee. *Reisen in das Orientalische Indien: Wissen über fremde Welten um 1600*. Cologne: Böhlau, 2016.

Sloan, Kim (ed.). *A New World: England's First View of America*. London: British Museum Press, 2007.

–. (ed.). *European Visions, American Voices*. London: British Museum Press, 2009.

Tise, Larry E. "The 'Perfect' Harriot/de Bry: Cautionary Notes on Identifying an Authentic Copy of the de Bry Edition of Thomas Harriot's *A Briefe and True Report* (1590)", in: Robert Fox (ed.). *Thomas Harriot and His World*. Farnham: Ashgate, 2012, pp. 201–29.

Bibliographical Details of the Original Volumes

Volume I
Admiranda narratio, fida tamen, de commodis et incolarvm ritibvs Virginiae. Anglico scripta sermone à Thoma Hariot, Frankfurt am Main, 1590.
John Hay Library, Brown University: Hay Military, v. 1.

Volume II
Indorvm Floridam provinciam inhabitantium eicones … ad vivum expressae à Iacobo Le Moyne … addita ad singulas brevi earum declaratione, duce Renato de Laudõniere … anno MDLXIIII. Qvae est secvnda pars Americae, Frankfurt am Main, 1591.
John Hay Library, Brown University: Hay Military, v. 2a.

Brevis narratio eorvm qvae in Florida Americæ provicia Gallis acciderunt: secunda in illam nauigatione, duce Renato de Laudõniere … anno MDLXIIII. Qvae est secvnda pars Americae, Frankfurt am Main, 1591.
John Hay Library, Brown University: Hay Military, v. 2b.

Volume III
Navigatio in Brasiliam Americae qua auctoris navigatio, quae memoriae prodenda in mari viderit, Brasiliensium victus & mores à nostris valde alieni, animalia etiam, arbores, herbae, & reliqua singularia nostris penitus incognita describuntur, Frankfurt am Main, 1592.
John Hay Library, Brown University: Hay Military, v. 3.

Americae tertia pars memorabile[m] provinciae Brasiliae historiam, Frankfurt am Main, 1592.
John Hay Library, Brown University: Hay Military, v. 4a.

Volume IV
Americae pars quarta. Sive, Insignis & admiranda historia de reperta primùm Occidentali India, Frankfurt am Main, 1594.
John Carter Brown Library, Brown University: J De Bry GV pt. 4 1594 Lat 1.

Volume V
Americae pars quinta: Nobilis … Hieronymi Bezoni secundae sectionis Hispanorum, tùm in nigrittas … tùm in Indos crudelitatem, Gallorumque piratarũ de Hispanis toties reportata spolia, Frankfurt am Main, 1595.
John Hay Library, Brown University: Hay Military, v. 5a and b.

Volume VI
Americae pars sexta: Sive, Historiae ab Hieronymo Bezono scriptae, sectio tertia, Frankfurt am Main, 1596.
John Hay Library, Brown University: Hay Military, v. 6a and b.

Volume VII
Americae Pars VII. Verissima Et Ivcvndissima Descriptio Praecipvarvm Qvarvndam Indiae regionum & Insularum, Frankfurt am Main, 1599.
Staats- und Stadtbibliothek Augsburg: 2 Gs 127.

Volume VIII
Americae Pars VIII. Continens Primo, Descriptionem Trivm Itinervm Nobilissimi Et Fortissimi Equitis Francisci Draken, Frankfurt am Main, 1599.
Staats- und Stadtbibliothek Augsburg: 2 Gs 127.

Volume IX
Americae Nona et postrema Pars. Qva De Ratione Elementorum: De Novi Orbis Natvra: De Hvivs Incolarvm Svperstitiosis cultibus: deq̃[ue] forma Politiae ac Reipubl. ipsorum copiosè pertractatur, Frankfurt am Main, 1602.
Staats- und Stadtbibliothek Augsburg: 2 Gs 127.

Pages 462/463
Text page alongside an alternative frontispiece, from: *America*, vol. VI

Pages 466/467
Adam and Eve each side of the tree of knowledge of good and evil, from: *America*, vol. I, plate 1

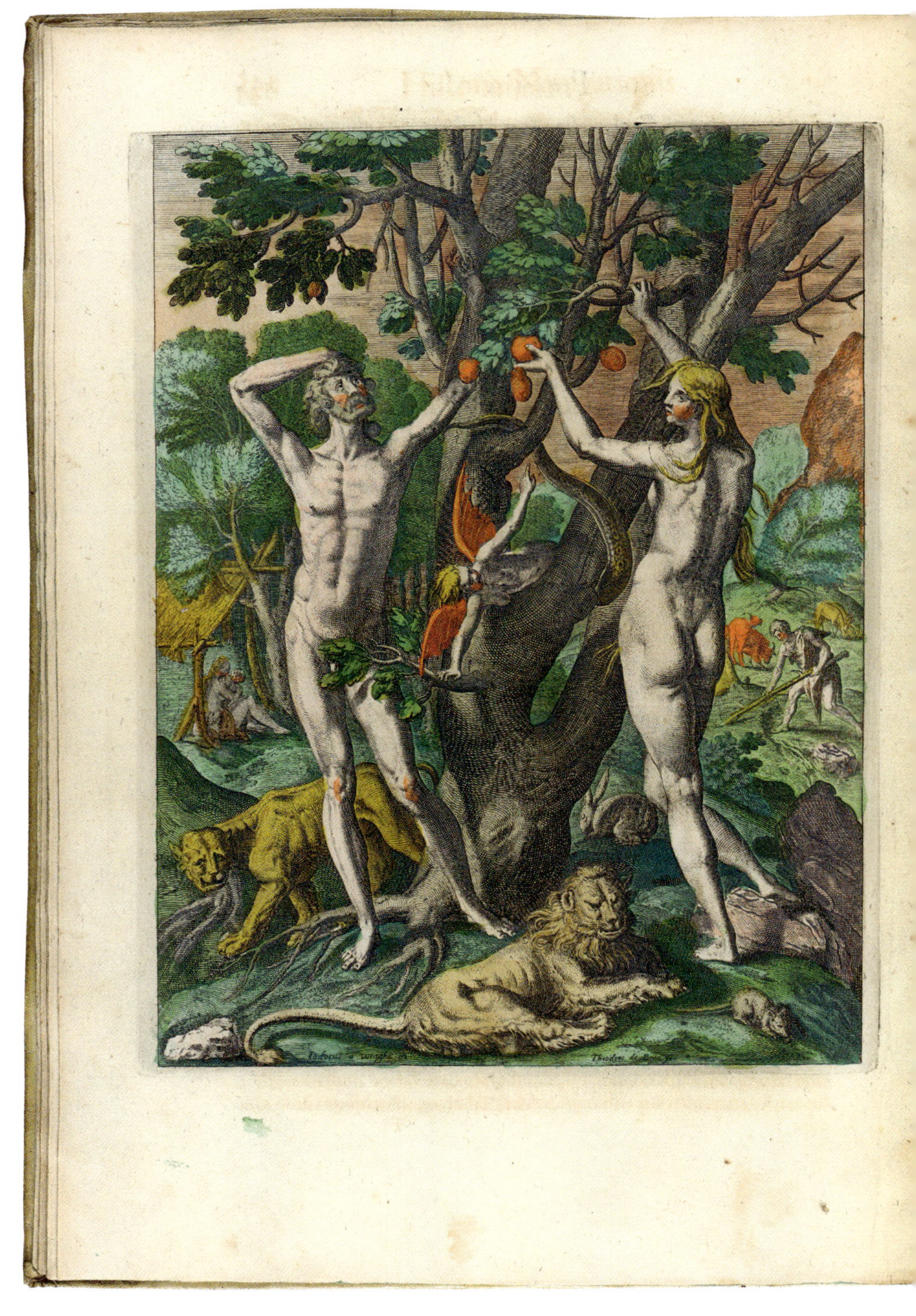

HISTORIA NAVIGATIONIS IN BRASILIAM AMERICÆ PROVINCIAM.

CAPVT I.

Auctoris scopus.

QVONIAM, quæ sit amœnitas, amplitudo, & vbertas, Quartæ Orbis terrarum sectionis, quæ *America* vulgo dicitur, cuius pars *Brasilia*; quibusque cingatur insulis, & regionibus antiquis penitus ignotis contineatur: quam multis item petita nauigationibus, annis abhinc octoginra, ex quo primum innotuit: plerique nostra memoria Cosmographi, in explicandisque rebus gestis versati homines docuerunt.

Illo itaque omni argumento longe lateque diffuso liberati, hac Historia duntaxat ea complecti decreuimus, quæ inter eundum & redeundum, & apud feros Americanos, quibuscum circiter annum vixi, experiendo ac obseruando, visu audituque, percepimus. Quod vt planius exponam, ab initio quænam fuerit hæc adeo longinqua difficilisque expeditio, explicandum.

CAP. II.

Ascensus in naues Juliobonæ: itemque occursus nauium & expugnatio: tempestates, littoraque & insulæ primum obuiæ.

CVM Boisius Villagagnonis nepos, qui ante Iuliobonam aduenerat, a pecunia regia tribus instructis nauibus, prouisaq; re frumentaria, pro imperio iuberet: 13. Cal. Decembr. anni 1556. in naues conscendimus. Ipse Boisius, ex nauibus vna, quæ Roberga minor appellabatur, octoginta nautis militibusque occupata, legati nomen imperiumque habuit. Alteram, duce Mario, Robergæ *Boisius classi præficitur.*

T

Index of Names and Places

The Authors

Michiel van Groesen is Professor of Maritime History at Leiden University, the Netherlands. He was previously Associate Professor of Early Modern History at the University of Amsterdam as well as Queen Wilhelmina Visiting Professor at Columbia University in New York. Van Groesen specialises in European representations of the early modern world. His work at the intersection of textual and visual sources had resulted in three books: *The Representations of the Overseas World in the De Bry Collection of Voyages (1590–1634)*, published in 2008, *Amsterdam's Atlantic: Print Culture and the Making of Dutch Brazil* (2017) and *An Ocean of Rumours: News and Information in the Atlantic World* (2026).

Larry E. Tise is a historian and author who has held senior posts with the North Carolina Division of Archives and History, the Pennsylvania Historical and Museum Commission and the Benjamin Franklin Memorial. From 2000 to 2015, he served as the Wilbur and Orville Wright Distinguished Professor at East Carolina University, thereafter continuing as adjunct Research Professor. His research centres on early modern exploration, particularly Thomas Harriot and Sir Walter Raleigh, and on the intellectual and technological origins of flight. From 2004 to 2025, he examined hand-coloured De Bry editions in major American and European research libraries.

Acknowledgements

The reprint of Theodore de Bry's *America* series (vols. I–IX) is based on the copies located at Brown University in Providence, USA (vols. I–VI) and the Staats- und Stadtbibliothek in Augsburg, Germany (vols. VII–IX). From Brown University we would like to express our thanks to Dr Thomas A. Horrocks, former Director of Special Collections and of the John Hay Library and his successor Jennifer J. Betts, as well as Dr Neil Safier, Director of the John Carter Brown Library.
We are most grateful for the excellent collaboration with Dr Karl-Georg Pfändtner, Director of the Staats- und Stadtbibliothek Augsburg, and his colleague Ursula Korber throughout the long and complex process of the digital reproduction of the volumes.
We would also like to extend our thanks to Dr Marieke van Delft, Curator of Early Printed Editions at the Koninklijke Bibliotheek/National Library of the Netherlands in The Hague, for providing us with additional plates.
Finally, we would especially like to acknowledge the contributions of our authors: Prof. Dr Larry Tise, in bringing these unique hand-coloured De Bry volumes to our attention; as well as Prof. Dr Michiel van Groesen, for his unrelenting support of our publication.

Pages 472/473
De Bry's foreword to volume IV, showing Columbus among nautical deities,
from: *America*, vol. IV

Exemplar Cæsarei Priuilegij.

RVDOLPHVS II. *Diuina fauente clementia electus Romanorum Imperator, semper Augustus, Germaniæ, Hungariæ, Bohemiæ Dalmatiæ, Croatiæ, Sclauoniæ, &c. Rex, Archidux Austriæ, Dux Burgundiæ, Styriæ, Carinthiæ, Carniolæ, VVirtembergæ, &c. Comes Tyrolis, &c. Recognoscimus & notum facimus tenore præsentium vniuersis, nobis & Imperio dilectum Theodoricum de Bry, ciuem Francofurti ad Mœnum, humiliter nobis exponendũ curasse, quod magna cura & magnis sumptibus Incolarum Americæ habitus, ritus & mores in æneas tabulas inciderit, quod opus libenter in lucem emittere cuperet, demisse etiam supplicasse (quandoquidem nemini id aduersum, sed multis gratum futurum sit, magniq; in eam rem sumptus sint ipsi faciendi) vt Cæsareo nostro priuilegio eum munire clementer dignemur, ne cuiquam alteri, qui suum commodum cum ipsius summo detrimento quærit, æneas istas tabulas aut icones vel hoc opus imitari aut exprimere liceat. Nos illius humilibus precibus annuentes, ex certa nostræ Cæsareæ Maiestatis scientia & autoritate hanc gratiam & priuilegium prædicto Theodorico de Bry cõcedimus, vt prædictos typos & icones in lucem edat, & ne intra quadriennium ab huius priuilegij concessione supputandum, quispiam, quicunq; tandem ille sit, istas icones ad imitationem excudat, aut sic impressas inuehat, importet aut vẽdat. Quapropter inhibemus singulis nostris & sacri Imperij subditis & fidelibus, cuiuscunque dignitatis, status & conditionis sint, præsertim autẽ omnibus Typographis, bibliopolis, aliisq; librariam negociationem exercentibus, nisi nostram indignationem & grauem pœnam incurrere velint; & vetamus, ne quis eorum, aut alius eorum nomine, prædictas æreas tabulas & icones quas sæpememoratus Theodoricus de Bry excudet, intra dictum quadriennium ad imitationem imprimat, aut sic impressas circumuehat, venales proponat aut quoquo modo distribuat, aliosve id facere permittat, sub pœna nostræ indignationis & amißionis singulorum exemplarium dictæ impreßionis, quæ sæpedictus Theodorus de Bry, vbicumq; locorum nactus fuerit, per se, vel suos, propria authoritate & sine impedimento sibi vendicare, atq; illis pro suo arbitrio vti poterit, libere, & sine detrimento.*

Debebit tamen sæpe præfatus Theodoricus de Bry, nisi hac nostra gratia & priuilegio priuari velit, tria præfatæ impreßionis exemplaria propriis impensis ad nostram Imperialem Cancellariam transmittere. Harum testimonio literarum manu nostra subscriptarum & sigilli nostri impreßione munitarum, Datum in nostra Regia arce Pragæ, vigesimaquarta Martij, Anno Domini Millesimoquingentesimo & nonagesimo, Regnorum nostrorum Romani decimoquinto, Hungarici decimooctauo & Bohemici etiam decimoquinto.

Rudolphus.

Ad mandatum sacræ Cæs. Maiest. proprium.

Iacob Kurz von Senfftenau.

A. Erstenberger.

No

AD LECTOREM.

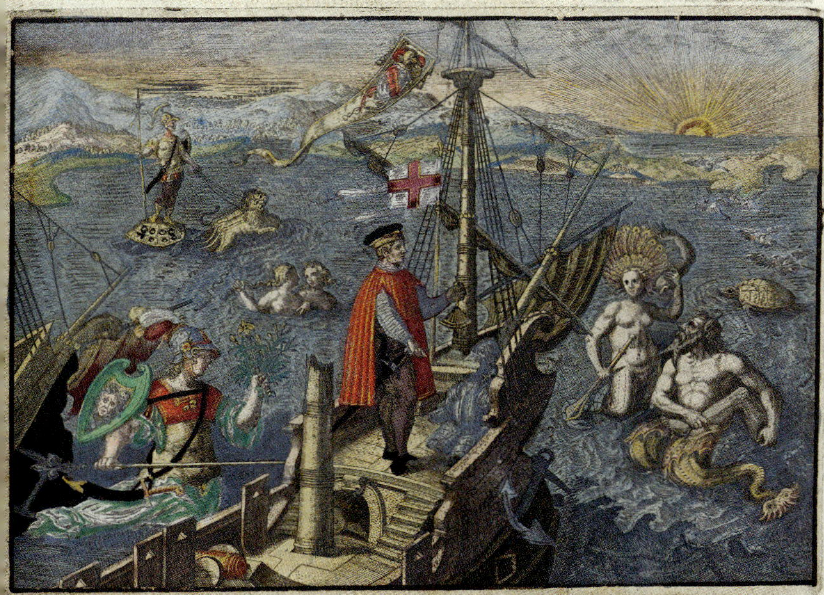

THEODORVS DE BRY BENEVOLO LECTORI.

NON existimo, candide lector, tibi ignotos esse tres illos priores libros, quos de noui orbis seu Indiæ
occidentalis tribus regionibus, nempe Virginia, Florida & Brasilia præteritis annis in lucem edidi
cum figuris & iconibus ad viuum expressis ac in æs incisis: in quibus barbarorum illorum tum cor-
poris cultus & ornatus, tum mores, tum deniq; fides & religio eleganter describũtur & exprimun-
tur, non minore cum legentis & contemplantis voluptate & delectatione quàm vtilitate. Cùm au-
em originem atq; initium inuentionis illarum terrarum noui orbis prætermittere mihi nec æquum nec deco-
um videretur, vt non tantum meo, sed & aliis bonis ingeniis satisfacerem, superioribus illis tribus libris, hunc
uartum adiicere visum est, in quo reperies primum tabulam chorographicam eius regionis quæ prima ab illu-
tri viro D. Christophoro Columbo Italo reperta est, in qua tabula loca ipsa ad quæ vir ille appulit quatuor illis
auigationibus quas in eas terras suscepit, accuratè notantur, adhibitis in eius rei diligentiorem inquisitionem
mnium maximè idoneorum authorum scriptis, atque in primis authoris nostri M. Hieronymi Benzoni Me-
iolanensis, qui in illis terris per 14. annos commoratus est. Inuenies præterea iconas complures tabulis æneis
nea filiorumq; meorũ opera incisas, quibus exprimuntur multa quæ ad incolarũ illius regionis mores, viuendi
ationem atq; religionem pertinent: ex quibus poteris videre quantum sit discrimen inter illos trium illarum
egionum superioribus libris descriptarum incolas, & hos de quibus in hoc libro fit mentio, præsertim in reli-
ione: siquidem hi non vnum solum Deum rerum omnium creatorem ac figura aliqua lignea repræsentatum
nstar Virginiæ incolarũ, nec solem aut Lunam sicut Floridenses, nec Maralea velut Brasiliani colunt, sed ipsum
Diabolum, qui sese ipsis omnis generis horrendis formis exhibet & ostentat, sicut ex figuris sequẽtibus, ac ipsius
bri lectione videbis & intelliges. Quod sanè horrendum est & maximè deplorandum, homines licet barbaros,
reatos tamen ad imaginem Dei, vt ad Angelorum imitationem eum perpetuò colerent & glorificarent, eò cæ-
itatis esse delapsos, vt loco creatoris ipsum iuratum Dei & generis humani hostem adorent. Veruntamen quid
niseros illos tantopere detestamur & damnamus? In nos ipsos descendamus, ac videamus num ipsis meliores

):( ):(3 simus,

Photo Credits

We are much indebted to the museums, libraries and all other institutions cited for their kind assistance in the publication of this volume.
All images, unless otherwise indicated, are based upon the editions of the *America* series located in the following libraries:

Vols. I–III, V/VI: © John Hay Library, Brown University, Providence.
Vol. IV: © John Carter Brown Library, Brown University, Providence.
Vols. VII–IX: © Staats- und Stadtbibliothek, Augsburg.

© akg-images: p. 16 right
bpk / Kunstbibliothek, Staatliche Museen zu Berlin / Dietmar Katz: p. 340–341
Bridgeman Images: © British Library Board. All Rights Reserved / Bridgeman Images, p. 9; Lebrecht History /Bridgeman Images, p. 12; Photo © GraphicaArtis / Bridgeman Images, p. 55 bottom
Houghton Library, Harvard University, Cambridge, US 19 095.88.14*: pp. 47 top, 60/61, front endpapers
John Carter Brown Library, J De Bry GV pt. 10 1618 Ger / Internet Archive: p. 20 left
Joyner Library, East Carolina University, Greenville: p. 59
KB National Library of the Netherlands, The Hague: 1712 A 12 [1], pp. 107–109, 113, back cover; 1712 A 12 [4], p. 55 top
The Mariners' Museum, Newport News, Virginia: front cover, pp. 40, 48, 63
© National Maritime Museum, Greenwich, London: pp. 10/11
The New York Public Library, Print Collection: p. 15
© Österreichische Nationalbibliothek, Vienna, E 34.403-C: p. 32
Princeton University Library General Manuscripts Bound (C0199); Manuscripts Division, Department of Rare Books and Special Collections: pp. 46 top, 53
Rijksmuseum, Amsterdam: pp. 8, 26, 27, 31
Rijksmuseum, Amsterdam / Purchased with the support of the Vereniging Rembrandt: p. 2
© The Trustees of the British Museum, London: pp. 14, 23, 37, 42 left, 51, 57, 58 left, 58 right
Virginia Cartographical Society, Norfolk; formerly owned by William C. Wooldridge and the Virginia Cartographical Society and reproduced with their permission: p. 62
© Wellcome Collection, London: 16 left
Wilson Library, University of North Carolina, Chapel Hill: p. 46 bottom

Imprint

Front cover
The Native Americans pray with rattles (detail)
From: *America*, vol. I, plate 17, Latin ed.
Newport News, Virginia, Mariners' Museum

Back cover
The true picture of a Pictish woman (detail)
From: *America*, vol. I, plate 2 of the five additional engravings, German ed.
KB National Library of the Netherlands, The Hague

Front endpapers
The Native Americans sitting to dine (detail)
From: *America*, vol. I, plate 16, French ed.
Cambridge, Harvard University, Houghton Library

Back endpapers
The Native Americans sitting to dine (detail)
From: *America*, vol. I, plate 16, Latin ed.
John Hay Library, Brown University, Providence

Page 1
Coat of arms, flanked by two lions
From: *America*, vol. I, Latin ed.
John Hay Library, Brown University, Providence

Page 2
Theodore de Bry
Self-portrait, 1597
Copper engraving, 18.5 x 16 cm (7¼ x 6¼ in.)
Amsterdam, Rijksmuseum

Pages 4/5
One of the chief ladies of Secota (detail)
From: *America*, vol. I, plate 4, Latin ed.
John Hay Library, Brown University, Providence

Page 64
The preparation of drinks (detail)
From: *America*, vol. III, plate 21, Latin ed.
John Hay Library, Brown University, Providence

Pages 476/477
The town of Pomeiooc
From: *America*, vol. I, plate 19, Latin ed.
John Hay Library, Brown University, Providence

Pages 478/479
The first voyage out of Lisbon
From: *America*, vol. III, plate 2, Latin ed.
John Hay Library, Brown University, Providence

Page 480
Allegorical figures representing peace, justice, truth, prudence, victory and strength, positioned among crests
From: *America*, vol. IV, Latin ed.
John Carter Brown Library, Brown University, Providence

EACH AND EVERY TASCHEN BOOK PLANTS A SEED!
Each year, we offset our annual carbon emissions with carbon credits at the Instituto Terra, a reforestation programme in Minas Gerais, Brazil, founded by Lélia and Sebastião Salgado. To find out more about this ecological partnership, please check: www.taschen.com/institutoterra.
Inspiration: unlimited.
Carbon footprint: (almost) zero.

Want to see more? Visit taschen.com to view our current publications, browse our latest magazine, and subscribe to our newsletter.

Project management: Mahros Allamezade, Cologne
Art direction: Anna-Tina Kessler, Los Angeles

Hohenzollernring 53, D–50672 Köln
www.taschen.com

Printed in Bosnia–Herzegovina
ISBN 978–3–8365–9853–8

XIX.

Oppidum Pomeiooc.

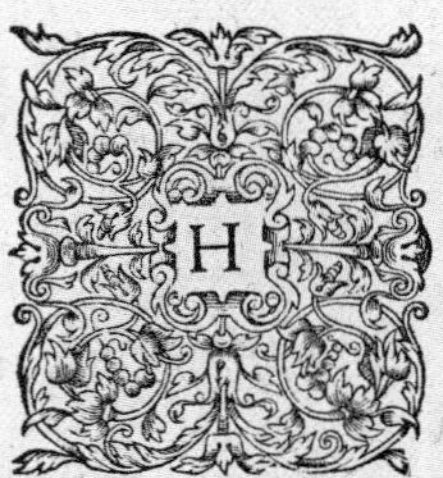

Hvivs regionis oppida iis fere similia sunt, quæ in prouincia Florida, non tamē adeo valida, neque tanta cura adseruata. Clauduntur quidem in orbem palis, firmiter in terram defixis, angusto aditu, sed infirmioribus, vt ex hac pictura videre licet, quæ ad exemplar oppidi POMEIOOC *expressa est. Pauca sunt in eo ædificia, præter ea, quæ Principi & proceribus sunt destinata: ab vno latere Templum est ab aliis ædificiis seiunctum, litera A. insignitum, rotunda forma exstructum, storeis tenuibus tectum, & veluti cortinis vndique cinctum, sine fenestris, & nullum lumen nisi per ianuam recipiens: ab altero sunt ædes Principis, signatæ litera B. Constructæ vero sunt eorum ædes palis satis tenuibus simul decussatim colligatis, & storeis tectæ, quibus in altum quantum lubet reflexis, lucem & aerem admittunt: nonnullæ etiam arborum ramis teguntur pro hominum arbitrio & voluntate. Festa sua celebrant & genio indulgent in media oppidi area, eo quo in XVII. figura dictum est modo. Cum porro oppidum satis procul a stagno distet, ingentem scrobem C. foderunt, ex qua necessariam aquam hauriunt.*

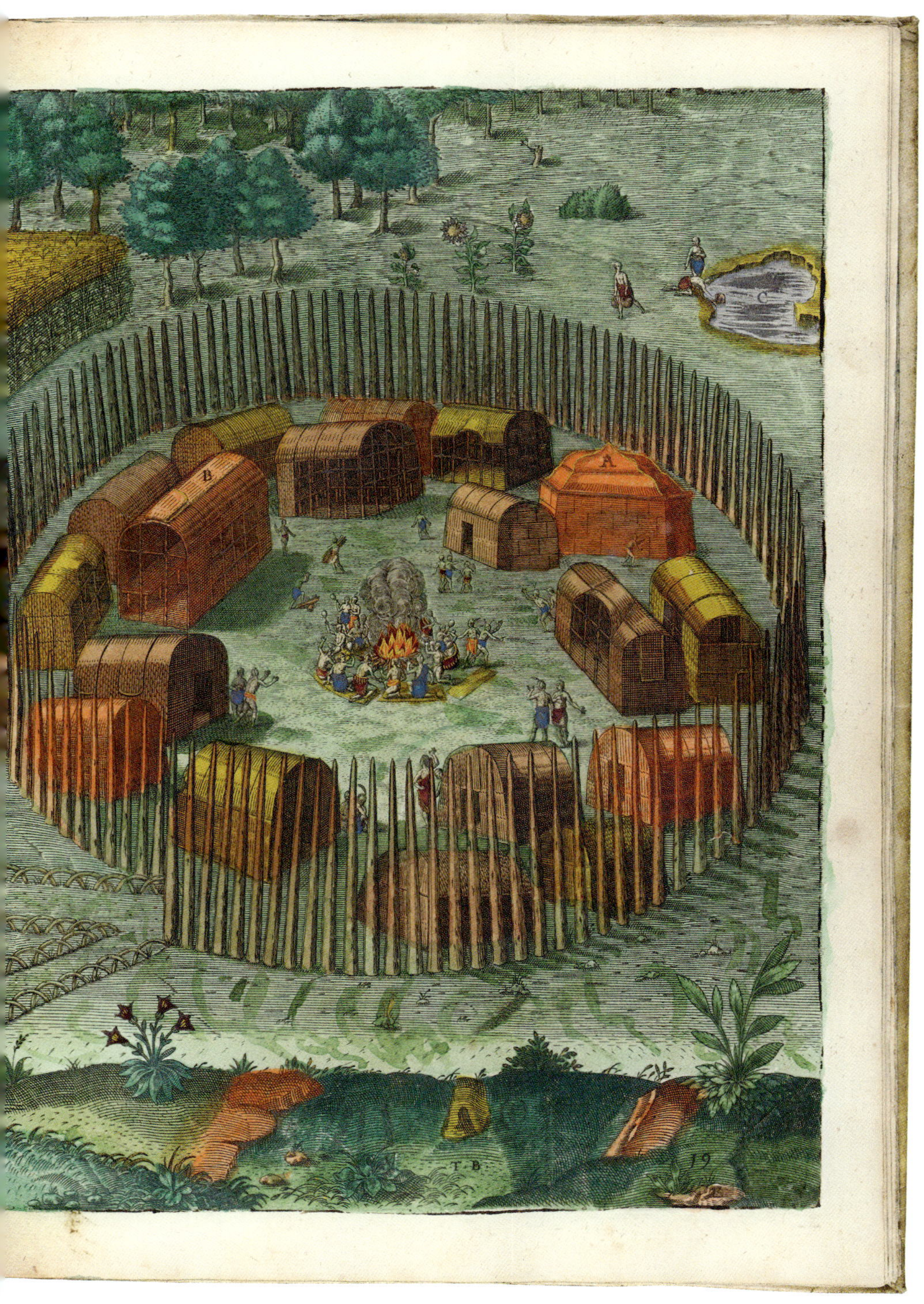
A
B
C
T B.
19

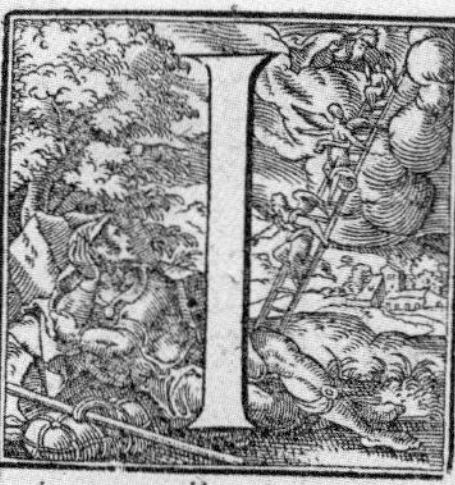

IOANNES ego cognomēto Stadius, patria Hombergensis, natione Hessus, Indiam perlustrare in animo meo proposueram. Bremam itaque Westphaliæ oppidum transiens, Hollandiam petii, eò delatus, offendi in vrbe Campensi naves, quæ salis inuehendi causâ in Portugalliam nauigabant: iis ego me socium adiungo, & mensem integrum continuando, ad tertium Kal. Maij Anni 1547. appello, ad vrbem Setubal dictam: Hinc emensis quinque milliaribus veni Vlyssibonam. Istic aliquandiu commoratus, hospiti meo, viro ex Germania oriundo, propositum meum expono, ex quo cum intelligo classem regiam iam ante aduentum meū soluisse, rogo, vt ad aliam me classem promoueat, vtpote cui idioma eius gentis familiare foret. Eius ope nauem conscendo, in qua sclopetarii vicem obirem. Capitaneus eius classis, qui Pintiadus erat nomine, negotiationis ergo Brasiliam petebat: illi potestas à Regia Maiestate naues, quas in Barbaria cum infidelibus commercia instituentes, & quæcunque Gallorum nauigia cum Brasiliensibus contrahentia offendisset, hostiliter adoriendi, atque deprædandi facta erat: adhæc captiuos secum ducebat quosdam Regios, qui capitis damnati, ad colonias in nouas illas prouincias deducendas deportandi reseruabantur. Classis nostra erat instructissima, ab omni apparatu bellico, qui in naualibus vsui esse solet. Tres autem omnino erant Germani inter ceteros in naui nostra, Ioannes videlicet Brachusius, Henricus Brandt Bremensis, & Ioannes ego Stadius.

CAP.

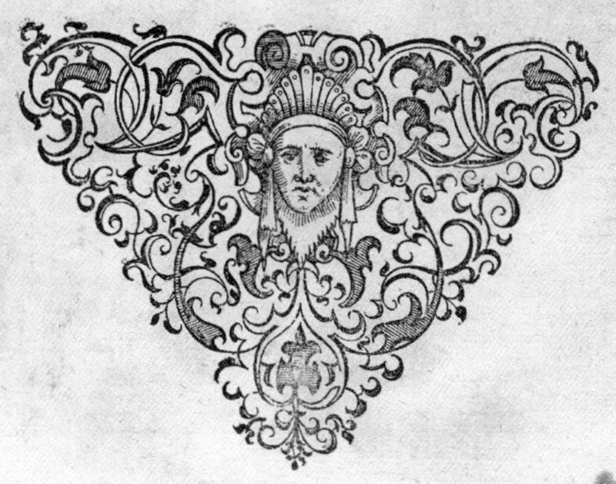

III. Pars. 3

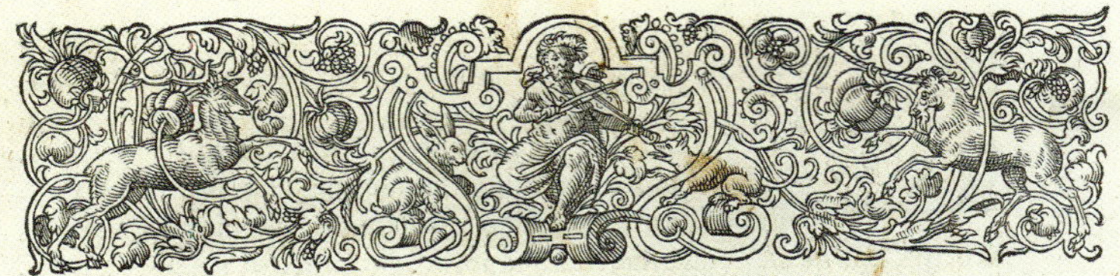

CAPVT II.

De ijs quæ acciderunt circa primam nauigationem.

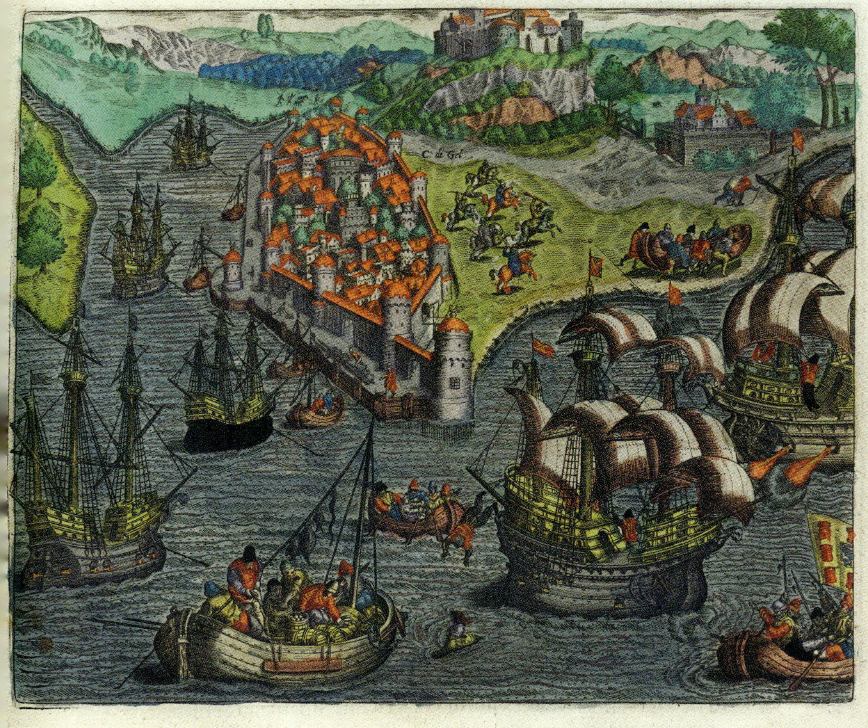

A 2

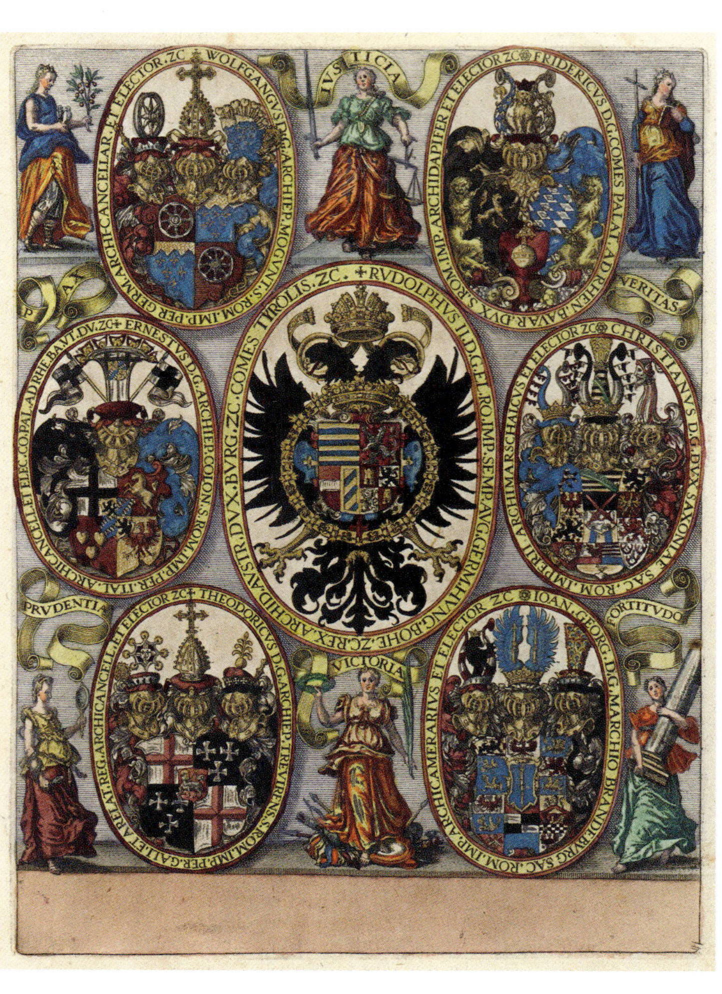
IVSTICIA
PAX
VERITAS
PRVDENTIA
VICTORIA
FORTITVDO